Composing with Confidence
Writing Effective Paragraphs and Essays

Alan Meyers
Harry S Truman College

Longman

New York   San Francisco   Boston
London   Toronto   Sydney   Tokyo   Singapore   Madrid
Mexico City   Munich   Paris   Cape Town   Hong Kong   Montreal

Vice President and Editor-in-Chief: Joseph Terry
Senior Acquisitions Editor: Steve Rigolosi
Development Manager: Janet Lanphier
Development Editor: Ann Hofstra Grogg
Senior Marketing Manager: Melanie Craig
Senior Supplements Editor: Donna Campion
Media Supplements Editor: Nancy Garcia
Senior Production Manager: Valerie Zaborski
Project Coordination, Text Design, and Electronic Page Makeup: Elm Street Publishing Services, Inc.
Cover Design Manager: Wendy Ann Fredericks
Cover Designer: Joseph DePinho
Cover Photo: ©Ryan McVey/PhotoDisc/PictureQuest
Photo Researcher: Photosearch, Inc.
Manufacturing Buyer: Lucy Hebard
Printer and Binder: Von Hoffmann Press, Inc.
Cover Printer: The Lehigh Press, Inc.

Library of Congress Cataloging-in-Publication Data

Meyers, Alan, 1945–
  Composing with confidence: writing effective paragraphs and essays / Alan Meyers. — 6th ed.
      p. cm.
  Includes index.
  ISBN 0-321-08831-X
    1. English language—Rhetoric. 2. English language—Grammar. 3. Report writing. I. Title.

PE1408.M519 2003
808'.042-dc21

2002025481

Please visit our website at http://www.ablongman.com/meyers.

ISBN 0-321-08831-X

1 2 3 4 5 6 7 8 9 10—VHO—05 04 03 02

In memory of the four B's

Brief Contents

v

Detailed Contents

UNIT I
Writing as a Composing Process   1

Rhetorical Contents

The following list classifies the reading selections and student essays according to the rhetorical modes they include. Many of the additional readings are mixed modes.

The Writing Process

Hints and Help for Writers

REFINING AND COMBINING SENTENCES

WORKING WITH VERBS

A WRITER SPEAKS

IF YOUR FIRST LANGUAGE IS NOT ENGLISH

Preface

While retaining the most popular features of previous editions, the sixth edition of *Composing with Confidence* is more engaging for students and versatile for instructors than ever before. For students, it presents high-interest content in exercises and readings, with a single theme (unusual facts about animals, the stories of Crazy Horse and Custer, the life of a man who was known as the Emperor of the United States, and so on) developed throughout each chapter. A new feature, "A Word About Words," graces the margins of every chapter, sparking interest in the roots and history of English as well as presenting fascinating etymologies of individual words. Sample paragraphs and essays, many written by students, provide lively and realistic models within each chapter on writing—as do the sixteen additional readings (including student essays) at the end of the book. Each chapter includes helpful tips in the margins, as well as advice for students whose first language is not English. A new chapter, "Writing on the Job," offers advice on and models for letter, résumé, and memo writing. And the answer key in the back of the book provides answers to all odd-numbered items in the exercises so that students may work independently. All sentence-level chapters now conclude with two Editing for Mastery exercises—the answers to the first also included in the answer key, so students may check their work before completing the second. A new graphic summary entitled "Synthesis for Success" concludes each unit, providing a quick reference to the most important elements of the unit.

Although *Composing with Confidence* provides guidance through the composing process, it does not aim to furnish empty organizational shells into which students pour content. Instead, the book stresses writing as a purposeful and social act, in which audience, occasion, and goal affect the outcome: the paragraph or essay. It is neither condescending in style nor attitude toward students. It regards them as writers—perhaps inexperienced (or inexperienced in writing in English)—but writers nonetheless. A feature entitled "A Writer Speaks" invites students to join the community of writers by hearing the advice and insights of experienced writers. These commissioned, original contributions from professional writers, editors, and professors confirm that the processes involved and the obstacles faced in shaping thoughts into meaningful messages for readers are universal.

For instructors, the book allows great flexibility. This new edition thoroughly explains the composing process in six steps, but not in a lockstep manner. The book emphasizes the rhetorical nature of writing: that each writing task is unique, depending on purpose, content, audience, and occasion; and that each writer is unique, depending on how he or she can best discover, plan, draft, revise, edit, and proofread his or her work. Each chapter includes one well-wrought writing assignment, as well as at least five alternatives, and allows the instructor to expand the paragraph into an essay at any point. Photographs and artwork provide visual prompts for writing, as do the numerous choices in end-of-chapter "Writing for Mastery" sections. And for instructors who favor student collaboration, the margins of each chapter are filled with optional activities allowing students to share ideas, peer review and edit, and help each other discover and strengthen their own talents as writers.

Previous users of the book will find a number of improvements on features. A unique feature entitled "Writing from Source Material" appears in each of the chapters in Units II and III, providing students with data to summarize, paraphrase, and quote in support of a topic idea without having to conduct independent research. Each chapter in Unit IV concludes with the two "Editing for Mastery" passages, the first with the answers supplied in the answer key, so that students may work independently. Additional readings afford more opportunities for integrating reading into the basic writing curriculum, as well as providing additional prompts for writing assignments. And a new quotation bank provides inspiration and prompts for even more writing. Key terms highlighted in the text are defined in a glossary at the back of the book.

CONTENT OVERVIEW

Composing with Confidence is designed for maximum flexibility. Instructors may choose to follow the book in sequence or to choose those chapters that best fit their students' needs.

- **Unit I: Writing as a Composing Process.** These four chapters motivate students to write and show them how it's done. Separate chapters focus on the reasons for writing; a six-step writing process that begins with discovery and ends with proofreading; the shape and form of the paragraph; and the shape and form of the essay.
- **Unit II: Strengthening Writing.** Chapters in this unit offer practice in developing a paragraph or essay through detail, illustration, and example; achieving coherence; writing directly and vividly; and fashioning a more concise and varied style.
- **Unit III: Composing Types of Paragraphs and Essays.** Instruction in both paragraph and essay writing is consolidated in this new unit on rhetorical modes. Each chapter includes at least one professional model and one student model, most new to this edition, and guides students through the composing process with explanations and a "blueprint" for organization. A chapter on writing the essay is designed to build student skills and confidence for this key to success in college. A new chapter, "Writing on the Job," offers advice on and models for workplace writing.
- **Unit IV: Troubleshooting.** This handbook-like section includes instruction and practice in sentence-level issues: fragments, comma-splices, and run-ons; coordination and subordination; subject-verb agreement; past-tense and past-participle verb forms; consistency in sentence structures; number and case of pronouns; placement of modifiers; use of apostrophes, hyphens, and capital letters; punctuation; and commonly confused words. Each chapter also provides advice on issues of concern to non-English-dominant, or ESL, writers.
- **Reading Selections.** These sixteen high-interest essays, arranged from most accessible to most challenging, represent a diversity of cultures and viewpoints. They also provide models of the rhetorical modes, practice in close reading, questions for discussion, and prompts for additional writing.

CONTINUING FEATURES

The following continuing features of *Composing with Confidence* make the text a valuable and flexible tool for both instructor and student:

- **Simple and Direct Explanations.** Discussions of the composing process, rhetorical modes for paragraphs and essays, grammar, and mechanics focus on what students should know to generate effective sentences, paragraphs, and essays, while increasing their facility with language and eliminating errors. Key terms are highlighted and explained in the text, and, for continuing reference, they are repeated in a glossary at the back of the book.

- **Clearly Outlined Composing Process Instruction.** The "Six Steps to Composing with Confidence" presents students with an easily mastered series of activities to perform in the writing process. Not only is the process thoroughly explained, but also outlining and writing topic sentences and thesis statements are highlighted in every chapter on the rhetorical modes.

- **High-Interest Exercises and Models.** Working with engaging materials in connected discourse, students gain skills in composing, revising, and editing sentences with meaningful content. Selections include odd and fascinating facts from history, animal behavior, and biographies of famous or unusual figures. This entertaining subject matter serves a more serious purpose: that people write to communicate ideas and that, if ideas are worth saying, they are worth saying well. As students read and then rewrite or revise an exercise, they discover that interesting ideas become clearer and even more interesting.

- **Mastery Learning Capabilities.** Unit IV of the book is designed to facilitate a Mastery Learning approach, in which students complete a section on grammar and mechanics, evaluate their understanding and application of the concepts, restudy parts of the section if necessary, and then engage in further evaluation. Two "Editing for Mastery" concluding exercises, as well as the parallel test forms in the ancillary testing package, all serve as useful tools in this approach.

- **Attention to Matters of Style.** Several chapters explore ways to make writing more lively, vivid, and direct. They offer practice in writing strong verbs, adjectives, and expressions; employing parallelism; eliminating unnecessary repetition of words and ideas; and avoiding clichés.

- **Chapter-Ending Summary Boxes.** These highlighted summaries help students identify and review the important points to learn and practice and serve as additional reference aids in revising and editing.

- **Multiple Opportunities for Collaborative Work.** For instructors who wish to encourage group work, *Composing with Confidence* offers a variety of options but does not require that they be followed. Each paragraph writing assignment includes **Revision Guidelines** that encourage peer response and editing. **Predicting activities** throughout the text provide additional opportunities for collaboration while stressing the interrelationship between writer and reader. **Collaborative activities**, presented as options in the margins of each chapter, guide students in sharing ideas, doing peer review and editing, and working in groups to improve their writing. Each sentence-level chapter concludes with an **Editing for Mastery** exercise, which can be done collaboratively or independently.

- **Full Integration of the Paragraph and Essay.** Each chapter in the rhetorical mode unit guides students in writing a paragraph and demonstrates the connection between paragraphs and essays. Additional assignments are provided for those students ready to put paragraphs together.

- **Multi-Faceted Writing Instruction.** Professional and student models exemplify the skills students should aim to achieve. Discussion questions focus attention on these models, followed by a step-by-step guide through a single, well-developed writing assignment. A section called **"Getting Ready to Write"** includes practice in formulating topic sentences, developing ideas, and organizing materials before students compose their own paragraphs. Each mode is not only described in text but also vividly illustrated through an easy-to-grasp blueprint of the essentials.

- **Readings.** Selections from contemporary writers stimulate student interest, exemplify rhetorical modes, guide analysis, and suggest topics for additional writing.
- **Writing from Source Material.** This unique feature provides data that students may employ as they gain experience with writing summaries, paraphrasing, quoting, and making attributions, but without requiring independent library research.
- **"A Writer Speaks."** These boxes feature writers, editors, and professors who give advice and encouragement to students by discussing their own composing practices and recounting their struggles and experience. All contributions are original and were commissioned solely for this book.
- **Chapter Goals.** These chapter openers address student aims instead of merely foreshadowing chapter headings.
- **Tip Boxes.** These boxes throughout the text provide helpful advice and mnemonic aids.
- **"If Your First Language Is Not English" Boxes.** These boxes provide helpful and timely advice for the specific needs of this growing segment of the student population. However, the boxes are not solely intended for non-English dominant, or ESL, writers; they are also useful to writers of all backgrounds and all ages.
- **Glossary.** Key terms are highlighted in the text and defined in a glossary at the back of the book.

NEW TO THE SIXTH EDITION

The sixth edition of *Composing with Confidence* has been revised with an eye toward increasing the emphasis on process, accessibility to students, ease of use for instructors, and adaptability to a variety of programs and teaching approaches.

- **Synthesis for Success.** This series of charts and graphics at the end of each unit provides students with a clear summary of and cross-reference to the unit's most important points.
- **A Word About Words.** Intended to engender in students a curiosity about and love for language, these boxes in the margins of each chapter present fascinating information about the roots of English and unusual etymologies.
- **Dual Editing for Mastery Exercises.** These chapter-concluding activities in Unit IV allow students to test their knowledge of the skills taught in the chapter, check their work in the answer key, and then apply their knowledge a second time.
- **New Visual Prompts.** Additional photographs and artwork provide subject matter for student writing.
- **Writing for Mastery.** Concluding each chapter in Unit III, this section offers multiple prompts for writing, including writing in response to readings.
- **New Chapter on Writing on the Job.** This chapter provides students with advice and models on three important types of workplace writing: the letter of application, the résumé, and the memo.
- **New Readings.** The number of readings at the end of the book has been increased to sixteen, and many of them are new, including several written by students and two separate renderings of a column by Bob Greene: the first as it originally appeared, the second as it was abridged in *Reader's Digest*.

- Quotations and Proverbs. This new quotation bank at the back of the book provides inspiration and prompts for even more writing.
- Answer Key. All odd-numbered items and answers to the first of each pair of "Editing for Mastery" exercises are listed here, allowing students to work independently and instructors to individualize instruction.

THE TEACHING AND LEARNING PACKAGE

Each component of the teaching and learning package has been crafted to ensure that the course is a rewarding experience for both instructors and students.

- The **Instructor's Manual** contains teaching tips, sources of additional information, sample course syllabi, and answers to all in-text questions. 0-321-08834-4
- The **Test Bank** contains a profusion of additional quizzes, tests, and exercises keyed to each chapter in the student text. The test bank is printed on 8 ½" × 11" paper and is perforated for easy removal and copying. 0-321-08833-6

For additional exercises, resources, and Internet activities, be sure to visit the **Companion Web site** at http://www.ablongman.com/meyers.

In addition to the book-specific supplements discussed above, a series of other skills-based supplements are available for both instructors and students. All of these supplements are available either free or at greatly reduced prices.

For Additional Reading and Reference

- The Dictionary Deal. Two dictionaries can be shrinkwrapped with this title either free or at a nominal fee. *The New American Webster Handy College Dictionary* is a paperback reference text with more than 100,000 entries. *Merriam Webster's Collegiate Dictionary*, tenth edition, is a hardback reference with a citation file of more than 14.5 million examples of English words drawn from actual use. For more information on how to shrinkwrap a dictionary with your text, please contact your Longman sales representative.
- Penguin Quality Paperback Titles. A series of Penguin paperbacks is available at a significant discount when shrinkwrapped with any Longman English title. Some titles available are Toni Morrison's *Beloved*, Julia Alvarez's *How the Garcia Girls Lost Their Accents*, Mark Twain's *Huckleberry Finn*, *Narrative of The Life of Frederick Douglass*, Harriet Beecher Stowe's *Uncle Tom's Cabin*, Dr. Martin Luther King, Jr.'s *Why We Can't Wait*, and plays by Shakespeare, Miller, and Albee. For a complete list of titles or more information, please contact your Longman sales consultant.
- *The Pocket Reader* **and** *The Brief Pocket Reader*, **First Edition**. These inexpensive volumes contain 50 readings and 80 brief readings, respectively. Each reading is brief (1–3 pages each). The readers are theme-based: writers on writing, nature, women and men, customs and habits, politics, rights and obligations, and coming of age. Also included is an alternate rhetorical table to contents. Ask your Longman sales representative for more information.
- *100 Things to Write About*. This 100-page book contains 100 individual assignments for writing on a variety of topics and in a wide range of formats, from expressive to analytical. Ask your Longman sales representative for a sample copy. 0-673-98239-4
- *Newsweek* Alliance. Instructors may choose to shrinkwrap a 12-week subscription to *Newsweek* with any Longman text. The price of the subscription is

57 cents per issue (a total of $6.84 for the subscription). Available with the subscription is a free "Interactive Guide to *Newsweek*"—a workbook for students who are using the text. In addition, *Newsweek* provides a wide variety of instructor supplements free to teachers, including maps, Skills Builders, and weekly quizzes. For more information on the *Newsweek* program, please contact your Longman sales representative.

Electronic and Online Offerings

- **[NEW] The Longman Writer's Warehouse.** The innovative and exciting online supplement is the perfect accompaniment to any developmental writing course. Created by developmental English instructors specially for developing writers, The Writer's Warehouse covers every part of the writing process. Also included are journaling capabilities, multimedia activities, diagnostic tests, an interactive handbook, and a complete instructor's manual. The Writer's Warehouse requires no space on your school's server; rather, students complete and store their work on the Longman server, and are able to access it, revise it, and continue working at any time. For more details about how to shrinkwrap a free subscription to The Writer's Warehouse with this text, please consult your Longman sales representative. For a free guided tour of the site, visit http://longmanwriterswarehouse.com.

- **The Writer's ToolKit Plus.** This CD-ROM offers a wealth of tutorial, exercise, and reference material for writers. It is compatible with either a PC or Macintosh platform, and is flexible enough to be used either occasionally for practice or regularly in class lab sessions. For information on how to bundle this CD-ROM free with your text, please contact your Longman sales representative.

- **GrammarCoach Software.** This interactive tutorial helps students practice the basics of grammar and punctuation through 600 self-grading exercises in such problem areas as fragments, run-ons, and agreement. IBM diskette only. 0-205-26509-X

- **The Longman Electronic Newsletter.** Twice a month during the spring and fall, instructors who have subscribed receive a free copy of the Longman Developmental English Newsletter in their e-mailbox. Written by experienced classroom instructors, the newsletter offers teaching tips, classroom activities, book reviews, and more. To subscribe, visit the Longman Basic Skills Web site at http://www.ablongman.com/basicskills, or send an e-mail to Basic Skills@ablongman.com.

For Instructors

- **Electronic Test Bank for Writing.** This electronic test bank features more than 5,000 questions in all areas of writing, from grammar to paragraphing, through essay writing, research, and documentation. With this easy-to-use CD-ROM, instructors simply choose questions from the electronic test bank, then print out the completed test for distribution. CD-ROM: 0-321-08117-X Print version: 0-321-08486-1

- **Competency Profile Test Bank, Second Edition.** This series of 60 objective tests covers ten general areas of English competency, including fragments; comma splices and run-ons; pronouns; commas; and capitalization. Each test is available in remedial, standard, and advanced versions. Available as reproducible sheets or in computerized versions. Free to instructors. Paper version: 0-321-02224-5   Computerized IBM: 0-321-02633-0   Computerized Mac: 0-321-02632-2.

- **Diagnostic and Editing Tests and Exercises, Fifth Edition.** This collection of diagnostic tests helps instructors assess students' competence in Standard Written English for purpose of placement or to gauge progress. Available as reproducible sheets or in computerized versions, and free to instructors. Paper: 0-321-11730-1. CD-ROM: 0-321-11731-X.

- **ESL Worksheets, Third Edition.** These reproducible worksheets provide ESL students with extra practice in areas they find the most troublesome. A diagnostic test and post-test are provided, along with answer keys and suggested topics for writing. Free to adopters. 0-321-07765-2

- **Longman Editing Exercises.** 54 pages of paragraph editing exercises give students extra practice using grammar skills in the context of longer passages. Free when packaged with any Longman title. 0-205-31792-8 Answer Key: 0-205-31797-9

- **80 Practices.** A collection of reproducible, ten-item exercises that provide additional practices for specific grammatical usage problems, such as comma splices, capitalization, and pronouns. Includes an answer key, and free to adopters. 0-673-53422-7

- **CLAST Test Package, Fourth Edition.** These two 40-item objective tests evaluate students' readiness for the CLAST exams. Strategies for teaching CLAST preparedness are included. Free with any Longman English title. Reproducible sheets: 0-321-01950-4. Computerized IBM version: 0-321-01982-2. Computerized Mac version: 0-321-01983-0

- **TASP Test Package, Third Edition.** These 12 practice pre-tests and post-tests assess the same reading and writing skills covered in the TASP examination. Free with any Longman English title. Reproducible sheets: 0-321-01959-8 Computerized IBM version: 0-321-01985-7. Computerized Mac version: 0-321-01984-9

- *Teaching Online: Internet Research, Conversation, and Composition, Second Edition.* Ideal for instructors who have never surfed the Net, this easy-to-follow guide offers basic definitions, numerous examples, and step-by-step information about finding and using Internet sources. Free to adopters. 0-321-01957-1

- *Teaching Writing to the Non-Native Speaker.* This booklet examines the issues that arise when non-native speakers enter the developmental classroom. Free to instructors, it includes profiles of international and permanent ESL students, factors influencing second-language acquisition, and tips on managing a multicultural classroom. 0-673-97452-9

- *Using Portfolios.* This supplement offers teachers a brief introduction to teaching with portfolios in composition courses. This essential guide address the pedagogical and evaluate use of portfolios, and offers practical suggestions for implementing a portfolio evaluation system in a writing class. 0-321-08412-8

- **[NEW] The Longman Guide to Classroom Management.** Written by Joannis Flatley of St. Philip's College, the first in Longman's new series of monographs for developmental English instructors focuses on issues of classroom etiquette, providing guidance on dealing with unruly, unengaged, disruptive, or uncooperative students. Ask your Longman sales representative for a free copy. 0-321-09246-5

- **[NEW] The Longman Instructor Planner.** This all-in-one resource for instructors includes monthly and weekly planning sheets, to-do lists, student contact forms, attendance rosters, a gradebook, an address/phone book, and a mini almanac. Ask your Longman sales representative for a free copy. 0-321-09247-3

For Students

- *Researching Online,* Fifth Edition. A perfect companion for a new age, this indispensable new supplement helps students navigate the Internet. Adapted from *Teaching Online,* the instructor's Internet guide, *Researching Online* speaks direct to students, giving them detailed, step-by-step instructions for performing electronic searches. Available free when shrinkwrapped with this text. 0-321-09277-5

- *Learning Together: An Introduction to Collaborative Theory.* This brief guide to the fundamentals of collaborative learning teaches students how to work effectively in groups, how to revise with peer response, and how to co-author a paper or report. Shrinkwrapped free with any Longman Basic Skills text. 0-673-46848-8

- *A Guide for Peer Response,* Second Edition. This guide offers students forms for peer critiques, including general guidelines and specific forms for different stages in the writing process. Also appropriate for freshman-level course. Free to adopters. 0-321-01948-2

- *Ten Practices of Highly Successful Students.* This popular supplement helps students learn crucial study skills, offering concise tips for a successful career in college. Topics include time management, test-taking, reading critically, stress, and motivation. 0-205-30769-8

- *Thinking Through the Test,* by D. J. Henry. This special workbook, prepared specially for students in Florida, offers ample skill and practice exercises to help students prep for the Florida State Exit Exam. To shrinkwrap this workbook free with your textbook, please contact your Longman sales representative. Available in two versions: with answers and without answers. Also available: Two laminated grids (one for reading, one for writing) that can serve as handy references for students preparing for the Florida State Exit Exam.

- [NEW] The Longman Writer's Journal. This journal for writers, free with any Longman English text, offers students a place to think, write, and react. For an examination copy, contact your Longman sales consultant. 0-321-08639-2

- [NEW] The Longman Researcher's Journal. This journal for writers and researchers, free with this text, helps students plan, schedule, write, and revise their research project. An all-in-one resource for first-time researchers, the journal guides students gently through the research process. 0-321-09530-8

- [NEW] The Longman Writer's Portfolio. This unique supplement provides students with a space to plan, think about, and present their work. The portfolio includes an assessing/organizing area (including a grammar diagnostic test, a spelling quiz, and project planning worksheets), a before and during writing area (including peer review sheets, editing checklists, writing self-evaluations, and a personal editing profile), and an after-writing area (including a progress chart, a final table of contents, and a final assessment). Ask your Longman sales representative for ISBN 0-321-10765-9.

ACKNOWLEDGMENTS

As always, I could not have achieved this result without the assistance, advice, and support of colleagues and students. I thank the administrators of Truman College and the City Colleges of Chicago, who granted me a sabbatical, part of which was devoted to revising this book. I thank my students, who continually teach me how the writing process works and should be addressed. I especially thank the students—some of them from my classes, others from other colleges—who have contributed paragraphs and essays to the text: Linder Anim, Tuyet-Ahn Van, Iman Rooker, Mirham Mahmutagic, Veronica Fleeton, Sara Sebring, Mark Schlitt, Jane Smith, Christine Mueller, and Amra Skocic. Again, Professor Patricia W. Kato of Chattanooga State Community College, Chattanooga, Tennessee, deserves my special thanks for providing several of the reading selections and student paragraphs for the book. And so does Professor Sherry F. Gott of Danville Community College, Danville, Virginia, who provided Jane Smith's student essay.

I thank the reviewers of the manuscript, whose invaluable criticisms and suggestions have helped shape this revision:

Joe Allen, Dutchess Community College
Robert Brannan, Johnson County Community College
Gail Caylor, Phoenix College
Cheryl Deward, Hawkeye Community College
Martha Funderburk, University of Arkansas
Judith Gallagher, Tarrant County Junior College
Sherry Gott, Danville Community College
Judy G. Haberman, Phoenix College
Lois Hassan, Henry Ford Community College
Kevin Hayes, Essex County College
Patricia Kato, Chattanooga State Technical College
Patsy Krech, The University of Memphis
Joan Mauldin, San Jacinto College South
Vincent Miholic, Southeastern Louisiana University
Beatrice Newman, University of Texas-Pan American
Sybil Patterson, Hillsborough Community College
Harvey Rubinstein, Hudson County Community College
Nancy J. Schneider, University of Maine at Augusta
Lisa Shucter, Naugatuck Valley Community College
James D. Suderman, Okaloosa-Walton Community College
Karean Williams, Miami-Dade Community College
Tricia Yarbrough, East Central University
Rose Yesu, Massasoit Community College

I also thank Brandi Nelson and her staff at Elm Street Publishing Services, Inc. for their outstanding work in the copyediting and production of the text. I thank my Acquisitions Editor, Steven Rigolosi, whose vision, insight, imagination, and flexibility made this whole project work. I also thank Valerie Zaborski, in-house production manager, for her many contributions; Donna Campion, for shepherding the ancillaries through their many stages, and Meegan Thompson for helping to keep track of the assorted pieces. But most importantly, I thank my Developmental Editor, Ann Hofstra Grogg, who once again has guided me so brilliantly through a revision of this text.

And the second Ann to whom I dedicate not only this book is my wife and companion for almost four decades. It is she to whom I attribute whatever small successes I have achieved in my adult life, and to whom I attribute my largest successes: our children Sarah and Bradley, who continue to make us proud of their achievements.

Alan Meyers

I
Writing as a Composing Process

Writing is communication—conveying your ideas to other people. That communication includes notes or e-mails to friends and relatives, essays and term papers to instructors in courses, memos and reports to colleagues and managers on the job, articles and letters to the editors of newspapers, and even books and novels for a larger audience. There's always a reason to write—and an audience to read the writing.

This book emphasizes writing as *composing*—as a process involving a number of concerns and a number of stages. Like music, the final product—the one the audience hears or sees—seems polished and effortless. But it emerges only after many hours of thought, discovery, practice, and revision. Writers (and composers) work hard to make their work look easy.

The four chapters in this unit show you how to compose in writing. They discuss the reasons for writing, how to explore and shape your ideas, how to capture them on the page or computer, and how to revise and rewrite them so they achieve your goals. These chapters suggest ways to make your writing interesting, direct, and clear. Above all, the chapters demonstrate that writing is a skill that, like all skills, improves with continual practice.

Don't worry if you're unsure about, or new to, the composing process. The chapters in this unit take you through it step by step. Just follow those steps and you can indeed write well—and with confidence. ■

1 The Reasons for Writing

Writing is speaking to those who, for one reason or another, can't—or shouldn't—hear you right now. Of course, writing is a talent, but it's mostly a *skill,* which improves with practice. Writing is also an *action*—a process of discovering and assembling your ideas, capturing them on paper, and reshaping and revising them. That process is called composing. We'll examine it in detail in Chapter 2. But first, we'll explore some basic options in the process and purposes of writing. We'll examine

- ways you can increase your confidence about writing
- different ways you can choose to write
- the variety of ways you can use your writing

WRITING AS COMMUNICATION

You communicate for many reasons—because you want to share an idea, supply information, express a greeting, state an opinion, or send a warning. In short, you communicate because you have

1. a set of circumstances for saying something: *an occasion*
2. something to say: *a subject*
3. a reason for saying it: *a purpose*
4. someone to say it to: *an audience*

Most often you communicate with others through speech. In doing so, you hear the responses of your listeners and respond to them. You answer their questions, clarify your ideas, and even change the subject if it doesn't interest them.

UNIT 1

Chapter 1

Composing with Confidence

©2003

GO ELECTRONIC!

Use the following electronic supplements for additional practice with your writing:

- For chapter-by-chapter summaries and exercises, visit the Composing with Confidence Companion Web site at: http://www.ablongman.com/meyers.
- For work with the writing process, visit The Longman Writer's Warehouse at http://longmanwriterswarehouse.com (password needed).
- For additional practice in grammar, use The Writer's ToolKit Plus CD-ROM

You enhance your communication with both your voice and body. You speak loudly or softly, quickly or slowly, and pause for effect. You shrug your shoulders, point with your hands, wink, smile, or grin. And as you communicate, you also discover and sharpen your thoughts. You both present and examine your ideas as you say them aloud.

But speaking isn't the only way to communicate, and writing is often a better one. In the free flow of conversation, you may say something brilliant—or foolish, and then try to repair the damage. Writing allows you the opportunity to get things straight beforehand. You can explore and organize your ideas, write them down, and then rewrite them. Moreover, when you have something important to say, you may choose to put it in writing. Readers can then consider it, reread it, and remember it. Sounds disappear into the air, but words on the page are more permanent.

"Write me a note," someone may say, "so I don't forget."

"Hold on a minute while I write down those directions," you may say, "so I don't get lost."

"Why don't you write me a memo," your supervisor may say, "so I can think about it carefully?"

"I just wanted to thank you for your kindness," you may write. "My family will be forever grateful."

WRITING AS A PROCESS

Unlike speaking, writing doesn't happen all at once. It's part of a *process* in which you sketch your ideas in a draft, then revise and improve them. Your readers aren't around for you to see and hear, so you must predict their reactions. You must choose a subject that interests you and try to present it in an interesting way so your readers will be interested, too. You must consider when an idea may be unclear to your readers and find a way to clarify it. You must anticipate their questions and try to answer them. You must present your ideas clearly, for, as a person with serious (or even humorous) things to communicate, you'd like yourself and your ideas to be taken seriously.

Your tools in writing, however, are more limited than in speech. You cannot rely on gestures and changes in your voice to emphasize a point, so you must pay greater attention to your language and the marks of punctuation that help convey your meaning. You must read what you write and then rewrite it until it says what you want it to say. You must choose your language carefully, arrange it carefully, and present it carefully.

You cannot achieve all those goals in one sitting. Any good paragraph or essay goes through many stages before it reaches an audience. You may begin by simply generating ideas as you put them into words, lists, or charts. Then you can write a first draft and let it sit for a while. Later you can question, challenge, and rewrite the draft. You can revise and polish your ideas and wording several times—until you feel confident that your audience will care about and understand your point. You must fine-tune the message before you communicate it.

That, precisely, is what this book will help you do.

COMPOSING WITH CONFIDENCE

"Composing" might seem like a strange word to find in the title of a book on writing. But it was chosen deliberately to convey the careful process involved in achieving solid paragraphs and essays. Composing in writing is like composing in music. In both cases, your audience may feel as if you produced the final product in a brief moment of inspiration, but that rarely happens. Instead, you start with an idea, an impulse, an emotion. You try to give it form, a pattern, a direction, a meaning. You experiment, shape, and reshape the parts. You engage in a fluid process until the finished product emerges. This book will guide you through the composing process.

Now in its sixth edition and in print since 1987, *Composing with Confidence* has helped thousands of people like you develop and improve their writing skills. Many of the model paragraphs and essays you'll see in the pages ahead were in fact written by students who used this book. They learned to compose with confidence, and so can you.

Perhaps you've had problems with parts of the process in the past—finding a subject, organizing your thoughts, choosing the right words, or correcting grammar and punctuation. Perhaps you've even struggled with writing in English if it's your second (or third, or fourth) language. This book is designed to maximize your chances for solving those problems. It will divide the composing process into a series of six small steps that you can master:

- ways to start thinking about your subject matter
- ways to explore your ideas freely
- ways to shape those ideas into a plan
- ways to compose a first draft
- ways to examine and revise the draft
- ways to edit and correct your work to produce the final copy

The later units of the book will provide you with further help. You'll find

- suggestions for strengthening your writing
- approaches for organizing paragraphs and essays
- methods for correcting problem sentences and structures
- advice on mastering grammatical and mechanical matters
- readings that serve as examples of effective writing and prompts for your own essays

The program in *Composing with Confidence* should convince you that, while writing is never effortless, it needn't be painful, and it can even be fun. Just flip through the pages of this book and look at the exercises that focus on unusual people, events, animals, and places. Some exercises take you step by step through the composing process. Others focus on one step in the process, perhaps helping you correct or polish sentences or a whole passage. Most exercises are designed for you to complete independently, and some can be done collaboratively with classmates. In either case, with repeated practice, you will compose with confidence.

You'll see something else in this book—professional writers discussing their own practices and offering you their help. Like you, they've encountered the challenge of the blank page. Like you, they've had to develop their skills. Like you, they're never quite satisfied with their work. They're always thinking they can do better. They draft, revise, edit, and revise again.

These professional writers care deeply about writing—and they care about helping beginning writers find their own voices—voices that are clear and powerful. So these professionals have contributed their stories and advice, which you'll find in every chapter throughout Units I, II, and III. No matter why they write, good writers follow one universal practice: they write a lot.

Here's the first writer speaking to you:

A WRITER SPEAKS

My most consistent piece of advice about writing is stolen from Nike's ads: Just do it. People find it hard to believe that writing is just like playing the piano or throwing a frisbee or learning to speak Spanish. The more you practice, the better you get. The distance between what you feel and the words that express it grows shorter. Your confidence increases. So stop fretting and do it.

Scott Turow, author of *Presumed Innocent, The Burden of Proof,* and *The Laws of Our Fathers,* and former teacher of creative writing at Stanford University

DISCOVERING THE RIGHT WAY TO WRITE

No two people follow exactly the same composing practices. So you need to determine the methods that achieve the best results for you. When do you work best—in the morning or at night? How do you work best—composing by hand, on a computer, or a combination of both? There is only one practice you must avoid: sitting down to write a paper the night before it's due. You *cannot* do your best under those circumstances. Composing requires time to think, reconsider, reread, and revise—and those can't happen when you rush.

Some writers are planners, who can envision where they're going and follow that route with only minor changes in plan. Other writers are discoverers, who arrive at their destination after composing and revising many times. Every composing task is different, so you may be a planner in one circumstance, a discoverer in another. Your primary objective, however, should be to begin with a plan and allow yourself the freedom to discover along the way. You needn't solve every problem before you begin. In fact, people who try to solve every problem often encounter "writer's block."

The first step in planning is to prepare a schedule. Set aside some time to list some topics, mull them over, and then choose one. Allow yourself time for ideas to occur to you as you walk the dog or ride the bus, and jot down those ideas whenever you can. (You'll see specific procedures for these practices in Chapter 2.) Build in time to do a first draft, put it aside, and return to it a day or two later. You may spend three hours in total on a writing assignment, but spread out in half-hour segments over a three- to five-day period. If you divide the composing process into small steps, you'll accomplish something in every session. That will build your confidence.

A Word About Words

The first use of the term "English" appeared about a thousand years ago. At that time, the language contained perhaps 30,000 words. Today *Webster's Third International* lists over 472,000 words.

WRITING FOR EVERY REASON

Let's return to the idea in the title of this chapter: the reasons for writing. Why do you write? The answer is both simple and complex. You write to communicate. And you need to communicate in everything you do throughout your life. That makes the reasons for writing more complex.

Writing for Work

Today's economy requires a literate workforce, for whom writing is more important than ever before. You'll need to write in almost every job you have, and you'll need to write often and well as you enter and maintain a professional career. You'll find a job partly by writing a solid résumé and letter of application. You'll keep a job by writing clear memos and reports. If you work in an office, you'll write letters, memos, and e-mails. If you work in a health care field, you'll keep records and prepare memos and orders. If you're a computer programmer, you'll write instructions in addition to computer code. If you're a teacher, you'll prepare lesson plans, write reports, and write notes to students and their parents. If you're a lawyer, you'll prepare legal briefs and documents. Virtually every twenty-first-century occupation and career will require that you express ideas and convey information *in writing*. Chapter 18, "Writing on the Job," is devoted exclusively to these practices.

Writing to Learn

As a student, your main job (or one of your main jobs) is getting through college. Writing is essential to your success. You must take notes and write reports, essays, and answers to examination questions—and maybe even an occasional letter home.

Taking notes is a critical learning activity. Take notes on lectures in your classes. The physical act of putting ideas into words will help you remember them. Take notes on your readings and mark up your books with reactions, reminders, and questions to pursue. Write down the instructions for assignments so you know what's expected of you and when. These practices will improve not only your writing but also your study habits.

You can further maximize your success in college by keeping a writing log or subject journal. Turn to your journal each day to record your progress in learning, thoughts about new concepts and materials, and questions to explore. Some students use a double-entry journal in which they summarize reading or lecture notes in one column or page and explore their reactions and questions to this material on the facing column or page.

And, finally, you can enhance your grade point average by writing well on examinations, a subject Chapter 17 will address. Knowing how to organize and present your ideas clearly and specifically is a skill that virtually every successful student has mastered.

Writing to Others

Writing keeps us in touch with other people. We write to communicate with relatives and friends. We write to preserve our family histories so our children and grandchildren can learn and appreciate their heritage. With computers and Internet connections in so many households, colleges, and businesses, people are e-mailing friends and relatives all the time—or talking to them in writing in online chat rooms. It's cheaper than calling long distance, and a lot more convenient than waiting until Sunday for the telephone rates to drop. Students are e-mailing their professors to receive and discuss their classroom assignments and to submit them. They're e-mailing classmates to discuss and collaborate on homework. They're also sharing information about concerts and swim meets, as well as jokes, gossip, and their philosophies of life.

Despite the growing importance of computers, however, there will always be a place and need for the personal letter. A handwritten note to a friend, a parent, or grandparent is and will continue to be the best way to communicate important thoughts at important times. No matter what the content of the message, its real point is, "I want you to know that I care about you." This writing practice brings rewards that can't be seen in bank accounts or grade point averages, but only in the success of human relationships.

Writing for Yourself

But there's another reason to write—for yourself—and this reason will last a lifetime. In this sense, all of us are writers. We write to explore our ideas, examine our plans, consider our dreams. We write to remind ourselves of what we learn or what we need to learn or do. We write for our own growth and enjoyment.

Many people maintain a daily journal. It can be a diary that summarizes your activities: "Took the big biology test and think I did all right, e-mailed Susan to see how her audition went, spent an hour with Tom at the coffee shop before heading off to work." But it can also be a place to record and explore your interests, plans, concerns, and questions—to capture what surprises or puzzles you, to express your anger or frustration, and to work your way through a problem.

Write for just ten minutes every day. Record amusing incidents, exciting or troubling thoughts, descriptions of interesting people or places. Even if you never look at these entries again, the act of writing them will give you personal satisfaction and continual practice in writing. But you can also use your journal as an excellent starting point for an essay. With so many ideas to choose from, you won't find yourself saying, "I don't know what to write about."

EXERCISE 1	Getting a Head Start

Start the composing process right now by listing topics for later writings. What has made you think, dream, or get angry? Jot down a few ideas. Then contemplate (but don't worry if you cannot yet answer) these questions on each topic: Why do I want to explore or explain these ideas? Whom would I like to read them?

_____

_____

_____

_____

_____

_____

_____

_____

2 The Composing Process

Composing is a process of exploring, organizing, and adjusting your ideas in writing until they express what you want them to say. And that process includes a number of steps. The page you're reading now, for example, is the finished product of many drafts and revisions over many hours of work. You don't see the papers that went into the wastebasket along the way: the notes, the false starts, the early drafts, and the later ones. You don't see the changes that occurred in response to the reactions and advice of students, professors who use this book in their classes, and editors. You see only the end product—the proof that composing does work.

The composing process will work for you, too. This chapter will show you

- procedures to follow during each stage of the process
- ways to determine what works best for you as a writer
- how a piece of writing takes shape and improves as you make your way through the process
- ways to put the composing process into practice

COMPOSING AS A PROCESS

No two writers approach composing in the same way. But they do tend to follow a sequence of actions that looks something like this:

Composing with Confidence in Six Steps
Step 1. Exploring your ideas
      a. Considering occasion
      b. Considering subject
      c. Considering purpose
      d. Considering audience

UNIT 1

Chapter 2

Composing with Confidence

©2003

GO ELECTRONIC!

Use the following electronic supplements for additional practice with your writing:

- For chapter-by-chapter summaries and exercises, visit the Composing with Confidence Companion Website at: http://www.ablongman.com/meyers.
- For work with the writing process, visit The Longman Writer's Warehouse at http://longmanwriterswarehouse.com (password needed).
- For additional practice in grammar, use The Writer's ToolKit Plus CD-ROM

Step 2: Prewriting—using one or more of these methods
    a. Brainstorming
    b. Clustering
    c. Freewriting
Step 3: Organizing your ideas
    a. Selecting
    b. Outlining
Step 4: Writing a first draft
Step 5: Revising the draft
    a. Reviewing
    b. Reading aloud
    c. Predicting
Step 6: Producing the final copy
    a. Editing
    b. Copying over
    c. Proofreading and copying over again

STEP 1: EXPLORING YOUR IDEAS

Remember that one of the ways writing imitates speech is in discovering ideas as you put them into words. So before you sit down to compose, allow yourself time and space for free exploration, both in your mind and on paper. Ideas will occur to you at unexpected moments—while taking a walk, boarding the bus, relaxing on the sofa. When inspiration appears, capture it. Make notes of your ideas as soon as you can, whether on scraps of paper, on napkins, in your journal, or on the back of your hand.

Then examine your ideas more systematically. You must consider what you are writing about and why, and to whom you are writing. Ask yourself four basic questions:

1. What is the occasion for writing?
2. What is my subject?
3. What is my purpose?
4. Who is my audience?

Take notes on your answers.

The Occasion

Ask yourself, *what is the occasion?* We write under many conditions and circumstances, and each calls for something a bit different. Are you composing a term paper, an essay examination, a letter of application for a job, a memo, a letter to a client, or a letter of complaint to a store manager? Are you writing a note to a friend, a newsletter for a business or community group, even an article for a newspaper or magazine? Each of these occasions involves choices about what to say, how much to say, and how to say it. A casual letter to a friend, for example, can take any form, be any length, and discuss any topic that you want to convey. A term paper, on the other hand, must take the form, length, and coverage of subject matter specified by your instructor. A memo must be short, perhaps with important points highlighted with bullets. You'll need to identify, and then meet, the expectations imposed by different occasions for writing.

Your Subject

Ask yourself, *what is my subject, and what can I say about it?* If you find the subject interesting, your audience will probably find it interesting, too. Draw from your own experiences. Choose a subject that you *know about* (or can find out about). Then you will have a lot to say, and you will say it clearly and confidently.

If the occasion is a work assignment or a letter of complaint, there won't be much choice in subject matter. But college assignments often give you some latitude, so choosing a subject may be more difficult. You often must select and narrow your subject from an assigned general topic. Try to work with material you know and understand.

Suppose a writing assignment for a business course stipulated that you describe a past or current job. Ask yourself

- What jobs have I done or do now?
- What do I know about these jobs? Which were most interesting and challenging, or repetitious and boring?
- Which jobs (or parts of one job) do I feel strongly about—that is, love, hate, get angry about?

Now explore your ideas. Choose one topic, and search for more detail.

- What tools or materials or skills do I use in my job?
- How do I perform each task?
- Which tasks are most interesting or boring?
- What kinds of people do I interact with at my job?
- What examples or little stories best illustrate these points?

Again, make notes of your answers, and refer to them later as you start to write.

Your Purpose

Ask yourself, *what is my purpose?* Purpose is more than just the occasion. It's the reason you are writing, the specific goal you want to accomplish with your audience. Are you trying to inform, persuade, or entertain readers—or maybe do all three?

- When you *inform*, you're explaining or describing an idea, a process, an event, a belief, a person, a place, or a thing. You're providing and analyzing facts, defining terms, and explaining causes. If you inform readers about your job, for example, you should mention aspects they don't know, describe routines they are unfamiliar with, or define job-related terms they haven't heard.
- When you *persuade*, you're trying to convince your readers to accept your viewpoint. You want readers to change their minds or behave differently, so you appeal to their reason or emotion or both. You might argue that your job at a carryout restaurant performs a useful role in feeding people who are too busy to cook or who simply want to eat out inexpensively.
- When you *entertain*, you're trying to make readers laugh, or be fascinated, surprised, or sometimes even angry. Of course, almost everything you write should be entertaining, as you always need to engage your audience. But when amusement is your primary goal, you need to focus, specifically, on the unusual and personal. For example, you could focus on funny moments or on cranky people you've encountered at your job.

EXERCISE 1	Analyzing Purpose

For each of the following opening sentences of a paragraph, label its main purpose: to inform, to persuade, *or* to entertain. *(There may be more than one possibility.)*

1. Jupiter is the largest planet in the solar system, and several of its sixteen moons are larger than the other planets. *to inform* _____

2. Few moments in the history of space flight were more dramatic than the night of July 16, 1969, when Neil Armstrong stepped onto the surface of the moon.

   _____

3. Cigar smoking may be fashionable, but it's just as unhealthy as cigarette smoking. _____

4. There are four uniform time zones in the continental United States, but prior to 1883, times varied by several minutes from city to city. _____

5. If milk is white, why is cheddar cheese yellow? _____

6. McGuire circled the bases as the crowd cheered wildly. _____

Your Audience

Ask yourself, *who is my audience?* The answer to that question will often determine a lot of the content and purpose of your writing. Suppose, for example, that you describe your part-time job at a carryout chicken restaurant, not for your business instructor, but for a feature article in the school newspaper. Your readers, other college students, already know such restaurants well, so you should focus on something they may not know: perhaps what happens behind the counter and in the kitchen. You can describe the steps in preparing the chicken: dipping it into those magical herbs and spices, popping it in the deep fryer, and laying it out on the trays. You can describe the crackpots and cranks who order you around as they order food. You can describe your coworkers who make the job harder—or actually fun. You can define the jargon you use on the job.

If, however, you write about the same topic in a memo to your boss, you would completely redirect the focus of your writing. Your boss already knows what happens behind the counter and in the kitchen, so you can discuss what he or she hasn't considered: your suggestions for improving working conditions for the employees, increasing efficiency and profits, or better satisfying the customers.

EXERCISE 2	Shaping Ideas for Audiences

For each topic provided, list two or three points you would include if you were writing persuasive letters to the various audiences specified.

1. The pros and cons of having two phone lines in the home
   a. parents of teenagers *Pros: children not tying up your phone, fewer arguments about their using the phone, no longer serving as the children's personal secretary for phone call messages. Cons: higher phone bills for you, lower grades for children*

who are always talking on the phone, and perhaps more arguments about talking on the phone.

b. teenagers _Pros: your parents not nagging you to get off the phone, making and_
receiving calls whenever you want. Cons: parents making you pay for the addi-
tional line.

2. The pros and cons of owning a car

   a. an adult who works some distance from home _____

   _____

   b. a high school student _____

   _____

3. The benefits of speaking more than one language

   a. a business major who wants to work in a foreign country _____

   _____

   b. a liberal arts major who doesn't want to work in a foreign country _____

   _____

4. The benefits of living in your city or town

   a. an unemployed person _____

   _____

   b. a person who wants to go to college _____

   _____

   c. a person with several children _____

   _____

| EXERCISE 3 | Analyzing a Paragraph |

Read the following passage, and then answer the questions.

People make language and the needs of people change over time, so the meanings
of words must change. A perfect example of this process is the word *awful*.
Consider it for a moment. What do its two syllables seem literally to mean? If you

guessed "full of awe," you are right. Originally, the word meant that something was impressive, powerful, even fear-inspiring. In these senses, the voice of God speaking to Moses through a burning bush was certainly awful, as was the eruption of Mount Vesuvius that destroyed Pompeii. But a poorly drawn painting or a tune sung off-key was not. However, sometime in the nineteenth century, the term came to mean not fear-inspiring, but unpleasant. A dictionary published in 1818 reported, "In New England, many people would call a disagreeable medicine *awful*." At about the same time, *awful* and a related form *awfully* began to show up as intensifiers—words such as *very* or *really* that add force or emphasis. In this new sense, people might say, "It was an *awfully* beautiful day." That is the meaning of the word today—if it has any meaning at all, for people now use *awful* and *awfully* so frequently that the words have lost their force. Why else would someone say, "That painting is *really* awful"—as if the word *awful* by itself doesn't say enough? *Awful* is now so far removed from its original heritage that people must express its former meaning through the words *awesome*. But even that word seems to be losing its force among teenagers, who use it to mean "interesting," "clever," or "admirable." Such is the nature of change in language.

1. What seems to be the occasion for this piece of writing? That is, would you expect to find it in a technical book, a business memo, or a magazine article? What evidence can you cite to support your answer?_____

_____

2. Who is the main audience for this piece? Does it seem addressed to English teachers or people with less knowledge about the history of words? Again, what evidence supports your answer? _____

_____

3. What is the primary goal of this paragraph: to inform, persuade, or entertain its audience? ___*to inform*___

_____

4. What point is the paragraph making? Why does it discuss the word *awful*?
b/c people doesn't use it right anymore

> ### Collaborative Activity 1
>
> **Reacting to Subject Choices**
>
> Share the topics you prepare in Exercise 4 with a group of four other classmates. Let them suggest which ones they find most promising.

EXERCISE 4	Choosing a Subject

List four or five topics relating to a job or jobs you do or have done. You could perhaps explain procedures, responsibilities, or difficulties in the work. You could relate amusing, frustrating, or frightening experiences. You could argue that the work is vital, or useful, or almost useless.

Then select one subject that seems most promising to develop.

STEP 2: PREWRITING

After considering the occasion, the subject, purpose, and audience, you'll already have ideas about what you want to say. You'll have thoughts about what you need to emphasize, what you need to explain, what you need to define. Now it's time to capture those ideas on paper.

Capturing your ideas is the second step of the composing process. Put down whatever you've thought of and whatever now enters your mind. Don't worry about spelling or punctuation or exact meanings, because you'll probably change your mind and your phrasing later anyway. This step, called **prewriting**, is a time to relax, to let the words flow, to see your ideas take shape. Enjoy yourself and be creative.

Brainstorming

One way to capture your thoughts is by **brainstorming**, or listing ideas as they come to you. Here's an example for the paragraph on the carryout restaurant:

> work behind the counter sometimes
>
> often prepare the food
>
> location: Washington Avenue and Main Street
>
> types of food: chicken, french fries, mashed potatoes and gravy, corn, rolls, coleslaw, potato salad
>
> hours: 4–9 three nights a week
>
> eat dinner at work–tired of the food
>
> my coworkers: Bill, LaVerne, and Tommie–funny people
>
> my boss: Mr. Williams, the warden in a prison
>
> cooking the chicken: unpacking it, washing it, adding the breading, putting it in the deep fryer, then putting it on the trays
>
> strange customers–Mrs. Bilge, she wants catsup, cheese, and gravy on her french fries, Mr. Stupor, the local drunk, he takes coffee with eight sugars, Mr. Blob, he orders 16 pieces of chicken with extra grease, Oscar the Grump, a charming guy
>
> packing an order: which pieces to include and how it's done

You can return to brainstorming at any time to generate more ideas. If you run into writer's block during the first draft, you can stop, do some brainstorming, and then start writing again.

Clustering

In **clustering**, you write your topic in a circle in the middle of the page, and then branch off from the circle, adding and circling related ideas as they occur to you. Here's how the diagram might begin:

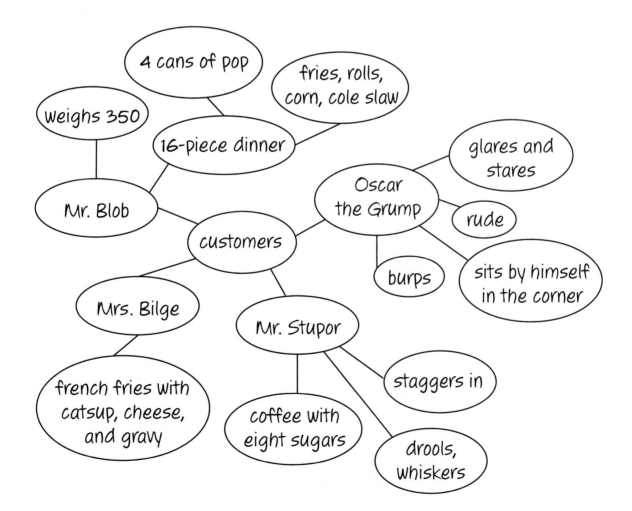

You can continue adding branches off of branches and filling up the page. At some point in the clustering process, however, you may discover (or stop to decide) that one or more main branches of the diagram is generating the most interesting details. Here, for example, is the part of the diagram with customers at the center:

This part of the diagram can form the basis of a new plan on a new page, centering on the word *customers,* so you have plenty of room to add branches.

Freewriting

Yet another way to get started is through **freewriting**. You simply write down your ideas about the subject without worrying about sentence structure, spelling, logic, and grammar. Write them as you would speak them. Use abbreviations and shortcuts so you can get your ideas down fast. Here is an example:

My part-time job. I'm a cook at a carry-out chicken place, on Washington and Main St. Don't like the hours—4 to 9, three nights a week. Travel is a pain—an hour each way on three buses. Hard to study later, I'm too tired. My job is to cook the chicken, fries, and onion rings. Sometimes work behind the counter. Funny people: Bill always telling the dumb jokes, which he thinks are hilarious, and LaVerne, who's always pretending to be offended. Tommie tries to act tough, but he's really a good guy. He has at least six tattoos, and has pierced his body in a lot of places, he talks tough, but he's really a good guy. Cooking chicken is really simple, just unpack the chicken from the crates, unwrap the plastic bags, and dump the whole mess in the sink. Then turn on the water and let drain. Take pieces and toss into big can of breading, turn on motor that shakes the can. Remove pieces and place in deep fryer. Eight minutes later, there it is, fast food at its finest. Customers are nice, but some weird. One lady, we call her Mrs. Bilge, because of the garbage she eats—always orders french fries with cheese and catsup. That's not so bad, but she also wants gravy on them, too. Yuk. The local drunk, Mr. Stupor, with his lovely drool and four-day-old whiskers, usually comes in about 8 P.M. to get some coffee—with eight sugars in it! Double yuk. And the all-time eating champ, Mr. Blob. Must weight 350. Every night, he orders a 16-piece dinner with extra grease and three or four cans of pop. Talk about cholesterol! Then there's Oscar the Grump, who's rude to everyone. Glares at everyone. Burps. Hate my boss, Mr. Williams, who should be a warden in a prison. Have only a half hour for dinner, but am tired of chicken, chicken, chicken.

Freewriting is disorganized, but that doesn't matter. It allows you to put ideas into words that you can look at later, develop, change, or delete.

EXERCISE 5	Prewriting a Paper

Return to the topic you chose in Exercise 4. Think carefully about your purpose: Will you inform, persuade, or entertain? Then do a brainstorming list, a clustering diagram, and a freewriting page so that you can sample each of these techniques. See which ones you find most useful.

A WRITER SPEAKS

Like most first-year college students, I lacked experience in writing and soon discovered I needed more time to revise than I thought. (That's still true.) I tried to finish all my other homework before starting to write, which usually meant I was tackling my toughest assignment late in the evening. Nonetheless, I wrote very slowly, spending a lot of time and effort trying to make my first drafts perfect. Writing exhausted me. The next night, when I read over my first draft, I found all sorts of things to change, add, or remove. Worse, if I didn't revise and edit my paper thoroughly—well, you know what happened.

Only later did I learn to do first drafts quickly, pushing my pen across the page without stopping to worry about the exact phrasing or order of ideas. I discovered—to my great delight—that the sentences would flow once I got going. I'd write on yellow legal pads, filling up page after page in an hour. When an idea occurred to me that I should have said earlier, I'd flip the page, jot it down, and then note in the margin where to insert it later. I began to write almost as if I were speaking. Now, writing exhilarated me. Much of the language of my first drafts never made it into the final version, but that was okay. I'd captured my ideas on yellow pages, and they were there for me to reconsider and change.

These practices have served me well through the years, even now as I compose on the computer. By the way, these three paragraphs went through three drafts, two sets of responses from an editor, and then some final revisions.

Alan Meyers, Professor of English, Harry S Truman College, and author of nine textbooks

STEP 3: ORGANIZING YOUR IDEAS

After capturing your ideas in words on paper, you can now select from and organize them. Consider what to include and what to leave out. In the limited space of a paragraph, essay, or memo, you can't say everything. So you must choose the most important, most relevant, and most interesting information. You must decide what to say first, second, third, and tenth. These decisions aren't final, but they do give you a point from which to start.

- Put a checkmark next to the best ideas in your brainstorming list. Then rewrite the list, grouping these ideas into some logical arrangement. Add more ideas as they occur to you. For example, the brainstorming list on the carryout restaurant contains too much information for a single paragraph or essay. You might therefore narrow its focus to one main idea—either how the chicken is made or a profile of the workers and customers. Then brainstorm additional details that develop that point.
- Select the part of the clustering diagram that seems most promising, and then do a second clustering diagram that expands on that part.

- Underline the parts of your freewriting that look most promising. Base a second or even a third freewriting on those parts. Focus more narrowly on your subject, and add more details.

Selecting

Once you've narrowed your focus and generated more ideas, you can choose the ones that fit the occasion, your purpose, and audience. For example, you can write an entertaining paper about the oddballs at the carryout restaurant, aimed primarily at people your age who also have part-time jobs—and to make the point that this job really isn't so bad. In this case, you select only the most humorous information about your coworkers (Bill, Laverne, and Tommie) and the customers (Mrs. Bilge, Mr. Stupor, Mr. Blob, and Oscar the Grump). You omit unimportant details or ones that drift off the point, such as how you prepare the chicken or how you travel to work. And you generate more details to develop the humor. On reflection, you decide that Oscar the Grump isn't funny, and you already have three customers to focus on, so you drop him.

Outlining

Now that you've focused your topic on people you meet at the carryout restaurant, you can make a rough outline, with examples and details in categories:

I. Setting
  A. Washington Avenue and Main Street
  B. Three nights a week from 4 to 9 P.M.
II. My boss: Mr. Williams, a warden of a prison
III. My coworkers
  A. Bill, the jokester, tells dumb jokes
  B. LaVerne, always pretending to be offended
  C. Tommie, tough and cool, but really a good guy
IV. Strange customers, especially the regulars
  A. Mrs. Bilge, who wants catsup, cheese, and gravy on her french fries
  B. Mr. Stupor, the local drunk, who takes coffee with eight sugars
  C. Mr. Blob, who orders a huge dinner with all the trimmings for himself every day

---

Other arrangements are possible: a time sequence, perhaps with each customer arriving on a typical night, or a comparison of the best and worst customers. There are many ways to organize paragraphs and essays, as later chapters in this book will explain.

EXERCISE 6	Selecting and Outlining

Return to the materials you generated in Exercise 5, and consider your purpose and audience. What point should you make, and to whom? Then select the relevant ideas by check-

ing, circling, or highlighting them. Arrange the ideas in an informal outline. If some parts of the outline need development, brainstorm, cluster, or freewrite more details for these parts.

STEP 4: WRITING THE FIRST DRAFT

TIPS

For Drafting by Hand

1. Write as fast as you can.

2. Leave wide margins and write on every other line so you have room for changes.

3. Use only one side of the paper so you can cut and paste changes.

4. Tape or staple additions where you want them to go.

5. If you have trouble expressing a thought, say it aloud before writing it. And expect to revise it later.

6. Circle or underline words you think you have misspelled or might change later.

You've done enough prewriting, selecting, and arranging your ideas to start writing a first draft. If you can think of a strong opening sentence, that's wonderful. But you really needn't worry. You can return to the opening at any point—in your second, third, or even your final draft. Never get stuck trying to fashion a "perfect" first draft; you will always rewrite and revise it later—adding to it, subtracting from it, changing some words and whole sentences. Here is an example of a first attempt based on the prewriting you saw earlier:

> I'm a part-time cook, and I work from 4 to 9 P.M. three days a week. My job is at a carryout chicken place on Washington and Main. My job is to cook the chicken, fries, and onion rings. I meet more interesting characters than the Colonel. I don't particularly like my boss, Mr. Williams, he should be a warden in a prison. But my coworkers are a riot. Bill goes to a local comunity college and considers himself another Eddie Murphy, he always has some dumb jokes to tell. LaVerne thinks that she's very sophisticated, so she always gets offended by Bill. Tommie has six tattoos, pierces in various body parts, and talks tough, but he's really a good guy. Some of our regular customers are a bit weird. One lady, we call her Mrs. Bilge, because of the garbage she eats, always orders french fries with cheese and catsup. That's not so bad, but she also wants gravy on them, too. The local drunk, Mr. Stupor, with his lovely drool and four-day-old whiskers, usually comes in about 8 p.m. to get some coffee-with eight sugars in it! And our all-time eating champ is the incredible Mr. Blob, who must weight 350. Every night, he orders a 16-piece dinner-with extra grease-and three or four cans of pop. Talk about cholesterol, fat, and sugar! I guess it's actually a good place to work, in fact, it's better than the zoo.

EXERCISE 7 | *Doing a First Draft*

Write a first draft based on your selecting and outlining in Exercise 6. If you write by hand, write on one side of the page only, leave wide margins, and skip every other line so that you have room for additional changes. If you use a computer, double space and leave wide margins as well. Then print out a copy of the paper for you to read.

STEP 5: REVISING THE DRAFT

After preparing your first draft, put it aside for a few hours or even a day. Allow yourself time before returning to it later so you can think about it with a clear

**For Drafting and Revising
on the Computer**

1. Write fast, and expect
   to revise later.

2. Save your work every
   five or ten minutes.

3. Use insert or cut-and-
   paste commands to add
   or move things around.

4. Print out a double-
   spaced copy for revi-
   sions; then revise in
   pencil.

head and see it with fresh eyes. You'll find sets of Revision Guidelines in this chapter (page 21) and in many other chapters, which help you to evaluate and reshape your earlier drafts.

Reviewing

Now review the first draft. Does the organization make sense? Is the wording clear? Are there enough—or too many—details? You'll probably find some things to delete, as well as some things to add. Don't be satisfied with making only minor changes. Substitute words, rephrase sentences, and rearrange sections. Write notes and new sentences in the margins and above the lines. Draft new material on separate pages so you can tape it in place on the original draft— or insert the material by computer. The amended draft may become so messy that you need to make a clean copy before going any further.

   Here, for example, is a bit of the first draft on the carryout restaurant after changes have been made:

For Revising

Print out a double-spaced or even triple-spaced copy of your first draft. Add your new ideas, details, and wording in the margins or between the lines. Then enter all these changes into the computer file and print out a copy once again.

> woman
>
> One ^lady (We call her Mrs. Bilge because of the garbage she eats) always
>   -and gravy!
> orders french fries with cheese and catsup^. ~~That's not so bad, but she~~
> ~~also wants gravy on them, too.~~ The local drunk, Mr. Stupor, ~~with his lovely~~
>   staggers
> ~~drool and four-day-old whiskers,~~ usually ^comes in about 8 P.M. to get some
> coffee—with eight sugars in it! And the all-time eating champ is the
>   weigh   pounds   16-piece dinner with fries,
> incredible Mr. Blob, who must ^~~weight~~ 350^. Every night, he orders a ^huge
>   tosses it down with
> ~~dinner with~~ slaw, and corn, and ^3 or 4 cans of pop. Talk about
> cholesterol, fat, and sugar!

Reading Aloud

Now read your work aloud—and listen carefully. You'll probably hear mistakes to correct and think of improvements to make. Read your work a second time— to another person if possible—and revise until you're satisfied that it's interesting and clear. Don't ask yourself, "Can this be understood?" Ask instead, "Can this be *mis*understood?" When the audience reads your finished product, you won't be around to explain, "Well, what I meant was. . . ." The words on the page must say what you mean.

Predicting

Readers aren't passive, like mere sponges absorbing information. They actively attempt to find meaning for themselves. They *predict* what will follow from your opening sentences and then verify or adjust their predictions as they read on. You can also benefit from predicting as you write and revise. Here is how to do it:

- Read your first sentence or two. Listen for keys words or phrases.
- Stop and consider those key words or phrases. What expectations do they create? Will those words or phrases be explained or defended? Will they be discussed in the same order they were introduced?
- Determine if the rest of the paragraph satisfies those expectations.
- Make notes on what should be added, removed, or shifted to satisfy those expectations.

Predicting is a valuable tool that should become a regular part of your revision practices.

Peer Review

Your writing is intended for other people to read, so a natural resource for you to tap as you revise is other people. Professionals—including professional writers—often ask for or expect comments on their drafts from colleagues, editors, friends, or even family members. In many offices, such collaborative writing and responding are routine.

What are the advantages of this collaboration? Other people don't live inside your head. They can't read your mind; they can only read your words. They can therefore raise questions, offer suggestions, notice problems you haven't considered, or resolve problems that have you stumped. And if, like many writers, you tend to read what you *think* you've written on drafts instead what's actually on the page, another pair of eyes can detect errors and omissions you hadn't seen.

Many colleges and universities provide writing centers and peer tutors for these kinds of help. But, if your teacher wishes, your classmates can be another resource. As they respond to the Revision Guidelines, they can offer you realistic and useful feedback. Don't expect two or three readers to agree on everything, though. No two readers will respond in precisely the same way. Their different backgrounds, expectations, vocabularies, and even reading abilities influence their responses. Nonetheless, if two or three people say that something you've said is unclear, illogical, or brilliantly written, then they probably have a point. If readers don't agree, then you must evaluate their responses and decide which, if any, make sense.

TIPS

For Peer Revision
Make three copies of your draft: two for classmates and one for your instructor. Keep the original for yourself. Staple a blank page to the right-hand side of each copy.

My draft is on this side

Have your classmates read the first two sentences, then predict, and write their predictions on the blank sheet. Next your classmates can read and comment on the rest of the draft, noting if their predictions were fulfilled and making suggestions for improvement. They can also write their responses to the draft according to the Revision Guidelines that follow here and in other chapters.

REVISION GUIDELINES | The Composing Process

1. What was the goal of this paper? Was the goal accomplished? If not, suggest ways to accomplish the goal.
2. What is the main point of the paper? Is the point clear? If not, suggest places where it could be clarified.
3. Who is the audience for the paper? Does the paper speak to the audience's knowledge and interests? If not, suggest ways it could do so.
4. Have any important ideas been omitted? If so, what are they, and where should they be included?
5. What other weaknesses does the paper have? Suggest ways of correcting these weaknesses.
6. List three strengths of the paper.

Producing the Cleaned-Up Version

Now pull all the revisions together in a second draft. Incorporate all the improvements and changes. Even as you do so, you'll discover more improvements to make. That's not a sign of indecisiveness. It's evidence that you've engaged in a true composing process and are letting the process work for you. Keep revising and copying over until you're satisfied with—or even proud of—the writing you've produced.

EXERCISE 8	Revising Your Paper

Now return to the draft you composed in Exercise 7. On the basis of your own analysis and the suggestions of your classmates, make changes to the original version (do cutting and pasting), and continue to make changes. As you reword sentences or sections of the paper, say or read them aloud so you can hear what sounds graceful and clear. If possible, read the amended draft to another person for additional predictions and comments.

STEP 6: PRODUCING THE FINAL COPY

TIPS

For Being Smarter Than Your Computer

1. Use the spelling and grammar checkers, but don't rely on them exclusively. They won't identify every mistake or distinguish between soundalike words such as *then/than*.

2. Use the computer's thesaurus (a dictionary of *synonyms*, or words that mean the same, such as "happy" and "joyful") to expand and vary your word choice. But select only words you know. Don't talk about "arachnids" at a picnic when you only mean "spiders."

3. It's easy to include extra words or to omit words when you revise on the computer. So print out a copy of your final draft and proofread it carefully.

Once you're satisfied with the content and form of your writing, you can begin producing the final copy. Like the other steps in composing, this one, too, involves several stages. Prepare your final copy according to the guidelines of your instructor, or the guidelines in the Tips box on page 23. Then take a good look at the fine points you may have ignored while capturing your ideas on paper and shaping them to fit your occasion, purpose, and audience.

Editing

You want people to judge your ideas, not your mistakes, so you must edit your work. **Editing** requires that you examine your writing carefully and look for errors. Too much attention to each sentence during early stages of the composing process can freeze your creativity. In the heat of writing and revising, you shouldn't have to stop and analyze every word, sentence, or comma. As you edit, however, you can examine your work coldly and make changes. Read what you actually said, not what you *think* you said.

Go over your paper slowly, checking for misspelled words, words omitted or repeated, errors in grammar, missing word endings, incomplete sentences, and incorrect punctuation. If you're uncertain about sentence structure, grammar, or punctuation, consult the chapters in Unit IV. Check your work more than once, and each time you make editorial corrections, copy the paper over or print it out again. The final copy should be neat and should represent your best work.

Proofreading

Students (and even some professional writers) tend to overlook or underestimate the last step in the composing process. **Proofreading** means carefully examining the next-to-last copy for errors and omissions. Read through the paper slowly. Place a ruler under each line to focus your eyes. Read the paper aloud. Read it again. Make a completely neat and legible copy—and then proofread that copy.

Here is the final typed copy of the paper on the carryout restaurant:

TIPS

For Preparing Final Copy

1. Use good quality 8½-by-11-inch paper: lined paper for handwritten work, unlined paper for typewritten or computer-printed work.

2. Include your name, the date, and assignment title according to the format your instructor requires.

3. Write or print clearly in black or blue ink—not in pencil.

4. Leave wide margins on both sides—at least an inch, and preferably 1½ inches.

5. Double space on the computer; skip every other line for handwritten work.

6. Number every page at the top or bottom as your instructor specifies.

7. Fasten the pages together with a paper clip or staple, whichever your instructor prefers.

Collaborative Activity 2

Peer Editing and Proofreading

If your instructor wishes, exchange papers with a classmate and check each other's work carefully. Consult with even another classmate when you aren't sure of your classmate's corrections. Ask for help—and give it—in both editing and proofreading. For example, have one classmate edit your paper, then a different student proofread it.

Your Name
Your Class
Your Instructor's Name
The Assignment
The Date

Tales from the Chicken Coop

As a part-time cook at a carryout chicken place, I meet much more interesting characters than the Colonel.

Although my boss, Mr. Williams, has the personality and charm of a prison warden, my coworkers make my three-night-a-week sentence tolerable. Bill, who goes to a local community college and considers himself another Eddie Murphy (Rodney Dangerfield is more like it), tells at least ten dumb jokes every night. LaVerne, who considers herself sophisticated, always pretends to be offended. She yells, "Bill, that's disgusting," as she turns her back and laughs. Tommie, who has six tattoos, pierces in various body parts, and the wardrobe of a biker, is really a good guy.

Some of our weird regular customers also keep us amused. One woman (we call her Mrs. Bilge because of the garbage she eats) always orders french fries with cheese and catsup—and gravy! The local drunk, Mr. Stupor, staggers in about 8 P.M. to get some coffee—with eight sugars—which drips on his four-day-old whiskers as he drinks. Finally, there's the all-time eating champ, the incredible Mr. Blob, who must weigh 350 pounds. Every night, he orders a sixteen-piece chicken dinner with fries, rolls, slaw, and corn—and then tosses it all down with three or four cans of pop. Talk about cholesterol, fat, and sugar!

Although I'm usually exhausted when I get home, I admit I really like my job. My coworkers and some customers make it fun. It's a short stay in a minimum-security prison.

Notice that this final copy is livelier than the original. It sticks to the point. Its sentences are clear. Its examples are developed with interesting details. It has turned one of its original ideas, that work is like prison, into a unifying theme.

You can achieve similar results by working your way through the steps in the composing process described in this chapter, which forms the core of the book. Refer to this chapter every time you write, until the process becomes a habit—even an instinct. You, too, can compose with confidence.

EXERCISE 9	Editing and Proofreading Your Work

Examine your revised paper from Exercise 8 carefully. Correct mistakes in spelling, grammar, and punctuation. Make a copy of the paper, and proofread it several times. Make a final clean copy, and proofread it, too.

IN SUMMARY   The Composing Process

1. Consider the occasion for your writing, your subject, your purpose, and your audience.
2. Discover your ideas by putting them into words through brainstorming, clustering, or freewriting.
3. Decide what to include in your writing and how to organize those details.
4. Compose a first draft (and don't worry about making it perfect).
5. Take a break and then revise the first draft several times, perhaps after getting the reactions of other people. When you're reasonably satisfied with your work, produce a clean copy.
6. Edit this copy, and make another if you find errors. Check your corrections and proofread the copy again, until your final copy is ready for your instructor or your intended audience.

3 Composing a Powerful Paragraph

Now that you've seen the steps in the composing process, put them to work. This chapter will show you how to compose a powerful paragraph. The process also applies to essays, but we'll start with paragraphs—the building blocks of essays. In this chapter you'll practice

- choosing the topic
- drafting the topic sentence
- developing the paragraph
- drafting the conclusion
- revising the paragraph for unity

WHAT IS A PARAGRAPH?

Paragraphs are the building blocks of all forms of writing—from essays, exams, and memos, on up to novels and textbooks. Learning to compose effective paragraphs is therefore an important first step in mastering all of these forms. **Paragraphs** develop the main idea of a longer work by breaking it down into smaller, easily understood parts. The first part leads logically to the second part, the second part to the third part, and so forth. These smaller divisions help readers understand complex ideas—and help writers express them.

In fact, you might think of the paragraph as an essay in miniature. While an **essay** is a group of paragraphs that discuss one large idea, a *paragraph* is a group of sentences that discuss a smaller idea. And, like an essay, the paragraph generally contains an introduction, a body, and a conclusion:

1. The **introduction** attracts the interest of the readers, and it often states the paragraph's main point in a **topic sentence**.

UNIT 1

Chapter 3

Composing with Confidence

©2003

GO ELECTRONIC!

Use the following electronic supplements for additional practice with your writing:

- For chapter-by-chapter summaries and exercises, visit the Composing with Confidence Companion Website at: http://www.ablongman.com/meyers.
- For work with the writing process, visit The Longman Writer's Warehouse at http://longmanwriterswarehouse.com (password needed).
- For additional practice in grammar, use The Writer's ToolKit Plus CD-ROM

2. The **body** supports the main point with specific details, explanations, and examples in five to perhaps ten sentences.

3. The **conclusion** summarizes or ties together the ideas of the paragraph as it brings it to a graceful end.

Thus, the form or pattern of the paragraph shapes its ideas so your readers can follow them easily. Here's the pattern for a paragraph, presented as a blueprint:

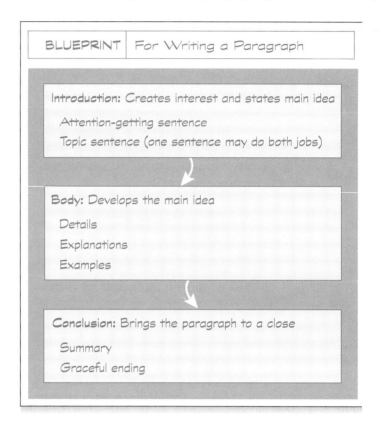

BLUEPRINT | For Writing a Paragraph

Introduction: Creates interest and states main idea

Attention-getting sentence

Topic sentence (one sentence may do both jobs)

Body: Develops the main idea

Details

Explanations

Examples

Conclusion: Brings the paragraph to a close

Summary

Graceful ending

All paragraphs share several other traits. First, a paragraph, such as the one you're now reading, normally begins with the first line indented about a half inch (or about five spaces on a typewriter). Second, each sentence follows the previous one on *the same line*, not on a new line. Third, the paragraph has **unity**. That means each sentence is related to and develops the topic idea or point. Fourth, the paragraph has **coherence**. That means each idea leads logically into the next, often with the help of transitional expressions (such as *first, second, third,* and *fourth* in this paragraph). We'll discuss transitions in Chapter 6.

The Topic

Although the final draft of a paragraph has a particular pattern or form, the process of shaping it is less tidy. Sometimes, you start with a clear plan in mind and then follow it closely; other times, your ideas become clear only as you write and revise.

In any case, as you saw in Chapter 2, the first step in composing is to explore ideas and choose a topic. For a single paragraph, that topic must be limited, or you'll be trying to say too much in too short a space. Suppose, for example, you want to describe a memorable experience in your life as a way of introducing yourself to your classmates. You could consider any number of important moments—a serious illness, a special trip, someone's death, your marriage, the birth of a child—each of which could be the subject of a long essay or even a book. Therefore, after choosing one topic—perhaps a special trip—you'll need to narrow it to a more manageable size. Begin by listing a few possibilities:

> my first airplane flight
> the moment when my grandparents met me at the plane
> dinner the first night
> the car ride through farm country
> staying with my grandparents

Then select one of these narrower topics—for example, your first airplane flight. Consider your attitude toward the subject. Were you nervous? Excited? Frightened? Your attitude will help you determine your purpose (in this case, probably to entertain, although probably not to amuse). You can then narrow the topic even further:

> Overcoming my fear of flying

Now you can brainstorm, cluster, or freewrite your ideas on the topic. How did you feel as you boarded the plane? How did you feel at takeoff? How did you react as you saw the buildings, farms, and mountains below? How did you feel when you landed? If your ideas about the topic aren't entirely clear at this point, don't worry. They'll become more focused as you work, and you can reconsider them later as you revise.

EXERCISE 1 | **Limiting Topics**

Suppose in a social science course you were asked to compose a short description of a contemporary problem that would provoke a lively debate. Limit each of the following broad topics so you could develop it in a single paragraph.

Collaborative Activity 1

Discussing Your Topics

In your collaborative group, list all the topics each member produced in Exercise 1. Briefly discuss each topic and choose the ones that would be best suited to the limited space of one paragraph. Which topics need to be narrowed further? How would you limit them? Report your findings to the entire class.

1. Problems created by taxes: *the unfairness of the sales tax for poor people*
   _____

2. Problems created by television: _____
   _____

3. Problems for college students: _____
   _____

4. Problems in modern family life: _____
   _____

5. Problems created by illegal drugs: _____
   _____

6. Problems created by the Internet: _____
   _____

THE TOPIC SENTENCE

A Word About Words

Many words in English come directly or indirectly from Latin. Most of these entered English during the Renaissance (c1480–1600 in England), when educated people wanted to study Latin and Greek.

Your topic sentence should guide the reader, who will be actively attempting to understand your ideas. Readers predict what will come based on what they have already seen. For example, suppose you read this sentence at the beginning of a paragraph:

Going to the beach on a Sunday afternoon is hardly a peaceful experience.

What would you expect the rest of the paragraph to say? _____

_____

_____

A logical answer might be, "an explanation of why the experience isn't peaceful." And the rest of the paragraph does explain precisely that:

It is everybody's day off, and the place is crowded, noisy, and busy. First, you have to maneuver through the mass of sand-covered blankets and sticky bodies to find a few square inches to spread out your blanket and set up your equipment. Second, you have to contend with the dueling boom boxes. Every blanket sports a radio or tape machine playing a different song, loudly enough to drown out the sounds from the other boom boxes, of course, but also loudly enough to make you want to drown their owners. Third, you have to put up with the thousands of preschoolers freed by their parents to terrorize everyone in the vicinity. They trample sand all over your blanket, spill water from their buckets on your head, and fight each other for possession of every toy on the beach. Fourth, you have to endure the macho morons who kick sand in your eyes as they dive for rubber footballs or Frisbees that land on your blanket. The whole experience is enough to make you want to pack up your boom box and Frisbee and take your own preschoolers somewhere else.

Each paragraph often contains one key sentence—usually, but not always, at or near the beginning of the paragraph—that presents the main point and suggests how the remaining sentences will relate to that point. This is called the **topic sentence**.

EXERCISE 2	Identifying Topic Sentences

Underline the topic sentences in the following paragraphs. Be careful: Not every topic sentence comes at the beginning. The topic sentence of the first paragraph has been underlined for you as an example.

The Counting Horse

Paragraph A. The talk of the town in 1904 in Berlin, Germany, was a mathematical genius—Clever Hans, the horse who could count. Not only could he count from one to a hundred, but he could also solve arithmetic problems, tap to identify letters of the alphabet, answer yes or no questions by nodding, and locate nearby objects. When tapping out an answer, Clever Hans used his right foot. When finished, the horse switched to his left foot for a single tap.

Paragraph B. Everyone wondered whether the horse was truly intelligent, capable of independent thinking, or whether Clever Hans was a clever hoax. The man who owned Clever Hans was Wilhelm von Osten, a German mathematics teacher. He welcomed investigations of the horse's abilities and never charged admission to the horse's theatrical demonstrations. It all seemed so believable that Clever Hans began to get an enormous amount of publicity, and his picture appeared on postcards and liquor labels.

Paragraph C. Two attempts were made to find out how the horse could count. The first of these was conducted by a special commission of respected Germans, including some scientists. Von Osten, who was sixty-five at the time, gladly cooperated with the members of the commission. Its final report stated that there was no evidence of trickery or fraud, but the commission had no idea how smart the horse was or how he was able to count. A second investigation was conducted by Oskar Pfungst of the Psychological Institute at the University of Berlin. He believed that Clever Hans was trained, on purpose or accidentally, to respond to body cues, intentional or unintentional. He devised a series of experiments to prove his theory, and he watched Von Osten as much as he watched the horse. In addition, more than forty other persons, including Pfungst, worked with the horse during the experiments.

Paragraph D. Pfungst noticed that the behavior of Clever Hans followed a consistent pattern. When the questioner knew the answer to a problem, Clever Hans was almost always correct. When the questioner didn't know the answer, the horse was usually wrong. If Clever Hans could actually see the questioner, he was usually correct. If the horse couldn't see the questioner, he was usually wrong. Pfungst also noted that when Clever Hans was wrong, he always overtapped and never undertapped.

Paragraph E. Pfungst believed that when the questioner gave a body cue, Clever Hans would begin to tap. The body cue—such as leaning forward to observe the horse's hoof—was the signal for the horse to start tapping. When the horse made the final tap of the correct answer, the questioner unintentionally straightened up—the unconscious signal for the horse to stop tapping. This second cue was the reason the horse always overtapped when he made an error. In short, according to Pfungst, the animal was responding to people, not actually counting on its own.

Paragraph F. Pfungst argued, but never proved, that Hans wasn't able to solve math problems independently. The horse was able to learn from the body language of one person and transfer that lesson to reading the body language of another person. Pfungst never claimed that any kind of fraud was taking place. The cues were "unconscious," and Pfungst was never able to explain how a variety of those unconscious cues, given by dozens of different people, could produce the same answers from Clever Hans. In addition, Pfungst never adequately tested his leaning forward and leaning back theory.

Paragraph G. When Pfungst's conclusions were published in 1907, von Osten was devastated. He and Clever Hans went into seclusion. The owner became so upset that he blamed his misfortunes more on the horse than on Pfungst, wishing that Hans would spend the rest of his life pulling hearses.

Paragraph H. After von Osten died in 1909, the reputation of Clever Hans declined even further. He was given to a horse trainer named Karl Krall, who was also experimenting with the idea that horses were capable of independent thinking. Krall hoped that Clever Hans would be able to teach what he knew to Krall's other horses, but when that idea failed, the public lost interest in Clever Hans. Unfortunately also lost in the hoax controversy was the fact that Clever Hans was an extraordinary animal with an amazing ability to learn.

Making a Point

The *topic* of a paragraph is different from its *topic sentence*. The topic is what the paragraph is about, but the topic sentence *makes a point* about the topic. A topic sentence, and the paragraph that develops it, should answer the question, "So what?" Notice that the following example doesn't answer that question:

> I flew for the first time when I visited my grandparents.

This sentence only announces the subject of the paragraph. It doesn't state or even suggest the writer's viewpoint toward the subject: that flying was horrifying, exciting, nauseating, or fun. The sentence simply doesn't inform readers of what the writer thinks about (or what they should think about) her experience. Here's the revised topic sentence, which makes a point at the end:

> My first airplane flight was both terrifying and exciting.

Now readers can predict what they'll encounter in the rest of the paragraph: details about the writer's feelings and how they changed throughout the experience.

Expressing an Attitude or Opinion

Another way to view the topic sentence is to think of its point as an *attitude* toward the topic. The words *terrifying* and *exciting* in the previous example express an attitude. Compare the following sentences:

No attitude:	Wolfgang Amadeus Mozart was a composer.
Attitude:	Wolfgang Amadeus Mozart was an amazing composer.
No attitude:	I'm taking business administration courses.
Attitude:	I'm enjoying my business administration courses.

Many topic sentences follow this pattern: subject + stated or implied attitude or opinion. Here are examples:

Subject	Attitude
Ms. Kim is	quite a *competent* attorney.
Returning to school has been	*wonderful*, but also *a bit frightening*.
Juan Gonzalez displays	*unusual* musical talent.

Getting Started

A strong topic sentence generally helps you write a strong paragraph because it lays out what you intend to say. In fact, some topic sentences act as organizers, providing the reader with an overview, or preview, of the specifics the paragraph will develop:

Wolfgang Amadeus Mozart was an amazing composer for three reasons.

The reader now knows that the paragraph will identify and explain three reasons. Some topic sentences are even more specific:

Wolfgang Amadeus Mozart was an amazing composer because he completed his first symphony when he was four, performed before kings when he was six, and wrote over 600 works before dying at the age of thirty-four.

But few writers get the topic sentence perfect on their first try. You'll probably revise the topic sentence later on, so don't worry about fashioning a flawless sentence now. The point of the paragraph (and, therefore, the topic sentence) usually emerges only during the process of composing—after you've examined your materials, put your ideas on paper, and revised them several times. While the finished product should be clear, the composing process itself is often far less tidy. At least three different options are available to you for getting started:

1. If you already know what you want to say, you can draft a preliminary topic sentence first and then add the supporting sentences.

2. If you need to discover your ideas, start with brainstorming, clustering, or freewriting. You can draft a preliminary topic sentence next and then organize the supporting ideas in the first draft of the paragraph.

3. If you want to draft and revise the entire paragraph without first writing the topic sentence, you can add the topic sentence (and revise it) later when you feel sure of your point and comfortable with the supporting ideas.

Of course, you needn't use the same method each time; most writers do what works best at the moment.

 TIPS

For Testing Topic Sentences

Test your topic sentence by disagreeing with it. A strong one expresses an attitude or opinion, so you should be able to challenge it. But a weak one merely announces the subject, so it won't make a point to argue against.

Strong: Ms. Kim is quite a competent attorney. (Well, perhaps you think so.)

Weak: Ms. Kim is an attorney. (Who can argue with that?)

EXERCISE 3	Revising Poor Topic Sentences

Each of these topic sentences fails to make a point, express an attitude, or allow you to predict what follows. Rewrite each one so that its point or attitude is clear.

1. This paragraph will discuss the Great California Gold Rush. *The Great California Gold Rush was a period of greed and near insanity.*

2. There are a lot of commercials on television. _____

3. The topic that I want to discuss is my job at a bank. _____

4. An issue that people argue over is capital punishment. _____

5. I have three cats. _____

6. Many people work part-time while attending college. _____

Collaborative Activity 2

Discussing Topic Sentences

Compare your revisions of the topic sentences from Exercise 3 in your collaborative group. List the most interesting revisions and report your findings to the whole class.

A WRITER SPEAKS

The first sentence of an essay can be the most horrifically hard one to write. A bad first sentence is like bad hair atop an otherwise good-looking head: it can wreck the first impression.

Try this: In your brainstorming stage, freewrite as many complete sentences as you can—random observations, stray thoughts, nutty opinions, brutally honest comments. Don't try to connect them; just let your mind wander. Then look over what you've written. Is there any one sentence that's an attention-grabber? Try putting that sentence first, no matter how improbable or out of place it looks.

Chances are the sentence will do more than seize the reader's interest; it will also set the tone—of anger or irony, of authority or scholarly inquiry, of sweet reasonableness or sheer silliness—that will carry you through the writing of the essay.

Robert Hughes, professor of English at Harry S Truman College and author of books and numerous feature articles

---

EXERCISE 4	Composing the Topic Sentence for Another Paragraph

Assume your instructor in an art history course has asked you to compose a short analysis of what the famous artist Edward Hopper was trying to "say" in the painting on page 33. Use your first reaction to the painting as a preliminary topic sentence expressing an attitude or point ("The café is . . ." or "The people in the café look . . ."). Then start brainstorming, freewriting, or clustering ideas to support the reaction.

Edward Hopper, *Nighthawks,* 1942. Oil on canvas, 84.1 x 152.4 cm. Friends of American Art Collection, 1942.51. Photograph © 2002, The Art Institute of Chicago, All Rights Reserved.

THE BODY

The body of the paragraph supports the point of the topic sentence with a series of details, explanations, or examples. Look for ways to group them. Does your preliminary topic sentence include *reasons, ways, methods,* or some similar categorizing word? If not, then supply three or four reasons, ways, or methods. Could the point of the topic sentence be made clearer or more interesting through examples? Then provide those examples. Do any ideas need explaining? Then explain them.

Before you draft the body, organize your materials in some appropriate way. You might sketch out a quick outline. Here, for example, is the beginning of an informal outline of a paragraph on the airplane flight. Notice it lists three general stages, along with several supporting details for each:

I. Boarding the plane
   Hugging my parents and then turning to wave to them
   Walking down the tunnel into the plane
   Finding my seat and, with trembling hands, putting
      my bag under the seat in front of me
II. Taking off
   Waiting on the runway and gripping the armrests
   Holding my breath as I felt the wheels leave the ground
   Looking down at the airport, the buildings, and the land as it
      quickly grew smaller
   Thinking—or did I say it?—wow

Continued

> III. Flying
>   Encountering turbulence-nervousness
>   Eating airline food
>   Wow! Peanuts!
>   Wow! A two-ounce rubber chicken breast!

Use such an outline only as a guide. Depart from it if a better organization or better details occur to you as you write. Composing is a process of self-discovery. Be open to new directions as you proceed. But remember, you're writing a first draft—which you'll revise later.

THE CONCLUSION

A paragraph's closing sentence often summarizes your main point. Sometimes you can return to the idea of the topic sentence, but don't merely repeat it in the same words. Change the language; make the ending graceful. And don't assume that every conclusion must summarize. You can also end with a punch—a quote, a joke, a final example, or a surprise:

> As I saw my grandparents at the arrival gate, I realized that flying wasn't so bad-as long as I don't have to eat airplane food.

In any case, expect to revise the conclusion later.

EXERCISE 5	Drafting Your Paragraph

Collaborative Activity 3

Exploring Topics

List five possible topics for a paragraph discussed in Exercise 5. Your collaborative group can then help you select the most promising topic. Then take five minutes to brainstorm, cluster, or freewrite ideas about the experience and to draft a preliminary topic sentence.

Select a topic for a paragraph about yourself—some amusing, frightening, exciting, or memorable event. You may not have climbed Mt. Everest or won the state ice cream eating contest, but you've probably taken a trip, seen or been involved in an accident, gone on a date, gotten married, or had a child. Take five minutes to brainstorm, cluster, or freewrite ideas about the experience and to draft a preliminary topic sentence. Then make an informal outline and write the first draft. The draft should include:

1. a preliminary topic sentence that makes a point, expresses an attitude, and/or previews what follows.
2. a body with details, explanations, or examples that expand on the point.
3. a preliminary conclusion.

You don't have to use all the details you've generated and outlined. Select the strongest and most relevant ones. Your purpose will be to inform, to persuade, or to entertain. Your audience will be your classmates. The occasion is, of course, a class assignment.

The first draft should be about one handwritten page or half a computer-generated, double-spaced page.

REVISING FOR UNITY

A paragraph is a small unit. It must be tightly organized, with each sentence related to or developing the topic idea or point. Once you have your first draft on paper, you can work on improving and refining the paragraph's **unity**.

First drafts often include some information that might be related to the subject but doesn't develop the topic idea. Eliminate that information, or recast it so it makes your point. In a well-unified paragraph, everything fits. Adjust your topic sentence and conclusion so that they, too, stick to the point.

Use the Revision Guidelines on pages 37–38 to help you evaluate and improve your paragraph.

EXERCISE 6	Examining Paragraph Unity

Read the topic sentence of the following paragraph, and then list five or six ideas you'd expect the paragraph to discuss.

The Origins of the Second Leaning Tower of Pisa

(1) Believe it or not, a man built a remarkable copy of the Leaning Tower of Pisa right here in the United States, and it still stands today.

_____

_____

_____

_____

_____

Now, read the remainder of the paragraph and identify the sentences that probably don't belong, that don't fulfill reasonable predictions.

Collaborative Activity 4

Developing Topic Sentences

Write a topic sentence that makes a point on a subject that interests you, and show it to your group. Each member will then predict—in writing—five or six details, explanations, or examples that the topic sentence suggests will follow. Compare these predictions. What do they suggest about the need for revising your topic sentence *after* drafting the body of the paragraph?

(2) The man was a Chicago millionaire, Robert A. Ilg, head of the Ilg Electric Ventilating Company, who constructed the tower in Niles, Illinois, in 1933. (3) He later retired and lived in the San Francisco area. (4) Ilg built his tower after seeing the Leaning Tower on a visit to the Italian town of Pisa. (5) The marble tower leaned because it had sunk seven feet below the ground at an uneven angle. (6) And, as many people know, it had been the site of Galileo's greatest experiment. (7) He proved that the pull of gravity is uniform when different sized stones that he dropped from the top of the tower landed at the same time. (8) Galileo also proved that the earth revolved around the sun, which seemed to contradict the Bible and caused him great trouble with the leaders of the Church. (9) At any rate, Ilg was so impressed with the beautiful 177-foot marble tower in Pisa that he was determined to construct a half-scale duplicate of it in Niles. (10) The copy was 96 feet tall and made of cement, not marble. (11) Ilg even added imported Italian bells like those in the massive Pisa original. (12) In 1960, he gave his tilted tower

to the Niles YMCA upon his retirement. (13) Although the tower has been closed to the public since the 1960s because of structural problems, Robert Ilg's love for the tower was recently consummated in an unusual marriage. (14) In 1991, Niles and Pisa formed an alliance as sister cities.

Which sentences don't belong? _____

Which of your predictions does the paragraph not fulfill? _____

_____

_____

_____

Did you predict that the paragraph would provide more specific information about the tower and its construction—for example, the cost of building the tower, the problems with making it tilt, the design of the tower, or the number of steps to the top? These are all valid predictions, and a more extensively developed paragraph might have fulfilled them.

Adjusting the Topic Sentence

In the final stages of unifying the paragraph, look at the topic sentence again. An overly general sentence won't give the readers a clear understanding of your point and may lead them to make false predictions. For example, the topic sentence of the following paragraph suggests too much:

> *Both the military personnel and the public have benefited from products designed for the military.* In the 1930s, the Army Air corps commissioned the optical firm of Bausch & Lomb to produce eyeglasses that would protect pilots' eyes from the dangers of the glare at high altitudes. The company's physicists and opticians perfected a special dark green lens that absorbed light. They also designed a slightly curved frame to shield pilots' eyes when they glanced downward toward the plane's instrument panel. Fliers were issued the glasses at no charge, and the public soon was able to purchase this model that banned the sun's rays when it was marketed as Ray-Ban Aviator sunglasses.

You predict the paragraph will discuss many products for many branches of the military, but it discusses only one—sunglasses for Army Air Corps pilots. The topic sentence is misleading and much too broad. Its idea requires a full essay, or even a whole book.

A topic sentence shouldn't be too specific, either, for it will also lead to false predictions, as in the following example:

> The first sunglasses were issued to Army Air Corps pilots for free.

This topic sentence doesn't suggest who invented the glasses or for what purposes.

Compose an appropriate topic sentence for the paragraph, one that is neither too specific nor too general. _____

_____

You probably wrote something like this: "Both the military personnel and the public benefited from a set of eyeglasses designed for the military."

You can change the topic sentence in another way: by adding a short phrase to preview what will follow. Let's return to a topic sentence you saw earlier in the chapter: "My first airplane flight was both terrifying and exciting." Suppose that while drafting the body of the paragraph, you thought of three moments that illustrated the terror and excitement. You could easily revise the topic sentence to preview these moments:

> My first airplane flight was both terrifying and exciting, especially when it took off, encountered turbulence in the air, and landed.

The topic sentences you saw on page 31 could be revised in similar fashion:

> Ms. Kim is a competent attorney in both criminal and civil cases.
>
> Returning to school has been wonderful, but also a bit frightening in several ways.
>
> Juan Gonzalez displays unusual musical talent as a composer, singer, and guitar player.

Sometimes these previewing phrases occur to you while drafting the preliminary topic sentence. At other times, they emerge in the late stages of composing. You needn't add a preview to every topic sentence, but previews are helpful when the ideas of the paragraph are complex.

Adjusting the Conclusion

Now look at the last sentence of your paragraph. Does it reinforce the topic idea? Does it end with a punch? Consider how you might revise it—but avoid obvious and corny endings like "I'll never forget that day as long as I live."

Collaborative Activity 5

Peer Review

If your instructor prefers, use peer review to help you revise the paragraph. Follow the procedures explained in Chapter 2, pp. 21.

EXERCISE 7   Revising Your Paragraph

Revise the paragraph you drafted in Exercise 5. Strive for unity. Eliminate material that doesn't fit, or recast the material to make it fit. Rework the body to further clarify or develop your point. Revise the topic sentence, adding a guiding phrase if possible. Adjust the conclusion so it's clear and emphatic.

REVISION GUIDELINES   Revising a Paragraph

1. Underline the topic sentence of the paragraph. Is it clear? Does it make a point? If not, suggest some possible revisions.

2. What word or words express the point of the topic sentence? Circle them. Are more needed, or should these phrases be revised? If so, suggest some possible revisions. If the point is not clear, how might it be clarified?

3. If the topic sentence is too specific or too general for the supporting details, how should it be changed?

4. Would adding a preview to the topic sentence increase the clarity and unity of the paragraph? If so, suggest some ideas to include.

5. Does the rest of the paragraph directly support the topic sentence? If not, what should be omitted or revised? If any ideas should be added, list them.

6. Is the conclusion effective? If not, what other conclusions might work for the paragraph?

EXERCISE 8	Revising, Editing, and Proofreading

Revise your paragraph from Exercise 7 one final time. Look for ways to make the paragraph even more focused and powerful. Edit, proofread, prepare a clean copy, and then proofread again. Submit the final copy to your instructor.

IN SUMMARY   Composing a Powerful Paragraph

A Paragraph

1. is a group of sentences that discuss one main idea, or topic.
2. begins with the first line indented, and each sentence follows the previous one directly.
3. generally includes at least seven sentences.
4. often states the main idea in a topic sentence, which usually (but not always) comes at the beginning of the paragraph.
5. has a body that explains and exemplifies the topic idea.
6. has a conclusion that reinforces the topic idea and may end with a punch.
7. has unity—all sentences develop the topic idea.

The Topic Sentence

1. states the main idea of the paragraph.
2. usually—but not always—comes at the beginning of the paragraph.
3. should make a point about the subject of the paragraph (not simply announce the subject).
4. should express an attitude toward the subject.
5. may offer preview phrases that allow readers to predict what follows.
6. should be limited—neither too general nor too specific.

The Body

1. supports the topic sentence with details, explanations, and examples.
2. develops the ideas previewed in the topic sentence.
3. is unified—all sentences relate to the topic sentence and to each other.

The Conclusion

1. summarizes the main point of the paragraph.
2. sometimes ends with a punch.

WRITING FOR MASTERY

Assume you are writing for a magazine published by students at your college. Compose an entertaining paragraph about a subject from the following list. Include a topic sentence and at least seven—but, if possible, even more—sentences that develop it. Limit the paragraph to the topic idea and unify the paragraph around it. Conclude the paragraph appropriately.

1. a description of the dog in the photograph below
2. a description of an interesting public place (a park with many people, a room in an art museum, an outdoor café, a beach, a skating rink, etc.)
3. a description of a rainstorm or a sunset
4. a description of a favorite place away from home
5. a description of an old building or part of the building

A shar-pei, an ancient breed of dog from China. Photo by Walter Chandoha.

4 Composing an Effective Essay

Now that you've stepped through the composing process and practiced with paragraphs, you can orchestrate all the skills you've acquired into **essays**—complex but unified pieces of writing containing many paragraphs. In this chapter, you'll see how the essay both resembles and differs from the paragraph. And you'll also write one or more essays in a process involving the familiar six steps. Specifically, you'll examine

- how the introduction to the essay connects subject, purpose, and audience
- how the body of the essay develops its ideas in a series of linked and unified paragraphs
- how the conclusion ties it all together

WHAT IS AN ESSAY?

Think of an essay as a complete intellectual meal. You wouldn't swallow all the courses at once. You'll eat them in smaller, more digestible parts. Each paragraph constitutes one course of the meal (and each sentence a single bite). A paragraph develops a smaller part of the main idea—in effect, giving your readers a chance to digest some information before moving on to the next part.

Furthermore, an essay must be arranged in an order that makes sense. The soup shouldn't come after the dessert.

The Elements of an Essay

So, like the paragraph, a typical essay includes an introduction, a body, and a conclusion.

1. The first paragraph or **introduction** attracts the readers' interest, states the essay's point in a **thesis statement**, and helps readers predict what will follow.
2. The **body** fulfills the readers' predictions by breaking down the thesis statement into smaller ideas, each of which may require one or more paragraphs to explain and illustrate. Each paragraph itself often includes a topic sentence; body sentences giving details, explanations, and examples; and a concluding sentence that often establishes a transition to the next paragraph.
3. The **conclusion**, the last paragraph (or two) of the essay, ties all the ideas together and gracefully ends the paper.

EXERCISE 1	Analyzing an Essay

Examine the following essay closely to see how it's put together. Then answer the questions that follow.

The Origins of Dr. Jekyll and Mr. Hyde

Paragraph A. Everyone who has read the novel by Robert Louis Stevenson or has seen a version of the movie knows about the fictional Dr. Jekyll and Mr. Hyde. Dr. Jekyll was a respectable physician in the daytime, but at night he swallowed a potion that transformed him into the brutal, evil Mr. Hyde. Although the story sounds impossible, it isn't. There really was a model for Dr. Jekyll and Mr. Hyde: Deacon William Brodie, who led a double life of criminal and respectable citizen in the mid-eighteenth century.

Paragraph B. Just like the fictional character, William Brodie changed identities in the nighttime. By day, he was a respected member of the community in Edinburgh, Scotland. He owned a successful cabinet-making business, served as a town councilman, and was the deacon of the town church, assisting the minister of the church in dealings with the cabinet maker's union. He usually wore white, lived quietly with his father and sister, and appeared to be a sober bachelor. But Brodie's dark side emerged when the sun set. In a black suit and a black mask, the deacon transformed himself into a gambler, a drunkard, and a thief who kept two mistresses and supported his five illegitimate children with part of his loot.

Paragraph C. Until Brodie let his ego overcome his caution, his many crimes went undetected for almost two decades. In 1786, at the age of twenty-seven, he committed his first burglary when he stole £800 from a bank. Then during the next eighteen years, he freely drank, stole, and carried on with women. But Brodie got ambitious—and careless. He dreamed of leading a gang of cutthroats, but his dream turned into a nightmare after he hired three robbers to assist him. The gang botched a robbery of the Scottish General Tax Office, and one of Brodie's partners confessed—and named names.

Paragraph D. With the police on his tail, Brodie tried to escape but didn't succeed. He made it to Amsterdam, Holland, and was about to sail for America when he was captured by local authorities, who found him hiding in a cupboard. They took him back to Edinburgh. In the same courtroom where he had served as a respectable juror six months earlier, he was sentenced to be hanged.

Paragraph E. Although this man of two lives plotted for a third, his attempt to cheat the hangman failed. Brodie made elaborate plans to soften the noose's impact, including consulting a doctor for help and wiring his body so it couldn't be jerked. An hour before he was to face the executioner on October 1, 1788, he even hid a steel collar under his neckerchief to prevent strangulation. Nevertheless, the gallows were not to be denied, and Brodie died of a broken neck—an unpleasant end for the real Dr. Jekyll and Mr. Hyde.

1. Which paragraph is the introduction? _____ Which paragraphs form the body? _____ Which serves as the conclusion? _____

2. Underline the thesis statement twice.

3. Underline the topic sentence of every paragraph.

4. Look at the introduction again. How does it connect with you, the *audience?* Where does it introduce the *subject* of the essay? Does the writer assume you already know something about the subject? How does the writer convey the *purpose?* _____

_____

5. The topic sentence of paragraph B introduces two main ideas. What are they? Which sentence later introduces the second part of the topic idea? _____

_____

6. Which sentence in paragraph E ties the ideas of the whole essay together? Does it introduce any new ideas? _____

_____

EXERCISE 2	Compressing the Essay

Transform the model essay into one paragraph by copying the key sentence in every paragraph of the original. Your first should be your topic sentence for the compressed paragraph. Follow it with three body sentences, and end it with a concluding sentence. Use the lines below. Don't read any further in the chapter until you've completed this exercise.

_____

_____

_____

_____

_____

_____

The Shape of an Essay

Is this the paragraph you wrote?

Topic sentence: *There really was a model for Dr. Jekyll and Mr. Hyde: Deacon William Brodie, who led a double life of criminal and respectable citizen in the mid-eighteenth century.* Just like the fictional character, William Brodie changed identities in the nighttime. Until Brodie let his ego overcome his caution, his numerous crimes went undetected for almost two decades. With the police on his tail, Brodie tried to escape but didn't succeed. Although the man of two lives plotted for a third, his attempt to cheat the hangman failed.

Notice how this compressed paragraph begins with the essay's thesis statement and proceeds with the topic sentence of each paragraph that follows. The last sentence of this revised paragraph creates a somewhat puzzling conclusion, though, because we don't learn how Brodie died.

This transformation should demonstrate the similarities between an essay and a paragraph. In a sense, an essay is a paragraph that has been exploded. The thesis statement is like a topic sentence for the whole essay. The body paragraphs—each with its own topic sentence—develop that thesis in the same way that sentences in the body of a paragraph develop its topic idea.

But is the paragraph you created effective? The answer is no. It serves as a summary, for its topic is too large to be developed in so short a space. In Chapter 3, you saw that narrowing a topic was an important first step in creating a unified paragraph. A topic that can't be narrowed enough to fit into one paragraph deserves fuller treatment in an essay.

Here's the pattern for an essay, presented as a blueprint:

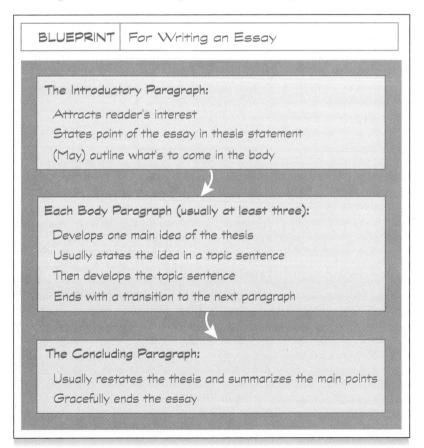

BLUEPRINT   For Writing an Essay

The Introductory Paragraph:

Attracts reader's interest
States point of the essay in thesis statement
(May) outline what's to come in the body

Each Body Paragraph (usually at least three):

Develops one main idea of the thesis
Usually states the idea in a topic sentence
Then develops the topic sentence
Ends with a transition to the next paragraph

The Concluding Paragraph:

Usually restates the thesis and summarizes the main points
Gracefully ends the essay

A CLOSER LOOK AT THE ESSAY

A Word About Words

Many Greek words entered English during the Renaissance. Examples include words ending in –*ics* (*politics, statistics*), or –*logy* (*biology, psychology*), and –*on* and its plural form –*a* (*phenomenon, phenomena; criterion, criteria*). Here are a few others: *Bible, catastrophe, magic,* and *idiot*.

Let's examine how the parts of another model essay are put together. The purpose of the following essay is to inform, and informative writing is called **expository** because it exposes—or explains—ideas. Expository essays (or themes) are common college assignments, in which, for example, you analyze the causes of the Civil War for your history instructor. But expository writing is even more common in work and community settings. You can discuss your qualifications for a job opening—or, once you have the job, explain the operation of a system for new employees. You can report the outcome of a block meeting to a community group, or tell a friend by e-mail why you think the home team lost a football game. In short, you'll see the need for expository writing throughout your life, and in every case you'll need to consider

1. the occasion for writing
2. your subject
3. your purpose
4. your audience

We'll look at the model essay part by part.

The Introduction and Thesis Statement

Except in school and work assignments, most people won't have to read your essay. You must make them want to read it—and, in fact, you should try to interest even a captive audience of classmates, instructors, or colleagues at work. Then you can introduce the main idea in the thesis statement. The introductory paragraph of the following model essay accomplishes both those tasks:

THE CLEAN TRUTH ABOUT PIGS

Paragraph A. What is the dirtiest animal? You would probably say the pig, which is known for wallowing in mud, eating garbage, and observing other practices of a less-than-genteel nature. However, this reputation for slovenly behavior is, pardon the expression, a lot of hogwash. The pig can't be blamed for its unsanitary practices and, in fact, is rather tidy in almost every way—from living quarters, to toilet habits, to bathing, to eating.

Look closely at the first two sentences. They're attention-getters—an attempt to engage the audience. The third sentence introduces the subject, states the thesis, and suggests the purpose of the essay. The fourth sentence is a preview, helping readers predict what the body of the essay will discuss: the pig's living quarters, toilet habits, bathing practices, and eating behavior. Examine the preview closely. The four topics are set off by a dash [—]. They could also be set off by a colon [:] or through linking words such as *because*, *since*, or *by*.

The Body

The body of the essay develops the ideas introduced in the first paragraph. There are four body paragraphs in the model essay, and each develops one topic mentioned in the introduction, and in the same order. Notice that each topic sentence refers back to the thesis statement:

Paragraph B. First of all, domestic pigs are supposed to "like" filthy living quarters: dusty pens, muddy areas, and smelly pigsties. *However, the charge that pigs enjoy such surroundings is not only undeserved but untrue.* In their natural state, wild pigs and boars roam the forests, never staying in one place long enough to create, let alone enjoy, such a mess. In captivity, however, the poor creatures are forced into slums against their wills. This practice began in early New England, where pigs were usually kept in the worst place on the farm—the sty under the barn, which was a small, dark, and dirty hole.

Paragraph C. *Second, even in close confinement, the pigs' toilet habits are among the best of domestic animals.* Pigs are actually rather tidy individuals, who defecate in only one spot. This behavior is far more civilized and refined than the practices of horses, cows, and other barnyard creatures. In fact, pigs are much more selective in their choices of where to relieve themselves than are most pet dogs, as many a frustrated owner of man's best friend can confirm.

Paragraph D. However, a third charge against pigs is true: They don't bathe, but instead wallow in the mud on hot days. *But the animals choose this activity out of necessity, not out of some defect in character.* They cannot perspire, and the cool mud lowers their temperature. Perhaps if swimming pools were readily available, pigs would avoid mud entirely. For, rumor to the contrary, their heavy hooves do not prevent them from swimming. Given the opportunity, they will dive into the water and paddle around with perfect ease.

Paragraph E. Fourth and finally, pigs can justifiably be accused of eating garbage, since they often do. *But pigs can't choose their menus; they must eat what they are served.* These four-legged gourmets actually prefer diets closest to those of human beings, but farmers take advantage of this desire by feeding pigs scraps from the dinner table. Perhaps this preference for such "garbage" is more a criticism of humans than the animals they call "hogs."

The Conclusion

The final paragraph—the conclusion—typically ties together the ideas in the essay and ends with a forceful or clever statement. A summary begins the last paragraph of the model essay, while a joke ends it:

Paragraph F. In short, pigs have taken a lot of undeserved ribbing. They want to be neat housekeepers, observe proper sanitary and bathing practices, and eat well-balanced meals, but they don't always receive courteous treatment from their hosts and keepers. Be careful, therefore, about calling someone "a filthy pig." You shouldn't slander a guiltless party by associating it with human beings.

The model essay is six paragraphs long. Essays can be of any length—even dozens of paragraphs long. But as you begin the process of composing essays, limit yourself to shorter ones of perhaps five paragraphs: an introductory paragraph, three or more body paragraphs, and a conclusion.

EXERCISE 3	Expanding a Paragraph Into an Essay

As a transition into composing essays, return to any paragraph you've written in an earlier chapter. Expand it into at least a five-paragraph essay. Include at least two sentences in the introductory paragraph: one that attracts the readers' interest and a second that states the thesis—essentially a revised topic sentence from the original paragraph.

Then consider ways to divide and develop your original supporting ideas into several body paragraphs. Can you explain your ideas further? Can you illustrate them through examples? Write a topic sentence that states each main idea, and then explain and illustrate that topic sentence in its own paragraph.

Finally, write a concluding paragraph that summarizes your ideas and brings the essay to a close. Don't worry if the essay is less than perfect. This is only a starting point.

COMPOSING AN ESSAY

You've already established your own composing habits and practices in previous chapters on paragraphs. Now, when composing an essay, follow the same six steps Chapter 2 outlined for you. In the remainder of this chapter, you'll see some additional suggestions about the composing process—as well as some exercises and collaborative activities to sharpen your skills.

A WRITER SPEAKS

My writing practices depend on the project. If I'm writing a letter or e-mail, I compose off the top of my head and rarely revise. If I'm writing a section of a textbook for students, I'm more deliberate: I focus on my topic, freewrite to get my basic ideas on paper and to discover new wrinkles or fresh connections to other ideas (I find it's only when I actually write that new, fresh "stuff" comes to mind); then I am ready to write a real draft. Depending on how that draft strikes me when I read it, I either revise right away or put it aside to revise (or leave alone) later.

One type of project almost always means I'm going to hit a "writing block." (You can imagine I try mightily to avoid such projects, but frankly it's impossible. So I tell myself it's "good for me" to face the block and push on.) What's this monster challenge? Writing an article or essay to be published in a professional, scholarly journal or book. Yes, I know this might sound strange, because as a professor I have to know a fair amount about my field. Added to that, I am an active researcher who tries to add to the collective knowledge of my field. But that's the truth—on such projects I'm way overly critical of my every word, sentence, and even idea. It's tough going for me to get the job done, but I can report that after thirty years of not giving up, I find my blocks are now less intense and shorter in duration. I'm proud of that.

Lynn Quitman Troyka, Ph.D., professor [emerita] of English, Queensborough Community College, CUNY, author of the *Simon and Schuster Handbook for Writers*, 6th ed. (Prentice Hall/Simon & Schuster, 2002)

Thinking and Planning

As always, begin by thinking about both the occasion for writing and your subject matter. Choose a topic you know well and can discuss comfortably. Consider your audience, too. Your purpose is to inform, so include only what your readers need to know.

EXERCISE 4	Analyzing Audiences

Suppose you've been asked to produce an informative brochure describing the most important features of your college to three different audiences: (1) young, incoming freshmen who have never been to a college anywhere, (2) transfer students, who have completed at least a year at another college, and (3) older students, who work full-time, have children, and may be taking only a few courses. Make your own list of the matters you can include in your description for each audience.

Young, incoming freshmen:

1. description of class schedules and explanation of course numbers

2. clubs, sports, and activities on campus

3. _____

4. _____

5. _____

6. _____

Transfer students:

1. comparison of class course numbers to those found at nearby universities

2. _____

3. _____

4. _____

5. _____

6. _____

Older students:

1. child care facilities

2. _____

3. _____

4. _____

5. _____

6. _____

Collaborative Activity 1

Compare the lists you prepared in Exercise 4 and discuss the differing needs of the various audiences. Appoint someone as a note taker as you prepare a master list, which you'll either submit to your instructor or report to the whole class.

Outlining

You can plan, draft, and revise a short paragraph in a day or two. But composing an essay is a more complex task. Allow yourself time to experiment, to walk away for a while, to return when you are inspired (and even when you aren't). Let yourself discover, play with, and organize ideas. When inspiration does strike, capture it on paper, even if that means keeping a pencil and notepad by your bed. Many a brilliant insight at midnight has disappeared by morning.

As you brainstorm, cluster, or freewrite, begin selecting and organizing. Then sketch out a rough outline. Outlining is even more important for an essay than for a paragraph, because an essay is longer. Divide your prewriting into topics, with each one serving as a paragraph in the body. If you can, draft preliminary topic sentences that shape the paragraphs.

The Preliminary Thesis Statement

Your most important task is to frame a preliminary thesis statement that, like a paragraph topic sentence, makes a point or expresses an attitude. But the thesis statement must also be broad enough to encompass the entire essay. And it may also include an overview, or preview, of the body paragraphs that will follow. You can attach that preview onto the thesis statement through linking words such as *because, since,* or *by,* or with a colon [:]. Or you can write an entirely separate sentence.

In fact, a preliminary thesis statement can help you organize and develop your ideas. The sample essay you read earlier in the chapter evolved in this way. The writer began by quickly jotting down a thesis:

Pigs actually have a lot of good traits.

Then, realizing that the phrases "a lot" and "good traits" were too vague, he revised the thesis statement. What, he asked himself, was his real point? What traits did he wish to discuss, and why? His questions led to this revision:

The reputation of a pig as a dirty animal is unfair; it's actually very clean.

The expanded thesis suggested a series of contrasts between myths and reality about the cleanliness of pigs, so he listed some points of contrast:

Main points: lives in filth, but actually clean in wild state
Doesn't defecate as other animals do
Sits in mud but does so to keep cool
Eats garbage, but prefers food we eat

Following this preliminary work, the writer considered his ideas even more carefully. He revised his thesis further, drafted preliminary topic sentences for each paragraph, and listed some possible support for the topic sentences:

Thesis: The pig can't be blamed for being dirty because in reality it is a rather clean animal.

1. Topic sentence: Farmers put pigs in filthy quarters.
   Possible development: discussion of reasons for pigsty
2. Topic sentence: Pig's toilet habits are good.
   Possible development: contrast to habits in the wild
3. Topic sentence: Pig does sit in mud, but not out of a desire to be dirty.

> *Possible development: inability to perspire*
> 4. <u>Topic sentence</u>: *Pig can swim and clean off the mud.*
>   *Possible development: myth about inability to swim*
> 5. <u>Topic sentence</u>: *Pigs do eat garbage, but only because they have no choice.*
>   *Possible development: diet closest to diet of humans*

Of course, the final version of the essay was tidier and more polished—as it should be. The writer added and discarded information. He revised sentences several times. And in the second or third draft, he revised the thesis statement to include a preview of the essay's main ideas. Compare the first and last versions of the thesis statement.

> **Preliminary thesis statement:** *The pig can't be blamed for being dirty because in reality it is a rather clean animal.*
>
> **Final version of thesis statement:** *The pig can't be blamed for its unsanitary practices and, in fact, is rather tidy in almost every way—from living quarters, to toilet habits, to bathing, to eating.*

EXERCISE 5	Considering Organization and Development

Examine each of the following thesis statements and predict the main supporting ideas you'd expect to find in the full essay—and the order in which they might be introduced. Report your findings to the whole class.

1. The methods of choosing the president and vice president have undergone three major changes throughout our country's history:

Paragraph 1. *A discussion of the original method of choosing the president and vice president*

Paragraph 2. _____

Paragraph 3. _____

Paragraph 4. _____

2. The Japanese elementary and secondary educational system differs from the American system not only in the length of the school year but also in the subjects emphasized in the curriculum, in the expectations placed on the students both by teachers and parents, and—most importantly—in the quality of the education itself.

Paragraph 1. _____

Paragraph 2. _____

Collaborative Activity 2

Discussing Organization

Compare the predictions you made for Exercise 5. Discuss the order in which each set of ideas should be presented and explain why the ideas should be presented in that particular order.

Paragraph 3._____

Paragraph 4._____

3. Despite what many people think, I believe pets are a waste of time, money, and affection that would be better directed toward our children and family.

Paragraph 1._____

Paragraph 2._____

Paragraph 3._____

Paragraph 4._____

EXERCISE 6	Choosing a Topic

Choose a subject for an essay from the following list. Explore your ideas through brainstorming, clustering, or freewriting. If your first choice meets a dead end, choose another topic and begin the exploration process.

1. For a magazine published by an international airline, explain to people from another country three reasons for (a) the popularity of an American sport, (b) the appeal of American popular music, or (c) the appeal of a particular sports star or entertainer.

2. In an article for a popular magazine, describe the three most important traits or behaviors of a group you know well: your parents; people in your neighborhood or community; people of your ethnic group; people of your faith or in your church, mosque, temple, or synagogue; or people in your field of study.

3. For a magazine about gourmet cooking, personal computers, photography, music, stamp collecting, running, travel—or any other hobby—give at least three tips on making the hobby more interesting, profitable, useful, or fun. Focus on one aspect of the hobby—for example, on warming up and stretching before or after a long run.

EXERCISE 7	Composing a Preliminary Thesis Statement and Topic Sentences

Return to the materials you explored in Exercise 6, and select from and organize them into an essay. Write a preliminary thesis statement, along with a topic sentence for each of three supporting paragraphs in the body of the essay.

Preliminary thesis statement: _____

Preliminary topic sentences: _____

1. _____

_____

2. _____

_____

3. _____

_____

Drafting the Introduction

The introduction to an essay has to work hard. It must state the thesis and preview the supporting topics that will follow. But a clear thesis won't do much good if you can't motivate your audience to read it. You'll need to experiment with ways to attract readers' interest, too. Here are some suggestions for strong attention-getters at the beginning of the essay.

A Question. An opening question actively involves readers, forcing them to consider an issue, as in the following paragraph. Notice that the thesis statement and preview immediately follow the question:

> *Is the biblical story of Jonah being swallowed by a whale just an ancient myth?* Don't be so sure. At the end of the last century, a human being was swallowed by a whale—yet he was rescued, and he survived.

Details or Examples. We're interested in people, things, and actions—not abstractions. So a surprising fact or example at the beginning of an essay can make us want to read on, as in the following paragraph:

> *The 1908 Sears, Roebuck and Company catalog included an unusual feature—a section on mail-order houses shipped by rail in large crates.* The build-it-yourself house kits included shingles, windows, precut lumber, and all the necessary building materials, along with blueprints and assembly instructions. As this example shows, Sears, one of the world's largest retailers, can and will market almost anything. Today it can not only supply your household goods; it can also fix your house, repair your car, and even provide you with eye and medical services.

A Story. We also enjoy stories, which transform abstract ideas into human terms, as in this example:

> *Former President Herbert Hoover recalled that when a small boy asked him for his autograph during a public gathering in Los Angeles, the lad requested and received three copies "because it takes two of yours to trade for one of Babe Ruth's."* Such was the fame and popularity of George Herman "Babe" Ruth, probably the greatest and certainly among the best-loved baseball players of all time.

A Misunderstood Fact or Belief. Contradictions create tension—and curiosity. So they're an excellent way to attract interest, as in this example:

> *Most people assume that Ping-Pong and table tennis are the same thing—but they aren't.* Ping-Pong is a registered trademark, and this accounts for the use of table tennis instead of the other term in publications. Trademarks such as Ping-Pong are official names or symbols registered with the government. Unlike copyrights or patents, trademarks last forever, and there are strict rules on how they may be used.

A Direct Statement of the Thesis. A strong, interesting thesis can stand on its own legs and may need no introduction at all. Here's an example:

> *Missouri once boasted the world's smallest town that human beings could walk through.* This miniature community, founded in 1925, was known as Tiny Town, for every structure was one-half the size of a normal building. The town occupied six acres of a public park in Springfield, Missouri. And it was designed, built, and run by students.

But in the best introductions, the attention-getter, the thesis statement and the preview of the topic ideas will work together. As you see, however, these elements needn't be entirely separate from each other. By the time you've finished revising your essay, they should blend together. One trait of effective writing is that it seems natural and effortless. Just as in a musical performance, the parts harmonize so well that you don't think about all the practice and rehearsals that led up to that moment.

EXERCISE 8   **Writing the Introduction**

Now write the first paragraph of your essay, using or experimenting with any attention-getting device you wish. Include a thesis statement and, if possible, a preview.

Drafting the Body

The body of an essay presents ideas in a logical order that's often previewed in the thesis statement. If a different order occurs to you as you write, adjust the thesis statement accordingly. In fact, a clear thesis may not come into focus until you've finished drafting the body. Expect, therefore, to make the body and thesis statement mesh as you revise, not in your first draft.

EXERCISE 9   **Writing the Body**

Write the first draft of a three-paragraph body of the essay you began in Exercises 7 and 8. Make sure each paragraph has a topic sentence.

Drafting the Conclusion

The traditional conclusion restates the thesis in different words. Let's briefly return to the essay about pigs. The thesis states that pigs are unsanitary through no fault of their own, and the preview lists four aspects of a pig's cleanliness. The conclusion restates these ideas:

> They want to be neat housekeepers, observe proper sanitary and bathing practices, and eat well-balanced meals, but they don't always receive courteous treatment from their hosts and keepers.

But the conclusion isn't concluded! It needs to end with a punch:

> Be careful, therefore, about calling someone "a filthy pig." You shouldn't slander a guiltless party by associating it with human beings.

Consider adding a punch line to your conclusion, too.

EXERCISE 10   *Writing the Conclusion*

Write a conclusion to the essay you've been working on throughout this chapter. Try to include a forceful or clever final sentence.

REVISING FOR COHERENCE

Just as in effective paragraphs, each sentence leads logically to the next, the links between paragraphs in an essay should be logical and clear. In part, that clarity results from a logical plan that begins with outlining. But, during revision, you should work to heighten that clarity even more. Consult the Revision Guidelines on page 54. And tighten the links between the thesis statement and the body paragraphs, as well as the links between the individual body paragraphs. That usually involves at least two elements:

1. repeating words or phrases (or substitutes for them) from the thesis statement
2. adding transitional words, phrases, or even whole sentences

These links give the essay **coherence**, an important quality we'll discuss at length in Chapter 6.

Adjusting the Thesis Statement

The body of a coherent essay clearly develops the central thesis. But if you find that not everything fits, you can revise the body, revise the thesis statement; or revise them both. Don't be satisfied with your preliminary thesis statement. Adjust it to account for all the information in the body. And don't be satisfied with the body, either. Add details that develop the thesis more fully, and remove parts that don't.

Repeating from the Thesis Statement

You can further strengthen coherence by making the preview attached to the thesis statement serve as a guide to the essay. The preview provides a road map for readers on their journey through the essay, and the topic sentence of each paragraph in the body signals the stops along the way. Notice how in the essay on pigs, the body paragraphs reuse or rephrase terms from the preview:

Preview:	In fact, the pig is rather tidy in almost every way—from living quarters, to toilet habits, to bathing, to eating.
Paragraph B:	First of all, domestic pigs are supposed to "like" filthy living quarters. . . .
Paragraph C:	Second, even in close confinement, the pigs' toilet habits are among the best of domestic animals.
Paragraph D:	However, a third charge against pigs is true: They don't bathe but instead wallow in the mud on hot days.
Paragraph E:	Fourth and finally, pigs can be justifiably accused of eating garbage. . . .

So look carefully at the preview, and revise it if necessary. Then repeat key terms (but vary them) in the topic sentences in the body.

Collaborative Activity 3

Peer Review

If your instructor prefers, use peer review to help you revise your essay, following the procedures explained in Chapter 2, pp. 21.

Adding Transitions

Yet another way to express complex relationships among paragraphs is through connecting expressions, or **transitions**. These transitional words or phrases, such as "therefore," "on the other hand," or "for example," tie what has gone before to what will come after. Notice, in the essay on pigs, that each of the body paragraphs begins with a transitional word or phrase: first of all, second, however, fourth and finally. We'll focus more directly on transitions in Chapter 6.

REVISION GUIDELINES | An Effective Essay

1. Underline the thesis statement and preview of the essay's main ideas in the opening paragraph. If either is missing or unclear, write suggestions for improving them on the blank sheet.

2. Does the first paragraph include an effective attention-getting introduction? If not, write some suggestions for an attention-getter on the blank sheet.

3. Underline the topic sentence of each body paragraph. If there is no topic sentence, is the point of the paragraph clear? If not, use the blank sheet to write suggestions for clarifying the point.

4. Examine the supporting explanations and details in each body paragraph. Are there enough? If not, brainstorm or freewrite ideas for support on the blank sheet. Does any supporting information seem to stray off the point? If so, circle it—or draw arrows to where it might more logically fit.

5. Examine the transitions between paragraphs. Are they clear? Graceful? If not, use the attached sheet to suggest transitions that might be included.

6. Does the final paragraph summarize the main ideas and end with a punch? If not, how should it be revised? Make your suggestions on the attached sheet.

EXERCISE 11 | Revising Your Draft

Now revise your own essay according to the following guidelines. Then make a clean copy of your work for further editing.

EXERCISE 12	*Editing and Proofreading Your Essay*

Then edit your essay, checking for correct spelling and punctuation, complete sentences, and clarity of ideas. Following that, make a clean copy and proofread it very carefully. Produce a final copy to submit to your instructor.

IN SUMMARY   Composing an Effective Essay

The Expository Essay

1. attracts the readers' interest with an introductory paragraph that includes a thesis statement. The thesis often previews—either explicitly or implicitly—the main ideas to be discussed in the body.
2. includes a body section of several—and often many—paragraphs, each of which develops a main supporting idea, often stated in a topic sentence.
3. includes transitions that serve to link paragraphs.
4. concludes with a paragraph that summarizes or echoes the main ideas of the essay, often by returning to—but not merely repeating—the thesis statement. The conclusion is strong, humorous, or upbeat.

A STUDENT MODEL ESSAY

Chang Rhiu is a student at Chattanooga State Technical Community College. As you read his essay, notice its parts and how they fit together. Notice how he develops each supporting point for his thesis in the body paragraphs, and notice how he ties the parts together in his conclusion.

Komerican
Chang Rhiu

* * * *

When I arrived in America, the first foreign country that I visited in my life, I never thought I would stay for a long time and become a part of the American society. People, cars, houses, language, and everything seemed so different that I felt as though I were on another planet. On the first day here, I already missed my family and friends in my country, Korea, and I wanted to go back to where I felt I belonged. Time passed just like a flowing river, and it has already been four years that I have been learning and practicing American culture. The person I am today is very different from the one who stepped off the plane in the Los Angeles International Airport four years ago. Komerican, a Korean who acts like an American, is my new identity, and there are several changes in my way of looking, thinking, and behaving.

First, my appearance has changed a lot since I arrived. I had a short hair cut, was clean shaven, and wore nice clothes in Korea. I needed to follow a certain order of fashion for people my age. I could not wear unusual clothes because I didn't want to look abnormal in society. When I came to America, I noticed that Americans look whatever way they want. People do not seem to care what anyone wears. Everyone has his/her own fashion and style. After a while, I started to let my hair grow; sometimes I grew a beard and wore more comfortable clothes than I did in my country. I quickly adopted the casual appearance of American fashion.

Second, my way of thinking changed a great deal. I used to be very concerned about what other people thought of me. For instance, at my friend's birthday party in Korea, even though I was bored and had other things to do, I stayed until the party was over. I worried that, if I left, my friends might think that I didn't like the party or that I was disrespectful to my friend. However, in America, I spend more time alone, so I think and care about my needs first before the needs of other people. I worry that I will become selfish, but I have become more independent and have gained more self-respect in America.

Finally, my behavior is less formal. When I was in Korea, if I met older people or teachers, I used to bow down to them out of respect, but here in America, I say "Hi" or just shake hands. In other words, I now treat older respected figures the same as I treated my peers in Korea. Sometimes I surprise myself in how drastically my behavior has changed.

I came to America to learn about a different culture and evaluate my own. However, while I was doing so, my looks, my thinking, and my behavior changed dramatically. I cannot say either is right or wrong, but when I finish my long journey here and go back to Korea, I hope I stay the same "Chang" on the inside as my family and friends used to know.

Questions for Analysis

1. In the first paragraph, which sentences are introductory? What sentence—or sentences—states Chang Rhiu's thesis? Where does he preview the body of the essay, and what three points does he promise to discuss? Underline these sentences.

2. What are the topic sentences of the three body paragraphs? How do you know?

3. In each of the three body paragraphs, Chang makes comparisons. Write a summary of each comparison in your own words. Don't copy the original wording.

4. Which sentence in the final paragraph summarizes the essay? Underline it.

5. Chang claims that he has changed a great deal since coming here four years ago. He stresses that in Korea, it was very important to conform to the expectations of the society. But he also says in the first paragraph that he has been "practicing and learning American culture." Consider that statement. Has he changed a great deal? Has he lost the cultural values of his native society?

WRITING FOR MASTERY

The following suggestions may stimulate your thinking as you choose subjects for expository essays of five or more paragraphs. Remember that the essay should be logically arranged, based on what your audience needs to know. Be sure that the final draft of your essay includes (1) an introductory paragraph, complete with an attention-getting opening and a thesis statement that encompasses the topic and previews or outlines the essay; (2) a body of several paragraphs that are organized in some logical way; (3) clear links between paragraphs; and (4) a concluding paragraph, complete with a summary of the essay's main ideas.

1. Have you, like Chang Rhiu, changed in a number of ways after entering a new environment, a new school, or a new culture? Discuss those changes.

2. As a social worker who counsels parents of adolescent children, describe one major problem that adolescents face, along with its consequences. Or give advice to the parents on how to deal with the problem.

3. As an executive of a large manufacturer of personal computers, write a memo to your marketing department suggesting several reasons why a typical American household needs a personal computer.

4. Write a letter to a prospective employer in which you describe the education, training, skills, and experience that qualify you for the position.

Composing in Six Steps

STEP 1	**EXPLORE**	
	Occasion . . . Subject . . . Purpose . . . Audience	
STEP 2	**PREWRITE**	
	Brainstorm . . . Cluster . . . Freewrite	
STEP 3	**ORGANIZE**	
	1. Select 2. Outline	
STEP 4	**WRITE A FIRST DRAFT**	
STEP 5	**REVISE**	
	Review . . . Read aloud . . . Predict	
STEP 6	**PRODUCE THE FINAL COPY**	
	1. Edit 2. Proofread 3. Finalize	

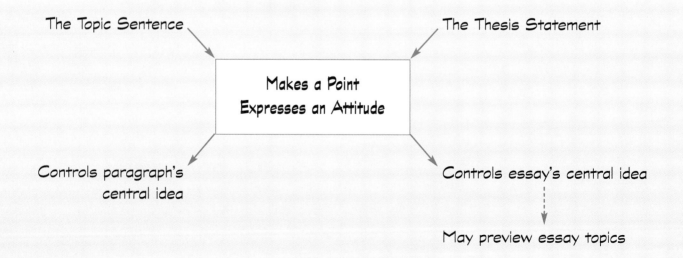

The Elements of a
Paragraph

The Elements of an
Essay

INTRODUCTION **(1-2 sentences)** Attention-getter Topic sentence	**INTRODUCTION** **(4-5 sentences)** Attention-getter Thesis statement Preview
	BODY PARAGRAPH Topic sentence
BODY **(5-7 sentences)**	**BODY PARAGRAPH** Topic sentence
	BODY PARAGRAPH Topic sentence
CONCLUSION **(1-2 sentences)** Return to topic sentence Wrap-up	**CONCLUSION** **(4-5 sentences)** Return to thesis Wrap-up

II
Strengthening Writing

The chapters of the previous units have introduced you to the composing process for both paragraphs and essays. You've seen that you write for a variety of purposes, audiences, occasions, and that these determine both the subject matter and the way you present it. You've explored the six steps in the composing process while learning to discover, shape, and present your ideas clearly. You've laid the foundation for composing with confidence.

Unit II strengthens and builds on this foundation. It shows you how to add details and examples to the framework of your ideas. It shows you how to make your sentences more direct, lively, and varied. And it shows you how to arrange and connect your ideas so your message and purpose are clear.■

5 Developing Ideas

As you know, a paragraph discusses one central idea or point, and an essay presents several points that develop a more complex idea. This chapter will show you how to develop these points in paragraphs and essays by looking at

- ways to explain, illustrate, and back up your general statements
- ways to use facts and figures to help prove your general statements

SUPPORT FOR GENERAL STATEMENTS

As you explore and then shape your ideas for a paragraph or essay, you'll essentially be looking at your general ideas. These **generalizations**—broad statements that express main ideas—form the structure or framework of your writing, and many will emerge as topic sentences or thesis statements. Think of them as a skeleton—bones without meat.

But to make your ideas clear, lively, and convincing, you need to flesh out these generalizations, putting specific meat on the bones. You can do precisely that by adding some or all of the following:

1. **explanations**, which clarify a general statement by discussing the reasoning behind it
2. **examples**, which illustrate a general idea, providing specific "for instances" that make the general statement easier to visualize or understand
3. **details** (from a French word that means "to cut something into pieces"), which quite literally show readers the small parts included within the larger idea

These specific statements provide the support for your generalizations.

Anticipate and Answer Questions

To recognize the kinds of support your general statements need—explanations, examples, and details—put yourself in your reader's place. Predict the questions your reader might reasonably ask. For example, what issues does the following paragraph raise in your mind?

> A French king once commanded an abbot to invent a ridiculous musical instrument for the amusement of his guests. After thinking about the possibilities for a while, the abbot came up with an ingenious solution: an apparatus for making hogs sing. The invention worked, and the king's friends were greatly entertained.

The *idea* of this paragraph is interesting enough, and, surely, the writer must know more about the subject than is expressed here. But you as a reader might justifiably ask: Which French king was it? Which abbot did he ask? When did he ask him? Who were the king's guests? What kind of apparatus did the abbot invent, and how did it make the hogs sing? These questions suggest the explanations, examples, and details that would flesh out the story.

How many explanations, examples, and details should you include? The answer depends on the answers to four other questions that relate to *subject, purpose, audience,* and *occasion*—the four concerns you must address as you begin (and continue) the composing process:

1. *How complicated is your subject?* The more complicated, the more you must explain and illustrate.
2. *How persuasive or entertaining should you be?* The more of either, the more lively the details you need.
3. *What don't your readers know about the subject?* The less they know, the more you must explain.
4. *How much (or little) space do you have?* Are you writing a paragraph or an essay? Of course, the more space you have, the more you can—and probably should—say.

Bringing your subject, purpose, audience, and occasion into focus will aid you in developing support for your general statements.

Provide Proof

Look back at the sample paragraph. The writer *claims* the abbot's solution to the problem was "ingenious" and that the guests were "greatly entertained," but how does he know? As a reader, you might justifiably ask for **proof**. The writer needs to back up these claims with evidence.

Here's another version of the paragraph, this time with the explanations, examples, and details that make it informative, interesting, and convincing. It names people and things. It defines terms. It describes and illustrates the ingenious process by which the hogs sang. And it shows how the writer knows the guests were greatly entertained:

> Around the year 1450, King Louis XI of France commanded an abbot from the monastery of Baigne to invent a ridiculous musical instrument for the amusement of the king's courtiers—noble men and women—at a party. After thinking about the possibilities for a while, the abbot came up with an ingenious solution: an apparatus for making hogs sing. He gathered a herd of hogs, ranging from nursing piglets to full-grown swine. He lined them up under a velvet tent with low-voiced porkers on the left, middle-range sows in the middle, and soprano piglets on the right. Then the abbot constructed a modified organ keyboard and attached the keys to a complicated device that ended with a series of small spikes, one poised over the rump of each pig. At the party, the abbot played his keyboard, causing the

Continued

> spikes to prick the pigs in sequence. The pigs naturally let out piercing squeals, each in its own particular voice range. The tunes were actually recognizable, and the courtiers applauded and congratulated the king on his fine entertainment.

This second version is a great improvement over the first, but not because it contains more words. It's simply more specific. The writer explains his reasoning, illustrates his points, and proves his claims.

EXERCISE 1	Sorting Out General and Specific Statements

Read the following sentences carefully. Your goal will be to rearrange them to create two paragraphs. But first you'll have to sort the general statements from the specific, supporting details. Identify two general statements that can serve as topic sentences. Then arrange relevant supporting details under each one. You may need to adjust sentence openings and pronouns to make the sentences flow. Write out the paragraphs completely, and indent the first line of each paragraph.

1. The camel is certainly odd-looking, with its big hump, matted fur, and twisted face.

2. The camel can go without liquids for as long as eight days in summer and eight weeks in winter.

3. After a long dry spell, the camel can consume as much as 100 quarts of water in ten minutes.

4. There is an old joke that the camel looks as if it had been made by committee.

5. Some people think the camel keeps water in the hump, but the hump contains fat that the camel converts to energy when needed.

6. Despite its appearance and reputation, the camel is very efficiently designed to cope with its environment.

7. The water the camel drinks goes directly into its system.

8. The camel moves awkwardly and is reputed to have a bad temper.

_____

_____

_____

_____

_____

_____

_____

_____

_____

_____

EXERCISE 2	Predicting Paragraph Development

Read each of the following topic sentences, and then record two or more questions you'd expect the rest of the paragraph to answer.

1. During the Civil War, the commanding generals of the Union army and the Confederate army differed in many ways, but they also had some surprising traits in common. _____

_____

2. Studying for a test involves far more than simply reading your notes. _____

_____

_____

3. The space shuttle is more than a rocket ship; it is a temporary house for seven astronauts. _____

_____

4. Recent advances in medicine have greatly altered traditional ideas about conceiving children, becoming biological parents, and delivering babies. _____

_____

_____

Collaborative Activity 1

Comparing Questions

In your group, select the best paragraphs from Exercise 1, and make a master list of the most likely questions from Exercise 2. Report your findings to the whole class.

TWO WAYS TO DEVELOP IDEAS

You'll develop your ideas most easily if you feel comfortable with both your subject and the way you capture your thoughts. Choose a subject you know well, and then explore your ideas freely during prewriting, without stopping to ponder each word.

As you organize ideas, separate general statements from supporting statements. The general statements are likely to become topic sentences or thesis statements—and many writers can draft them in the beginning stages of the composing process. But other writers (or the same writers at other times) focus on the specifics first, before deciding what general ideas the specifics convey. We'll examine both methods.

From Topic Sentence to Supporting Materials

Suppose that you're writing about a college student's lifestyle for a popular magazine. Part of the article might describe your bed at home or in a dormitory. Look at the bed, and jot down your first reaction:

> It's a mess.

This preliminary topic sentence can now guide you in developing that idea. For example, you can brainstorm or freewrite a few specifics that explain your reaction:

> I use my bed as a dining room table.
> I dump my clothes on the bed.
> I spread out my books and papers on it to study.

You can generate details—exactly what you see—that illustrate the reaction:

> it's unmade, dirty sheets, covered with school books, clothes, and a banana peel in a rolled-up napkin
> it's old (I've had it since I was three), light brown wooden headboard, spongy mattress, a red-and-white checked spread that never gets put on, a gray blanket, clothes on the bed: pair of jeans, blue shirt, red sweater

If some of these details don't fit, you can discard them:

> ~~it's old (I've had it since I was three), light brown wooden headboard, spongy mattress~~

Then you can compose a first draft that develops the topic sentence. Here's part of the draft that focuses on one point. Notice that the first sentence makes a general statement and the second gives a specific example.

> I use my bed as a dining room table. Right now, for example, there's a banana peel in a rolled-up napkin on top of the bed, left over from a snack I had earlier.

Eventually, this exploration, planning, and drafting will result in a final draft such as the one that follows. Notice that it begins with a topic sentence and then supports its generalizations with explanations, examples, and details:

> My bed, like the beds of so many college students my age, is a mess because it serves as my temporary clothes closet, informal dining room, and study area. It is always unmade, and the sheets are usually dirty. The faded red-and-white checked bedspread lies on the floor and hasn't been put on the bed since my grandmother came to visit last fall. Instead, the bed is covered with a variety of objects. As my temporary

clothes closet and fashion display case, it holds the clothes I have taken off after returning from school or work. At the moment, for example, some grungy jeans, a blue shirt, and a red crew-neck sweater lie at the foot of the bed, and two pairs of clean slacks and a couple of shirts are laid out across the middle. As a makeshift dining room table, it holds the remains of whatever snacks I have eaten as I read, study, or listen to music. Right now, for example, a banana peel in a rolled-up napkin rests on top of my pillow. And as my study area, it holds the books and papers I have used to complete my homework assignments. Of course, the bed isn't messy all the time. I must remove some of this junk before I go to sleep.

A WRITER SPEAKS

In high school and college, my writing process could best be described as a sweatbox—staring a lot at a blank page and sweating out ideas word by word. It was sometimes agonizing, but I learned early on how much forward progress I could make by going backward, by rereading what I'd already written. If I stuck with my efforts for a period of time, I usually produced an acceptable paper.

Some years later when I began doctoral work in composition, I learned about the prewriting process and its many idea-generating activities—freewriting, clustering, listing, brainstorming, and others. I used them all and found I really could write on almost any subject. Nothing has proved more valuable to me now than focused freewriting paired with what I call focused thinking—consciously putting the subject I want to write about in my head and forcing myself to consider it off and on over time. If a new idea occurs to me, I try to be prepared to write it down. I keep pen and notepad or laptop handy, but I will write on anything: margins in a book, magazine, or newspaper, or even my shirt tail.

Several years ago, I took up serious walking for exercise. While walking rapidly on the wooded trail around the college golf course, I soon discovered that great ideas were entering my mind, most of which I lost by the time I finished. So I purchased one of those small voice-activated tape recorders to carry in a shirt pocket. Then I'd verbalize my thoughts, and the recorder would pick them up. Now if something I'm writing is important and I need fresh ideas, I don't hesitate to hit the outdoor trail with my recorder.

Once I capture the ideas in a quickly written first draft, I work at revising to shape them into effective prose. For me, the hard part is finding good content. When I have the material, I don't mind going over it once or twice a day for several days or weeks to whip it into shape.

Mark Reynolds, professor of English, Jefferson Davis Community College, Brewton, Alabama, and former editor of *Teaching English at the Two-Year College,* published by the National Council of Teachers of English.

<table>
<tr><td>EXERCISE 3</td><td>Generating Specifics</td></tr>
</table>

Assume you're composing a note to prepare a friend for what he or she will encounter when visiting your home. Draft a preliminary topic sentence for each of the following subjects to guide you in listing supporting explanations, examples, and details. (The first topic has been completed as an example.)

Subject A. The kitchen table

Topic Sentence: Our kitchen table after lunch is usually a disaster. 1. half-eaten food 2. example: my son's plate with the peanut butter and jelly sandwich sliced in fours, only one side of which has been nibbled at 3. example: my daughter's plate with 3/4 of the hot dog bun left, dripping mustard 4. spilled drinks 5. examples: a small puddle of juice next to my son's orange juice cup, and the ring of apple juice left by my daughter's cup 6. wrappers, containers, and garbage 7. examples: ice-cream bar wrappers and leaky push-up containers on the plates, peach pits, banana peels, and empty yogurt container in front of my place

Subject B. A possible guest room

Topic Sentence: You should probably stay in _____

because _____

_____

_____

_____

_____

Subject C. Your house or apartment building

Topic Sentence: The _____ looks (seems, feels, is)

_____

_____

_____

_____

Subject D. A place to visit while in town

Topic Sentence: A (*or* The) _____ is interesting (fun, exciting,

beautiful) because _____

_____

_____

_____

_____

EXERCISE 4	Drafting a Paragraph

Now draft a paragraph based on one of the topic sentences and lists you compiled in Exercise 3. Expand on your explanations, examples, and details. Then revise the paragraph.

EXERCISE 5	Drafting from a Preliminary Topic Sentence

Write a letter to a friend in which you describe the terrible state of the house in the picture. Record your initial reaction as a preliminary topic sentence. Then list the details you observe that explain or illustrate your reaction.

Photo by Charlie Wunder/Photo Researchers, Inc.

From Supporting Materials to Topic Sentences

Sometimes your ideas may not be clear as you begin. But don't worry. Just as with music, the composing process for writing always involves experiment and change. The final performance comes later. So feel free to explore your ideas—by brainstorming, clustering, or freewriting—before you arrive at some initial topic sentence. You can then reorganize the details, explain more ideas, and adjust the topic sentence as these things become clearer. This approach isn't very tidy, but remember that only results count, not how you arrive at them.

EXERCISE 6	Starting with Details

Write a short interpretation that will be placed on a label next to the following painting by Salvador Dali at the local art gallery. Your purpose is to interpret and help viewers understand the artist's message.

Collaborative Activity 2

Continuing Your Interpretation

With your group, discuss and compare what you see in Dali's painting. Try to arrive at some conclusions about its meaning (that won't be easy!). What clue does the title provide about the artist's message?

Start by listing the details you observe in the painting. Look over your list to see if the details lead to an interpretation of the picture. Jot down that interpretation, no matter how awkward or rough it sounds.

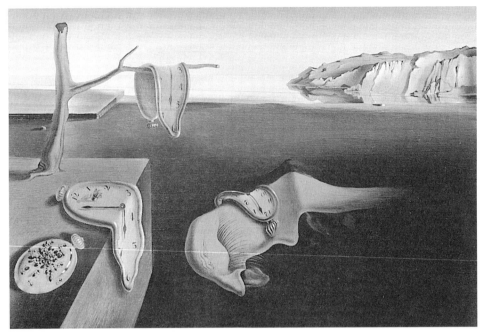

Salvador Dali, *The Persistence of Memory*, 1931. Oil on canvas, 9½ x 13 in.
© MoMA/Scala/Art Resource, NY.

EXERCISE 7   **Writing Your Interpretation**

Draft the label for Dali's painting, using the ideas and specific details you developed in Exercise 6 (and Collaborative Activity 2, if your instructor assigned it).

FACTS AND FIGURES

Many of the details and examples in the sample paragraphs you've seen throughout this book are specific statements of **fact**—that is, they're statements that can be proven. Facts often come from personal observations. But many come from outside sources such as books, magazines, and pamphlets. Some sample paragraphs you've read also include **figures**—numbers and statistics—which can be especially persuasive because they sound scientific and authoritative. Notice how the figures in the following paragraph dramatically support the point of the topic sentence:

> *There are more insects in the world than people.* More than 80 percent of the animals in the world are insects, according to Simon Goodenough, in *15,000 Fascinating Facts* (1983). The current population of the world is over six billion (6,000,000,000) people. Yet, in one year a single cabbage aphid can produce sixteen full generations of offspring—more than 1,560,000,000,000,000,000,000,000 little bugs—to easily surpass that total. While a queen termite may live only a few weeks, she lays one egg every

two seconds, 24 hours a day during her lifetime—that is, more than 600,000 eggs. Other insects produce similar numbers of descendants, and only the opposing forces in the ecology—disease, predators, and so on— keep these crawling, flying, stinging, and biting creatures from overrunning the planet.

As you support general ideas with specifics, you may find useful facts and figures in outside sources, which lend authority to your writing. Be sure to record them accurately, but don't copy the *language* of the original sources. **Paraphrase** it: restate it in your own words and sentence structure. Copying another writer's words is a form of academic dishonesty called **plagiarism**. Acknowledge each source by including the author, title, and date of publication if appropriate.

Here are some guidelines for using facts, figures, or other material from books, magazines, the Internet, or interviews—whether in this class or others.

1. *Know your stuff.* Choose a subject you're familiar with so you can judge the accuracy of outside facts (and be more confident writing about them).

2. *Control the material; don't let it control you.* Present your own ideas. If you choose to support these ideas with facts and figures, do so in your own words.

3. *Acknowledge your sources; tell where you found the information.* Acknowledging the source is not only a courtesy you owe the original author but is also required by the copyright laws. You don't have to use footnotes if you mention the author and title of the work (and possibly publication information) somewhere.

To help you gain experience in using outside sources, writing assignments at the end of this and other chapters supply facts and figures that you can use.

EXERCISE 8   Adding Facts and Figures

If your instructor directs you to include outside source material in your interpretation of the Dali painting, do the following.

Predict the questions a visitor to the art gallery might reasonably ask about what you've written on the label. What else might a visitor want to know? Who was Dali? When and where did he live and paint? What was his style? What were his ideas about memory and time? Consult at least one encyclopedia article, an art history textbook, or an Internet source to find facts and figures that can answer these questions and provide proof. Revise your label (it may now be two or three paragraphs) incorporating these new details. Be sure to acknowledge your sources.

EXERCISE 9   Revising Your Label

Now revise your label. The Revision Guidelines that follow will help you. Then make a clean copy of your work for further editing.

REVISION GUIDELINES | Developing Ideas

---

1. Underline the thesis statement or topic sentence(s). Does each make a point? Is each clear? If not, suggest some possible revisions.

2. Which sentences explain the main ideas? Enclose them in brackets. If more explanations are needed, list a few possibilities.

3. Where are the examples? Circle them. If more examples are needed, list a few possibilities.

4. What details support the main ideas? Underline them with a squiggly line.

5. What supporting evidence, or proof, is offered for the main idea? Underscore the evidence with dots.

6. Are any facts and figures included? Underline them twice. Are they presented clearly? Are their sources identified? If not, suggest some possible revisions.

7. Is the paragraph or essay unified? (That is, do all the explanations, examples, details, facts, and figures develop the topic sentence?) If not, which explanations or examples should be omitted, or where should the connections between ideas be clarified?

Collaborative Activity 3

Peer Review

If your instructor prefers, use peer review to help you revise your label. Follow the procedures explained in Chapter 2, pp. 21.

EXERCISE 10   Polishing Your Work

After completing the revision, edit the label, checking for correct spelling and punctuation, complete sentences, and clarity of ideas. Then make a clean copy of the paper and proofread it carefully for errors. Submit your final draft to your instructor.

IN SUMMARY   Strengthening Writing

1. Use specific explanations, examples, and details.
2. Support your ideas with evidence or proof.
3. Include facts and figures, which may be from outside sources.

WRITING FOR MASTERY

Here's an opportunity to gain more experience with developing ideas. For each of the following topics, write a paragraph that includes a topic sentence and supporting details. Alternatively, if your instructor prefers, you may expand one of the topics into a full essay, complete with thesis statement, topic sentences in the body paragraphs, and—again—supporting details.

1. Compose another label for a museum. Select your subject by visiting a museum, looking through magazines or books, or picking from your own collection. Prewrite. Sort generalizations and supporting details. Then compose the label. The final draft that you submit to your instructor should contain (1) a topic sentence, (2) supporting details, (3) facts and figures from outside sources if necessary, and (4) a concluding statement. Provide a photograph or photocopy of your subject if possible.

2. Describe and interpret
   a. the photograph of the room on page 73
   b. a painting or piece of sculpture, or an unusual object
   c. something hanging on the wall in your room

Photo by Walker Evans for the Farm Security Administration, first reproduced in *Three Tenant Families: Let Us Now Praise Famous Men,* **1941. Library of Congress.**

d. a family souvenir

e. any other unusual object you have collected

3. *Writing from Source Material.* Compose a paragraph for an article in *National Geographic,* based on some—but not all—of the facts and figures supplied here. (You might base it only on those about the elephant's trunk or the comparative sizes of elephants, but these aren't the only possibilities.) Read through the material several times before you begin composing. Then draft a preliminary topic sentence that states the topic and an opinion about it, such as, "The elephant's trunk is a very unusual object." Arrange the supporting details logically and then *paraphrase* them. Restate them in your own words. This may take several revisions. Then edit and proofread the paragraph. Produce a final copy and submit it to your instructor.

locale: Africa and Asia

size: African elephant generally bigger than Asian elephant

tusks: rare in female Asian elephants

ears: large on African elephant; small on Asian elephant

tusks: large on African elephant

skin: darker on African elephant

trunk: more wrinkled on African elephant

trunk: end functions almost like fingers; is very sensitive

height: about eleven feet tall at shoulder of average African male

weight: as much as 14,000 pounds for average African male

trunk: as much as six feet long; weight as much as 300 pounds

use of trunk: to carry food and water to mouth, to take a shower, to measure temperature, to feel objects, to fight, and to show affection

tusks: ivory

trunk: can grasp peanut, carry a 650-pound log, or drag two tons

tusks: used for fighting, digging, and carrying objects

Source: David Wallechinsky and Irving Wallace, *The People's Almanac 2* (1978).

6

Achieving Coherence

Now that you've practiced ways to develop and support your ideas, you can look at ways to strengthen the links between ideas. This chapter will show you how to carry the composing process further to create a smooth and easily understood logical flow. You'll practice

- ways to form links with repetitions and substitutions
- ways to highlight the relationships between ideas

WHAT IS COHERENCE?

A topic sentence and unified supporting sentences go a long way toward helping readers understand and appreciate your ideas. But readers must also see how these ideas *cohere*—or, literally, "hold together." **Coherence** is the logical arrangement of ideas so that each leads deliberately to the next.

Coherence emerges primarily from planning and revising. In prewriting, you select ideas, discard others, and organize what remains. You draft and revise until the paragraph or essay takes on a logical form. We'll examine a different form of paragraph organization in every chapter of Unit III. Here we'll focus on ways to make your writing—in whatever form it takes—hang together.

PARALLELISM

One way to achieve coherence is through **parallelism**, or **parallel construction**. You arrange words in a certain way and then repeat the arrangement. Parallelism signals to readers that ideas are closely related and equally important—and, just as in music, it often adds a pleasing rhythm to your writing.

Recognizing Parallel Structures

Parallel structures often have a rhythm you can hear in your head (or literally hear, if you read your papers aloud). Recall, for example, Abraham Lincoln's unforgettable conclusion to the Gettysburg Address:

UNIT 2 Chapter 6 Composing with Confidence ©2003	GO ELECTRONIC! Use the following electronic supplements for additional practice with your writing: • For chapter-by-chapter summaries and exercises, visit the Composing with Confidence Companion Website at: http://www.ablongman.com/meyers. • For work with the writing process, visit The Longman Writer's Warehouse at http://longmanwriterswarehouse.com (password needed). • For additional practice in grammar, use The Writer's ToolKit Plus CD-ROM

A Word About Words

English is classified as a Germanic language because of its Anglo-Saxon roots, but many words from German came into English later on. Here are a few: *lobby, hamster, waltz, zigzag, iceberg, poodle, protein, poker, ouch, beer,* and, of course, *kindergarten.*

> . . . and that government of the people, by the people, and for the people shall not perish from the earth.

The passage is memorable because it is simple, elegant—and parallel.

Because parallel structures call so much attention to the sounds and shapes of ideas, they help you recognize the important details, such as those supporting the topic sentence in the following paragraph:

> The original designers of the American flag were quite casual in their attitude toward it. *Some stars came with five points. Some stars came with six. Some stars came in white. Some came in silver.*

Some + came line up all the ideas in a neat sequence.

Parallelism works not only between sentences but also within them. Notice how easily you can see the relationships among a series of ideas in the following examples:

> During the American Revolution, Samuel Adams gained fame as an inspirational *writer, speaker,* and *leader.* (repeated nouns)
>
> His personal life was less glamorous. He *wasted* his inheritance, *ruined* his father's brewery, and *failed* as a tax collector. (repeated past-tense verbs)
>
> This hot-headed member of the famous Adams family was far better at *brewing* rebellion than *brewing* beer. (repeated *–ing* words)
>
> Adams signed the Declaration of Independence *during the war,* held a variety of state offices *after the war,* and disappeared from the national scene *after that.* (repeated time expressions)

Here, parallelism emphasizes the main themes of the life of Samuel Adams: he was a notable public figure but a miserable private failure.

EXERCISE 1   Identifying Parallel Structures

Underline the parallel structures between and within sentences in Paragraphs B through D.

It's a Grand Old Flag—Sort of

Paragraph A. We <u>salute</u> our flag, <u>fly</u> it proudly, and sing to it at the beginning of sports events. It's an almost sacred symbol of patriotism today, but it <u>was far from sacred</u> to our country's first citizens. In fact, many Americans—including top government officials—didn't know what it looked like. More than a year after Congress officially adopted it, Benjamin Franklin and John Adams, in a joint letter to the king of Naples, said it "consists of thirteen stripes, alternately <u>red, white, and blue.</u>"

Paragraph B. We can forgive these famous Americans for their ignorance, for they rarely had the chance to see the flag. It didn't fly from buildings, wasn't put in the schools, wasn't reproduced in the newspapers, and didn't appear in any pictures painted at that time. One historian, who searched all major catalogs of art from the Revolutionary War, says he could not find a single picture of the American flag.

Paragraph C. We think that Old Glory appeared everywhere during the Revolution because it appeared everywhere in the paintings of the Revolution done a century afterward. But the fact is that not a single land battle of the Revolutionary War was fought under the Stars and Stripes. In fact, American soldiers first fought under Old Glory during the Mexican–American War—seventy-five years later. Even then, the flag didn't often show up in battle. The Marines didn't adopt the flag until 1876. The U.S. Cavalry didn't adopt it until 1887. And those pictures of George Custer and the Stars and Stripes during his famous last stand? Forget them. His men never carried that flag.

Paragraph D. Soldiers did not fight without flags, of course. They carried battle flags to keep up their spirits. But today we're not interested in those flags. What we want is Washington crossing the Delaware with the Stars and Stripes. And what we want was exactly what the artists in the nineteenth century gave us. Those pictures including American flags have always sold well.

Revising for Parallel Structures

If you feel confident in your ideas and writing voice, parallelism will flow naturally from your pen, pencil, typewriter, or word processor. But if you don't find any parallelism during revisions, you might look for equal ideas to rewrite in repeated sentence structures. For example, suppose you begin a paragraph with this topic sentence and second sentence of supporting detail:

> There wasn't much to do on Saturday night in my tiny home town, so almost every teen-age kid ended up in the town square. <u>The male bikers were there</u> in their black leather jackets, <u>looking</u> tough as they circled around the fountain in the center of the square.

As you continue to compose the first draft, you can repeat the pattern of the second sentence ("The bikers were there, . . . looking . . ."):

> <u>The greasers were there, cruising</u> in their twelve-year-old cars around the square. Their radios blasted away and horns honked at the people who sat around or gathered in groups on the sidewalks. <u>The preppies were there, discussing</u> Friday night's game, who was dating whom, or where they'd meet for hamburgers or pizza later in the evening. <u>The girls were there, standing</u> in groups or <u>driving their parents' cars</u>. They were the main reason that boys hung around. At least some of the girls would pair up with boys, and the square would empty out.

EXERCISE 2 | Writing Parallel Structures

Complete each of the following paragraphs by drafting at least three more sentences of supporting detail. Read the sentences already supplied and find a pattern you would expect to be repeated. Then repeat that pattern in the sentences you write.

1. *My English classroom is typical of the rooms in the college.* There are windows along the left wall. There is a row of coat hooks on the right wall. *There is a blackboard on the front wall. There is a clock above the chalkboard. There is an instructor's desk in front of the chalkboard. There are movable student desks arranged in rows in the middle of the room. And there are twenty-five brilliant students sitting at those desks, eagerly awaiting the wise pronouncements of our instructor.*

2. *During the summer months, I try to be outdoors as much as I can.* I walk along the river or pedal down the bike paths. _____

   _____

   _____

   _____

3. *My morning routine is about the same each day.* I wake up slowly, dragging my reluctant body out of bed. _____

   _____

   _____

   _____

   _____

4. *The behavior of* _____ *is full of contradictions.* (Establish your own pattern and repeat it.) _____

   _____

   _____

   _____

   _____

Collaborative Activity 1

Examining Parallelism

Examine each other's answers to Exercise 2 by writing them on a separate sheet of paper and passing it to the left. If you can strengthen the parallelism of a sentence, revise it. Then discuss your answers and suggestions for revisions within the group.

EXERCISE 3 | Drafting a Paragraph

Draft a paragraph about your hometown or community for a magazine article about life in various cities and towns in the United States or other countries. For example, you could discuss what people did on weekends, at night, during particular seasons, or on special occasions such as weddings or festivals. Draft a preliminary topic sentence that states the point, such as, "On Friday night, my friends and I mostly traveled in packs from one person's house to another, watching videos, emptying the refrigerator, calling everybody on our cell phones, and finding ways to stay up until 4:00 A.M." or "On Saturdays during the summer, my friends and I usually ended up at the beach for tanning, loafing, people-watching, or even swimming." Develop the topic sentence through specific details arranged in parallel structure.

REPEATED WORDS AND IDEAS

Aside from repeating sentence structures, you can link ideas by repeating key words or substituting other words for them. There are a number of options to choose from: pronouns, repeated nouns, synonyms, and substitutions.

Pronouns and Repeated Nouns

As their name suggests, **pronouns** often replace nouns. And pronouns often refer back to their **antecedents**, the nouns or other pronouns they replace. Because of the link between pronouns and antecedents, correctly used pronouns are a useful tool in achieving coherence. They keep the reader's focus on the person, place, or thing you're discussing, and they sharpen your focus on the subject as you write and revise. Using them correctly involves two simple rules:

1. A pronoun such as *he, she, it,* or *they* must have an antecedent;
2. The pronoun must agree in number with its antecedent (that is, a plural pronoun such as *them* cannot refer to a singular antecedent).

Let's look at an example. In the model paragraph you read earlier, the pronoun *they* refers to *preppies:*

> The preppies were there, discussing Friday night's game, who was dating whom, or where they'd meet for hamburgers or pizza later in the evening …

✓ TIPS

For Using Pronouns

For pronouns and their antecedents to mesh, they have to agree. That is, a singular pronoun (*he/she/it; him/her; his/her/its*) must refer to a singular noun (*a man, a woman, a chair*). And a plural pronoun (*they, them, their*) must refer to a plural noun (*men, women, chairs*). Look carefully at pronouns and antecedents as you edit to make sure they match.

EXERCISE 4	Adding Pronouns

Improve the coherence in the following paragraph by circling the antecedent of each missing pronoun, and then supplying a pronoun that agrees with its antecedent.

Oh, Say: Was the Flag Still There?

(1) The popularity of the song "The Star-Spangled Banner"—if this unsingable song can still be said to be popular—is due as much to the unusual circumstances under which *it* _____ was written as to the appeal of its lyrics. (2) Very few people can recite _____, but many people know the story behind the song. (3) _____ composer, Francis Scott Key, actually watched the bombardment of Fort McHenry (which guarded Baltimore) in the War of 1812, and Key actually waited through the night to see if "our flag was still there."

(4) However, two common beliefs about the song aren't quite accurate. (5) Many people are sure _____ was adopted as the national anthem within a few years.

(6) The actual date of its adoption was 1931. (7) Many people also think that the tune came from an old English drinking song. (8) That belief is partially true. (9) The lyrics did discuss the glories of wine—but _____ also described love-making in a rather explicit way. (10) If Francis Scott Key ever felt embarrassed about the origins of his creation, he never said so.

Collaborative Activity 2

Examining Pronoun-Antecedent Relationships

Photocopy a fairly long paragraph from a novel. Then rewrite the paragraph, replacing every pronoun with the noun it represents. (Don't replace *I*, *we*, and *you*.) Exchange the paragraph with a classmate, and rewrite it again, replacing the nouns with the pronouns. Then compare the original to the second rewrite. Do the pronouns clearly refer to and agree with the antecedents?

Repeated Key Terms

Don't overuse pronouns, for not every pronoun establishes a clear link. In the model paragraph, the pronoun *they* could refer to any of three antecedents:

> The girls were there, gathering in groups or driving their parents' cars. They were the main reason that boys hung around.

Did the boys hang around because of the cars or the girls (or groups of them)? Repeating the appropriate noun eliminates any confusion:

> The girls were the main reason that boys hung around.

There's another reason not to overuse pronouns: to avoid monotony. So try to blend pronouns and repeated key words in equal measure. Notice, for example, how repeated words (in italics), along with a few pronouns, neatly tie ideas together in the following paragraph:

> (1) Did *the flag* that Francis Scott Key saw at "dawn's early light" during the War of 1812 fly through *the night*? (2) Probably not *that flag*, which is now on display at the Smithsonian Institution in Washington. (3) *The night* was stormy, windy, and rainy—and the banner at the Smithsonian is massive. (4) It's thirty feet by forty-two feet. (4) The stars alone measure two feet across from point to point. (5) That the *flag* could have survived the tempest of the previous *night* seems unbelievable. (6) Only *another, smaller flag* would have withstood the tempest.

Vary your word choice. Don't overload a passage with pronouns or repeated words, but use enough of each to establish coherence. In fact, as you'll soon see, there are even more ways to repeat ideas gracefully.

Repeating Across Paragraphs

Repeating a term or idea from the last sentence of a paragraph is a good way to establish connections between paragraphs. Look at how expressions (in italics) tie the following paragraphs together.

Paragraph A. In Rochester, New York, in 1820, Susan B. Anthony was born into a world of every privilege except one. Women did not have the right to vote. She battled throughout her life to ban alcohol and to end slavery, but her greatest contribution to the cause of *social justice* was to gain the right to vote for women.

Paragraph B. Anthony's passion for *social justice* did not come from poverty; it came from the moral principles of her family. Her father, Daniel Anthony, was a Quaker who gave young Susan the best schooling available. Then, as a matter of principle, he insisted that she earn her own living. She worked as a schoolteacher at a salary of eight dollars a month, while male schoolteachers were receiving from three to four times that amount. But unequal pay did not make her as angry as *unequal treatment*.

Paragraph C. In the summer of 1849, Anthony experienced an *inequality* she never forgot. She tried to serve as a delegate to the New York Men's State Temperance Convention, but the male reformers would not allow her to join them. At the convention, Anthony met Elizabeth Cady Stanton, who had been similarly rejected when she had tried to attend an antislavery convention in 1840. Together they vowed to fight for equal rights for women, especially the right to vote. For the rest of their lives they attended political conventions, state legislatures, and other gatherings that affected the legal status of women. Sixty years later, after both women had died, their goal was achieved.

EXERCISE 5 — Identifying Repetition

Find the repeated key terms in the following passage. Circle the term the first time it is used, and underline it the second time.

(1) If there was a banner on the pole in the morning following the bombardment of Fort McHenry—and there undoubtedly was—it was probably hoisted up the pole that morning. (2) And that is precisely what an eyewitness says happened. (3) According to Midshipman Robert J. Barrett, as the British fleet sailed away after the battle, the Americans "hoisted a most superb and splendid ensign on their battery." (4) If a banner did fly all through the previous night, it must have been the fort's so-called storm flag, a small flag designed for use in bad weather. (5) In fact, it's doubtful that Key could have even seen the storm flag in the darkness. (6) He was eight miles away—possibly near enough to see the large banner, but not the smaller one.

EXERCISE 6 — Editing for Coherence

The following passage is incoherent in places because of carelessly used pronouns (in italics). Replace these pronouns with repeated key terms.

The Beginnings of the Revolutionary War

(1) The colonists hated the taxes Britain imposed on them, and *it* that hatred eventually led to the Revolutionary War. (2) "Taxation without

representation is tyranny," they protested when the British Parliament passed the Stamp Act in 1765. (3) Then two years later, *they* _____ placed additional taxes on key imports—especially tea. (4) Even when *they* _____ were collected, British tea was still relatively cheap. (5) But the colonists opposed *them* _____ on principle, and some angry residents of Massachusetts dumped 342 cases of *it* _____ into Boston Harbor in 1773—an act that came to be known as the Boston Tea Party. (6) The British Parliament promptly responded to *it* _____ by closing the port of Boston. (7) When further rebellions and punishments led to actual battles in 1775, *they* _____ chose "liberty or death" rather than "slavery" as part of the British Empire. (8) Therefore, armed with high principles and deadly rifles, *they* _____ banded together in the modern world's first revolutionary war against a mother country.

Synonyms and Substitutes

You've seen two ways to repeat ideas, through pronouns and repeated key terms. Now let's expand your choices to include synonyms and substitutions. A **synonym** is a word with approximately the same meaning as another. "Physician" is a synonym for "doctor." "Courage," "boldness," "fearlessness," and even "valor" are synonyms for "bravery." A **substitute** word or phrase, while not a synonym, clearly represents an earlier idea. "This tiny device," or "handy apparatus" are substitutes for "a pager." Notice how synonyms and substitutions (in italics) refer to the two most important ideas—George Washington and his handwritten will (both boldface)—in the following paragraph:

> **George Washington** was an extremely precise man, and his **handwritten will**—*composed* without the help of a lawyer—demonstrates this trait by its almost maddening neatness. *The former first president penned* it on fifteen sheets of personal watermarked *parchment*. He filled both sides, numbered and signed each page, and, apparently concerned with the *document's* artistic appeal, *engineered* every line to be precisely the same length. He used dashes to extend short lines and hyphens to break a long line's last word irrespective of proper syllabication. *The text* looks computer-set, with perfectly aligned margins.

Notice the synonyms and substitutions:

Original term	Replacement
handwritten	penned, composed, engineered
George Washington	the former first president
will	parchment, document, text

✓ TIPS

For Choosing Synonyms

If you look up synonyms in a dictionary or thesaurus, select only words you already know, and know will fit your meaning. A misused synonym invites confusion, not coherence—and maybe even unintentional humor if you don't know what you're really saying!

EXERCISE 7 | Writing Synonyms and Substitutions

Improve the coherence of the following passage by filling in appropriate synonyms or substitutions for the italicized words.

The Man Behind the Legends of George Washington

(1) Everyone knows that *George Washington* chopped down a cherry tree when ___the young man_____ was only six years old. (2) But most Americans don't know that this story of ___the future president's___ honesty is simply imaginary—the invention of a man named Mason Locke "Parson" Weems (1760–1825). (3) The cherry tree *tale* is only one of the _____ in Weems's biography, <u>Life of George Washington; with Curious Anecdotes, Equally Honorable to Himself; and Exemplary to His Young Countrymen</u>. (4) This _____ is a largely fictional—or at least largely exaggerated—account of Washington's life and times. (5) *Weems* knew what the reading public loved. (6) _____ wasn't necessarily a liar; he just got carried away with his own *enthusiasm*. (7) As an ordained minister in Maryland for eight years, he expressed that strong _____ in his sermons. (8) But Weems was unhappy with his life, so he took up a new *occupation* as a traveling bookseller for Matthew Carey, who published religious books in Philadelphia. (9) Weems loved his _____ and soon also began to write a number of "improvement *books*" such as the _____ about George Washington.

EXERCISE 8	Revising Your First Draft

Revise the first draft of the paragraph you wrote in Exercise 3. Make sure that pronouns clearly refer to antecedents, and that neither pronouns nor key terms are repeated too often. Include some synonyms and substitutions as well.

TRANSITIONS

A final method for achieving coherence is through **transitions**, words or phrases that establish logical connections among ideas. They add ideas together, contrast ideas, locate ideas in a time or space sequence, or show one as the cause or result of another.

Transitions can be single words such as *therefore, also, however, later,* or *finally.* Or they can be short expressions such as *in the center, at the top, as a result.* Either way, they cement relationships among ideas. Notice how the italicized transitions in the following paragraph help you identify each supporting idea of the topic sentence:

THE CAREER OF PAUL REVERE

Paul Revere is notable for a number of reasons. First, of course, he is best known from Longfellow's poem about his midnight ride—during which, in 1775, he supposedly alerted the American colonists that the British were coming. *Second,* he is well known as a silversmith, the man who founded the company that today makes Revereware pots and pans. *Third,* he is perhaps less well known as a manufacturer of teeth, a manufacturer of guns, and an artist and engraver. *Fourth,* and what is least known about him and most surprising, is that, as an artist, he forged other artists' pictures.

The following list of common transitions, arranged according to meaning, may provide a useful reference as you draft and revise.

TRANSITIONS

Enumeration (or Counting)
first, second, third, next, then, after that, finally

Space
above, around, behind, below, beneath, beyond, close by, farther away, in front of, in the front (back, rear), in the middle (center), inside, on the inside (outside), nearby, next to, to the left (right), to the north (south), on the right (left, bottom, top), outside, over, under, underneath

Time
In sequence: after, after a while, afterward, and then, an hour (a day, a week) later, eventually, finally, first (second, third), later (on), next, soon, still later, the next day (week, year), tomorrow
Simultaneous or close in time: as, as soon as, at that moment, during, immediately, meanwhile, suddenly, when, while
Previous time: before, earlier, last night (month, year), yesterday
At a stated time: in March, in 1983, on July 8

Addition
additionally, also, and, furthermore, in addition, moreover, too

Comparison
in the same way (manner), likewise, similarly

Concession
as you probably know, certainly, naturally, no doubt, of course

Contrast
although, but, despite, even though, however, nevertheless, nonetheless, on the contrary, on the other hand, yet

Emphasis
above all, especially, indeed, in fact, in particular, most important

Illustrations
as an example (illustration), for example, for instance, in particular, such as

Qualification
maybe, perhaps, possibly

Reasons
as, because, because of, for, one reason for this is, since

Summary/Conclusion
and so, in other words, in short, in summary, to summarize, to sum up, thus, therefore

---

EXERCISE 9 | Locating Transitions

The following passage tells a story, so it is organized in a time sequence. Underline each transition that indicates a time relationship.

The Origins of Our Nation's Capital

Congress had an important reason for meeting in June 1783 to relocate the nation's capital from Philadelphia. The War of Independence had just ended in February, and the new nation was flat broke. It had no credit, still lacked a strong central government, and was heavily in debt to soldiers for back pay. As a result, a large and angry mob of soldiers invaded Philadelphia on June 20 to demand that Congress pay them. The members of Congress were so frustrated and frightened that they decided to move out of town. At their meeting in the Old City Hall that day, they began to discuss creating a federal city in an isolated, inconvenient area where lawmakers could conduct the business of government without being bothered by its citizens.

The debate about where to place this new city continued for many years. New Englanders, led by Alexander Hamilton of New York, wanted a capital in the North. Southerners, represented by Thomas Jefferson of Virginia, argued for a location in the South. In 1790, the recently elected president, George Washington, attempted to satisfy both sides. He chose a site eighteen miles up the Potomac River from his home in Mount Vernon—midway between the North and South at that time. No one denied, however, that the ten-mile-square site was a swamp.

Too many transitions are annoying, so don't overuse them. As you revise, consider the logical relationships between ideas. You may need to add a few transitions, change some that seem illogical, and substitute for some transitions you have repeated.

To see how transitions can firmly cement an otherwise coherent piece of writing, let's return once more to the final draft of the model paragraph on page 77. Not only has its word choice been improved, but its coherence has been strengthened by some short transitional expressions (underlined):

> There wasn't much to do on Saturday night in my tiny hometown, so almost everyone ended up in the town square. The male bikers were there in their black leather jackets, looking tough as they circled around the fountain in the center of the square. The greasers were there, cruising in their twelve-year-old cars around the square. Their radios blasted away, and horns honked at the people who sat on the steps of town hall, stretched out on the grass around the fountain, or stood on the sidewalks in groups of three, four, or more. The preppies were there <u>as well</u>, discussing Friday night's high school basketball or football game, who was dating whom, or where everyone would meet for hamburgers or pizza

Continued

later in the evening. And the girls were there, congregating in groups or driving their dads' cars. Naturally, the girls were the main reason that the bikers, the greasers, and the preppies hung around. At least some members of one sex would eventually pair up with members of the other, and by 2:00 A.M. the square would empty out.

EXERCISE 10	Predicting Transitions

Read each passage, and then list four or five transitions you would expect to find in the remainder of each passage.

Passage A. The steps involved in registering for classes are rather complicated. First, you must request a packet of materials from the Office of Admissions. *Second, Third, Fourth, Finally*

_____

Passage B. After playing on the muddy ground and in the wet leaves, the six-year-old boy was a mess. First, his shoes were caked with mud. Second, his pants were ripped and grass-stained at the knees. _____

_____

_____

Passage C. Friday was extremely busy for Serina Johnson. In the morning, she had a conference call with sales representatives in five cities on the East Coast.

_____

_____

Passage D. The new three-story auditorium is large and beautiful. On the ground floor, the seats nearest the stage are covered with a plush red velvet material, and the wide spaces between rows allow plenty of leg room. The seats farther from the stage are equally plush, but the rows are closer, leaving less room for the legs. _____

_____

Passage E. (Write your own topic sentence about the following picture. Then list the transitions you would most likely need.) _____

_____

_____

_____

Claude Monet, *La Grenouillere, A Resort on the Seine River, Paris,*
1869. Oil on canvas, 29⅜ x 39¼ in. The Metropolitan Museum of Art,
H. O. Havemeyer Collection, Bequest of Mrs. H. O. Havemeyer, 1929
(29.100.112). Photograph © 1989 The Metropolitan Museum of Art.

EXERCISE 11	Adding Transitions

*Insert transition words or phrases regarding time, space, or contrast in the following
paragraph so the relationships among ideas are clear. Consult the list of transitions on
page 84 for suggestions.*

Betsy Ross: The Designer of the American Flag?

(1) We know that the American flag did not have a single dramatic moment of
birth. (2) *In fact,* _____ the star-spangled banner evolved over a long
period and was shaped by many hands. (3) This evolution raises the question
whether a tailor named Betsy Ross was actually involved in creating it.
(4) According to legend, General Washington came to her shop in Philadelphia in
June of 1776. (5) They discussed various flag designs until they settled on one
she suggested: seven red and six white stripes, and thirteen five-pointed white
stars arranged in a circle. (6) The general left, and the seamstress began stitching
the American flag. (7) _____ many historians have several
problems with this explanation. (8) _____ not a single one of
the many flags during the Revolutionary War carried Betsy Ross's design.
(9) _____ the tale was told by Betsy Ross herself—on her
deathbed in 1836—and to an eleven-year-old boy, William J. Canby, who was her
grandson. (10) _____ Canby didn't relate this account until
1870 at a meeting of the Pennsylvania Historical Society. (11) It was thirty-four

Collaborative Activity 3

Looking at Transitions
Compare your answers to
Exercises 10 and 11. Where
the answers differ, discuss
the effect these differences
make on the meaning of a
passage. Are you able, as a
group, to reach consensus
on the best choices? Report
your results to the whole
class.

Collaborative Activity 4

Peer Review

If your instructor prefers, use peer review to help you revise your paragraph or essay. Follow the procedures explained in Chapter 2, page 21.

years after he had heard the story as a boy, and almost 100 years after the events had supposedly occurred.

(12) Historical records show that George Washington was in Philadelphia in June of 1776. (13) _____ his written records don't mention a meeting with a local seamstress, and his diary doesn't include a single word about creating an official American flag. (14) In fact, Congress hadn't even discussed the need to replace the flag in use at that time. (15) _____ many historians believe that the Betsy Ross story is a charming legend, but probably untrue.

EXERCISE 12 — Doing a First Draft

Draft a paragraph based on the material from one of the passages from Exercise 10. Be sure to include all (or most) of the transitional expressions you have listed.

REVISING FOR COHERENCE

If you've planned and organized your paragraph or essay carefully, its coherence should already be apparent. But, during revision, you can increase the coherence even more. Tighten the links between ideas by adding transitions, repeating key terms, choosing synonyms carefully, employing parallelism, and checking for agreement between pronouns and their antecedents. Consult the Revision Guidelines that follow for help.

REVISION GUIDELINES — Tightening Coherence

1. Is the topic sentence clear? If not, how should it be changed?
2. Is the paragraph developed adequately? If not, list some suggestions for additional explanations, examples, details, proof, or facts and figures.
3. Underline parallel structures. If you see any places where parallelism is needed, list those on the blank sheet.
4. Circle the pronouns. Are there too many? Are the antecedents of any unclear? Is so, list terms that could be repeated in place of the pronouns.
5. Bracket the repeated terms. Are there too many? If so, list some synonyms or substitutions that the writer could use.
6. Look at the transitions. If any are missing, make a list of possible additions to the paragraph.

EXERCISE 13 — Revising Your Draft

Now revise your paper according to the following guidelines. Then make a clean copy of your work for further editing.

EXERCISE 14 — Polishing Your Work

After revising your paper, edit this draft for errors. Make a clean, proofread copy to submit to your instructor.

IN SUMMARY	Achieving Coherence

1. Use parallelism, or repeated sentence structures.
2. Use pronouns.
3. Repeat key terms.
4. Use synonyms and substitutions for key words.
5. Use transitional expressions.

WRITING FOR MASTERY

Now put your knowledge of coherence to work. For each of the following topics, write a paragraph that includes a topic sentence and supporting details. Alternatively, if your instructor prefers, you may expand one of the topics into a full essay, complete with thesis statement, topic sentences in the body paragraphs, and support. Try to achieve coherence through the repetition of sentence structures, the use of pronouns, the repetition or substitution of key words, and the use of transitional expressions.

1. A description of the building in one of the following photographs. Use transitions such as "at the top," "to the right," and "below the dome" to locate details, and make sure your pronoun references are clear.
2. A story about a time when you did something funny, heroic, or difficult. Use transitions such as "first," "later that day," and "soon afterward" to indicate the time sequence.
3. A comparison of your activities on a typical weekday with your activities on a Saturday or Sunday. Use repeated sentence structures to emphasize the comparisons.

Taj Mahal, Agra, India, 1632–48. Brian Vikander/CORBIS.

Imperial Heavenly Vault, Temple of Heaven, Beijing, 1530, restored 1752 and later. Dean Conger/CORBIS.

4. A short character sketch of someone close to you—a parent, a friend, a sibling, or another person you know well. Emphasize what makes this person special. Use pronouns, synonyms and substitutions to refer to the person.

5. A description of your favorite meeting place (or hangout) when you were younger. Discuss the typical activities at that place, focusing on the behavior of particular people. Make sure your pronoun references are clear. And include transitions indicating locations and the sequence of time.

6. *Writing from Source Material.* Write an informative paragraph (or essay) about the early history of the nation's capital in Washington, D.C. Using the information supplied, develop a coherent paragraph that develops the topic sentence. Organize the material logically before you begin to write. Then draft and revise the paragraph so each sentence relates to the ones preceding it. Use parallelism, pronouns, repeated key terms, synonyms and substitutions, and transitions.

Do not copy any of the language, aside from names, dates, and the material in quotation marks. State the ideas in your own words, and revise the paper until you're sure the words are clearly yours—and clearly stated.

capital expands quickly as many more offices built

September 1793, President Washington lays cornerstone for first U.S. Capitol building

1790, Washington announces the site for the capital

1800, government moves headquarters from Philadelphia to Washington upon seeing the first buildings of the new city, senators and members of Congress call it "capital of miserable huts" and a "mud hole"

President Washington at time of announcement: "a city of magnificent distances"

August 1814, British invade Washington, burn president's mansion, the Capitol Building, and Navy arsenal

national tragedy changes attitude toward capital

1814, Jefferson donates his books to replace burned books of the Library of Congress

the burned wood of president's mansion painted bright white, and building called the White House

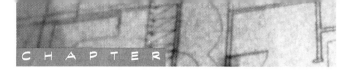

7 Writing Directly and Vividly

Strong writing goes beyond sound organization. It's musical: rhythmic, lively, and direct. That music comes from listening to your writing voice and then revising to strengthen that voice. It also comes from deliberate choices during the process of composing, especially during revising. This chapter will help you

- choose strong verbs and adjectives
- eliminate wordiness and meaningless expressions
- employ lively comparisons

WHAT IS STRONG WRITING?

Add power to your sentences. Make them say a lot in just a few words. Choose language that's specific, fresh, graceful, and trim.

Weak sentences are vague, stale, repetitious, and wordy. Compare these examples:

> 1. In my opinion, a good place to get good food which is not too expensive is a restaurant named the New Café, which is located on the corner of Franklin Street and Second Avenue.
> 2. The New Café, on the corner of Franklin Street and Second Avenue, serves delicious food at reasonable prices.

The second sentence states the point directly in just eighteen words, while the first sentence squanders many of its thirty-four words. Let's examine the waste:

> *In my opinion* (You're recommending a restaurant, which is obviously an opinion. So why state the obvious?)
>
> *a good place to get good food* (Why repeat the flabby adjective *good*? And isn't a restaurant obviously a place?)
>
> *which is not too expensive* (Why state your recommendation negatively? State it affirmatively: the prices are reasonable.)
>
> *is a restaurant named the New Café* (Why waste the words *restaurant* and *named?* The New Café is obviously the name of a restaurant.)
>
> *which is located on the corner of Franklin Street and Second Avenue.* (Why say *located?* The words *on the corner of Franklin Street and Second Avenue* indicate location.)

In short, the first version is filled with *deadwood:* lifeless and useless language. It states the obvious, repeats dull words unnecessarily, overrelies on the linking verb *is*, and stuffs two *which* clauses into the pile of debris.

Strong writing puts every word to work. It's direct, colorful, concrete, and action-filled. You can compose in a confident voice; then revise to prune the deadwood and fortify what remains.

A WRITER SPEAKS

I guess I'm lucky that I don't have much trouble writing. I sit down at the computer, and the words simply flow. The problem is that too many of them flow. If I stop and try to edit myself while I'm writing, I just get frustrated and lose track of what I want to say. So I let the floodgates open, and when I'm done writing, I go back and cut out as many words as I can. (I've noticed, for example, that I greatly overuse the word "really.") As an editor, I firmly believe that every sentence is at least three words too long—so I look on the revision phase as time to get rid of the excess baggage. In fact, I think it's very rare to find a long sentence from which three words can't be cut.

Steve Rigolosi, senior editor, Addison Wesley Longman

ELIMINATING WEAK VERBS

A Word About Words

Many words change in meaning over time. Here's an example. Today *brokers* sell real estate or stocks. But *brokieres,* from old French, were people who opened up wine casks to bottle and sell the wine. Eventually the word referred to wine salespeople, and finally to anyone who sold anything at all.

Don't worry about each word during first drafts. Let your ideas and words flow. But pay special attention to verbs during revisions. Look for ways to replace vague and overused verbs such as *is/are/am, go, get, have, make, do, run, put, take, see, use,* and *talk.* The verb *get,* for example, expresses countless meanings:

get an idea, get a present for someone or from someone, get a job, get home, get an A, get sick, get married, get a raise, get angry, get up, get off, get on, get in, get out, get over, get around, get down, get through, get to work, get to sleep, get finished, get lost, get ahead, get away with, get together, get even with, get done with this list

You can't completely eliminate common and bland verbs, but don't overuse them. Circle weak verbs and substitute verbs or phrases that more precisely express your meaning. These replacements needn't be fancy, just more exact. Here are a few alternatives for *get:*

TIPS

For Choosing Strong Verbs

If you can't think of a substitute verb, check a *thesaurus:* a dictionary of synonyms. In fact, you can access the thesaurus in most word-processing programs with a keystroke or click of a mouse. *But let the thesaurus remind you of synonyms you already know.* Don't try impressing readers with fancy words you don't fully command. You may amuse them instead—at your expense!

got to sleep:	I	fell asleep / nodded off / drowsed off	at midnight.
got angry:	The coach	exploded / roared / fumed	at the players.
got home:	He	arrived home / staggered in the door / burst into the house	at 9:30.

Like *get*, the verb *have* shows up all the time. When it expresses possession, it often wastes an entire sentence, whose meaning can be expressed in one word. Look for ways to replace *have* with **possessive pronouns**—*my, our, your, his, her, its,* and *their*—and with **possessive nouns**, formed by adding *'s* to singular nouns or *'* after the *–s* in plural nouns—*Maria's piano, the Wilsons' horse's stable.*

Poor: I have a good friend named Bill. We hang out together all the time.

Better: My good friend Bill and I hang out together all the time.

Poor: Maria has an instructor who gives wonderful lectures.

Better: Maria's instructor gives wonderful lectures.

EXERCISE 1   **Writing Strong Verbs**

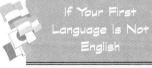

If Your First Language Is Not English

Many languages contain only one verb to express the ideas of the English verbs *do* and *make.* Compare the two verbs

- **Make** means *to create something—in the physical world, in our imagination, or in our minds:* make a dress, make a dinner, make a decision.

- **Do** means *to perform an action or a job:* do work, do (wash) the dishes, do (the work on) your homework.

Therefore: A teacher makes an assignment; the students do it.

Write three to five different verbs that express the idea in parentheses, and be prepared to discuss the differences in meaning among the verbs.

1. (move slowly)   Black Bart   ambled / strolled / swaggered / staggered / crawled   into the saloon.

2. (move fast)   The runner   _____   past the cheering crowd.

3. (removal)   The thief   _____   the woman's purse.

4. (see)   I   _____   the document for several

                           _____   minutes.

                           _____

                           _____

                           _____

5. (make)   She   _____   a wonderful dessert.

                           _____

                           _____

                           _____

                           _____

6. (do)   He   _____   his homework just before

                           _____   class.

                           _____

                           _____

                           _____

EXERCISE 2	Tightening Sentences

Combine each of the following pairs of sentences or clauses, eliminating the verb have.

1. Bill has a crazy friend. He is always getting into trouble.

Bill's crazy friend is always getting into trouble.

2. She has a used car. It barely runs during the winter.

_____

3. When I was a child, I had a cat. She slept on my bed every night.

_____

4. We have some homework. We must finish it by Friday.

_____

5. My father has a favorite chair that he sits in every night.

_____

6. William has a blue coat that he wears to church on Sunday.

_____

EXERCISE 3	Replacing Verbs

The following passage overuses the verbs go *and* get. *Rewrite the passage, substituting more exact and interesting word choices.*

I leave the house around 7:30 and go to pick up my friend, and then we go to
school. At 2:00 I get out of school and go home. Then I get started on my

homework. I usually eat dinner about 5:00, and after I get finished with dinner, I go out with my friends. We usually go to someone's house or go to a game room nearby for an hour. But I try to get home by 11:00 so that I can get my clothes ready for the next day, and then I go to bed.

I leave the house around 7:30 to pick up my friend on the way to school.

EXERCISE 4	Revising Your Own Sentences

Write five sentences, each of which includes a verb from the following list: put, do, make, have, take, run, move, say, talk, give, look, use, *and* go. *Then revise each sentence, substituting a stronger, more precise verb.*

1. *My counselor gave me some advice on which classes to choose next semester.*

   Revision: *My advisor advised me on which classes to choose next semester.*

2. _____

   _____

   Revision: _____

   _____

3. _____

   _____

   Revision: _____

   _____

4. _____

   _____

   Revision: _____

   _____

5. _____

   _____

   Revision: _____

   _____

6. _____

   _____

Collaborative Activity 1

Comparing Your Work

Discuss and compare your answers to Exercises 1–4. List all the action verbs your group has produced. Refer to the list as you revise drafts for the rest of the term.

Revision: _____

ELIMINATING VAGUE EXPRESSIONS

Like common verbs, the most common adjectives are often sickly and dull. As you revise, circle overused adjectives such as *good, bad, nice, different, interesting,* and *pretty*—and substitute more vivid adjectives and expressions:

Weak:	One scene in the movie was *very interesting.*
Better:	One scene in the movie was *astonishing,* or *fascinating,* or *horrifying.*
Better:	One scene in the movie made me want to dive under my seat and hide.

Vague expressions such as *what they did, the things he does, what he said,* and *we saw a lot of things* communicate virtually nothing. Try to replace them with specific details:

Weak:	What the man did next scared me to death.
Better:	I closed my eyes when the man in the mask swung his axe at the knight's head.
Weak:	I don't like Jim because of the things he does.
Better:	I don't like Jim because he constantly insults people, mooches money from me, and bullies little children.

EXERCISE 5	Revising Weak Sentences

Rewrite each of the following sentences in more vivid and exact language.

1. The things my brother does at the dinner table are disgusting. *When my brother eats with his hands, talks with his mouth full, and belches, I would like to break a plate over his head.*

2. On my last vacation, I did some interesting things. _____
_____
_____

3. What the man did wasn't too nice. _____
_____
_____

4. A strange cat was doing weird things in my yard. _____
_____
_____

5. I saw a dude today who really looked bad. _____
_____
_____

Collaborative Activity 2

Strengthening Sentences
Write five deliberately vague sentences. Exchange papers by passing to the left, and revise the sentences you receive. Circle the weak verbs, adjectives, and other expressions, and then replace them with stronger, more direct language. Discuss your changes.

6. My father gave me all sorts of stuff to do in the yard over the weekend. _____

_____

_____

ELIMINATING WORDINESS

Look carefully at long phrases. Can you express their meaning in a single word?

Phrase	Replacement
in this day and age	*now*
due to the fact that	*because*
She dances *with a great deal of grace.*	She dances *gracefully.*

Flabby verbs often borrow strength from modifiers and tacked on phrases. Can you find a more muscular replacement?

Weak verb and attachment	Replacement
He *looked* at her *in an angry manner.*	He *scowled* at her.
He *has the ability* to swim well.	He *can* swim well.

Empty phrases often insult the intelligence of readers, explaining what needn't be explained or placing ideas in empty or obvious categories. Throw away the empty containers—but retain the core meaning:

Poor:	*As far as intelligence is concerned,* Bill is very *smart.* (What else could *smart* refer to but *intelligence?*)
Better:	Bill is *very intelligent.*
	Bill is *brilliant.*
Poor:	My father is *the type of man who* never misses work. (Why say that your father is a *man* unless readers might think he's a woman? And why mention that he is *a type?*)
Better:	My father never misses work.
Poor:	August *was a month that* caused several *different kinds of* problems for me. (Why say that August was *a month?* And why mention both *different* and *kinds,* since one implies the other—and *several* implies both.)
Better:	August caused several problems for me.

EXERCISE 6 | *Revising for Conciseness*

Replace each of the following phrases with a single word or two.

1. in this day and age   *now* _____

2. talked in an extremely loud voice   _____

3. has the ability to write   _____

4. the reason why   _____

5. a blue color   _____

6. 9 P.M. at night _____

7. true facts _____

8. during the same time that _____

EXERCISE 7	Tightening Sentences

Rewrite each of the following sentences, eliminating unnecessary words and empty phrases.

1. When my instructor returned my test back this morning, I saw that I had made a lot of careless mistakes that came from not being careful. *When my instructor returned my test this morning, I saw that I had made a lot of careless mistakes.*

2. In today's modern world, there are always new innovations in home electronics.

_____

_____

Collaborative Activity 3

Tightening Sentences
Now write five deliberately wordy sentences—in fact, as wordy as you can make them. Exchange papers by passing to the left, and revise sentences you receive. Circle the wordy expressions and replace them with tighter phrasing. Discuss your changes.

3. The kinds of imported cars that come into the country from Japan and Europe have a reputation of being better than the types of American cars made in the United States. _____

_____

_____

4. The reason why I like the Black Tie Club is because I see people who are dressed in the wildest kinds of clothes I have ever seen people wear. _____

_____

_____

5. In my opinion, I feel that today's athletes are overpaid and making too much money for the kind of jobs they do. _____

_____

_____

6. The story had a lot of specific details that created a feeling of true-to-life reality.

_____

_____

ELIMINATING UNNECESSARY REPETITION

Not all repetition weakens a paper. As you saw in Chapter 6, intentional repetition solidifies coherence. And parallelism—the repetition of sentence structures and language—can create a pleasing rhythm. Repetition can even create tension and build to a climax.

But unintentional repetition of a word (even in a different form or with a different meaning) can result in boredom. Repeat a word or phrase only for emphasis or clarity. Notice how the following sentences can be pruned of deadwood:

Poor:	A good athlete is a hard-working athlete.
Better:	A good athlete works hard.
Poor:	I had problems solving the math problems.
Better:	I struggled to solve the math problems.
Poor:	When the magician pulled the rabbit out of the hat, it was the only trick that tricked me.
Better:	I was tricked only when the magician pulled the rabbit out of the hat.
Poor:	He had a reasonably good reason for his tardiness.
Better:	His tardiness was justified.

EXERCISE 8 | Removing Weak Repetition

Rewrite each of the following sentences to eliminate unnecessary repetition.

1. My break time at work really breaks up the monotony. *My break time at work relieves the monotony.*

2. My boss, Mr. Carson, is the best boss I could ever want. _____

3. Not too many of my coworkers work hard at work. _____

4. Our center, Stretch Everest, is always the center of attention when he walks onto the basketball court. _____

5. A large truck crashed into the rear of the automobile. This truck caused considerable damage. _____

6. I usually have a bite to eat in the afternoon. After I finish eating, I then start my homework. _____

EXERCISE 9 | Revising a Paragraph

Rewrite the following passage to eliminate unnecessary repetition of words and ideas. Your revision should be about half as long as the original.

Collaborative Activity 4

Comparing Revisions
Compare your revisions of the passage in Exercise 9 until the group arrives at a single version that compiles the most concise and vivid sentences. Share your results with the whole class.

Collaborative Activity 5

Writing Badly for Fun
Make several photocopies of a paragraph you've written for a previous class assignment. Share it with your collaborative group, brainstorming ways to express the ideas of the paragraph in less colorful, less graceful, less precise, and more repetitious ways. See who can produce the worst version of the paragraph. (That person might qualify to become a college administrator—or at least a government bureaucrat!)

As we arrived at the amusement park, I was very excited to ride the most exciting and scariest ride, which was called the Whirl Around. It was the only ride I really wanted to ride, for I had heard so many things about how scary it was. I stood in line and waited anxiously. After I had waited for twenty or thirty minutes, I reached the entrance, and it was my turn to get strapped into one of the cars. I got into a little red-colored car. Then the attendant strapped me in. After everyone was strapped into the cars, we began our ride. First the cars began slowly, and then they began to pick up speed. It was beginning to become scary to me. The cars went around and around in a circle. They even went upside down, and they even went sideways. They finally went at a very fast speed. But after a while, the speed began to decrease, and the cars pulled back into the platform. Finally, the ride was over, and it had been very exciting and scary.

As we arrived at the amusement park, I was excited to try the most thrilling and frightening ride, the Whirl Around.

EXERCISE 10 — Tightening Your Own Writing

Compose a six- to ten-sentence paragraph describing a typical activity you perform. Then circle words and ideas you have repeated and consider each one. Is the repetition necessary? Could it be eliminated, perhaps by a substitute, perhaps by combining ideas or even sentences? Make your changes on the original draft and then revise the paragraph.

ELIMINATING TIRED COMPARISONS

Comparisons serve many useful purposes. They can clarify your meaning, especially in helping readers visualize or understand something unfamiliar by showing its resemblance to something familiar. And comparisons can enliven your writing, especially when they are colorful and original. But use comparisons with care. If they're forced, your writing will seem artificial. Or if they're dull and unoriginal, your writing will be, too.

Avoiding Clichés

A **cliché** is an overused expression that strikes readers with the force of a half-empty balloon. Clichés originated as colorful expressions. But we use them so often that they rarely convey their meaning. Does "quick as a wink," for example, make you think about how fast a blink of an eye is?

Avoid these wasted words. Look for them during revisions, and try to substitute fresher expressions:

Cliché: I like to do my own thing.
Better: I am independent.

Cliché: last but not least
Better: finally

EXERCISE 11   Substituting Fresh Expressions

Rewrite each of the following sentences to eliminate clichés.

1. I had the time of my life visiting friends in Austin, Texas. *I loved my visit with friends in Austin, Texas.*

2. He was as happy as a lark. _____

3. Every day my father is up at the crack of dawn to go to work. _____

4. True blue friends are few and far between. _____

5. Once in a blue moon, something happens that makes my blood boil. _____

6. After Ralph blows his top, it is over and done with, and he lets bygones be bygones. _____

7. I worked like a horse outside today from sunup to sundown. _____

8. Last but not least, this exercise should teach you to avoid clichés like the plague.

TIPS

For Avoiding Clichés

Let following list of clichés serve as examples of what to avoid:

a chip off the old block
at this point in time
avoid it like the plague
bored to tears
butterflies in my stomach
easier said than done
few and far between
more fun than a barrel of monkeys
one in a million
sleep like a log
the time of my life
up at the crack of dawn
where you're coming from

Using Fresh Expressions

Clichés have lost their power to surprise and delight, but fresh similes and metaphors have that power. A **simile** is a figurative comparison of one thing to another using *like* or *as.* The comparison draws a sharp image for readers and often adds richness of meaning to a passage:

> His temper is *like popcorn in hot oil.*
>
> She is as angry as *an arsonist without a match.*

A **metaphor** is a comparison without the words *like* or *as.* A metaphor often creates pleasing, unexpected similarities between your subject and something quite different. It allows you to discuss your subject in terms of another subject. Look at these examples:

> The top of his desk was *a swamp of papers and books.*
>
> He *slithered* into the room and *coiled up* next to me.

In the first example, the desk is discussed in terms of a swamp. In the second, the movement of a person is discussed in terms of a snake—that is, the verbs indicate snakelike actions.

Experiment with similes and metaphors; they can greatly enliven your writing. But don't overuse them. Too many in a paper can overwhelm your readers.

Collaborative Activity 6

Listing Clichés
Brainstorm and list as many clichés as your group can think of. Add more to the list each time you meet. Include all the clichés you encounter in each other's writing throughout the term. Try to compile at least 100, and share your lists of what to avoid.

EXERCISE 12	Composing Similes and Metaphors

Complete each of the following sentences with an appropriate simile or metaphor.

1. Gloria's laugh is _contagious_____ ; it _infects even the most serious people_ _around her._____

2. Life in my neighborhood is as exciting as _____
   _____
   _____

3. When Fred hears about a sale on DVD movies, he arrives at the store as fast as
   _____
   _____

4. He _____ his food like a _____

5. Life is a _____

6. Television is a _____

REVISING FOR DIRECT AND VIVID LANGUAGE

Now try enlivening the language of your previously written paragraphs or essays. Replace weak verbs and adjectives with strong ones. Shorten lengthy expressions. Cut empty words and unnecessary repetition. Strike out clichés, and strive for lively expressions and metaphors. Consult the Revision Guidelines on page 104 for help.

EXERCISE 13	Revising Your Own Work

Look at a paper you are writing now or return to one you have written previously, and revise it to eliminate weak verbs, adjectives, and other expressions, wordiness, unnecessary repetition, and clichés. Add a few similes and metaphors if you can. Use the following Revision Guidelines to aid your revision.

EXERCISE 14	Polishing Your Paper

Edit the paper, checking for correct spelling and punctuation, complete sentences, and clarity of ideas. Then make a clean copy of the paragraph and proofread it carefully for errors before submitting it to your instructor.

REVISION GUIDELINES | Writing Direct, Vivid Sentences

1. Do you see any weak verbs that might be replaced? Circle them, and on the blank sheet suggest replacements.
2. Do you see any vague expressions that could be more specific? Underline them, and on the attached sheet suggest revisions.
3. Do you see any wordy expressions? Any unnecessary repetition? Bracket these expressions, and on the attached sheet suggest revisions.
4. Do you see any clichés? Underline them twice and suggest fresh ways to express the writer's ideas. Use similes and metaphors if you can.

IN SUMMARY | Writing Directly and Vividly

To Write with Strong Verbs and Adjectives
1. During revisions, circle weak verbs and empty expressions.
2. Substitute words that more vividly and exactly express your meaning.

To Avoid Wordiness and Weak Repetition
1. Shorten clauses to phrases or phrases to single words whenever possible.
2. Eliminate empty categorizing words, needlessly repeated words, and words whose meaning other words express.
3. Violate the above advice when the revision is unclear or awkward.

To Avoid Tired Comparisons
1. Circle them during revisions and rewrite the passage in your own words.
2. Look for fresh and unusual ways to express comparisons through similes and metaphors.

WRITING FOR MASTERY

Now that you've practiced ways to strengthen your writing, put that strength to the test. After drafting a paragraph on a topic from the following list, revise the draft to avoid weak verbs, vague expressions, wordiness, needless repetition, and clichés. Try to include similes and metaphors, too. Your audience will be your classmates, your purpose to entertain. Alternatively, if your instructor prefers, you may expand one of the topics into a full essay, complete with thesis statement, topic sentences in the body paragraphs, and support.

1. Narrate any ritual you perform on a typical day: awakening, dressing, and eating in the morning; getting your children or younger siblings out of bed and off to school; studying for a test (or finding ways to avoid studying); laundering three weeks' worth of dirty clothes strewn all over your bedroom; or washing the dishes. Include specific details, lively verbs, and fresh language.

2. Describe the antics of a friend, sibling, or neighbor in a moment of foolishness, anger, or less than brilliant activity. Include strong verbs and, if possible, similes and metaphors.

3. Tell the story of an amusing experience with a pet. Include specific and lively verbs and adjectives.

4. Choose an activity you've often done or witnessed, and describe it through similes. Here are a few examples to stimulate your thinking: dinner at my house is like feeding the lions at the zoo; my younger sister (or brother) prepares for a date like an artist working on a masterpiece.

5. Describe a room in your house, apartment, or dorm after a party. Include plenty of specific details, and draw comparisons to a battlefield, boxing arena at the end of a match, or any other appropriate place.

6. *Writing from Source Material.* Read the following information about the game *Monopoly* several times, and then write a paragraph (or essay) based on the information as a feature article in the "Contemporary Living" section of a newspaper. Arrange the information in any way you wish. You don't have to use it all, and probably shouldn't. Make your writing as concrete, direct, and lively as you can.

Monopoly

best-selling copyrighted game ever

sales of 90 million sets in 1985

Game first marketed: 1935

inventor Charles Darrow, an unemployed heating engineer from Philadelphia

Darrow eventually sold idea to Parker Brothers

company had initially rejected idea in 1933, claiming it contained "52 fundamental playing errors"

at age forty-six, Darrow retired a millionaire

spent time traveling and growing exotic orchids

street names taken from Atlantic City, New Jersey

in 1974, attempt by Atlantic City council to change two street names of city provoked massive protest

hundreds of letters from all over the United States and Canada

group of Princeton University students in committee called "Students to Save Baltic and Mediterranean Avenues"

threat by students to cover city with *Monopoly* money if the ordinance passed

300 protesters at committee meeting

testimony from executives of Parker Brothers

failure of ordinance

in 1975, amount of real money printed by United States Bureau of Engraving: $22 billion in 1975, amount of *Monopoly* money printed by Parker Brothers: $40 billion

most expensive *Monopoly* set: $5,000, made by Alfred Dunhill

cost of edible version of game, "the Christmas present with a difference,"
made of milk chocolate or butterscotch: $600

Sources: John May, *Curious Trivia* (London: Dorset Press, 1980); *Chicago Tribune,* January 2, 1985.

8 Creating Sentence Variety

Make your writing more interesting and engaging by varying your sentences. The more options you select, the more interesting and powerful your writing will be. This chapter will help you

- vary the length and beginnings of sentences
- vary the types of sentences
- vary sentence structures

WHY WORK FOR SENTENCE VARIETY?

Sentence variety brings maturity to your writing; it provides opportunities for drama, tension, and surprise. It also brings music to your message, through rhythm, repetition, and release. Think for a moment about a musical beat: *dum-da-dum bop! dum-da-dum-bop! dum-da-da-dum bop bop!* The power of the *bops* derives from the *dums* and *das* that precede them. Without this variety, writing is monotonous and flat, as in the following passage where all the sentences are approximately the same length.

> In ancient Rome, the upper classes and lower classes ate with their fingers. All the Europeans did the same thing. The practice changed in the fourteenth century. This period is called the Renaissance. It was the beginning of concern for "genteel" behavior. There was a right way and a wrong way to pick up food. People also picked up food in a polite or an impolite way. A low-class person grabbed his food with five fingers. A high-class person did it differently. He politely lifted it with three fingers. He didn't want to get his ring finger or pinkie dirty.

The style is childishly simple and lacks the graceful flow of one idea into the next. Here's a revision:

UNIT 2

Chapter 8

Composing with Confidence ©2003

GO ELECTRONIC!

Use the following electronic supplements for additional practice with your writing:

- For chapter-by-chapter summaries and exercises, visit the Composing with Confidence Companion Website at: http://www.ablongman.com/meyers.
- For work with the writing process, visit The Longman Writer's Warehouse at http://longmanwriterswarehouse.com (password needed).
- For additional practice in grammar, use The Writer's ToolKit Plus CD-ROM

FINGER FOOD FOR EVERYONE

The upper and lower classes of ancient Rome ate with their fingers, as did all the Europeans. But that changed with the beginning of concern for "genteel" behavior during the Renaissance in the fourteenth century. There was a right and a wrong way, a polite and an impolite way, to pick up food. A lower-class person grabbed at his food with five fingers, while a person of breeding politely lifted it with three. He would never soil his ring finger or pinkie!

This version is faster paced, more lively, and rhythmic—and it sets up the punch line at the end.

VARYING SENTENCE LENGTH

Varying the length of sentences often serves to emphasize ideas. Notice how short and long sentences alternate in the following paragraph:

FROM PITCHFORK TO TABLE

The word *fork,* which comes from the Latin term for a farmer's pitchfork, is an ancient tool. Miniature pitchforks dating back to 4000 B.C. were discovered during an archaeological dig in Turkey. Although no one knows what function these tools served, it probably wasn't as tableware. What we do know is that the first forks as eating utensils appeared in eleventh-century Tuscany, Italy. We also know that they were unpopular. In fact, the priests condemned them outright. The clergy argued that only human fingers created by God were worthy of touching the food given to us by God. Nevertheless, two-pronged forks of gold and silver continued to be custom-made for wealthy Tuscans. Somebody must have liked the things.

The long sentences establish a rhythm that sets up the punch lines found in the short sentences in the middle and at the end:

We also know that they were unpopular.
In fact, the clergy condemned them outright.
Somebody must have liked the things.

Experiment with differing sentence lengths and word order as you do first drafts—and especially as you revise—until you hear the music in your words.

EXERCISE 1	Revising Short Sentences

Rewrite the short sentences in the following passage, trying out different sentence lengths and arrangements of words. Combine and reword sentences as you wish, but be sure to maintain the same meaning of the passage.

The fork was a shocking invention. That shock lasted at least a hundred years. For example, an Italian historian wrote about a dinner. A noblewoman from Venice ate with a fork at it. She had designed the fork. Several priests condemned her "excessive sign of refinement." The woman died a few days after the meal. It was

Collaborative Activity 1

Revising the Revisions

Exchange the passage you composed in Exercise 1 with a person in your collaborative group. Experiment with improving the passage further— or at least changing it further. Rewrite sentences or parts of sentences on a blank sheet of paper. Then discuss the changes.

supposedly from the plague. Clergymen claimed that her death was a punishment from God. The punishment warned other people. They shouldn't show off by using a fork.

For at least a hundred years, the fork remained a shocking invention.

_____

_____

_____

_____

_____

_____

VARYING SENTENCE BEGINNINGS

Don't fall into a pattern of sameness: "I did. She did. He did." Vary the beginnings of sentences. Start some with time expressions, others with *-ing* words, others with *if* or *as* or *whether*. That way, you'll involve your readers, surprise them, please them.

A WRITER SPEAKS

I learned to write by teaching it. Early in my career, I encountered a book called *Telling Writing* by Ken Macrorie. One chapter in particular (Chapter 4, "Tightening"—I can cite it from memory) affected me profoundly, showing me how to cut, combine, vary—and find the power in my own voice. I conveyed my enthusiasm over this revelation to my senior colleagues, one of whom sneered, "So, you don't care what the students say as long as their style is pretty."

That wasn't the case at all.

Once a writer falls in love with language, cares about language, and wants that language to count with readers, then the writer cares deeply about saying something important.

Let me quote Macrorie: "You may think that wasting words is a form of dishonesty. No writers mean to do it; but when they do it, they risk losing both their reader's attention and trust."

I didn't say that to my senior colleague, but I should have.

Alan Meyers, professor of English, Harry S Truman College, and author of nine textbooks

Time Expressions

"Once upon a time" begins the fairy tales from our youth—and time expressions begin many a story for adults. In fact, time expressions throughout a passage establish graceful **transitions** from one important moment to the next.

A Word About Words

Goodbye was actually a blessing, for it comes from the words *God be with you.* The earliest written appearance of the expression was in a letter from 1573. Why is *good* instead of *God* in the expression? Probably because the new word was influenced by the expression *good day.*

Time expressions are an especially good way to begin a sentence because they offer a break from the usual word order. Notice how each of the following examples begins with the subject and the verb:

Subject	Verb	Remainder of Sentence (with time expression italicized)
Thomas à Becket	was	the archbishop of Canterbury *during the mid-twelfth century.*
He	left	England *in 1164* to escape a trial for treason.
He	returned	*six years later* with some forks from Italy.
Noblemen	may have used	them for dueling *soon afterward.*

Too much of this predictable order may lull readers to sleep. So add variety and emphasis by starting some—but not all—of your sentences with time expressions:

Time expression	Subject	Verb
During the mid-twelfth century,	Thomas à Becket	was the archbishop of Canterbury
In 1164,	he	left England to escape a trial for treason.
Six years later,	he	returned with some forks from Italy.
Soon afterward,	noblemen	may have used them for dueling.

Many time expressions are **prepositional phrases**— a group of related words that include a preposition followed by an object, usually a noun:

Preposition	Object
After, before, during	the start of the show
Around, about, at, by, since, until	midnight
In	1985
On	November 22
Within	a short time

Most introductory time expressions are followed by a comma, except for short ones such as *now, then, soon, sometimes,* and *next week.*

EXERCISE 2   Revising Time Expressions

Shift the time expression to the beginning of each sentence that follows. Use commas as needed.

1. The fork was still nothing more than an expensive ornament in England by the fourteenth century. *By the fourteenth century, the fork was still nothing more than an expensive ornament in England.*

2. King Edward I had thousands of royal knives and hundreds of spoons but only seven forks: six silver and one gold, in 1307. _____
_____

3. King Charles V of France owned only twelve forks, most of them decorated with precious stones, later in the century. _____
_____

4. None of these forks were used for eating even at that point. _____
_____

5. Customs slowly began to change then. _____
_____

6. A fork would appear at the table of a lord or lady sometimes. _____

EXERCISE 3 | *Drafting a Short Narrative*

Draft a paragraph of perhaps eight sentences about an experience that happened to you over a period of time. Begin the first sentence by stating when the experience started ("Three years ago," "Last Thursday evening," "When I was sixteen," etc.). Then mark the transitions between events with time expressions in the body sentences. The list in the tips box at the top of this page should be helpful.

Expressions of Space

Like time expressions, expressions of location can launch a sentence, as in this example:

> *In Italy*, the country of the fork's origin, the implement was still laughed at all the way into the seventeenth century.

And, like time expressions, most expressions of location are prepositional phrases. These phrases don't have to begin sentences, and if overused, they will become tedious as well. So experiment with the placement of prepositional phrases until a sentence sings—gracefully, emphatically, and clearly.

Adverbs

Varying the placement of adverbs will also help create variety. The normal position of **adverbs**, words that usually end in *–ly* and describe an action, falls between the subject and verb, or between the first two words of a verb phrase:

Subject	Verb	Adverb	
Forks	were	*typically*	considered effeminate and unworthy of men.
Fork users	were	*often*	subject to ridicule and insults.

But these adverbs gain emphasis if you shift them toward the beginning of sentences or to other places in the sentences:

> *Typically,* forks were considered effeminate and unworthy of men.
>
> Forks, *typically,* were considered effeminate and unworthy of men.
>
> *Often,* fork users were subject to ridicule and insults.

Notice the punctuation, which should echo the sounds of the sentences. Listen for the pauses in rhythm. A comma follows the adverb that begins the first and third sentences, and two commas enclose the adverb that breaks the rhythm of the second sentence. (But don't punctuate entirely by ear! Know the rules for comma use, which you'll find in Chapter 27.)

EXERCISE 4	Revising Sentences

Underline the adverbs and prepositional phrases in the following sentences. Then rewrite each sentence twice with the adverbs or prepositional phrases in different positions. Add commas where necessary.

1. Women who used forks before the eighteenth century were often ridiculed as well.

   a. *Often, women who used forks before the eighteenth century were ridiculed as well.*

   b. *Before the eighteenth century, women who used forks were often ridiculed as well.*

2. A printed report describes with disgust the behavior of the wife of an important politician in Venice in 1626.

   a. _____

   _____

   b. _____

   _____

3. According to the report, she stupidly ordered a servant to "cut her food into little pieces" and ate with "a two-pronged fork" instead of eating properly with knife and fingers.

   a. _____

   _____

   b. _____

   _____

4. In the 1650s, a popular book on manners thoughtfully gave this advice on something that was not yet obvious: "Do not try to eat soup with a fork."

   a. _____

   _____

   b. _____

   _____

EXERCISE 5	Writing Your Own Sentences

Compose five of your own sentences that begin with expressions from the following list: cautiously, angrily, cleverly, stupidly, happily, without thinking, last year, after a long time, in the next few weeks, before the end of the decade, except for a few lucky people, on a perfect spring day. *Add commas when necessary.*

1. _____

   _____

2. _____

   _____

3. _____

   _____

4. _____

   _____

5. _____

   _____

Collaborative Activity 3

Revising Sentences

As in collaborative activities 1 and 2, exchange your sentences from Exercise 5 with a member of your group and experiment with improving the sentences. Rewrite the sentences on a blank sheet of paper. Then discuss the changes.

USING SPECIAL TYPES OF SENTENCES

You've seen how to create variety by alternating sentence lengths and rearranging sentence elements. But there are even more options. Sentences come in different varieties, too. Here are three you may wish to use occasionally: rhetorical questions, commands, and exclamations.

Rhetorical Questions

Why not ask a question from time to time? A **rhetorical question** engages your readers in the subject matter by making them think about the answer, which should be clear. In fact, you can express the topic idea of a paragraph in a rhetorical question:

> *When did forks finally become fashionable—and why?* The change occurred in eighteenth-century France, partly to emphasize differences in social class. With the French Revolution about to begin, and with revolutionaries shouting "liberty, equality, and fraternity," the rich people used their forks more often—especially the four-tined variety. The fork became a symbol of luxury, refinement, and status. Suddenly, touching food with even three bare fingers was rude and vulgar.

EXERCISE 6	Writing a Paragraph

Choose one of the following topics and draft a question as the topic sentence of a paragraph, as does this example:

Topic: the benefits of slowing down and enjoying life

Topic Sentence Question: ___Will Americans ever learn to slow down and enjoy themselves?___

Then draft a paragraph that answers (that is, develops) the question.

Topics:

1. the wasteful use of packaging

2. the benefits (or insanity) of eating (or not eating) certain foods

3. a problem with professional sports (or one professional sport)

4. a problem with (or benefit of) video games

5. the ideal job

Commands

Mix an occasional command into your writing. Commands, or **imperative sentences**, give readers advice or instructions efficiently. An imperative sentence addresses your readers directly but omits the implied subject *you*, as in these examples:

> *Affirmative command:*   *Pick up* your food with three fingers.
> *Negative command:*   *Do not try* to eat soup with a fork.

Notice that these imperative sentences (and the sentence you're reading right now) give suggestions, directions, or warnings.

EXERCISE 7	Writing a Paragraph of Instructions

Draft a paragraph that gives advice or instructions. Make every sentence imperative.

Example: Blend the ingredients in a blender or mixer until the batter is smooth but not watery.

Exclamatory Sentences

Add power to passages! An **exclamatory sentence**—which ends in an exclamation point—will do the job. It dramatizes an idea, as in this revised example from a passage you read earlier in the chapter.

> A lower-class person grabbed at his food with five fingers, while a person of breeding politely lifted it with *three*. He would never soil his ring finger or pinkie!

Experiment with questions, commands, and exclamatory sentences as you draft and revise, but don't overuse them.

EXERCISE 8	Writing Exclamations

Follow each sentence provided with an exclamatory sentence.

1. People say that Americans don't work as hard as they used to. This is nonsense!

2. First, medical researchers tell us not to eat red meat; then they tell us the opposite. _____

3. Is camping in Yellowstone or Yosemite National Park really worth the effort?

   _____

4. A developer wants to tear down another 100-year-old house and replace it with a high-rise steel and glass building.   _____

   _____

5. Tom lost his temper and told off his boss.   _____

   _____

6. Jill crashed her bike, sprained her ankle, scraped her elbows, and tore her new baggy jeans in four places.   _____

   _____

JOINING SENTENCES

Listen to the rhythm of your sentences. Are they too short, too herky-jerky? Then try combining ideas. You can combine subjects that carry the same verb or verbs that attach to the same subject. You can also streamline your writing by joining related ideas instead of laying them out in separate sentences.

We'll look at four ways to join sentences: by combining subjects, combining verbs, repeating and renaming nouns, and transforming verbs into modifiers.

Combining Subjects

Consider these short and needlessly repetitious sentences:

> Spoons have a long history. They were never ridiculed. Their users were never ridiculed, either.

The verb—*were ridiculed*—appears twice, each time with a separate subject. You can therefore join the subjects with *and,* creating a **compound subject** with only one verb. Here's a revision:

> **Compound subject**
> Over their long history, *spoons and their users* were never ridiculed.

Notice that you needn't repeat the exact language of the original sentences as you revise and combine.

EXERCISE 9	Forming Compound Subjects

Combine each of the following groups of sentences to form a single sentence with a compound subject.

The Origins of the Spoon: 20,000 Years Ago

1. The earliest known spoons were found in Asia during archaeological digs. Evidence of their use was found at the same time.   *The earliest known spoons and evidence of their use were found in Asia during archaeological digs.*

2. These spoons date back at least 20,000 years. Primitive bowls also date back that far. _____

_____

3. Thick porridge that couldn't be sipped from a bowl was eaten with a spoon. Thick soupy foods were also eaten with a spoon. _____

_____

4. Wooden spoons have been recovered from ancient Egyptian tombs. Stone spoons have been found in these tombs. Ivory spoons have been recovered from them as well. Gold spoons have also been recovered from these ancient burial sites. _____

_____

5. Upper-class Greeks used spoons of bronze and silver. Upper-class Romans used spoons of bronze and silver, too. Poorer people carved spoons from wood.

_____

EXERCISE 10	Completing Sentences

Complete each of the following sentences, supplying a compound subject.

1. __High intelligence__ and __good looks__ are my two most obvious traits.

2. _____ and _____ will pay off in the end.

3. _____ and _____ enjoy each other's company.

4. _____ and _____ always arrive ten minutes late for class.

5. Bill's _____ and _____ make him popular with just about everyone.

6. [Supply two *–ing* words as subjects] _____ and _____ won't change the facts.

Combining Verbs

Like compound subjects that share the same verb, a **compound predicate**—which states the action of the subject—links two or more verbs that share the same subject. Here's an example:

Original:	In ancient times, poor folks carved spoons from wood. Then they used the spoons for eating.
Revision:	In ancient times, poor folks *carved* spoons from wood and then *used* them for eating.

You can form compound predicates with other joining words such as *but*. You can also combine more than two verbs:

Knives *date back* to the cave dwellers era *but have changed* very little since that time.

Early people *killed, sliced, and raised* their food to their mouths with the same knives.

EXERCISE 11	Creating Compound Predicates

Combine each of the following groups of sentences to form a single sentence with a compound predicate. Join the verbs with and *in every sentence except one, in which you should use* but *or* yet.

1. Spoons from the Middle Ages were carved from wood. They were also fashioned from bone. And some were hammered from tin. *Spoons from the Middle Ages were carved from wood, fashioned from bone, or hammered from tin.*

2. In Italy during the fifteenth century, wealthy people bought silver "apostle spoons." They gave the spoons to children as baptismal gifts. _____

_____

3. The spoons cost a fortune. They were highly popular. _____

_____

4. The handle of a typical spoon was shaped like the child's patron saint. It would supposedly protect the child from harm._____

_____

5. The expression "born with a silver spoon in his mouth" came from this custom. It meant that a family could afford to have such a spoon made as a gift.

_____

EXERCISE 12	Completing Sentences

Complete each of the following sentences, supplying a compound predicate. Be sure to include two verbs (three in sentence 5)—and don't repeat the subject.

1. The spaghetti slipped off the plate and *slid inside Mr. Gottbuck's money belt.*

_____

2. The cat crept up to the large round bowl and_____

_____

3. Ralph tried to pick up the egg rolls with chopsticks but _____

_____

4. Sally washed her hair thoroughly yet, it _____

_____

5. Chef Roland whipped the batter in a large bowl, _____

_____, and _____

Repeating and Renaming Nouns

These two sentences are crying out to be combined:

> Perhaps 1.5 million years ago, *Homo erectus* made the first stone knives for killing prey. *Homo erectus* was an early ancestor of modern humans.

There's a neat way to combine them, with an **appositive**. It's a word or phrase that renames or defines the noun that comes before it:

> Perhaps 1.5 million years ago, *Homo erectus, an early ancestor of modern humans,* made the first stone knives for killing prey.

The appositive—"an early ancestor of modern humans"—defines *Homo erectus* in the combined sentence. But you can also reverse the noun and its appositive:

> . . . an early ancestor of modern humans, *Homo erectus,* . . .

Notice that, in both cases, the appositive always comes directly after its partner noun and is enclosed in two commas.

In general, use commas when a proper noun comes first in an appositive. But don't use commas when the proper noun comes second. Here are some examples:

No commas	Commas
my older brother Bill	Bill, my older brother,
their good friend Raoul	Raoul, their good friend,

EXERCISE 13 | *Combining Sentences*

Join each pair of sentences by creating an appositive, and punctuate each with the correct number of commas.

1. *Apostle spoons* were very fashionable in fifteenth-century Italy. They were spoons with handles in the shape of patron saints. *Apostle spoons, spoons with handles in the shape of patron saints, were very fashionable in fifteenth-century Italy.*

2. Thomas à Becket brought the two-pronged fork to England in the thirteenth century. He was the archbishop of Canterbury. _____

   _____

3. Our word "fork" comes from the term *furca*. This is Latin for a farmer's pitchfork.

   _____

   _____

4. Dining customs changed during the Renaissance. The Renaissance was a period of great growth in culture beginning in the fourteenth century. _____

   _____

   _____

5. According to legend, Duc de Richelieu greatly reformed table manners. He was

cardinal and chief minister to the king in seventeenth-century France. _____

_____

_____

EXERCISE 14	Completing Sentences

Complete each of the following sentences, including an appositive and commas, if necessary.

1. You'll be competing *in the pie-eating contest* _____ against Polly Saturated, *the* _____
heavyweight champion of the world. _____

2. Tommy Teacup _____ has _____

_____

3. I'll _____ the largest amusement park in the region _____

_____

4. My _____ owns _____

_____

5. The Vietnam War Memorial_____

_____

6. _____ the winner of last year's championship _____

_____

Transforming Verbs into Modifiers

Another way to add music to your message is by changing verbs into **modifiers**—a word or group of words that function as an adjective or adverb—thereby streamlining and combining ideas. We'll look at two types of these modifiers: *–ing* words and *–ed* words.

–ing **Modifiers.**   Sometimes a verb can be transformed into an *–ing* form. Consider these two sentences:

> For centuries, a single knife was an all-purpose tool. It hung from a man's waist.

If you change *hung* to *hanging* and combine the sentences, here's the result:

> For centuries, a single *knife hanging from a man's waist* was an all-purpose tool.

Combine the following two sentences, changing the verb *disgusted* to an *–ing* word.

1. During meals, noblemen used the point of their knives to pick their teeth.

2. This disgusted the Duc de Richelieu.

_____

_____

And combine these sentences, this time changing *attempted* to an *–ing* word.

3. Richelieu attempted to stop this crude practice.

4. He changed the shape of dinner knives.

_____

_____

Did your sentences resemble these?

During meals, noblemen used the point of their knives to pick their teeth, *disgusting the Duc de Richelieu.*

Attempting to stop this crude practice, Richelieu changed the shape of dinner knives.

Note that the *–ing* modifier can follow or precede the word(s) it relates to. Note, too, that the two subjects of the separate sentences have become one.

An *–ing* modifier can also follow some transitions indicating time:

$$\left. \begin{array}{l} \text{While} \\ \text{Before} \\ \text{When} \\ \text{After} \end{array} \right\} \text{attempting to stop this pracitce . . .}$$

An *–ing* modifier at the beginning of a sentence requires a comma, while most *–ing* modifiers later in the sentence do not:

Sitting by the pond, I watched a mother duck and six little ducklings.
I saw a mother duck and six little ducklings *swimming past the dock.*

The one exception to this rule occurs when the *–ing* modifier and the word(s) it describes are separated. A comma clarifies the meaning:

I sat by the pond, *watching a mother duck and six little ducklings.*

Placement is crucial. If an *–ing* modifier doesn't immediately precede or follow the word it describes, the result can be misleading:

Incorrect: I watched a duck and six little ducklings *sitting by the pond.*
(The duck and ducklings weren't sitting—you were!)

Correct: *Sitting by the pond,* I watched . . .

EXERCISE 15	Combining Sentences

Join each of the following pairs of sentences by changing one into an –ing modifier. Place the modifier either before or after the word(s) it relates to, and add commas as needed.

Duc de Richelieu's Crusade for Rounded Knives

1. The round-tip dinner knife supposedly originated in France in the 1630s. It followed one man's attempt to end a common but impolite practice. *The round-tipped dinner knife supposedly originated in France in the 1630s, following one*

man's attempt to end a common but impolite practice or *Following one man's at-tempt to end a common but impolite practice, the round-tip dinner knife sup-posedly originated in France in the 1630s.*

2. Armand Jean du Plessis was known as the Duc de Richelieu. He served King Louis XIII as cardinal and chief minister. _____

_____

_____

3. Richelieu was disgusted by the noblemen at the dinner table. They picked their teeth with the pointed end of a knife. _____

_____

_____

4. He was able to stop the behavior. He ordered his chefs to file the points off his table knives. _____

_____

_____

5. Soon French women began to follow his example. They placed orders for knives with rounded ends. _____

_____

_____

EXERCISE 16	Completing Sentences

Add a phrase beginning with an –ing *modifier (and, if you wish, a preposition of time) to each of the following sentences. Supply commas as needed.*

1. *After finishing his seventh helping of banana cream pie,* Albert burped content-edly and wiped his mouth on his sleeve.

2. _____ Chef Louis served the apricot-flavored sushi.

3. Tom tossed the salad in a large wooden bowl _____

_____

4. Several knives and forks fell to the floor _____

_____

5. _____ the dinner guests left after midnight.

–ed **Modifiers.** Just as with *–ing* words, verbs with *–ed* endings can be modi-fiers. Consider these two sentences:

The knife *was invented* in cave dweller times. It joined the spoon as an eat-ing implement 20,000 years ago.

If you drop was and combine the two subjects into a single subject, here's the result:

Invented in cave dweller times, the knife joined the spoon as an eating implement 20,000 years ago.

or

The knife, invented in cave dweller times, joined the spoon as an eating implement 20,000 years ago.

Note that *invented,* formerly part of the verb *was invented,* now stands by itself as a modifier.

The punctuation rules for the *–ing* modifier and *–ed* modifier are the same. Use a comma when the modifier begins a sentence, no comma when it doesn't— unless the modifier is separated from the word it describes. And, make sure to place the *–ed* modifier in a spot where its meaning is clear:

Unclear: *Grilled over hot coals,* most people enjoy almost any kind of meat. (The meat—not the people—is grilled.)

Clear: Most people enjoy almost any kind of meat *grilled over hot coals.*

Here's another point that you may have already considered: not all *–ed* modifiers end in *–ed.* They're officially called **past participles**, and many are irregular (for example, *seen, done, cut, driven,* and *gone*). You'll see a full list of them in Chapter 21.

EXERCISE 17	Combining Sentences

Combine each of the following groups of sentences by changing one –ed verb into an –ed modifier and eliminating the original verb. Include commas as needed.

The Origins of the Napkin

1. Small napkins are used today to dab our lips and protect our laps. They would never have been adequate centuries ago. *Small napkins used today to dab our lips and protect our laps would never have been adequate centuries ago.*

2. A seven-course meal was eaten entirely with the fingers. That custom made a napkin the size of a towel essential. _____

_____

3. They were later called "serviettes." Towel-like napkins were used by the ancient Egyptians, the Greeks, and the Romans to wipe food from their hands. _____

_____

_____

Collaborative Activity 4

Drafting Sentences

List five *–ing* modifiers and five *–ed* modifiers. Exchange lists by passing them to the left. Write a sentence using each modifier. Be careful to place and punctuate the modifiers correctly. Then exchange sentences with the person to your left, and check over the work. Discuss any problems with the whole group. Here are a few examples to get you started: *amazing, boring, exhausted, excited.*

4. And to further clean the hands during a meal, all three cultures used finger bowls. They were filled with water. It was scented by flowers and herbs. _____

_____

_____

_____

5. In Egypt, the scents—almond, cinnamon, or orange blossom—were chosen according to the courses. The courses were eaten by the people at the table. _____

_____

_____

_____

EXERCISE 18 | *Completing Sentences*

Add a phrase beginning with an –ed modifier to each of the following sentences. Supply commas as needed.

1. *Known for its excellent roasted ants and fried caterpillars,* _____

   the Petite Crawler is a popular place for dining and passing out.

2. _____ coffee bars are appearing throughout the city.

3. We enjoy a flourless chocolate cake _____

   _____

4. Rare roast beef _____ is the specialty of the house.

5. _____ the guests thanked their host for the wonderful meal.

6. _____ the host faced a mound of dirty dishes and utensils.

REVISING FOR SENTENCE VARIETY

Now try sharpening the language of your previously written paragraphs or essays. Vary sentence length. Combine sentences. Add rhetorical questions, imperatives, and exclamations if they're appropriate. Shift time and space expressions and adverbs. Consult the Revision Guidelines that follow for help.

REVISION GUIDELINES | Sentence Variety

1. Do you see any opportunities to vary sentence length? Bracket the sentences and suggest revisions.
2. Do you see any time expressions, expressions of space, or adverbs that might be shifted to create variety or more graceful sentences? Circle them, and on the blank sheet, suggest revisions.

3. Do you see two or more sentences that might be combined in any way? Underline them, and on the blank sheet suggest how.

4. Do you see any sentence structures that can be recast as rhetorical questions, imperative sentences, or exclamatory sentences? Bracket them, and on the blank sheet, suggest ways they can be recast.

5. Do you see any opportunities to combine sentences by changing verbs into *–ing* or *–ed* modifiers? Underline the sentences twice, and on the blank sheet, draft the combined sentence.

EXERCISE 19	Revising for Sentence Variety

As a way of summing up all you've done in this chapter, completely rewrite the following passage. Include long and short sentences, compound subjects and predicates, rhetorical questions, imperatives, and exclamations. Begin some sentences with time expressions, adverbs, or prepositional phrases. And combine sentences with appositives, –ing modifiers, or –ed modifiers.

The Rise and Fall of the Napkin

It was the sixth-century B.C. Roman nobles found a second use for the napkin. It was as a sort of doggie bag. Guests at a banquet were expected to use serviettes. They used them to wrap up goodies from the table. Then they were expected to take them home. It was not good manners to leave empty-handed.

Documents have been preserved. They came into Italy in the 1680s. They reveal the elegance of the serviette. There were twenty-six favorite shapes for folding dinner napkins. These depended on the guests. They also depended on the occasion. The shapes included Noah's Ark (for members of the clergy). They also included a hen (for the noblewoman of highest rank present). Other shapes were chicks (for the other women), plus carp, tortoises, bulls, bears, and rabbits.

A book of etiquette discusses the large serviette. The book was published in 1729. The serviette had many uses: "For wiping the mouth, lips, and fingers when they are greasy. For wiping the knife before cutting bread. For cleaning the spoon and fork after using them." The same book then makes an important point. "When the fingers are very greasy, wipe them first on a piece of bread, in order not to spoil the serviette too much."

The large serviette was finally undermined by the fork. It also undermined the finger bowl. Forks handled food. They left fingers spotless. The large napkin became unnecessary. Napkins were still used. They were smaller. They were used to wipe the mouth.

Collaborative Activity 5

Discussing Your Rewrite

Compare your revisions for Exercise 19. How many ways have the group members been able to add variety to their writing? See if you can arrive at a single version that incorporates the best work of everyone in the group. Share it with the whole class.

The size of the serviette is shown in the origin of the word *napkin*. The function is also shown. The word comes from the Old French *naperon*. The word means "little tablecloth." The English borrowed the word *naperon*. They used it to name a large cloth. It was tied around the waist. It protected the front of the body. The hands were also wiped on it. They called it a *napron*. A shift in pronunciation also occurred. A single letter was dropped. A *napron* became "an apron." So the napkin at one time or another has been a towel. It has also been a tablecloth. It has also been an apron. It had a colorful history. The history was also complicated. The napkin was once regarded as noble. It has fallen to the lowly status of a throwaway today.

IN SUMMARY | ## Creating Sentence Variety

1. Employ long and short sentences.
2. Begin sentences with time expressions, adverbs, or prepositional phrases.
3. Combine subjects and verbs.
4. Use occasional rhetorical questions, imperatives, or exclamations.
5. Use appositives to combine sentences.
6. Transform verbs into *–ing* modifiers or *–ed* modifiers.

EXERCISE 20 | Revising Your Own Work

Return to a paper you are writing now or to one you have written previously. Revise to achieve greater sentence variety, employing the strategies you have practiced in this chapter. Use the following guidelines to aid your revision.

WRITING FOR MASTERY

You've practiced a number of ways of creating sentence variety; now employ them in your own writing. Draft and revise a paragraph from the following list, varying the length of your sentences, varying sentence beginnings, and employing rhetorical questions, imperative statements, and exclamatory sentences. Use transitions of time and space to improve coherence. Make sure your final draft includes a topic sentence and at least five supporting sentences that develop the topic idea.

1. Describe the following scene, using a variety of sentence structures, locating objects within the scene, and conveying a clear sense of the action.
2. Imagine what led up to the scene in the picture on p. 126, and tell the story of what happened and why.
3. Discuss a time when an older person demonstrated through example how or how not to behave in a difficult circumstance. Convey the action specifi-

Vietnam War protest march on the Pentagon, October 1967.

cally—what happened and when?—and build toward a dramatic climax. Vary your sentence structure, and include specific details.

4. Has any object—a kitchen utensil, an appliance, a VCR, a computer, or anything else—changed your behavior in some way? Write about that change, contrasting your actions prior to acquiring the object and after acquiring it. Has your behavior continued to change as a result? If so, discuss those changes as well.

5. Many individuals claim that people are rude, inconsiderate, and ill-mannered today. What manners do you think are most important? Write about at least three, illustrating each with real or hypothetical examples, and perhaps contrasting them with examples of bad manners.

6. *Writing from Source Material.* Draft a paragraph based on the following information from an outside source. Pose a question at or near the beginning, and include at least one imperative sentence and one exclamatory sentence. Use time expressions as transitions. Work for sentence variety. Don't change the meanings of the material, but arrange and reword it in any way you wish.

before eighteenth century: most people still shared bowls, plates, and even drinking glasses

each aristocrat had full set of cutlery, plates, and glasses

fork now part of that set

today everyone uses separate knives, forks, and spoons

beginning of eighteenth century: upper class in Europe used individual place settings

from etiquette book of that period: "When everyone is eating from the same dish, you should take care not to put your hand into it before those of higher rank have done so."

from an etiquette book of mid-seventeenth century: "Do not try to eat soup with a fork."

mid-eighteenth century; almost everyone owned and used two pieces of tableware: the knife and the spoon

spoon older than the fork, used for thousands of years

just before the French Revolution, fork became a symbol of luxury, refinement, and status

just before the French Revolution, to touch food with fingers became bad manners

SOURCE: Charles Panati, *Extraordinary Origins of Everyday Things* (New York: Harper & Row Publishers, 1987).

Three Ways to Strengthen Ideas

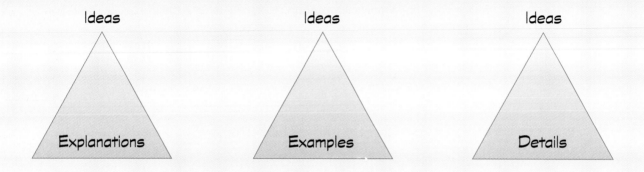

Ideas

Explanations

Ideas

Examples

Ideas

Details

Three Ways to Hold Ideas Together

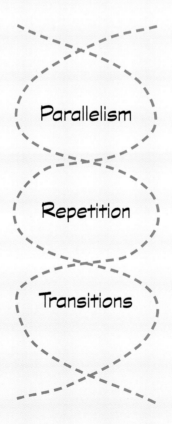

Parallelism

Repetition

Transitions

Strengthen by Replacing . . .

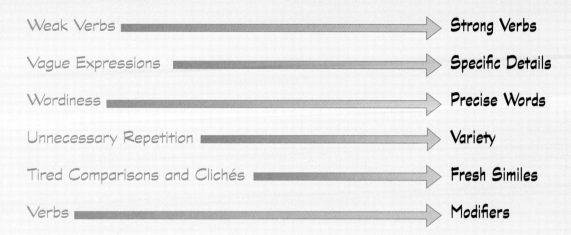

Weak Verbs ➞ **Strong Verbs**

Vague Expressions ➞ **Specific Details**

Wordiness ➞ **Precise Words**

Unnecessary Repetition ➞ **Variety**

Tired Comparisons and Clichés ➞ **Fresh Similes**

Verbs ➞ **Modifiers**

Strengthen by Combining . . .

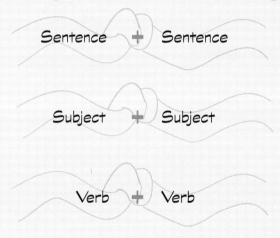

Sentence + Sentence

Subject + Subject

Verb + Verb

Add Variety by Varying . . .

Sentence **Length**

Sentence *Beginnings*

Sentence Type

Word Choice

Word **Order**

III
Composing Types of Paragraphs and Essays

Now that you've gained practice in the composing process and strengthened your writing skills, this unit will help you apply those skills in a variety of ways. Although the six steps in the composing process remain essentially the same no matter what you write, this unit will demonstrate that differing purposes, occasions, and audiences govern the organization of a paragraph or essay. You'll be introduced to eight organizational structures—from narration through persuasion. Each structure is different because each aims at achieving a different goal for a specific audience. And you'll see how to write effectively within two additional contexts: in essay examinations and in the workplace.

Seeing those differences and learning how to address them will help you communicate your message in virtually any situation, for any purpose, for any reader. That's the ultimate goal of this book—to give you the versatility to compose with confidence. ■

9 Composing a Description

Good description is clear, well organized, and, above all, specific. Through strong details, imaginative word choice, and sound organization, you draw a picture in your readers' minds. You don't just *tell* them that something or someone is remarkable, unusual, or pretty. You *show* them so they can see the uniqueness, rare qualities, or beauty for themselves.

This chapter will help you compose paragraphs and essays of description. You'll

- examine a model paragraph of description
- analyze its structure and learn how it was written
- practice generating and arranging descriptive details
- write a paragraph and/or an essay of description

A MODEL PARAGRAPH: DESCRIPTION

Description draws a picture of someone or something through words. It allows your readers to visualize the subject matter clearly, and it may involve the senses of sound, touch, motion, and smell in addition to the sense of sight.

Here's a model paragraph based on firsthand experience: a description of the Grand Canyon. As you read it, look for the specific details that support the topic sentence.

A View of the Grand Canyon

* * * *

On my visit to Arizona, I saw one of the earth's greatest natural wonders, the Grand Canyon. It is a massive hole in the ground covering much of the northwestern part of the state. In all, the canyon is over 270 miles in length (although Grand Canyon National Park includes only 100 miles) and between 4 and 18 miles in width. It is also monstrously deep, over a mile in spots, but a visitor can see all the way to the bottom. The walls are far from flat; they are filled with cliffs, ridges, hills, and even valleys. The multicolored rocks ring the canyon walls in layers, beginning at the top with a sand color, then red, then lavender, then blue-brown, then bright red, and then black at the very bottom. These colors change according to shifts in light; at noon they blend into a bright red, but at sunset they turn dark red and brown. Finally, at the bottom is the Colorado River, which looks like a tiny snake winding through the canyon, although the roar of its current can be heard in places even at the top. In fact, that powerful current has carved out much of the canyon over a two-billion-year period, and it has left huge towers of rock, like Aztec temples, that rise from the middle of the canyon floor. This massive natural excavation project has also exposed fossils of prehistoric man, dinosaurs, and the earliest forms of plant and animal life that lie within the canyon's walls.

Questions for Analysis

1. What is the topic sentence? Underline it.
2. What sentences provide general information about the canyon?
3. Where are the specific details introduced?
4. Circle every transitional word that serves to locate things in the canyon. Look carefully at the placement of these words. What kind of organization do they reveal—right to left, top to bottom, center to sides?
5. The end of the paragraph seems to depart from purely a description of the canyon. Why?

The Structure of Description

Notice how the paragraph on the Grand Canyon helps you visualize the canyon by providing a general overview and then filling in the specific details according to a plan. The description moves from top to bottom: with the writer, you look down from the upper edge, to the walls, to the river at the bottom.

The most logical way to organize descriptive details is in **spatial order**—that is, arranged in space from top to bottom, left to right, nearest to farthest, or the like. Even a description that involves people or animals can establish the setting or full scene first and then present details in a spatial order.

A blueprint of a typical paragraph of description might look like this:

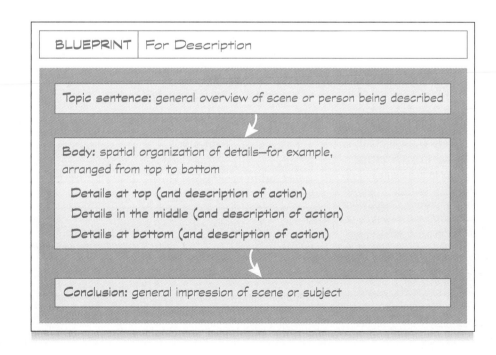

BLUEPRINT | For Description

Topic sentence: general overview of scene or person being described

Body: spatial organization of details—for example, arranged from top to bottom

   Details at top (and description of action)
   Details in the middle (and description of action)
   Details at bottom (and description of action)

Conclusion: general impression of scene or subject

The Process of Composing Description

Description is different from other kinds of writing because of its focus on details. Notice the many specific details in the paragraph on the Grand Canyon—its size measured in miles, the colors of the rocks, the sound of the river, the time it took for the canyon to form.

The best descriptions are based on firsthand experience. Writers observe the subject closely and take notes on what they see, hear, feel, smell, or even taste. But, of course, that's not always possible. Some descriptions are based on memory. To describe something or someone from the past, writers must take time to recall important details. They close their eyes, put themselves back into the scene, and visualize the experience. Then they write down what they've remembered, recording as many specific details as possible. And sometimes they use helpful facts and figures from outside sources. The writer of the paragraph on the Grand Canyon found information on the canyon's size in a brochure.

A WRITER SPEAKS

Some books on writing give the impression that there are just two styles: good and bad. It is often helpful to remember that there are many good styles—and there is no doubt good and bad writing in all of them. Good writers rarely use just one; the best writers choose a style that fits the situation. Even the mindless, impersonal, repulsive prose of bureaucracy is suitable for some situations, those in which you don't want to take responsibility for saying anything because you have no idea what you're talking about, but you got stuck with writing the memo, for example.

There are no universal virtues in writing. Not even clarity is a virtue in every style. In diplomatic style, vague and ambiguous treatment of some issues may allow agreement in others. In such cases, clarity can be a vice, if not a disaster—it can lead to war.

Francis Noel Thomas, coauthor, with Mark Turner, of *Clear and Simple as the Truth: Writing Classic Prose* (Princeton, N.J.: Princeton University Press, 1994).

Thomas and Turner maintain a Website on writing prose style: classicprose.com

Now let's see how the writer of the description of the Grand Canyon actually composed his paragraph. Here are the steps involved:

1. Observe and Take Notes.   The writer of the paragraph on the Grand Canyon began recording details about what he saw—along with some facts and figures he found in brochures. Here's a small part of his brainstorming list:

> It's huge—hundreds of miles long, and deep incredible beauty—many colors of rock at different levels brochure: over 270 miles long, width varies from 4 to 18 miles, and over a mile deep in places (over 100 miles of canyon inside Grand Canyon National Park)

A Word About Words

There are many Italian words in English, including most of our musical terms. Additional common words with roots in Italian include *alarm, million, race, umbrella, bankrupt, balcony,* and *ghetto. America* itself, named after the explorer *Amerigo Vespucci,* could also be said to be an Italian word.

2. Draft a Topic Sentence.   After gathering and recording the information, the writer drafted a topic sentence that summarized his attitude—his dominant impression about the canyon:

> The Grand Canyon is an amazing sight.

Now his task was to show what makes the canyon so amazing.

3. Outline in Spatial Order.   The writer then selected from and shaped his observations, facts, and figures into an outline. As in the diagram you saw earlier, his plan begins with a general overview of the canyon, followed by specific details, arranged spatially from top to bottom:

> I. General Information
>   Canyon located in northwestern Arizona
>   a massive hole in the ground
>   brochure: over 270 miles long, width varies from 4 to 18 miles, and
>   over a mile deep in places (over 100 miles of canyon inside Grand
>   Canyon National Park)
>   from brochure: canyon 2,000 million years old, with fossils in the rock
>   of prehistoric man, dinosaurs, and the earliest forms of plant and
>   animal life
> II. Specific Details
>   incredible beauty-many colors of rock all along its sides from the top,
>   the layers of rock are sand-colored, then red, then lavender, then
>   blue-brown, then bright red, then black colors change in the light-
>   very red at noon, but dark red, purple, and blue at sunset
>   sides of the canyon have cliffs, ridges, hills, and even valleys at the
>   bottom, huge towers of rock carved out by the river, look like
>   Aztec temples
>   Colorado River runs along the bottom, looks like a snake from above,
>   but sounds noisy
>   from brochure: the powerful currents of river carved out much of the
>   canyon

4. Draft and Revise.   Following this preliminary work, the writer drafted the paragraph and revised it several times. He kept searching for strong, specific, and lively language to emphasize his main impressions about the beauty and size of the canyon:

TIPS

**For Establishing
Relationships in Space**
Here's a list of the most
common expressions for
showing spatial relation-
ships: *over, above, at the top
(or bottom), in the middle, in
the center, below, behind, beneath, under(neath), on (to)
the left (or right), on one side,
around, in the front (rear), in
front (back) of, next to, beside, nearby. close by. far
away, farther away, beyond,
inside, outside, on the inside
(outside), within, to the north
(south, east, west)*

incredible beauty

massive hole

powerful currents

huge towers

over 270 miles long

over a mile deep in places

He also added transitions to give coherence to the paragraph, helping readers visualize the placement of details—in this case, from the rim of the canyon to its base. Notice the transitions in just one sentence:

The multicolored rocks ring the canyon walls in layers, beginning at the top with a sand color, then red, then lavender, then blue-brown, then bright red, and then black at the very bottom.

That's how the paragraph of description took shape. It's a simple process. You can do it, too.

GETTING READY TO WRITE

As you prepare to write a paragraph of description, try these warm-up exercises. They'll help you focus on generating specific details that support the topic sentence, arranging the details in spatial order, and working from firsthand observations to make the description concrete.

EXERCISE 1   *Generating Details*

For each of the following topic sentences, list at least three supporting details that you predict would follow.

1. *Topic sentence:* The produce section of the grocery store was filled with beautiful, fresh items:

   a. red, firm apples, stacked in uniform rows

   b. _____

   c. _____

   d. _____

2. *Topic sentence:* The swimming pool was crowded and filled with activity.

   a. _____

   b. _____

   c. _____

   d. _____

3. *Topic sentence:* The ticket buyers for the Rotten Peaches concert were dressed in a wild array of outfits.

a. _____

b. _____

c. _____

d. _____

4. *Topic sentence:* The picnic area in the woods was a perfect setting.

a. _____

b. _____

c. _____

d. _____

5. *Topic sentence:* Jawon's room is a shrine to pro basketball.

a. _____

b. _____

c. _____

d. _____

6. *Topic sentence:* Maria's new minivan is sleek, modern, and very well equipped.

a. _____

b. _____

c. _____

d. _____

EXERCISE 2	Arranging Details in Spatial Order

Each of the following groups of sentences should be arranged in a consistent spatial organization, but the sentences are out of order. Number the scrambled sentences in each of the following groups to establish a logical arrangement. Pay attention to key words and transitional phrases, which should help you decide on the arrangement.

Paragraph A:

Topic Sentence: Abraham Lincoln may not have been our most handsome president, but his face was certainly among the most memorable.

_____ His dark hair and beard formed a frame around his long, angular face.

_____ Lincoln's bushy eyebrows that arched in quarter moons shielded his deep-set, almond-shaped eyes.

_____ The lips of his broad mouth were badly matched: a narrow upper lip and fleshy lower one.

_____ The wavy hair shot up like lava from a volcano, exposing his deeply lined high forehead, but it did not cover his enormous jutting ears.

_____ Finally, his short and neatly trimmed beard covered his chin but did not extend to a mustache.

_____ But his most prominent feature may have been his long, straight nose that widened at the tip and nostrils.

_____ To the sides were his high, bony cheeks, and midway down the right side was a large bump—probably a birthmark, though not discolored or hairy.

_____ To most Americans, the face of our sixteenth president is instantly recognizable.

Paragraph B:

Topic Sentence: Of all the extinct species of birds, the most incredible was the ridiculous dodo.

_____ It was discovered on an island in the Indian Ocean but died out by the end of the seventeenth century.

_____ The bird resembled a fat and strangely shaped dove (and it was, in fact, a member of the dove family), the size of a large turkey.

_____ In the center were the tiny useless wings, and at its rear was the tail, a tuft of feathers that curled over backward like a question mark.

_____ Its head was odd looking, with tiny round eyes near the top, and beneath them a long, lumpy upper beak that hooked over the much smaller lower beak.

_____ The dodo's neck formed an s, ending at its body, which looked like a large egg that had short feathers glued on it.

_____ It was about three feet tall, fat, and heavy-footed, with a belly that scraped the ground when it waddled, but it could not fly.

_____ Under its body were clawed feet that seemed barely able to support the weight of the body.

EXERCISE 3	Observing, Evaluating, Arranging, and Writing

Read the model paragraph below, and then draft a paragraph of your own that describes the room you're in right now. Use the paragraph as an inspiration for the kinds of details to record and the spatial organization that will help readers see what you're seeing. After looking around and jotting down details, state your impression of the room in the topic sentence, jot down an outline, and then write.

A Vision of Chaos

My room at home is cramped and messy. Its dimensions are small, nine feet by ten feet, and furniture is crowded into almost every available space. Next to the door is a long chest of drawers, all of which are crammed full. The top of the chest is covered with more clothes, letters, magazines, and personal effects that I cannot put anywhere else. A small mirror is attached to the wall over the dresser, but photographs, invitations, and pictures from magazines are taped over much of its surface. In fact, all of the walls are filled with posters, photos torn from magazines, and unframed pictures. On the left side of the room is a small old desk, covered with papers, books, magazines, pens and pencils. A short, four-shelf bookcase occupies the space just to the right of the desk, and it, too, is overflowing with books, some of them stacked sideways in piles on top of the other books. A wicker wastepaper basket filled with papers, tissues, and candy wrappers lies under the desk, and I often kick it when sitting in the desk chair. My bed occupies almost the entire wall opposite the door, partially blocking the only window in the room. The sheets, blanket, and bedspread hang over the right side of the bed in disarray. On the left of the bed is a nightstand I picked up at a garage sale, and on it are placed my telephone, answering machine, clock radio, jewelry case, keys, wallet, and balled up pieces of paper. On the wall to the right of the bed is a small bench, on which I have placed a nine-year-old, fourteen-inch TV and a cheap stereo system. There isn't enough room on the bench for both speakers, so I have placed one of them on the floor, next to the tiny closet that never has enough room or hangers for my clothes.

Topic Sentence: The room I'm writing in is _____

_____

PARAGRAPH WRITING ASSIGNMENT

Assume the instructor of a world history class has asked you to describe this scene from eighteenth-century England, based on the following engraving. Consider the title of the engraving, *The Sleeping Congregation,* and the point that the artist William Hogarth is trying to convey. Include the details that support your interpretation.

The following questions may guide you in recording details:

1. Where is the location?
2. How large or small are the objects or details in the scene?
3. What are the most important features of the objects or details?
4. Where is each object or detail—on the right, in the middle, above something else, close, or far away?
5. Where are people in the scene? What do they look like? What are they doing?

State your first reaction to the engraving in a preliminary topic sentence to guide you in selecting from and organizing the details. Arrange them in a rough outline, and then write your description. Supply transitions that cement the relationships between ideas.

Revise your description one or more times, making it unified, coherent, and clear. Pay attention to word choice—strong verbs and adjectives—sentence variety,

William Hogarth, *The Sleeping Congregation,* **1736. The Charles Deering McCormick Library of Special Collections, Northwestern University.**

and lively language. Engage your readers, and yourself, in an interesting and specific piece of writing.

The Revision Guidelines that follow may help guide the revision. Your instructor may designate this activity as peer review work to be discussed in your collaborative group, as described in earlier chapters.

After you've completed the revision, edit the paragraph, checking for correct spelling and punctuation, complete sentences, and clarity of ideas. Then make a clean copy of the paragraph, and proofread it carefully for errors. Submit the final copy to your instructor.

REVISION GUIDELINES   Writing a Descriptive Paragraph

1. Is the point of the topic sentence clear? If it is not clear, suggest some phrases to include in a revision.

2. Does the beginning of the paragraph provide a clear, general overview of the scene? If not, suggest additions or changes.

3. Do the details support the topic sentence? Are there enough? If not, suggest additions, deletions, or changes.

4. What principle of spatial organization does the paragraph use in arranging the details (for example, top to bottom, center to outside, or nearest to farthest)? Does the paragraph depart from that organizing principle at any point? If so, sketch briefly a possible rearrangement.

5. Are transitions lacking or too vague at any point in the paragraph? If so, suggest transitional phrases.

6. Does the conclusion summarize the scene and the writer's impression of it? How can it be improved? Suggest any punch lines that occur to you.

WRITING FOR MASTERY

Paragraphs

The following list of topics should provide you with ideas for writing other paragraphs of description. Include a topic sentence in each paragraph. Provide a general outline of the subject matter, followed by specific details arranged in a consistent spatial order. Tie your ideas together in the concluding sentence.

1. Describe an animal, perhaps a pet. Supply general details about the animal first—its overall size, weight, color, and shape. Then provide the specifics, arranged in spatial order—perhaps front to rear end, or face to feet. Include transitions.

2. Describe the person in the painting on page 142. What point do you think the artist James Gillray was trying to make about the upper class in 18th-century England? Support your analysis with specific details.

3. Describe an unusual-looking public figure, such as an athlete, movie star, or politician.

4. Describe a scene at the beach, in a park, or anywhere outdoors.

5. Describe something truly ugly.

6. *Writing from Source Material.* Write a description of the Loch Ness monster (or "Nessie") for *Nature* magazine. Craft a topic sentence and then specific details to support it. Use the following information to support the topic sentence. Do not copy the exact wording, except for the numbers indicating dimensions. Restate, or paraphrase the wording. You may need to make several revisions.

Scotland's Loch Ness monster: no conclusive proof

eyewitnesses construct a clear picture

skin: like a snail's

size of body: at least thirty feet long and twelve feet wide

skin color: gray, silver, or black

tail: rather flat, blunt at the end

neck: about four to seven feet long, gracefully curved, about as thick as an elephant's trunk

length from head to tail: more than fifty feet

head: like a snail's and very small compared to body

SOURCE: Simon Goodenough and others, *1,500 Fascinating Facts* (London: Octopus Books, 1983).

James Gillray, *A Voluptuary under the Horror of Digestion.* **Courtesy of the Samek Art Gallery, Bucknell University, Lewisburg, PA (#657/2500.).**

FROM PARAGRAPH TO ESSAY

Remember that an essay is essentially an exploded paragraph. It begins with a large idea, or thesis, stated in the introductory paragraph. It develops that idea specifically in the body paragraphs. And it brings the discussion to a close in the concluding paragraph.

A MODEL ESSAY: DESCRIPTION

Here's a model essay of description taken from Gilbert Highet's Talents and Geniuses, *a collection of essays based on his radio talks.*

Before beginning to read the essay, use your dictionary to look up the following words:

1. benumb   *5. congeal*
2. perfunctory   *6. dubious*
3. leprous   *7. debris*
4. defile   *8. abominable*

The Decadent
Gilbert Highet

* * * *

1   I have been traveling on the New York subway system for nearly twenty years. Probably by this time I look just as benumbed as all my fellow-sufferers. Yet the other day I had a strange mystical experience on the subway, which changed the place, and changed me, and illuminated for me the transforming power of the spirit.

2   Standing in a subway station, I began to appreciate the place—almost to enjoy it. First of all, I looked at the lighting: a row of meager electric bulbs, unscreened, yellow, and coated with filth, stretched toward the black mouth of the tunnel, as though it were a bolt hole in an abandoned coal mine. Then I lingered, with zest, on the walls and ceiling: lavatory tiles which had been white about fifty years ago, and were now encrusted with soot, coated with the remains of a dirty liquid which might be either atmospheric humidity mingled with smog or the result of a perfunctory attempt to clean them with cold water; and, above them, gloomy vaulting from which dingy paint was peeling off like scabs from an old wound, sick black paint leaving a leprous white undersurface. Beneath my feet, the floor was a nauseating dark brown with black stains upon it which might be stale oil or dry chewing gum or some worse defilement; it looked like the hallway of a condemned slum building. Then my eye traveled to the tracks, where two lines of glittering steel—the only positively clean objects in the whole place—ran out of darkness into darkness above an unspeakable mass of congealed oil, puddles of dubious liquid, and a mishmash of old cigarette packets, mutilated and filthy newspapers, and the debris that filtered down from the street above through a barred grating in the roof. As I looked up toward the sunlight, I could see more debris sifting slowly downward, and making an abominable pattern in the slanting beam of dirtladen sunlight. I was going on to relish more features of this unique scene: such as the advertisement posters on the walls—here a text from the Bible, there a half-naked girl, here a woman wearing a hat consisting of a hen sitting on a nest full of eggs, and there a pair of girl's legs walking up the keys of a cash register—all scribbled over with unknown names and well-known obscenities in black crayon and red lipstick; but then my train came in at last, I boarded it, and began to read. The experience was over for the time.

3   Still, it lingered in my mind. It had been very peculiar. For me, it had been unique. But since then I have been able to repeat it, almost at will. . . . With a slight adaptation of my sensibility, I find that I can actually relish this experience.

Questions for Analysis

1. What sentence states the main idea of the essay? Draw a box around it.
2. What pattern of spatial arrangement does Highet follow in the second paragraph? What transitions establish that arrangement? List them.
3. Compare Highet's organization to the diagram of a typical description you saw earlier in the chapter. You might try diagramming Highet's structure in the same way. Does it resemble the diagram of a paragraph? Note the way the structures of essays and paragraphs are similar.
4. Highet gives details that show the deterioration in the subway station. List them.

5. Many of Highet's adjectives convey the unpleasantness of the things he observes. Underline these adjectives. Some of his adjectives also show his fascination, even joy, at observing these things. Circle those adjectives.

6. Summarize the way Highet's experience in the subway affected him. What sentences seem most directly to express that idea?

A STUDENT MODEL ESSAY: DESCRIPTION

Max Rodriguez-Reyes composed this essay in a composition class for foreign students at Truman College in Chicago. He is a native of Guatemala and has a wife and child. As you read the essay, notice how Max describes the town at different times of the day or week. Notice, too, how he includes sounds and tastes in addition to the sights of the town.

Before beginning the essay, use your dictionary to look up the following words:

1. *counterpoint*
2. *innumerable*
3. *serene*
4. *artifacts*
5. *savory*

The Beauty of My Town
Max Rodriguez-Reyes

* * * *

1   I come from a small town called Coban, far from Guatemala City, with a population of about 2,000 people, mostly of Mayan Indian descent. The beauty of green villages and mountains and the spiritual culture of the Mayan Indians are preserved almost intact from the region of their birth.

2   In the morning when I am there, I enjoy the cool mountain breezes and the pure golden sunlight as a refreshing counterpoint to the endless ticking of the clock. When I leave my house, the first things that strike my senses are the smell of fragrant wildflowers and the sight of Mayan Indians riding their horses up the mountain on the way to work. In the afternoon, I walk along the woodland trails amid the tall trees and the singing of innumerable birds, exchanging endless greetings with the Mayans passing by. Then I wander along the river, where the clear blue water running serenely down the mountains never fails to make me yearn for an evening swim.

3   On Saturdays, I visit the local plaza and drink in the sights and sounds of Indians wearing and selling their traditional costumes and artifacts made by hand with clay, a phenomenon almost unique to the town. On Sunday mornings the plaza looks quiet and almost deserted because virtually the entire population is in church. But by noon of the same day the village square is alive with flocks of brightly costumed children at play under the tolerant eyes of their parents and elder siblings, while on the main stage of the *zocalo* (the town square), the *marimbas* (the national instrument of Guatemala) are casting their magical spell while people of all ages dance and sing around them, and I enjoy such savory appe-

tizers as Guatemalan tamales and *atole de elote* (the delicious corn soup for which the Mayan are renowned through the world).

4   As the magnificent evening sunset filters slowly down through the magically changing blues and greens of the mountain rivers, I reflect once more on the inestimable treasures of spiritual beauty with which our humble people have been blessed.

Questions for Analysis

1. What is the main point that Max Rodriguez-Reyes makes?
2. Max includes several Spanish words, which he then defines or describes in parentheses. Would the description be less effective with the Spanish words removed?
3. Max mixes action along with description. Identify several places in which he does this.
4. Examine the organization of each paragraph. What transitions help you follow the organization? Underline them. How is the whole essay organized?

WRITING FOR MASTERY

Essays

The following list presents some broad topics for descriptive essays. Be sure your essay includes a thesis statement and topic sentences. Be sure it has adequate detail and clear transitions. Be sure, also, that you arrange the details in a consistent spatial order.

1. Return to the paragraph you wrote on the Hogarth engraving and expand it into a full essay. Consider the main points—or the separate parts of the engraving you describe in the paragraph—and make each into a paragraph in the essay, perhaps three body paragraphs. Include an introductory paragraph and a concluding paragraph.
2. Expand any of the paragraphs you wrote from Writing for Mastery on page 141 into a full essay.
3. Assume you are composing a letter to an out-of-town friend. Describe one interesting place, as Max Rodriguez does, depicting the activities there at different times of the day, week, or season and conveying a main point about the place.
4. Have you, like Gilbert Highet, ever been fascinated by something ugly? Have you ever been revolted by something ugly? Write an essay in which you describe the subject and express your feelings.
5. Describe a place of great natural beauty, like the Grand Canyon. Be specific.
6. Describe the scene in the painting on page 146. It is *A Sunday on La Grande Jatte*, by Georges Seurat (1859–1891). Painted in 1884–1886, it shows people in a public park on an island in the Seine River near Paris.

Georges Seurat, *A Sunday on La Grande Jatte*, 1884–86. Oil on canvas, 81½ x 120¼ in. Helen Birch Bartlett Memorial Collection, 1926.224. Photograph © 2002, The Art Institute of Chicago, All Rights Reserved.

10 Composing Narratives

A narrative tells a story that makes a point—and often in dramatic fashion. Therefore, the details must develop that point, as well as create a sense of realism and tension. This chapter will help you compose narrative paragraphs and essays. You'll

■ examine a model narrative paragraph

■ analyze its structure and learn how it was written

■ practice gathering and organizing narrative details

■ write a narrative paragraph and/or a narrative essay

A MODEL PARAGRAPH: NARRATION

As you read the following narrative paragraph, look at how it establishes the setting while carrying the action forward. Look, too, at how the inclusion of just a small amount of dialogue creates a sense of immediacy—putting you there, witnessing the event.

A Race to Eternity

* * * *

The day that "marathon man" James Worson accepted a challenge to race was the day the proud, athletic shoemaker screamed once and then mysteriously vanished from the earth. On September 3, 1873, Worson bragged to two friends that he had often raced from one town to another in record time. His friends challenged him to prove his ability, and Worson happily accepted. He would show them, he said, with a twenty-mile run from the city of Leamington to Coventry. Worson put on his running clothes and set out. His friends, Hammerson Burns and Barham Wise, carried a camera and trailed close behind him in a horse-drawn buggy. A quarter of the way through the race, Worson was running effortlessly and turning occasionally to exchange words with his friends. But then

UNIT 3

Chapter 10

Composing with Confidence

©2003

GO ELECTRONIC!

Use the following electronic supplements for additional practice with your writing:

• For chapter-by-chapter summaries and exercises, visit the Composing with Confidence Companion Website at: http://www.ablongman.com/meyers.

• For work with the writing process, visit The Longman Writer's Warehouse at http://longmanwriterswarehouse.com (password needed).

• For additional practice in grammar, use The Writer's ToolKit Plus CD-ROM

Worson suddenly stumbled in the middle of a dirt road, pitched forward, and emitted a piercing scream. Wise said later, "It was the most ghastly sound either of us had ever heard." That terrible cry was their last memory of him. Worson's body never struck the ground, for he vanished in the middle of his fall. The road itself provided evidence of what they had witnessed. Burns's pictures of the long-distance runner's tracks show clear footprints suddenly ending as if Worson had crashed into a stone wall. When the men returned to Leamington, a massive hunt began. Searchers combed every inch of the trail without success. Bloodhounds were strangely unwilling to approach the spot where Worson's footprints ended. And for years after his disappearance, there were reports of a ghostly green runner at night on the road from Leamington to Coventry.

Questions for Analysis

1. What is the topic sentence? Underline it. Does it make you want to read on? Why or why not?
2. What is the setting of the action? Where and when was it? Who was involved?
3. Which words and phrases indicate the passage of time? Are all of these expressions located at the beginning of sentences?
4. What is the climax of the story? Where does it occur?

The Structure of Narrative

Narration is storytelling. Unlike physical description, which organizes details in space, narration usually proceeds in **chronological order**—in a time sequence. Notice how the model paragraph on James Worson moves the action forward to a dramatic end. The paragraph is unified, focusing on one event. And it's coherent, with transitions that indicate the passage of time and place. It shares the traits of all good narratives:

1. It establishes the four Ws of a setting—*who, what, where,* and *when*—within the context of the action.
2. It's specific, putting readers on the scene so they can observe and listen to the action.
3. It begins at the beginning and ends at the end.
4. It builds toward a climax, bringing the action to a dramatic close.

A WRITER SPEAKS

I was searching through a pile of magazines in a doctor's office when I saw the cover of *Time*. It was the photograph that caught my eye. The child on the cover looked so much like one of my sons that I found myself gaping at it. Then I noticed the headline: "Children Who Kill." Quietly hysterical, I combed through the pages until I got to the lead story of a child in England who had smothered a smaller child.

Time passed, and though I had no inkling of it, I was still fixed on that image. When I sat down to write a few months later with six weeks off from teaching and the intention of starting a new novel, there it was: the cover of *Time*. Suddenly I knew what my subject had to be. A flood of language began to transform that picture of a stranger into the subject for my new novel: woman's son has (accidentally?) killed the neighbor's child. What does it feel like to be that woman? During my six weeks off, I wrote the first seventy-five pages of my novel, *A Boy in Winter*.

Maxine Chernoff, novelist and poet, and Chair of the Department of Fiction, San Francisco State University

A blueprint of a narrative paragraph might look something like this:

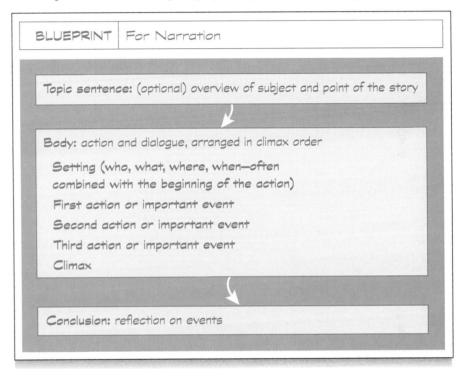

BLUEPRINT | For Narration

Topic sentence: (optional) overview of subject and point of the story

Body: action and dialogue, arranged in climax order

  Setting (who, what, where, when—often combined with the beginning of the action)

  First action or important event

  Second action or important event

  Third action or important event

  Climax

Conclusion: reflection on events

The Process of Composing a Narrative

Let's examine the steps the writer might have gone through in composing the narrative paragraph. Here are the steps:

1. Record Details.   The writer first recorded details about the events of the story of James Worson—in this case, by reading interviews of the people who witnessed the event. He gathered far more information than he could use in a single paragraph, knowing he'd probably summarize or omit some of it later.

Because the writer found his materials in printed sources, he decided to record it all in a brainstorming list. If he had been writing from firsthand experience, he might have used freewriting to create a continuous flow of ideas in complete—or nearly complete—sentences.

2. Draft a Topic Sentence.   After gathering his materials, the writer looked for a leading idea—a common theme—he could state in a topic sentence. He wanted to emphasize the mystery of the story while not revealing the ending. In fact, for that reason, many writers end the narrative with the topic sentence.

A Word About Words

Here's a little narrative about the birth of a word. In the morning hours of an all-night card game on August 6, 1762, John Montagu, fourth earl of Sandwich, a notorious gambler, decided that he was hungry but wouldn't dare leave his cards for a meal. Instead, he ordered a servant to bring him some cold, thick-sliced roast beef between two pieces of toasted bread. This was the origin of the sandwich.

✓ TIPS

For Choosing Transitions to Show Time Relationships

Here's a guide to help you mark the movement in time:

Consecutive time: after, after a while, afterward, and then, an hour (a day, a week) later, finally, first (second, third), later (on), next, soon, still later, the next day (week, year)

Same time: as, as soon as, at that moment, during, immediately, meanwhile, suddenly, when, while

Specific time: in October, in 1975, on January 9, at noon, at 8:30

But don't be mechanical in using transitions. Sometimes you'll need full sentences to gracefully connect the ideas and establish time relationships.

Just as a reminder, here's the topic sentence that begins the story:

> The day that "marathon man" James Worson accepted a challenge to race was the day the proud, athletic shoemaker screamed once and then mysteriously vanished from the earth.

3. Outline in Chronological Order. Now the writer organized his materials in a time sequence. He also worked toward a dramatic **climax**—when the tension is greatest and the outcome is revealed.

The writer outlined the materials as follows:

> I. Worson's challenge from friends
> 20-mile run from Leamington to Coventry
> beginning the run
>   friends in buggy
>   carrying a camera
> first one-fourth
>   effortless running
>   talking to friends
> dramatic moment
>   stumble, fall, scream
>   disappearance of Worson
> II. search for Worson
> photos showing end of footprints
> massive search
> bloodhounds not willing to go to spot of disappearance
> III. ghostly reappearance of Worson

4. Drafting and Revising. Now the writer drafted the story, adding and removing details in revisions, and supplying transitions to strengthen the chronological order for his readers. He ended the story on a powerful note:

> And for years after his disappearance, there were reports of a ghostly green runner at night on the road from Leamington to Coventry.

He avoided a cliché like, "It was a day no one will forget." That corny ending merely elbows the reader in the ribs as if to say, "Get the point? Get it?"

That's how the narrative paragraph was composed. You can follow similar procedures in composing your own narrative.

GETTING READY TO WRITE

As you prepare to write a narrative paragraph, try these warm-up exercises. They'll give you practice organizing details chronologically so that they can build to a climax.

EXERCISE 1	Arranging Details in Chronological Order

Number each of the sentences in the following groups so that each group makes a coherent, chronologically organized paragraph.

Earth Making (A Cherokee Legend)

Paragraph A:

_____ Although living creatures existed, their home was up there, above the rainbow, and it was crowded.

___*I*___ In the beginning, water covered everything.

_____ "We are all jammed together," the animals said.

_____ Wondering what was under the water, they sent Water Beetle to look around.

_____ "We need more room."

Paragraph B:

_____ Water Beetle skimmed over the surface, but couldn't find any solid footing.

_____ Someone Powerful then fastened it to the sky ceiling with cords.

_____ Magically, the mud spread out in the four directions and became the island we are living on—this earth.

_____ So Water Beetle dived down to the bottom and brought up a little dab of soft mud.

Paragraph C:

_____ At first, the earth was flat, soft, and moist.

_____ But the birds all flew back up and said there was still no spot they could perch on.

_____ Therefore, they kept sending down birds to see if the mud had dried and hardened enough to take their weight.

_____ All the animals were eager to live on the earth.

Paragraph D:

_____ Then the animals sent Grandfather Buzzard down.

_____ When he swept up his wings, they made a mountain.

_____ But when he glided low over what would become Cherokee country, he found that the mud was getting harder.

_____ It's because of Grandfather Buzzard that we have so many mountains in Cherokee land.

_____ By that time, Buzzard was tired and dragging.

_____ So when he flapped his wings down, they made a valley where they touched the earth.

_____ The animals watching him from above the rainbow said, "If he keeps on, there will be only mountains," and they made him come back.

_____ He flew very close and saw that the earth was very soft.

Paragraph E:

_____ The crawfish had his back sticking out of a stream, and Sun burned it red.

_____ The animals couldn't see very well because they had no sun or moon.

_____ Now they had light, but it was much too hot because Sun was too close to earth.

_____ Then someone said, "Let's grab Sun from up there behind the rainbow! Let's get him down, too!"

_____ At last the earth was hard and dry enough, and the animals descended.

_____ His meat was spoiled forever, and the people still won't eat crawfish.

_____ Pulling Sun down, they told him, "Here's a road for you," and they showed him the way to go—from east to west.

Paragraph F:

_____ They pushed him up as high as a man, but it was still too hot.

_____ They tried four times and then, when they had Sun up to the height of four men, he was just hot enough.

_____ So they pushed him farther, but it wasn't far enough.

_____ Everyone asked the sorcerers, the shamans, to go put Sun higher.

_____ Everyone was satisfied, so they left him there.

EXERCISE 2	Generating Details

Complete each of the topic sentences, and then list at least four supporting details in chronological order.

1. *Topic sentence:* When I _____, I had a big surprise.

    a. _____

    b. _____

    c. _____

    d. _____

2. *Topic sentence:* Adjusting to _____ can be difficult.

    a. _____

    b. _____

    c. _____

    d. _____

3. *Topic sentence:* My first _____ was particularly exciting.

    a. _____

    b. _____

    c. _____

    d. _____

4. *Topic sentence:* _____ once had a lucky moment (or a narrow escape).

    a. _____

    b. _____

    c. _____

    d. _____

5. Topic sentence: _____ benefited from an unexpected act of kindness.

    a. _____

    b. _____

    c. _____

    d. _____

PARAGRAPH WRITING ASSIGNMENT

Write an entertaining narrative paragraph for a young audience, perhaps children in sixth or seventh grade, on the following topic: a legend or frequently repeated story from your family, your community, or your native country if it was not the United States. Or tell a dramatic or amusing story in which you or someone in your family was involved.

Generate the details in whatever way feels most comfortable: brainstorming, clustering, or freewriting. Look for a leading idea to state in a preliminary topic sentence, which you may choose to place at the end of the narrative. Select details that best support the topic idea and discard details that aren't particularly relevant.

Then arrange the details in chronological order and draft the story. Establish the setting, and let the action unfold toward a climax. If halfway through the draft you recall a detail that belongs earlier in the story, don't say, "Incidentally, something happened earlier that I forgot to mention." Jot down the detail on a separate piece of paper for use in your next draft. Or, if you're composing on a word processor, scroll to the spot where the detail should go and insert it.

As you revise, work for unity, coherence, and clarity. Is the setting established? Is the movement between events clearly established? Is there sufficient detail? Are the verbs and adjectives strong, the sentences varied, the language lively?

The Revision Guidelines below can guide your revision. Your instructor may designate this activity as peer review work in your collaborative group, as described in Chapter 2.

Edit your work, checking for correct spelling and punctuation, complete sentences, and chronological order. Then make a clean copy of your paper, proofread it carefully, and submit the final copy to your instructor.

REVISION GUIDELINES | Composing Narratives

1. Is the point of the story clear? If not, suggest language that would clarify the point.
2. Does the beginning of the paragraph establish all the important information about the setting? If not, what could be added?
3. Do all the details develop the point? If not, list what should be eliminated, revised, or added.
4. Is the paragraph organized chronologically? If not, make a numbered list of ideas arranged in the proper order. Does the narrative lead to a climax? If not, rework the organization or reword the sentences to create a dramatic conclusion—but avoid clichés.
5. Is the narration unclear in any spots? If so, list the spots where it lacks clarity.
6. Are transitions lacking or too vague at any point? If so, suggest some transitions showing time relationships, and draw an arrow to the place where each might be inserted.

WRITING FOR MASTERY

Paragraphs

The following list of topics should provide you with ideas for writing other paragraphs of narration. In each paragraph you write, include a topic sentence that states the main idea but doesn't reveal the climax. Arrange the details in chronological order, and include transitions that show time relationships. Build toward a climax, and end your paper with a conclusion that ties everything together but avoids clichés like, "I'll never forget that day as long as I live."

1. Discuss a mysterious or unusual event that happened to you or someone you know.
2. Relate a story that you heard from one of your parents or grandparents about one of their experiences as children or young adults.
3. Tell the story of a trip to the dentist or doctor when you were young.
4. Tell the story of some loss of an innocent childhood belief: of discovering that Santa Claus wasn't real, that there wasn't a tooth fairy, that people couldn't fly like Superman or Peter Pan, or any other moment when you discovered some disappointing truth.
5. Tell about your first haircut—or taking a child or sibling for a haircut.
6. Relate the story of a wedding—yours, a sibling's, a relative's, a friend's—in which you participated.
7. Tell the story of taking your first cigarette, or beer, or other taboo—or of refusing to smoke, drink, or do something you found unpleasant or wrong.

FROM PARAGRAPH TO ESSAY

A narrative paragraph relates a single action. A narrative essay relates a series of actions, each in its own paragraph, that develop one main idea or thesis. The paragraphs themselves are arranged in chronological order, building toward a climax.

Here are two models of narrative essays, both written by students. Notice how each story is developed through a series of scenes involving different locations, times, or characters. These scene changes largely determine the paragraph divisions in the essays. Notice, too, how each narrative begins in the midst of the action, therefore sparking your interest. Neither begins with a corny "I'll never forget the time that . . ."

A STUDENT MODEL ESSAY: NARRATION

Bunny Dewar was a student at Truman College in Chicago. She had been an acupuncturist and then returned to school for additional training. As you read her story, notice how she establishes the setting within the context of the action. Notice, too, how she builds toward a climax. And notice her use of transitions to show the movement in time.

The Footsteps in the House
Bunny Dewar

* * * *

1   The first time I walked through the door of the old house I could feel its presence. The house had five floors with twelve-foot ceilings. It was built in 1890 and, like most old houses, it was drafty. But an unmistakable warmth hovered over me as I did some exploring.

2   The first night I slept there, a strange thing happened. At around one o'clock I woke up to some noise. I'm a very light sleeper, so it could have been anything. I lay there in the dark listening to all the creaks and moans that an old house can make. It was then that I heard the footsteps. They were slowly coming up the stairs, not heavy steps but rather light and steady. They turned right at the top of the stairs and hesitated outside of the bedrooms at the end of the hall. As I listened, I heard

them start toward my door. I felt my heart pounding as I waited to see the doorknob turn. After a moment of silence, the footsteps continued down to the other end of the hall. I don't know how long I listened, but I must have fallen back to sleep because the next thing I knew it was morning.

3   I knew Bob hadn't heard a thing because, like all men, he sleeps like a baby, so I decided not to say anything. The next night I awoke to the sound of steps again. I wish I could have been brave enough to open the door, but I'm no dummy. I've seen all the horror movies where the audience knows the heroine shouldn't open the door, and she does anyway and pays for her stupidity by running right into the monster. Again, I lay there in the dark listening and waiting, but nothing happened.

4   The third time was the strangest. I heard the footsteps as usual, but this time I knew to whom they belonged. I have always been a little psychic. Sometimes I just know things. I don't have any control over it; it just happens. As the footsteps walked by my door, I knew who this person was—or I should say who she was when she was alive. She and her family had built this house. I didn't know her name and couldn't see her face, but I knew she was wearing a long robe and carrying a candle. She was making her nightly check on the children before she retired to her bedroom at the other end of the hall. This explained the pauses I had heard in front of each doorway and why the footsteps never returned once they reached the end of the hall.

5   Actually, her presence made me feel quite safe. You might think such noises in an old house would be a little spooky, but they seemed to bathe my house in a warm glow. Even other people would comment on the comfort during their visits. The darkest recesses held no threat, and I was at ease with my nightly visitor.

6   Bob had gone out of town, and this was the first time I would be alone in the house. That night as I went upstairs to bed, I had an overwhelming urge to talk to her. I stood in the hallway and told her I knew she was there and that I loved this house as much as she did. I was glad no one could see me now, or they would have thought I had gone off the deep end. Suddenly I was surrounded by a warm breeze. The hair on my arms and neck stood on end. She was there! I could smell a touch of lavender, and her warmth swept over me like a cloud. I regained my composure and continued my conversation with her. I'm not sure how long I went on because the encounter became so intense. As I went to bed that night, I knew I really belonged in this house.

7   We are doing construction on our second floor right now, so I'm not hearing her on her nightly rounds. But I can still feel her in every corner of the house, and maybe if you come to visit sometime you'll be able to feel her too!

Questions for Analysis

1. Why does the first sentence of the first paragraph refer to "its presence" rather than naming the object that was present?
2. Which paragraphs begin with topic sentences? Why doesn't every paragraph contain a topic sentence?
3. Transitional expressions of chronological order are very explicit in this story. Underline them.
4. What is Bunny Dewar's attitude toward the strange being who occupies her house? What statements and details reveal that attitude?
5. Bunny's details touch on several of the five senses. Locate these details. What effects do they create?
6. At what points in the story are the details most specific and dramatic? How do these details contribute to the central idea and mood of the story?

AN ADDITIONAL STUDENT MODEL: NARRATION

Jillian Wright, a student at Truman College in Chicago, had lived for a while in Martha's Vineyard, where the following events occurred. As you read her essay, notice the precise details and word choice. Notice, too, how Jillian departs from chronological order as she engages in flashbacks, but how she guides us easily through the time shifts via transitions.

A Death
Jillian Wright

* * * *

1   She died in February. I found her on a cold afternoon late in winter, in her cabin. The lake lay still and the chimney stood smokeless. The door was open, a seemingly empty hole in the wall. I was the one who closed the door. I was the one to lower myself into the silence, onto the floor, next to her. I was the one to close her eyes and hold the gray face. I wrapped her in blankets and huddled in the gloom of the cabin as the snow fell to the ground.

2   The room was dim behind drawn curtains as I surveyed the surroundings where she had died. Seeing nothing of interest, I looked to the body. Her slender torso was stiff and awkward upon the floor. Her limbs were rounded and hard, their once easy suppleness gone. She was now altogether like a statue. I felt someone should keep her company now—for what reason I did not know. But I was the one who simply knelt and stroked her dry hair, as if she would suddenly wake from a deep sleep and fix herself a cup of tea.

3   A shadow was creeping across the landscape. A cloud had moved in front of the sun, and the cabin's interior took on a thick foreboding feeling. I left her body resting on the dry planks of the floor, stood and opened the door to let the breeze blow the feeling of the moment away in a gentle flurry.

4   Walking back to the body . . . her body, I lifted it from its resting place on the dry planks. Taking her into my arms, I lifted her to the bed and gently set her down.

5   Then turning around, I walked to the door. I left it open and walked out onto the patio. Strained squeaks from old wood sounded underfoot as I looked to the lake. The water was calm and black as the snow fell. The air was dry, but nonetheless heavy. As the sun sank behind the clouds, I lit a cigarette and returned to the cabin. I looked to the bed and noticed how weighted and dull she looked, as if bored. I wasn't saddened. It was enough to be there, not asking questions, not doing anything. I simply stood and looked at her for a moment. It was enough.

6   I had seen her many times in town, the first when I was sixteen. It had been the summer I worked at the Farmers' Market. She had come in for groceries, all quiet and mysterious. She had long brown hair and hazel eyes that seemed to look right into you, into your very insides every time she looked your way. She walked calmly, barefoot and strong, with her arms gently swinging by her side.

7   Without saying a word, she brought her items to the counter and pulled out some wadded money from a pocket in the side of her dress. Clumsily I bagged her goods and gave her change. She smiled slowly, looking me in the eye, and left, it seems, much more quickly than she arrived. More than anything, I felt a deep sense of curiosity.

8   She had a certain youthful arrogance to her posture that made her seem wondrously spirited, yet she tempered her youth with an uncanny elegance that kind of threw you off guard every time you saw her. You almost felt clumsy just being around her. I hardly remember seeing her with another soul. I guess she seemed perfectly content with her own company.

9   The winter that year was unusually mild. The snows came late, around January and February. Once the snow arrived, I noticed that she hadn't come into town for groceries. As the snow accumulated, I had the notion to leave some things beside her front door.

10   It had been a long walk up that dirt road, and I had to stop along the way to catch my breath. I thought about how carefree she seemed when she would walk into town and wondered what I would look like upon returning—most likely worn out and haggard.

11   When I came to the final turn, the snow had increased a bit, and I felt relieved at finally spotting her cabin. It stood on a grassy knoll, now white with snow, and the first thing I noticed was the front door ajar.

12   As I neared the open door, I thought about her face and if it would show how surprised she was to see me. And I hoped she would be able to understand the small amount of sign language I knew and she would respond. I knew she was deaf and I was told by others that she had never spoken a word, but could if she wanted to. I often wondered what her voice would have sounded like, the tone, the subtle gestures of it.

13   I walked back to town that day and told the police what I had found. Later that evening I called the coroner. He told me that she had frozen to death.

14   Alone at twenty-three.

Questions for Analysis

1. The climax of a story normally occurs at the end, yet Jillian Wright begins her story by announcing the death of the young woman. Why? What effect does that announcement have on you? Where are the actual climactic moments, when dramatic details are revealed?

2. Only in a few places does Jillian discuss her feelings about the young woman's death. What details in the action of the story suggest how Jillian felt?

3. Jillian fills the story with description of the woman's body and of the natural surroundings. What effects do these descriptions create?

4. Contrasts establish much of the interest and tension in this story. What contrasts do you see? How do they affect you?

5. The narrative frequently shifts back and forth in time. What expressions help you identify the shifts?

6. Underline all the topic sentences in the story. Does every paragraph contain a topic sentence? Why or why not?

WRITING FOR MASTERY

Essays

According to the directions of your instructor, you may compose a paragraph or a full essay for one or more of the following topics. Or you can return to the topics suggested for paragraphs and develop one into a full essay. For each, assume you are writing for the college literary magazine and your primary purpose is to entertain.

1. Like Bunny Dewar, tell the story of an odd or mysterious experience that you or someone you know has encountered. Gather material for and compose the first draft of a story, organizing the paragraphs in climax order. Be sure to save the most important or most dramatic events for last.

2. Like Jillian Wright, have you ever witnessed or participated in a sad event? Tell the story.

3. Tell about a time when you or someone else was a hero. (Acts of heroism can be large or small.) Again, organize the sentences or paragraphs to build to a climax.

4. Describe the experience of gaining a new brother, sister, son, daughter, or friend.

5. Tell the story of a dangerous or embarrassing experience.

6. *Writing from Source Material.* Jillian Wright's story is obviously about death, but it's about much more than that. Make four columns on a sheet of paper with the following headings: (1) isolation and loneliness, (2) inability to communicate, (3) physical handicaps, (4) nature. Then return to the story, locate any details that fit into these categories, and list them in the columns.

Then consider what you've found. What point or points do you think Jillian Wright was trying to communicate? Write a paragraph that interprets the story. State your interpretation in a topic sentence about one or more of these categories. You don't have to deal with all of them.

Explain your ideas, and illustrate them with details from the story. Don't copy from the story; describe the action in your own words. Or, if you decide to use any of the exact language of the story, put quotation marks around that language. Place a comma inside the end quotation mark, and identify the source of the quote with a phrase such as *Jillian Wright says,* or *Ms. Wright recalls.* (Don't refer to the writer by her first name; that's reserved for me— her teacher!)

Revise this paper one or more times, making sure that your sentences sound clear and natural.

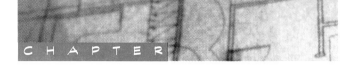

11 Explaining a Process

People are eager to learn—and need to learn—how to do things and how things work. Giving and receiving directions are essential for you and others to acquire knowledge, learn skills, and perform daily tasks. These are the reasons for process analysis, in which you explain procedures and give directions to your readers. This chapter will direct you through the process of composing a process analysis. You'll

- examine models of process analysis paragraphs
- analyze their structure and how process analysis is written
- practice generating the details for and arranging the steps in a process analysis
- write a paragraph and/or an essay of process analysis

MODEL PARAGRAPHS: PROCESS ANALYSIS

*Every set of instructions for assembling a new toy is a process analysis. So is every operating manual for a VCR, recipe in a cookbook, and orientation handbook for new students or workers. So, in fact, is much of what you learn in college: an explanation of photosynthesis, or of Newton's third law, or how to create a computer database, or how to compose a paragraph. These are all examples of **process analysis**—explanations of how to do something or how something works.*

Here's an example. As you read it, consider its goal. What are readers to do with the information?

GO ELECTRONIC!

Use the following electronic supplements for additional practice with your writing:

- For chapter-by-chapter summaries and exercises, visit the Composing with Confidence Companion Website at: http://www.ablongman.com/meyers.
- For work with the writing process, visit The Longman Writer's Warehouse at http://longmanwriterswarehouse.com (password needed).
- For additional practice in grammar, use The Writer's ToolKit Plus CD-ROM

A Matter of Gravity

* * * *

If you travel to the moon someday, be prepared for some surprises, for the moon's gravity is only one-sixth as strong as the earth's. This reduced gravitational pull affects your weight, strength, and the moon's own atmospheric conditions. Your first surprise will be your sudden weight loss—although you won't be slimmer. You'll be five-sixths lighter than you'd be on earth. Or, to put it another way, a 180-pound person on the mother planet will weigh only 30 pounds on the moon. Your second surprise will be your sudden gain in strength. On the moon, without a strong gravitational pull holding you to the surface, you could easily surpass the Olympic high jump record. The current mark of about 8 feet would translate into 48 feet on the moon. Finally—and this may not be a surprise—because the moon's gravity is too weak to capture and hold an atmosphere, you'd find no weather at all: no wind, rain, or snow. And without an atmosphere to regulate climate, you'd also find no stability in temperature. During the day the surface is hot enough to boil water, but at night it drops to 260 degrees below zero. That's why the astronauts needed their own oxygen supplies and insulated space suits. You'd need them, too, for no matter how light and strong you felt, without protection, you wouldn't live more than a few seconds to enjoy these feelings.

Questions for Analysis

1. What is the topic sentence of the paragraph? Underline it.
2. The writer addresses the readers directly and seems to be giving them advice on what to expect when they go to the moon. Does the writer expect them to go to the moon—and if not, why does he mention this possibility?
3. The paragraph labels each step in the process as a "surprise." How many steps does the paragraph discuss? What are they?
4. Process analysis often explains unfamiliar ideas or concepts through comparisons to familiar ones. What comparisons does this paragraph make?

Here's another example, with quite a different goal—to instruct readers on how to perform a task. Notice the inclusion of the tools needed to perform the task, the step-by-step instructions, and the transitions that introduce each of the steps.

Photographing Wild Animals

* * * *

If you are interested in animals and photography, you can put the two together by photographing wild animals—not in a zoo, but out in their natural environment, the woods. Six steps are involved in taking pictures of wildlife in the woods. First, you will need clothing that blends into the background of the woods. (Combat fatigues from any army surplus store are good.) Second, you need a good camera—and that excludes digital cameras, which don't yet achieve the clarity of 35-millimeter film. The camera should allow you to bypass its automatic features. Automatic cameras tend to give an "average" reading of the subject—a sort of compromise between the subject in the background, and the light and dark shading. But you don't want to compromise.

Furthermore, you want to be able to zoom in or out on your subject, as well as to adjust both the time that the lens is open (called the shutter speed) and the width of the lens (called the lens opening). A lens that is open too long will produce a blurred image of a quickly moving animal, and a lens that is opened too widely will produce muddy images caused by the darkness of the woods. Third, you need to find a spot in the woods where animals are likely to come— probably around water or food (fruit, leaves, and the like). Experienced hunters or nature photographers can offer you advice on where to go. Fourth, after arriving at the spot, you will need to make final preparations: choosing a place to conceal yourself and adjusting your camera's lens opening and shutter speed for the conditions. Fifth, you must wait patiently. You may have to sit for many hours—and be willing to accept the possibility that no animals will come at all. Finally, if one does appear, you will need to act quickly. You must aim your camera and take as many pictures as you can, for under these conditions only a few shots will be interesting or even clear.

Questions for Analysis

1. Who is the audience for this paragraph? What does the writer expect the audience to do with the information provided?
2. What is the topic sentence of the paragraph? Underline it. How many ideas does it preview in the body of the paragraph? What tools does the writer specify?
3. What terms does the writer explain or define? Circle them.
4. How many steps are involved in the process? What transitions help you identify the steps? Bracket them.

The Structure of Process Analysis

The purpose of process analysis is usually to inform, and it always breaks the process down into a series of steps that are presented in **sequential order**. This arrangement is much the same as chronological order, except that chronology usually describes a series of events in the past (a narrative), while sequence describes a series of typical or characteristic actions that may take place in the past, present, or future.

Basically, there are two types of process analysis:

1. *Explanations of how something works*—for example, gravity, a printing press stamping out copies of a newspaper, a mixture of chemicals producing a powerful drug, or a tadpole developing into a frog. Drawings or photographs often accompany such explanations. They are usually written in the third person (*it* or *they*), but can be written in the second person, as the paragraph on gravity was. Remember, **person** is divided into three categories: first person (*I* and *we*); second (*you*, both singular and plural); and third (*he, she, it*, and *they*).

2. *Explanations of how to do something*—for example, how to photograph animals in nature, bake a flourless chocolate cake, use a fax modem, or travel by car from St. Louis to Minneapolis. These directions are usually written in the second person (addressing the audience as *you*) or in the **imperative** ("First do this. Then do that.") For a review of the imperative, see Chapter 8.

A blueprint of a process analysis might look something like this:

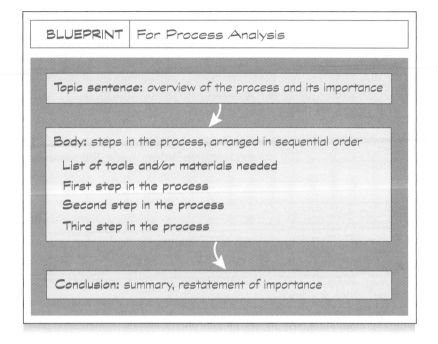

The Process of Composing a Process Analysis

Because the success of a process-analysis paragraph depends on a clear, well-organized presentation, the paragraph should be planned with special care. How did the writer compose the paragraph on taking photographs? Here are the steps involved.

A WRITER SPEAKS

Many of my family and colleagues think I put writing off to the last minute. They're right, but they're also wrong. Because writing the final product is not particularly enjoyable to me (I'd rather read than write), I do postpone the actual time in front of the computer screen until a deadline looms. However, in another sense, I've been writing from the moment I received the assignment. I write in my head—planning the most appealing way into the subject, how best to organize the material, how to genuinely conclude and not just end. My writing process—prewriting, composition, and revision—is almost all mental. When I finally sit down to write, I know where I'm going and how I'll get there; seldom does discovery happen while I'm composing at the computer. I may agonize over the turn of a sentence or whether I need another piece of evidence to make a point clear, but I seldom do a real revision on paper. My peer readers are mostly an editing group, not suggesting global changes, but sentences that could be clarified or paragraphs that could be divided, for example. I've tried composing on the screen before having the paper worked out in my head, but it just doesn't work for me. That's what I tell my students—find a process that works for you and stick with it.

Trisha Yarbrough, Ph.D., professor of English, East Central University, Ada, Oklahoma

1. Limit the Topic.   The writer's first task was to limit the topic. She knows a great deal about photography and could discuss types of lenses and special filters to use under different lighting conditions. She could also discuss techniques for developing negatives and making prints in the darkroom. All this information, however, is very technical and would require a long essay or even a book-size manual to explain.

2. Plan and Outline.   After limiting the topic, the writer explored her ideas, keeping in mind that her readers probably don't know much about cameras and photographic techniques. She did some freewriting and clustering, followed by more systematic planning. She established his goal, then listed terms to define, the tools needed, and the steps in the process. She included all these ideas in an informal outline:

Goal: readers to perform the task

Terms to define: none

Tools or materials needed:
1. a good camera
2. clothing that blends into the background of the woods

Steps in the process:
1. preparation: loading the camera
2. finding spot where animals are likely to frequent: place where there is water or food
3. waiting quietly with camera ready
4. aiming quickly and taking several pictures in rapid succession

---

Later, she realized her readers might not understand what she meant by a "good" camera. She needed to introduce and define the terms *lens opening* and *shutter speed*. She also realized that the photographer should load the camera *after* finding a good spot in the woods, not before. So she returned to his word processor and changed the outline:

Terms to define:
1. lens opening (for amount of light exposure)
2. shutter speed
Tools or materials needed:
1. a good camera that can be adjusted manually for the lighting conditions and the speed of moving objects
2. clothing that blends into the background of the woods
Steps in the process:

✔ TIPS

For Generating and Organizing Materials
Use the outline mode of a word processing program (or simply generate ideas in a brainstorming list). Then you can easily add or delete items and reorganize by cutting and pasting.

Continued

TIPS

For Choosing Transitions to Show Sequence

You can help readers identify each step in the process you're describing by adding appropriate transitions to the beginnings of sentences:

Consecutive order: first, second, third, after that, next, then, later, as soon as, until, when, once

Simultaneous: at the same time, during, meanwhile, while

Conclusions: finally, last (of all), most important, to finish

---

1. finding a spot where animals are likely to frequent: a place where water is found

2. final preparation: loading the camera and setting the lens opening and shutter speed

---

3. Draft a Topic Sentence. The writer experimented with several versions of a topic sentence in the first draft of the paragraph and in revisions:

Anyone can take good pictures of wildlife in the woods if he or she observes these steps.

You can become a good wildlife photographer if you follow this advice.

Four steps are involved in taking good pictures of wildlife in the woods.

Taking good pictures of wildlife in the woods involves four steps.

None of these versions appear in the final draft.

4. Draft and Revise. Then the writer drafted the paragraph and revised it several times as she worked to make the explanation as clear as possible. In deciding what was clear and what wasn't, she had to put herself (an experienced photographer) in the place of her reader (a first-time nature photographer). Process analysis requires that you pay special attention to the audience. You need to anticipate what readers will want or need to know.

This writer discussed a technical subject, photography. But in a process analysis you can discuss anything you do or have done at home, work, school, or play. If your goal is to have your readers *do* the process, you'll probably address them directly—in the second person or in the imperative. If your goal is to have your readers understand the process, you might use the third person or the second person.

GETTING READY TO WRITE

Here are some warm-up exercises to help you practice organizing paragraphs of process analysis.

EXERCISE 1 | Arranging the Steps in a Process

Each of the following groups of sentences can be organized into a paragraph that develops the topic sentence. Number the sentences in each group in a logical order.

Paragraph A:

Topic Sentence: Look at the mailboxes in any rural area, or even in big cities, and you will see a great many mistakes in one of the simplest and most straightforward rules of grammar—the formation of plurals of proper names.

_____ All you need to do is add *s* to the name or *es* if the name already ends in *s* or an *s* sound, and you never use an apostrophe before or after this final *s* or *es*.

_____ Yet few grammatical processes in English are easier than making proper nouns plural.

_____ Therefore, the proper plurals ought to be *the Robinsons, the Smiths, the Joneses,* and *the Marxes.*

_____ On many mailboxes or signs, you will find such misspellings as *the Robinson's, the Smith's,* or even *the Jone's's.*

Paragraph B:

Topic Sentence: The blood is composed of three different elements—red corpuscles, white corpuscles, and plasma—each of which has a different function.

_____ White corpuscles fight disease in the body by crowding around bacteria and digesting them.

_____ These red, disk-like objects are very small, and there may be several million of them in a single drop of blood.

_____ However, the disks wear out quite quickly—within a few weeks—and must be remade in the bone marrow.

_____ The red corpuscles carry oxygen through the blood.

_____ White corpuscles are much larger and are rather shapeless, and there are far fewer of them than red corpuscles, which usually outnumber them 500 to 1.

_____ The plasma, in which both the red and white corpuscles float, carries food and chemicals throughout the body while collecting carbon dioxide that will be passed through the lungs.

_____ Therefore, when necessary, the body makes more of them to combat attacks from germs.

EXERCISE 2	Generating and Organizing the Steps

Complete each of the following topic sentences, and list at least four steps in the process the topic sentences introduce.

1. *Topic sentence:* There are _____ to register for classes at this college.

   a. _____

   b. _____

   c. _____

   d. _____

2. *Topic sentence:* If you want to enjoy yourself in the evening, _____

    a. _____

    b. _____

    c. _____

    d. _____

3. *Topic sentence:* The best way to travel with children _____

    a. _____

    b. _____

    c. _____

    d. _____

4. *Topic sentence:* There are several ways to get along with _____

    a. _____

    b. _____

    c. _____

    d. _____

5. *Topic sentence:* If you really want to avoid studying, here are _____

    a. _____

    b. _____

    c. _____

    d. _____

EXERCISE 3	Shifting Person

The following paragraph explains a process using the third person (he, she, it, they). Recast it entirely in the second person (you). Some sentences may require more than simply switching pronouns. When you've finished, evaluate the difference that person makes.

The World's Smallest Medicine Men

In South America, a first-aid kit or medicine cabinet might well include a jar of ants—doctor ants, that is. (2) These tiny six-legged medicine men from the forests of South America have sharp, viselike jaws that allow a swarm of ants to strip an entire citrus grove overnight. (3) However, the Brazilian Indians have found a use for the ants to stitch up incisions during surgery. (4) Here is how the Brazilians do it. (5) They first press the edges of the wound together. (6) Then they apply the doctor ants along the seam. (7) After the ants have bitten the wound closed, they snap off the ants' bodies, leaving the jaws in place. (8) Later, after a suitable healing period, the Brazilians remove the heads, leaving the patient with a cleanly stitched incision— and probably a low medical insurance bill.

_____

_____

_____

_____

_____

_____

_____

_____

PARAGRAPH WRITING ASSIGNMENT

List four or five topics that you know how to do or have done: for example, changing a car's spark plugs, reconciling a checkbook with a bank statement, changing a child's diaper, training an animal, performing some task at work, or getting along with your neighbors. You can include topics from Exercise 2 in your list. Then choose the topic you can best explain, and limit the topic so you can explain it in one paragraph.

Consider these issues as you plan:

1. Do you want your readers to perform the process or just to understand it?
2. Will you use the second person or the third person? Your answer to question 1 will help you decide. If you want your readers to *do* the process, you should probably address them in the second person—as *you*—or in imperative sentences, as explained on page 162.
3. What do your readers already know about the process, and what don't they know? What will you need to explain?
4. What tools or materials are involved?
5. What terms need to be defined, explained, or illustrated through examples?
6. How many steps are involved in the process, and what are they?

Draft and revise the paragraph until the explanation is clear and complete. The following Revision Guidelines may aid you in revising or may be used as a guide for peer review in your collaborative group, as described in Chapter 2, page 21.

Edit your work, checking for correct spelling and punctuation, complete sentences, and clarity of ideas. Then make a clean copy of the paper, proofread it carefully, and submit it to your instructor.

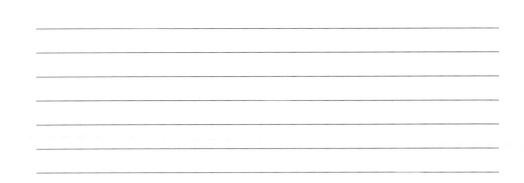

REVISION GUIDELINES   Explaining a Process

1. Does the topic sentence make clear what process is being described? If not, how could it be revised?
2. Is the second person, or third person, or imperative used consistently? If not, decide which suits the subject best, and recast the sentences that are inconsistent.
3. Does the paragraph include all the tools and materials needed? Does it mention them in appropriate places? If not, list the tools and materials, and show where they should be introduced.

4. Do any terms need to be defined for the intended audience? If so, list which ones.

5. Are all the important steps in the process explained? Are the steps explained chronologically? If not, list (and number) the steps.

6. Is the explanation unclear at any point? If so, list the points at which clarification is needed.

7. Are transitions lacking or too vague at any point in the paragraph? If so, where should they be added? Suggest some transitions showing sequence.

WRITING FOR MASTERY

Paragraphs

The following list of topics should provide you with ideas for writing other paragraphs of process analysis. In each paragraph you write, include a topic sentence that makes your purpose clear—that is, whether you want your audience to perform the process or merely understand it. Arrange the details in sequential order, and include transitions that show ideas in a sequence. List tools and materials needed, and define terms your readers won't know.

1. Assume that you are writing for a humor magazine; compose an explanation of how to wake up slowly in the morning.

2. Again for a humor magazine, compose an explanation of how to write an F paper.

3. Compose a letter to a friend who is planning a visit. Advise him or her on how to do any of the following tasks: locate your home or dormitory; be safe from street criminals (or from local drivers); or dress for the climate (or according to the styles in your circle of friends and acquaintances).

4. Assume you are a coach of an athletic team and are writing a short instruction manual for players in your sport. Describe one of the following—or any other activities your players should know how to do: how to steal a base, swim the butterfly stroke, serve a tennis ball, shoot a jump shot, or warm up before exercising.

5. Advise your readers on how to break a bad habit such as smoking, nail biting, or cursing.

A Word About Words

African languages are probably the sources for a number of the most colorful words and phrases in English. They include *banjo, bad mouth, hip, jazz, jitterbug, tote, voodoo, yam, zombie, mumbo jumbo, sweet talk,* and *speak softly and carry a big stick.*

FROM PARAGRAPH TO ESSAY

Whenever the process you want to describe is too complex for a paragraph, compose an essay, using the same method for composing described in this chapter. The first paragraph introduces the thesis (the *point* of the essay), names the tools and materials needed, defines terms if necessary, and previews the steps. Then each step becomes the topic idea of one of the following paragraphs. A concluding paragraph can comment on the process and its significance.

The following two essays examine a multistep process in more detail than the model paragraphs you have read. Each step is developed in a separate paragraph. Together, they constitute a process analysis essay.

A MODEL ESSAY: PROCESS ANALYSIS

Garrison Keillor is a well-known humorist, radio personality, and author of Lake Woebegone Days. *As you read his instructions on performing a simple task, notice how he addresses you, the reader, and connects with you. Notice how he establishes the reason for learning the process. Notice his use of details, of examples, of names. Notice each step in the process. And notice how he encourages you to perform it without fear or hesitation.*

How to Write a Personal Letter
Garrison Keillor

* * * *

1   We shy persons need to write a letter now and then, or else we'll dry up and blow away. It's true. And I speak as one who loves to reach for the phone and talk. The telephone is to shyness what Hawaii is to February, it's a way out of the woods. *And yet:* a letter is better.

2   Such a sweet gift—a piece of handmade writing, in an envelope that is not a bill, sitting in our friend's path when she trudges home from a long day spent among wahoos and savages, a day our words will help repair. They don't need to be immortal, just sincere. She can read them twice and again tomorrow: *You're someone I care about, Corinne, and think of often, and every time I do, you make me smile.*

3   We need to write, otherwise nobody will know who we are. They will have only a vague impression of us as A Nice Person, because, frankly, we don't shine at conversation, we lack the confidence to thrust our faces forward and say, "Hi, I'm Heather Hooten, let me tell you about my week." Mostly we say "Uh-huh" and "Oh really." People smile and look over our shoulder, looking for someone else to talk to.

4   So a shy person sits down and writes a letter. To be known by another person—to meet and talk freely on the page, to be close despite distance. To escape from anonymity and be our own sweet selves and express the music of our souls.

5   We want our dear Aunt Eleanor to know that we have fallen in love, that we quit our job, that we're moving to New York, and we want to say a few things that might not get said in casual conversation: *Thank you for what you've meant to me. I am very happy right now.*

6   The first step in writing letters is to get over the guilt of *not* writing. You don't "owe" anybody a letter. Letters are a gift. The burning shame you feel when you see unanswered mail makes it harder to pick up a pen and makes for a cheerless letter when you finally do. *I feel bad about not writing, but I've been so busy,* etc.

7   Skip this. Few letters are obligatory, and they are *Thanks for the wonderful gift* and *I am terribly sorry to hear about George's death.* Write these promptly if you want to keep your friends. Don't worry about the others, except love letters, of course. When your true love writes *Dear Light of My Life, Joy of My Heart,* some response is called for.

8   Some of the best letters are tossed off in a burst of inspiration, so keep your writing stuff in one place where you can sit down for a few minutes and—*Dear Roy, I am in the middle of an essay but thought I'd drop you a line. Hi to your sweetie too*—dash off a note to a pal. Envelopes, stamps, address book, everything in a drawer so you can write fast when the pen is hot.

9   A blank 8" × 11" sheet can look as big as Montana if the pen's not so hot—try a smaller page and write boldly. Get a pen that makes a sensuous line, get a comfortable typewriter, a friendly word processor—whichever feels easy to the hand.

10   Sit for a few minutes with the blank sheet of paper in front of you, and let your friend come to mind. Remember the last time you saw each other and how your friend looked and what you said and what perhaps was unsaid between you; when your friend becomes real to you, start to write.

11   Write the salutation—*Dear You*—and take a deep breath and plunge in. A simple declarative sentence will do, followed by another and another. As if you were talking to us. Don't think about grammar, don't think about style, just give us your news. Where did you go, who did you see, what did they say, what do you think?

12   If you don't know where to begin, start with the present: *I'm sitting at the kitchen table on a rainy Saturday morning. Everyone is gone and the house is quiet.* Let the letter drift along. The toughest letter to crank out is one that is meant to impress, as we all know from writing job applications; if it's hard work to slip off a letter to a friend, maybe you're trying too hard to be terrific. A letter is only a report to someone who already likes you for reasons other than your brilliance. Take it easy.

13   Don't worry about form. It's not a term paper. When you come to the end of one episode, just start a new paragraph. You can go from a few lines about the sad state of rock 'n' roll to the fight with your mother to your fond memories of Mexico to the kitchen sink and what's in it. The more you write, the easier it gets, and when you have a True True Friend to write to, a soul sibling, then it's like driving a car; you just press on the gas.

14   Don't tear up the page and start over when you write a bad line—try to write your way out of it. Make mistakes and plunge on. Let the letter cook along and let yourself be bold. Outrage, confusion, love—whatever is in your mind, let it find a way to the page. Writing is a means of discovery, always, and when you come to the end and write *Yours ever* or *Hugs and Kisses,* you'll know something you didn't when you wrote *Dear Pal.*

15   Probably your friend will put your letter away, and it'll be read again a few years from now—and it will improve with age.

16   And fifty years from now, your friend's grandkids will dig it out of the attic and read it, a sweet and precious relic of the ancient Eighties that gives them a sudden clear glimpse of the world we old-timers knew. You will have then created an object of art. Your simple lines about where you went, who you saw, what they said, will speak to those children and they will feel in their hearts the humanity of our times.

17   You can't pick up a phone and call the future and tell them about our times. You have to pick up a piece of paper.

Questions for Analysis

1. Keillor is known primarily as a humorist. Is the purpose of his essay to entertain? How would you characterize his attitude toward his subject? Why does he take that attitude?

2. Who is the audience for the essay? Why does he feel that writing letters is important for them? What person—second or third—has he used throughout the essay?

3. Keillor doesn't label most of the steps involved in writing the letter. What are the steps he does explain? Which ones doesn't he explain? Why did he choose the steps he did?

4. Keillor tends to break the "rules" concerning punctuation and sentence fragments. How does his rule-breaking affect your reaction to the essay? Are any of his rule-breaking sentences unclear?

5. Is any of Keillor's advice useful to people attempting other kinds of writing (maybe to you and your classmates writing papers for school)?

A STUDENT MODEL ESSAY: PROCESS ANALYSIS

Margot Reynolds, who wrote the following essay, was a student at Truman College in Chicago before receiving her bachelor's degree from DePaul University in the same city. Her story is painful, but it addresses a serious problem with honesty and insight. Notice how, as she narrates her experiences, she also describes a number of processes she, her siblings, and her mother engaged in.

Let's Talk About It
Margot Reynolds

* * * *

1   I was watching television in my apartment in 1982 when a commercial interrupted the program. I stared in disbelief at the advertisement. The commercial was stating that alcoholism was a disease, that it affected many people in the American population, and there was treatment available—"just call." Societal beliefs about alcohol abuse had changed dramatically from the time when I was growing up in the 60s and 70s.

2   "Shh, be quiet, someone will find out," my brother hissed at me. "Well, what are we going to do?" I whispered. "Take her upstairs and we'll run the Cub Scout meeting," he said. "Yeah, right," I thought. "Like I can lift her." Finally, I propelled my mother from the kitchen, where she had passed out, into the den. I tried to get her on the couch, but she rolled off. So I pushed her close to the couch and left her on the floor. I threw a blanket half over the couch and half over her to cover her up. "That will have to do," I sighed. "Hopefully she won't wake up and start wandering around."

3   That afternoon was my mother's turn to host my two younger brothers' Cub Scout troop. There were mothers at our kitchen door waiting to drop off their kids for the meeting. My older brother Mark told them our mother was in the basement getting everything ready, and the mothers happily left their children with us for the afternoon. My brother took the kids to the basement to play games. I made lemonade, and we all had a snack. My two younger brothers had been panicked and in tears when we got home from school, and they saw the condition of our mother. Now they were happy. The moms came back and picked up their children around dinner time. Mark and I were exhausted, but relieved. We had covered up for our mother (and literally, covered *her up*), and no one found out that it was one of those days when Mom was not feeling well.

4   Every day was different. Arriving home from school, my brothers and I would hold our breaths, brace ourselves, and open the kitchen door. Some days we would be greeted by a version of Carol Brady from the *Brady Bunch*. My mother would be friendly, overly cheerful, and involved in something domestic. When Mom had these good days and tried so hard to be nice to us, I felt uneasy and guilty. Other days, we would be greeted by a woman who didn't know why we were there or what our names were. But on these days, my brothers and I could exhale and even relax. We knew how to handle this situation; this was *normal*. Sometimes, however, we would arrive home to a silent house. We were a little scared, but we usually found her safe and alive in the laundry room, in the closet, or perhaps in the bathroom with a bottle of vodka. The only days we really worried were when we saw the car was gone. If Mom was behind the wheel, that could be dangerous.

5   No matter what the day, the one constant in our lives was that *no one outside of the family could know that our mother had a drinking problem.*

6   When I was growing up, alcoholism wasn't openly discussed. Adults might speak in hushed tones among themselves about someone who had a little problem. Alcoholism was not considered an addiction, and no one believed it had a

genetic component. Someone who drank too much lacked self-control or, in some vague way, moral fiber. People were not called alcoholics. They had "a little problem" or were "heavy drinkers," "drunks," "boozers," or "lushes," depending upon their social class.

7   On trips to New York City as a child, I would see through the car window the men living on the Bowery. They were the Skid Row bums, and in no way was I to associate them with my mother. She was well educated, well turned-out, part of the middle class, and a loving mother of ten children. However, the men on the Bowery always made me queasy. It seemed to me, at that young age, that the only difference between them and my mom was that she had nice clothes to wear and a nice house to live in.

8   While covering up for my mother and hiding her "little problem," we did not consider ourselves "enablers" or "codependents" (in fact, these terms had yet to be invented). We simply followed the unspoken code. We were upholding the family image. As young children, we thought our mother's behavior was normal. As we got older and began visiting our friends' homes, we realized that something was not quite right in our house. We learned the words. Mom had a "drinking problem." But we pretended everything was fine. As adolescents, my brothers and I became experts at covering up. If the manager of the supermarket called to tell us that our mother was asleep in her car in the parking lot, we would call the high school so one of our older siblings could drive over to get her. When my father's boss was coming for dinner and we found Mom passed out in the hallway cradling a frozen pot roast, we simply cooked dinner and sobered her up. On nights we woke up to her screaming in the throes of the "DT's" (she occasionally tried to stop drinking), we would simply remove all hazardous objects from her room and lock the door. The next day, we would act as if nothing happened. We let Mom out of her room, ate breakfast, and went to school.

9   My mother tried Alcoholics Anonymous without much success. She also went to "dryout clinics," which in our family were referred to as "little vacations to get some rest." When Mom came home from her "vacations," she would make a valiant effort not to drink. She would be bright and cheerful, and try to be the perfect mother. In reality, her guilt and shame always drove her to despair—and back to the bottle. My brothers and I could see how bad she felt underneath this cheerful facade, but we didn't possess the emotional capabilities to counsel her. She couldn't talk to her peers, because everyone pretended she had just come back from a vacation. In those days, treatment facilities didn't involve family members and friends as a support group.

10   Now, in 1982, I was watching a commercial on television that said that alcoholism was a disease, not a moral failing and not a little family secret. Many people, from all walks of life, were battling an addiction. They didn't have to feel ashamed, and they could get help, and enlist the support of their family and friends. After I saw the commercial, I wanted to jump up and call my mother. We didn't have to pretend anymore. She didn't have to feel guilty or ashamed. We could talk openly and seek real help.

11   Unfortunately, my mother had died the week before from alcohol abuse.

Questions for Analysis

1. Margot Reynolds never states her main point, or thesis, but lets her readers determine that for themselves. Explain in your own words the point she makes.

2. Find the paragraphs that describe the processes the children went through in hiding their mother's drunkenness or addiction to alcohol. List the steps involved in these processes.

3. What steps did the mother undergo in trying to overcome her addiction? Why didn't she succeed?

4. Look at the paragraph that begins, "Every day was different." How many differences does it discuss? What transitions introduce these differences?

5. Why does Margot use the third person, and not the second person, in this essay?

WRITING FOR MASTERY

Essays

The following list can serve as topics for paragraphs or essays. For each topic provided, state your point in a topic sentence or thesis statement. Then explain the process step by step. Think about what your audience knows or needs to know. Include whatever transitions are necessary to show the sequence of steps. If you wish, you can expand one of the subjects from the section on Writing for Mastery on page 169 into a full essay. State the main idea, list tools, and define terms in the first paragraph. Then explain each step in the process in a separate paragraph.

1. Assume that, like Garrison Keillor, you are writing advice to others about performing a simple, familiar task in a way that would make it very special: how to make a dinner party a wonderful experience for your guests, how to have a truly romantic date, how to bring a story to life for children as you read it out loud, how to plan an exciting birthday party, or any other commonplace task. Write about it with practical, specific, and imaginative suggestions, and illustrate your advice as does Keillor.

2. Have you ever had to take care of someone in a personal crisis—either once, or repeatedly? Write an essay in which, like Margot Reynolds, you introduce the issue and describe the processes involved in taking care of that person.

3. Have you or has someone you know ever recovered from an injury or a sickness—or had an addiction? (Smoking is a good example.) Write an essay in which you describe the process of recovery and the steps involved.

4. Assume you are writing for a humor magazine. Compose a caption to be placed under the cartoon on page 175, in which you explain the process.

5. Like Rube Goldberg, design your own complex and crazy machine for performing a simple task: opening a door, turning on a light, fanning yourself, pouring dry dog food into a a bowl, and so on. Then explain how the contraption works, including your own crude drawing of the apparatus.

6. *Writing from Source Material.* Assume you have to explain the Electoral College to a high school history class. Draft and then revise a paragraph or essay based on the information provided, although you don't have to use all the information.

Electoral College, described in the United States Constitution of 1787

Reasons for Electoral College: (1) fear that uninformed public could not be trusted (2) inability to inform public of issues and candidates for a national office at time Constitution written

The number of electors = combined number of U.S. senators and members of the House of Representatives

Each state has 2 senators (today total of 100)

Total number of representatives today is 435

Self-Watering Palm Tree

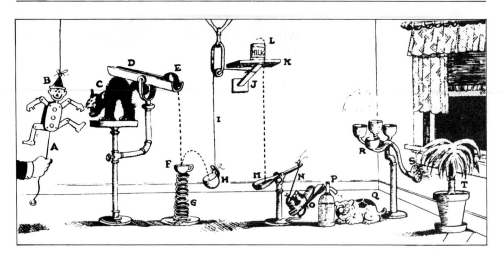

Rube Goldberg, *Self-Watering Palm Tree*. Reprinted with special permission of King Features Syndicate, Inc.

Twenty-third Amendment to Constitution in 1961 adds 3 electors for the District of Columbia

Total Electoral College vote = 538

Winner of presidency must receive an absolute majority (270) of the electoral votes cast. If no majority, the House of Representatives picks winner from the top three, with each state delegation in the House casting only one vote. Only two U.S. elections have been decided this way (1800 and 1824).

If no vice-presidential candidate receives a majority, Senate picks the winner from the top two, each senator voting as an individual. The Senate has not made the choice since 1836.

When voters vote for president, they are actually voting for the electors pledged to a presidential candidate.

Electors are named by state party organizations.

Election day is first Tuesday after the first Monday in November

Electors meet in their state capitals in mid-December to cast their ballots

Results of balloting sent to the presiding officer of U.S. Senate

In January, vice-president supervises the count in Congress

Vice-president announces the results

Electoral College today is a formality

Electors not required by Constitution to vote for the presidential candidate they are pledged to

But they usually do

Sources: *The League of Women Voters of California Education Fund, Choosing the President—1992* (New York: Lyons and Burford, 1992), pp. 91–97; Thomas R. Dye et al., *Politics in America*, 2nd ed. (Upper Saddle River, N.J.: Prentice Hall, 1997), pp. 270–71.

12 Drawing Comparisons and Contrasts

You constantly make choices: what to buy, where to live or work, what to study, which candidate to vote for, and even what to eat for dinner. Virtually every choice requires that you consider the similarities and differences among places, people, things, and activities. This chapter will show you how to write paragraphs and essays that explore such similarities and differences. You'll

- examine two model paragraphs that show similarities and differences
- analyze two ways to structure these paragraphs
- practice generating and arranging material for comparison and contrast
- write a paragraph and/or a full essay that explores similarities and differences

MODEL PARAGRAPHS: COMPARISON AND CONTRAST

Each day, you encounter new subjects in school, new discoveries and beliefs, new fashions or fads, new practices in the business world, and new products and inventions. Each day, you also make decisions about what is better, faster, or more valuable. In other words, you compare and contrast things—usually to evaluate them and decide which is better. A **comparison** *is an examination of similarities. A* **contrast** *is an examination of differences.*

Here is a model paragraph that contrasts and compares the practices of a fast-food restaurant chain with the practices of several competitors. As you read it, note each of the contrasts, as well as the similarities.

White Castle's Unorthodox Success Story

* * * *

In the competitive world of fast-food hamburgers, White Castle is the odd man out. It does everything "wrong" and yet it has been successful since 1921. Here are just a few of the ways in which White Castle differs from the bigger players on the block. While McDonald's, Burger King, and Wendy's earn much of their income from selling franchises to individual owners, all White Castle stores are owned by the parent company. While the Big Three have tried to expand their businesses quickly and widely through franchising, White Castle has been content to maintain operations in the Midwestern states, as well as in Kentucky, New Jersey, and New York. While other fast-food restaurants have expanded their menus, offering gourmet sandwiches, and salad bars, White Castle has stuck with the staples. Yes, it does serve breakfast. It does offer french fries, onion rings, and a couple of other sandwiches. But hamburger sales account for a full 60 percent of its gross profit, a much higher figure than any other major hamburger chain's. While the other fast-food outfits emphasize the large size of their patties, White Castle sticks with its tiny, inexpensive burgers. What customers get is a patty that is two inches square and very thin. White Castle is like its competitor Wendy's in one respect: serving square burgers (and, in White Castle's case, square buns). Unlike Wendy's, however, which chose the square shape for marketing reasons, White Castle packs thirty square patties onto its square grills for quick, efficient cooking. Another major difference between White Castle and its competitors is the way the burgers taste and feel. There is no delicate way of stating it: White Castle burgers reek of onions and have a soggy texture. Far from an insult, these are the reasons White Castle fans love them. Devotees call the little burgers "sliders," undoubtedly because the bun and patty are soggy enough to slide down the throat without chewing. The final and most striking difference between White Castle and its competitors is that each White Castle patty has five little holes. As usual with White Castle, these holes serve a totally practical function. They allow steam and grease from the grill to rise to the upper bun, which sits on top of each patty. The meat therefore cooks evenly without having to be flipped over. In sum, White Castle doesn't think there is anything fancy about the hamburger business. It has taken a soggy, smelly burger that MBA types would probably consider impossible to sell and created a mini-empire.

Questions for Analysis

1. What is the topic sentence that introduces the comparisons? Underline it.
2. What sentence introduces the contrasts and comparisons in the body of the paragraph?
3. What transitional expression is repeated in the introduction to each contrast in the first half of the paragraph? What transitions show contrasts in the second half?
4. Where are the paragraph's main ideas summarized? How do you know?
5. Although many comparisons evaluate the things being compared, this paragraph doesn't say that White Castle is better than its competitors. State in your own words the point of the paragraph.

The next model paragraph describes an imaginary new car, contrasting it to typical cars of today—and evaluating why it is better. As you read it, note the expressions that introduce contrasts.

Why Settle for an Ordinary Car?

* * * *

The car of the future is available today: the revolutionary Omicron. Although in appearance and seating capacity it resembles a conventional car, the Omicron differs dramatically in every other aspect. Unlike the front-mounted gasoline motor in a conventional car, the Omicron's powerful rear-mounted electric motor emits no pollution and runs far more economically. Its cost in electricity translates to an amazing seventy-five miles per gallon of gasoline three times the mileage of the average car. Yet despite this economy, the Omicron is a powerful driving machine, achieving a top speed of 140 miles per hour, compared to 100 mph in most other cars. Other advances in technology make the Omicron virtually maintenance-free. It never requires a tune-up or an oil change. And, perhaps most important of all, the Omicron is the safest car you can drive. The reliability and stability of its magnetic braking system far exceed those of disc-brake systems in conventional cars. The Omicron's patented reinforced plastic alloy frame and panels—four times stronger than the steel found in conventional cars—provide unsurpassed protection against injury in collisions. Don't wait until the next century to ride in the comfort, safety, and economy of the Omicron. See your local Omicron dealer and test-drive the car of the future today.

Questions for Analysis

1. What is the purpose of this paragraph? Who is the intended audience?
2. In what ways does the Omicron resemble typical cars?
3. List all the ways in which the Omicron differs from typical cars. List all the transitions that establish contrasts.
4. The writer of this paragraph attempted to build to a climax. Where does the climax occur?
5. Which sentence summarizes the main ideas?

The Structure of Comparison-Contrast

Comparisons and contrasts need to proceed in a consistent way: whole-to-whole or part-to-part. We'll examine both.

Part-to-part.   The paragraph on the Omicron emphasizes the differences between this new car and a familiar, conventional automobile. Because much of the information about the Omicron is new and complex, readers may not understand or appreciate all of these features if they're presented at the same time. A part-by-part organization sharpens the focus. It alternates between the Omicron and conventional cars while discussing the features one by one—first the similar features and then the different ones. And it builds to a climax at the conclusion, where it urges readers to test drive the Omicron. A diagram of a typical part-to-part organization might look like the first blueprint on page 179.

Whole-to-whole.   This organization first discusses one subject of comparison completely, then the other. A whole-to-whole organization is most appropriate with simple and easily understood material. For example, suppose the paragraph about the cars contrasted two familiar autos: the Slugmobile and Panther EX-LE. It could describe every important feature of the first car (its large size, quiet operation, and ease of handling in city traffic) and then describe these same features of the second car (its smaller size, roaring motor, and handling on the open road)—in the same order, while drawing comparisons and contrasts. Again, the comparisons lead up to a climactic concluding statement that recommends one car—or both of them, but for different types of driving. A diagram of a typical whole-to-whole comparison might look like the second blueprint on page 179.

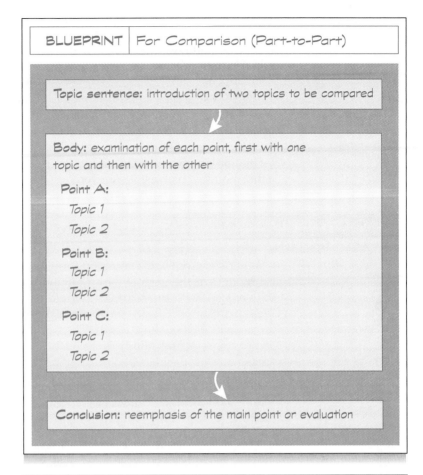

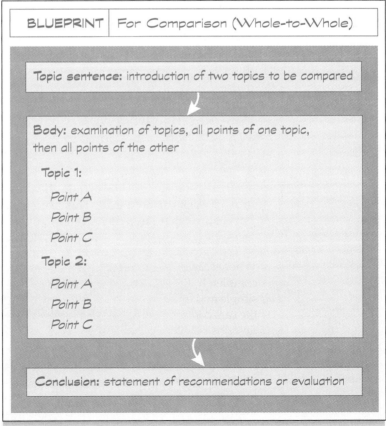

The Process of Composing Comparison-Contrast

Let's examine how the writer of the comparison of the Omicron and conventional car might have composed the paragraph. Here are the steps involved.

1. Plan.   The writer's first task was to consider his subject, purpose, and audience—and the conclusion he wanted to draw from the comparison. He was recommending a revolutionary new car for prospective automobile buyers. He therefore wanted to emphasize each feature, showing its superiority to a similar feature on a conventional automobile. That seemed to suggest a part-by-part organization, but he wasn't sure yet.

A WRITER SPEAKS

Comparison/contrast, a common form of the student essay, was my "rhetorical model" in this sonnet, "In the Suburb of the Spirit." My idea was to be very explicit with the contrast. I would oppose the idea of staleness with the idea of freshness: death and birth, experience and innocence. All are contained within this short poem. The point is that the writer's attention (his composing eye and mind) gives birth to the world. It is the writer's job to "make it new," permanent, and amazing.

Everything has happened. Nothing is quite new.
Summer is so old it wrinkles at the edges.
Nothing is surprising. Nothing should alarm.
It's the same old rain over and over.
The sun is old, and the light is so decrepit
it lies flat on the ground and can't get up again.
Even your anger is old. It's large or small,
but all of your life it's been the same. Then
everything is new. Nothing ever ages. There
was no wind until just now, no glacier until you
thought of it. Fish change every second. Every glance
makes a new landscape, and the sea has a stiff new shine
as it moves around on crutches. Clouds are shaped
like typewriters. Things amaze. Nothing dies.

Paul Hoover, poet, novelist, and editor of *Postmodern American Poetry*

A Word About Words

The meanings of words change over time. For example, the dignified words *lord* and *lady* evolved from their relationship to a loaf of bread. The *lord,* or head of the household, was the loaf-protector (in Old English *blaford*). The lord's wife was the "loaf-kneader" (in Old English *blafdige*), or maker of a loaf of bread.

2. Generate Ideas on a Grid.   In the prewriting stage, the writer listed the features of each car on a grid. This process not only highlighted the comparisons but ensured that the writer wouldn't overlook any of them:

Features	Omicron	Conventional car
1. seating	5 people	5 people
2. appearance	normal	normal
3. motor	rear-mounted electric	front-mounted gasoline
4. mileage	75 mpg	25 mpg
5. top speed	140 mph	100 mph
6. maintenance	no tune-ups or oil changes	tune-ups, oil changes
7. brakes	magnetic	disc
8. body	plastic alloy	sheet metal and plastic

The writer decided to use part-to-part organization, so he read across the grid. But if he'd decided to use whole-to-whole organization, he would simply read down the grid—finding all the information about one car, then the other car.

3. Draft a Topic Sentence and Try Out an Organization.   Now the writer drafted the topic sentence and paragraph—and, in this case, the concluding sentence, since it makes his most important statement. His decision to use part-to-part organization turned out to be a good one. But sometimes writers experiment with one organization, discover it isn't working, and then recast the paragraph in another way. And, in fact, some writers discover that their comparisons are most effective if they use a little bit of both organizations.

4. Draft and Revise.   The writer then revised the paragraph several times. He rearranged his details to lead up to a climax that presented the most important reasons for buying the Omicron. He added transitions that labeled each comparison and created a smoother flow between ideas. Finally, he edited his work and proofread it for errors.

That's how the process worked for this writer. You'll go through a similar process in composing your own comparison-contrast paper.

GETTING READY TO WRITE

The following warm-up exercises will give you practice in choosing an organization for a comparison-contrast paragraph, generating supporting details for topic sentences, and working with both comparisons and contrasts.

EXERCISE 1   *Arranging Details*

Assume you were writing the answers to essay questions based on the points in the following list from outside sources. Decide on a whole-to-whole or part-to-part organization, and write your choice in the space after the topic sentence. Then, on the lines that follow, write the numbers of the supporting points (such as A1, B4) in the order that most effectively develops the topic sentence.

Paragraph for a Psychology Course

psychiatrists

A1. are always M.D.s

A2. may treat patients face to face across desk

A3. may not personally have undergone therapy

A4. may use variety of techniques: medication, behavior modification, electric shock, Freudian analysis, or other therapy

A5. may also be psychoanalysts if they have undergone psychoanalysis

psychoanalysts

B1. have personally undergone psychoanalysis

B2. use classical Freudian analysis or other methods of exploring a patient's past life

B3. most often treat patients who lie on a couch

B4. are not necessarily M.D.s

B5. always have formal training as analysts

Topic sentence: *Although many people think psychiatrists and psychoanalysts are the same, the two are more different than they are alike.*

Organization: _____

_____

_____   _____

_____   _____

_____   _____

_____   _____

_____

EXERCISE 2   Generating Details for Comparisons

Assume that for a sociology class you have been asked to write a paragraph discussing the different responsibilities and behavior of people in various roles. Complete each of the following lists by supplying additional similarities and differences, and then draft a preliminary topic sentence stating the comparison. Finally, indicate whether you'll use a whole-to-whole or part-to-part organization.

Comparison A

a typical single person

1. lives alone or with roommate
2. _____
3. _____
4. _____
5. _____
6. _____

a typical married person

1. lives with spouse
2. _____
3. _____
4. _____
5. _____
6. _____

Topic Sentence: _____

Organization: _____

Comparison B

a tourist

1. visits popular places
2. stays in hotels or motels
3. _____
4. _____
5. _____
6. takes many photographs or videos

an explorer

1. goes to hard-to-reach places
2. _____
3. _____
4. _____
5. _____
6. _____

Topic Sentence: _____

Organization: _____

Comparison C

a parent

1. responsible for feeding, care, etc.
2. _____
3. _____
4. _____
5. _____
6. _____

a dog owner

1. responsible for feeding, care, etc.
2. _____
3. _____
4. _____
5. _____
6. _____

Topic Sentence: _____

Organization: _____

EXERCISE 3	Generating Details for Contrasts

Assume you are composing a magazine advertisement for a brand of detergent, an automobile, cereal, artificial sweetener, or egg substitute, or any other real or imaginary product. List the superiorities of your product over the competitor, and then supply a topic sentence and method of organization as explained in Exercise 2. Also draft a conclusion that emphatically states your sales pitch.

your product

1. _____
2. _____
3. _____
4. _____
5. _____
6. _____

its competitor(s)

1. _____
2. _____
3. _____
4. _____
5. _____
6. _____

Topic Sentence: _____

Organization: _____

Conclusion: _____

PARAGRAPH WRITING ASSIGNMENT

For an audience of your classmates, write a paragraph in which you compare and contrast the ways in which your attitudes or behaviors toward your parents or toward studying have changed since you've been in college. Your purpose will be either to entertain your classmates or stimulate discussion of the topic.

Begin by narrowing your topic and considering what period of your life— early childhood? adolescence? last week?—you will compare to the present time. Explore your ideas by freewriting, clustering, or brainstorming, and then prepare a grid like the one you saw earlier in the chapter. As you plan and then write the paper, keep these guidelines in mind:

1. *Make a point.* Don't just say that your behavior or attitude is different. Argue that the difference is better (or worse), and explain why. You can state the

point at the beginning, or you can state the point in your concluding sentence using climax organization.

2. *Whenever possible, supply examples and explanations to support your comparisons.* Don't say merely that your behavior toward your parents used to be a bit angry, intolerant, or irrational. (Of course, you wouldn't ever have acted that way, would you?) Tell how you acted (if it's not too incriminating).

Then write a draft of the paper, including a topic sentence that states your main point. You may choose to place the topic sentence at the end of the paragraph if you wish to lead up to a climax.

Revise the draft, using the questions in the Revision Guidelines, below, as a guide. Or you may use them to structure a peer review in your collaborative group, as described in Chapter 2, page 21.

After completing the revision, edit the paper, checking for correct spelling and punctuation, complete sentences, and clarity of ideas. Then make a clean copy of the paragraph and proofread it carefully for errors.

REVISION GUIDELINES | Composing Comparison-Contrast

1. Is the topic sentence clear, and does it suggest the reason for the comparison? If not, how should it be revised?

2. Does the paragraph follow a consistent whole-to-whole or part-to-part organization? If not, should the organization be changed?

3. Do the details all support the topic sentence? If not, should the organization be eliminated, revised, or added?

4. Do the details build to a climax? That is, are the comparisons or contrasts arranged from the least to most significant one? If not, would this arrangement improve the paragraph?

5. Are the similarities and differences unclear at any point? If so, how could they be clarified?

6. Are transitions lacking or too vague at any point in the paragraph? If so, what should be added or revised?

7. Is the conclusion strong and clearly derived from the points of comparison and contrast in the body of the paragraph?

WRITING FOR MASTERY

Paragraphs

The following list of topics should provide you with ideas for writing other comparison-contrast paragraphs. In each, begin by drafting a topic sentence and conclusion, and listing points of comparison on a grid. Decide on a whole-to-whole or part-to-part organization, and then write and revise the paragraph.

1. Assume you're a writer who evaluates cars, electronics, or computers for *Consumer Reports, Car and Driver, Audio, Video,* or *PC Magazine.* Compare the main features of two such items, recommending one as the better buy.

2. Assume you're writing for a fashion magazine. Describe a new style in clothes by comparing it with an earlier style.

3. Write a comparison of your choices of friends at two different times of your life. (Don't use real names.) Your purpose may be to amuse or to make a serious point. Your audience will be your classmates.

4. Write a comparison of your choices of entertainment at two different times of your life. Your purpose and audience will be the same as in the previous topic.

5. Write a comparison of careers you are or have been considering. Your purpose will be to inform or persuade your classmates of what career seems best for you—or them.

FROM PARAGRAPH TO ESSAY

Comparisons and contrasts are built by assembling points. If each point must be explained and illustrated in a full paragraph rather than just one sentence, the result will be an essay. The introductory paragraph engages the reader, introduces the thesis, and previews its treatment. In part-to-part organization, each part—compared or contrasted across both subjects—occupies a full paragraph. In whole-to-whole organization, one or more paragraphs focus on one subject; then one or more paragraphs focus on the other subject. The final paragraph in either organization presents the conclusion or makes a recommendation.

The following essays expand their comparisons or contrasts over several paragraphs. Most of these paragraphs examine a single point of comparison, explaining and illustrating it. Together, the paragraphs in each essay develop the larger point—the thesis.

A MODEL ESSAY: COMPARISON-CONTRAST

The following essay by the professional writer Robert Hughes discusses his experience appearing in a "starring role" in a movie. (See his advice in A Writer Speaks *in Chapter 3.) As you read the essay, notice that much of its humor comes from the comparisons, as well as the contrasts between what he claims to be true and the real truth of the experience he describes.*

Matinee Idler
Robert Hughes

* * * *

1   I don't mind admitting that in my gray fedora, I look like Harrison Ford.

2   My wife and my friends are too shy to point this out to me, but give me a square jaw, hair on the top of my head, and a look in the eye like I know what I'm doing and I could be his double. Yes, I know I look exactly like a middle-class, middle-aged, middle-American dad wrestling candy out of the hands of his sons (ages five and seven) at the supermarket checkout counter. But look closer. Don't you see a kind of Indiana Jones charisma? An air of sexy danger?

3   A psychiatrist might say that I am suffering from a common mental delusion, and that if you scratch beneath the surface of any typical harried father you will find a glamorous alter ego trying to claw its way out.

4   I don't deny that this syndrome is a problem for many men. My own father was a victim of it. I remember the day, sometime during the 1960s, that he surprised us all by coming home from work sporting what he called his "Rex Harrison hat." I realized with a twinge of boyish embarrassment that my dad actually thought he looked like the distinguished bachelor Henry Higgins in *My Fair Lady*. Now, my dad was a handsome man. But I knew Rex Harrison. I had seen Rex Harrison on TV. Dad was no Rex Harrison.

5   Fortunately for me, my resemblance to Harrison Ford is a matter of simple fact. Therefore, it seemed only natural that when the opportunity arose last year to be an extra in Ford's movie *The Fugitive,* which was filmed here in Chicago, I would seize it.

6   On the set, I quickly discovered that in the movie world, the status of extras is roughly equivalent to the status of chairs at a church pancake breakfast—necessary, but ranked far below actual people. My scene, in which I play a guy sitting next to another guy among 200 or so spectators in the courtroom where Dr. Richard Kimble is being tried for the murder of his wife, brought out my most profoundly chairlike qualities. My nuanced performance adds a note of stunning invisibility that is rare in film history. An extra is just a star with a smaller part.

7   But that's not really the point. The point is that for a whole day, I worked with Harrison Ford. Like me, Harrison Ford sat. Like me, he had lunch in the cafeteria. Like me, he made wisecracks to break the tedium between takes. Together he and I listened to the state's case against Dr. Richard Kimble. We registered shock, fear, anger, sorrow. We smiled understandingly as an actor flubbed his lines. We looked up in concern when a technician slipped while adjusting a light.

8   It's true that Harrison leveraged a bit more talent into his role than I did. And yes, he was paid more. But the outline of our day was absolutely identical.

9   After twelve hours or so of work, I called home to let my wife know that the director planned to film past midnight.

10   "Past midnight?" In the background I recognized the telltale sounds of barely controlled sibling mayhem.

11   "I'm sorry, honey, but we're talking Hollywood blockbuster here."

12   "Okay. But you owe me." She said this playfully, yet with a hint of menace.

13   As I walked back to the set, I tried to imagine how Harrison Ford would react to the script direction "playfully, yet with a hint of menace." He'd give a sly half-smile followed by a mock-fearful grimace, then move on confidently.

14   When we get *The Fugitive* on video, I'll hit the pause button when we reach the courtroom scene.

15   "See, boys, there I am. Next to the fat guy in the tenth row."

16   "The fat guy near the door, Dad?"

17   "No, the other fat guy, the one behind the woman in the blue dress next to the man with the plaid sport coat. See, that's me! That's your dad in the same movie as Indiana Jones!"

18   Then, to avoid the twinge of boyish embarrassment, I'll cock my fedora over my eyes and hit the rewind button for one more glimpse of cinematic glory.

Questions for Analysis

1. At the beginning of the essay, Robert Hughes compares and contrasts two ideas: his own claim that he looks just like Harrison Ford and his father's claim that he looked like Rex Harrison. What point is Hughes making?

2. Hughes compares his actions to those of Harrison Ford throughout the essay. In what ways are they alike? In what ways are they different?

3. Much of the humor in Hughes's essay arises from the contrasts between his tongue-in-cheek fantasy world and his actual experiences. Identify several of these contrasts. What is Hughes's attitude toward himself?

4. Aside from his comparisons to Harrison Ford, what other comparisons does Hughes make? Why?

5. Hughes is obviously pretending that he plays an important role in the movie. How does he actually feel about the experience? (The answer to this question is complex.)

A STUDENT MODEL ESSAY: COMPARISON-CONTRAST

When Lynne Sparberg was enrolled at Truman College in Chicago, she was not the age of a typical first-year or second-year student. She had witnessed many changes in technology over many years, and her years of experience influenced her point in the following essay. While reading the essay, note its specific details and examples. Consider its organization: Is it whole-to-whole or part-to-part?

Lady in the Telephone
Lynne Sparberg

* * * *

1   The phone on my bedroom dresser was installed today, bringing memories from childhood forty-five years ago. I remember having a family telephone: short, black, thin on top, and stout on the bottom. Its home was the family's end table, located in the living room.

2   Looking at my new telephone, my eyes rest upon the square, numbered buttons on the telephone's white face. All sorts of buttons appear: redial, the mute button, the ringer on/off button, and—of course—the "O" button (for operator).

3   This beautiful piece of machinery is indeed a wonder, except for the lack of one thing I long for—a telephone operator. In all, this phone does not compare to my childhood phone. That phone was unexciting by itself, but very lovable, because of the voice on the other end.

4   Lifting the receiver, I heard the sweet voice of the telephone operator speaking, but that live speaking voice is now a dying breed.

5   I imagined what that person uttering those sounds may have looked like. She was plain-looking, not too young, yet not too old. She was probably somebody's grandmother, wearing a dark-colored dress with cap sleeves, and a white collar. She wore black, cat's eyeglasses and heavy red lipstick. This telephone operator looked quite different from the operators of today. "May I help you?" she asked. What has become of that special person who directed calls?

6   Today's modern technology has murdered my friend's voice. What was once a simple project has been turned into a time-consuming nightmare. My kingdom for a live telephone operator!

7   Today's version of the telephone operator is called Directory Assistance. This is indeed a challenge. Lily Tomlin, where have you gone? Who turned you into a computer, or—worse yet—a computer with a male voice? Who asked for this change?

8   Today the telephone operator resembles something like a voice that is a cross between a *Star Wars* character and a chipmunk. These voices talk through their noses. The nasal voices ask for the city and state, and then for the name of the business or person. This procedure is followed by a moment of silence, not a meditational experience, followed by a Morse Code-like series of clicking noises. Then another inaudible voice comes on, again asking for the city, state, and name.

9   Asleep by this time, the caller needs to have the question repeated. "City, state and name," shrieks the computer. Again, given the same response, the telephone explodes with a series of sounds, perhaps clicking, gum chewing, throat clearing, coughing, sandwich munching, and at least fifty other animal-like noises. After what seems like a lifetime, the caller hears a sentence coming from another planet, followed by the number from yet another computer.

10   The first operator was not broken, so why fix her? Let's bring back the old days. One walks to the telephone, dials "O" for operator, and zap! A real operator

comes to the telephone. "May I help you?" "Yes, I need the XYZ Company's telephone number, located in blah-blah-blah."

11   "One moment, please," says the golden-throated telephone operator. Thirty seconds could pass, and a human operator—clearly, and simply—tells you the telephone number.

12   Pick up your picket signs and join me outside of AT&T's offices. Sit with me until the telephone operator appears. Let us e-mail our senators, telling them to bring back the live lady in the telephone. She is sorely missed.

Questions for Analysis

1. What organization does Lynn Sparberg use—whole-to-whole or part-to-part? What transitions show the contrasts?
2. Ms. Sparberg is older than most students. Is she addressing only an older audience? How do you know?
3. What is her purpose in the essay—to entertain, inform, or persuade?
4. What is her point—her thesis—and where does she state it? Why?

WRITING FOR MASTERY

Essays

This list of topics may help you formulate ideas, essays (or paragraphs) of comparison or contrast. For each topic, first consider your main point. What will the comparison or contrast establish? How will it conclude? Then arrange the information according to a whole-to-whole or part-to-part structure, and insert appropriate transitions when necessary. Be sure the purpose of the essay or paragraph is clearly stated or implied, and be sure to develop each idea fully.

1. Like Lynne Sparberg, consider a change in behavior or technology you've witnessed over the years. Do you approve or disapprove of the change? Contrast the current and past situation. Make your point clear.
2. Compare yourself to someone you admire, famous or otherwise. Your comparison doesn't have to be humorous like Robert Hughes's essay. (In fact, his accomplishment would be very hard to duplicate.)
3. Assume you are a music, television, or movie critic for your campus or local newspaper. Write an informative classification of the newest trends in popular music, television, or movies.
4. Assume you teach child development courses and are preparing your students for dealing with the typical behavior of 2- to 3-year-old children in a day-care center. Describe several types of behavior. Or, for the same audience, write an analysis of the behavior of the parents of the children.
5. Assume you are composing a paper for a music appreciation class. Evaluate a new musical performer, a new group, or a new musical style by comparing it with an older, more familiar one.
6. The 18th-century English artist William Hogarth (1697–1764) does more than simply "draw" the scenes in *Gin Lane* and *Beer Street*. He is making social commentary on the differences between the effects of alcohol on poor people (in *Gin Lane*) and wealthy people (in *Beer Street*) at the time. Write an essay in which you compare the two engravings, arguing for what you think Hogarth was trying to "say" in them.

**William Hogarth, *Gin Lane*, [no date]. Metropolitan Museum of Art.
New York, Harris Brisbane Fund, 1932.**

7. *Writing from Source Material.* Assume you're writing a paragraph comparing a beehive to a factory for either a biology or business management course. Base your comparison on the following information. Use the topic sentence provided, draft a conclusion, and decide on an organization. Then write and revise the paragraph. As usual, paraphrase the information; don't copy it.

a beehive

houses workers who perform different tasks

is responsible for two activities: making honey and producing more bees

has older workers that bring materials—pollen and nectar—to make honey

has younger bees that receive and transfer pollen and nectar into open cells in the honeycomb

has drone bees to impregnate the queen bee

has queen bee that lays eggs in cells while tended to by worker bees

William Hogarth, *Beer Street*, 1751. Engraving. Art Resource, NY.

    has worker bees that make major decisions: when to get rid of drones, when
       to increase the number of queen bees, or when to kill the existing ones

a human factory

houses workers who manufacture products

receives materials that are used in manufacturing

is responsible for one activity: making a product

usually has highly organized division of labor

has workers who perform different tasks

has workers who unload and store materials

has managers and supervisors who make decisions

Topic Sentence: <u>In many ways, the operation of a beehive is like the operation of a</u>
<u>modern factory.</u>

Concluding Sentence: _____

_____

Organization: _____

_____

13 Making Classifications

Look at any college, and you'll find students grouped in categories according to their year of study: first-year students, sophomores, juniors, and seniors. You'll also find them grouped according to their major fields of study: engineering, art, business administration, computer information systems, English, communications, and so on. And you'll find them grouped in yet another way: part-time and full-time students. The more you look, the more groupings you'll find: by age, by place of birth, by ACT and SAT scores, by gender, or by race.

We place things, people, and ideas in categories so we can identify and examine them. This chapter will show you how to write papers that establish such groupings. You'll

- examine a model paragraph that divides its subject matter into categories
- analyze the structure of this type of paragraph
- practice arranging material into your own categories
- write a paragraph and/or a full essay

A MODEL PARAGRAPH: CLASSIFICATION

The process of placing people or things into categories is called **classification**— *or* division, *since it divides people or things into separate groups. The following paragraph is an example. As you read it, notice the categories it establishes and the order in which each is discussed.*

UNIT 3
Chapter 13

Composing with Confidence
©2003

GO ELECTRONIC!

Use the following electronic supplements for additional practice with your writing:

- For chapter-by-chapter summaries and exercises, visit the Composing with Confidence Companion Website at: http://www.ablongman.com/meyers.
- For work with the writing process, visit The Longman Writer's Warehouse at http://longmanwriterswarehouse.com (password needed).
- For additional practice in grammar, use The Writer's ToolKit Plus CD-ROM

Making Sense of Academic Titles

* * * *

Students in colleges or universities are sometimes puzzled about how to address their teachers, for not everyone who gives grades is a professor. Academic titles are, in fact, as rigid in what they represent as ranks in the military. In terms of prestige (and often pay), teachers on American campuses can be classified from highest to lowest as follows. The generals, colonels, and captains are the *full professors, associate professors,* and *assistant professors.* Although the reasons for these rankings are not consistent, most professors have Ph.D.s, and full professors are typically senior faculty members who have taught for many years and published many articles or books. The associate professors are generally less experienced and have published less material. And the assistant professors are usually the least experienced and least published. Nevertheless, you can properly address all three as "professor." Next come the sergeants—the *instructors*—followed by the foot soldiers in the academic hierarchy—the *fellows* and *assistants* (or *teaching assistants, graduate assistants,* or some similar title). Instructors may or may not hold Ph.D.s, and they are usually relative newcomers to the faculty. Fellows and assistants are graduate students in the university who teach while they complete their studies. You should probably address all of them as "Mr.," "Mrs.," "Miss," "Ms.," or, if they prefer, "Dr." (assuming they have Ph.D.s). One final category can be added to this list—*lecturer,* an academic title in some colleges and universities, although its meaning varies. Most often it is the title for a part-time teacher who ranks somewhere around instructor.

Questions for Analysis

1. What is the topic sentence that introduces the classification? Underline it.
2. Who is the likely audience for this paragraph?
3. On what basis are college teachers classified?
4. Although no single sentence states the reason for classifying teachers in colleges and universities, several sentences imply it. What is the reason?
5. What order are the types of teachers presented in? Why is order important?
6. Does the classification include all types of college teachers? Why is the category of *lecturer* introduced separately at the end of the paragraph?
7. What comparison does the writer use to clarify the ranking of teachers?
8. Based on the description of the teachers' educational background and experience, what other criteria could be used for classifying the teachers? How would the categories then change?

TIPS

For Making Valid Classifications

Don't oversimplify. Make careful distinctions, include exceptions, and explain the categories. There are too many negative stereotypes in the world already—false classifications that separate us and reinforce prejudices rather than celebrate our individuality.

The Structure of Classification

A classification makes sense only if it's consistent. So the categories must be based on only one **criterion**, or standard. For example, a natural criterion for describing how people behave could be the age of the people, with such categories as infancy, childhood, adolescence, adulthood, middle age, and old age. But the criterion could just as easily be people's personalities: introvert, extrovert, and so on.

Therefore, follow these guidelines in your paragraph:

1. *Stick with one criterion for classifying.* Group cats according to their breed, or color, or age, or gender. Don't attempt, in a paragraph, to group them according to more than one criterion. Otherwise the groupings will overlap with, for example, the same cat fitting into the categories of domestic cat, short hair, white, mature, and female.

2. *Make the classification complete.* A classification of Americans according to religion should include Protestants, Catholics, Jews, Muslims, and Buddhists, but it should also include *other religions* (or *religions with fewer than 10,000 members*) and *no religion*.

3. *Explain or illustrate all the categories.* Don't just list categories; clarify and explain them. For example, explain that the category *no religion* probably includes those who claim no formal relationship with a church or synagogue or who refuse to discuss their religion. Or explain that the category *Protestant* includes many denominations, such as Baptist, Methodist, Episcopalian, and Lutheran.

4. *Arrange the categories in some consistent order.* Start, for example, with the largest groups and end with the smallest, or start with the most expensive and end with the cheapest.

A diagram of a typical paragraph of classification might look like this:

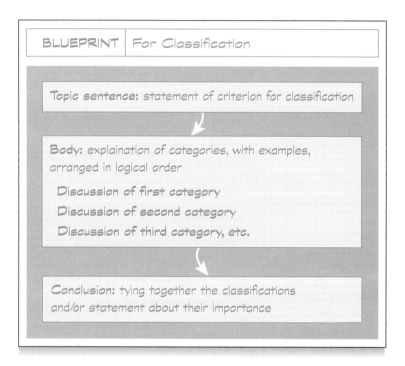

BLUEPRINT | For Classification

Topic sentence: statement of criterion for classification

Body: explaination of categories, with examples, arranged in logical order

Discussion of first category
Discussion of second category
Discussion of third category, etc.

Conclusion: tying together the classifications and/or statement about their importance

The Process of Composing a Classification

In composing a classification paragraph, focus on establishing logically separate categories and presenting them in a logical order. Suppose, for example, that you want to advise students on the best ways to study. Here's how the composing process might work.

1. Generate Ideas and Select a Criterion.   First, using brainstorming techniques, list all the topics or ideas you might classify—in this case, study practices. These might include reading and underlining or highlighting, note taking, keeping a journal, asking questions in class, outlining textbook chapters, reviewing and discussing notes, restating main points, memorizing, and anticipating test questions. Then experiment with different ways to classify them. You could group types of study behavior according to *when* they occur (before class, in class, and after class), or *where* they occur (at home, in class, or in the library), or *how often* they occur (daily, weekly, or only before tests). Select the most promising criterion—in this case, when they occur.

2. Outline on a Grid.   Now arrange the practices according to the time they take place. It's often helpful to plot your ideas on a grid, like this one that classifies study behavior according to time. Your computer may have a function that allows you to create a grid easily:

Time	Activities
Before class	Reading, highlighting, and outlining textbooks
During class	Note taking, questioning, and determining what the instructor means
After class	Reviewing and discussing notes
Prior to examination	Reviewing notes and texts, restating main points in writing or orally

Because in this case the criterion for classification is a time sequence, the categories should be presented from first to last. But with other topics and other criteria, the arrangement could be from largest to smallest, most frequent to least frequent, or safest to most dangerous. The arrangement could also be in climax order, with the important category last.

3. Draft a Topic Sentence.   Your topic sentence should include or imply the criterion used in determining the categories. The sentence will then guide both you in writing the paragraph and your audience in reading it. Here's an example of a topic sentence:

> You should develop four sets of study habits, based on when they occur: before class, during class, after class, and directly before a test.

Notice that the sentence states the behavior it discusses (study habits), the number of categories (four), and the criterion for classifying them (when they occur).

4. Draft and Revise the Body.   Now you can write the first draft of the paragraph. Present each category, and then explain, illustrate, and interpret it. As you revise, sharpen the categories. Be sure your classification system includes all the groupings; if it doesn't, adjust the categories. Arrange your presentation in some consistent order. Follow your usual procedures for turning your rough initial attempt into a finished product. Shift ideas around. Clarify them. Expand on them. Strengthen your language. Add transitions that will clarify relationships among ideas.

✓ **TIPS**

For Choosing Transitions

Here's a short list of transitions to help readers see the relationships among ideas in the classification paragraph:

For introducing categories: first, second, third, next, finally, last

For illustrating categories: as an example (illustration), for example, for instance, to illustrate

For explaining categories: in other words, that means

GETTING READY TO WRITE

The following warm-up exercises will help you hone the skills involved in writing classification. You'll work on generating categories, selecting a criterion for classification, arranging the categories, and formulating the topic sentence.

EXERCISE 1	Selecting Criteria for Classifying

On the line after each of the following classifications, write the criterion used to determine the categories.

Classification A: slow workers, workers of average speed, and fast workers

Criterion: speed of the workers _____

Classification B: bicycles without gear shifts, three-speed bicycles, five-speed bicycles, ten-speed bicycles, and bicycles with more than ten gear ratios

Criterion: _____

Classification C: ostriches and monkeys, cows and cats, and fish and snakes

Criterion: _____

Classification D: doctors and lawyers, nurses and teachers, mechanics and technicians, and factory workers and fast-food workers

Criterion: _____

Classification E: superstition, religion, and science

Criterion: _____

EXERCISE 2	Arranging Categories

Each of the following classifications is based on more than one criterion, so the categories within the classification overlap. Choose a single criterion for classification, state the criterion, and then rearrange and rewrite the information to fit within a clear outline. (You don't have to use all the information.)

Classification A: types of dressers

Original arrangement

the fancy dresser

the plain dresser

the fashionable dresser

the conservative dresser

the practical dresser

the impractical dresser

the sexy dresser

Revised arrangement

Criterion: degree of concern with popular fashions

I. The conservative dresser

    A. plain

    B. practical

II. The fashionable dresser

    A. fancy

    B. impractical

    C. sexy

Classification B: types of students

Original arrangement

lazy students

hard-working students

Revised arrangement

Criterion: _____

_____

_____

intelligent students   _____

unintelligent students   _____

well-organized students   _____

disorganized students   _____

successful students   _____

unsuccessful students   _____

Classification C: types of houses

Original arrangement   *Revised arrangement*

                                        *Criterion:*_____

expensive houses   _____

inexpensive houses   _____

moderately price houses   _____

two-bedroom houses   _____

three-bedroom houses   _____

four-or-more-bedroom houses   _____

new houses   _____

old houses   _____

middle-aged houses   _____

EXERCISE 3	Predicting Paragraph Development

After each of the following topic sentences, list at least three categories you expect the paragraph to develop.

A. Animals can be classified according to their intelligence.

1. highly intelligent animals _____

2. moderately intelligent animals _____

3. somewhat unintelligent animals _____

4. primitively intelligent animals _____

5. animals unable to think _____

B. Most adults choose their leisure-time activities according to how much mental and physical effort they wish to expend.

_____

_____

_____

_____

_____

C. On weekends, this city offers a variety of activities in all price ranges.

_____

_____

_____

_____

_____

EXERCISE 4	Drafting a Topic Sentence

Draft a topic sentence of classification for each of the following subjects and their categories. Be sure to include the criterion for classification.

A. **Subject:** homicide

Categories: murder, manslaughter, government-sponsored killing, and killing of the enemy in war

Statement: There are at least four ways of viewing homicide, based on the punishment or reward given to the person who commits the killing.

B. **Subject:** clocks

Categories: pendulum-operated, battery-powered, powered by household current, and mainspring-operated

Statement: _____

_____

_____

_____

C. **Subject:** elementary schools

Categories: public, private religious, and private nonreligious

Statement: _____

_____

_____

D. **Subject:** thieves

Categories: armed robbers, burglars, con artists, and embezzlers

Statement: _____

_____

_____

PARAGRAPH WRITING ASSIGNMENT

Classify the students in your writing class into groups. Working collaboratively, brainstorm a one-page questionnaire for each student to complete anonymously. It might include any, but not all, of the following: the age of students, their gender, their college majors, their full- or part-time status, the number of hours they work in jobs, their native country or place of birth, their hobbies, their marital status, the number of children they have. You should decide on what to ask. But the questionnaire shouldn't ask too many questions, or the amount of information will be too extensive to discuss in a single paragraph. Then, as a class, tabulate the results with your instructor or one student recording them on the chalkboard.

After the tabulation is complete, decide on your own means for classifying students (kindly) into categories, and arrange them on a grid. Examine the information. Does it encompass everyone in the class? If not, adjust or expand the categories. Include a topic sentence that identifies the categories and the criterion for classification. Introduce them in a consistent order, and explain and illustrate each one.

Before or while drafting your paper, consider ways of giving each category life and fullness through examples, details, or even contrasts. By now, you should know your classmates well enough to determine this information, but if you don't, interview a few classmates who represent different categories to find it.

You may wish to use the following questions in the Revision Guidelines, below, to guide your revision, or use them to structure peer review in your collaborative group, as described in Chapter 2, page 21.

After completing the revision, edit the paragraph, checking for correct spelling and punctuation, complete sentences, and clarity of ideas. Then make a clean copy of the paragraph and proofread it carefully for errors.

REVISION GUIDELINES   Classifications

1. Is there a clear formal statement of classification? If the statement is not clear, how should it be revised?
2. Are the categories determined by a single criterion? If not, what should the criterion be, and how should the categories be changed?
3. Are the categories arranged in a logical order? If not, how should they be arranged?
4. Are all the categories sufficiently explained and illustrated? If not, what should be changed or added?
5. Are transitions lacking or too vague at any point in the paragraph? If so, what should be added or revised?
6. Does the conclusion tie together or state the point of the paragraph? If not, how could it be improved to do so?

WRITING FOR MASTERY

Paragraphs

The following list of topics should provide you with ideas for writing other classification paragraphs. In each, begin by deciding on a criterion for classification, arranging the categories on a grid, and drafting a topic sentence and conclusion. The final draft should present the categories in a consistent order and explain and illustrate each one.

1. Write a classification based on any of the material you generated in Exercises 3 or 4. Decide on your purpose and point.
2. Describe several types of bosses. Arrange your categories in climax order so you introduce the best type of boss last. Your purpose might be to inform.

3. Describe several types of doctors you've encountered. Again, arrange the categories in climax order. Your purpose might be to recommend a certain type of doctor.

4. Classify the behavior of people at a party. Your purpose might be to entertain.

5. Classify types of music, types of singers, or types of concerts. Your purpose might be to inform.

FROM PARAGRAPH TO ESSAY

Moving from a classification paragraph to the essay is relatively easy. Each category becomes the subject of its own paragraph, to be illuminated through explanations, examples, and details. Remember that the introductory paragraph must introduce the thesis while stating the criterion for classification and previewing the categories. The concluding paragraph summarizes the classification.

A MODEL ESSAY: CLASSIFICATION

The following essay of classification by Harold Krents, a lawyer, appeared in The New York Times *in May 1976. As you read it, determine his purpose in writing the classification, the categories he establishes, and the examples he provides.*

Before you begin reading, look up the following words in your dictionary:

1. narcissistic	4. retina	7. mandate
2. enunciate	5. disposition	
3. invariable	6. cum laude	

Darkness at Noon
Harold Krents

* * * *

1   Blind from birth, I have never had the opportunity to see myself and I have been completely dependent on the image I create in the eye of the observer. To date it has not been narcissistic.

2   There are those who assume that since I can't see, I obviously also cannot hear. Very often people will converse with me at the top of their lungs, enunciating each word very carefully. Conversely, people will also often whisper, assuming that since my eyes don't work, my ears don't either.

3   For example, when I go to the airport and ask the ticket agent for assistance to the plane, he or she will invariably pick up the phone, call a ground hostess and whisper, "Hi, Jane. We've got a seventy-six here." I have concluded that the word "blind" is not used for one of two reasons: either they fear that if the dread word is spoken, the ticket agent's retina will immediately detach, or they are reluctant to inform me of my condition of which I may not have been previously aware.

4   On the other hand, others know that of course I can hear, but believe that I can't talk. Often, therefore, when my wife and I go out to dinner, a waiter or waitress will ask Kit if "*he* would like a drink" to which I respond that "indeed he would."

5   This point was graphically driven home to me while we were in England. I had been given a year's leave of absence from my Washington law firm to study for a diploma in law degree at Oxford University. During the year I became ill and was hospitalized. Immediately after admission, I was wheeled down to the X-ray room. Just at the door sat an elderly woman—elderly I would judge from the sound of her voice. "What is his name?" the woman asked the orderly who had been wheeling me.

6   "What's your name?" the orderly repeated to me.

7   "Harold Krents," I replied.

8   "When was he born?"

9   "November 5, 1944," I responded.

10   "November 5, 1944," the orderly intoned.

11   This procedure continued for approximately five minutes at which point even my saint-like disposition deserted me. "Look," I finally blurted out, "this is absolutely ridiculous. Okay, granted I can't see, but it's got to have become pretty clear to both of you that I don't need an interpreter."

12   "He says he doesn't need an interpreter," the orderly reported to the woman.

13   The toughest misconception of all is the view that because I can't see, I can't work. I was turned down by over forty law firms because of my blindness, even though my qualifications included a cum laude degree from Harvard College and a good ranking in my Harvard Law School class.

14   The attempt to find employment, the continuous frustration of being told that it was impossible for a blind person to practice law, the rejection letters, not based on my lack of ability but rather on my disability, will always remain one of the most disillusioning experiences of my life.

15   Fortunately, this view of limitation and exclusion is beginning to change. On April 16 [1976], the Department of Labor issued regulations that mandate equal-employment opportunities for the handicapped. By and large, the business community's response to offering employment to the disabled has been enthusiastic.

16   I therefore look forward to the day, with the expectation that it is certain to come, when employers will view their handicapped workers as a little child did me years ago when my family still lived in Scarsdale.

17   I was playing basketball with my father in our backyard according to procedures we had developed. My father would stand beneath the hoop, shout, and I would shoot over his head at the basket, attached to our garage. Our next-door neighbor, aged five, wandered over into our yard with a playmate. "He's blind," our neighbor whispered to her friend in a voice that could be heard distinctly by Dad and me. Dad shot and missed; I did the same. Dad hit the rim; I missed entirely: Dad shot and missed the garage entirely. "Which one is blind?" whispered back the little friend.

18   I would hope that in the near future when a plant manager is touring the factory with the foreman and comes upon a handicapped and nonhandicapped person working together, his comment after watching them work will be, "Which one is disabled?"

Questions for Analysis

1. Harold Krents establishes three categories in his essay. What are they, and what is his criterion for determining them?

2. How does he illustrate each category?

3. How would you describe Krents's tone in the essay: angry? sarcastic? amused? What evidence supports your response? Is Krents serious when he mentions his "saint-like disposition"?

4. What is Krents's purpose in writing this essay? What is his point, and where does he state or imply it?

A STUDENT MODEL ESSAY: CLASSIFICATION

Michael Brotonel was a student at Truman College in Chicago. As you read his essay, notice the categories of behavior he discusses, his examples of each type, and his attempt to explain why these behaviors occur.

A Wake
Michael Brotonel

* * * *

1   Who attends a wake? The recent passing of my girlfriend's stepfather provoked this question. I decided there are three different types of mourners: immediate family, acquaintance of deceased, and friend of an immediate family member. Are there differences in the way these people mourn? How does the death affect their lives? While one might be thinking about how empty his or her life will be without the deceased, another may be wondering whether it'll be beef or chicken at the reception after the funeral. These contrasts of emotions (or lack of) piqued my curiosity.

2   My definition of immediate family is different from most people's. I feel that a person's family has nothing to do with blood or a last name. A person in my family is someone who spends time (in person or over the phone) with me because he or she enjoys my company. Real friends are family. These people feel the purest form of loss. It's as if a physical piece of them is gone. They're ones at the wake who try to smile and say, "Thank you for coming." But while they try to be almost hostlike, they seem very distant, never quite in focus with the present situation. Maybe they're thinking about moments in the past with the deceased. Maybe they're wishing they had a chance to say something to the deceased and are now regretting their procrastination. For these people, the loss of the person never heals. Although memories of special moments may help minimize their immediate pain (crying, headaches, nausea), the physical absence of the person who has passed will have an emotional effect on the rest of their lives.

3   Bud, my girlfriend's stepfather, was a carpenter who worked with many different people over the years. His wake was filled with men who hadn't seen him since the last job they did together. Some of these men talked about past jobs they did with Bud. Others were trying to play catchup with family members. At other wakes I've attended, I've heard people say "God, I didn't know 'so-and-so' was that sick," or "He looked so well the last time I saw him." Others ask questions about the general past of the deceased. For this group, the acquaintance of the deceased, the loss isn't as emotionally deep. Rather, it's more of a surface wound. The death of the person may leave a scar in the future of these mourners, but the wound will heal with time.

4   I've been to a couple of wakes where I had no relationship with the deceased but knew a close member of the family. In those few scenarios, my mind would jump from one observation to another. At one wake, I was looking at the floor of the casket viewing room and noticed how worn out the carpet looked. The next second, I was thinking about how many times this particular room was used a week. "Is this place that busy?" I remember asking myself. Then questions about my own life started drifting into my head. I began thinking about my goals and whether or not I was doing anything to achieve them. The more questions I asked myself, the more I realized that the questions were about myself. Basically, I was focusing more on my own life and what I needed to do to make it complete instead of reflecting on the lost life of the stranger in the coffin. This may sound like a selfish thing to do, but it's hard to mourn for a person you didn't really know. I feel many people who attend wakes and funerals of people they didn't really know turn inward and try to find answers to questions in their own lives. The best thing to do is to keep your introspective questions and affirmation to yourself and be a shoulder for your friend to lean on.

5   Who attends a wake? The answer stretches to many corners of the life and family of the person who has passed away. The gathering, to some, is a time to reflect on a person who was and will always be loved, but is now gone. To others, it's a time to think about their own lives and where they're going.

Questions for Analysis

1. What sentence in the first paragraph states the classification? The sentence implies but does not state the criterion for establishing the categories. What is it?

2. In the second paragraph, what is Michael Brotonel's definition of "immediate family"? Why does he include the definition?

3. In the same paragraph, what reasons does Michael suggest to explain the behavior of the immediate family?

4. In the third paragraph, identify the examples he provides of how the acquaintances of the deceased behave. According to Michael, why do they behave this way?

5. Who is his example for the last category in the fourth paragraph? What explains that person's behavior?

6. Compare the opening and concluding paragraphs. How does he reinforce the main idea of the essay without repeating the language that introduced that idea?

WRITING FOR MASTERY

Essays

The following topics can serve as subjects for essays (or paragraphs). For the topic you choose, follow the procedures you've practiced in this chapter. Introduce the topic, state the criterion for classification, and preview the categories in the opening paragraph. Arrange the categories in a consistent order (perhaps leading to a climax) and present each category in a separate paragraph. Develop this paragraph with explanations, examples, and details. Conclude the essay with a summary, or a climactic statement endorsing the category you've shown to be best.

1. Does the background, appearance, or any other special circumstance make you or someone you know unusual in any way? Like Harold Krents, establish three categories that describe the way people have treated or still treat you or the person you know because of this unusual trait. Illustrate each category with examples. Your audience will be readers of a popular men's or women's magazine.

2. Like Michael Brotonel, classify people at an event—a school football game, a study table in the library, a rock concert, or other place or happening of your choice. Give examples of each type, or develop the characteristics of each type through descriptive details.

3. Write a guide for visitors to a local zoo. Place the animals into categories, and explain where at the zoo each grouping can be found. If you wish, draw a map of the zoo to accompany your essay.

4. Assume you are a music, television, or movie critic for your campus or local newspaper. Write an informative classification of the newest trends in popular music, television, or movies.

5. Assume you teach child development courses and are preparing your students for dealing with the typical behavior of two- to three-year-old children in a day-care center. Describe several types of behavior. Or, for the same audience, write an analysis of the behavior of the parents of the children.

6. *Writing from Source Material.* Assume you are describing national parks in the United States for a social science class. The following information has already

been arranged in four categories for you. Use the first set to write the introduction. Then, based on the other information provided, construct a unified essay. You don't have to use all of the information. Include a formal statement of classification, transitions between categories of the classification, and explanations of the classifications.

General information

1. an abundance of natural parks for citizens to enjoy in United States
2. more than 330 sites in National Park system
3. sites protected and preserved for benefit and enjoyment of public

Areas preserved for their beauty or other natural features

1. balance of nature cannot be disturbed
2. fishing permitted, but not hunting, mining, or logging
3. examples: Yellowstone, Grand Canyon, Mammoth Cave, Grand Teton, Everglades, Yosemite, Hot Springs, Badlands, Glacier Bay, Hawaii Volcanoes, Death Valley
4. scientific research encouraged
5. visitors may not harm the areas

Areas preserved for historical reasons

1. include forts, monuments, historic buildings and bridges
2. the original appearance preserved or restored
3. examples: Lincoln's birthplace, Fort Bowie, Fort Laramie, Vanderbilt Mansion, Washington Monument, Gettysburg Battlefield, Vietnam Veterans Memorial, Arlington National Cemetery, the White House
4. lectures and tours for visitors
5. most free to public

Areas preserved for recreation

1. include parks, beaches, rivers, trails, mountain areas
2. swimming, hiking, horseback riding, sailing, fishing, and snorkeling allowed
3. examples: Lake Mead, Blue Ridge Parkway, Wolf Trap Farm Park for the Performing Arts, Indiana Dunes, Rio Grande Wild and Scenic River, and Cape Cod
4. visitors may not remove or destroy plants
5. visitors may not touch or feed wild animals

SOURCE: *The World Book Encyclopedia.*

14 Composing Definitions

The most important goal of every writer is to be clear. And clarity requires explaining terms readers don't know, or terms being used in a special way. This chapter will show you how to define terms in the way you want them to be understood. You'll

- examine two model paragraphs of definition
- analyze their structures and see how they were written
- practice different ways of explaining the meanings of terms
- write a paragraph and/or a full essay in which you explain a term

MODEL PARAGRAPHS: DEFINITION

*As you predict your audience's response to your writing, you must be alert to the times they might ask, "What do you mean?" Suppose, for example, that in a letter to your local school board suggesting changes in the curriculum, you use the term "good students." The board members might wonder whether you mean quiet students or inquiring students, competitive students or collaborating students, students who can recite what they learn or students who can apply it. You need a **definition**—an explanation of how you're using the term. That explanation can be short, but it can also be long—an **extended definition** requiring an entire paragraph. In fact, an extended definition may be the subject of an informative essay that describes, explains, and illustrates the term it defines.*

Here's a model paragraph of an extended definition. As you read it, note that it defines and contrasts two terms:

What Are Assault and Battery?

* * * *

The words *assault* and *battery* are linked in many people's minds, but they do not mean the same thing at all. *Assault,* in legal terms, is an attempt or threat to

GO ELECTRONIC!

Use the following electronic supplements for additional practice with your writing:

- For chapter-by-chapter summaries and exercises, visit the Composing with Confidence Companion Website at: http://www.ablongman.com/meyers.
- For work with the writing process, visit The Longman Writer's Warehouse at http://longmanwriterswarehouse.com (password needed).
- For additional practice in grammar, use The Writer's ToolKit Plus CD-ROM

use force or violence and doesn't have to involve actual physical contact. *Battery* is the actual use of force. The distinction is important. Without it, a person who fails in a holdup and doesn't harm his victim might not be charged with a crime. Another example comes from everyday life. Shaking your fist at your neighbor in a threatening manner is assault—if he or she wants to press charges. It is not battery unless you follow it up by punching your neighbor in the nose, at which point it becomes assault and battery.

Questions for Analysis

1. What is the topic sentence of the paragraph? Underline it.
2. What sentences define each term? Circle them. Look at their structure, the way the words are arranged. What pattern do they have in common?
3. The paragraph contains several examples. Bracket them. Now reread the paragraph, ignoring the examples. Are the definitions still as clear?
4. The paragraph also contrasts assault and battery. Would the definition of either term be as clear without the contrast?
5. What words, phrases, or sentences serve as transitions in the paragraph?

Here's a second paragraph of extended definition, intended for quite a different audience and using quite a different approach. Notice that it tells a story, provides one definition, and contrasts that definition with another.

Is Chauvinism Bad?

* * * *

The expression "male chauvinism" is now a part of everyday American vocabulary. The man who inspired the word *chauvinism,* however, had nothing against women. Nicholas Chauvin was a soldier in Napoleon's French army at the beginning of the nineteenth century. Poor Chauvin was wounded badly no fewer than seventeen times. He was eventually too scarred to continue fighting and had to retire. This poor man received nothing more for his efforts than a medal, a ceremonial sword, and a pension of 200 francs (about $40). Other men might have become bitter, but not Chauvin. Instead, he became obsessed with Napoleon, ranting and raving constantly about the greatness of France. Even after Napoleon's downfall, Chauvin remained his supporter. Chauvin's hero worship grew so intense that he became the laughingstock of his village. Two French playwrights, Jean and Charles Cogniard, heard of the patriotic madman and used him as a character in a comedy. After several other playwrights followed their example, Chauvin's name came to represent extreme devotion to a name or cause. Today, of course, the women's movement uses the term *chauvinism* to describe the excessive defense of men's "privileges." What would the battle-bruised, faithful soldier have thought if he heard the expression "male chauvinist pig"?

Questions for Analysis

1. The paragraph tells the story of how Nicholas Chauvin became the source of the term "chauvinism." What purpose does the story serve in the paragraph?
2. Chauvin was extremely loyal to his leader and country. Why did he become a "laughingstock"?
3. There are two formal definitions of chauvinism in the paragraph. Underline them. How are they alike in structure and meaning? How do the meanings of chauvinism differ?

4. Why don't the formal definitions appear at the beginning of the paragraph?

5. Chauvin himself and the term chauvinism have represented several ideas since the beginning of the nineteenth century. What do these differences suggest about the relationship between words, history, and society?

The Structure of Definition

Some terms can be defined in a few words or even a single word. But, as you've seen, many terms require full explanations or examples. Although specific methods of developing a paragraph of definition vary, most paragraphs include two parts: (1) a single sentence that defines the term, and (2) a body section that expands on the definition.

Many definition paragraphs begin with the statement of definition, but others begin with the discussion and lead up to, in climax order, the statement of definition at the end. Let's examine both parts of a definition paragraph first.

The Statement of Definition. The statement of definition can be expressed either by a **synonym**—a word with virtually the same meaning as another word—or in a more formal way. Here are examples of definitions by synonym:

> A CRT is computer terminology for a *monitor* or *television screen.*
> The *aardvark*—or *anteater*—is found in southern Africa.
> *To eschew* means *to avoid.*

The synonym and the word it defines must be the same part of speech (noun and noun, infinitive and infinitive, adjective and adjective) so that one term can substitute for another.

When the meaning of a term is too complex for a single synonym, it then requires a formal statement of definition, the method most often used in dictionaries. The statement begins by placing the term into a larger category, or class:

Word	Category or class
A psychiatrist	is a medical doctor. . . .
Manslaughter	is an unlawful killing. . . .

Then the statement distinguishes the term from others in the same category:

Word	Category or class	Distinguishing characteristics
A psychiatrist	is a medical doctor	who specializes in the study, diagnosis, treatment, and prevention of mental illnesses.
Manslaughter	is an unlawful killing	without the clear intent to do harm to the victim.

You can quote the definition from a dictionary—if that definition fits your meaning and you cite your source. But many writers define a term because they want to use it in a way that dictionaries don't specify. You'll see an example shortly.

If you do write your own definition, keep these guidelines in mind:

1. *Don't make the category too broad.* It's not enough to say that a *psychiatrist* is a "person," or even a "doctor." A psychiatrist is a *medical doctor;* there are many Ph.D.s who are psychologists, but they aren't psychiatrists.

2. *Don't make the distinguishing information too vague.* It is not enough to say that a psychiatrist *treats* mental illnesses; he or she *studies, diagnoses, treats,* and *prevents* them as well.

3. *Don't make the definition circular.* Don't repeat the term in a slightly different form as part of the definition. It's not enough to say that a *psychiatrist* practices *psychiatry;* explain what that practice involves.

Development of a Definition.   The rest of the paragraph provides examples, contrasts closely related ideas, or gives the historical origins and development of the term. Each method requires a particular structure that previous chapters in this unit have discussed.

1. *Examples.* Examples make a definition more concrete and lively, especially when you want to show what a term means to you personally or means within the context of an essay. Chapters 9 and 10, on description and narration, show how to present these examples.

2. *Contrast.* One way to sharpen a definition is to say not only what it is but what it is not. Chapter 12 shows how to organize a contrast. Let's look at an example here, though. In an argument to college administrators that residents of a nearby nursing home be allowed to take free adult education courses, the writer defines maturity in a way that contradicts the dictionary definition:

> *Maturity* is not, contrary to what most dictionaries say, "a state of development in which all growth has been completed." To my mind, maturity is exactly the opposite: a state of mental development in which people understand the need for much more growth. Mature people realize that they will stop learning only when they die.

Then the writer establishes a series of part-to-part contrasts:

> Mature people aren't know-it-alls; they admit their ignorance. Mature people don't close their minds; they change their minds often. Mature people don't live only for today; they plan for tomorrow as well. Thus, an elderly person can be mature in the best sense of the word: still inquisitive about, involved in, and interested in learning.

3. *Historical process.* Sometimes you can best explain a term's meaning by tracing its origin and development over time—for example, the paragraph on chauvinism. That requires a narrative structure, discussed in Chapter 10. Or it may require a process analysis structure, discussed in Chapter 11.

Paragraph Order.   The paragraph can begin with the statement of definition or end with it, depending on your audience, purpose, and topic. For example, is the definition simple and straightforward, something easily understood by your readers? Then you can state the definition first and develop it in the remainder of the paragraph. Is the definition complex or controversial, something your readers won't easily understand or accept without some explanation, historical background, or examples? Then you should lead up to the definition in climax order. Or you might define a term in a simple way at the beginning of the paragraph and redefine the term with all its nuances and complexities at the end.

The diagram of a definition paragraph—accounting for all these possibilities—might look like this:

A Word About Words

The word "panties" can trace its roots to the name of a saint. In Venice, a Christian doctor named Pantaleone who treated the poor for free was condemned to death by the Romans in 305 A.D. Through some miracle, he survived six execution attempts before he was finally beheaded. This courageous man (*Pantaleone* means "all lion") became patron saint of doctors, and many Venetian parents named their boys after him for centuries. As a result, a comic character in a 15th-century play took the name. This skinny old man Pantaloon wore trousers that billowed out above the knees. Trousers thus became known as *pantaloons*—or *pants,* for short. From there came its recent use as *panties,* or women's underwear. Oddly enough, in Britain, *pants* refers to men's underwear—and is not a synonym for trousers (or saints).

```
┌─────────────────────────────────────────────────────────────┐
│  BLUEPRINT │ For Definition                                  │
├─────────────────────────────────────────────────────────────┤
│                                                               │
│  ┌─────────────────────────────────────────────────────────┐ │
│  │ Topic sentence: introduction of term and statement of   │ │
│  │ definition                                              │ │
│  └─────────────────────────────────────────────────────────┘ │
│                            ↓                                  │
│  ┌─────────────────────────────────────────────────────────┐ │
│  │ Body: examination of traits, with examples              │ │
│  │    1. Examples and explanations                         │ │
│  │                    or                                   │ │
│  │    2. Contrast (whole-to-whole or part-to-part)         │ │
│  │                    or                                   │ │
│  │    3. Historical process                                │ │
│  └─────────────────────────────────────────────────────────┘ │
│                            ↓                                  │
│  ┌─────────────────────────────────────────────────────────┐ │
│  │ Conclusion: restatement or definition                   │ │
│  │ (or, in climax organization, first statement of         │ │
│  │ definition)                                             │ │
│  └─────────────────────────────────────────────────────────┘ │
│                                                               │
└─────────────────────────────────────────────────────────────┘
```

The Process of Composing a Definition

Finding the right words for defining a complex term or idea is difficult. That will take time. Don't expect to draft and revise the definition in one sitting; finding the right words may be the last thing you do.

A WRITER SPEAKS

Rather than giving you advice, Michael Raleigh decided to exemplify—and have fun with—a definition. Notice that he starts with a rhetorical question, elaborates through contrast, builds through three paragraphs of details, and concludes with a convincing statement of definition.

Why I Hate My Garden

What is a garden? To most people, a garden is a harmless and even a pleasant place. I do not share this view. I hate my garden. My garden is a place where man jousts with nature and comes in a distant second.

First, my garden is hot, a little square desert, often twenty degrees warmer than the rest of the city. I sweat in my garden; I lose weight. Once I fainted among the green beans and had to be rescued by a neighbor's dog, who now believes himself to be a hero. I also get sunburned in my garden.

As if the sunburn and the humiliation were not enough, my garden provides me with backbreaking labor. I must dig in my garden. For a hundred years my ancestors dug ditches, and I'm still digging them. Also, I have to pound stakes into the ground, tie knots, carry large stones, and get mud all over my clothes.

Finally, my garden is a place of terror. It is overrun by insects, by spiders, probably by bats, even though I have never seen any. Some of the insects in my garden haven't even been named yet, and the spiders are as big as my tomatoes. They know my name, these spiders, they know when I'm coming to work in the garden, and they know I'm afraid of them.

Other people's gardens might be havens from the world. Mine is a place of peril.

Michael Raleigh, author of *In the Castle of the Flynns* and the Paul Whelan mystery novels

1. Explore Your Meaning.   The first step in composing an extended definition is exploring your own ideas about the term. If you can't think of a synonym or a good formal definition, look in a dictionary—or in several. You might find a definition that closely expresses your views. The dictionary or encyclopedia might also explain the historical origins of the term. If you disagree with the definition, however, then elaborate on your disagreement. Heighten the contrast, as, for example, Michael Raleigh does in A Writer Speaks, above. You can also ask others what they think the term means. Their responses may help you anticipate your readers' responses and therefore refine your definition while planning the organization of your paragraph. Capture all these ideas through brainstorming, clustering, or freewriting.

2. Draft the Topic Sentence.   The topic sentence often includes the definition of a term, but not always. The most important function of the topic sentence is to make clear to readers why (or at least by what method) you're defining the term. Here are a few examples:

> Computer-assisted instruction is any kind of teaching that occurs with the help of a computer, but it must always be a supplement to normal instruction by teachers or tutors, as these examples will demonstrate.
>
> In my experience, the traits of an effective teacher go far beyond what can be measured on teacher evaluation forms.
>
> My family and old friends call me Rolly instead of Rawley, and there is an interesting story about how I got the nickname.

3. Outline the Supporting Material.   Pick up examples, contrasts, or stories of origin you captured in brainstorming, clustering, or freewriting. Classify them into categories, and produce a rough outline. Here's an outline for the paragraph on *chauvinism*:

> I. Nicholas Chauvin as war hero
>   French soldier in Napoleon's army
>   wounded 17 times
>   too scarred to continue fighting

Continued

> II. His retirement
>
> total rewards: a medal, a sword, and small pension
>
> III. His devotion to Napoleon
>
> emotional and unstoppable
>
> eventual subject of ridicule
>
> IV. Chauvin as character in plays
>
> first by Jean and Charles Cogniard then others
>
> V. Thus definition: Chauvinism = extreme devotion to a name or cause
>
> change of meaning because of women's movement = men who
>
> believe in and defend their superiority to women

TIPS

For Choosing Transitions for Definition

For examples: as an example (illustration), for example (for another example), for instance, in particular, such as

For contrasts: although, but, even though, however, nevertheless, on the other hand, on the contrary, yet

For historical process: as a result, consequently, so, soon, later, afterward (or any other time expression)

Notice how the writer has arranged the details on historical process in chronological order, then concluded with a statement of definition.

4. Draft and Revise.   Decide whether the statement of definition will have the greatest impact at the beginning of the paragraph or at the end in a climax organization. Then draft the body, citing examples, making contrasts, or tracing the history of the word. In revising, supply transitions that will help your readers see the flow of ideas within the paragraph. And, as you revise, be open to the possibility of refining the wording of your definition, and perhaps moving the statement of definition from the beginning to the end—or the end to the beginning—of the paragraph.

GETTING READY TO WRITE

Before you begin writing your definition paragraph, the following warm-up exercises should help you draft statements of definition, choose a method of development, and arrange the information in the paragraph.

EXERCISE 1	Defining by Synonym

Draft sentences that define each of the following words by synonyms. Use your dictionary if necessary, but don't copy.

1. bison _____

2. elated _____

3. to masticate _____

4. infinite _____

5. prevaricator _____

EXERCISE 2	Composing Formal Definitions

Define each of the following terms by placing it in a category and specifying its distinguishing characteristics. You may use a dictionary, but restate the definition in your own words.

Term	Category	Distinguishing Characteristics
1. An *impresario*	*is a sponsor or a producer of entertainment*	*most often, of an opera company*
2. A *mantra*		
3. A *satellite*		
4. A *taboo*		

Also define two slang words you use with your friends, or two specialized terms you use at work or in a class on a technical subject, such as biology, accounting, or computer science.

| 5. _____ | | |
| 6. _____ | | |

EXERCISE 3	Predicting Paragraph Development

After each of the following topic sentences, write the method of development you expect to find in the paragraph—example, contrast, historical process, or a combination of these—and list two or three examples of each.

1. The meaning of the word *villain* has changed considerably over the last thousand years.

Method of development: __*historical process*__

Details: __*its first meaning, any later meaning, its current meaning*__

2. Although the dolphin lives in the sea, it is unlike most other marine-dwelling creatures.

Method of development: _____

Details: _____

3. Since the process of conceiving, carrying, and giving birth to a child has taken new forms in recent years, biological motherhood is not easily defined.

Method of development: _____

Details: _____

4. For me, true heroism goes way beyond merely risking one's life.

Method of development: _____

Details: _____

EXERCISE 4	Organizing a Definition Paragraph

Number each of the following sentences so they make a logical and coherent paragraph of definition. Put a check mark next to the sentence that formally defines the term.

_____ Few legal concepts are more widely misunderstood than circumstantial evidence, which many people believe means suspicion without proof.

_____ Since in our legal tradition a person accused of a crime is considered innocent until proved guilty, he or she might confess or be convicted on the basis of testimony—which is often unreliable—or circumstances.

_____ Mistakes in convictions, however, are much more likely to result from false testimony, since people tend to lie or misinterpret what they have seen.

_____ Without it, no legal system can possibly work.

_____ An example of a murderer who must be convicted on the basis of circumstantial evidence is the one caught while bending over the dying victim.

_____ No one has actually seen him commit the crime.

_____ As a matter of fact, all evidence except that given by witnesses or victims is circumstantial—that is, based on the conditions, weapons, or facts relating to the crime.

PARAGRAPH WRITING ASSIGNMENTS

Choose one or more of the following assignments for your definition paragraph.

Defining by Examples

As part of a proposal to a community or neighborhood sports league, ask the league officials to establish (or modify) a children's summer athletics program that stresses the best qualities of sportsmanship. Define what *sportsmanship* means in this context. State a formal definition, using your dictionary if you wish. Then illustrate the definition, either with several examples or by telling the story of one person who meets the criteria you establish.

Defining by Contrast

As a member of a committee chosen to hire a new elementary school principal, establish what you mean by the term *academic leadership*. Define the term, and contrast the traits of a leader to those of someone who is not. (For example, should a leader simply dictate policies, or should the leader consult the people whom the policies most affect? Is the first practice justified at times and, if so, when?)

Defining by Historical Process

Every family or religious or ethnic group uses nicknames or other words and phrases that have special meanings for members of the family or group. The terms may be formal or playful, but their meanings are generally understood only within the family or group. Explain to an interested friend how such a term evolved in your family.

Revising Definitions

After drafting your paragraph, revise it, using the following questions from the Revision Guidelines, below, as a guide. Or use these questions to structure peer review in your collaborative group, as described in Chapter 2, page 21.

After completing the revision, edit the paragraph, checking for correct spelling and punctuation, complete sentences, and clarity of ideas. Then make a clean copy of the paragraph and proofread it carefully for errors.

REVISION GUIDELINES | Composing Definitions

1. Is there a clear definition by formal statement? If the definition isn't clear, how should it be expanded or revised?
2. Is the definition developed sufficiently by examples, contrast, or historical process? If not, what should be added or changed?
3. Is all the material in the paragraph relevant to the definition? If not, what should be eliminated, revised, or added?
4. Is the paragraph unclear at any point? If so, how should it be revised?
5. Are transitions lacking or too vague at any point in the paragraph? If so, suggest transitions that will work.

WRITING FOR MASTERY

Paragraphs

The following list of topics should provide you with ideas for writing other definition paragraphs. For each, formulate a definition, decide where to position it, and develop the definition according to the method specified.

1. Define *natural resources* through examples.
2. Define *community service* through examples—and perhaps through contrast. Is a paid employee doing community service?
3. Define *family values* through contrast. What criteria show a real commitment to a family?
4. Define *self-interest* through contrast.
5. Define *utopia* through historical process. (This will require some research).
6. *Writing from Source Material.* Many Americans use the terms *Britain* and *England* interchangeably. This is incorrect and sometimes offends the British themselves. Write a paragraph in which you define Great Britain (or Britain) using the information supplied. Begin by drafting a statement of definition. Develop the definition through examples, contrast, and/or historical process.

England

1. a country
2. one of three (England, Scotland, and Wales) on same island

Great Britain (or Britain)

1. an island with three countries on it
2. the largest of the British Isles (Britain, Ireland, the Isle of Man, and the Channel Islands)
3. member of the United Kingdom, which includes all countries in the British Isles, with the exception of part of Ireland
4. Wales, located on western part of island; politically united with England in 1536
5. Scotland, located on northern part of island; politically united with England and Wales in 1707

SOURCES: Tom Burnam, *The Dictionary of Misinformation* (New York: Thomas Y. Crowell Company, 1975); *Columbia Encyclopedia,* 5th ed.

FROM PARAGRAPH TO ESSAY

Some definitions are so complex, so important, so thought provoking, or so amusing that they demand a full examination of their thesis in an essay. But almost any important term that requires a full paragraph of definition can be defined in an essay, too, by using all three methods of development. For example, one body paragraph can give examples, one contrasts, and one historical origins. The following models should serve as illustrations and inspirations.

A MODEL ESSAY: DEFINITION

Here's an example of a short essay of definition from Bill Cosby's book Fatherhood. *As you can guess, he defines the term* father—*but not in the way it's defined in a dictionary. Notice that Cosby's essay lists a number of traits of a father.*

Play It as It Lays
Bill Cosby

* * * *

1   It is no profound revelation to say that fathering has changed greatly from the days when my own father used me for batting practice. However, the baffling behavior of children is exactly the same today as it was when Joseph's brothers peddled him to the Egyptians. And in the face of such constantly baffling behavior, many men have wondered: Just what *is* a father's role today? As a taskmaster, he's inept. As a referee, he's hopeless. And as a short-order cook, he may have the wrong menu.

2   The answer, of course, is that no matter how hopeless or copeless a father may be, his role is simply to *be* there, sharing all the chores with his wife. Let her *have* the babies; but after that, try to share every job around. Any man today who returns from work, sinks into a chair, and calls for his pipe is a man with an appetite for danger. Actually, changing a diaper takes much less time than waxing a car. A car doesn't spit on your pants, of course, but a baby's book value is considerably higher.

3   If the new American father feels bewildered and even defeated, let him take comfort from the fact that whatever he does in any fathering situation has a 50

percent chance of being right. Having five children has taught me a truth as cosmic as any that you can find on a mountain in Tibet: There are no absolutes in raising children. In any stressful situation, fathering is always a roll of the dice. The game may be messy, but I have never found one with more rewards and joys.

4   You know the only people who are *always* sure about the proper way to raise children? Those who've never had any.

Questions for Analysis

1. What is the purpose of Bill Cosby's essay? Who is his likely audience?
2. In the first paragraph, Cosby in part defines the new American father by saying what the term doesn't mean. What shouldn't a father do? What does Cosby say a father should do?
3. Cosby also cites an example of old-fashioned fathers, implying that their behavior is unacceptable today. What did they do?
4. In the second paragraph, what does Cosby say is the main role of a father? What does Cosby think about setting down rigid rules?
5. Cosby compares diaper changing to waxing a car. Why?
6. What does Cosby say are the pitfalls of fatherhood? What are the rewards?
7. Cosby doesn't provide a formal definition of a father but advises readers on how to be good fathers. From his advice, try composing a statement of definition, beginning with, "A father is a man who . . ."

A STUDENT MODEL ESSAY: DEFINITION

Regina Manikowski was a student at Truman College in Chicago. As you read her definition of marriage, notice that it identifies a number of traits of a strong marriage and then discusses each one.

What Is a Strong Marriage?
Regina Manikowski

* * * *

1   Marriage is a powerful word for a contract between two people who are pledged to each other for a lifetime. Most people marrying for the first time have an idealistic view of the partnership. Sometimes this view is a little naive because they don't realize that marriage evolves and changes through the years. A lot of things are needed to make a marriage successful such as commitment, compromise, common goals, the ability to maintain individuality, and, through it all, laughter.

2   The mutual attraction part of a marriage is very potent at first, and it's what leads people to commit. But that attraction changes and can even diminish. What comes afterward is more important.

3   The marriage vows signify a commitment to each other, that no matter what problems arise, the relationship will survive the outcome. At any given time, outside influences can put a serious strain on the marriage and in many of these instances, walking out the door would seem easier than staying to work things out. But the bond to each other should be strong enough to withstand these problems. The survival of the marriage is worth that commitment.

4   Compromise and commitment go hand-in-hand. Marriage joins two people with their own individual personalities, neither one of them necessarily wanting to give in or lose in a disagreement. They must not let pride get in the way of the ability to compromise because marriage is not a battle, but a union. The overall success of the marriage is more important than any single issue that comes up.

5   The married couple is a family of their own, working as a team. They should have common goals that could range from having children to maintaining a certain lifestyle. Striving for something allows the marriage to develop because people need challenges in order to grow. If husband and wife don't share common goals, the relationship would stagnate or die.

6   It's also important to maintain individuality within the marriage. Even though a person is now part of this "team," he or she is still an individual who should have interests outside the marriage. These interests could include friends, sports, the arts, or music. These things make people more appealing as individuals and allow them to continue to bring that extra individuality to the marriage. People change, but they should strive to change for the better, making for a better marriage.

7   The most important quality two people can share in a marriage is their ability to laugh, a lot. When strains in the marriage occur, the laughter allows the people to release the tension. Too much seriousness can be devastating.

8   The most important thing to remember about marriage is that the relationship between the two people involved constantly changes. If on the day the vows were taken, the people knew what would happen later, they might have had doubts about saying "I do." But sharing your life with someone you love is really wonderful—someone who will support and encourage the very best parts of you and, hopefully, ignore the worst.

Questions for Analysis

1. Where does Regina Manikowski state her formal definition of marriage? Which sentence previews the traits of marriage she'll discuss in the body of the paragraph?
2. What key terms from the preview are repeated in the topic sentences of each body paragraph? Underline them.
3. In the fourth paragraph, what contrast does Regina introduce? Why?
4. The fifth paragraph doesn't include any key terms from the preview. Does the paragraph stray off topic? Why or why not?
5. What ideas in the concluding paragraph reflect back on the opening paragraph?

WRITING FOR MASTERY

Essays

The following suggestions can serve as topics for essays of definition. They'll also work for paragraphs. In each, include a statement that defines the term, and develop the definition through illustration, contrast, or historical process.

Development by Examples (or Other Method)

1. Define the role of a modern-day college student, grown son or daughter, coach, worker, manager, or any other role you are familiar with. Explain and illustrate several different "duties," behaviors, or attitudes that you associate with the role. Assume you are writing a short article for a magazine that is read by people who have roles similar to the one you describe.
2. Assume you are preparing a one-page handout about the company you work for (or would like to work for) to be distributed at a college or high school career day. Define and describe a term important to potential job applicants.

3. Assume that, as a summer camp administrator or senior counselor, you are preparing an informational brochure for the parents of children who might attend the camp. Choose an important term associated with the camp's programs, rules, or activities to define and illustrate.

Development by Contrast

4. Assume you are representing an advertising agency for an automobile manufacturer. Define and describe a *sport utility vehicle* by comparing it with a van or station wagon.

5. Assume that, because of controversy about student cheating, your college has asked you to serve on a committee, which will consider the issue. Define *cheating* and contrast it to legitimate student collaboration.

6. Assume that, in a world history class, your instructor has asked you to write a short definition of a *dictator*. Define the term and contrast it to a leader in a democracy.

Development by Historical Process

7. *Writing from Source Material.* Assume your English teacher has asked you to write a short paper defining one of the following terms that were originally the names of persons or places. Consult encyclopedias, etymological dictionaries, or other reference books for information about their origin and development. And consult more than one source for each term you define; you'll find more information that way—and some differences in information as well. Some good ones include Eric Partridge, *A Dictionary of Word Origins* (New York: Greenwich House, 1983); Joseph T. Shipley, *Origins* (Totowa, N.J.: Littlefield, Adams, 1970); and Robert Hendrickson, *QPB Encyclopedia of Word and Phrase Origins* (New York: Facts on File, 1997). Do not copy the information; compose the definition in your own words. Include references to your sources in your essay.

   a. August

   b. July

   c. hero

   d. bedlam

   e. guillotine

   f. boycott

   g. Caesarean section

   h. gerrymander

   i. nicotine

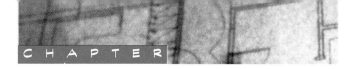

15 Examining Causes or Effects

People are problem solvers. When they see a problem (cancer, unemployment, or pollution), they explore its causes in hopes of finding a solution. When they see a change in society (the Internet, managed health care, or unemployment), they try to predict its results in hopes of adjusting to the change. Once they've found the causes or results, people become communicators. They want to share their information—sometimes to inform, other times to warn, and other times to stir people to act.

You're also a problem solver and communicator, so you should know how to write an explanation of why something happened, is happening, or could happen. This chapter will show you how. You'll

- examine two model paragraphs that explain reasons or results
- analyze their structures and how each was written
- practice generating and organizing information about reasons or results
- write a paragraph and/or an essay presenting causes or effects

MODEL PARAGRAPHS: CAUSES OR EFFECTS

*Cause-effect paragraphs usually work in one of two ways. After stating the practice or problem, the paragraph might look backward to examine the reasons it exists—its **causes**. Or the paragraph might look forward to examine its results— its **effects**.*

Here's a paragraph that examines the historical causes of a common practice today:

UNIT 3

Chapter 15

Composing with Confidence

©2003

Why Is June So Popular for Weddings?

* * * *

June is the month when most schools break for vacation and when the weather is appropriate for most outdoor weddings, but these truths don't explain why June has long been a popular month for weddings. The explanations can be found in ancient mythology. The first reason relates to the actions of a Roman goddess for whom the month was named. As the goddess of marriage and young people, Juno supposedly insisted that couples marry during "her" month. So an ancient Roman proverb said, "Prosperity to the man and happiness to the maid when married in June." But there is a second, more important reason that so many weddings are performed in June. May has been long considered the unluckiest month for marriage, as shown by the superstitious rhyme, "Marry in May, and rue the day." The superstition itself originated in Roman mythology. The month of May honors *Maia,* a Roman earth goddess and the mistress of the fire god Vulcan, who signified danger. Maia was also the goddess of the elderly, and therefore not the best symbol for young people who wished to marry. Consequently, the superstitions about May marriages have caused June to fill its own quota, and some of May's postponed weddings as well.

Questions for Analysis

1. What is the topic sentence of the paragraph? Underline it.
2. Who is the audience for this paragraph? What is the writer's purpose?
3. How many causes for June weddings does the paragraph provide? Is one more important than the other(s)?
4. Underline the transitions in the paragraph. Do they signal a chronological organization or a climax organization?
5. What is the function of the last sentence?

This next model paragraph looks at effects. As you read the paragraph, notice its topic sentence and careful use of transitions.

The Benefits of Exercise

* * * *

Many people have grown tired of hiding their flabby thighs, sucking in their stomachs at the beach, and trying one fad diet or another. The only solution to weight reduction is a serious program of aerobic exercise. Regular exercise for twenty minutes three times a week provides at least five physical and mental benefits. First, the body tends to become slimmer. Typically, a person engaged in aerobics loses one or more inches around the waist and sheds a large amount of body fat. The reason for this loss of body fat is that the body uses more calories than the person has consumed up to that moment, so it begins to burn the calories stored in fat cells. Second, the exercise strengthens much of the body—arms, shoulders, chest, legs, thighs, back, and stomach. Exercisers therefore feel more fit and look it, too. Third, aerobic fitness generally results in better health. Most physically fit people probably decrease their chances of suffering a heart attack or stroke, and, in addition, suffer from fewer colds or cases of influenza. In fact, many people who exercise regularly also sleep better as a result. Fourth, aerobic fitness also increases stamina. Physically fit people can play many sports without tiring, can lift heavy weights, and don't get sleepy in the late afternoon. Finally, aerobics improves people's mental condition. They feel more relaxed and self-confident, for physical strength seems to lead to mental strength. They feel in better control of their lives and consequently give up smoking and eat less junk food. All of these benefits are more than enough reason to engage in some form of aerobic activity.

Questions for Analysis

1. What is the topic sentence of the paragraph? Underline it.
2. Who is the audience for this paragraph? What is the writer's purpose?
3. How many effects does the paragraph discuss? Find and underline the transitions introducing each one.
4. Does the paragraph discuss any causes? If so, where, and why?
5. Are the effects arranged chronologically or in climax organization?

The Structure of Cause-Effect

Whether a paragraph examines causes or effects, it usually begins by establishing the topic. Then it examines the reasons for its occurrence or the results of its occurrence. This examination is usually organized in one of two ways:

1. In **climax order**, moving from the least to most important reason or result. This may lead to a **call for action**—a persuasive appeal to the reader to do something. For example, once the reader knows the effects of the issue, you can ask him or her to remedy those effects.
2. In **chronological order**, moving from the first cause or effect in time to the last. Unlike the chronological organization of a narrative, however, a cause-effect paragraph also includes interpretation and examples.

Think of the causes or effects as steps on a ladder, leading up or down to the event you're analyzing. A diagram of the paragraph might therefore look like this:

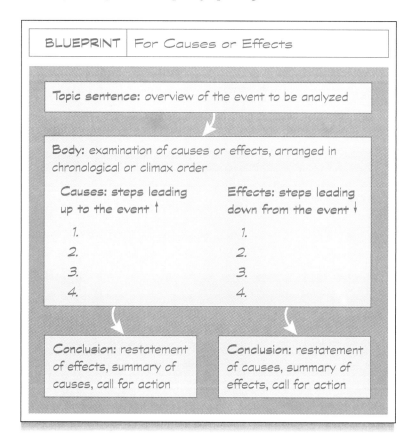

BLUEPRINT | For Causes or Effects

Topic sentence: overview of the event to be analyzed

Body: examination of causes or effects, arranged in chronological or climax order

Causes: steps leading up to the event ↑
1.
2.
3.
4.

Effects: steps leading down from the event ↓
1.
2.
3.
4.

Conclusion: restatement of effects, summary of causes, call for action

Conclusion: restatement of causes, summary of effects, call for action

The Process of Composing Cause-Effect

After selecting the topic and determining whether to describe its causes or effects, you can begin the composing process. Let's look at the steps involved in how a cause–effect paragraph took shape and how it might take shape for you. We'll return to the model paragraph you read earlier on the benefits of exercise.

1. Examine Causes or Effects.   The writer—in this case, a fifty-seven-year-old college professor who has refused to settle into comfortable geezerhood—chose a subject he knows well: exercising. He began thinking about exercise in light of the following:

1. *His audience:* probably students reading this book who've spent too many years watching their bodies grow in directions they hadn't intended
2. *His purpose:* to inform and persuade them of the benefits of exercise

   Then he began brainstorming effects:

---

slimmer waist (most people lose one to two inches)

less body fat

much more stamina

sleep better

increased strength in legs, back, and stomach muscles

fewer colds and other common illnesses

increased self-confidence; physical strength leads to mental strength

think more about other habits of good health-eating better or not
  smoking

time to think, relax, solve problems

fellowship with others engaged in aerobics

negatives: get sweated up, some days must force yourself to do it,
  possible injury from improper warm-ups or carelessness

---

2. Sort and Structure.   As he looked over his list, he sorted specifics into general categories, which became six effects:

---

increased strength

loss of weight

increased stamina

improved outlook on life

better health

negatives

Next, he challenged the details. Was each necessary or important? Which needed explanations or examples? He added an explanation:

> When the body uses more calories than a person consumes, it then begins to burn the calories stored as fat.

And he supplied this example:

> Physically fit people can play many sports without tiring. They can lift heavy weights. And they don't get sleepy in the late afternoon.

He then sorted and shaped the details to support the effects and arranged the effects in climax order:

> slimmer body
> increased strength
> improved health
> increased stamina
> improved mental condition

✓ TIPS

For Choosing Transitions to Heighten Causes or Effects

These transitions can signal chronological or climax order.

For showing causes: because, because of, since, for, one cause (reason) is, another (a second) reason is

For showing effects: as a result, consequently, later, a (one) result of this is, another (a second) result of this is, so, therefore, thus

For items in a series: first, second, third, finally, for one thing, for another

3. **Draft a Topic Sentence.** Having amassed and outlined the effects of exercise, the writer was more convinced than ever of its benefits. He wanted to write a strong topic sentence, one that not only introduced his subject but conveyed his enthusiasm for it. Here's the original topic sentence, which changed several times during revisions:

> A regular program of aerobic exercise three or more times a week may result in a great many physical and mental benefits and has very few drawbacks.

But notice how the topic sentence did change—in fact, becoming two sentences. This should serve to remind you that no experienced writer attempts to compose a perfect first draft. You shouldn't either; just put your ideas into words and expect to change them later.

> The only solution to weight reduction is a serious program of aerobic exercise. Regular exercise for twenty minutes three times a week provides at least five physical and mental benefits.

4. Draft and Revise. Then, following his outline, the writer wrote the entire first draft. In revising, however, he decided to drop all discussion of negative aspects of exercise and to focus entirely on the benefits. He added some transitions that introduced each of the five remaining effects, and he reworked his concluding sentence that tied all the benefits together.

A WRITER SPEAKS

Once again, Michael Raleigh has chosen to write a humorous model essay on causes, rather than give you advice. Notice that he states his thesis in the opening paragraph, develops it in three support paragraphs, each of which is signaled by a transition, and then binds the ideas together—with a twist—in the final paragraph:

The True Fate of the Dinosaurs

No one will ever really know what became of the dinosaurs, but it is possible that they were killed off by the least likely suspect: themselves. Yes, it seems that the ugly beasts themselves were the cause of their own demise.

First, they made each other ill. As prehistoric species migrated from place to place, one scientist has explained, they exchanged microbes and viruses with one another and literally gave each other colds and other unpleasant conditions.

Second, they behaved badly: they ate each other—a practice now frowned upon throughout the world—and what is worse, they ate each other's young. Think about that.

Finally, they were gluttonous: they ate a lot, and what they ate was often unhealthy. For one thing, many of the dinosaurs are believed to have been scavengers; that is, they ate what we would call "road kill." What happens when we eat old meat? And if we eat it raw? And two hundred pounds of it?

Any of these factors might have been enough to set a species back a few million years, but all of them taken together explain why we don't share the planet with the dinosaurs.

Michael Raleigh, author of *In the Castle of the Flynns* and the Paul Whelan series of mystery novels

GETTING READY TO WRITE

Before you compose a cause-effect paper, the following warm-up exercises will help you determine an organization, generate details, formulate topic sentences, and arrange the information.

EXERCISE 1	Predicting Paragraph Development

After each of the following topic sentences, place a check mark next to the most likely development of the paragraph that follows. Will it discuss causes or effects? Will it be arranged in chronological or climax order?

1. Picasso is considered a major artist for three important reasons.

   ✔ a. causes   ___ a. chronological order

   ___ b. effects   ✔ b. climax order

2. A job in health care—whether as doctor, nurse, technician, or aide—offers several important benefits.

____ a. causes   ____ a. chronological order

____ b. effect   ____ b. climax order

3. A series of changes in my life led to my decision to return to school.

____ a. causes   ____ a. chronological order

____ b. effects   ____ b. climax order

4. A child who runs away from home can—and should—expect to encounter some serious and even dangerous problems.

____ a. causes   ____ a. chronological order

____ b. effects   ____ b. climax order

5. The war of 1898 between Spain and the United States broke out as the result of many foolish and selfish acts, not out of any real threat to our safety or well-being.

____ a. causes   ____ a. chronological order

____ b. effects   ____ b. climax order

6. The reduction of college tuition scholarships for the poor is causing a number of serious changes in our society.

____ a. causes   ____ a. chronological order

____ b. effects   ____ b. climax order

EXERCISE 2	Generating and Selecting Details

Assume you're composing a letter for admission to a program in a field that interests you (for example, in computer science, nursing, law, medicine, or business). Name the program, and develop each topic idea that follows by listing some causes or effects, explaining these causes when necessary, and illustrating them through examples. Put a check mark (✓) next to the material you would most likely include in your letter. Finally, draft a topic sentence for each topic.

Type of Program: _____

Topic A: why you deserve admission to the program

_____

_____

_____

_____

_____

_____

Topic Sentence: _____

Topic B: how you would benefit from the program

_____

_____

_____

_____

_____

_____

_____

Topic Sentence: _____

Topic C: how you would contribute to society after completing the program

_____

_____

_____

_____

_____

_____

_____

Topic Sentence: _____

EXERCISE 3	Arranging in Chronological Order

Number the following sentences in each paragraph so they trace the causes of an effect in chronological order.

The Earliest Origins of American Football

Paragraph A:

_____ Then, shortly after the Danes were defeated in 1042, an Englishman dug up the skull of a buried Danish soldier and kicked it around his field.

___1___ If it weren't for the forces of civilization, we might call the game "headball" instead of football because the forerunner of football used human skulls as the ball.

_____ The Danes occupied England in the early eleventh century.

_____ Therefore, they looked for other choices of sporting equipment.

_____ Others dug up Danish "headballs" and enjoyed the pastime of kicking them around until they found the object to be rather hard on the foot.

_____ They quickly found the obvious choice: inflated cow bladders, of course.

Paragraph B:

_____ The game began when a bladder was dropped between two neighboring towns.

_____ Finally, however, King Henry II (who reigned from 1154 to 1189) outlawed the sport, not only to eliminate uncontrolled vandalism and violence but to eliminate a security threat.

_____ A later version of the game became popular and created large-scale insanity.

_____ A team won if it managed to kick the bladder into the center of the other's town.

_____ The reason was that his soldiers were playing futballe instead of practicing their archery. So, for the next 400 years, futballe was against the law, but continued to be played anyway.

_____ The game became increasingly violent. Although the players never touched the ball with their hands (indeed, they called the game futballe), they were quite willing to use their fists to hit each other.

Paragraph C:

_____ And the game became even more polite when round balls replaced cow bladders.

_____ The ban against futballe was lifted by James I (who reigned from 1603 to 1625), who honored the wishes of sportsmen.

_____ This game became known as Association Football.

_____ The game developed formal rules by placing it in standard-size playing fields and awarding points for passing the other team's goal.

_____ The shortening of Association to Assoc. led to the slang expression "soccer," which is the sport's modern name in the U.S.

Paragraph D:

_____ The name of his college was Rugby.

_____ Although his action was not rewarded, his college became notorious for its unsportsmanlike behavior.

_____ The next important historical development in the history of football occurred in 1823.

_____ He scored a touchdown, but it was illegal.

_____ (And now you know why this is the only sport whose name is often capitalized, at least when it refers to English Rugby.)

_____ During a game in England, a college student named William Ellis became frustrated, picked up the ball, and ran with it.

_____ Eventually, the games of soccer and Rugby came to American colleges, where they evolved into modern-day football.

EXERCISE 4	Arranging in Climax Order

Read the introductory and topic sentences for the following paragraph, and then number the supporting sentences in climax order, with the most important reason coming last. The paragraph should include four reasons for the end of Prohibition, and each reason should be developed specifically by other statements. Add transitional expressions (such as second, third, finally, therefore, *and* for example) *to the beginnings of sentences.*

After a long campaign against alcohol by ministers, the Woman's Christian Temperance Union, and others, a Constitutional amendment banned the production and sale of all alcohol throughout the country in 1920. However, the ban, known as Prohibition, lasted only thirteen years for several reasons.

_____1_____   _First_   Prohibition was unable to prevent people from drinking.

_____   _____   "Distilleries" in out-of-the-way factories, in people's basements, and even in bathtubs produced illegal booze.

_____   _____   The illegal use of alcohol was widespread throughout society, from average citizens to politicians, who drank at home or at liquor-serving night clubs, called speakeasies.

_____   _____   The desire for even more liquor created a whole new class of gangsters, who became rich from making and selling alcohol.

_____   _____   In 1933 another Constitutional amendment was passed, reversing the earlier one and ending the era of Prohibition in the United States.

_____   _____   Prohibition eliminated too many jobs.

_____   _____   At the beginning of the Depression in the 1930s, there were many claims that the legal manufacture and sale of alcohol would create badly needed work for honest citizens.

_____   _____   Prohibition was unable to eliminate the manufacture of alcohol.

_____   _____   A great deal of liquor was manufactured in Canada and then smuggled into the United States.

PARAGRAPH WRITING ASSIGNMENT

Here are two choices for paragraphs.

1. Consider an important decision you've made: quitting a job; returning to school; getting married, beginning a relationship with someone, or ending the marriage or relationship; moving to another neighborhood, city, or country. What events caused you to make the decision, and did one event lead to another?

2. Or, if you wish, examine the effects of your decision. In what ways did your life change as a result? Discuss several.

Your purpose for either 1 or 2 will be to advise or warn people who might be contemplating a similar decision. Would you recommend they follow your example?

Explore your ideas through brainstorming, freewriting, or clustering. Then determine several general causes or effects and list supporting details under each. Outline the paragraph either in chronological or climax order. Draft a topic sentence that introduces the subject and makes a point about it. Then discuss the reasons or results in the body of the paragraph. Add explanations and examples that clarify and strengthen each one. Draft a conclusion that pulls everything together.

Use the following questions from the Revision Guidelines, below, to guide your revision. Or you may use them to structure a peer review in your collaborative group, as described in Chapter 2, page 21.

After completing the revision, edit the paragraph, checking for correct spelling and punctuation, complete sentences, and clarity of ideas. Then make a clean copy of the paragraph and proofread it carefully for errors. Turn in a final copy to your instructor.

REVISION GUIDELINES   Examining Causes or Effects

1. Is the topic sentence clear, and does it make a point? If not, how should it be revised?
2. Do all the reasons or results support the topic sentence? If not, what should be eliminated, revised, or added?
3. Is the paragraph well organized, either chronologically or in climax order? If not, how can the organization be strengthened?
4. Are the connections between causes and effects logical and clear? If not, what sentences should be revised, or where should transitions be added? Suggest appropriate transitions.
5. Does the conclusion summarize or reinforce the point of the paragraph? If not, how can it be improved?

WRITING FOR MASTERY

Paragraphs

The following list of topics should provide you with ideas for writing other cause-effect paragraphs. For each, draft a topic sentence establishing the event or happening you'll discuss. Then trace its causes—or effects—and develop each one with explanations and examples. Include transitions that show the relationships among the causes or effects. And end the paragraph with a concluding sentence that ties all the ideas together. Discuss

1. Your decision to go to the college you're attending—what caused it, or what has resulted from it.
2. The high rate of divorce in this country—what causes it, or what has resulted from it.
3. The practice of unmarried couples living together—what causes it, or what has resulted from it.
4. The high rate (or decrease) in violent crime in the United States—what causes it, or what has resulted from it.
5. Human cloning—what might result from it.

FROM PARAGRAPH TO ESSAY

Recall the process of composing a cause-effect paper. After generating details, you arrange them in several general categories. If each category becomes the topic of a paragraph, you have "exploded" a paragraph into an essay. The first paragraph introduces the thesis, stating your attitude toward or opinion about it. Each body paragraph, in turn, examines a single cause, or effect, with supporting explanations, examples, and details. The concluding paragraph summarizes and reinforces your opinion.

The following models should provide you with inspiration and examples.

A STUDENT MODEL ESSAY: EXAMINING CAUSES

April Harkness was a student at Truman College in Chicago. As you read her essay, notice that she recounts, in chronological order, stages in her developing awareness of her identity and examines the causes of each.

Don't Worry, Be Hapa
April Damasco Harkness

* * * *

1   "What are you?" was a question I was asked frequently at different stages of my life. My answer would have varied from white to Filipina. I now consider myself Hapa, which is a Hawaiian term that refers to people of Caucasian and Asian descent.

2   I grew up in Erie, Pennsylvania, as the product of a Filipina mother and a Scottish-German father. I didn't know I was different until I attended school. My classmates would insist I was Chinese or Japanese. At other times I was told to go back to my country. Worst of all was my fourth grade teacher who praised my grasp of the English language. Of course I could speak English. I was born here.

3   During high school, the harassment continued. Every day I could count on someone calling me a chink or a gook. At this point in my teenage years, I was ashamed to be Asian. I hated my dark black hair and the way my eyes were shaped. I hated being the only Asian in school. I just wanted to be like everyone else.

4   Moving to Chicago felt like a breath of fresh air. For the first time no one stared at me as if I didn't belong. Chicagoans actually guessed I was a Filipina. I eventually met other Asian-Americans in my new city. It felt great to belong to a group where I didn't stick out like a sore thumb.

5   Unfortunately, there were some Filipinos who snubbed their noses at me for being mixed and not knowing my mother's native language.

6   I have come to accept and take pride in both the cultures that reside inside me. Reading an article, I learned that the number of biracial people is multiplying rapidly. The image of America is changing. I am a Hapa, but after all, I am an all-American girl.

Questions for Analysis

1. What sentence in the first paragraph describes the final effect—or result—of the stages April Harkness describes in the body of her essay? Underline it.

2. Each body paragraph describes a stage in April's developing awareness of her identity. What organizational principle does she use for presenting these stages? What transitions introduce each stage?

3. Explain in your own words the causes of her unhappiness at each stage.

4. What are the causes of her current happiness with and pride in her identity?

5. How does her conclusion summarize and extend the points developed in the body paragraphs? She ends her essay with a punch. What is it?

A STUDENT MODEL ESSAY: EXAMINING EFFECTS

Patrick Ingram is a former marine, guitar player in two rock bands, a bouncer—and a former student at Truman College. In the following essay, he demonstrates the unpleasant effects of what he thought was a pleasant experience. As you read the essay, notice its chronological organization, the precise attention to detail, and his purpose, which he states at the end.

Liquid Revenge
Patrick Ingram

* * * *

1   It's six A.M., BEEP, BEEP, BEEP, BEEP, my alarm clock alerts me that I must face another day. I quell this incessant racket by slapping the convenient yet deceiving snooze button. The noise is gone, and now I can return to that wonderful dream of winning the state lottery and . . . , BEEP, BEEP, BEEP, BEEP!!

2   "THAT'S IT!!" I think to myself as my eyes jerk open, and I consider the violent acts I am going to enact upon an otherwise unfeeling instrument of technology. I'm prepared to deliver the first blow when I am knocked flat on my back by a bright white flash, and a sound like a thousand alarms blasting in unison; very similar to the intro of the Pink Floyd song "Time." All my violent thoughts are replaced by my shivering body, rocking back and forth as I grab my head, which seems to have gained a few pounds. My brain is reeling from the force of one thousand devils, with pitchforks and pickaxes, jumping up and down and around. There is a mosh pit going on in my head, and I am powerless to stop it. This is just the beginning of my agony. I realize, as I attempt to walk/crawl to the porcelain god and pay homage, that I have been flung headfirst into the merciless void of a hangover.

3   I'm still agonizingly trying to perform some sort of locomotion to the temple of relief. My life of the past twenty-four hours is replaying in my mind. I am reliving the ultimate sin of overindulgence. My body is enduring a harsh penalty for my incompetent actions. "You buffoon! You drank yourself into a stupor!!" my angered conscience screams. My only response is to whimper in agreement as my struggle continues toward what I hope will be my salvation. The actions of the previous night replay themselves in my mind like a broken record that keeps skipping at the same verse. I'm reminded of shot after shot of Jack Daniel's and an unspecified amount of beers. I'm reminded of my arrogant belief that I could defy the body's rejection of poison. This agonizing penance I am attempting to perform is a testament to my wickedness.

4   I'm feeling very, very sorry for angering the cosmic forces now unleashing their wrath upon me. I'm slowly getting closer to the temple door of salvation. I swear to myself, as many a soul in my position has done before, that I will never perform such wanton sacrilege again. I do this in the hopes that somehow, somewhere, this agony will end. My body, now on autopilot, continues to push me closer to the end of the hall. I reach the door and open it, falling flat at the foot of the porcelain face of benevolence. I lift myself up and perform the ritual, leaving my offering for the approval of my master of the moment. It's not over yet, as I am

still left to fend off the pounding, spinning mosh pit that seems to ravage and rage endlessly inside my head.

5   I am forced to stare at my weakened features in the mirror, a window of self-revelation. I reach into the medicine cabinet, seeking an elixir of relief. The gods have forgiven me, for the remedy I seek is, mercifully, within my grasp. I gratefully accept the gift of forgiveness, a bottle of aspirin that is blessedly full. I swallow the pills and perform a cleaning ritual. I revel in the coolness of the water as it splashes my face in baptism. Eventually, the ordeal ends, leaving me with the small throbbing of my head and a mind full of regrets.

6   What I have just described is the result of not recognizing and heeding my limitations. A hangover can happen and has happened to most of us at one time or another. Perhaps for some people, the effects are not as dramatic, but many can attest that a real head-banger can leave them crying like babies. Should we thrust ourselves into the throes of pain that a hangover can bring?

Questions for Analysis

1. Patrick Ingram doesn't state the point of his essay at the beginning. Why? Where does he state the point?
2. In each paragraph except the last, Patrick describes the effects of his overindulgence in alcohol. What determines the paragraph divisions? That is, what is the unifying idea of each paragraph?
3. In your own words, list three or four effects of alcohol that Patrick is experiencing. Why do you think he decided not to organize his essay according to general effects?
4. Patrick describes his experience in the present tense. Why? How would your reaction to the story change if he described it in the past tense?
5. Throughout the description, Patrick uses a metaphor—an implied comparison to something else. What is the metaphor, and why does he use it?

WRITING FOR MASTERY

Essays

The subjects that follow may help you generate ideas for essays (or paragraphs) that explore causes or effects. For each topic, include a thesis statement or topic sentence(s). Arrange the causes or effects in chronological or climax order, and show that order through appropriate transitions.

1. For a student literary magazine, examine how your early experiences (at home, in school, in your community, or in your ethnic background) affected your feelings about yourself or possibly your behavior. Like April Harkness, explore some incidents that illustrate the experiences.
2. For a psychology course, describe what you think to be the most important reasons that adolescents do one of the following things: smoke, drink, or take drugs. Be sure to limit your topic, for this is a complex subject.
3. For the same class, discuss the influences—good or bad—that professional athletes have on teenagers.
4. In an article for *TV Guide,* discuss the effects that television has on elections.
5. In an editorial for your campus newspaper, discuss the problems that unprepared or unmotivated students cause for themselves and their classmates.
6. *Writing from Source Material.* Prepare a short brochure about the origins of margarine for members of the American Dairy Association. Write a cause-effect

paragraph based on the following information. Pay special attention to the dates, which will help you organize the information. Include transitional expressions and qualifying words as necessary.

after popularity in France, margarine spread throughout Europe

butter shortage in United States during World War I in Europe (1914–1918); margarine arrived

butter spoils in heat

during Franco-Prussian War in 1870–71, butter substitute needed by France; had to be stored on ships

Emperor Napoleon III of France sponsor of contest with prize for best substitute

butter expensive in second half of nineteenth century

winner: the Frenchman Hippolyte Mege-Mouries

his formula: combination of beef fat and milk

Mege-Mouries called product oleomargarine because mistakenly believed beef fat possessed margaric acid

margarine cheaper than butter

margarine doesn't spoil as quickly as butter

SOURCE: David Wallechinsky and Irving Wallace, *The People's Almanac* (New York: Doubleday and Company, 1975).

16 Persuading an Audience

Now comes the most challenging but most fascinating composing task: persuasion, in which you attempt to change the minds or behavior of your audience in some way. Persuasion is not easy, but this chapter offers you advice and practice on how to achieve some success. You'll

- examine two models of persuasion
- recognize the elements of persuasion
- practice shaping ideas into effective arguments
- write a persuasive paragraph and/or a persuasive essay

MODELS OF PERSUASION

Persuasion is a central part of everyday life. Each day you see and hear thousands of ads and commercials enticing you to buy goods and services. Each day in conversation, you make requests, pleas, demands, or even threats—for example, that a friend lend you some money; that your professor allow you more time to complete an assignment; or that your son, roommate, or spouse put the dirty dishes in the sink. And less often—but far more importantly—you make written requests or demands that employers consider you for a job, clients buy your products, senators and representatives support or oppose a law, or the automobile dealer fix your car properly if that dealer ever wants your business again.

Here's an example of a persuasive paragraph written by Christopher S. Linbarger, a student at Chattanooga State Technical Community College in Tennessee. Notice the statement of his point and the evidence he cites to support that point.

Just Who Are the Victims?
Christopher S. Linbarger

* * * *

Smokers are being persecuted. It's now politically correct to look down at, make fun of, and badger smokers. When a person cannot smoke without being

UNIT 3

Chapter 16

Composing with Confidence
©2003

made out to be a fool, something is wrong. Smokers can put up with having to sit in the back of restaurants and not smoking on planes or anywhere in public for that matter. However, they cannot and should not have to accept the harsh comments, mean looks, and personal humiliation that nonsmokers give them. People start smoking for many reasons, but one of those reasons is certainly not to be made fools of in public. The next time you give a dirty look to a smoker or mumble something under your breath, think about it. You may be practicing your own form of discrimination.

Questions for Analysis

1. Who is the likely audience for this argument?
2. What evidence does Christopher Linbarger offer to support his claim that smokers are being persecuted?
3. Do you accept the argument? If not, why not?
4. What direct appeal does he make to his readers? Why?

A single paragraph can be persuasive. But a controversial and complex topic requires more extensive treatment in a full essay. Here's an essay on one such controversy, written as a letter to the readers of the People's Almanac *by Mrs. Marsha Phillips. As you read her argument, consider these issues: Who is her audience? How does she think they feel about her argument? What evidence does she cite to back up her argument? And how does she answer the objections to her argument?*

Let's Legalize Heroin
Marsha Phillips

* * * *

1   It may seem strange to suggest that a drug as evil as heroin be legalized, but please hear me out. If I had my way, no one would take heroin. But, in reality, lots and lots of people use it and many of them become addicts. And these addicts need large amounts of money, every day, to support their habits. To get this money, many heroin addicts become thieves, preying on innocent people so the addicts can afford the outrageous prices that pushers are able to charge since they deal in an illegal, underground substance which they sell to customers who have to have it.

2   If heroin were legal, the price would go way down, addicts wouldn't have to steal to support their habit, and the rest of us wouldn't be victimized. Who would lose if heroin were legal? Only the pushers and the crime syndicates. It makes you wonder why politicians have allowed the heroin trade to go on as long as they have. If heroin were legal, the police would have more time to deal with other crimes. I have heard that over 50 percent of the crime in New York City is committed by heroin addicts.

3   The victims of heroin addiction are both rich and poor. Last summer, three blocks from my suburban home, two darling teenagers were shot to death when they came home from school and surprised a burglar. That burglar turned out to be a heroin addict with a $300-a-day habit. Four days later my housekeeper came to work crying because her brother was in critical condition in the hospital, having been stabbed by an intruder. Fortunately, he survived, but this intruder, too, was a heroin addict.

4   Perhaps it is true that legalizing heroin would cause there to be more addicts, but those addicts would commit far fewer crimes than the ones in the system we now have. When I told my friends about my idea to make heroin legal, one of

them said that she had heard the idea before on the radio. And she said that some well-known lawyers and even judges supported it. If this is so, then why is heroin still illegal? Are the politicians afraid that if they support legal heroin, people will think they are pro-drugs? Or is organized crime so strong that it can buy off the politicians or otherwise convince them not to act?

Questions for Analysis

1. What is the purpose of the opening two sentences in the first paragraph?
2. Where in the first paragraph does Marsha Phillips define a problem?
3. Where does she propose a solution to the problem, and what is that solution?
4. What does she predict would result if her solution were adopted? Does she predict any negative results and, if so, where?
5. Where does she cite statistics to support her argument? Where does she cite respected members of the community?
6. Why, in the third paragraph, does she mention that the victims of heroin addiction are both rich and poor?
7. What, according to Phillips, seems to prevent her solution from being enacted?
8. Does she directly call upon people to act? If not, what actions do you think she would suggest?

The Elements of Persuasion

Persuasion is an attempt to convince others that they should accept your point of view or do your bidding. People believe they're rational animals—and they are. But they also have many irrational opinions based on fear, anger, prejudice, and ignorance. They don't easily change their minds—especially about long-held beliefs—so, to be convincing, you must answer their counterarguments, questions, and doubts. You must base a persuasive argument on reasons and explanations, proof (through facts, figures, and examples), and emotional appeals.

Your presentation must be carefully directed to its audience. That means consciously deciding on your **tone**: the attitude you take toward your readers. You can be informal and animated with a friend, loud and angry with a teenage son, polite but firm with a repair person, or humble and soft-spoken with a professor. In short, your appeal must actually be a *persuasive strategy* based on the subject, the reason for persuading, and the audience's attitude toward you and the subject.

The Subject Matter.   The subject you discuss must be one you know about and care about. You cannot be convincing without knowledge of the facts, the arguments for and against your position, and a viewpoint on the subject you can affirm and defend. Furthermore, what you say, when you say it, and how you say it depends on how controversial your subject is. With a noncontroversial subject, such as persuading your classmates to register early, you can state your point, then develop and support it. But with a controversial subject, such as encouraging students to boycott classes, you may state your point only at the end of your argument—after explaining your reasoning and presenting your evidence. If you state the point too early, your audience may simply dismiss you as a radical—or a kook.

The Reason for Persuading. A persuasive goal can be modest (for example, a request that people reconsider an opinion), or it can be an ambitious **call for action** (for example, a demand that people boycott a store, vote for a candidate they oppose, repair your car for free, or quit their jobs). The more you ask of an audience, the more difficult the task of persuasion becomes. You'll need to marshal your evidence, anticipate and respond to counterarguments, and decide when to state your point. You may need to lead up to your point in climax organization, after showing your audience the facts, dispelling their fears, and winning their trust.

The Attitude of the Audience. Some readers can be easily persuaded; others can't. Audiences can generally be classified into three types according to their attitudes toward you and your arguments.

1. *A Friendly Audience.* These readers are the easiest to convince because they already agree with your arguments and trust (or at least don't distrust) you. With this audience, you can make a straightforward presentation: state your point and then support it. Your tone may be angry, urgent, or calm, depending on the subject matter.

2. *A Neutral Audience.* These readers have an open mind about the subject. You can make a straightforward presentation to them also, but probably must answer their questions or objections. You may not choose to address them in an angry or urgent tone until late in the argument, when you've won them over to your side.

3. *An Unfriendly Audience.* These readers oppose your point of view and perhaps don't trust you. You must therefore win them over, softening their hostility and mistrust. Your tone must be reasonable, must acknowledge their feelings, must accept some of their conclusions—and should perhaps state your point at or near the end of your essay.

No matter who your readers are, be sure to respect them.

- Don't underestimate the intelligence of your audience, so make your arguments logical and fair.

- Appeal to emotions, but don't attempt to manipulate them. The result can backfire, turning your audience against you.

- Don't reduce an argument to personal attacks on opponents. Not only is this tactic unfair and beside the point, but it can also turn your audience against you.

- Above all, don't distort the truth. Not only will you lose the trust of your readers, but you will lose any hope of succeeding in your goals—and you *should* lose!

The Structure of Persuasion

A persuasive argument can be structured with the thesis statement (or topic sentence) first, followed by its support—or in climax order with the point stated at the end. Your choice should depend on the subject matter, the reason for persuading, and the audience's attitude. A diagram of a persuasive argument might include all or most of the following elements, but not necessarily in the order presented here:

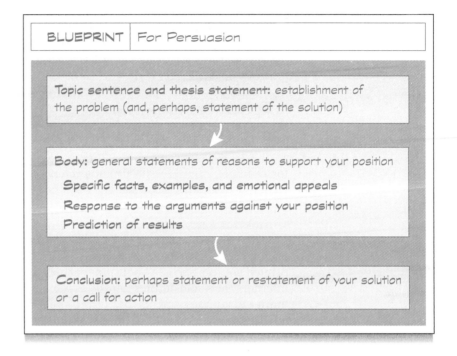

The Process of Developing a Persuasive Strategy

A persuasive argument must be crafted with care. The more effort you put into planning—before you begin to write—the more successful your argument will be.

First, you'll need to define the problem. Draft a statement of it. Maybe it will be self-evident, maybe not—in which case, you will have to convince your audience. Can you show that there is a problem?

Then, draft a solution. Can you show why it will (or might) work?

Here are other matters to consider:

- What questions or objections will your audience raise—and how you will answer them?
- When should you state your point—at the beginning or end of your argument?
- What reasons will you state for your point of view? List them.
- What evidence will support each point most effectively? List your evidence.
- How will you interpret the evidence? How will you convince your audience that they should accept your reasoning?
- How will you gain your audience's trust? How will you win their confidence in you?

There are no "right" answers to these questions, but you must take them seriously. Here are steps to follow in shaping a strategy.

1. Prepare a Preliminary Statement of Your Point.   Make the statement clear and direct; let your readers know exactly what you want them to believe or do. This statement may become your topic sentence or thesis statement at the beginning of the argument. Or it may be the climactic statement at the end. But you should know what you want to say and aim toward proving it, no matter where it appears. Since you're recommending or demanding something, the statement will probably include the verbs *should, ought,* or *must,* as in these examples:

> Anyone interested in American history should visit Boston and its surrounding areas, where our independent nation was really founded.
>
> You ought to be eating more foods with high fiber content, while cutting down on eggs, red meats, and whole-milk dairy products.
>
> If we want our children hope to survive in the future, we must stop the destruction of the ozone layer.

2. Discuss the Issue in Human Terms.   Relate the issue to people's lives. Recall, for example, how Marsha Phillips refers to two neighborhood teenagers who were killed, and her housekeeper's brother who was stabbed, by heroin addicts.

3. Look for Facts and Figures—and Use Them Wisely.   Whenever possible, provide evidence—facts and figures—to support your point. As you may recall from Chapter 5, **facts** are statements that can be proven, and many come from printed sources such as books, magazines, pamphlets—or, these days, from the Internet. Facts and figures can be especially persuasive because they lend authority to your arguments. But record them accurately; read over the source material more than once to be sure you understand it. Then either **paraphrase** the material (that is, restate it in your own words and sentence structures) or quote it (which means you cannot change a word of the original). Acknowledge your source by citing the author, title, publisher, and date of publication. (Your instructor may provide you with guidelines on formatting this acknowledgment.)

And take control of the material. Interpret the facts; don't just list them. Here's an example. To support his argument that overwork is literally killing the Japanese, journalist Pete Hamill cites and compares statistics, then quotes a Japanese friend's reaction to them:

> Japan works harder than any nation on earth. According to 1989 figures from the Ministry of International Trade and Industry, the Japanese worker puts in 2,246.8 hours of work the year before—300 more than the average American, 600 more than the West Germans and the French.
>
> "That's too low," one Japanese editor friend said, making calculations with a pencil. "They must be leaving out overtime. If I could work 2,500 hours a year, I'd feel as if I was on vacation."

4. Cite Authorities.   People and organizations that readers respect also add weight and prestige to an argument. Again, recall Marsha Phillips referring to well-known lawyers and judges who support making heroin use legal. Here's another example. The writer summarizes and quotes a respected organization's research into the public's mixed feelings about abortions:

> According to the National Opinion Research Center, a nonprofit group affiliated with the University of Chicago, a large majority of Americans support abortion only when the woman's health is seriously endangered, when the pregnancy is the result of rape or incest, or when the baby is likely to be born with a serious birth defect. But if a woman wants an abortion because she is unmarried or does not want more children or is too poor to support them—the circumstances under which most abortions take place—slightly less than half of Americans think a legal abortion should be available.

TIPS

For Choosing Transitions in Persuasion
Because the relationships among ideas are complex, the transitions must reflect those complex relationships. Here are a few more that may apply to your persuasive strategy:

To make a concession to readers: of course, surely, naturally, to be sure, no doubt

To qualify a statement: perhaps, maybe, possibly

To predict results or consequences: therefore, thus, as a consequence, as a result

To cite an authority: according to, as says (demonstrates, argues, shows)

5. Predict the Results.   Show how people will benefit if your solution is adopted, or warn them against the dangers if it is not. Recall again that Marsha Phillips predicts a reduction of crime if heroin use is legalized.

6. Predict Counterarguments.   Consider what your readers know—and how they feel—about your subject matter. What questions will they raise? What objections will they make? What authorities do they trust? And how will you answer these questions, objections, and authorities? Sometimes you'll confront them head-on, other times you'll concede a point or two, and still other times you'll need to dissect the counterarguments point by point, showing the fallacies behind them. The task may be easy, challenging, or irrelevant. It depends on the topic, your goal in persuading, and the audience.

7. Draft Your Argument.   You've developed a persuasive strategy by marshaling your evidence and authorities, appealing to the feelings of your audience, anticipating their opposing arguments, predicting consequences, and considering whether to call for action or to propose a solution. Now, you're ready to outline and write. Draft your argument, and revise it carefully. Allow yourself time to think about the issue between revisions.

A WRITER SPEAKS

> Stop while you're ahead. That's my best advice to those of you embarking on essays, term papers, and other long writing assignments. Few long and complex assignments can be completed in one sitting. Drafting paragraphs and pages may take several days. Each time you're getting ready to end a drafting session, try to stop before you're tired and frustrated. Instead, stop when you know where you'll go next. You might even sketch a little outline of the next paragraphs or topics. That way, when you come back to writing, you'll be able to start right in with confidence.
>
> Ann Hofstra Grogg, editor

GETTING READY TO WRITE

Before tackling the task of persuasion, try these warm-up exercises. Not only will they give you practice in persuasive skills, but they'll get you started on the paragraph or essay you choose to write.

EXERCISE 1	Predicting Persuasive Organization

After each of the following topic sentences, list the matters you would expect the writer to address—or the questions you want the writer to answer.

Topic Sentence A: Let's replace the current public educational system with a voucher system so that parents may freely choose the type of private school their children will attend.

1. Explanation of a voucher system 2. Problems with the current educational system

3. Ways that the voucher system would solve these problems 4. What do we do with the currently employed teachers and administrators? 5. How do we make sure that all children are educated in the basics? 6. Should we pay for education in a religious school?

Topic Sentence B: I propose that every homeless person be provided with free housing.

_____

_____

_____

_____

_____

Topic Sentence C: The legal age for drinking alcohol should be lowered from twenty-one to eighteen.

_____

_____

_____

_____

_____

Topic Sentence D: The legal age for obtaining a driver's license should be raised from sixteen to eighteen.

_____

_____

_____

_____

_____

EXERCISE 2	Composing Topic Sentences

Assume you're writing an editorial for your college newspaper. Choose a topic that most interests you from those listed here, and draft a topic sentence that best reflects your position on the topic.

1. the grading system
2. required courses
3. college sports

4. tutoring and academic support services
5. smoking or tobacco use

*Topic Sentence:*_____

_____

EXERCISE 3	Supporting Topic Sentences

List evidence to support each of the following statements based on the type of supporting material indicated. You needn't write complete sentences.

1. The elderly need better care than we are currently providing them. (facts)
   Poor food and sanitary conditions in nursing homes. Not enough services to allow sick elderly to live at home. Not enough useful activities for retired persons to do.

2. The cafeteria in this college needs improvement (or is quite adequate). (facts)

   _____

   _____

3. In this era of big government, big business, and computer records about everyone, Americans must protect their right to privacy. (specific example from someone's life) _____

   _____

4. The air everyone breathes and the water everyone drinks must be protected against polluters. (name of specific authority or type of information authority would give) _____

   _____

5. This country needs to step up the search for cheap, practical sources of solar energy. (prediction of results)_____

   _____

EXERCISE 4   Identifying Effective Persuasive Strategies

Label each of the following introductory paragraphs as effective or ineffective for their audience, and say why.

Paragraph A:

Audience: a group of working-class people opposed to welfare

There have been, and will continue to be, isolated cases of welfare fraud. Nevertheless, anyone who seriously believes that most people on welfare are cheating the public is either an idiot or a hypocrite. Everybody, everywhere, cheats. People lie on their income tax returns. Clergy steal from collection boxes. Even President Nixon lied all the way through the Watergate scandal, President Clinton lied about Monica Lewinsky, and President Bush lied about his arrest for D.U.I.

Label: _____

*Why:*_____

_____

Paragraph B:

Audience: parents of juvenile delinquents

No one is in favor of juvenile crime, and surely no parent teaches his or her children to be drug dealers, thieves, pimps, prostitutes, or killers. We as a society, however, must take a stand against teenagers who control the streets in our neighborhoods and terrorize so many decent people. We must get these punks and thugs off the streets and into constructive activities so they can become useful members of our communities.

Label: _____

Why: _____

_____

Paragraph C:

Audience: college seniors

Has it ever occurred to you that you have been wasting your time in college? There is plenty of evidence to support that theory. The time, hard work, and money you have spent so far could have been invested in activities that would already have profited you in far more significant ways. Countless studies, in fact, have shown that it is not education that makes success but hard work, the right kind of personality, and the courage to seize opportunities when they arise.

Label: _____

Why: _____

_____

Paragraph D:

Audience: anti-abortion or pro-life groups

No one could quarrel with someone who opposes murder. And I know that you believe that abortion is murder. It is a serious position, a moral position, and I respect it. I ask only that you respect me enough to hear my case: that individuals must have the opportunity to choose for themselves, based on their own circumstances, beliefs, and religious teaching.

Label: _____

Why: _____

_____

PARAGRAPH WRITING ASSIGNMENT

Consider this statement as the topic for your persuasive argument: "You and I need to be treated more as individuals and less as faces in the crowd." Modify the topic in any way you wish. You can be more specific about the circumstances: "In college." You can be more general about the people involved: "Teenagers need to be treated . . ." or "Working mothers . . ." or "Part-time college students . . ."

As you shape the topic, explore your ideas—and marshal evidence, examples, and facts to support them. Consult outside sources if necessary. Arrange your materials in a plan that carries out an effective persuasive strategy. In planning the paragraph, specify an audience for your argument and consider what questions or objections they would raise.

Then write a first draft.

Use the following questions from the Revision Guidelines, below, to guide your revision. Or use them to structure peer review in your collaborative group, as described in Chapter 2, page 21.

After completing the revision, edit the paragraph, checking for correct spelling and punctuation, complete sentences, and clarity of ideas. Then make a clean copy of the paragraph and proofread it carefully for errors. Submit the final copy to your instructor.

REVISION GUIDELINES   Persuading

1. Does the paragraph define the problem to which it offers a solution? If not, how can the definition of the problem be improved?

2. Is the statement of the point clear? If not, how should it be clarified? Does the statement come too early—or late—in the paragraph? If so, where should it be placed?

3. Are the organization and the persuasive strategy effective for their intended audience? Does the argument show respect for the audience? Has it worked to build their trust? If not, what should be revised, eliminated, added, or shifted?

4. Are the persuasive appeals effective? If not, what should be eliminated, revised, or added?

5. Are transitions lacking or too vague at any point in the paragraph? If so, what should be added or revised?

6. Does the paragraph end on a strong note—restating its main point or calling on its reader to act?

WRITING FOR MASTERY

Paragraphs

The following list of topics should provide you with ideas for writing other persuasive paragraphs. For each, begin by drafting a statement of your point, then listing your evidence, examples, facts, and figures. Decide on a persuasive strategy, especially the strategy of when you will state your point—at the beginning or end. Then draft and revise the paragraph.

1. Argue for or against fraternities and sororities. (audience: college administrators)
2. Argue for laws restricting the sale of handguns or the right to bear arms. (audience: members of Congress)
3. Argue whether high government officials should have the right to personal privacy. (audience: editor of newspaper)
4. Argue whether college students should be required to take general education core courses. (audience: college administrators)
5. Argue whether the telephone solicitations should be restricted or regulated. (audience: government officials)

FROM PARAGRAPH TO ESSAY

As you've no doubt understood, writing to persuade is a complex undertaking. It requires familiarity with and facts about the subject, an understanding of your audience, and a willingness to present your argument forcefully but fairly, to appeal to reason and to human emotion. This isn't an easy task, and it probably can't be accomplished in a single paragraph. Because you'll need to develop at least three reasons to persuade your audience, give each one its own paragraph. Support each one with evidence—with examples, facts, and figures. Engage your readers in an introductory paragraph that perhaps states your thesis. Conclude your essay in a final paragraph that does more than summarize. State or restate your thesis and make a particularly strong appeal. Or tell your audience what action they should take.

The two models that follow demonstrate the different approaches you can take when you discuss a noncontroversial topic or a controversial topic.

A MODEL ESSAY: PERSUASION

Robin Roberts, a member of major league baseball's Hall of Fame, was one of the finest pitchers of his era. The following article, which appeared in Newsweek *magazine, makes a strong argument that few people have considered. As you read it, note his reasoning and evidence, as well as his appeals to the audience.*

Strike Out Little League
Robin Roberts

* * * *

1   In 1939, Little League baseball was organized by Bert and George Bebble and Carl Stotz of Williamsport, Pa. What they had in mind in organizing this kids' baseball program, I'll never know. But I'm sure they never visualized the monster it would grow into.

2   At least 25,000 teams, in about 5,000 leagues, compete for a chance to go to the Little League World Series in Williamsport each summer. These leagues are in more than fifteen countries, although recently the Little League organization has voted to restrict the competition to teams in the United States. If you judge the success of a program by the number of participants, it would appear that Little League has been a tremendous success. More than 600,000 boys from eight to twelve are involved. But I say Little League is wrong—and I'll try to explain why.

3   If I told you and your family that I want you to help me with a project from the middle of May until the end of July, one that would probably disrupt your dinner schedule and pay nothing, you would probably tell me to get lost. That's what Little League does. Mothers or fathers or both spend four or five nights a week taking children to Little League, watching the game, coming home around 8 or 8:30 and sitting down to a late dinner.

4   These games are played at this hour because the adults are running the programs and this is the only time they have available. These same adults are in most cases unqualified as instructors and do not have the emotional stability to work with children of this age. The dedication and sincerity of these instructors cannot be questioned, but the purpose of this dedication should be. Youngsters eligible for Little League are of the age when their concentration lasts, at most, for five seconds—and without sustained concentration organized athletic programs are a farce.

5   Most instructors will never understand this. As a result there is a lot of pressure on these young people to do something that is unnatural for their age—so there will always be hollering and tremendous disappointment for most of these players. For acting their age, they are made to feel incompetent. This is a basic fault of Little League.

6   If you watch a Little League game, in most cases the pitchers are the most mature. They throw harder, and if they throw strikes very few batters can hit the ball. Consequently, it makes good baseball sense for most hitters to take the pitch. Don't swing. Hope for a walk. That could be a player's instruction for four years. The fun is in hitting the ball; the coach says don't swing. That may be sound baseball, but it does nothing to help a younger player develop his hitting. What would seem like a basic training ground for baseball often turns out to be a program of negative thoughts that only retards a young player.

7   I believe more good young athletes are turned off by the pressure of organized Little League than are helped. Little Leagues have no value as a training ground for baseball fundamentals. The instruction at that age, under the pressure of an organized league program, creates more doubt and eliminates the naturalness that is most important.

8   If I'm going to criticize such a popular program as Little League, I'd better have some thoughts on what changes I would like to see.

9   First of all, I wouldn't start any programs until the school year is over. Any young student has enough of a schedule during the school year to keep busy. These programs should be played in the afternoon—with a softball. Kids have a natural fear of a baseball; it hurts when it hits you. A softball is bigger, easier to see and easier to hit. You get to run the bases more and there isn't as much danger of injury if one gets hit with the ball. Boys and girls could play together. Different teams would be chosen every day. The instructors would be young adults home from college, or high-school graduates. The instructor could be the pitcher and the umpire at the same time. These programs could be run on public playgrounds or in schoolyards.

10   I guarantee that their dinner would be at the same time every night. The fathers could come home after work and relax; most of all, the kids would have a good time playing ball in a program in which hitting the ball and running the bases are the big things.

11   When you start talking about young people playing baseball at thirteen to fifteen, you may have something. Organize them a little, but be careful; they are still young. But from sixteen and on, work with them really hard. Discipline them, organize the leagues, strive to win championships, travel all over. Give this age all the time and attention you can.

12   I believe Little League has done just the opposite. We've worked hard with the eight- to twelve-year-olds. We overorganized them, put them under pressure they can't handle and made playing baseball seem important. When our young people reach sixteen they would appreciate the attention and help from the parents, and that's when our present programs almost stop.

13   The whole idea of Little League baseball is wrong. There are alternatives available for more sensible programs. With the same dedication that has made the Little League such a major part of many of our lives, I'm sure we'll find the answer.

14   I still don't know what those three gentlemen in Williamsport had in mind when they organized Little League baseball. I'm sure they didn't want parents arguing with their children about kids' games. I'm sure they didn't want to have family meals disrupted for three months every year. I'm sure they didn't want young athletes hurting their arms pitching under pressure at such a young age. I'm sure they didn't want young boys who don't have much athletic ability to be made to feel that something is wrong with them because they can't play baseball. I'm sure

they didn't want a group of coaches drafting the players each year for different teams. I'm sure they didn't want unqualified men working with the young players. I'm sure they didn't realize how normal it is for an eight-year-old boy to be scared of a thrown or batted baseball.

15   For the life of me, I can't figure out what they had in mind.

Questions for Analysis

1. Who is the audience for this argument? What is the goal of the argument—that is, what does Roberts expect the audience to do?
2. What main problem does Robin Roberts establish for his audience? What problems does Little League create for families and children? Underline each statement of a problem.
3. What transitions introduce these problems? Bracket each transition.
4. What point does Roberts make through the comparison in the third paragraph?
5. What solution to the problem does Roberts propose? What transitional sentence introduces this solution?
6. What is the effect of the parallel sentence structure in the next-to-last paragraph?
7. Compare the first and final paragraphs of the essay. What device is Roberts using, and what is its effect?

A STUDENT MODEL ESSAY: PERSUASION

Raphael Beita, a former student at Truman College in Chicago, chose a noncontroversial subject and addresses his argument to a friendly or neutral audience. As you read his essay, note his straightforward thesis statement and the type of evidence he uses to support the thesis.

The Schick Protector
Raphael Beita

* * * *

1   If you are a man who takes pride in a closer, more comfortable, bloodless shave right after your early morning shower, then this is the shaving instrument for you! The Schick *Protector* shaving tool has become my face protector after years of ugly dried blood spots. As a former U.S. Marine, I still take pride in the closest, smoothest, cleanest shave physically possible after a hot shower. As Drill Instructor Staff Sergeant Avara used to say: "Your face should look and feel as smooth as a baby's butt!"

2   Over the last few years, it became harder for me to acquire the same results without countless, minuscule, bloody cuts all under my chin. This happened repeatedly with brand new twin razor blade cartridges, no matter how slowly I shaved. I have always believed that one should not have to spend over $150 in a quality electric shaver to avoid cuts.

3   I have tried every single shaver in the market—from inexpensive plastic disposables, to sophisticated high-end shavers. When Gillette's *Sensor Excel* came out it became my choice. It proved to be above the rest. But, little by little, the cuts on my face returned. Apparently it all depends on the manufacturing lot from which the blades come. One razor cartridge would last up to three weeks without losing its comfortable sharpness, while the next one would leave a trail of countless bloody cuts on the first use! Knowing that *Sensor Excel* was the highest

quality shaver available, I had no choice but to subject myself to the uncertainty of each individual blade cartridge.

4   The other day while waiting at the supermarket checkout line, I saw a metallic blue casing. Inside sat the most aerodynamic, sporty red shaver I had ever seen. I quickly recognized all the features of an expensive quality razor blade shaving system:

- Rubberized grip for "precise handling and control"
- Pivoting blades which "contour the face in multiple directions"
- "Ultra Glide TM" strip for smoother skin travel
- Hair-lifting forward strip to ensure closer shave
- Protective sliding cover to ensure sharpness between shaves
- Watertight blade cartridge compartment for safe refill storage
- Upright holding stand for storing the razor and refill compartment
- Safety wires to protect the skin and eliminate cuts

5   The last feature stood out from all the others. This particular shaver contained tiny safety wires running vertically across the edges of the twin blades in the shaving cartridge! A total of ten hair thin filaments vertically wrapped twin blades at ⅛-inch intervals.

6   The Schick *Protector* beats the competition in performance and price. When I tried it for the first time, I could not believe my eyes. It shaved my chin closer than Gillette's *Sensor Excel,* and with no cuts! I usually need several strokes to shave my chin. With the Schick *Protector,* one stroke was sufficient. Even after a week of continued daily use, the first of the two twin blade cartridges included continues to smoothly shave my face, and still no cuts! This represents a very good example of how a simple technological innovation can improve such an old model. Priced at $3.49, this shaver has become the best shaving instrument for everyone. If its manufacturing quality does not decline, it will remain on top for many years to come.

Questions for Analysis

1. Who is the intended audience for this essay? How does Raphael Beita connect with his audience in the first paragraph?
2. Why has Raphael been dissatisfied with other razors?
3. What initially attracts him to the Schick *Protector?*
4. What advantages does he claim this razor provides?
5. Describe, in as much detail as you can, the persuasive strategy Raphael has adopted.
6. Evaluate Raphael's argument. List his personal appeals and his references to facts and figures.
7. How has Raphael organized his essay? How else could he have organized?
8. What appeal does Raphael make in his conclusion? Does he tell the reader what to do? Why or why not?

WRITING FOR MASTERY

Essays

As this chapter has stressed, you will be most persuasive when writing on topics you care about and know well. Therefore, the first suggestion in the following list, although very general, is intended to spur your thinking about such a topic.

1. Like Raphael Beita, write a consumer review. Argue for or endorse a particular device, practice, or behavior you've found useful or effective. Address your essay to a neutral audience.

2. Like Robin Roberts, choose a policy or practice that you disagree with, something you feel is wrong or unfair. It could be something in school, in an organization you belong to, in your dormitory, or in society at large. Then compose a letter to the people most responsible for the policy (the school administration, the leaders of the organization, the governing body of the dormitory, or members of Congress), suggesting or demanding that they change the policy. Don't just criticize the existing policy; recommend specific changes.

3. Write a letter to your high school principal identifying a weakness in the high school education you received that is the fault of the school administration (not your own). Now that you're in college, you have the authority and experience to explain how high school did not prepare you. Point out the problem, and then offer a solution. In your concluding paragraph, suggest a plan for action.

4. Recommend that sex education, consumer education, environmental concerns, or evolution should or should not be taught in elementary schools. (audience: students, teachers, parents, or specific interest groups)

5. Argue whether parts of the Internet should be regulated or censored. (audience: parents of adolescents)

6. Identify a problem in your college community, and write an open letter to the student or local newspaper about it. Attempt to persuade your readers to respond to the problem as you do and take the action you recommend. The problem can be anything from pot to potholes, but it should be something you care about and would like to see changed.

CHAPTER

17 Writing Essay Exams

The essay examination is a fact of college life. In the classroom, in a limited amount of time, you must plan and write essays that demonstrate your knowledge and abilities. Tests do put you under a lot of pressure. But you can write confidently under such conditions by following the composing practices you've learned in this book. This chapter will show you how to transfer those practices to the in-class writing experience. You'll

■ examine a model essay examination answer

■ see how to prepare to write in class

■ look at the process of writing the essay

■ practice the skills involved in the process

■ apply those skills to writing essays

A Word About Words

You know what an *essay* exam is. You may be interested, then, to know what *essay* means as a verb.

Essay: 1. to put to a test 2. to make an often tentative or experimental effort to perform; try.

—*Merriam Webster's Collegiate Dictionary,* 10th ed.

A MODEL ESSAY: AN ESSAY EXAM

All writing is done for a purpose and for an audience, and the essay examination or impromptu theme is no exception. An **essay examination** *asks that you demonstrate your knowledge of the subject matter by answering test questions, in writing, in class.*

Here's an example of an essay examination question and response. Notice that it directly answers the question, sketches the outline of its organization, and develops each point specifically.

Question: In what ways were explorers of the fifteenth and sixteenth centuries like or unlike the early astronauts?

The explorers in the fifteenth and sixteenth centuries resembled astronauts in three important ways and differed from them in one important way. The similarities involved the relatively great

Continued

UNIT 3
Chapter 17

Composing with Confidence
©2003

GO ELECTRONIC!

Use the following electronic supplements for additional practice with your writing:

- For chapter-by-chapter summaries and exercises, visit the Composing with Confidence Companion Website at: http://www.ablongman.com/meyers.

- For work with the writing process, visit The Longman Writer's Warehouse at http://longmanwriterswarehouse.com (password needed).

- For additional practice in grammar, use The Writer's ToolKit Plus CD-ROM

distances both traveled, the dangers in both journeys, and the unknown conditions both faced. The difference involved the ability of the astronauts to communicate with many technicians on earth who could support their efforts. I'll discuss those similarities and differences below.

First, both the explorers and the astronauts traveled great distances, relative to the times in which they lived. In the fifteenth and sixteenth centuries, the known world was limited to Europe and parts of Asia and Africa. The longest journeys up to that point were only a few hundred miles, and most of those were over level ground or in calm seas. However, Columbus, Magellan, and other early explorers set out to travel thousands of miles in uncharted waters, using ships that were untested for journeys of that length. Similarly, before the astronauts went into space, the distance of journeys was limited to the face of the earth, which the astronauts would orbit many times during their voyages in the air or which they would leave completely as they traveled the quarter of a million miles to the moon.

A second similarity between the explorers and the astronauts is that both encountered many dangers. For the explorers, there were the high seas and storms, the possibility of meeting dangerous animals or hostile natives, and the possibility of running out of food and water far from land. For the astronauts, there were the unknown conditions of outer space, the extreme heat generated by friction as the rocket left and reentered the earth's atmosphere, and the possibility of running out of oxygen in space.

Third, both explorers and astronauts faced unknown conditions on the oceans or in outer space. The explorers took their journeys during a time of almost complete ignorance of the conditions they would face, but during a time when there were many superstitions about those conditions. While most educated people didn't believe in the possibility of sailing off the edge of the earth or being attacked by sea monsters, no one knew for sure what would happen. Furthermore, there were no accurate maps to guide the explorers, who could only estimate the distances involved (which, incidentally, turned out to be completely wrong). No one knew what the climate would be like, what food the explorers would find, or even how long the journeys would take. The astronauts knew more than the explorers: they had very precise measurements of distances to be traveled, the amount of food and oxygen they would need, and so on. Nevertheless, no one knew whether anything would happen to the body during long periods of weightlessness, whether there were objects or even living beings they would encounter in outer space or on the surface of the moon, or whether the surface of the moon would be rock hard or powdery soft. No one knew whether the moon might contain unusual types of bacteria that could be harmful to life forms on earth.

However, the astronauts had one major advantage over the early explorers: they could communicate with technicians on earth, who supported their efforts. These technicians were equipped with the most sophisticated technology available: computers, measuring devices, and so forth. Therefore, when something unexpected did happen, both the astronauts and hundreds of specialists on earth could devise ways of dealing with the problem. On the other hand, the early explorers were on their own, and many of them died or simply disappeared, never to be heard from again.

Questions for analysis

1. Compare the question and the first sentence of the response to the question. How are they similar?
2. What is the function of the first paragraph?
3. What is the function of the first sentence in each body paragraph? How do those sentences relate back to the first paragraph?
4. Underline the transitions at the beginning of each body paragraph. What function do they serve?
5. Why did the writer arrange the essay to show three similarities first, then one difference? How does this difference serve as a conclusion?
6. What grade would you give this essay? Why?

PREPARING FOR AN ESSAY EXAMINATION

How can you prepare to write on a topic you won't see until the moment it's revealed? You do so in a prewriting stage at home. It begins with studying, continues with studying, and ends with studying.

But many students don't understand how to study for an examination. They think—wrongly—that reviewing their notes and their textbook chapters is enough. The preparation should be much more systematic and thorough. Here's what to do.

Identify and Restate Main Points

As you read your textbook chapters during the term, identify the information you might need to know for the examination. Underline or highlight all of these sections:

- previews, summaries within chapters, and summaries at the ends of chapters, which state the main points of each lesson
- headings within the text (usually capitalized and in darker print), which outline the chapter for you
- the topic sentences that introduce the main ideas that support the headings and summaries

Then throughout the term, and especially before the examination, reread the underlined or highlighted material as well as your classroom notes—but don't stop there. Reread one small section at a time—perhaps four or five main points from your text or a page or more of notes. Then state the main points aloud in your own words, and do it more than once. If you can't explain the ideas the day before the examination, you certainly won't be able to do so during the examination. After restating several sections, stop to review them all until you can explain the entire body of material in your own words. You may also find it helpful to outline a chapter. The physical and mental act of transferring the author's ideas into your words will help you retain them. And, of course, study your outline until you can repeat its ideas by heart.

Many chapters end with study questions. Use them as prompts for writing practice essays, or at least outlines of essays. These should increase both your knowledge of the material and confidence in your ability to convey that knowledge.

If possible, have someone quiz you on the material. Or study with another person and take turns explaining the material to each other. Often the best way to learn a subject is by teaching it.

Memorize

Make a list of important facts and definitions to commit to memory. Citing specific information will convince your instructor that you really know your stuff—and, in fact, you do.

Help yourself out by using memory games. In a physics course, for instance, you can memorize the colors of the light spectrum by remembering the name ROY G. BIV, which stands for red, orange, yellow, green, blue, indigo, and violet. Or, in a music course, you can represent the notes of the lines of the treble clef by remembering the sentence, "Every good boy does fine," which stands for E G B D F. Make up your own phrases or sentences to represent important details.

Anticipate Questions

Study your instructor as well. Most instructors are fair, so they base their examinations primarily on material stressed in class, or on the study questions in the chapters. Instructors may even tell you what to expect on the examination, so you should practice answering typical questions. You'll feel good if you find the actual examination question similar to one you've practiced the night before.

WRITING THE ESSAY ANSWER

If you're well prepared, you should be reasonably confident and relaxed in the classroom. Keep a clear head so you can read the directions, budget your time, organize your ideas, and write, develop, and then briefly revise and edit them.

Read the Directions

As soon as your instructor hands out the directions for the examination, don't just jump right in and write. Take time to look through the entire test. Get an overview of all its parts.

Then read the specific directions and be sure to note everything the directions ask for. Underline key words. Be sure you know exactly what to do and how much time you have to do it in. For example, the directions may tell you to compare two concepts or things. If you simply write about both without comparing them, your grade will suffer.

Budget Your Time

Determine how much time you can devote to each question on the examination. Most directions indicate how much each question is worth, so a typical three-part exam might divide its 100-point total in this manner:

Part I   20 points
Part II   40 points
Part III   40 points

If you budget the time in a fifty-minute class period according to those percentages, you'd allow yourself ten minutes for the first part and twenty minutes for each of the second and third parts.

Stick to those time limits. Don't spend half the class period answering a question worth twenty points, then try to earn eighty points in the second half of the period.

Answer the Easiest Question First

On an essay examination, start with the question you can answer most comfortably. It will help you overcome your test-taking jitters and probably make you more confident when answering the other questions. You'll also invest your time wisely, earning full credit for what you know, instead of partial credit because you didn't have time to show your stuff.

Organize Your Response

Even though you're writing in class, you'll still be using the methods of development you've practiced throughout this book. The language of the examination question should reveal the method of development. Underline the verbs and key words in the question. Try it with this example:

> Define the terms *synchronous* and *asynchronous communication* on the Internet and compare the advantages and disadvantages of each.

Did you underline *define* and *compare?* These familiar verbs suggest the two methods of paragraph development to employ in your answer. But, since the two types of communication apparently have both advantages and disadvantages, a rough outline of your answer would take this form:

> I. Definition of synchronous and asynchronous communication
>
> II. Advantages and disadvantages of synchronous
>
> III. Advantages and disadvantages of asynchronous

You'll often find familiar verbs that reveal the method of development needed to answer other examination questions, but not always. In fact, the question or topic sometimes implies rather than states the method of development. Here's a short list of synonyms for the verbs and phrases you already know:

KEY TERMS IN TEST DIRECTIONS

Familiar verb	Synonyms
Describe	(from, happened because of)? Trace the results, show, indicate, discuss, summarize.
Narrate	Tell, trace the development of (or history of), explain. What happened?
Analyze (a process)	Explain, describe, or discuss (especially with the phrases *the process of* or *the steps in*). How does it work?
Compare	Show the similarities, draw parallels, make a comparison. How are they alike (similar)? What are the similarities between?
Contrast	Show the differences, establish the points of difference. How are they different? What are the differences between?
Compare and contrast	Evaluate, judge, show (explain) the similarities and differences between.
Define	Explain the meaning of, identify. What is the meaning of?
Classify	Identify, group, categorize. What are the kinds (types) of?
Illustrate	Provide (cite) examples (illustrations, instances) of, exemplify, demonstrate.
Show causes	Explain (trace) the reasons (causes). What created (brought about, produced, gave rise to, led to, determined)? What are the reasons for?
Show effects	What were the results of (resulted from, sprung)?

Plan Your Essay

Remember: *you won't have time to revise the essay,* so you need to plan it carefully. Spend a few minutes structuring your ideas. Jot down or outline the main points you wish to cover—on the back of the exam booklet, on the instruction sheet, or on a piece of scratch paper (if the instructor allows you to use one). Then follow the outline as you write. Skip this step only when you're sure of your organization and can begin writing immediately.

Draft the Essay

Once you've settled on an approach and an outline to follow, you can write the essay itself. Because time is limited, you must handle each step efficiently, with almost no changes of mind or plan.

Begin with a Thesis Statement.   Your instructor will be reading many booklets or essays—and probably reading them quickly. So make your main points almost jump off the page. Begin your answer with a straightforward thesis statement (or topic sentence for a one-paragraph answer) and, if possible, a preview.

Use the language of the question or topic as your guide. You can often repeat much of that language in your opening sentence, as in this example:

> Question: What were the major stages of the civil rights movement in the 1950s and 1960s?
>
> Opening sentence of essay: There were three major stages of the civil rights movement in the 1950s and 1960s.

If possible, add a preview of your answer to the thesis statement:

> There were three major stages of the civil rights movement in the 1950s and 1960s: (1) early legal challenges to discrimination in the early and mid-1950s, (2) nonviolent protests in the first part of the 1960s, and (3) the Black Power movement of the mid- and late 1960s.

Label Each Important Point.   Whether or not you include a preview, you can still highlight the main points of your essay. Begin each paragraph with a topic sentence and transition. Here are the opening sentences for the body paragraphs of the essay on the civil rights movement:

> The first stage of the civil rights movement, which took the form of legal challenges to unjust laws, occurred in the early and mid-1950s.
>
> The second stage, at the beginning of the 1960s, was characterized by nonviolent protests against both unjust laws and unofficial practices of discrimination throughout the South.
>
> The third stage, the Black Power movement, occurred in the mid- and late 1960s.

There's nothing fancy about these topic sentences; they repeat much of the language of the preview. But they clearly identify each main point in your essay while helping you maintain control of your answer as you compose quickly.

Conclude with a Wrap-up.   Last impressions count. By the time you finish answering the essay question, you should be able to pull together all your thoughts into a strong summary or powerful conclusion. It will reinforce what you've said and maybe even call attention to a point your instructor may have missed in reading through your answer.

Edit and Proofread.   You've budgeted a few minutes at the end of the class period to read over your essay. Now force yourself to do it. You may discover

TIPS

For If You Run Out of Time

What can you do if you don't have time to finish your essay? Take another minute to jot an outline of the main points you wanted to include. This will show the instructor that you studied and could have said more. Many instructors will give full or partial credit for this outline.

phrases that make no sense or remember things you should have said. Cross out the errors and write above the lines or in the margins. Instructors expect such revisions and won't penalize you for them. But do try to make your work legible.

GETTING READY TO WRITE AN EXAM

The following warm-up exercises will give you practice in writing essay examination answers, as well as leading you into the actual writing of one or more answers.

EXERCISE 1	Preparing for the Examination

Read the following textbook passages several times, and then restate their main points (including definitions of important terms) in your own words. Try not to look back at a passage until you have restated as many points as possible.

Passage A (from a psychology textbook):

Paragraph 1: Although there is much that psychologists do not know about memory, they are fairly well agreed that there are three different memory systems within the overall system of remembering and recalling information: sensory memory, short-term memory, and long-term memory. Sensory memory preserves fleeting impressions of sensory stimuli—sights, sounds, smells, and textures—for only a second or two. Short-term memory includes recollections of what we have recently perceived; such limited information lasts only up to twenty seconds unless special attention is paid to it or it is reinstated by rehearsal. Long-term memory preserves information for retrieval at any later time—up to an entire lifetime. Information in long-term memory constitutes our knowledge about the world.

Restatement: There are three basic types of memory: (1) sensory memory—very short impressions of sights, sounds, and the like; (2) short-term memory—slightly longer memories of what we see or hear; (3) and long-term memory—those things that we can remember even throughout our lives and that give us our real knowledge of life.

Paragraph 2: For examples of these three kinds of memories, imagine that as you are passing a movie theater, you notice a distinctive odor and hear loud sounds from inside (fleeting sensory memories). When you get home you decide to check the time of the next show, so you look up the theater's number and then dial the seven digits. Your short-term memory holds these digits for a brief period between looking up the number and dialing it; however, you will probably have to look up the number again if the line is busy because your memory of the number will fade very soon unless you work at remembering it. Once you are given the show times, you will have to rely on your long-term memory to get you to the theater on time.

Restatement: _____

_____

_____

_____

Paragraph 3: These three memory systems are also thought of as stages in the sequence of processing information. They differ not only in how much information they can hold and how long they can hold it but also in how they process it. Memories that get into long-term storage have passed through the sensory and short-term stages first. In each stage, the information has been processed in ways that made it eligible for getting into the next one. Sense impressions become ideas or images; these, in turn, are organized into patterns that fit into existing networks in our long-term memory.

Restatement: _____

_____

_____

_____

Passage B (end-of-chapter terms summary from a business textbook):

1. A *business* is a competitive, profit-seeking organization that produces and sells goods or services.

2. *Goods and services* are produced by transforming inputs into outputs. The most basic inputs are the factors of production: labor, capital, and natural resources.

3. *Profits* are calculated by subtracting a firm's costs from the revenues it brings in by selling the goods or services it produces. To earn a profit, a firm must turn inputs into outputs that are worth more than the inputs were worth at the beginning. Profits serve a number of useful functions: they signal the best places to put resources to work, provide incentives to use resources wisely, and screen out mistakes.

Restatement: _____

_____

_____

_____

4. All firms compete both in selling outputs and in buying inputs. A firm that faces no competitors in the marketplace where it sells its outputs is called a *monopoly.* In the real world, pure cases of monopoly are rare, if they exist at all.

5. Successful competition requires a constant search for product improvements and better production techniques. The art of competition is known as *entrepreneurship.*

Competition is not limited to business firms. Not-for-profit firms and government agencies also compete, both in buying outputs and in serving clients.

6. Business managers have a duty to obey the law and to fulfill the terms of contracts they enter into. They have a duty to earn as much profit as they can for the owners of their firms. Businesses have responsibilities toward the environment, employees, and consumers.

7. The major responsibility of government toward business and society is to establish a set of rules that minimize conflicts between profits and social responsibility. Ideally, a business would be able to do well only by doing good.

Restatement: _____

_____

_____

_____

EXERCISE 2 Anticipating Questions

Return to the textbook passages from Exercise 1 and formulate three or four questions based on each passage using one of the following methods of development: description, process analysis, cause-effect, comparison-contrast, definition, or classification.

Passage A:

1. Define and illustrate the three types of memory.

2. _____

3. _____

4. _____

Passage B:

1. Describe the process of calculating the profits of a business.

2. _____

3. _____

4. _____

EXERCISE 3 Outlining Essays

After each of the following questions, write a thesis statement. Then, based on the information supplied as well as your own knowledge of the subject, write several topic sentences introducing main points.

1. Identify the three branches of the U.S. government and explain the role of each.

a. legislative branch (Congress): makes laws

b. executive branch (president and cabinet departments): enforces laws

c. judiciary branch (the courts): interprets laws

Thesis statement: _____

_____

Topic sentences: _____

_____

_____

_____

_____

2. Contrast the reproduction system of a single-celled organism with that of a mammal.

    a. sexual differentiation: none in single-celled organism, male and female in mammals

    b. sexual mating: none in single-celled organism

    c. birth: single-celled organism duplicates itself, mammal produces embryo/infant

Thesis statement: _____

_____

Topic sentences: _____

_____

_____

_____

_____

3. Discuss the role of advertising in marketing a new product, using one such product as an example.

    a. create consumer awareness

    b. establish need for product

    c. differentiate product from others

Thesis statement: _____

_____

Topic sentences: _____

_____

_____

_____

_____

ESSAY WRITING ASSIGNMENT

Choose one of the examination questions from Exercise 3 and write a full answer to it. Don't worry about getting all the facts right; concentrate on clear organization and development. Be sure to begin with the thesis statement and add a preview of the main ideas if possible. Use a topic sentence at the beginning of each paragraph in the body of your answer. Conclude with a wrap-up. Don't write for longer than half an hour.

Give yourself five or ten minutes for the analysis and revision. Quickly reread the examination answer and respond to each of the questions in the Revision Guidelines below—not in writing but in your head. Use the responses for revising your answer, and then make the revisions above the lines and in the margins.

REVISION GUIDELINES | Answering Essay Questions

1. Is the thesis statement clear? If not, how should it be revised?
2. Is the method of development logical? Is its organization clear? If the organization is not clear, what transitions are needed?
3. Are the main ideas supported with details and examples? If not, what details or examples could you add quickly?
4. Is the meaning of every sentence clear? If not, what should be revised?
5. Does the essay conclude with a summary of the main points?

WRITING FOR MASTERY

Essays

Use any of the following examination questions for more practice in identifying specific instructions, outlining answers, writing thesis statements and topic sentences, or (if you are familiar with the subjects) writing examination answers themselves.

1. What major effects did the Crusades have on religious practices, everyday life, and the relationship between the nobility and serfs during the Middle Ages?
2. Explain the process by which the quadratic equation is derived.
3. Compare the views of the Imperialists with those of the Anti-Imperialists before and after the Spanish-American War of 1898.
4. Define and describe the process of *photosynthesis.*
5. What are the major effects of insufficient sensory stimulation of infants? Describe each.
6. Compare and contrast *common stock* and *preferred stock.*
7. What are the *humanities,* and why are they important?

18 Writing on the Job

The key part of the word *business* is *busy*. In the world of work, people don't have the time to read long letters that wander around the point. Workplace writing must be short, clear, and precise. This chapter will give you some advice and some examples. You'll gain some insights into the writing that will get you a job in the first place and the writing you'll most likely need on the job. You'll

- examine a job application letter
- develop a résumé
- prepare a memo

WRITING IN THE WORLD OF WORK

You need to get down to business in the business world. Your correspondence—letters, résumé, memos, and e-mails—must be direct and to the point. Audience, purpose, and occasion are critically important: you must be able to assess the concerns of your reader, state and develop your point directly, and do so in the format that your reader expects.

Since things happen fast in the world of work, you must be able to draft and revise your correspondence quickly. The steps in the composing process get compressed. But editing and proofreading your work are essential; success on the job—not just a grade in a course—is at stake. Most businesses won't tolerate errors in correspondence going out to their clients, or even to the managers and coworkers within the organization.

Therefore, the time to become proficient in the writing process is now—while you're in college—so you can compose with confidence as you make the transition to the world of work.

UNIT 3

Chapter 18

Composing with Confidence
©2003

GO ELECTRONIC!

Use the following electronic supplements for additional practice with your writing:

- For chapter-by-chapter summaries and exercises, visit the *Composing with Confidence* Companion Website at: http://www.ablongman.com/meyers.
- For work with the writing process, visit *The Longman Writer's Warehouse* at http://longmanwriterswarehouse.com (password needed).
- For additional practice in grammar, use *The Writer's ToolKit Plus CD-ROM*

THE JOB APPLICATION LETTER

The **job application letter** (and accompanying résumé, which we'll discuss later in this chapter) won't get you a job; its purpose is to get you in the door for a job interview. Therefore, the letter must be clear and direct, reflecting your confidence and professionalism—or at least your ability to work and learn while working. Its tone must be confident but not arrogant. And it must be error free. When fields of applicants are crowded, those reviewing the applications are looking for people to eliminate, and grammatical errors or typos are likely to do just that.

The letter itself follows the model for virtually all business correspondence. The first paragraph should make clear why you are writing and introduce the most important information your reader needs to know. The body of the letter should state your major points, with each paragraph unified around a single idea. And the conclusion should reinforce your message and ask the reader to respond in some way.

Begin the job application letter by identifying the title or position you're applying for and where you learned about it, including the date and location of the advertisement or notice. Then introduce your thesis: a statement of your ability to do the job.

In the body of your letter, supply information about your qualifications: relevant degrees or courses you've completed, and jobs you've had or still have. Each of your body paragraphs should discuss one aspect of your qualifications: your work history; your education; and your special talents, experiences, and personality traits. Emphasize your strong points and show how they relate to the job you're applying for.

Conclude the letter by saying that you have enclosed your résumé. State when you're available for an interview and how you can be contacted.

Here's an example of the job application letter. Note that all its elements are single spaced, with double spaces between paragraphs. Note also that the letter is brief, its tone is confident, and each paragraph focuses on a single point.

✓ **TIPS**

For Formatting a Business Letter

Most word processing programs include default style sheets and templates for use in business letter writing, résumés, and memos. You can examine the style sheets in the lists and previews and then choose one to use.

Heading with return address

```
Alex Johnson
1145 N. Maple Street
Columbus, OH   43227
```

Date

```
June 9, 2003
```

Name, title, and address

```
Julie Smith
Personnel Director
Acme Pharmaceuticals
10 W. Broad Street
Columbus, OH   43251
```

Salutation

```
Dear Ms. Smith:
```

Opening paragraph identifies the job the writer is applying for, where the information about the job was found, and the writer's thesis.

```
I am writing in response to your advertisement for a pharma-
ceutical trainee in the Columbus Daily Journal on Sunday, June
7. I believe that my academic background and previous experi-
ence make me highly qualified for this position.
```

Second paragraph summarizes and highlights academic experience.

```
I have completed my A.S. degree with honors from Columbus
Technical College. My study has included a variety of courses
in the sciences, including organic chemistry and microbiology.
```

I have also taken several computer courses and am familiar with database programs such as *Excel* and *Access*. In addition to my course work, I participated in several service learning projects involving health care for young children.

Third paragraph summarizes job experience.

My job experience has greatly familiarized me with the pharmaceutical industry. While putting myself through school over the past three years, I worked part-time as a pharmacy technician at Walgreen's, and last year I passed my certification examination. My supervisors always complimented me on my work and rewarded me with frequent raises in salary.

Fourth paragraph makes clear when the applicant can be interviewed and how he can be reached.
Fifth paragraph concludes on a positive, confident note.

I have enclosed a résumé for your consideration. I am available for an interview every afternoon except Fridays. You may reach me at 999-555-1234 or by e-mail at ajohnson@aol.com.

Thank you for your consideration. I look forward to hearing from you soon.

Conventional closing, which leaves space for signature and name typed beneath.

Sincerely yours,

Alex Johnson

Alex Johnson
List of enclosures.   Enc.: Résumé

EXERCISE 1   Composing a Job Application Letter

Consult the help wanted section of your local newspaper (Sunday has the largest number of job listings), and choose one listing that you might like to apply for. (The closer the job fits your real employment goals, the better.) Then compose the job application letter.
Revise the letter several times so it is clear, well organized, and confident sounding. Then proofread the final draft to ensure that it is error free.

THE RÉSUMÉ

TIPS

For Formatting a Résumé
Most word processing programs also contain—you guessed it—default style sheets for résumé. So you can select the one with the categories and layout you find most appropriate and attractive.

A **résumé** is an outline. In separate categories, it lists information about your education, previous jobs, other experiences, and personal interests. There's no set format for a résumé, so you should include the information most relevant to the job you want, emphasizing your strengths and accomplishments. For example, if you have paid for your college education or worked in a similar job, include this information.

You can list the information on your résumé in **reverse chronological order**, beginning with your more recent educational and work experience and working backward. Or you can list the information in **emphatic order**, first presenting the job or educational experience that will most impress your prospective employer. But in either case, try to limit the résumé to one page so potential employers can get a quick overview, and include the following sections:

- A *heading*, that includes your name, address, telephone number, and e-mail address

- An (optional) *statement of your career objective*—that is, the kind of job you would like to have
- An *education section*, including all the schools you've attended (excluding high school) and degrees you've earned or will be earning
- An *employment section*, including your most recent job and moving backwards
- An *activities, interests, or special skills section*, listing your most important interests, volunteer work, membership in organizations, travels—anything you feel will set you apart from other job applicants
- An optional *awards or honors section*—depending on whether you've received any special recognition
- A *reference section*, listing the names and addresses of at least three people who can recommend you (if your résumé is already one page long, you may simply state that the references are available upon request)

Begin the composing process for the résumé by brainstorming. What schools have you attended? What activities have you participated in? What honors or awards have you received? What skills or talents do you have? What experiences have you had that set you apart from others? While the basic categories of a résumé are fairly set—education, job experience, awards, and honors—you can create categories that highlight your qualifications and experiences: for example, if you have been in the military, list that under a separate heading; or if you've traveled extensively or lived in other countries, list that under separate headings. Be creative so you set yourself apart from the other job applicants.

Here's an example, arranged in emphatic order with the objectives stated first and the most relevant work history following. Notice that all dates are chronological, beginning with the most recent:

Alex Johnson
1145 N. Maple Street
Columbus, OH 43227
999-555-1234
ajohnson@aol.com

Objective
To obtain entry-level employment with a pharmaceutical company that offers opportunities for additional training and professional growth

Education
2003 A.S. Degree with Honors, Columbia Technical College
  Major: Pre-pharmacy

Relevant Work History
Walgreen Drugs, 1111 W. Main Street, Columbus, Ohio,
  2000-present, Pharmacy Technician, certified in 2003
Wal-mart, 2222 W. Broadway, Columbus, Ohio, 1998-2000, stock
  boy in pharmacy department

Other Work History
Municipal Pool, Columbus, Ohio, 1997-1999, Lifeguard
Wilkens Day Camp, Columbus, Ohio, Summer 1996, Assistant
  Counselor

Activities and Awards
Vice President, Chemistry Club, Columbus Technical College,
    2002
Service Learning Coordinator, Columbus Boys and Girls Club,
    2002
Dean's List, 2001-2002

Interests and Special Skills
Proficiency on both PC and Macintosh in Word, Excel, and
    Access, as well as Photoshop and Quark Express
Photography, Computer Graphics

References
Available upon request

EXERCISE 2	Preparing a Résumé

Compose a résumé that targets the same job listing you selected for Exercise 1, Revise—and edit—the final product so it is absolutely clear and error free. And do the final draft on a computer. If you are entering a profession, then make your work look professional.

THE BUSINESS MEMO

Once you have a job, you'll be writing and receiving memos: messages of a paragraph or two—or even longer if necessary—that report on activities, make proposals, or ask for clarification or changes in procedures. All memos are public records, not just chat among friends, so they should be clear and direct. As you write the memo, think of how you would make an important phone call. Consider what needs to be said—and what does not.

Audience, purpose, and occasion play important roles in memos. Some memos are to a single person in the organization, while other memos are to a group of people. If you write to a supervisor or manager, your memo will be formal. But if you write to coworkers on less important topics, the memo can be conversational. And because the purpose of the memo must be apparent, you must state that purpose or main point first. Depending on your subject matter and purpose, you may structure the memo to explain a process (Chapter 11), draw comparisons and contrasts (Chapter 12), make classifications (Chapter 13), examine causes or effects (Chapter 15), and—especially—persuade an audience (Chapter 16).

No matter what case, however, the memo deserves some planning, drafting, editing, and proofreading. It does, after all, carry your name; it places you on public display.

The format of a memo always includes these elements:

- A heading with four categories:
  1. The person(s) receiving the memo
  2. The person sending the memo
  3. The subject of the memo
  4. The date of the memo

A Word About Words

The business and scientific world uses many terms specific to individual fields (as many as 5–10 million technical and scientific terms). You'll probably learn a lot of new words in the workplace—words not found in a typical dictionary.

TIPS

For Formatting a Memo
Aside from style sheets for memos, many word processors also contain an autotext feature that allows you to retain the information contained in the heading so you can reuse it.

- The opening sentence, which clearly states the main point of the memo
- The body of the memo, which should include short paragraphs or bulleted items
- The conclusion, which either specifies the action the reader should take or ends on a positive note

For example, a formal memo to a supervisor might include the full name and title of both the person who wrote it and the person receiving it. But an informal memo to coworkers announcing plans for an office party might simply include your and their first names.

Here are two sample memos, one formal, the other informal:

Formal Memo

Acme Pharmaceuticals
Columbus, OH

Heading

To: All Employees
From: Ricardo M. Garcia, Senior Vice President
Subject: New Parking Regulations
Date: October 30, 2003

Opening sentence, stating purpose of the memo

Due to several recent accidents in the parking lot, we are enacting the following new regulations effective immediately.

Body, with bulleted main points

- Speed limits in the parking lot will be reduced to 20 mph.
- Cars exiting from the east side of the lot must yield to cars going north. A traffic officer will be present at the beginning and end of the workday to facilitate this change in traffic flow.
- No left turns will be permitted onto Reagan Blvd. Cars will be permitted to turn left only at the stoplight one block west of the building.
- SUVs and vans will use the right lane only so as not to block the view of drivers in conventional cars.

Conclusion, ending on positive note.

We realize that these new policies will cause some inconvenience, but we hope they will lead to a safer environment as we enter and leave the parking area.

Informal Memo

Heading, using only first names

To: Judy, Elisha, Raphael, Jonnie, Michelle, Laverne, Charlie, and Sung Hee
From: Alex
Subject: Holiday Party
Date: December 11, 2003

Opening paragraph, with main point stated in first sentence	As we've already discussed, let's get together for dinner and fun at my place on December 22, perhaps around 8:00 P.M. Bring your spouse, your significant other, or a guest. Or just come alone; the main thing is that we relax and enjoy the occasion.
Body, with specific actions requested stated on separate lines	I'll supply the main course, but I'm hoping you can all pitch in and bring the other things. Let's divide up the responsibilities this way:
	People whose last name begins with "a" through "g," bring hors d'oeuvres.
	People whose last name begins with "h" through "o," bring something to drink (soda, wine, or beer is fine).
	People whose last name begins with "p" through the end of the alphabet, bring a dessert—nothing too fancy.
Conclusion, stating final action requested	Let me know by December 15 if you can attend so we can plan accordingly

---

EXERCISE 3	Writing a Memo

Choose an issue that you'd like to discuss with a classmate, the entire class, or your instructor: for example, the best time to meet and study together, request for advice on formatting an assignment, an invitation to a campus gathering, and so on.

Then, if you wish, actually send the memo to the intended audience.

TYPES OF PARAGRAPHS AND ESSAYS

Description

NARRATION

PROCESS ANALYSIS

Comparison and contrast

Classification

Definition

Causes or effects

Persuasion

WAYS TO ORGANIZE

Spatial order

Chronological order

Sequential order

Climax order

Part-to-part
or
whole-to-whole

TYPES OF TRANSITIONS

To show space:
over, above, at the bottom, next to, in the center, to the right

To show time:
after, before, later, the next day, soon, then, a month later

To show sequence:
first, second, then, next, after, finally

To show comparison and contrast:
like, similarly, in the same way, unlike, by contrast,
on the one hand . . . on the other hand

To establish classification categories:
first, second, finally

To elaborate on a definition:
(example) for instance, for example
(contrasts) although, however
(historical process) as a result, consequently, afterward

To heighten causes or effects:
because, since, as a result, consequently

To support persuasion:
(concession) of course, no doubt
(qualification) perhaps, probably
(results) therefore, consequently
(citing an authority) according to, as _____ says or demonstrates

IV
Troubleshooting

Previous units of this book have discussed the composing process, ways of strengthening, and ways of organizing and developing paragraphs. This final unit addresses grammar, punctuation, and the mechanics of written presentation. You may want to study the whole unit, just individual chapters, or even the parts of the chapters that cover your particular concerns. You may also use the unit as a reference as issues arise.

Specifically, the chapters will troubleshoot the following matters:

1. Making sentences complete
2. Joining sentences correctly, logically, and gracefully
3. Getting the forms right for nouns and verbs
4. Getting the forms right for pronouns
5. Maintaining consistency in word forms and sentence structures
6. Gaining control over apostrophes, hyphens, and capitalization
7. Mastering punctuation marks
8. Keeping the sound-alike and look-alike words straight

Take what you need from the unit so your writing will exhibit the polish and clarity that inspire confidence.■

19 Writing Complete Sentences

You've already seen, in Chapter 7, how to make sentences strong. But no sentence will be strong, no matter how streamlined, specific, and original, unless it's also complete. It takes a complete sentence to express a complete idea. This chapter shows you how to make sure your sentences are complete. It examines

■ how to recognize whether a sentence is complete

■ ways to fix fragments—or incomplete sentences

WHAT IS A SENTENCE?

Most of the time, even without realizing it, you express your ideas in complete sentences. Every **sentence** makes a complete statement, and that's the only way people can make sense of what you say. There are two main parts of a sentence, which together are called a **clause**:

• a **subject** (someone or something that the sentence discusses)
• a **predicate** (the discussion of the subject, beginning with a verb)

A **fragment** is an incomplete statement—only a partial sentence. Many fragments are missing a subject, verb, or some other part of the predicate. Some fragments contain a subject and predicate but are incomplete for reasons we'll explore later in this chapter.

Some writers employ an occasional fragment for emphasis and variety—if its meaning is clear in the context of other sentences. But if you write unintentional fragments, you may be confusing or annoying your readers. Why, then, do these fragments occur? There are several reasons:

• You may be struggling to express yourself and therefore produce awkward and unnatural expressions—half thoughts in half sentences.
• You may punctuate (or mispunctuate) by ear, hearing a pause and marking the pause with a period—signaling the end of a sentence that hasn't ended.

A Word About Words

In fact, the words *sentence* and *sense* come from the same root word, which entered English from French and Latin and means a *perception* or a *meaning*.

GO ELECTRONIC!

Use the following electronic supplements for additional practice with your writing:

• For chapter-by-chapter summaries and exercises, visit the Composing with Confidence Companion Website at: http://www.ablongman.com/meyers.

• For work with the writing process, visit The Longman Writer's Warehouse at http://longmanwriterswarehouse.com (password needed).

• For additional practice in grammar, use The Writer's ToolKit Plus CD-ROM

- You may be omitting subjects or writing only partial verbs.
- You may not know how to correctly use joining words such as *because, although,* or *which.*

You can work on eliminating fragments, therefore, by following these steps:

1. Choose a topic that you feel comfortable discussing, and write and revise the draft several times.
2. Read the paper out loud and listen for only partially expressed ideas. This practice helps—but don't rely on it completely. Remember: many fragments occur because writers mispunctuate, placing periods where commas should go.
3. Revise once again, this time identifying the subjects and verbs of each statement and examining the way you punctuate them. This chapter will show you how to revise in this way. Practice, and with experience, you'll compose complete sentences even in first drafts.

Identifying Subjects

Since every sentence contains at least one complete clause, you should learn to identify the subject and verb of every clause. And since subjects and verbs must go together, you can most easily identify the subject when you look for the verb at the same time.

For a moment, however, let's look at the subject. The subject

- tells *who* or *what* the predicate makes a statement about
- usually (but not always) comes *at or near the beginning of a sentence*—before the verb, which begins the predicate and tells what the subject *does* or *is*
- is often a **noun**—a person, place, idea, or thing
- or a **subject pronoun**—a word that replaces a noun

Subject (who or what) + *verb*

For example, the following sentence makes a statement about *Deborah Sampson.* Notice that the verb *was* begins the predicate, or statement about the subject:

Deborah Sampson was a very unusual Revolutionary War heroine.

Underline the subjects at the beginning of each of the following sentences:

1. Miss Sampson was born in Plympton, Massachusetts, on December 17, 1760.
2. She came from a long line of Puritans, all the way back to the *Mayflower.*
3. However, her father had lost all of his money and deserted the family.
4. Deborah and her mother could not survive on their own.
5. Teaching infant school became Deborah's only alternative.

Are these the words and phrases you underlined? Each one reveals an important trait about subjects.

1. <u>Miss Sampson</u> (This subject is a **proper noun**—a name that is capitalized.)
2. <u>She</u> (This is a **subject pronoun**. The complete list includes *I, we, you, he, she, it,* and *they.*)
3. <u>father</u> (This subject is a **common noun**—a noun that is not a name and therefore is not capitalized. Note that the possessive word, *her,* is technically not part of the subject.)
4. <u>Deborah</u> and her <u>mother</u> (These are two subjects joined by *and.*)

5. <u>Teaching</u> (This subject is an *-ing word*—a verb turned into a noun.)

Note that these sentences contain many other nouns and pronouns that don't function as subjects. These other nouns and verbs aren't in the subject position—before the verb—and the sentences don't make statements about them.

EXERCISE 1	Identifying Subjects

Underline the subjects of each of the following sentences.

1. <u>Deborah Sampson</u> taught for a short time in an infant school.

2. Nonetheless, she longed to travel and see the world.

3. Freedom was her goal—the kind of freedom only allowed young men.

4. Therefore, she decided upon a bold project.

5. A tailor made her a gentleman's suit.

6. In this disguise, Deborah went to a nearby village and enlisted in the Continental Army under the name of Timothy Thayer.

7. That night, her joyous drinking and loud singing in a tavern caused a scene.

8. Out of embarrassment, she crept back home, hid her man's suit, and resumed her post as a schoolteacher.

9. The authorities found her and made her refund her army pay.

Identifying Verbs

Now let's turn our attention to the verbs in clauses. A **verb**

- usually comes right after the subject and begins the predicate (that is, the statement about the subject)
- tells what the subject *does* (an action verb) or *is* (a *be* verb)
- often has a tense (past, present, future, and so on)
- can be a **phrase**—a group of two or more words

Action Verbs. An **action verb** expresses the action of the subject. Here are some examples in a variety of tenses and in two-word, three-word, and four-word phrases:

Subject: Tom
Verbs: works, slept, walked, is talking, will go, could have driven, should have been working

Locate and circle the action verbs in each of the following sentences.

1. Deborah's neighbors ridiculed her behavior.
2. They were criticizing her behind her back and to her face.
3. She didn't like the criticism.
4. Deborah wanted to avoid embarrassment.
5. Therefore, she again dressed herself as a male and left.
6. She went to the coast, looking for a job on a ship.

TIPS

For Identifying Fragments

Change the tense of the verb: *Original (a sentence)* Deborah Sampson *served* in the Revolutionary War.

With tense change: Deborah Sampson *serves* in the Revolutionary War.

If the change sounds more like Martian than English, perhaps you've found a sentence fragment.

Original (a fragment) Deborah Sampson in her *fighting* gear.

With tense change: Deborah Sampson in her *fought* gear. [huh??!!]

Are these the words you circled? Again, each reveals a trait about action verbs:

1. <u>ridiculed</u> (a *past-tense* verb)
2. <u>were criticizing</u> (a *two-word verb phrase*)
3. <u>did</u> . . . <u>like</u> (The adverb *not* comes between these words.)
4. <u>wanted</u> (Did you circle *to avoid?* See below.)
5. <u>dressed</u> . . . <u>and left</u> (There are two action verbs, joined by the word *and.*)
6. <u>went</u> (Did you circle *looking?* See below.)

Sentence 4: *To avoid,* an action word preceded by *to,* is an **infinitive**. It's formed from a verb but cannot function as a verb.

Sentence 6: *Looking,* an *–ing* word that's also formed from a verb, can't function as a verb either—with one exception, which we'll discuss shortly.

Although infinitives and *–ing* words are formed from verbs, they normally function as other parts of speech. (Remember "Teaching infant school" in Sentence 5 of the sample sentences for subjects? *Teaching* serves as a noun in that sentence.) So pay attention to infinitives and *–ing* words. Confusing them with verbs is a major cause of sentence fragments.

Helping Verbs.   Remember that verbs can be phrases—groups of two, three, or even four words. The last word of the phrase is called the **main verb**; it conveys the main action. The words preceding the main verb are called **helping verbs**; these help the main verb express its meaning in a variety of tenses and circumstances. In the examples below, the main verb is *go,* and there are one, two, and three helping verbs:

go	am going	will be going	must have been going
goes	is going	would have gone	should have been going
went	has gone	might be going	could have been gone
	did(n't) go	must be going	would have been gone
	may go	may be going	
	will go	could be going	
	had gone	might have gone	

Here's the one exception to the rule about about *–ing* words. They can be verbs—*if and only if* some form of the helping verb *to be* precedes them:

is going, am going, are going, was going, were going, will be going, etc.

Collaborative Activity 1

Writing Verbs—and Sentences

Write ten action verbs. Then exchange lists by passing to the left. Write a complete sentence for each verb, pass your list to the left, and check over the list. Discuss any problems in the full group.

EXERCISE 2   Identifying Subjects and Action Verbs

Underline the subjects and circle the complete action verbs in each of the following sentences. Some of the verbs can be helping verbs; circle them twice.

1. A boat <u>captain</u> (offered) Deborah a job as a waiter.

2. But his friendliness on land changed to cruelty at sea.

3. She quit the job and continued northward.

4. After arriving in Bellingham, Massachusetts, she enlisted in the Continental Army again and used the first and second names of her brother, Robert Shurtleff Sampson.

5. Her second enlistment began on May 20, 1782.

6. By that time, the war had practically ended.

7. Consequently, new recruits did not expect to receive combat assignments.

EXERCISE 3	Writing Sentences

Compose five sentences of your own using at least one helping verb, along with any of the following verbs: stumble, smile, wish, come, wiggle, hold, need, like, sleep, take, buzz, holler, snuggle.

1. _____

_____

2. _____

_____

3. _____

_____

4. _____

_____

5. _____

_____

Linking Verbs (or *Be* Verbs).   Some verbs do not express action. Instead, they link the subject to words that describe or name the subject in some way. The most important linking verb is *to be* (*is, am, are, was, were*). The others represent the five senses (*look, smell, taste, feel, sound*) and also include *become, appear, seem, remain, get, act,* and *stay.* Here are examples:

Subject	Linking verb	Descriptive words
Tom	*is, was, will be, became, stayed, remained*	a doctor/sad.
Judith	*appears, became, got, seems, acts, looks, feels, sounds*	sad.
The soup	*tastes, smelled*	bad.

EXERCISE 4	Identifying Linking Verbs

Underline the subjects and circle the linking verbs (some also have helping verbs, so circle those, too) in each of the following sentences.

1. Private Deborah's <u>uniform</u> (was) a handsome blue coat with white trimmings.

2. In it, she appeared quite masculine.

3. Her normal female bulges looked flat in their tight corsets.

4. Her movements were quick and strong.

5. Her deep voice sounded manly.

6. Thus, she felt quite confident in her disguise.

EXERCISE 5	Composing Sentences

Write five sentences with a different linking verb in each, followed by any of these descriptive words or phrases: weird, wet, a bit strange, embarrassing, impossible to understand, dazzling, uncontrollable, 300 pounds overweight, impressive, challenging, cuddly, affectionate. *You may add additional words to the predicate.*

1. _____

_____

2. _____

_____

3. _____

_____

4. _____

_____

5. _____

_____

EXERCISE 6	Making Sentences Complete

Supply a subject or a verb, along with any other words needed to form a complete statement, in each of the following sentences.

1. Blue ice cream _____

_____

2. _____ circled _____

3. A large, slobbering dog _____

4. _____ could have taken _____

5. Grinning broadly, my younger brother _____

_____ and _____

EXERCISE 7	Composing Complete Sentences

Write five sentences of your own and then underline the subjects and circle their verbs.

1. _____

_____

2. _____

_____

3. _____

_____

4. _____

_____

5. _____

_____

SIMPLE FRAGMENTS

Collaborative Activity 2

Checking Sentences

Exchange the lists of sentences you composed in Exercises 5 and 7 with a member of your collaborative group. Check each other's work, and consult the rest of the group if you're unsure about any sentence.

During the final stages of revising and editing your papers, look for and try to eliminate fragments by identifying the subjects and verbs of your sentences. If you discover that a subject, verb, or both are missing, supply the words that will make the statement complete. There are four main kinds of simple fragments:

1. fragments missing a subject
2. fragments missing a verb or part of a verb
3. fragments beginning with infinitives or *–ing* words
4. fragments that add details or examples

Missing Subjects

In this first case, a fragment may be missing a subject because of incorrect punctuation, especially when a subject performs two actions. You may end a sentence after the first action, leaving the second verb hanging without a subject, as in this example:

Sentence	Fragment
Deborah disguised herself as a man.	And fooled her fellow soldiers.

The fragment contains a verb, *fooled,* but doesn't have a subject. You could fix the fragment either by combining the fragment with the sentence preceding it or by supplying the missing subject:

Combining:	Deborah disguised herself as a man and fooled her fellow soldiers.
Adding a subject:	Deborah disguised herself as a man. *She* therefore fooled her fellow soldiers.

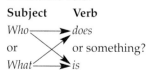

TIPS

For Identifying the Subject and Verb

In every sentence *someone* or *something does* something or *is* something. One simple question will help you spot the subject and verb.

Who or *what does* something or *is* something? *Who* or *what* reveals the subject of the sentence. *Does* or *is* reveals the verb.

Subject	**Verb**
Who	*does*
or	or something?
What	*is*

Missing or Incomplete Verbs

In this second case, part of the verb—usually the helping verb—is missing. Most often, that helping verb is a form of *to be (is, am, are, was, were)* or *to have (has, have, had):*

Incomplete verbs	Complete verbs
She *fighting* in the war.	She *is* (or *was*) *fighting* in the war.
She *gone* to Massachusetts.	She *has* (or *had*) *gone* to Massachusetts.

Infinitives and –*ing* Words

Infinitives and –*ing* words are formed from verbs, so they express an action. However, they usually don't function as verbs but only introduce or continue a sentence. If they aren't attached to that sentence, they'll hang loose as fragments. Here are examples:

Sentence	–*ing* word fragment
Deborah enlisted in the army.	Using the name Timothy Thayer.

Infinitive fragment	Sentence
To join the army.	She had to disguise herself as a man.

You can fix the fragments by attaching them to the complete sentences:

Deborah enlisted in the army, using the name Timothy Thayer.
To join the army, she had to disguise herself as a man.

Hanging Details or Examples

Some fragments are simply details that should be attached to the previous sentence. The detail fragment that follows the following sentence doesn't contain a verb:

Sentence	Detail fragment
A doctor discovered her identity while treating her injury.	A bullet wound in the thigh.

You can simply add this detail fragment to the sentence:

A doctor discovered her identity while treating her injury, a bullet wound in the thigh.

EXERCISE 8 | Identifying and Eliminating Fragments

Label each of the following groups of words F (for fragment) or S (for sentence). Then revise each fragment to form a full statement.

1. __S__ The Continental Army fought the British. __F__ Often suffering great losses. _The Continental Army fought the British, often suffering great losses._

2. _____ Battles were bloody. _____ With hundreds of people wounded or dying.

_____

_____

3. _____ Many fights were terrible to witness. _____ And even more terrible to participate in. _____

_____

4. _____ A barrage of cannon fire, an exchange of rifle fire, and enemies charging each other on horses. _____

_____

5. _____ The number of dead and wounded seemed enormous. _____

_____

6. _____ The war was a horrible waste of young lives! _____ But it had to happen for the colonies to gain their freedom. _____

_____

_____

7. _____ The Revolutionary War ended in 1783. _____ With the defeat of the British. And the victory of the thirteen colonies. _____

_____

_____

COMPLEX FRAGMENTS

You've seen that every sentence contains at least one subject and a verb, which form the core of a clause. But you often write **complex sentences**. They contain two clauses, and one depends on the other to complete its meaning. If these clauses are not joined properly, the dependent clause may be a fragment. Let's look at two types of these fragments:

1. those beginning with words like *although, because, if* and *when*
2. those beginning with words like *who, which,* and *that*

Dependent Clauses with Joining Words

Read the following clause. Notice that it does contain a subject and a predicate. But is the statement complete?

> Although the soldiers bathed in the river together.

You're probably asking, "What happened?" That's because the clause is a fragment, called a **dependent clause**. It cannot stand alone but must be attached to another clause to form a complete sentence:

> Although the soldiers bathed in the river together, *Deborah would always remain apart from the others.*

Notice that this second clause can stand alone as a complete sentence, so it's called an **independent clause**. The dependent clause can come last or first in the combined sentence:

> Deborah would always remain apart from the others, *although the soldiers bathed in the river together.*

TIPS

For Using *Although*

Don't confuse *although* with *however. Although* is a conjunction, so it joins sentences and isn't followed by a comma. *However* is a transitional word (see Chapter 20); it doesn't join sentences and is followed by a comma.

Some other dependent clause fragments follow. Their joining words (called **conjunctive adverbs**)—*if, when, because,* and *after*—demand that the clauses be attached to an independent clause. Make each clause into a complete statement.

If I am not busy, _____

When you really enjoy yourself, _____

Because Juan received a scholarship, _____

After we went to the movies, _____

EXERCISE 9	Identifying Clauses in Combined Sentences

Collaborative Activity 3

Analyzing Fragments and Finding Solutions

Compare and discuss your answers to Exercise 9 in your collaborative group. If you've determined that a sentence was incomplete, explain why. Compare the ways in which you fixed the problem.

Underline the subject and circle the verb of each clause in the sentences provided. Then put a box around the word that combines the clauses. One sentence has three clauses.

1. The fighting continued after Deborah's enlistment, when she saw plenty of action.

2. After the British in New York raided some farms for food, the farmers complained to the American army.

3. Some people protected the British soldiers because these people did not believe in the war.

4. Such raids were difficult to stop, since the soldiers needed stolen food to survive.

5. Although Deborah received several wounds on one of these expeditions, she could still conceal the secret of her sex.

6. When her thigh was pierced by a bullet, causing her right boot to fill with blood, she pulled the bullet out with a penknife and recovered from the wound.

EXERCISE 10	Correcting Fragments

 TIPS

For Creating Dependent Clauses

These frequently used conjunctive adverbs begin dependent clauses:

For Time Relationships: *After, As, As soon as, Before, Once, Since, Until, When, While*

For Reasons: *Because, Since*

For Contrast: *Although, Even though, Whereas*

For Establishing Conditions: *If, Unless*

Revise each of the following dependent clause fragments into a complete sentence by adding an independent clause.

1. Although Deborah Sampson disguised herself as a man, *no one in the army de-tected the disguise.*

2. When a country goes to war, _____
_____

3. _____
_____

   because the British Army had more soldiers and guns.

4. After Deborah was wounded in battle, _____
_____

5. If Deborah's disguise had been discovered, _____
_____

6. _____

although Deborah was a woman.

EXERCISE 11	Composing Sentences

Write five complete sentences of your own that include a dependent clause after the joining word supplied. Be sure that each clause contains its own subject and verb.

1. Our family always goes downtown on July 4 because the fireworks display is spectacular.

2. Although _____

_____

3. If _____

_____

4. When _____

_____

5. Because_____

_____

6. _____

after _____

Collaborative Activity 4

Comparing Sentences
Exchange the sentences you composed in Exercise 11 with a classmate. Check and discuss each other's work.

Dependent Clauses with Pronouns

Another type of dependent clause sometimes sneaks its way into people's writing as a fragment. Look at this clause, for example:

Which could uncover her secret.

This clause makes no sense by itself; it is a fragment. It has to be attached to an independent clause that completes its meaning:

Deborah avoided medical examinations, which could uncover her secret.

Almost every clause beginning with *which, who,* or *that* is dependent and by itself will be a fragment. Here are some further examples of dependent clause fragments, which are themselves attached to only partial clauses—the verbs are missing. Make each of them a complete sentence.

The woman *who smiled at you* _____

The issue *that interests me most* _____

A complete physical examination, *which people over thirty-five should have each*

year, _____

Note that *who, which,* and *that* can also begin independent clauses.

1. Under certain conditions, *which* and *who* can begin questions that consist of a single independent clause:

Who has joined the armed forces?
Which army wears brown uniforms?

2. *That*, when it refers to an idea in a previous statement, can also begin an independent clause:

The soldiers destroyed crops and other private property. *That behavior* is not permitted in war.

EXERCISE 12 | *Correcting Fragments*

Label each of the following groups of words S (for sentence) or F (for fragment). Then revise the sentence fragments. Add an independent clause to make them complete sentences.

1. ___F___ Deborah Sampson, who was born to a wealthy family. *Deborah Sampson, who was born to a wealthy family, lived a difficult life as a soldier.*

2. _____ Her father lost all of his money in an investment. _____ Which proved unlucky. _____
   _____

3. _____ Deborah, who could have remained a teacher. _____
   _____

4. _____ A bullet that wounded her in the thigh still did not betray her disguise.
   _____
   _____

5. _____ The doctor who treated her. _____
   _____

6. _____ The army officers who eventually discovered the true identity of their recruit. _____ They were astonished. _____
   _____

Collaborative Activity 5

Comparing Sentences
Exchange the sentences you composed in Exercise 12 with a classmate. Check and discuss each other's work.

EXERCISE 13 | *Writing Sentences with Dependent Clauses*

Write five complete sentences of your own that include a dependent clause beginning with the joining word or pronoun supplied. Be sure that each clause contains its own subject and verb.

1. *The Revolutionary War,* _____ which *began in Massachusetts, soon spread throughout the thirteen colonies.*

2. _____
   who _____

3. _____
   that _____

4. _____

if _____

5. _____

because _____

6. Although _____

_____

IN SUMMARY   Writing Complete Sentences

A Fragment

1. may be missing a subject, a verb, or both.
2. may contain an incomplete verb.
3. may be a hanging detail or example.
4. may be a dependent clause beginning with a joining word.
5. may be a dependent clause beginning with a pronoun.

Revise Fragments to Make Them Complete by

1. adding the missing subject.
2. completing the verb.
3. attaching the hanging detail or example to another sentence.
4. attaching the dependent clause to an independent clause.

EDITING FOR MASTERY

Mastery Exercise 1

The next passage contains twelve fragments, in addition to another that has been corrected for you as an example. Find and eliminate the fragments by following this procedure:

1. Underline the subject(s) and circle the verb(s) in every clause.
2. Make any necessary changes above the lines. These changes can include
   a. supplying the missing subject or a missing (or incomplete) verb
   b. joining an incomplete sentence to another sentence (usually by removing a period between two sentences)
   c. eliminating a word from a dependent clause to make the clause independent

The Discovery of Deborah Sampson's Secret

(1) In June 1783, Deborah Sampson was sent with some troops to put down a mutiny of soldiers (2) *who* ~~Who~~ were demanding their pay. (3) Here she developed a terrible fever. (4) After she had been carried to a hospital. (5) She was examined by a doctor. (6) He put his hand on her bosom to feel her pulse. (7) And found a tight corset pressing down on her chest. (8) After tearing it off, he was even more shocked. (9) Not only that the soldier was alive, but that he was quite obviously a

female. (10) The doctor concealed his discovery from everyone but the nurse. (11) Who helped bring Deborah back to health. (12) When Deborah left the infirmary. (13) The doctor gave her some words of caution. (14) He also gave her a letter. (15) Which was addressed to her commander at West Point.

(16) The letter contained the news of his discovery. (17) The good general, who was amazed at this information. (18) He summoned Private Deborah to his quarters and addressed her. (19) "Because you have continued in my service and have always been vigilant, vivacious, faithful. (20) And, in many respects distinguished from your fellows. (21) I would only ask one question. (22) 'Does that martial attire, which now glitters on your body, conceal a female's form?'"

(23) As he finished his sentence. (24) Tears came to his eyes, and Deborah fainted.

(25) The general gave Deborah an honorable discharge in October 1783, and she returned to Massachusetts. (26) Still in men's clothing. (27) She spent the winter doing farm work in a village, where she finally assumed the role of a woman once again. (28) Here she met a hard-working farmer, Benjamin Gannett. (29) Who stirred some long silenced emotions in her heart. (30) She married Gannett on April 7, 1784.

Scorecard: Number of Errors Found and Corrected _____

Collaborative Activity 6

Comparing Corrections

Appoint someone in the group to read the entire passage from Mastery Exercise 1 aloud so you can hear where errors occur. Make corrections, discuss them in your group, and report them to the entire class.

Mastery Exercise 2

The next passage contains twelve fragments, in addition to another that has been corrected for you as an example. Find and eliminate the fragments by following this procedure:

1. *Underline the subject(s) and circle the verb(s) in every clause.*
2. *Make any necessary changes above the lines. These changes can include*
   a. *supplying the missing subject or a missing (or incomplete) verb*
   b. *joining an incomplete sentence to another sentence (usually by removing a period between two sentences)*
   c. *eliminating a word from a dependent clause to make the clause independent*

Heroines of the Battlefield

(1) A classic dispatch written by Union Army Col. Elijah H. C. Cavins during the U.S. Civil War (2) It is revealing in its simplicity:

(3) A corporal was promoted to sergeant for gallant conduct in the Battle of Fredericksburg, since which time the sergeant has become the mother of a child.

(4) It a little-known fact (5). That hundreds of American women have fought and even died in combat. (6) In fact, women served in America's wars. (7) Even before the existence of the United States. (8) It was not unusual to see women on the battlefield during the American Revolution.

(9) Margaret Corbin is an example. (10) When her husband joined the Continental Army in 1776. (11) She accompanied him as a camp follower. (12) Which was a common practice back then. (13) At the Battle of Fort Washington in 1776. (14) A terrible British artillery barrage rained down on the Colonial forces. (15) When the bombardment stopped and the smoke began to clear, Margaret Corbin became aware of the devastation around her. (16) She ran to her husband's cannon and found his body lying there among the debris. (17) With tears streaming down her face. (18) She stepped up, fired his cannon, and then began reloading it.

(19) Inspired by her bravery, artillerymen along the line lifted themselves from the rubble. (20) Straightened their weapons, and joined in the battle. (21) A cannonball hit Margaret Corbin. (22) She was severely wounded and remained an invalid for the rest of her life. (23) When she died, was buried with full military honors at West Point.

(24) Deborah Sampson Gannett was another Revolutionary War heroine. (25) While disguising herself as a man. (26) She enlisted in the Continental Army and showed incredible bravery in combat. (27) When the war ended, she became the first American woman to go on the lecture circuit. (28) After her death, Congress voted to give her husband a pension. (29) As the surviving spouse of a Continental soldier.

(30) Mary Hays also distinguished herself on the battlefield. (31) At the Battle of Monmouth in June of 1778, she raced through a hail of gunfire. (32) To get ammunition for her fellow soldiers. (33) As she ran, a cannonball ripped away part of her dress, barely missing her legs. (34) She ignored the close call, grabbed the ammuni-

tion, and ran back to the line. (35) A loud cheer went up from the soldiers. (36) Who recognized true heroism when they saw it.

(37) There are many long-forgotten stories of women. (38) Who played roles in the struggle for American independence. (39) Sadly, historians have generally ignored their exploits.

Scorecard: Number of Errors Found and Corrected _____

20 Joining Sentences Through Coordination and Subordination

Chapter 8 showed you the importance of sentence variety and explained some simple ways of combining sentences to achieve this variety. This chapter examines more complex ways. You'll practice

- ways to combine equally important ideas
- ways to combine unequal ideas

COMBINING EQUALS

Some sentences contain two subjects, some contain two verbs, and some contain two clauses that are grammatically equal—and equally important. Here are examples of sentences with two such clauses:

> During the nineteenth century the Sioux lived on the Northern Great Plains, but they had earlier lived to the north and east.
>
> The hostile Ojibwa had forced them to migrate, and the Sioux gradually adapted to life on the great plains.

These are **compound sentences**. Each contains two subject-verb combinations called **independent clauses**—clauses that can stand alone as complete sentences.

The following sections will show you several ways to combine independent clauses into compound sentences.

Combining with Conjunctions

The grammatically equal structures that make up compound sentences are *coordinate* (*co* = equal, *ordinate* = level). The words that join them are therefore called **coordinating conjunctions** (like a *junction* that joins two roads).

There are only seven coordinating conjunctions: *for, and, nor, but, or, yet, so.* The expression FAN BOYS will help you remember them:

For	But
And	Or
Nor	Yet
	So

Coordinating conjunctions can also join words or short phrases, but here we'll look at how they join two sentences into one.

In each of the following examples, notice that the coordinating conjunction not only joins two independent clauses, but also *explains the relationship between the clauses:*

A Native American boy was born sometime around 1842 into the Sioux confederation, *and* he was known as Curly. (*And* adds the second clause to the first.)

His mother was the sister of Chief Spotted Tail of the Brule tribe, *but* his father was a medicine man for the Oglala tribe. (*But* contrasts the second clause to the first.)

His childhood should have been happy, *yet* tragedy struck when his mother died. (*Yet* signals an unexpected contrast between the two clauses.)

Fortunately, Curly's father married his late wife's sister, or the infant would have had no one to take care of him. (*Or* signals that the second clause is an alternative to the first.)

Before he was twelve, Curly showed his bravery in killing a buffalo, *so* he received a horse as a reward. (*So* signals that the second clause results from the first.)

He soon developed a hatred toward whites, *for* they killed a tribal leader, destroyed Sioux villages, and grabbed Native American land. (*For* signals that the second clause explains the first.)

These white men couldn't have known the fierceness of their future opponent, *nor* could they guess at the fame of the boy who would later be known as Crazy Horse. (*Nor* presents the second clause as a negative alternative to the first.)

In many combined sentences, the content of the independent clauses determines which conjunction to use:

Crazy Horse was only a boy, *but* he fought like a man. (The ideas obviously contrast.)

But in other combined sentences, the conjunction you use determines the logical relationship between the two independent clauses. Different conjunctions convey different messages:

> Crazy Horse was a ruthless fighter, *and* the white soldiers greatly respected him. (*And* merely adds the second idea to the first.)
>
> Crazy Horse was a ruthless fighter, *so* the white soldiers greatly respected him. (*So* establishes that Crazy Horse's fighting ability created the soldiers' respect.)
>
> Crazy Horse was a ruthless fighter, *yet* the white soldiers greatly respected him. (*Yet* establishes that the soldiers respected Crazy Horse in spite of his ruthlessness.)

Notice that a comma comes before the coordinating conjunction in these combined sentences. You can omit the comma in very short combined sentences:

> I like you and you like me.

But you can't omit the conjunction. The conjunction, not the comma, joins the two clauses. We'll return to that issue shortly.

EXERCISE 1	Combining Sentences

Rewrite each of the following pairs of sentences, joining them with a coordinating conjunction, preceded by a comma. Use each conjunction (for, and, nor, but, or, yet, so) at least once.

1. Soon after the killing of the tribal leader, Curly had a strange experience. He went on a vision quest in which he dreamed about a horseback rider in a storm.
   Soon after the killing of the tribal leader, Curly had a strange experience, for he went on a vision quest in which he dreamed about a horseback rider in a storm.

2. The rider had flowing long hair. Drawings of lightning and hail decorated his body. _____

3. The rider was clearly a warrior. He didn't carry any scalps. _____

4. The storm faded. A red-backed hawk flew over the rider's head. _____

5. Curly's father was a medicine man. He understood the meanings of dreams. _____

6. His father said that the dream predicted his son's future greatness in battle. The boy should now take his father's name, Crazy Horse. _____

7. Four years later, Crazy Horse must have been highly respected. He couldn't have fought with the adults in a battle against the Crow Indians. _____

8. As in his dream, his long hair flowed freely. He wore a red hawk feather in his headdress. _____

_____

9. His face was painted with a lightning bolt. Dots like hail decorated his body.

_____

_____

10. Crazy Horse fought bravely. He was wounded in the leg because, as his father said, he had ignored the dream and taken two scalps. _____

_____

11. Crazy Horse never again took a scalp. He never again was wounded in battle. (Use *nor*, and adjust the word order of the second sentence.)_____

_____

EXERCISE 2	Writing Combined Sentences

Add a second independent clause to each of the sentences that follow. Be sure that the clause is complete: that it contains both a subject and a verb, not just a verb.

1. Many jobs are available in high-tech industries, *so many students are majoring in fields such as computer programming and engineering.*

2. Well-trained programmers often start at good salaries, but_____

_____

3. Several high-tech companies come to college campuses to recruit employees, and _____

_____

4. In today's competitive job environment, new workers had better be well pre-pared, or _____

_____

5. Modern corporations will not tolerate inefficient employees, nor _____

_____

6. One very popular high-tech field is health care, for _____

_____

7. More than half of today's college students want to major in business or high-tech fields, yet _____

_____

8. Companies also look for employees with well-rounded backgrounds, so_____

_____

_____

Combining with a Semicolon

A Word About Words

Columbus probably called Native Americans *Indians* because he thought he had landed in the Indies of Asia—the first of many mistakes Europeans made regarding the indigenous people of the Americas.

When independent clauses are closely related in meaning, you can combine them with a punctuation mark: the **semicolon (;)**. Notice that the semicolon is a combination of a period and a comma—sort of a halfway mark between the two. It signals the end of the first clause while joining it to the second:

> A treaty finally ended the conflict; the army left the Bozeman Trail in exchange for an end to the fighting.
>
> Red Cloud retired from his warrior role; Crazy Horse was soon to take his place.

The two clauses make one sentence, so the first word after the semicolon is not capitalized (unless it is the pronoun *I* or a proper noun).

EXERCISE 3	Writing Sentences

Complete each of the following sentences by writing a second independent clause after the semicolon. Base the second clause on the words in parentheses.

1. The Black Hills of South Dakota are famous for their Native American history; (home/Oglala and Brule/branch of Sioux) *they were home to the Oglala and Brule branches of the Sioux.*

Collaborative Activity 1

Writing and Checking Sentences

Write seven compound sentences, using a different coordinating conjunction in each. Then copy the sentences over, eliminating the coordinating conjunction. Exchange sentences with a member of the group by passing to the left and restore the missing coordinating conjunctions. Then discuss the revisions. Are the clauses complete? Is the relationship between ideas logical?

2. Native Americans and whites fought many battles; (whites/most often/winners)

_____

_____

3. Whites traveled through Native American territory along the Oregon Trail; (for California/hunting for gold)_____

_____

4. Wagon trains created many problems for the Native Americans; (ruined land/garbage) _____

_____

5. The army and the Native Americans signed many treaties; (army/not honor)

_____

_____

6. To the Northern Plains Native Americans, the buffalo was extremely important; (many uses) _____

_____

Adding Transitional Words

Unlike the coordinating conjunctions (*for, and, nor, but, or, yet, so*) that both join and explain the relationship between independent clauses, a semicolon merely joins the clauses. But the relationship between the clauses may need explaining. Look, for example, at this sentence:

> Crazy Horse was a member of the Sioux Nation; he married a woman from the Cheyenne Nation.

The ideas are connected by a semicolon, but the logical connection isn't clear. There's no transition from one clause to the next; something else must be added:

> Crazy Horse was a member of the Sioux Nation; *nevertheless*, he married a woman from the Cheyenne Nation.

The added **transitional word** *nevertheless* is called a **conjunctive adverb** because it's partly a conjunction and partly an adverb. But it's not a true conjunction that joins the two clauses; the semicolon joins them.

Here are a few more examples of combined sentences with transitional words after the semicolon. Notice that, like the coordinating conjunctions, each one implies a different relationship:

> Crazy Horse gained many friends and followers among the Cheyenne; *consequently*, they supported him in later battles.
>
> The whites called the Battle for the Bozeman Trail a massacre; *however*, it was actually a brilliant victory by the Native Americans.

Notice, too, that a comma always follows the transitional word.

The following box lists the most common transitional words and compares their meanings to those of coordinating conjunctions:

Transitional word	Compares to the conjunction	And means
also, additionally, furthermore, moreover	and	in addition
however	but	in contrast
nevertheless	yet	in contrast
therefore, consequently, thus	so	as a result
instead, otherwise	or	as an alternative

You can place other transitional words after the semicolon, especially if the transitions express logical relationships that a coordinating conjunction cannot. Here are two more examples:

> The famous warrior was given the name Curly at birth; *later*, he took the name Crazy Horse. (*Later* expresses a time relationship.)
>
> The memory of Crazy Horse is greatly respected by the Sioux Nation; *in fact*, members of the nation are constructing an enormous monument to him in South Dakota. (*In fact* introduces more specific information.)

Semicolons and transitional words slow down the reader, emphasizing the relationship between the ideas they join. But too many semicolons clog a passage and restrict the flow of ideas, so don't overuse them.

EXERCISE 4	Combining Sentences

Combine each pair of sentences with a semicolon. Then insert an appropriate transitional word followed by a comma.

1. Crazy Horse desperately wanted to protect the Black Hills area from white settlers and travelers. He joined in every major battle fought by the Oglala Sioux.

   Crazy Horse desperately wanted to protect the Black Hills area from white settlers and travelers; therefore, he joined in every major battle fought by the Oglala Sioux.

2. Several tribes signed a treaty in 1868 that would send them to a reservation in western South Dakota. Crazy Horse, Sitting Bull, and other Native American leaders refused to sign. _____

   _____

   _____

3. After Red Cloud's retirement, Crazy Horse became warrior chief of the Oglala. He joined with his wife's people, the Cheyenne, in attacks against whites._____

   _____

   _____

4. The warrior chiefs would not allow the Northern Pacific Railroad to build a new line through the Native Americans' only remaining buffalo range. The railroad immediately sent a team of surveyors to the Sioux and Cheyenne lands._____

   _____

   _____

5. The Native Americans were not heavily armed. The surveyors were accompanied by 1,500 soldiers, including a lieutenant colonel named George Armstrong Custer. _____

   _____

   _____

6. Several fights broke out. The surveyors completed their work without many casualties on either side._____

   _____

   _____

7. General Philip Sheridan would not honor the treaty of 1868. He built an army fort in the Black Hills, right in the middle of the Great Sioux Reservation. _____

   _____

   _____

| EXERCISE 5 | Joining More Sentences |

*Combine each pair of sentences, but vary the combinations. Use coordinating conjunctions (*for, and, nor, but, or, yet, so*) in some sentences, semicolons and transitional words (*however, therefore, nevertheless, and so on) in others.*

1. Scientists and geologists were also exploring for gold. General Sheridan sent Lieutenant Colonel Custer to the Black Hills in 1874 to protect them. *Scientists and geologists also were exploring for gold, so General Sheridan sent Lieutenant Colonel Custer to the Black Hills in 1874 to protect them.*

2. The Native Americans didn't oppose this expedition. Most of them did not even know what was happening until it was all over. _____

3. By then, their last hope of keeping the Black Hills for themselves was doomed. The expedition had found gold. _____

4. Custer, who loved to brag, greatly exaggerated the size of the gold deposits. The whole country was burning with gold fever. _____

5. The U.S. government could not keep its citizens out of Sioux lands. Government officials brought the chiefs to Washington and offered to buy the Black Hills. _____

6. The meeting was unsuccessful. The government tried again the next year. _____

7. A distinguished group of commissioners arrived at the Sioux Reservation to negotiate. The commissioners came close to being the central figures in a massacre. _____

Copyright © 2003 by Addison Wesley Longman, Inc.

Collaborative Activity 2

Comparing Sentences
Exchange the sentences you wrote in Exercise 5 with a member of your collaborative group. Rewrite each other's sentences, substituting coordinating conjunctions for semicolons and transitional words or vice versa. Then discuss your changes. Which create more graceful sentences? Consider the flow of ideas in the whole passage. If you used a semicolon in one sentence, should you use a coordinating conjunction in the next?

Avoiding Errors in Combining Equals

Be careful to join independent clauses with either a conjunction or a semicolon. Incorrectly joined sentences are confusing and annoying. Here are two examples:

✓ TIPS

For Avoiding Sentence-Joining Errors

Be careful when using *then* and *also*. They explain relationships between ideas, but they don't join sentences.

Incorrect: Crazy Horse's mother died, then his father remarried.

Correct: Crazy Horse's mother died, *but then* his father remarried.

Incorrect: The young warrior was brave, also he was a great leader.

Correct: The young warrior was brave, *and* he was also a great leader.

The Oglala Sioux had a great leader his name was Crazy Horse.

The Sioux and Cheyenne Native Americans won a famous battle, they killed General Custer and all of his troops.

- In the first sentence, *nothing* separates the two clauses—a serious error called a **run-on sentence**.
- In the second sentence, only a comma joins the two clauses—another serious error called a **comma-spliced sentence**.

Rewrite both sentences to include both a comma and a coordinating conjunction:

1. _____

2. _____

Don't fall into the trap of reaching for a semicolon every time you want to link independent clauses. Remember that the semicolon implies a special, close relationship between the clauses. Semicolons are forceful, and they're not always appropriate. They should never be used as quick cures for run-on or comma-spliced sentences.

EXERCISE 6	Correcting Errors in Coordination

*Label each of the following sentences as a comma-spliced (C.S.) sentence or a run-on (R.O.) sentence. Then join each sentence correctly. Insert the logical conjunction (*and, but, or, nor, for, so, yet*) preceded by a comma.*

If Your First Language Is Not English

Be careful with comma-spliced sentences. In some languages, especially Spanish, joining independent clauses with a comma is correct. But in English, commas don't join ideas; they separate them. So be sure you include an actual joining word—the coordinating conjunction—between the clauses:

Incorrect: Crazy Horse had a dream, later it came true.

Correct: Crazy Horse had a dream, *and* later it came true.

The Beginnings of the War

_C.S._ 1. In 1848, gold was discovered in California, ^*and* trouble soon brewed between the United States government and Northern Plains Native Americans.

_R.O._ 2. Within a year, thousands of fortune hunters called "forty-niners" took the Oregon Trail through South Dakota ^*, and* their wagons were ruining the Sioux hunting grounds.

_____ 3. Garbage, dead animals, and disease fouled the land, white hunters drove away the buffalo.

_____ 4. In 1851, the American government and a united council of tribes signed a treaty for the rights to the Oregon Trail, suspicion and bad will between the two parties continued.

_____ 5. Then in 1854, a Native American killed a settler's cow, a foolish lieutenant named Grattan and thirty soldiers went looking for the Sioux.

_____ 6. A good-natured Indian leader tried to settle the matter the soldiers shot and killed him.

_____ **7.** A battle broke out, Native Americans killed Grattan and all but one of his men.

_____ **8.** The following summer, 1,300 troops raided a small village, they slaughtered 86 Sioux, including many women and children.

_____ **9.** Gold was discovered in Montana, the army began building the Bozeman Trail through South Dakota in 1866.

_____ **10.** The Oglala tribe, led by Chief Red Cloud, attacked and killed the entire army, Crazy Horse gained fame for his courage and brilliant battle tactics.

COMBINING UNEQUALS

Some sentences contain two complete clauses, but the clauses are not equal. One may serve as an introduction, an identifying structure, or a source of incidental information. In other words, these less important ideas are **subordinate** (*sub=lower; ordinate=level*). They belong in dependent clauses, which cannot be sentences by themselves. They must be attached to a more important idea in an independent clause to form a complete sentence.

That combination of a dependent clause and independent clause is called a **complex sentence**. We'll look at two types of dependent clauses in complex sentences, which not only sharpen the relationships between your ideas but also add variety to your writing:

- adverb clauses (when-why-where)
- adjective clauses (who-which-what)

Adverb Clauses

Adverbs typically answer the questions *when? why?* or *where?* in a sentence. So a dependent clause that explains when, why, or where functions as an adverb. Suppose, for example, you want to join these two sentences:

> The commissioners arrived. Several armed and angry Native Americans surrounded them with guns aimed at their heads.

Would you use *and,* which suggests that both ideas are equally important? Probably not. The idea in the second sentence is clearly more important than the first. A better solution would be to begin the first clause with the word *when,* making the clause dependent on the second:

> When the commissioners arrived, several angry Native Americans suddenly surrounded them with guns aimed at their heads.

When is one of the subordinating conjunctions, which create dependent clauses that attach to independent clauses and form complex sentences. Here are two more examples:

After the Native American leader Little Big Man announced that this was as good a time as any to start a war, the U.S. cavalry responded by drawing their guns.

Bloodshed was avoided because cooler heads were able to prevail.

The following list includes the most common subordinating conjunctions and the logical relationships they express:

When conjunctions: after, as, before, since, until, when, while, as soon as
  Example: After the battle had ended, . . .
Why conjunctions: Because, since
  Example: Because the Native Americans wanted to keep their lands, . . .
Where conjunctions: Where, wherever
  Example: Wherever gold was found, . . .
Contrast-Concession Conjunction: Although, even though, whereas
  Example: Although the Sioux wanted to live in peace, . . .
Conjunctions Establishing Conditions: If, unless
  Examples: If the tribes wouldn't live on the reservations, . . .
    Unless the tribes moved onto the reservations, . . .

Punctuating Adverb Dependent Clauses. Punctuate adverb dependent clauses according to these rules:

1. When the dependent clause begins a sentence, follow the clause with a comma (as in this sentence).

2. Don't use a comma when the dependent clause comes last (as in this sentence).

You can place a comma before final *although* or *since* clauses if you hear a pause before them.

If Your First Language Is Not English

In some languages (especially Chinese and Urdu), *although* and *but* begin both clauses in a combined sentence. In English, however, you may use only one of the conjunctions:

Correct: Although Crazy Horse was just a boy, he fought like a man.

Correct: Crazy Horse was just a boy, *but* he fought like a man.

EXERCISE 7	Combining Sentences

Combine each pair of sentences by placing a subordinating conjunction before the less important idea. Insert a comma where necessary.

1. The nerves of the government commissioners must have been rattled. They sat down with Red Cloud to discuss the purchase of the Black Hills. *The nerves of the government commissioners must have been rattled when they sat down with Red Cloud to discuss the purchase of the Black Hills.*

2. Red Cloud calmly proposed that $600 million seemed like a fair price. The region was so valuable to the commissioners. _____

3. The Native Americans discussed the matter further. They suggested a $6 million price tag. _____

Collaborative Activity 3

Joining Sentences

Write five complex sentences, one using each of the types listed in the box on page 297. Then copy the sentences over, this time eliminating the subordinating conjunction. Exchange sentences with a member of the group and restore the missing subordinating conjunctions. Then check over the results. Are the sentences correctly joined and complete? Is the relationship between ideas logical?

4. The commissioners were too intimidated to negotiate. They angrily returned to Washington. _____

_____

5. The government ordered all Native Americans to come onto the reservation at once. Most of them never even heard about the illegal order. _____

_____

_____

6. The deadline came. One small band of Native Americans had come in. _____

_____

_____

7. General Philip Sheridan was sent to fight the Sioux and Cheyenne. They had never violated a treaty or actually attacked a U.S. citizen. _____

_____

_____

✔ TIPS

For Recognizing Dependent Clause Fragments

Read your writing aloud. If your voice falls at the end of a sentence, it's probably a complete statement. If your voice rises at the end, you may have written a fragment.

Complete statement: The Sioux lost many of their lands after the last battle had ended.↓

Incomplete statement: After the last battle had ended↑

Adverb Fragments.   When you subordinate one clause, you intentionally create a sentence **fragment**: a dependent clause with nothing to depend on. This less important clause cannot stand on its own. Be sure you combine it with an independent clause.

Incorrect:	When General Sheridan planned his strategy of attack. He expected an easy victory.
Correct:	*When General Sheridan planned his strategy of attack*, he expected an easy victory.
Incorrect:	The Native Americans overwhelmed the army forces. When Crazy Horse led his men into battle with his famous war cry: "Come on, Dakotas; it's a good day to die."
Correct:	The Native Americans overwhelmed the army forces *when Crazy Horse led his men into battle with his famous war cry: "Come on, Dakotas; it's a good day to die."*

Adjective Clauses

Adjectives are modifiers. They supply details about a noun in a sentence. These details can come in a single word, a phrase, or a clause. Look at the following two sentences. Which one is a likely modifier?

Crazy Horse won the battle. It would bring him everlasting fame.

The second sentence supplies details about the battle. Note that the sentence begins with the pronoun *it*, which refers to the battle. To combine the second sentence with the first by subordinating the modifier, replace the pronoun with another one, *that:*

Crazy Horse won the battle *that would bring him everlasting fame.*

You've now created a complex sentence, with one independent clause and one dependent clause. The pronoun you've used as the subject of the dependent clause—*that*—relates the information of the clause back to *the battle.* Therefore, *that* is called a **relative pronoun,** and the dependent clause is also a **relative clause**. Since the clause describes a noun—the battle—it functions as an adjective. Here are two more combined sentences with relative clauses:

> For many years, workers on a South Dakota mountain have been carving an enormous monument, *which will be the largest statue in the world when completed.*
>
> The monument depicts a warrior *who represents the famous Crazy Horse.*

In the first sentence notice the relative pronoun *which* refers to *monument,* and in the second the relative pronoun *who* refers to *warrior.*
That, which, and *who* are all relative pronouns.

- Use *which* or *that* to refer to things.
- Use *who, that,* or *whom* to refer to people.

Notice that a relative clause comes directly after the noun it describes:

> . . . monument, *which will be the largest statue in the world when completed.*
> . . . *warrior who represents the famous Crazy Horse.*

An incorrectly placed relative clause often creates confusion.

> *Poor:* Many people have viewed the statue near Mt. Rushmore that memorializes Crazy Horse. (What memorializes Crazy Horse—the statue or Mt. Rushmore—which memorializes three presidents?)
>
> *Better:* Near Mt. Rushmore, many people have viewed the statue that memorializes Crazy Horse.

EXERCISE 8 | **Combining Sentences**

Combine each of the following pairs of sentences by making the second sentence into a dependent clause beginning with who, that, *or* which. *Place this clause directly after the noun it describes.*

TIPS

For Using Commas with Relative Clauses

1. When in doubt, leave the commas out.
2. Never place commas around a clause beginning with *that,* because the clause always introduces clauses with essential information.

1. After the first battle, the man considered his strategy for the next day. He had led the forces against Crazy Horse. *After the first battle, the man who had led his forces against Crazy Horse considered his strategy for the next day.*

2. But Brigadier General George Crook didn't realize he had entered into a new kind of warfare. It differed completely from the Native Americans' charge-and-run tactics of the past. _____

_____

_____

3. The Sioux and Cheyenne nations had developed a new spirit of cooperation. It led to a surprising victory against the stronger government troops. _____

_____

_____

4. General Crook devised a strategy. It would send one group of soldiers up the Little Bighorn River and the Seventh Cavalry down and around the river from the south.

_____

_____

5. The action had been used successfully many times before. It would trap the Native Americans between the two forces. _____

_____

_____

6. The leader of the Seventh Cavalry had often bragged his unit could whip all the Native Americans on the plains. He was a hotheaded and arrogant lieutenant colonel named George Armstrong Custer. _____

_____

_____

Punctuating Relative Clauses.   To punctuate relative clauses correctly, you have to evaluate their importance. Look at the following sentence:

> Lieutenant Colonel George Armstrong Custer, who at twenty-three was temporarily promoted to brigadier general during the Civil War, further improved his reputation for fearlessness during the Indian Wars.

If you remove the *who* clause, the reader still knows the identity of the man it describes:

> Lieutenant Colonel George Armstrong Custer . . . further improved his reputation for fearlessness during the Indian Wars.

The information in the *who* clause isn't essential. Therefore, the clause is enclosed in two commas, which function almost like parentheses.

But the next sentence presents a different situation:

> The man who died in 1876 in the Battle of Little Bighorn had earlier gained fame in the Civil War.

If you remove the *who* clause, the sentence no longer identifies the man it discusses:

> The man . . . had earlier gained fame in the Civil War.

In this case, the *who* clause contains essential information, so it shouldn't be enclosed in commas. The same rules apply to *which* or *that* clauses: If the meaning is essential, use *that* instead of *which* with no comma; if the meaning isn't essential, use *which* with the comma.

Collaborative Activity 4

Joining Sentences

Write three sentences using the relative pronouns *that, who,* and *which* without commas, and two sentences using *who* and *which* with commas. Then copy the sentences over, this time eliminating both the relative pronouns and the commas. Exchange sentences with a member of the group and restore the missing words and punctuation. Then check over the results. Are the sentences correctly joined and complete? Is the relationship between ideas logical?

EXERCISE 9   Adding Punctuation to Relative Clauses

Underline each relative clause in the following sentences. Then place commas around the relative clauses that need punctuation.

Custer's Last Stand

1. In 1876, Lieutenant Colonel George Armstrong Custer's regiment joined troops <u>that had been ordered to find the Sioux and Cheyenne Native Americans and force them onto reservations</u>.

2. On June 22, as Custer left with the Seventh Cavalry before the other troops that would meet him on June 26, Colonel Gibbon called out to him, "Now, Custer, don't be greedy; wait for us."

3. Early on June 25, Custer's scouts discovered a Native American village that was located in a valley along the Little Bighorn River about fifteen miles away.

4. Custer who commanded 650 troops expected to find about 1,000 warriors in the village, but he was convinced his men could easily encircle and capture them.

5. However, this group which included Crazy Horse, Sitting Bull, and other great leaders was probably the largest gathering of Native American warriors of all time, numbering at least 2,000 and perhaps as many as 5,000.

6. Deciding to attack at once, Custer split his regiment into three divisions which were led by Captain Frederick W. Benteen, Major Marcus A. Reno, and himself.

7. After the divisions headed in three directions, Custer lost contact with his commanders who could not join or rescue him.

8. Reno's troops were badly defeated by the Native Americans and withdrew to the other side of the river. Benteen's group who still had not seen or heard from Custer joined Reno's men there.

9. They asked why Custer had deserted them. The answer to their question came later that day. Scouts reported finding the dead bodies of Custer and all of his troops in a field that lay about four miles away.

10. They had probably been killed in fighting that lasted less than an hour.

Adjective Fragments.   Remember that when you subordinate a clause, you create a fragment unless you attach it to an independent clause. Don't let it hang.

> . . . that lost the Battle of Little Big Horn . . . (What was or did what?)

Be sure the dependent clause fits in, and is joined to, the independent clause:

> *Unjoined:* The man that lost the Battle of Little Bighorn. Was General George Armstrong Custer.
>
> *Joined:*   The man that lost the Battle of Little Bighorn was General George Armstrong Custer.

IN SUMMARY	Joining Sentences

To Combine Sentences That Are Equals

1. Place *coordinating conjunctions (for, and, nor, but, or, yet, so)* between independent clauses
   Example: Crazy Horse was a great warrior, but he never was a tribal chief.
2. Place *a semicolon and transitional word (however, therefore, nevertheless, etc.)* between independent clauses.
   Example: Crazy Horse was a great warrior; however, he never was a tribal chief.

To Combine Sentences That Are Not Equals

1. Place a *subordinating conjunction (after, before, because, although, as, if, etc.)* before the less important clause.
   Examples: Although Crazy Horse was a great warrior, he was never a tribal chief.
   Crazy Horse was never a tribal chief although he was a great warrior.
2. Make one clause dependent with a *relative pronoun: who, which,* and *that.*
   Example: Crazy Horse was a great warrior who never was a tribal chief.

EDITING FOR MASTERY

Mastery Exercise 1

Correcting Errors in Coordination and Subordination

The following passage contains fifteen errors related to joining sentences—in addition to the first error, which has been corrected as an example. Some sentences use inappropriate conjunctions or relative pronouns to join clauses. Some sentences are fragments. The passage also contains comma-spliced or run-on sentences and sentences with other punctuation errors, including missing commas or incorrectly used semicolons. Correct each error by writing your changes above the lines.

The Death of Crazy Horse

(1) After they had won the Battle of Little Bighorn,the (2) The Native American bands split up, and Crazy Horse led his people back to the Rosebud River. (3) As the government troops wore the Native Americans down and starved them out; many of the reservation Native Americans returned to their agencies. (4) Nevertheless; Crazy Horse, Sitting Bull, and most of the other nontreaty Native Americans continued their hopeless fight for freedom and independence. (5) On January 8, 1877, when Crazy Horse and 800 braves attacked the troops in southern Montana. (6) The troops opened fire with cannons and then counterattacked. (7) The Native Americans withdrew to the hills then they retreated in a blinding snowstorm.

(8) Finally, General Crook who the Native Americans respected for his integrity, proposed a deal. (9) Crook promised Crazy Horse that if he surrendered, his people would have a reservation of their own. (10) The proud warrior agreed on May 5, 1877, he led his 800 followers into the Red Cloud Agency in northwestern Nebraska.

(11) Although General Crook tried to secure a reservation for Crazy Horse, but he was unable to make good on his promise. (12) Crazy Horse remained at the Red Cloud Agency, but he soon grew to hate his life behind walls. (13) After some false rumors spread, that he was planning another rebellion, Crazy Horse left with his family for the Spotted Tail Agency on September 4, 1877. (14) When Crook sent some Native American scouts to stop him; Crazy Horse agreed to return, and he entered Camp Robinson the next day.

(15) Crazy Horse had surrendered peaceably, nevertheless soldiers and their Native American helpers took him to a stockade instead of letting him rejoin his own people. (16) Which was the beginning of a terrible tragedy. (17) What happened as they entered the stockade is not entirely clear. (18) Crazy Horse apparently realized that he was about to be locked up and tried to break away. (19) According to some accounts, he grabbed a knife from his belt and lunged through the door; however, an army captain seized his left arm, and Little Big Man seized his right arm. (20) As Swift Bear and other Brule Native American police rushed to help Little Big Man, and one of the soldiers plunged a bayonet into Crazy Horse's abdomen.

(21) The Native Americans, who had helped the soldiers, immediately released Crazy Horse, but he died on September 7, 1877. (22) After asking his parents that his heart be returned to his homeland. (23) They were given his body the following morning, and soon vanished into the hills. (24) To this day, no one knows where the great Oglala warrior lies buried.

Scorecard: Number of errors found and corrected _____

Collaborative Activity 5

Comparing Corrections

Appoint someone in the group to read the entire passage from Mastery Exercise 1 aloud so you can hear where errors occur. Make corrections, discuss them in your group, and report them to the entire class.

Mastery Exercise 2

Correcting Errors in Coordination and Subordination

The following passage contains sixteen errors related to joining sentences—in addition to the first error, which has been corrected as an example. Some sentences use inappropriate conjunctions or relative pronouns to join clauses. Some sentences are fragments. The passage also contains comma-spliced or run-on sentences and sentences with other punctuation errors, including missing commas or incorrectly used semicolons. Correct each error by writing your changes above the lines.

Booze on the Battlefield?

(1) The rumor has persisted for well over a century. (2) Were Gen. George A. Custer's soldiers either drunk or suffering a collective hangover that fateful day~~,~~

when

(3) ^~~When~~ they were slaughtered at Little Big Horn?

(4) The speculation began when Native American veterans of the legendary battle reported finding numerous canteens containing whiskey instead of water on the bodies of Custer's soldiers. (5) Supposedly, because the U.S. Army was already embarrassed from criticism about the massacre; it covered up the fact that the men of the 7th Cavalry had been drinking the night before the battle.

(6) Many questions about the events of that day remain unanswered, however, this much we do know.

(7) As Custer and his 7th Cavalry approached on the campsite, but he ignored reports from scouts that a large number of Sioux and Cheyenne were ahead—far larger than he could have guessed. (8) If he could strike first; his reward would be a great victory—and perhaps a presidential nomination afterward. (9) He was afraid that the Sioux might flee from him and get away. (10) He therefore split his command, he sent about 300 troops under Maj. Marcus Reno to circle around the encampment and cut off any retreat. (11) Although, retreat was the last thing the Sioux had in mind.

(12) When Custer and the remaining 264 cavalry under his direct command entered the camp, 4,000 or 5,000 angry Native Americans attacked and killed them all. (13) Afterward, the victors looted the battlefield, they took many canteens full of whiskey.

(14) The handsome and dashing Custer permitted just about anything in his camp, except desertion. (15) Even though, he himself had once been court-martialed and temporarily suspended when he deserted to visit his wife. (16) Drinking in the ranks appears to have been widespread. (17) Just four days before the Battle of Little Big Horn, Custer's troops met a supply ship on the Rosebud River. (18) Where they renewed their supply of whiskey.

(19) Everyone agrees that Custer's second in command, Major Reno, was a heavy drinker, he brought a full keg of whiskey with him when the 7th Cavalry set out to locate the Sioux. (20) Was his conduct on day of the battle influenced by drunkenness? (21) As soon as Reno and his men were attacked; he immediately retreated to a defensive position. (22) He ignored pleas to go to Custer's aid, refusing to budge from his position. (23) He supposedly was drinking heavily that day, plus the night before he was intoxicated to the point of being irrational.

(24) At the time that Custer began his campaign against the Sioux, he was a national folk hero. (25) His reckless and sometimes foolish actions caused his superiors to cringe, however, the public and the newspapers adored him. (26) As he began that final campaign, Custer seriously was considering a candidacy for president of the United States. (27) The only blemish on his record was the court-martial for desertion, he was determined to erase that with a victory over the Sioux. (28) Custer was convinced that only one impressive victory in the field would boost him into the White House. (29) Instead of being cheered on Pennsylvania Avenue, Custer and his ambitions were drowned in a chorus of war cries on a remote hillside overlooking the Little Big Horn River.

Scorecard: Number of errors found and corrected _____

21 Checking Subject-Verb Agreement and Noun Plurals

Good writing ought to be transparent. Readers should focus on the ideas beneath your words and not be distracted by unexpected and confusing matters on the surface. One issue that can cause trouble comes when subjects and verbs don't match. This chapter will show you how to make them match. You'll learn

■ how to make subjects and verbs fit together

■ how to recognize and master the exceptions to the rules

WHAT IS SUBJECT-VERB AGREEMENT?

You know that subjects can be nouns or pronouns. You know, too, that they can be **singular**: representing one person, place, or thing. Or they can be **plural**: representing more than one. In other words, nouns and pronouns have **number**. Verbs also can have singular or plural forms. A singular subject goes with a singular verb, and a plural subject with a plural verb. That's **subject-verb agreement**, and without it, some sentences can sound pretty odd.

Look, for example, at the following two sentences written in the **present tense**, which discusses habitual actions or states, or actions that are happening now:

> *I work* part-time as a sky-dive instructor.
> My friend *works* part-time as the parachute folder.

These sentences probably look fine to you; they meet your expectations about the forms of words you see in edited written English. When the subject is *my friend*, the verb form is *works*—with an –s ending. When the subject is *I*, the verb form is *work*. Therefore, the subject and verb are said to *agree* when their forms are the ones most readers would expect to find together in written English.

UNIT 4

Chapter 21

Composing with Confidence

©2003

GO ELECTRONIC!

Use the following electronic supplements for additional practice with your writing:

• For chapter-by-chapter summaries and exercises, visit the Composing with Confidence Companion Website at: http://www.ablongman.com/meyers.

• For work with the writing process, visit The Longman Writer's Warehouse at http://longmanwriterswarehouse.com (password needed).

• For additional practice in grammar, use The Writer's ToolKit Plus CD-ROM

But look at another sentence:

One of the parachutes *are* torn.

According to the sentence, how many parachutes are torn? The sentence proba-bly confuses you momentarily because the verb *are* agrees with the wrong word, *parachutes*. Correct subject-verb agreement clears up the problem:

One of the parachutes *is* torn.

Subject-verb agreement isn't an issue in every verb tense. It's limited to tenses that deal with the present, and to only one verb in the past tense, which we'll dis-cuss in Chapter 22. Right now, we'll focus on the present-tense agreement.

AGREEMENT WITH NOUN SUBJECTS

The form of the verb depends on the subject, which can be singular or plural. A singular noun almost never ends in –*s*, but the present-tense verb after every sin-gular noun subject does end in –*s*.

Mr. Wilson teaches yoga and Tibetan cooking.
My friend plays bass guitar in a rock group.
Exercise builds strong muscles.

Placing –*s* Correctly

Most plural nouns end in –*s* or –*es* (*cars, birds, cities, potatoes, knives,* and thou-sand-dollar *bills*). But the verb after a plural noun subject never ends in –*s:*

The Wilsons both *teach* yoga.
My friends play guitar in a rock group.
Certain *exercises build* strong leg muscles.

EXERCISE 1 | Establishing Verb Agreement

Write the appropriate present-tense form of the verb supplied in each of the following sentences.

A Mouthful of Crocodiles

(1) A popular myth (hold) _holds_____ that crocodiles (eat)

_____ their young. (2) Although incorrect, the belief (come)

_____ from the unusual practices of the mother crocodile. (3) After the

young crocs (hatch), their mother gently (take) _____ them into her huge

jaw and (shake) _____ them down into a special pouch in the floor of

her mouth. (4) The mother (create) _____ a strange picture with such a

mouthful. (5) Perhaps eighteen baby crocodiles (peer) _____ out from

between her teeth as she (travel) _____ along. (6) Mommy finally (carry)

_____ them down to the water, where the babies (try) _____ out their swimming skills.

Irregular Noun Plurals

A few nouns do not form their plurals by adding *-s*. Here's a list of some of the most important **irregular nouns**:

Singular form	Different plural form
child	children (not childs or childrens)
man	men (not mans)
woman	women (not womans)
foot	feet (not foots)
medium	media (not mediums)

Singular form	Same plural form
deer	deer
fish	fish (or fishes)

EXERCISE 2   *Correcting Noun-Plural Errors*

Some of the noun-plural forms in the following passage are missing or incorrect. (Not every noun is the subject of a sentence.) Find and correct the errors.

The World's Best Dad

(1) The temperature during the long Antarctic winter plunges as low as 80 degree^s Fahrenheit. (2) Under these conditions, only an amazing combination of patience and acrobatics allows the emperor penguin to hatch its eggs. (3) The emperors are magnificent bird, with feather covering most of their bodies. (4) The female lays a single egg in midwinter and immediately goes on a long fishing trip, leaving her mate in charge of the egg. (5) The egg would freeze almost immediately in the bitter cold if it touched the ground. (6) To protect it, the male stands for sixty day on one foot, holding the egg next to his warm underbelly with the other foot. (7) Occasionally, he switches feets, but throughout this period he eats nothing at all. (8) Finally, when the chick is about ready to hatch, the female returns to take over the child rearing, and the very hungry male waddles off to the ocean to find some fishs of his own.

AGREEMENT WITH PRONOUN SUBJECTS

Pronouns substitute for nouns, and only the third-person-singular subject pronouns (*he, she, it*) agree with verbs that end in *s*.

	Singular + verb		Plural + verb	
First person	I	work	we	work
Second person	you	work	you	work
Third person	he	*works*	they	work
	she	*works*		
	it	*works*		

EXERCISE 3   Forming Agreement with Pronoun Subjects

Fill in the appropriate present-tense verb form after each pronoun.

1. She (go) *goes* _____ to Hawaii every winter for a month.

2. Therefore, I (admire) _____, (respect) _____, and (despise) _____ her greatly.

3. You (need) _____ only two things for a trip to Hawaii: a lot of suntan lotion and a lot of money.

4. It (sound) _____ like a wonderful place to visit.

5. We (wish) _____ you luck with raising the funds to get there.

6. Why not check with John? He (make) _____ money the old-fashioned way; he (print) _____ it in his basement.

SUBJECTS JOINED WITH *AND*

TIPS

For Determining Agreement in Compound Subjects: The Rule of *And*

When two subjects are joined by *and,* the verb needs to be plural.

Subject *and* subject = verb without -*s*:

Love *and* marriage *go* together like an old-fashioned carriage.

A second kind of plural subject is the **compound subject**—two or more subjects combined by *and,* whether nouns, pronouns, or nouns and pronouns. Here are some examples:

> John *and* I
> plants *and* animals
> Sam, Pam, Bill, Will, Judy, *and* Trudy

These subjects always take a present-tense verb form without -*s* because they are plural:

> Swifty and I *run* together weekly in marathons.
> My eighteen dogs and cats *get* along fine—as long as they're in separate rooms.

EXERCISE 4   Forming Agreement with Compound Subjects

Write the appropriate present-tense form of the verb supplied in each of the following sentences:

Facts About Aging

(1) Instead of occurring suddenly when someone (reach) _reaches_____ sixty or seventy, old age and its complications (come) _____ about in gradual steps. (2) As adults, you and I (die) _____ a little every day. (3) Most tissues, organs, and physical processes (begin) _____ to deteriorate when we (become) _____ about twenty-five years old, but these body parts and functions (decline) _____ at different rates. (4) The blood that (flow) _____ to the brain of a seventy-five-year-old is 20 percent less than the amount the same person had at age thirty. (5) Furthermore, the older person's brain weight (equal) _____ only 56 percent of what it was. (6) During short bursts of activity, old people (work) _____ at less than half of their former maximum speed. (7) An elderly man and a woman (lose) _____ almost two-thirds of the taste buds they had at age thirty. (8) Why he and she (experience) _____ such a dramatic decline in the ability to taste is a mystery.

Collaborative Activity 1

Checking Agreement

List five subjects—nouns, pronouns, and compound subjects. Exchange papers by passing them to the left and write a sentence in the present tense for each of the subjects. Then pass the papers to the left again so a third student can check your work. Discuss your answers.

IRREGULAR PRESENT-TENSE VERBS

The verbs *to be, to do,* and *to have* deserve special attention for two reasons: (1) you use them more often than most verbs, and (2) you use them as **helping verbs** in verb phrases—that is, as the verbs that come before main verbs.

To Be

To be (is, am, are) is the most common verb in the English language. As a helping verb, it always precedes *–ing* words in verb phrases:

I *am counting* my millions right now.
My friend Lionel *is taking* a vacation in Pago Pago for a month.

And it often serves as a linking verb, linking the subject to the words that describe or rename the subject in some way:

Those spotted green sandwiches *are* very appetizing.
The university *is* a great fountain of knowledge where many students come to drink.

Here are the present-tense forms of *to be* and their **contractions** (that is, their shortened forms with **apostrophes** ['] replacing omitted letters):

Subject	Verb	Contractions	Negative contractions
I	*am*	*I'm*	
he, she, it (or singular noun)	*is*	*he's, she's, it's*	*isn't*
we, you, they (or plural noun)	*are*	*we're, you're, they're*	*aren't*

| EXERCISE 5 | Forming Agreement with To Be |

TIPS

For Remembering Contractions

An *apostrophe* ['] always replaces the letters that have been omitted in a contraction. Examine *be* verbs carefully to avoid two common errors with contractions:

1. Leaving off the *–'s*, the *–'m*, or the *–'re.* Check your sentences during revisions, and if you see, for example, "He a tall man," change it to "He's a tall man."

2. Confusing the contractions with sound-alike or look-alike words: *we're* with *were, you're* with *your, it's* with *its,* and *they're* with *their* or *there.*

Write the present-tense form of to be *in each sentence. Some sentences are missing the verb altogether. Others are missing the helping and/or linking verb.*

A Belly Full of Information

(1) Your stomach growls because a lot of physiological activity ^*is* ~~are~~ taking place. (2) As you eating, drinking, or swallowing saliva, you also swallow gas. (3) Imagine that your stomach and intestines like a front-loading washing machine in a laundromat. (4) Instead of clothes, water, and detergent whooshing around, there solid foods, liquids from your diet, water, digestive fluids, and gas constantly churning and contracting. (5) This churning important because it kneads and mixes the food and enzymes as part of the digestive process. (6) But just as it necessary to eliminate excess water and suds from the washer, the food left in your stomach moves into the intestines, where it made ready for disposal. (7) As the bubbles of gas and liquids mixed together and then pushed out of the stomach, the result gurgling, splashing, and squeaking of all kinds—which you describe as "growling." (8) The stomach seems to growl more when you hungry because the muscular activity in the abdomen increases as it anticipates a new meal.

| EXERCISE 6 | Editing To Be Forms |

Many—but not all—of the following sentences contain errors in the use of to be. *In some sentences* to be *is missing. In other sentences, the form of* to be *doesn't agree with its subject. And in still other sentences, there's an incorrect contraction using* to be. *Correct each error above the line.*

The Bear Facts

1. ^*We're* ~~Were~~ used to thinking of humans as left-handed or right-handed, but we don't think of animals in those terms.

2. Strangely enough, however, all polar bears is left-handed.

3. When their attacked, they use only their left paws to strike out or defend themselves.

4. A fully grown polar bear weighs as much as 1,000 pounds, and its often nine feet tall.

5. Very high concentrations of vitamin A is in the livers of polar bears.

6. In fact, all the members of a nineteenth-century Arctic expedition we're poisoned by eating the liver of a polar bear they'd killed.

7. The koala bear and the panda is not members of the bear family.

8. The panda is actually a type of giant raccoon.

9. The koala is more closely related to the kangaroo, since there both marsupials

(animals that carry their young in pouches).

To Do

Aside from functioning as a main verb, *to do (do, does)* serves as the helping verb in most present-tense questions or negative statements:

> *Do* you like my pet snake?
> *Does* she ever pet her snake?
> I *don't* want two elephants—only one!
> She *doesn't* drive a car, but she has a pilot's license.

Here are the present-tense, affirmative and negative forms of *to do,* including the negative contractions:

Subject	Verb	Negative verb	Negative contractions
I, we, you, they	*do*	*do not*	*don't*
he, she, it	*does*	*does not*	*doesn't*

EXERCISE 7	Forming Agreement with To Do

Supply the appropriate present-tense form of to do *in each of the blank spaces.*

The World's Most Boring Animals

(1) Sloths may be the laziest land animals in the world; they ___do___n't do anything fast—but there isn't very much that they do anyway. (2) For all intents and purposes, a sloth _____n't have any reflexes. (3) Sloths _____n't even flinch, let alone jump, at a sudden loud noise. (4) A sloth that falls from a tree _____n't try to stand up; instead, it sags to the ground like a bag of flour.

(5) Furthermore, only a female sloth can maintain a constant body temperature, and it _____ that only when pregnant. (6) The animals can turn their breathing on and off at will, and they _____n't suffer any ill effects. (7) Even when sloths eat, their food _____n't get digested fast. The process takes at least two weeks. (8) _____ this animal sound like the kind you would want to invite to a dinner party?

EXERCISE 8	Writing Negatives with To Do

Write the appropriate negative contraction of to do *(doesn't or don't) in each sentence. You'll first need to determine whether the subject is singular or plural.*

1. Lions may attack other animals, but they usually ___don't___ bother each other.

2. They're actually rather social animals. A lion _____ live alone but in a group of two to forty others, called a *pride.*

3. However, one male rules the pride, and the rest of the animals certainly _____ share equal rights with him.

4. He is first in mating, and other lions _____ eat until he's had his portion.

5. Lionesses are chiefly responsible hunting for food. The females _____ receive this assignment because the male is lazy. His big mane is simply too easy for prey to recognize.

6. In the wild, a 350-pound lion will eat 45 pounds of food daily. However, a lion _____ eat nearly as much in captivity—usually only 10 to 15 pounds a day.

7. The biggest threat to lions _____ come from other animals; it comes from human hunters and poachers.

Collaborative Activity 2

Writing Irregular Verbs

Write six affirmative sentences in the present-tense: two using *be,* two using *have,* and two using *do.* Exchange papers and rewrite each sentence twice. The first time, change the sentence into a negative statement. The second time change a singular subject to a plural or a plural to a singular. Exchange papers again, check the answers, and discuss any problems.

To Have

In addition to functioning as a simple verb, *to have* often acts as a helping verb.

They *have fulfilled* all the certification requirements to become lifeguards in the desert.
Albert *has eaten* the whole pizza.

Here are the present-tense affirmative forms, contractions, and negative forms of *to have:*

Subject	Verb	Contractions	Negative contractions
I, we, you, they	have	*I've, we've, you've, they've*	*haven't* or *don't have*
he, she, it	has	*he's, she's, it's*	*hasn't* or *doesn't have*

EXERCISE 9   Forming Agreement with To Have

Fill in the appropriate present-tense form (affirmative or negative) of to have *in each of the following sentences.*

A Few Swift Facts

(1) The European bird called the *swift* _has_____ a number of unique and extraordinary behaviors. (2) It eats only flying insects and _____ never been seen on land or in trees except when nesting. (3) Apparently it also _____ real talent as a weather predictor. (4) The birds _____

been observed flying hundreds of miles to the north or south well in advance of an approaching cyclone. (5) Swifts know that they _____n't a chance of finding insects in the air during the storm. (6) Meanwhile, their young, who _____ to be left in the nest, immediately hibernate until their parents return.

SPECIAL PROBLEMS WITH SUBJECT-VERB AGREEMENT

Certain kinds of sentences or words present tricky issues with subject-verb agreement. We'll examine those issues next.

Collective Nouns

Collective nouns represent a group of two or more persons, things, or ideas:

class	family	Sears, Roebuck, and Company
audience	team	jury

Deciding whether a collective noun is singular or plural presents problems for even the most experienced writers. Here are a few useful guidelines.

Collective nouns are singular when they represent the whole group of persons, things, or ideas acting together:

> My *family* (together) *has* a reunion each year in May.
> The baseball *team* (together) *practices* at 3 o'clock.

But when collective nouns represent a group of people, things, or ideas acting individually, the collective nouns are plural:

> The *family* (individual members) *are* seated around the table.
> The baseball *team* (individual members) *come* from all over the world.

To avoid confusion—and the impression that your grammar is in error when it's not—rewrite the sentences with plural subjects:

> The *members* of the family *are* seated around the table.
> The *players* on the baseball team *come* from all over the world.

A few collective nouns are always plural: words such as *police, faculty,* and *staff;* all team names—even if they don't end in *s,* such as the *Chicago Fire;* and all nationalities:

> The *police patrol* this area regularly.
> The *Atlanta Braves* usually *have* a strong team.
> The *French are* proud people.

In most cases, **uncountable nouns** (*wine, sugar, homework, furniture,* and so on) are always singular. They cannot end in *-s,* and the verb that agrees with them should end in *-s.* Of course **countable nouns** (*one lamp* or *three lamps,* and so on) can be singular or plural.

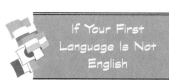

If Your First Language Is Not English

Be careful if you were educated in a British school system. British English tends to treat collective nouns as plurals: "Harrod's Department Store are having a sale." American English tends to treat collective nouns as singular: "Marshall's is having a sale."

EXERCISE 10	Forming Agreement with Collective Nouns

Write the appropriate present-tense form of each verb in parentheses.

1. The jury (have) *has* _____ reached a decision.

2. The class (meet) _____ at 9 o'clock.

3. The police (come) _____ into this area often.

4. The Dutch (produce) _____ beautiful tulips, delicious chocolate, and wonderful beer.

5. The New York Yankees (win) _____ most of their games year in and year out.

6. The audience (be) _____ enjoying the play.

Questions

The subject normally begins a sentence and therefore alerts you to the form of the verb that follows. But in questions, the verb comes first. To avoid errors in agreement, especially with compound subjects, you need to anticipate what the subject will be as you write the verb. Here's an example:

Incorrect: *Does Maria and Tom* expect their baby soon?

You may think that the verb agrees with *Maria,* the word that immediately follows. But then poor Tom is left without a verb—or a baby. The sentence needs to be rewritten:

Correct: *Do Maria and Tom* expect their baby soon?

There Is/Are

A similar issue occurs when *there* starts the sentence: you must decide whether to use *are* or *is* before stating the subject. If the subject is singular, use *is*. If the subject is plural, use *are:*

There's *a player* on the basketball team who *is* eight feet tall.
There *are three players* who *are* over seven feet, two inches.
There *are a center, two forwards, and two guards* on the team.

But don't overuse *there is/are,* which waste words and bury grammatical subjects in the middle of sentences. You can often revise a sentence to omit these constructions:

Poor: *There are* some students in Professor Booring's class *who never understand* his lectures.

Better: Some students in Professor Booring's class *never understand* his lectures.

EXERCISE 11	Forming Agreement with Questions and There

Complete each of the following sentences with the appropriate present-tense form of the verb in parentheses.

The Problems with Wine Buying

(1) Although many wealthy adult Americans buy wine, there (be) _are_____ very few sales of wine to people of moderate incomes. (2) Why (do) _____n't these people buy much wine? (3) People would probably say there (be) _____ only one reason: Wine is too expensive. (4) But (be) _____n't these the same folks who are quite willing to spend $1.50 for a bottle of imported water? (5) The real reason is that there (be) _____ too much rigmarole surrounding wine, so the average person is afraid of it all. (6) At a fancy restaurant, for example, (do) _____ a man and woman on a date understand all those French names of wines—and which wines go with which foods? (7) "(Do) _____ that white wine go with fish? And what (do) _____ we order if I get steak and she orders fish—pink wine? Come to think about it, there (be) _____ a pink wine, _____n't there?" (8) And then there (be) _____ that embarrassing and awkward moment when the server pours the wine into the patron's glass for inspection. (9) (Do) _____ the customer, who can't even pretend to be judging the quality of the wine, want to look like an idiot? (10) There (be) _____ good reasons to stick with soda and beer.

Phrases between Subject and Verb

A phrase that comes between the subject and the verb may distract you from the actual subject and lead to an agreement error. Most of these phrases begin with a preposition—a small word such as *in, with, to, of,* or *from*. For example, what verb form is required in the following sentences?

The box of crayons (is/are) on the table.
The answers to the question (is/are) not difficult.

You should have chosen first *is* and then *are*. With the prepositional phrases removed, the sentences appear like this:

The box . . . is on the table.
The answers . . . are not difficult.

When you aren't sure of the verb form as you proofread, try drawing a line in pencil through the prepositional phrase so you can locate the true subject of the sentence:

> The box of crayons is on the table.
> The answers to the question are not difficult.

Cross out the prepositional phrases in the following sentences and then circle the correct verb form:

> The top and bottom of the carton (have/has) to be handled carefully.
> A female dog with seven puppies (make/makes) quite a mess.

Were these your answers?

> The top and bottom . . . have to be handled carefully.
> A female dog . . . makes quite a mess.

EXERCISE 12   Working with Prepositional Phrases

Draw a line through the prepositional phrase after the subject of each sentence and then fill in an appropriate present-tense verb.

Dust and Skin

(1) Pieces of skin (make) _make_____ up seventy percent of common household dust, according to Dr. Raymond Clark of London's Clinical Research Centre. (2) Dr. Clark claims that 5,000 flakes of skin (be) _____ shed by the human body every minute. (3) In all, forty pounds of skin (be) _____ shed during the average person's lifetime. (4) The entire outside layer of our bodies (be) _____ replaced every seven to ten days. (5) The pieces of discarded skin from this shedding action (be) _____ small enough to pass through most forms of clothing. (6) Columns of rising hot air (surround) _____ the body, (lift) _____ these tiny particles above a person's head, and (create) _____ household dust.

Expressions of Parts

Some words express parts of a whole: *some, many, all, most, one-half,* and so forth. When they're used with prepositional phrases beginning with *of,* they present an exception to the rule about prepositional phrases:

> Some of the glasses . . .
> All of the material . . .
> All of the students . . .
> Most of the students . . .
> One-half of the flowers . . .

Collaborative Activity 4

Working on Agreement
Prepare six sentences—two with collective nouns, two with prepositional phrases after the subject, and two with part markers and *of.* Write the sentences in the past tense or the future tense. Exchange papers and rewrite the sentences in the present tense. Exchange papers again by passing to the left, check over the sentences, and discuss any problems.

To determine whether the verb should be singular or plural, draw a line through the part markers. You can then see the true subject—and the form of the verb it should agree with:

Part markers	True subject	Verb	
Some of	the glasses	are	broken.
All of	the material	is	here.
All of	the students	are	here.
Most of	the students	are doing	very well.
One-half of	the flowers	are damaged	by the frost.

EXERCISE 13	Establishing Agreement

Write the correct form of the verb in each of the following present-tense sentences.

Age and Skin

(1) Why (do) _does_____ all of our skin become dried with age? (2) As we grow older, all of the dead skin cells from the outer layer—the epidermis—(be) _____ replaced more slowly by new cells from the layer below, the dermis. (3) Most of the dermis gradually (shrink) _____ and (harden) _____ . (4) Some of the secretion from sweat and oil glands also (decrease) _____ . (5) As a result, a lot of our skin (begin) _____ to dry out and crack.

IN SUMMARY	Checking Subject-Verb Agreement

In Present-Tense Subject-Verb Agreement

1. Only the pronoun *he*, *she*, and *it* and all singular nouns agree with verbs ending in *-s*.
2. All other subject pronouns (*I*, *we*, *you*, and *they*) and all plural nouns agree with verbs without *-s* endings.
3. Almost all plural nouns end in *-s*, but the verbs that agree with them do not; very few singular nouns end in *-s*, but the verbs that agree with them do; and all compound subjects (two or more subjects joined by *and*) are plural and take verbs without *s* endings.
4. The verbs *be*, *do*, and *have* take special forms.
5. Collective nouns, with a few exceptions, are singular.
6. Questions and statements with *there is/are* as sentence-starters require that you find the complete subject after the verb.
7. Prepositional phrases between subject and verb don't determine agreement.
8. Part markers with or before the subject don't determine agreement.

EDITING FOR MASTERY

Mastery Exercise 1

Correcting Errors in Subject-Verb Agreement and Noun Plurals

The sentences that follow contain twenty errors, in addition to the first error, which has corrected for you as an example. The errors include incorrect subject–verb agreement, incorrect noun plurals, missing verbs, and incorrect contractions with the verb to be. *Find and correct each error by making your changes above the lines.*

Food for Thought

1. A gourmet service in England offer^(s) this dish: a dormouse, electrocuted and then skinned, which are prepared either by braising in honey or wine or lightly frying in butter. The mouses are said to be delicious.

2. There is a live-minnow-eating festival that held every year in a town in Belgium. The contestants drop minnows into a silver goblet full of red wine and then drinks them.

3. Every year in Japan, about 200 people dies from eating the fu-gu, a fish that is considered a delicacy. The fish have poison in its guts, and a cook who don't have a license is not allowed to prepare it.

4. Chicken feathers is 97 percent protein, and researchers at the University of Georgia has found a way of turning them into a fine white powder they claim is easy to digest. A panel who have tasted cookies made from this powder describes them as "pretty good to eat."

5. In 1868, a horse meat banquet for 160 peoples was held at London's Langham Hotel. The highlight of the meal was a 280-pound slab of horse carried on the shoulders of four chef.

6. In 1978, the movie director Herb Robbins held a worm-eating competition at Rialto College, California, to promote his movie *The Worm Eaters*. The winner, Rusty Rice, ate 28 worm.

7. A cookbook by Martha Wapensky describe the correct way to cook African Flying Ants. There's several steps in the process. First, a cup of ants are fried in a dry pan. The next step in preparing the ants are to remove the pan and dry the ants in the sun. After their dry, any wing and stones are removed. Then the ants is fried again, with or without a little oil, and a bit of salt is added. When the ants are fully prepared, there served over a bed of rice.

Scorecard: Number of Errors Found and Corrected _____

Collaborative Activity 5

Comparing Corrections
Appoint someone in the group to read the entire passage from Mastery Exercise 1 aloud so you can hear where errors occur. Make corrections, discuss them in your group, and report them to the entire class.

Mastery Exercise 2

Correcting Errors in Subject-Verb Agreement and Noun Plurals

The sentences that follow contain twenty errors, in addition to the first error, which has corrected for you as an example. The errors include incorrect subject-verb agreement, incorrect noun plurals, missing verbs, and incorrect contractions with the verb to be. *Find and correct each error by making your changes above the lines.*

Odd Animals and Their Behavior

1. Goby fish ∧is found in tropical rivers. They has gills and a supplementary breathing system that allow them to draw oxygen from either water or air. They certainly don't act like other fish since they prefer "walking" on land to swimming.

2. All snakes shake their tails when their emotionally aroused, but only the rattlesnake have a noisemaker.

3. Reptile purchased as pets and later flushed down toilets have been found alive and well in the sewer system of New York City.

4. Ostriches don't care too much about family togetherness. They sometimes lays their eggs in a community nest, and the first-hatched babies is fed the unhatched eggs.

5. A chameleon is a tree-dwelling reptile with a strange habit. It changes color whenever the animal becomes emotionally excited.

6. Whales are the best high jumpers; they can leap more than twenty feets into the air.

7. Hornets and wasps are great paper maker. They mixes their saliva with wood pulp that they have eaten and form a paste that dry into stiff paper.

8. An elephant have superior hearing; it can easily detect the footsteps of mouses.

9. Three-wattled bell birds of Costa Rica makes a call that can be heard for three miles.

10. The hiccup fish of Brazil don't get its name for nothing. It swallows huge gulps of air and then release them to make a sound like a hiccup. When the fish is fully grown to twelve inch, its hiccup can be heard a mile away.

11. One kind of earthworm that found in Australia don't exactly qualify as one of earth's tiny creatures. The little fellow has a diameter of almost an inch and is ten feet long.

12. Woodpecker finches lives in the Galapagos Islands. These birds have the very humanlike ability to use tools. They hunt for insects by poking holes in tree trunks with cactus thorns and twigs.

Scorecard: Number of Errors Found and Corrected _____

22 Checking Past-Tense and Past-Participle Forms

The past tense and its close relation, the past participle, are among the trickiest verb forms in English. That's partly because they come in many varieties, and partly because they combine with other verbs in a variety of ways. This chapter will show you how to use all these verb forms. You'll learn about the following:

■ varieties of the past tense

■ the verb forms to select in discussing the past

■ ways to use verb forms as adjectives

THE PAST TENSE OF REGULAR VERBS

You write in the **past tense** to discuss actions or events that occurred before the present. Over the many centuries that English has evolved, the past-tense verb forms have become increasingly simplified. Today, most verbs in the past tense share a common ending: *–ed,* no matter what their subject, and are therefore called **regular verbs.** Here are some examples:

> The Soviet Union *launched* the first satellite into space on October 4, 1957.
>
> Its Russian name, *Sputnik,* immediately *entered* the vocabulary of the United States.
>
> A month later, *Sputnik II orbited* the earth and *carried* a little dog, Laika.

Remember that **infinitives**—words formed from verbs by adding *to* before them—function as adjectives, adverbs, or nouns and do not take a tense.

A Word About Words

One theory about the origins of the past tense is that long ago *did* was added to verbs, such as in the sentence "The man walk did." Later, this addition was shortened to *–ed.*

GO ELECTRONIC!

Use the following electronic supplements for additional practice with your writing:

- For chapter-by-chapter summaries and exercises, visit the Composing with Confidence Companion Website at: http://www.ablongman.com/meyers.

- For work with the writing process, visit The Longman Writer's Warehouse at http://longmanwriterswarehouse.com (password needed).

- For additional practice in grammar, use The Writer's ToolKit Plus CD-ROM

EXERCISE 1	Identifying Past-Tense Verbs

✔ **TIPS**

For Spelling Regular Past-Tense Verbs

1. When the verb already ends in *–e*, just add *–d:*
   like + *d* = *liked*
   smoke + *d* = *smoked*
2. When the verb ends in a consonant *–y*, change the + *–y* to *i* before adding *–ed:*
   reply = *replied*
   deny = *denied*

Write Pr *before each present-tense sentence and* P *before each past-tense sentence.*

Pr _____ **1.** Rockets launched into space are routine occurrences.

_____ **2.** The Russian Yuri Gagarin circled the earth in a space capsule on April 12, 1961.

_____ **3.** The American Alan Shepard piloted a space capsule beyond the earth's atmosphere soon afterward but did not orbit the earth.

_____ **4.** John Glenn accomplished the feat of orbiting the earth almost a year later.

_____ **5.** Then, in 1998, Glenn orbited the earth again, and at seventy-seven years old, was the oldest person to do so.

_____ **6.** From its headquarters in Colorado Springs, Colorado, a government agency called NORAD tracks satellites and assorted junk left in space from previous launches.

EXERCISE 2	Transforming Verb Tenses

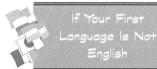

If Your First Language Is Not English

Past-tense endings of regular verbs end in *–ed*, but are most often pronounced like *–t* or *–d*. That makes hearing and saying them difficult. So use your eyes and ears to recognize past-tense verb endings. Be careful, though, to focus only on true verbs, not infinitives (which usually begin with *to*—such as *to go* or *to make*—and never take a tense).

The following passage is written in the present tense. Change it to the past tense by writing the proper past-tense form of each verb above the line. Be careful not to place –ed endings on infinitives.

The Beginnings of Manned Space Flights

(1) The flights by both Russian and American astronauts ^ ~~convince~~ *convinced* scientists that a weightless environment presents no serious dangers to humans over long periods of time. (2) People enter orbits around the earth, conduct useful observations and experiments, and then return home to report on their findings. (3) The American Gemini and Russian Voskhod manned programs demonstrate the ability of humans to maneuver a spaceship and dock with another vehicle. (4) The programs also allow humans to walk and work in space. (5) These flights provide the experience and knowledge that prepares the United States' program for manned landings on the Moon.

THE PAST TENSE OF IRREGULAR VERBS

Not all past-tense verbs take the regular *–ed* ending. Some simply refuse to give up their ancient **irregular** forms. We'll examine these irregular verbs, beginning with the three most important ones: *to be, could,* and *would.*

To Be

By far the most common irregular verb is *to be.* It's also the only verb that agrees with its subject in the past tense. As you saw in Chapter 21, that means it changes its form depending on whether the subject is singular or plural:

Subject	Verb
I He She It Singular nouns	} *was* or *wasn't*
We You They Plural nouns	} *were* or *weren't*

Notice that, as in the present tense, *to be* ends with *-s* to agree with third-person singular subjects—and also with the pronoun *I*. You may want to review the discussion of *to be* in Chapter 21 before completing the following exercises or consult that chapter as you go along.

EXERCISE 3	Forming Agreement with To Be

In each of the following sentences, write the proper past-tense form of to be.

1. I _was_____ amazed at Albert's ability to fill up space—in his body.

2. Once he _____ even able to limit himself to a mere three slabs of ribs.

3. _____ you able to keep his plate full for more than a few minutes?

4. There _____ large crowds that gathered to watch him eat.

5. _____ the police ever called to control the crowds?

6. The jury _____ unanimous in its verdict—gross!

Could and *Would*

Could is the past tense of *can*, so *could* refers to ability in the past. Compare these clauses:

Past ability
In 1969, the United States *could afford* to send manned missions to the
Present ability
Moon, but now we *can* only *talk* fondly about those missions.

Would is the past tense of *will*, so *would* refers to the future from a point in the past. Compare these clauses:

	Past
At Christmas time in 1968, an American manned spacecraft *circled* the	
Future from a point in the past	
Moon in preparation for a flight that *would take place* the following year.	

If Your First Language Is Not English

Pay close attention to *could* and *would*. Some languages, such as those spoken in the Philippines, don't have past-tense forms of *can* and *will*. Check these verbs carefully as you revise.

Would also appears in statements in which *if* is stated or implied. Notice that *if* introduces a condition that is contrary to fact, a remote possibility, or a very polite request:

If I were on the Moon, I *would* weigh a lot less. (contrary to fact, since I cannot be on the Moon now.)

If I went Mars, I *would take* along a good camera. (an unlikely possibility)

Tom *would like* to be an astronaut. (*if* it is possible)

Would you please *help* him? (*if* you don't mind)

EXERCISE 4	Transforming the Tenses of Can and Will

Rewrite each of the following sentences in the past tense.

1. We hope that the landing on the Moon will be successful. *We hoped that the landing on the Moon would be successful.*

2. The astronauts can walk in space. _____

3. They can live outside the earth's atmosphere for extended periods of time. ____

4. They realize that there will be many dangers._____

5. On July 20, 1969, astronauts Neil Armstrong and Buzz Aldrin can land their space vehicle on the Moon's surface just a few seconds before their fuel supply will run out. _____

The Other Irregular Verbs

Here's a list of the other most common irregular verbs. You probably know most of them, but read them all and put a check mark next to the ones you need to memorize. The last category on the list is the past participle, which we'll discuss later in the chapter.

Simple form	Past tense	Past participle
be	was, were	been
beat	beat	beaten
become	became	become
begin	began	begun
bend	bent	bent

Continued

Simple form	Past tense	Past participle
bet	bet	bet
bind	bound	bound
bite	bit	bitten
bleed	bled	bled
blow	blew	blown
break	broke	broken
breed	bred	bred
bring	brought	brought
build	built	built
burst	burst	burst
buy	bought	bought
cast	cast	cast
catch	caught	caught
choose	chose	chosen
come	came	come
creep	crept	crept
cut	cut	cut
dig	dug	dug
do	did	done
draw	drew	drawn
drink	drank	drunk
drive	drove	driven
eat	ate	eaten
fall	fell	fallen
feed	fed	fed
feel	felt	felt
fight	fought	fought
find	found	found
fit	fit (or fitted)	fit (or fitted)
flee	fled	fled
fly	flew	flown
forget	forgot	forgotten (or forgot)
forgive	forgave	forgiven
freeze	froze	frozen
get	got	gotten (or got)
give	gave	given
go	went	gone
grind	ground	ground
grow	grew	grown
hang	hung	hung
have	had	had
hear	heard	heard
hide	hid	hidden
hit	hit	hit
hold	held	held

A Word About Words

Irregular verbs probably evolved because they were easier to pronounce. Compare *leave did* with *left*, or *send did* with *sent*, for example.

Simple form	Past tense	Past participle
hurt	hurt	hurt
keep	kept	kept
know	knew	known
lay	laid	laid
lead	led	led
leave	left	left
lend	lent	lent
leap	leapt (or leaped)	leapt (or leaped)
let	let	let
lie	lay	lain
lose	lost	lost
make	made	made
meet	met	met
pay	paid	paid
put	put	put
quit	quit	quit
read	read	read
ride	rode	ridden
ring	rang	rung
rise	rose	risen
run	ran	run
say	said	said
see	saw	seen
sell	sold	sold
send	sent	sent
set	set	set
shake	shook	shaken
shed	shed	shed
shine	shone (or shined)	shone (or shined)
shoot	shot	shot
shut	shut	shut
sing	sang	sung
sink	sank (or sunk)	sunk
sit	sat	sat
slay	slew	slain
sleep	slept	slept
slide	slid	slid
slit	slit	slit
speak	spoke	spoken
speed	sped	sped
spend	spent	spent
spin	spun	spun
spread	spread	spread
spring	sprang (or sprung)	sprung

Continued

Simple form	Past tense	Past participle
stand	stood	stood
steal	stole	stolen
stink	stank (or stunk)	stunk
strike	struck	struck
strive	strove (or strived)	striven (or strived)
swear	swore	sworn
sweep	swept	swept
swim	swam	swum
swing	swung	swung
take	took	taken
teach	taught	taught
tear	tore	torn
tell	told	told
think	thought	thought
throw	threw	thrown
thrust	thrust	thrust
understand	understood	understood
wake	woke	woken
wear	wore	worn
weave	wove	woven
win	won	won
wind	wound	wound
write	wrote	written

Whenever you're unsure of a verb form, refer to this list or look up the verb in a dictionary. You'll find it under its simple form, and the past tense and past participle follow immediately before the definitions. (If you see no such forms, that means the verb is regular.)

EXERCISE 5	Writing Past-Tense Verbs

Fill in the correct past tense of each verb in the following passage. Consult the list above if necessary.

The First Tragedy in the Space Program

Collaborative Activity 1

Writing Irregular Verbs
Look over the list of the irregular verbs and write
the simple forms of the ten
you find most difficult.
Then exchange papers by
passing to the left. Write a
past-tense sentence for
each of the verbs. Return
the papers and check them
over.

(1) For almost a decade the safest form of transportation in history (be) _was_____ the space capsule. (2) Dozens of American astronauts and Soviet cosmonauts (ride) _____ into space in giant rockets. (3) They (spin) _____ around the earth, covering millions of miles. (4) They (go) _____ outside the capsule for space walks but always (make) _____ it back inside. (5) They (come) _____ back to earth in fiery capsules, splashing into the ocean or parachuting to land with amazing accuracy. (6) The United States and the Soviet Union (build) _____ space vehicles that (withstand) _____ every challenge.

(7) A failure (have) _____ to happen, however, and it finally (do) _____ on January 27, 1967, during a test run for the Apollo project. (8) The project (will) _____ try to land the first men on the Moon, and the crew of the first *Apollo* spacecraft, Virgil "Gus" Grissom, Ed White, and Roger Chaffee, (know) _____ how to handle a spacecraft.

(9) All three men (rise) _____ early that morning to rehearse their up-coming flight inside the space module at the Kennedy Space Center near Cocoa Beach, Florida. (10) They (spend) _____ five long hours in their space suits as they (keep) _____ repeating their drills. (11) Gus Grissom, a forty-year-old veteran of two previous space missions, (lie) _____ on his back strapped to his seat as he (give) _____ responses to the ground control's request for information.

(12) Then a ground control technician (catch) _____ the first sign of trouble. (13) The inside of the module suddenly (become) _____ pure white and then (grow) _____ dark on his television monitor. (14) He soon (hear) _____ a voice screaming over the headphones: "Fire . . . I smell fire!" (15) There (be) _____ a short silence, and then Ed White (speak) _____: "Fire in the cockpit!"

(16) The three men in the capsule (beat) _____ on the hatch before the voice of Roger Chaffee (can) _____ be heard: "We're on fire . . . get us out of here!" (17) Following that, there (be) _____ silence.

(18) In just four minutes, an emergency crew (burst) _____ from the control room on the ground level and (shoot) _____ up to the entrance to the capsule by high-speed elevator. (19) They (tear) _____ open the main hatch of the burning hot capsule. (20) But the billowing smoke and gases (make) _____ entry impossible, so they (draw) _____ back from the hatch.

(21) Meanwhile, as the smoke (blow) _____ out of the hatch, the pic-tures on the television cameras in ground control (become) _____ clearer. (22) Technicians (see) _____ the motionless bodies of the three astronauts. (23) The crew of the *Apollo* (lose) _____ their lives in a matter of seconds: the victims of the first space disaster—right here on earth.

THE PERFECT TENSES

The close relatives of the past tense are the present-perfect and past-perfect tenses, which also refer to the past in more complex ways. We'll examine both tenses.

The Present-Perfect Tense

Compare these two sentences:

> The United States *placed* a communications satellite in orbit in 1958.
> The United States *has placed* communications satellites in orbit since 1958.

Which tells you that the United States still launches communications satellites?

You should have identified the second sentence. It's an example of the **present-perfect tense**, which describes an idea that began in the past but continues up to the present.

The present-perfect tense is formed from two verbs:

1. the present-tense helping verb *have* or *has*
2. the main verb—a **past participle**—which ends in *–ed* for regular verbs but has a variety of forms if irregular

Remember that a **helping verb** helps the main verb express its tense and meaning. (See Chapter 19.) The past participle functions as the main verb in perfect tenses, but, as you'll see later, it has other functions. Also notice that the words *for* and *since* show when the action began:

> The Hubble space telescope has been orbiting the earth *since April 18, 1990.*
> The Hubble space telescope has been orbiting the earth *for several years.*

There's a second way in which you use the present-perfect tense. You can discuss a completed action in the indefinite past—you don't specify the time—that relates to the present. Here are some examples:

> Astronauts *have brought back* Moon rocks that *are* on display at the Air and Space Museum in Washington.
> The Mariner space project *has gathered* a great deal of data about Mars that *we're studying* today.

Statements about actions that ended just before the present often include the word *recently, already,* or *yet:*

> The prices of home satellite dishes have *recently* dropped dramatically.
> Satellite-based communications media have *already* changed the way we gather and exchange information.
> Have you created your own Web page *yet?*

When revising, look carefully at each use of *have* or *has* to see if it triggers the present-perfect tense—and if the past participle that follows is correct.

EXERCISE 6	Transforming Verb Tenses

Change each past-tense sentence into one using the present-perfect tense. Then compare the difference in meaning between the two versions of each sentence.

1. We took two courses in astronomy. *We have taken two courses in astronomy.*

2. I memorized only half of the dictionary so far. _____

_____

3. My friend Claudio flew to Ecuador twice this month. _____

_____

4. He saw several of his relatives on each trip. _____

_____

5. Elmer took a bath every Saturday, whether he needed to or not. _____

_____

6. My little brother grew six inches this year. _____

_____

The Past-Perfect Tense

In the following sentence, which actions happened long before the other action started?

> Both Germany and the Soviet Union *had begun* their rocket research programs ten years before the United States *started* its program.

Obviously, the actions of Germany and the Soviet Union happened first. They're stated in the **past-perfect tense**. This tense always describes an action that occurred *before* another time in the past—usually in a combined sentence that discusses both times. Like the present-perfect tense, the *past-perfect tense* is a combination of two words:

1. *had* (the past tense of *have*)
2. the past participle

However, the past-perfect tense is a *past* tense. Here's one more example in a combined sentence:

> Several German scientists, who *had worked* for Hitler during World War II, *continued* their rocket research in the United States after the war.

Both actions happened in the past. But the past-perfect-tense action happened earlier.

✓ **TIPS**

For Keeping the Past-Perfect and Present-Perfect Tenses Straight

Remember these differences:

1. The present-perfect tense relates the past to the present. Its helping verbs are *has* and *have*.
2. The past-perfect tense relates an earlier past action to a more recent one. Its helping verb is *had.*

EXERCISE 7   **Writing Perfect Tenses**

Write either the present-perfect or past-perfect-tense of the verb supplied in each of the following sentences.

1. After the Soviet Union (launch) _had launched_____ the first satellite, called *Sputnik I*, in 1957, the United States accelerated its space program.

2. The United States grew more jittery after a Russian named Yuri Gagarin (fly) _____ in space on April 12, 1961.

3. After President Kennedy (take) _____ office in 1961, he announced that a man from the United States would walk on the Moon by the end of the decade.

4. He talked about what the Soviet Union already (accomplish) _____.

5. Although U. S. astronauts (walk) _____ on the Moon two years earlier, the Russians launched the first space station in 1971.

6. After it (pass) _____ Jupiter in July 1979, *Voyager II* went on to fly past Saturn, Uranus, and Neptune for the next ten years.

Pay special attention to the past participle of *to be*—the word *been*. Notice its use in these present-perfect-tense sentences:

People have probably *been interested* in space travel since they first gazed at the stars.
The existence of an atmosphere on Mars *has already been proven*.

Been by itself cannot be a verb; it always requires *have, has,* or *had* as its helper. Check carefully for errors with *been* as you revise your papers.

EXERCISE 8	Writing Sentences with Been

Complete each of the following sentences with a verb phrase in the present-perfect or past-perfect tense using been.

1. The space shuttle *has been* _____ operating since April 12, 1981.

2. All the shuttle flights _____ manned.

3. The flights were suspended for a long time after all seven crew members _____ killed in the explosion of the Challenger on January 28, 1986.

4. The flights resumed after the o-rings on the rocket boosters of the shuttle _____ redesigned and thoroughly tested.

5. Unmanned launches of satellites _____ successfully accomplished by many countries.

THE OTHER ROLES OF THE PAST PARTICIPLE

Aside from its use in perfect tenses, the past participle also functions as part of a verb phrase or as an adjective.

After *Have*

Most three- and four-word verb phrases contain *have* plus the past participle:

could have gone	may have been	could have been working
could have seen	might have stolen	should have been gone
must have done	would have driven	might have been sleeping

When *have* is a helping verb, the main verb following it must be a past participle. The only exception is *have to,* meaning *must: We have to go.*

EXERCISE 9	Writing Phrases with Helping Verbs

Complete each of the following sentences using have *and an appropriate past participle.*

1. Maria had an accident. She should *have been more careful.*

2. I don't know what happened to my notebook. I could _____

_____

3. If I had known that you had to walk to school, I would _____

_____

4. Phu Nguyen got another perfect score on an examination. He must_____

_____

_____

5. Homer wore a striped tie, a polka-dot shirt, and checked polyester slacks. He

might _____

_____

6. The streets look very wet. Last night, it may _____

_____

After *To Be*

The past participle follows *to be* in the **passive voice**, in which the subject of a sentence does not perform the action but instead receives the action:

> The sound barrier *was first broken* by a pilot named Chuck Yeager.

Notice that the subject of the sentence—the sound barrier—didn't break a thing! A pilot named *Chuck Yeager* did the breaking. In other words, the subject of the sentence was passive; it did not act but was acted upon. Here's the same sentence in the **active voice**, in which the subject performed the action:

> A pilot named Chuck Yeager *broke* the sound barrier first.

Don't confuse *voice* with *tense*, for passive voice ideas can occur at any time in the past, present, or future. Compare the following sentences:

Tense	Passive voice	Active voice
Past	The flying saucers *were seen* by several people.	Several people *saw* the flying saucers.
Present	New satellites *are launched* every month.	We *launch* new satellites every month.
Future	Our society *will be transformed* by this new technology.	This new technology *will transform* our society.

As you edit your work, check for correct past-participle forms after the verb *to be*. And if you find a passive-voice sentence, consider whether to restate it in the active voice, which is usually less awkward and more direct. Use the passive voice only when the action you describe is more important than the person performing it:

Tickets for the Moon flight will be sold on a first-come, first-served basis. (The sentence does not—and need not—mention who will sell the tickets.)

EXERCISE 10	Writing Passive-Voice Sentences

Complete each of the following sentences in the passive voice by supplying an appropriate verb phrase. Be sure the verb tense is logical for the context of the action.

1. The sound barrier *was first broken*_____ by Chuck Yeager in October 1947.

2. Seven astronauts _____ when the Challenger Space Shuttle exploded on January 28, 1986.

3. Mars probably _____ by people from earth in the next two decades.

4. Water _____ on Mars several years ago.

5. An application to become an astronaut must _____ by the first week of next month.

6. One of the space shuttles _____ repaired now.

As an Adjective

Sometimes a past participle doesn't express an action. Instead, it functions as an adjective describing a noun or even a pronoun. Adjectives tend to appear in three places: after linking verbs, before nouns, and even after nouns.

After Linking Verbs.   Remember that **linking verbs** such as *is/are, become, feel, sound, taste, appear,* and *seem* link or join their subjects to adjectives. Here are examples with past-participle adjectives:

Subject	Linking verb	Past participle
Sammie	looks	tired.
That rooster	sounds	worn out.
Everyone	is	excited about the big game.

These are sentences of description; nothing *happens* in them. The subject does not act, and the past participle does not act upon the subject.

Before Nouns.   Like all adjectives, past participles often appear before nouns:

That is a *stolen* watch; don't buy it.
Used cars are cheaper than new ones.

Errors in past-participle forms before nouns can confuse or annoy readers, as demonstrated by the following example:

> He was a tire man.

Is this sentence supposed to mean that the man was tired or that he sold tires?

After Nouns.   A single-word adjective comes before the noun it describes. But an adjective phrase (two or more words that function as an adjective) comes after the noun. Many of these phrases begin with a past participle:

	Adjective phrase	
A man	*named John*	called a while ago.
	Adjective phrase	
I've just received a letter	*written by Mr. Lampley.*	

Look carefully at the words preceding and following nouns. Are they past participles? Have you used them correctly?

EXERCISE 11 | Writing Past-Participle Adjectives

Write the past-participle adjective form of a verb from the following list in each of the sentences. Do not use the same past participle twice.

do	prejudice	disgust
know	shake	satisfy
annoy	shock	encourage
disappoint	please	sadden
thrill	delight	amuse
enrage	offend	frighten

1. I waited for a long time, so I was quite _annoyed_ when Willie didn't show up.

2. Everyone is _____ about the good news.

3. Don't be _____ if you don't win; there are a lot of talented people in the competition.

4. He is well _____ for his acting ability.

5. I was _____ to hear the news.

6. Paulo says he is not upset, but he certainly acts _____.

EXERCISE 12 | Writing Past Participles with Nouns

Write an appropriate past participle in each of the following sentences.

1. When you visit Washington, be sure to see the Tomb of the _Unknown_ Soldier.

2. Roland can't walk; I think he has a _____ leg or ankle.

3. I usually have _____ eggs, but the rest of my family likes _____ eggs.

4. The _____ bear chased after the camper.

5. That _____ old suit looks terrible on you.

6. Mr. Gonzalez is a businessperson _____ for his honesty.

7. At all the clubs, everyone is doing a dance _____ the Sloppy Shuffle.

8. At the Ritz restaurant, you will enjoy food _____ by Chef Rudolfo.

9. Don't eat the meat _____ on the counter for three days.

IN SUMMARY | Checking Past-Tense and Past-Participle Forms

To Form the Past Tense and Past Participle
1. Add –ed to all regular verbs.
2. Study the irregular verb forms so you can use them correctly.

To Form the Perfect Tenses
1. For the present-perfect tense, use *have/has* as the helping verb.
2. For the past-perfect tense, use *had* as the helping verb; then add the past participle.

To Use the Past Participle
1. In most three- or four-word verb phrases, use this combination: *could, should, must, may, might, would + have + past participle (+ –ing).*
2. Use the past participle after a form of *be* in passive voice.
3. The past participle is used as an adjective after linking verbs, before nouns, and after nouns.

EDITING FOR MASTERY

Mastery Exercise 1

Correcting Errors in Past-Tense and Past-Participle Forms

The following passage contains twenty errors in past-tense and past-participle verb forms, in addition to the first error, which has been corrected for you as an example. Find and correct each remaining error by making the changes above the lines.

The First Moon Walk: July 29, 1969

(1) It ^begun on July 16, 1969, when three astronauts—Neil Armstrong, Michael Collins, and Edwin Aldrin—lifted off from the earth in *Apollo 11,* a spaceship power by the *Saturn V* rocket. (2) They was on their way to the Moon, where humans will set foot on its surface for the first time. (3) The spacecraft shooted along eventually reaching a speed of 24,300 miles per hour. (4) On the second day of the flight, the

astronauts sent a live television picture back to earth. (5) Over 500 million people watched the three men in action.

(6) Three days later, the astronauts had travel 244,930 miles, and the ship reached an orbit around the Moon. (7) It circle the Moon twice before moving closer to the surface. (8) Then the astronauts undocked the Lunar Module *Eagle* from the Command Module *Columbia.* (9) Armstrong and Aldrin, who would walk on the Moon while Collins flied the *Columbia,* crawled through the tunnel between the two modules and entered the *Eagle.* (10) Soon Armstrong announce to the earth, "*Eagle* has wings." (11) The Lunar Module was free from *Columbia.*

(12) The *Eagle* then drawed to within 500 feet of the Moon's surface. (13) Armstrong and Aldrin watched the terrain for the best place to land. (14) When they seen that the on-board computer had began to fail, the astronauts turned off the semiautomatic pilot and steered the ship themselves. (15) In a tense moment, as the *Eagle* was headed for a rocky crater, Armstrong fire the engines to carry the ship four miles farther along. (16) The maneuver worked. (17) When the Lunar Module touch down on the surface, Armstrong can see a sheet of Moon dirt blowed upward by the rocket exhaust. (18) He shut off the engine and reported, "The *Eagle* has landed." (19) He seemed calm, but his heart beated at twice the normal rate.

(20) The two men were suppose to spend eight hours checking the ship out, eating, and then resting, but they were too excited to wait. (21) Houston agreed and letted them skip the rest period. (22) After putting on his equipment, Armstrong lead the way down the nine-rung ladder. (23) When he reached the second rung, he turn on a television camera. (24) A moment later, his foot maked contact with the Moon's surface. (25) It was July 20, 1969, at 10:56 p.m. Eastern Daylight Time. (26) The world then heard Armstrong's now famous words, "That's one small step for man, one giant leap for mankind."

Scorecard: Number of Errors Found and Corrected _____

Mastery Exercise 2

Correcting Errors in Past-Tense and Past-Participle Forms

The following passage contains twenty errors in past-tense and past-participle verb forms, in addition to the first error, which has been corrected for you as an example. Find and correct each remaining error by making the changes above the lines.

John Glenn's Return to Space

(1) On February 20, 1961, a forty-one-year-old Marine Corps pilot ^*named* ~~name~~ John Glenn, Jr. climb into a tiny capsule on top of an Atlas-6 rocket and blasted into orbit around the earth. (2) His journey lasted 4 hours, 55 minutes, and 23 seconds before splashdown in the ocean. (3) When he lefted the space capsule, Glenn became the first American to orbit the earth and an instant national hero. (4) He will continue to work with NASA until 1964. (5) Then he entered the business world as a successful executive, and was elected to the United States Senate from Ohio in 1974, where he has continued to serve. (6) These accomplishments would have being enough for just about any person—but not John Glenn.

(7) On Friday, January 16, 1998, NASA choosed the seventy-seven-year-old Senator to return to orbit—more than thirty-six years after he had first flew in space. (8) The announcement had came at Glenn's request. (9) He asked NASA if he can fly again on the Space Shuttle *Discovery* to conduct space-based research on aging, but only if he meet the agency's physical and mental requirements. (10) These requirements was rigorous and demanding, but he done them all—and better than men half his age.

(11) Back on February 20, 1961, when Glenn had took off in his Friendship 7 Mercury capsule, the largest mystery facing the young NASA space program were whether humans could even survive in the hostile environment of space. (12) In the 121 space missions since Glenn's flight during the Mercury, Gemini, Apollo, Skylab and Shuttle programs, more than 200 Americans have went—and thrived—in space. (13) Glenn, who had inspired many current astronauts to pursue space flight as a career, continued to inspire people of all generations as he prepare for a return to space.

(14) So, on October 29, 1998, Senator John H. Glenn, Jr. shooted into orbit as part of a multi-national crew with the launch of Space Shuttle Discovery. (15) Watching a broadcast of the takeoff at John Glenn Elementary School with local school children in Seven Hills, Ohio, were Vice President Al Gore.

(16) The flight involved more than eighty scientific experiments investigating mysteries than span the realm from the inner universe of the human body to studies of our own Sun and its solar activity. (17) After the crew had did eight days of experiments and observations, the Discovery come back to Earth, and John Glenn, Jr. was once again hailed as a national hero.

Scorecard: Number of Errors Found and Corrected _____

23 Achieving Consistency

Chapter 6 showed you the importance of coherence in presenting your ideas clearly to readers. This chapter expands on a related idea—consistency.

Remember that your readers are actively attempting to understand your ideas. But despite their efforts, illogical shifts in pronouns or tenses will be confusing. As you focus on consistency in this chapter, you'll practice locating and correcting

- inconsistencies in pronoun forms
- inconsistencies in the tenses of verbs
- illogical shifts in sentence structure
- illogical shifts in reporting or quoting speech

PRONOUNS

A Word About Words

English used to have a second-person pronoun—*thou*—used for family and loved ones. Its forms correspond exactly to modern first-person singular pronoun forms:

Thou   thee   thy   thine   thyself

I   me   my   mine   myself

A **pronoun** stands for the noun it replaces or represents. **Personal pronouns** represent specific people—and, in some cases, specific things. Chapter 24 will discuss other kinds of pronouns and further issues related to pronoun use. Here, we'll focus on keeping personal pronouns consistent in two ways: person and number.

Person means whom the pronoun represents. You're the *first person—I*. The person you address is the *second person—you*. And someone you and the second person discuss is the *third person—he, she* or *it.* **Number** simply means that the pronoun is singular or plural. Here is the list of the personal pronouns that serve as subjects, objects, and possessive words:

	Singular	Plural
First person	I	we
Second person	you	you
Third person	he, she, it	they

Person

Read the following sentence. Do you notice an illogical shift?

I won't eat Papa Mangiano's spicy meatballs because they make *you* sick.

How did the meatballs magically transfer from the writer's body to yours? Revising the sentence to maintain the same person eliminates the confusion:

I won't eat Papa Mangiano's spicy meatballs because they make *me* sick.

Shifts in person are not only confusing; they can even be insulting:

Security is so poor in Goodman's Department store that *you* could steal just about anything.

Readers will be thrilled to learn that the writer thinks they're thieves! The problem can be fixed if an appropriate noun replaces the pronoun:

Security is so poor in Goodman's Department Store that *a thief* could steal just about anything.

Number

A pronoun also needs to agree in number with its **antecedent**, a word or phrase that precedes the pronoun. Here's an expanded list of the third-person pronouns as subjects, objects, and possessive words, plus the antecedents they refer to:

Singular antecedent	Subject	Object	Possessive
a man	he	him	his
a woman	she	her	her
a car, the committee	it	it	its
Plural antecedent	**Subject**	**Object**	**Possessive**
people			
wages	they	them	their
the rain and snow			

Here's another sentence with an illogical shift. Can you find it?

A person on vacation should carry their money in traveler's checks.

Does the writer intend to discuss one person or more than one? Here is a revised sentence with third-person plural throughout:

People on vacation should carry *their* money in traveler's checks.

Revise the next sentence yourself:

These days, a mother has to be careful about all the violence and sex that television exposes their children to._____

TIPS

For Avoiding Shifts in Number

Instead of falling into the *"a person . . . they"* pronoun-antecedent trap, express the idea with plurals: *"many people . . . they."* Most of the time the plurals will work.

Your revision could have taken either of these forms:

... a mother ... her children
... mothers ... their children

The main point, therefore, is that clarity requires consistency. Choose one pronoun and number—*we, you,* or *people*—and stick with it unless you have a logical reason to switch.

EXERCISE 1	Maintaining Consistency with Pronouns

Write appropriate pronouns in the blank spaces. When the antecedent is third-person singular, use either he *or* she *(or* his *or* her*).*

Just Who Is the Mother Fish?

1. Some fish in India, called the mouth-breeding bettas, mate and create offspring in unusual ways. Each of the parents plays *its* _____ own strange role in the process.

2. When the female lays her eggs, the male catches _____ in _____ rear fin and fertilizes_____.

3. The female then gathers the eggs in _____ mouth and spits each one at the male, who catches _____ in _____ mouth.

4. He will occasionally return an egg to _____ mate, and the ball game between the two might continue for several throws.

5. The female expects the male to take care of all the eggs, however, so eventually _____ stuffs them all into _____ mouth, where _____ will incubate for the next four or five days.

6. During this time, nothing else can make _____ way into the male's mouth, including food.

7. Even after the eggs hatch, the entire group of offspring will seek protection in the parents' mouths when anything threatens _____.

Collaborative Activity 1

Revising Sentences
Look over each other's sentences from Exercise 1, choose the five most interesting or amusing ones, and then change their singular subjects to plural subjects. Do the changes affect the humor or impact of the sentences in any way?

EXERCISE 2	Composing Sentences

Complete each of the following sentences, maintaining the same person and number in pronouns and nouns.

1. A dog is the most popular pet in America because *the animal gives unconditional love to its masters.*

2. We should attempt to save endangered species if _____ want _____

3. The average owner of seventeen cats _____ when _____

Collaborative Activity 2

Correcting Pronoun Use
Write sentences with deliberate mistakes in pronoun agreement. Then exchange papers with another member and correct each other's errors. Discuss any areas of disagreement.

4. Alligator breeders and snake lovers _____

_____

5. One should avoid placing _____ inside the mouth of a hungry python

unless _____

6. The average TV talk show host _____ if _____

_____

EXERCISE 3	Editing for Errors in Person and Number

Several sentences in the following passage contain illogical shifts in person or number. Eliminate these shifts by making changes above the lines.

Wake Me When Winter Is Over

(1) Hibernation is one of nature's most baffling tricks. (2) A wild bear, for instance, can sleep for up to five months, and all during that time ^*it doesn't* ~~they don't~~ eat, drink, urinate, or defecate. (3) For about a month before a bear goes into winter sleep, they are incredibly hungry. (4) It eats twenty hours a day and gains more than 100 pounds. (5) A bear's temperature during hibernation drops by only four degrees, which is why they sleep quite lightly and why it is liable to attack people if you disturb it.

(6) Woodchucks, ground squirrels, and many reptiles also hibernate, and it can experience a drop in temperature of more than sixty degrees. (7) One of these animals can sleep so soundly that a person can pick them up and toss them around and you won't awaken it. (8) Hibernation is therefore more than mere sleep, but we don't fully understand how it occurs.

Collaborative Activity 3

Comparing Revisions
Discuss your revisions of Exercise 3. Arrive at a final version with completely consistent person and number throughout. Should the bears and other animals be treated as singular or plural? Decide.

TENSE

Like pronouns, which must be consistent in person and number throughout a passage, verbs must be consistent in **tense**—the form of verb that shows when an action or idea occurs or occurred.

Reviews and Discussions of Literature

As you become absorbed in composing first drafts, you may unconsciously shift from one tense to another, especially when discussing literature, movies, or plays—which require the *present tense*. Look at the following passage. Do you see where the tense shifts illogically?

> The book *includes* a shocking scene in which several dolphins *are* caught in the nets of a tuna fishing boat. When the sailors *raised* the nets and *dumped* their contents onto the deck, many of the dolphins *would die* from strangulation in the ropes.

1. Many languages don't have past-tense forms of *can, will,* and *is/are*—especially languages spoken in the Philippines and in parts of Africa. Here, as a reminder, are those forms:

Present tense	Past tense
am, are, is	was, were
can	could
will	would

2. Also, some Asian languages don't indicate time through verb tense—but only through adverbs. A rough translation of a sentence into English might therefore be, "I *am* sick yesterday," instead of "I *was* sick yesterday."

Notice that the passage begins in the present tense but then slips into the past tense with *raised, dumped,* and *would die.* The passage needs to be revised:

> The book *includes* a shocking scene in which several dolphins *are* caught in the nets of a tuna fishing boat. When the sailors *raise* the nets and *dump* their contents onto the deck, many of the dolphins *die* from strangulation in the ropes.

Narratives or Histories

When telling a story about the past—whether a story about yourself or some event in history—you should maintain consistency in the *past tense.* In this next example, an illogical use of *would* creates a problem:

> The ancient Egyptians *worshipped* cats, *protected* them from harm, *would embalm* them, and *buried* them in elaborate caskets when the animals *died.*

The shift is annoying, for the sentence establishes a pattern of past-tense verbs that readers expect to continue:

> *. . . worshipped . . . protected . . . embalmed . . . buried . . . died*

The longer the paragraph (or essay) you compose, the more likely you are to shift tenses accidentally. Therefore, look carefully at your verb tenses as you revise and correct any inconsistencies. Reading your paper aloud may help you identify illogical tense shifts.

EXERCISE 4	Revising Verb Tenses

Each of the following sentences contains an illogical shift in tense. First read each sentence carefully, and then clarify its meaning by correcting the verb tense error.

A Dark History of Black Cats

1. Fear of cats, especially black ones, began in Europe in the Middle Ages, when the cities ^became ~~would become~~ overpopulated with the animals.

2. The cats were independent, stubborn, and quiet, so they make people uneasy.

3. People in the cities were superstitious and would distrust anything they don't understand.

4. Fear of witches spread throughout Europe, and people say that the homeless old ladies who fed alley cats are practicing black magic.

5. Naturally, the cats (especially black ones) would be thought to be four-legged witches.

6. The witch scare turns into a frenzy, and many innocent women and their harmless pets were burned at the stake.

7. A tremendous campaign to exterminate cats begins in France, and thousands of the animals were burned to death each month until King Louis XIII stops the practice in the 1630s.

8. Amazingly, even though black cats were slaughtered throughout Europe for centuries, the color does not disappear from the species.

EXERCISE 5	Composing Sentences

Complete the following sentences, using verbs in the appropriate tenses.

1. Because I overslept this morning, I had to skip breakfast and ___*rush to school.*___

2. Every day when class begins, our instructor _____

   _____

3. We'll meet you at 8:30, and we _____

   _____

4. Did you know that _____

   _____

5. He has been absent from school this week because _____

   _____

6. The repairman said that _____

   _____

EXERCISE 6	Revising Verb Tenses

The following passage contains illogical shifts in tense. Correct any errors by rewriting the verb above the lines.

It's No Sweat Off Their Tongues

(1) A dog does not "sweat with its tongue," as many people ^*believe*/believed. (2) A dog has some sweat glands, but the largest glands will be on the soles of its feet. (3) There are no sweat glands anywhere in a dog's mouth. (4) When a dog needs to cool itself, it breathes rapidly, which is why it panted after running. (5) But when a dog's tongue becomes moist, the animal would stick it out to let the air dry it off—not because the dog needed to sweat.

SENTENCE STRUCTURE

The following sentences sound odd, somehow out of balance:

He *is* very tall, *weight* 185 pounds, *and brown eyes.*
They enjoyed *swimming, to fish, and the beach.*

These sentences sound odd because they join similar ideas but don't employ similar grammatical structures. They need to be revised:

> He *is* very tall, *weighs* 185 pounds, and *has* brown eyes. (This sentence repeats verbs ending in -*s*.)
>
> They enjoyed *swimming, fishing,* and *lying* on the beach. (This sentence repeats –*ing* words.)

Now the ideas are clear because of the repeated structures. This repetition of sentence structures is called **parallelism** or **parallel construction** (discussed briefly in Chapter 6). Use parallelism to balance subjects with subjects, verbs with verbs, phrases with phrases, and clauses with clauses. Here are more examples:

> The cat *arched* its back, *bared* its teeth, and *hissed* loudly. (past-tense verbs)
>
> Our dog is *gentle, affectionate,* and incredibly *dumb.* (adjectives)
>
> The wind blew the papers *off the desk, onto the floor,* and *out the back window.* (prepositional phrases)

When you link together a string of equally important ideas, consider making them parallel.

EXERCISE 7	Identifying Parallel Structures

Circle the structure that's not parallel in each group.

1. lying on the beach

   a relaxing day

   getting a suntan

   swimming in the ocean

2. a man of few words

   a man with strong character

   a man without fear

   a man who knows what to do

3. take a vacation

   get a rest

   calm your nerves

   to be refreshed and ready to go

4. taken their time

   known the procedures

   seen the solutions

   understand the directions

5. a popular girl

   smart

   witty

   friendly

6. writes with pen

   adds with pencil

   copies with carbon paper

   satisfied with an old-fashioned approach

EXERCISE 8	Composing Sentences

Complete each of the following sentences, using parallel construction.

1. Tom is handsome, athletic, *and extremely conceited.* _____

2. During the spring break, I intend to _____, _____, and _____.

3. Senator Foghorn was greeting the crowd, _____, and _____.

4. Have fun and _____, but _____.

5. She's tall, _____, and _____.

6. Mr. Williams _____ the door, _____ his wife, and _____ the dog.

EXERCISE 9	Editing for Parallelism

Parallelism may occur throughout a paragraph, not just within a sentence. Revise the italicized parts in each of the following paragraphs to use parallel construction.

The Truth About Some Animals

Paragraph A:

(1) An opossum doesn't "play possum"—that is, play dead when endangered. (2) If cornered, it will hiss and snap. (3) If chased, it will run away. (4) *It will bite if you handle it.* (5) Occasionally, an opossum may collapse and appear motionless, but scientists don't think the reaction is deliberate. (6) Instead, *it is compared to the shock suffered by a human accident victim.*

Revised: *(4) If handled, it will bite.*

(6) Instead, they compare it to the shock suffered by a human accident victim.

Paragraph B:

(1) Poets—and most other people—have always assumed that birds sing to attract the opposite sex, to show off, *or simply expressing joy.* (2) But all of these theories are probably wrong. (3) The more likely reason that birds sing is to stake out their territories *and announcing their domains.* (4) No one has determined why birds sing more in some seasons than in others, and at some times of the day than in others. (5) One naturalist observed a bird that seemed to be staking out territory in the

morning instead of the evening—perhaps because the bird was less tired and more ambitious in the morning.

Revised: (1) _____

(3)_____

Paragraph C:

(1) The behavior of wolves is greatly misunderstood. (2) Wolves don't normally form large packs when they hunt. (3) They don't howl when they hunt. (4) *And other animals aren't frightened by them when they howl.* (5) Like most animals, wolves get their food the easiest and safest way they can. (6) They prey on mice, squirrels, rabbits, *and they also kill lambs and calves.* (7) Wolves form packs to hunt larger animals only in winter. (8) These packs are usually small—usually a family group consisting of mother, father, and their grown children.

Revised: (4) _____

(6)_____

Paragraph D:

(1) Only a few creatures inspire such a mixture of awe, fear, and *are as fascinating as snakes.* (2) And only a few creatures are so often the subject of misunderstandings. (3) One of the oldest misunderstandings is that a "snake" tempted Adam and Eve in the Garden of Eden. (4) The book of Genesis actually calls the tempter a "serpent." (5) In ancient times, the word serpent could refer to any creeping animal, especially a poisonous or dangerous one. (6) *And in the fifteenth and sixteenth centuries, many creatures could be referred to by the word serpent, including both salamanders and crocodiles.*

Revised: (1) _____

(6)_____

QUOTATIONS AND REPORTED SPEECH

In writing persuasive arguments, you may find it helpful to refer to or quote experts or authorities to support your position. In writing narratives, you may want to incorporate dialogue. Whenever you present the words or ideas of others, there is potential for illogical shifts in tense and in sentence structure. You can relate what someone else says or said in two ways:

1. by directly quoting the person's words
2. by indirectly reporting the person's words

A **direct quotation** reproduces *exactly* what the speaker says or said—in the same words and in the same verb tense. It encloses the speaker's words in quotation marks:

> *Direct Quotation:*
> Susan asked Tom, "Does your dog have a pedigree?"
> Tom replied, "No, it's a mutt that came from the city animal pound."
> "Can you tell me where the pound is?" she inquired.

Notice that the speaker's words are in the present tense—the tense the speaker used when he or she spoke. But the words identifying the speaker and introducing the quotation are in past tense, because that's when the words were said. These tenses are accurate; they don't represent illogical shifts. Notice, too, that commas, periods, and question marks go inside the quotation marks; see Chapter 15 for a full discussion of how to punctuate quotations.

Reported speech, as its name suggests, reports but does not quote what the speaker says or said. It *never* uses quotation marks and usually begins statements with *that,* or with *if* or *whether* with questions:

> *Reported Speech:*
> Susan asked Tom if his dog had a pedigree.
> Tom told her that it was a mutt that came from the city animal pond.
> She asked Tom to tell her the location of the pound.

Notice that the verb tenses of the reported speech are in the past tense, as are the words identifying the speaker and introducing the reported speech.

Whether you quote or report a speaker's words, you must be consistent.

> *Inconsistent:*   Susan asked could I tell her where I got it?
> *Consistent:*   Susan asked, "Can you tell me where you got it?"
> *Consistent:*   Susan asked if I could tell her where I got it.

EXERCISE 10 | *Composing Quotations and Reported Speech*

Rewrite the direct quotations as reported speech or vice versa, changing tense, person, and word order as necessary.

Direct quotation

1. Juan said, "I'm sure you are correct."

2. Every weekend, my brother asks me, "Can I borrow your car?"

3. _____
   _____

Reported speech

1. *Juan said that he was sure I was correct.*

2. _____
   _____

3. Dr. Smith told Bill that he could turn in the paper on Tuesday.

Direct quotation

4. The new student asked, "Where is the counseling office?"

5. The doctor warned me, "Don't go to work until tomorrow."

Reported speech

4. _____
   _____

5. _____
   _____

6. "I'll see you later," said Gloria.   6. Gloria _____

_____

| EXERCISE 11 | Writing Quotations or Reported Speech |

Suppose you are telling the story of a disagreement between your friends Maria and Tomas, who are fraternal twins. Use your imagination and, based on the information supplied, compose sentences that quote or report what each of them said.

1. Tomas to Maria: can't find dictionary/thinks she has taken it   *Tomas told Maria,*
"I can't find my dictionary. Did you take it?"

or

Tomas told Maria that he couldn't find his dictionary. He asked her if she had
taken it.

2. Maria to Tomas: denies she took it/says he's always blaming her _____

_____

3. Tomas to Maria: accuses her of always taking pens, paper, stapler, and tape

_____

_____

4. Maria to Tomas: denies the accusation/says he always swipes her compact disks

_____

_____

5. Mother to both: stop arguing and learn to share _____

_____

6. Maria and Tomas both apologize _____

_____

| EXERCISE 12 | Editing Quotations or Reported Speech |

Correct any errors in quotations or reported speech by writing your changes after each paragraph.

Cats on the Post Office Payroll

Cats have been on the official payroll of the British Post Office for more than a century. They're not hired to sort or deliver mail, of course, but to keep it from being eaten by mice. The problem was especially bad in London in the mid-1800s, when mice invaded the sorting rooms to gnaw at mail, money orders, and employees' sandwiches. Traps and poisons didn't work, so in 1868 the secretary of the post office approved the hiring of three female cats at an allowance of four pence per week. But he cautioned, "If the mice are not reduced in number in six months, he would have to stop a further portion of the allowance."

Revised: _____

_____

Within months, the rodent population had shrunk dramatically, and post offices received the go-ahead to hire more cats. Many did, and as the number of feline employees increased, so did their pay. In 1953, the assistant postmaster general assured the House of Commons "that female mouse-hunters received very adequate maternity benefits and he gives them the same wages and employment opportunities as male cats."

Revised: _____

_____

As of the mid-1980s, cats were on the payroll at three postal sites in London. A terror named Kojak at London's Nine Elms postal garage was, at £1.80, among the top-paid mousers in the land. Bill Woodford, the officer in charge, said that most weeks, Kojak leaves a couple of rats on my desk as well as an array of mice.

Revised: _____

_____

IN SUMMARY   Achieving Consistency

To Avoid Confusing Shifts in Person or Number
1. Decide which person—first, second, or third—and number—singular or plural—is most appropriate for your audience and purpose, and then consistently use that person and number unless you have a logical reason to change.

To Correct Illogical Shifts in Tense
1. Read over your early drafts (and read them aloud), looking specifically at the tenses of the verbs.
2. Identify illogical tense shifts.
3. Correct the tense shifts as you revise.

To Join Similar Ideas by Using Parallel Construction
1. Repeat the same grammatical structure (for example, noun and noun, present-tense verb and present-tense verb, –*ing* word and —*ing* word, and so forth).

To Correct Inconsistencies in Quotations
1. Quote the exact words of a speaker—using the same tense, word order, and pronouns that the speaker employs or employed.
2. Do not include the identification of the speaker in the quote.

To Correct Inconsistencies in Reported Speech

1. Introduce the reported speech with *that* for statements or *if* or *whether* for questions.
2. Do not use quotation marks.
3. Use verb tense and word order that is consistent with the sentence that reports the speaker's ideas.

EDITING FOR MASTERY

Mastery Exercise 1

Correcting Inconsistencies

The first error in the following passage has been corrected as an example. Find and correct the remaining twenty illogical shifts in the person and number of pronouns, in tense, in parallelism, and the handling of quotations or reported speech. (The first error has been corrected as an example.) Above each line, make the necessary changes to eliminate these shifts and errors.

Charles Waterton: A Most Daring Naturalist

(1) An Englishman named Charles Waterton (1782–1865) was among the strangest naturalists who ever lived. (2) He was constantly involved in weird and wild adventures, all of which ^stemmed ~~stem~~ from his love of nature. (3) After completing school in 1800, he decided to live in South America. (4) Then, in 1812, he made his first trek into parts of the Brazilian jungle where no person would ever risk their lives by entering before. (5) His goal is to search for a certain poison that was supposed to cure an illness. (6) On this and three later trips to the region, he will perform many truly odd feats. (7) Everyone who learned of his exploits did not believe what they hear.

(8) For example, after someone reported that they had spotted a large python in the area, he dashed off barefoot to capture it. (9) He never wore shoes or putting on boots in the jungle. (10) After the natives have pinned the snake's head to the ground, Waterton threw himself onto the python's body and tied the creature's mouth with his suspenders. (11) The safari returned to Waterton's hut, where the natives deposited the python in a large sack, closed the opening with a knotted rope, and would place the sack in a corner of the hut. (12) You could hear the snake thrash around violently in the sack all night long, but Waterton apparently does not object to sharing his sleeping quarters with a python.

(13) On another occasion, he was trying to capture a crocodile, but his helpers can't pull the creature from the river. (14) Waterton said that "he sees the animal is in a state of fear." (15) Finally, when they got the crocodile within a few yards of the bank, Waterton sprang from the boat and jumps on the animal's back. (16) "I seized his forelegs," he says, "and twisted them on the animal's back, where he could use

Collaborative Activity 5

Comparing Corrections
Review your corrections in Mastery Exercise 1 with your group. Report your findings to the entire class.

them for a bridle." (17) With Waterton riding the crocodile, his helpers dragged it onto the bank. (18) He remarked that it was the first and last time I was ever on a crocodile's back.

(19) On another of his trips into the jungle, Waterton learned that vampire bats liked to suck human blood, so he would decide to let them drink some of his. (20) He brought one of the creatures into his quarters and purposely was sleeping with one foot exposed. (21) Yet in spite of his best efforts, Waterton is frustrated. (22) The vampire bat ignored him and instead sank its teeth into the big toe of an Indian who slept nearby.

Scorecard: Number of Errors Found and Corrected _____

Mastery Exercise 2

Correcting Inconsistencies

The first two errors in the following passage have been corrected as an example. Find and correct the remaining twenty illogical shifts in the person and number of pronouns, in tense, in parallelism, and the handling of quotations or reported speech. Above each line, make the necessary changes to eliminate these shifts and errors.

Charles Darwin and The Origin of Species

(1) Charles Darwin's father, a 350-pound jolly gentleman, said that his son cared

for nothing but shooting, raising dogs, and ^ ~~he liked to catch rats~~ *rat-catching*. (2) Like many fa-

mous men, Charles as a child didn't act like a person who ^ ~~will~~ *would* become great in the

future. (3) He was lazy, and he was a poor student. (4) However, he did like to col-

lect things—bugs, shells, and he also collected coins. (5) His father's comment on

this was that Charles will "mess up the house with this everlasting rubbish."

(6) When Charles was sixteen, his father decides to make a doctor out of him

and sending him off to Edinburgh University. (7) But Charles could not bear to

watch operations, and two years later he had gone to Cambridge to become a

parson. (8) There one of his teachers recommended him for an unpaid job on

HMS *Beagle*, which was bound for South America for a two-day scientific expedi-

tion. (9) (It will last five years.)

(10) During the voyage on the *Beagle,* Charles kept a diary in which he ex-

pressed his wonder at his growing collection of fossils, plants, and he also found

animals. (11) Every place the ship stopped, he went exploring and then was taking

his discoveries back to his laboratory to examine.

(12) All along, Darwin noticed patterns. (13) In the Galápagos Islands, there were

fourteen different species of finch like birds with different-sized bills. (14) You also saw a resemblance, too, between the species on the South American mainland and this island. (15) And mice on one slope of the Andes were different from those that are on the other. (16) He later wrote that these facts and many others could only be explained if species gradually changed over many generations, and the subject haunted me.

(17) In November 1859, Darwin's Book—*On the Origin of Species, by Means of Natural Selection, or the Preservation of Favored Races in the Struggle for Life*—was published. (18) The publisher was nervous about the manuscript and they suggested that Darwin rewrite it and confining it to pigeons, because "everybody is interested in pigeons." (19) Naturally, Darwin refused.

(20) On the first day of publication, the entire print run of 1,250 copies immediately sold out. (21) Of course, it was controversial, and everyone had their own opinion about its scientific accuracy. (22) The Church was against the book. (23) They said it contradicted the first chapter of Genesis. (24) It also suggested that man had an ancestor in common with the ape, which you immediately misinterpreted to mean that man was descended from the monkeys. (25) The theory soon became known as "Darwin's 'monkey theory.'"

(26) The man around whom the furor raged was a gentle, sickly, kindly person, with blue eyes, a balding head, and he also had a long, shaggy beard. (27) He listened to the criticisms, was evaluating them, and revised his work in light of his evaluations. (28) He said, "If he is wrong, the sooner I am knocked on the head and annihilated, so much the better."

Scorecard: Number of Errors Found and Corrected _____

24 Using Pronouns

Pronouns are useful and versatile tools in writing. They help you avoid weak repetition, create coherence, emphasize ideas, and combine sentences gracefully (see Chapters 6–8). So using them correctly is important. We'll look at a variety of ways to use them in this chapter:

- as replacements for nouns
- as part of comparisons
- as ways to increase clarity and unity
- as ways to emphasize ideas

CHOOSING THE RIGHT PRONOUN

A Word About Words

The word *pronoun* (*pro =
for* + noun) literally means
"for a noun."

Pronouns, which act as substitutes for nouns, are among the most common words, and most people employ them effectively most of the time. But when pronoun forms are misused or when their **antecedents**—the words they refer to—are unclear, the result can be confusing. Let's take a look at those pronouns and how they function.

As Subjects and Objects

Unlike nouns, which over the centuries have lost many of their complex original forms, pronouns retain a variety of ancient forms—or cases—to indicate whether they serve as subjects or objects. Here, again, is a list of subject-case and object-case pronouns, arranged according to **person** (first, second, or third), and **number** (singular or plural):

	Singular subject	Plural subject	Singular object	Plural object
First person	I	we	me	us
Second person	you	you	you	you

Continued

GO ELECTRONIC!

Use the following electronic supplements for additional practice with your writing:

- For chapter-by-chapter summaries and exercises, visit the Composing with Confidence Companion Website at: http://www.ablongman.com/meyers.
- For work with the writing process, visit The Longman Writer's Warehouse at http://longmanwriterswarehouse.com (password needed).
- For additional practice in grammar, use The Writer's ToolKit Plus CD-ROM

	Singular subject	Plural subject	Singular object	Plural object
Third person	he	they	him	them
	she	they	her	them
	it	they	it	them

As their name suggests, **subject-case pronouns** function only as subjects. Likewise, **object-case pronouns** function as objects of action verbs, of words formed from verbs, or of prepositions:

After action verbs	{ He hit *me*. You saw *them*.
After –ing words	After seeing *him*, they ran away.
After prepositions	{ Bradley picked up the puppy without hurting *it*. some of *us* with *her*

Determining the appropriate pronoun case is easy when a clause contains only one subject or object:

Incorrect:	Her *is busy.*
Correct:	She *is busy.*
Incorrect:	Bill gave it to *I.*
Correct:	Bill gave it to *me.*

But when a clause contains more than one subject or object, choosing the appropriate pronoun case may be more difficult. The following sentences contain pronoun case errors, but do they sound incorrect?

> *Me and him* like to play ball.
> *You and her* can do this.
> Let's keep this a secret between *you and I.*

TIPS

For Keeping *I* and *Me* Straight

Sometimes your ear for grammatical mistakes can deceive you. "*Me and my friend* like to play ball" might sound better than "*I and my friend* like to play ball." Here's why. In the second version, the subject pronoun *I* occupies the wrong position. It should come second—not first—after *and*: "*My friend and I* like to play ball."

If your eye or ear doesn't pick up the errors, here's an easy way to detect them. Temporarily remove all but one subject or object, and look at the pronoun that remains:

Incorrect:	Me . . . like to play ball. Him . . . like to play ball.
Incorrect:	. . . her can do this.
Incorrect:	. . . between . . . I.

Then rewrite the full subject or object:

Correct:	He and I like to play ball. You and she can do this. Let's keep this a secret between *you and me.*

If Your First Language Is Not English

Many languages include the pronoun in the verb, but not English. In Spanish, for example, the verb *está* means "it is." English requires the pronoun. So, while editing your work, make sure you haven't omitted the pronoun in a clause and created a fragment.

| **EXERCISE 1** | *Correcting Pronoun Case* |

Some—but not all—of the following sentences use incorrect pronoun case. Cross out each error and write the correct form above the line. If a sentence has no errors, don't make any changes.

1. The Hendersons have always been friends with my wife and ^*me* I.

2. When we were kids, me and my brother swam almost every day during the summer.

3. My parents always knew that he and I were at the beach.

4. You and her are welcome anytime.

5. Call me or him whenever you want.

6. There will never be a problem between you and I.

In Comparisons

Notice in the following comparisons that a simple clause—a subject pronoun and a helping verb—comes after the word *than* or *as:*

> My brother is older than *I am.*
> Judith's brother takes the same classes as *she does.*

You can drop the verb from these clauses, but you still must retain the subject pronoun after *than* or *as,* especially in formal writing:

> My brother is older than *I (am).*
> Judith's brother takes the same classes as *she (does).*

But suppose you compare objects instead of subjects:

> Bob talked to *her* as much as *you.*

Now the pronoun *you* is not only inappropriate but perhaps misleading. Does the sentence say that *Bob* talked to *you* or that *you* talked to *her?* You can clear up the problem by repeating the preposition *to:*

> Bob talked to him as much as *to you.*

| **EXERCISE 2** | *Using Pronouns in Comparisons* |

Write a sentence making a comparison based on the information supplied.

1. Tom is 6 feet tall, but she is 5 feet 6 inches tall. *Tom is taller than she is.*

2. Norma is very patient. He is not so patient. _____

_____

3. José runs fast. They run more slowly. _____

_____

Collaborative Activity 1

Writing and Checking Pronouns

Write ten sentences (including some comparisons) that use pronouns, but omit the pronouns and draw a line in each pronoun slot. Exchange papers with a classmate and then select the correct pronouns. Have a third student check your answers. Discuss any difficulties or debatable choices.

4. Jerold is very friendly. She rarely says hello. _____

_____

5. Mom always liked you a lot. She didn't like me as much. _____

_____

6. Lonnie is very short. He is also very short. _____

_____

With Antecedents

Pronouns must refer clearly to their *antecedents,* the words that the pronouns represent or replace. They must also agree with their antecedents in person and number. Here are some examples:

Antecedent	Pronoun
Juan and I	we
Juan and me	us
Someone	he/she; him/her
He and Katrina	they
Katrina and him	them
Carlos and you	you

Repeating an antecedent or its **synonym**—a word that has the same meaning as another—is sometimes a better choice than substituting a pronoun. Too many pronouns can be monotonous, and a pronoun with more than one antecedent can be confusing. Note the repeated words or substitutions for them (both in italics) in the following paragraph:

The Amazing Guru

(1) In India, a religious brotherhood of warriors called the Sikhs tell the story about one of their early *leaders,* a *guru* named Gobind *Singh,* who lived in the seventeenth century. (2) *He* gathered the Sikhs together during a crisis and said that the times required supreme loyalty. (3) Drawing *his* sword, *he* asked for volunteers to give *him* their heads. (4) There was a long silence. (5) Finally, one man stepped forward and was led into the *guru's* tent. (6) *Singh* reappeared soon after—alone, and with a bloody sword. (7) *He* asked for a second volunteer, and then a third and a fourth and a fifth. (8) Each time, a man was led away and, each time, the *guru* returned with blood on *his* sword. (9) "Now," said the *leader* to *his* followers, "you have proven your courage and devotion to our cause, so I will restore the men to life." (10) *Singh* returned to *his* tent and brought the five men back, unharmed—the result of either a miracle or a trick, for some say that a goat had been sacrificed in place of the men.

After the first sentence, which identifies Gobind Singh as a leader, or guru, his name can serve as the antecedent for most pronouns in the remainder of the paragraph. But look at sentence 8:

> Each time, *a man* was led away and, each time, the *guru* returned with blood on *his* sword.

The sentence discusses two people: *a man* and *the guru*. Inserting the pronoun *he* would create a problem:

> Each time, *a man* was led away, and each time, *he* returned with blood on *his* sword.

Just who was it that carried the sword—Singh or the man?

Remember, when there are two potential antecedents to a pronoun, don't use the pronoun. Repeat the noun or use a synonym instead. In this paragraph, *Singh, guru,* and *leader* are synonyms. They serve as substitutes in sentences 5, 6, 9, and 10 of the paragraph.

A sentence may also be unclear if its pronoun has no antecedent. What, for example, does *they* refer to in the following sentence?

> *They* are replacing the curbs on my block this week.

The writer probably means "city workers" or "the city" but doesn't mention either. So the sentence should be reworded using one of these nouns:

> *City workers are* replacing the curbs on my block this week.
> *The city is* replacing the curbs on my block this week.

Don't begin a new paragraph with a pronoun; always use a noun to identify the subject the paragraph will discuss.

EXERCISE 3	Revising for Pronoun Variety

The following passage repeats the same words too often. Create more variety by substituting nouns or pronouns for the italicized words. Write your substitutions above the line.

The Amazing Boy General

1   When *Galusha Pennypacker*, a U.S. Civil War hero of the Union army, was awarded the rank of major general, he was too young to vote. *Pennypacker* ^The tall recruit first joined the army in 1861 as a quartermaster sergeant at the age of sixteen. That August, he was elected captain of the Ninety-seventh Pennsylvania Volunteers. *Pennypacker* was a colonel by 1864, for his men loved their brave leader. At Fort Gilmer, *Pennypacker* led troops across a mile of brush in full view of the *Confederate army*. Though the *Confederate army* killed *Pennypacker's* horse and wounded *Pennypacker*, *Pennypacker* kept on fighting. *Pennypacker's* twentieth birthday was spent convalescing from three battle wounds, but *Pennypacker* was soon back in action.

2   On January 15, 1865, at Fort Fisher, North Carolina, *Pennypacker* led a brigade across the Confederate army's defenses and was the first to reach the top of the hill where *Pennypacker* triumphantly planted his brigade's flag. Standing in plain sight of the Confederate army, Pennypacker watched as a *Confederate army* soldier took aim, shot, and badly wounded *Pennypacker* in the side and hip. A month later, the twenty-year-old *Pennypacker* was appointed brigadier general. *Pennypacker* was the youngest soldier to achieve that rank on either side in the Civil War. In March 1865, *Pennypacker* was appointed a major general, and *Pennypacker* was still not twenty-one.

3   The rest of *Pennypacker's* career was uneventful. Throughout the Reconstruction period after the war, *Pennypacker* remained in the army. *Pennypacker* later refused an opportunity to run for governor of Pennsylvania and lived out a lonely retirement in Philadelphia, where *Pennypacker* died on October 1, 1916.

When Referring to Pronouns

As you can guess from their name, **indefinite pronouns** don't refer to a specific person, place, or thing:

For people		For things	For places	For people, things, or places	
everyone	everybody	everything	everywhere	each	either
someone	somebody	something	somewhere	one	neither
anyone	anybody	anything	anywhere	any	
no one	nobody	nothing	nowhere		

Indefinite pronouns as antecedents present difficulties for the pronouns that refer back to them. For example, which pronoun should refer to *everybody* in the following sentence?

Everybody has turned in _____ paper.

The most obvious choice is the plural pronoun *their*, which avoids **sexual bias**—that is, it doesn't refer to a male or a female. But *everybody*, like all indefinite pronouns, is grammatically singular. (Notice that the verb after *everybody* is *has*, a singular verb.) Therefore, while *their* is becoming increasingly common, it may not be appropriate in formal writing.

Another choice is *his*, which seems to exclude women. And a third choice is *his or her*, but the phrase sounds awkward, especially in longer passages:

Everybody has turned in *his or her* paper. *He or she . . .*

So what do you do? One solution is to avoid using the pronoun altogether, and another solution is to use a female pronoun:

Everybody has turned in *a* paper.
Everyone has turned in *her* paper.

Collaborative Activity 2

Comparing Revisions

Compare your revisions of the passage in Exercise 3 and create one version that provides the most variety and clarity.

TIPS

For Identifying Singular Indefinite Pronouns

Here's a handy way for remembering that pronouns are singular. Look at the root words that most indefinite pronouns contain—*one* and *body*. It's simple arithmetic: *one* = one, *body* = one body. If you're writing in the present tense, look at the verb, which should also be singular:

Everybody has, no one does, someone is, and so on.

Yet another solution is to rewrite the sentence with a plural subject:

> *All of the students* have turned in *their papers*. (Note that *papers* is plural to establish consistency throughout the sentence.)

Since the handling of indefinite pronoun antecedents is controversial, you may want to discuss the issue in class with your instructor.

EXERCISE 4	Avoiding Sexual Bias

Revise each of the following sentences, using a plural subject and making all other appropriate changes.

1. Everyone in the class has improved his grade.

   Revised: All the students in the class have improved their grades.

2. Everyone has reduced his or her weight during this exercise program.

   Revised: _____

   _____

3. Everybody involved is doing their best to make the party successful.

   Revised: _____

   _____

4. Anybody who uses this type of savings account can withdraw her money at any time.

   Revised: _____

   _____

5. Nobody has left their books on the desk. (Hint: start the sentence with *None*.)

   Revised: _____

   _____

6. Every man is entitled to a trial by jury.

   Revised: _____

   _____

With Collective Nouns

Most **collective nouns**, which represent a group (for example, *a club, a team,* or *a class*), are singular. Therefore, careful readers expect you to refer to a collective noun by using *it* or *its*:

> The *class* meets in room 214 on Monday, but *it* meets in room 210 on Wednesday.
> My hockey *team* won all of *its* (not *their*) games this season.

Some collective nouns are treated as plurals:

> the police
> the Chinese, the British, etc.
> the staff
> the faculty
> the New York Yankees

Again, you can look for clues in the verb. If it is singular, the noun is singular, and any pronouns referring to it will need to be singular, too.

EXERCISE 5 — Using Pronouns After Collective Nouns

Collaborative Activity 3

Working with Pronouns
Write four sentences: two with indefinite pronouns as subjects and two with collective nouns as subjects. Exchange papers. Write a second sentence after each of the four, using a pronoun that refers to its antecedent. Pay attention to agreement and to sexual bias. Exchange papers again and revise—or entirely rewrite the first and/or second sentence or any awkward sounding pairs. Discuss these revisions in your group.

Complete each of the following sentences, referring back to its subject with an appropriate pronoun.

1. The police sent *five of their patrol cars to the scene of the crime.*
2. The group is _____
3. The committee has voted _____
4. Wal-Mart doubled _____
5. The Giants won _____
6. The faculty are _____

SPECIAL PRONOUNS

Pronouns perform a variety of functions. Not only do they refer to antecedents, but they can also join clauses, emphasize ideas, and make statements more specific. We'll examine those functions here.

Relative Pronouns

Who is a subject-case pronoun; *whom* is an object-case pronoun. Use *whom* when it receives the action of the verb or is the object of a preposition. Both *who* and *whom* often begin questions.

But when *who* and *whom* appear as **relative pronouns** in relative clauses, their use becomes more complicated. You may recall from Chapter 19 that *who* serves as the subject of a relative clause in a complex sentence:

> Juan was the man *who spoke to you.*
> The woman *who left her package* will be back to get it soon.

However, many people insist that in formal writing you use *whom* when it's the object in a relative clause:

> O   S   V
> Juan was the man *whom you spoke to.*

Most of the time, you can eliminate *whom* from such clauses:

> S   V
> Juan was the man [whom] *you spoke to.*

But you cannot eliminate *whom* when it follows a preposition (a somewhat rare and very formal structure):

> P   O   S   V
> Juan was the man *to whom* you spoke.

EXERCISE 6	Combining Sentences with Relative Pronouns

Join each pair of sentences, using who, whom, or no relative pronoun.

1. Mr. Bailout is the administrator. He handles student loans and grants. *Mr. Bailout is the administrator who handles student loans and grants.*

2. Dr. Freud is the counselor. Students consult with her when they need advice on personal matters. _____

3. You must talk to the person. She sets the policy for admissions. _____

4. Washington and Lincoln were the presidents. Historians consider them our greatest. _____

5. We all need a close friend. We can discuss our problems with him. _____

6. Wilber Smith is the manager. He's in charge of giving out million-dollar loans for college tuition. _____

Reflexive Pronouns

In some sentences, the same person or thing is both the subject and the object:

> The wicked witch looked at *herself* in the mirror.
> I talk to *myself* when I want to have an intelligent conversation.

The objects in these sentences are called **reflexive pronouns** because they reflect back to the subjects like mirrors. Note that all the singular reflexive pronouns end in *–self;* all the plurals end in *–selves.* Like other pronouns, reflexive pronouns must match their antecedents in person and number:

	Singular	Plural
First person	myself	ourselves
Second person	yourself	yourselves
Third person	himself (not hisself)	themselves (not theirselves)
	herself	themselves
	itself	themselves

You can also use a reflexive pronoun to repeat and thus emphasize a subject or object:

> I *myself* don't want to skydive into the volcano, but my best friend insists that we do it.
> If you want to exchange this parachute for one that works, you will have to talk to the manager *himself.*

But you can't use a reflexive pronoun as the subject of a sentence:

> *Incorrect:*   Rudolfo and *myself* would like to thank you for your help.
> *Correct:*   Rudolfo and *I* would like to thank you for your help.

EXERCISE 7   Writing Reflexive Pronouns

Write the correct pronoun in each of the following sentences.

1. Does John ever do any of the laundry by *himself* _____?

2. You and Sheila should help _____ to whatever you want to eat.

3. Thanks. We can prepare it _____.

4. My children walk to school by _____.

5. My parents, my brothers, and _____ manage to arrange our schedules so that we actually eat dinner together every Sunday.

6. Maria _____ cooked the entire dinner.

Demonstrative Pronouns

This/that and *these/those* are called **demonstrative** words because they demonstrate or point out what they refer to. You can use demonstratives alone as pronouns:

✓ TIPS

For Using *This*

This by itself is often vague and unclear. So, whenever possible, attach *this* to a noun.

Poor: Some of my friends always want to copy my homework. *This* bothers me.

Better: Some of my friends always want to copy my homework. *This dishonesty* bothers me.

This is the one I want.
I like *these* but not *those*.

Or you can place the demonstratives before nouns as adjectives:

This wallet is very heavy.
Would you hand me *those $100 bills,* please?

Note that the demonstratives have both singular and plural forms:

Singular: this, that
Plural: these, those

As a general rule, use *this/these* to refer to things physically close, and use *that/those* to refer to things farther away:

These stacks of money (close by) belong to me; *those* rolls of pennies (farther away) must belong to you.

But don't use *this* when you mean *a:*

Incorrect: I have *this* friend who always gets into trouble.
Correct: I have *a* friend who always gets into trouble.

EXERCISE 8	Writing Demonstrative Words

*Write the correct word—*this, that, these, *or* those*—in each blank space provided.*

1. As a child, I swam in the pond near our house in the country. I loved ____those____ times.

2. Would you give _____ letter to Mr. Turner and bring _____ one to Ms. Green?

3. _____ chairs in the other room might look nice in _____ spot.

4. Who was _____ masked man? I wanted to thank him.

5. Keep _____ in mind: The test will begin at 9 A.M. sharp.

6. I have my books. But who owns _____ books?

EXERCISE 9	Editing for Errors with Demonstratives

Eliminate the error in the use of this *in each passage by revising the appropriate section of the passage.*

1. I saw this movie last night that was terrific.

   Revised: _I saw a movie ..._

2. The underground wells do not have enough water to supply all the houses in the area. This is a problem.

Revised: <u>This water shortage is a problem.</u>

3. This car in front of me had a flat tire.

Revised: _____

4. I saw this dog biting this man right in front of this crowd of people who just stood and watched.

Revised: _____

5. People should not charge more on their credit cards than they can afford to pay each month. This would solve a lot of financial problems.

Revised: _____

6. Some people want to eliminate the different tax brackets and have a single flat tax rate. This would favor the rich and discriminate against the poor.

Revised: _____

IN SUMMARY   Using Pronouns

To Choose the Correct Pronoun

Check all pronouns to be sure they agree with antecedents in person and number.

To Choose the Correct Pronoun with More Than One Subject or Object

Temporarily remove all but one subject or object from the sentence to see if the remaining pronoun is correct.

To Determine the Correct Pronoun Case after *Than* or *As* in a Comparison

1. Temporarily insert the omitted words after *than* or *as.*
2. Then remove the words you inserted, or leave them in, to avoid possible confusion.

When the Antecedent of the Pronoun Is Unclear

Replace the pronoun with a noun.

When You Use Pronouns to Refer to Indefinite Pronouns

1. Remember that indefinite pronouns are singular.
2. Recast the pronouns in the plural to avoid sexual bias with *he/him/his* or *she/her/her.*

When You Use Pronouns to Refer to Collective Nouns

Make sure they agree in number—which is usually singular.

When You Use Relative Pronouns

Select *who* as the subject of the relative clause, *whom* as the object of the clause.

When You Use Reflexive Pronouns

1. End singular pronouns with *–self* and plural pronouns with *–selves* (for example, *yourself* = singular, *yourselves* = plural).
2. Never use reflexive pronouns as subjects—only as objects—but you can emphasize a subject or an object by repeating it with a reflexive pronoun.

When You Use Demonstrative Pronouns

1. Use *this/these* to refer to things physically close, and *that/those* to things farther away.
2. Avoid sentences beginning with *this* standing alone; attach it to a noun to make its reference clear.

EDITING FOR MASTERY

Mastery Exercise 1

Correcting Errors in Pronoun Use

The following passage contains twelve errors related to pronoun use in addition to the first three errors, which have been corrected as examples. Find and correct each error by making your changes above the lines.

The Amazing Machine

(1) Perhaps the most famous robot in history was the Terrible Turk, ^who ~~whom~~ was a robot chess player. (2) ^All the people ~~Everyone~~ who saw this fantastic adult toy ^were ~~was~~ amazed, but they were the victims of a brilliant fraud. (3) Baron Wolfgang von Kempelen built this for Maria Theresa, the empress of Austria. (4) The robot looked like a wooden man with a mustache. (5) It wore Oriental robes and a turban and sat at a chest, that had a built-in chessboard. (6) They opened the doors of the robot to reveal brass machinery inside.

(7) After the baron died in 1804, the robot was sold to Johann Nepomuk Maelzel. (8) Him and the robot then went on tour, first in Europe and then in America. (9) People were amazed that it could play so much better than them. (10) However, while they were in France in 1809, Napoleon Bonaparte seemed to frustrate it by deliberately making false moves. (11) The robot swept the pieces from the board in a very unmachinelike display of temper. (12) On a second tour in 1826, Maelzel took the robot across the United States accompanied by a friend,

chess champion William Schlumberger, who had suspiciously stooped shoulders. (13) It was a big hit, with whirring and rackety machinery, rolling eyes, and its cry of *"Echec!"* ("Check!"). (14) They wondered, however, why Schlumberger was so often absent when the Turk played.

(15) In 1834, the secret workings of the automation were revealed. (16) He was not a robot at all. (17) Jacques Mouret, a chess player from Paris who had worked for Maelzel, explained that once they closed the doors, a human player (usually Schlumberger) concealed hisself inside it, behind the display machinery. (18) He could see the chess pieces and move it with rods leading to the robot's arms. (19) This had been kept a secret for nearly sixty years. (20) After Schlumberger and Maelzel both died in 1938, the machine ended up in Philadelphia's Chinese Museum but was destroyed by fire at age eighty-five.

Scorecard: Number of Errors Found and Corrected _____

Collaborative Activity 5

Comparing Corrections
Review your corrections in
Mastery Exercise 1 with
your group. Report your
findings to the entire class.

Mastery Exercise 2

Correcting Errors in Pronoun Use

The following passage contains twelve errors related to pronoun use in addition to the first error, which has been corrected as an example. Find and correct each error by making your changes above the lines.

Ferdinand Demara: The Great Imposter

(1) Ferdinand Waldo Demara Jr. may or may not have been history's cleverest impostor, but no one assumed more false identities than ^him. *(he did)* (2) He changed his name and profession so often no one can say with certainty whom Demara was. (3) They only know that he often helped others—and was often successful in doing so.

(4) Born in Lawrence, Massachusetts, on December 12, 1921, Demara left home at sixteen to join a monastery and stayed there two years until he quit to join the army. (5) But he quickly disliked the life that him and the other soldiers led, so he masqueraded successfully as a military orderly. (6) It was the first of the many fakeries, that he committed.

(7) Over the next three decades, Demara taught college classes in psychology as Dr. Robert Linton French, passed hisself off as a zoologist named Cecil Haman, served as dean of the School of Philosophy at Pennsylvania's Gannon College, taught science at a Catholic boys' school, did cancer research in Seattle, worked as a civil engineer in Mexico, and directed a student counseling center. (8) Demara, whom had never finished high school, was always able to learn enough about each profession to perform it competently and credibly. (9) However, his deceptions did lead to trouble when they found about them.

(10) Once, for example, Demara, posing as "Martin Godgart," was hired to teach Latin, English, and French at a high school on an isolated island off the Maine coast. (11) They liked the job he was doing. (12) But his lack of formal credentials was discovered, and he was fired and briefly jailed. (13) Another time, when authorities learned of his desertion from the navy, he was sentenced to eighteen months in prison (after he had, of course, conducted his own defense). (14) Demara learned enough from this to give a believable performance as a law student and as the assistant warden of a Texas prison.

(15) Demara carried off his biggest deception during the Korean War aboard the Canadian destroyer *Cayuga*. (16) Posing as Dr. Joseph Cyr, which was a lieutenant surgeon in the Royal Canadian Navy, he read medical texts and journals, braced himself with heavy drink, and successfully operated on dozens of wounded South Korean servicemen and civilians. (17) Under less than ideal conditions, Demara removed a bullet lodged less than an inch from one patient's heart. (18) He was soon known as the "miracle doctor," and many people owed their lives to he and his skill. (19) But the real Dr. Cyr, who's credentials Demara had stolen, soon learned of the fraud, and Demara was kicked out of the navy.

(20) In his later years, Demara lived under his own name and counseled terminal patients at Good Samaritan Hospital in Anaheim, California. (21) Most likely, this new career wasn't entirely voluntary: a magazine story and, later, a movie about him called

"The Great Imposter" (starring Tony Curtis) blew his cover. (22) Stripped of the power to deceive, Demara became "about the most miserably unhappy man I have ever known," according to his physician, Dr. John Zane. (23) He died on June 7, 1982.

Scorecard: Number of Errors Found and Corrected _____

25 Strengthening Modifiers

Chapter 7 explained several ways to make your writing vivid and direct. One additional way is through the varied use of modifiers—descriptive words or phrases. But modifiers must be employed carefully and correctly. This chapter will show you how to

■ identify modifiers

■ condense long modifiers into short ones

■ attach modifiers to the nouns and action words they describe

WHAT IS A MODIFIER?

A **modifier** is a descriptive word or group of words. It gets its name from the fact that it changes—or modifies—the meaning of the word or words it describes. Let's look at two types of modifiers: adjectives and adverbs.

Adjective Modifiers

Adjectives are words or groups of words that describe a noun. Suppose, for example, you want to describe the noun *apartment*. You can place single-word adjectives before the noun:

> a *large* apartment   a *large modern* apartment

You can place *adjective phrases* after the noun:

> an apartment *with all the latest conveniences*
> an apartment *facing the lake*
> an apartment *built by Henderson and Company*
> an apartment *to rent*

UNIT 4
Chapter 25

Composing with Confidence
©2003

GO ELECTRONIC!

Use the following electronic supplements for additional practice with your writing:

• For chapter-by-chapter summaries and exercises, visit the Composing with Confidence Companion Website at: http://www.ablongman.com/meyers.

• For work with the writing process, visit The Longman Writer's Warehouse at http://longmanwriterswarehouse.com (password needed).

• For additional practice in grammar, use The Writer's ToolKit Plus CD-ROM

Or you can follow the noun with *adjective clauses:*

an apartment *that a famous movie star once owned*
the apartment *where the Thompsons live*

Adverb Modifiers

Adverbs tell *when, how, where, why,* or *how often* an action occurred. So, for example, you can explain when the action of a past-tense verb happened by adding a word, a phrase, or a clause:

| Verb | Adverb |
John *came* to work *late.*

| Verb | Adverb |
John *came* to work *yesterday.*

| Verb | Adverb phrase |
John *came* to work *on time.*

| Verb | Adverb phrase |
John *came* to work *after a long, frustrating drive.*

| Verb | Adverb clause |
John *came* to work *when he had recovered from his illness.*

| Verb | Adverb clause |
John *came* to work *before he left for his dentist appointment.*

CONDENSING CLAUSES TO PHRASES

Every modifier—whether a word, a phrase, or a clause—serves a purpose, but too many long modifiers will weaken your writing. So strengthen your modifiers by streamlining them. You can often condense clauses to phrases.

Adjective Clauses

You may recall that adjective clauses usually begin with *who, which,* or *that* (see Chapter 20). For example, consider the following sentences:

The oil painting *that is hanging over the mantelpiece* was a wedding present.
The teacher *who is with those students* is Professor Harrison.

If you remove the subjects and verbs—*that is* and *who is*—from both clauses, the result is both tighter and more direct:

The oil painting *hanging over the mantelpiece* was a wedding present.
The teacher *with those students* is Professor Harrison.

Here's another example, which converts a clause into an **appositive**—or renaming—phrase:

> My favorite professor, *who is Ms. Johnson,* teaches English literature.
> My favorite professor, *Ms. Johnson,* teaches English literature.

You can't condense every adjective clause to a phrase, but if the result saves words and sounds graceful, do it.

EXERCISE 1 | Condensing Adjective Clauses

Whenever possible, draw a line through who, which, *or* that *and any form of* to be *in the following sentences. Do not change the sentence if the result sounds awkward.*

1. Phineas Taylor (P. T.) Barnum (1810–1891), ~~who was~~ the world's most successful creator of sideshows and exhibitions, made a fortune from manipulating and fooling the public.

2. According to Barnum, there was no difference between displaying a monkey to the public and presenting an opera to a prince, for all show business is "trade," which is the practice of buying cheap and selling at a profit.

3. He got his start in show business by exhibiting a black woman named Joice Heath, who was supposedly the oldest living person at 161 years of age.

4. Upon examining Ms. Heath after her death, however, a doctor said that she was far younger, which was a claim Barnum insisted could never be proven.

5. Barnum, who was touring with a circus in 1836, met several ministers who were denouncing his activities as immoral.

6. In 1841, the American Museum, which was purchased after a series of schemes and maneuvers, became Barnum's permanent exhibition hall in New York.

EXERCISE 2 | Combining Sentences

Combine each of the following groups of sentences by changing one sentence into a descriptive phrase or an adjective clause. Insert commas as needed.

1. At the end of August 1843, the New York newspapers announced a "Grand Buffalo Hunt, Free of Charge." It was to take place in Hoboken, New Jersey, on a Thursday afternoon. *At the end of August 1843, the New York newspapers announced a "Grand Buffalo Hunt, Free of Charge," to take place in Hoboken, New Jersey, on a Thursday afternoon.*

2. The beasts would be lassoed and hunted as part of the entertainment. They would be placed behind strong fences to protect the public. (Hint: Begin the combined sentences with *Enclosed,* and place it before *behind strong fences.*)

_____

_____

3. What the newspapers did not say was that the buffalo were old and weak animals. They were hardly able to move, much less commit violence. _____

_____

_____

4. Barnum wisely decided to make admission free. He knew that the spectacle might not be all the audience anticipated. (Hint: Change *knew* to an *–ing* word.).

_____

_____

5. He didn't say that he had made a deal with the ferryboat owners. The owners agreed to take the public from Manhattan to New Jersey and give Barnum a percentage of the fares. _____

_____

_____

6. All through the day, boatloads of spectators crossed to New Jersey. They hoped to see shows scheduled for different times. _____

_____

_____

7. When the second batch of spectators arrived, they passed the boats filled with the first batch. The returnees called out that the hunt was the biggest humbug imaginable. _____

_____

_____

8. However, the eager audience showed no disappointment. They gave three cheers for "the author of the humbug, whoever he might be." (Hint: Change *gave* to an *–ing* word preceded by *instead*.) _____

_____

_____

Adverb Clauses

Adverb clauses (see Chapter 20) begin with joining words such as *after, if, although,* and *because,* as in the following example:

> *Because he understood that American audiences enjoyed clever tricks,* Barnum constantly entertained them with other spectacular but phony stunts.

You can easily condense these clauses to phrases. In this example, remove the subject from the clause and change the verb *understood* into an *–ing* word:

> *Understanding that American audiences enjoyed clever tricks,* Barnum constantly entertained them with other spectacular but phony stunts.

You can also make phrases from many adverb clauses beginning with time words such as *when, while, as, after, before,* or *whenever.*

> *When people looked at Barnum's mermaid,* they realized it wasn't an object of beauty.

You can express the *when* idea in different words and forms:

> *Looking at Barnum's mermaid,*
> *When viewing Barnum's mermaid,* } people realized it wasn't an object of beauty.
> *After a glance at Barnum's mermaid,*

But whenever you condense an adverb clause into a phrase, pay careful attention to the subject. It must be the same in both dependent and independent clauses. If it is, you should move it (or leave it) in the independent clause:

> *Clause:*   After *Barnum* had acquired an odd or spectacular exhibit, he couldn't resist the chance to make it a bit more unusual than the actual truth allowed.
>
> *Phrase:*   After acquiring an odd or spectacular exhibit, *Barnum* couldn't resist the chance to make it a bit more unusual than the actual truth allowed.

If the subject isn't the same in both clauses, the result may be unclear:

> *Dependent clause:*   Although *Barnum* never completely understood the reasons for his success, *other people* considered him a genius at promoting events and exhibitions.
>
> *Phrase:*   Although never completely understanding the reasons for his success, other people considered . . .

The second version seems to state that *other people*—not Barnum—didn't understand the reasons for his success, and that is not what the writer intended.

EXERCISE 3 | *Condensing Clauses to Phrases*

Whenever possible, change the adverb clause into a phrase in the sentences that follow. Cross out the subject in the adverb clause, and write your changes above the line. Some of the adverb clauses cannot be changed.

1. ^Hearing of ^~~When Barnum heard of~~ a dead mermaid from the Fiji Islands, ^Barnum ~~he~~ decided to buy it as an exhibit.

2. After a man named Moses Kimball had gotten the mermaid from a sailor, he offered to share profits (and costs) of the exhibition with Barnum. (Hint: Begin with *Having.*)

3. Because Barnum refused to part with any money so quickly, he talked to a naturalist, who said that the object was a fake.

4. When the naturalist was asked why he gave this verdict, he replied, "Because I don't believe in mermaids."

5. Since the naturalist didn't offer definite proof of a fraud, Barnum decided to ignore this opinion.

6. When Barnum sent letters to newspapers across the country, he claimed that a British naturalist named Dr. Griffin had found the mermaid in the "Feejee Islands."

7. Although Dr. Griffin was an impostor whose real name was Levi Lyman, no one knew that at first.

EXERCISE 4	Condensing Clauses to Phrases

Revise each of the following sentences, changing the clause into a phrase that uses the words in parentheses.

1. Because the Feejee mermaid consisted of the body of a fish connected to the head and hands of a monkey, it was quite a sight. (With . . .) *With the body of a fish connected to the head and hands of a monkey, the Feejee mermaid was quite a sight.*

2. Since the black dried-up animal had an open mouth, a tail twisted at an odd angle, and arms thrown up in the air, it appeared to have died in great pain. (With its . . .)

_____

_____

3. Because Barnum wanted to emphasize the mermaid's natural origins, he put up "Dr. Griffin" in a New York hotel and then arranged for reporters to call and examine the mermaid. (To . . .) _____

_____

_____

4. Although the reporters were suspicious at first, they soon became convinced the mermaid was genuine. (Despite . . .) _____

_____

_____

5. Barnum then delivered a picture of the mermaid to all the newspaper publishers, because he wanted to explain that Dr. Griffin would not let the mermaid be exhibited. (In order to . . .) _____

_____

_____

6. After the public demanded to see the mermaid, Dr. Griffin "reluctantly" allowed Barnum to exhibit it at the American Museum. (As a result of . . .) _____

_____

_____

Collaborative Activity 1

Shortening Sentences
Write ten sentences: five with adjective clauses and five with adverb clauses. Then exchange sentences with another group member. If possible, revise each sentence, changing the clauses to phrases. Then discuss your revisions. Are they clear, graceful, grammatically correct?

7. When evidence surfaced that the mermaid was a fraud, Barnum absolutely denied any responsibility for the hoax. (In the face of . . .) _____

_____

_____

EXERCISE 5	Combining Sentences

Make each of the following groups a single sentence. Use modifying phrases whenever possible. (One combined sentence cannot use a modifying phrase.)

1. Barnum hoped to acquire a sacred white elephant from Burma. He bribed the king of that country to send him one. *Hoping to acquire a sacred white elephant from Burma, Barnum bribed the king of that country to send him one.*

2. Barnum's men boarded the ship from Burma. They found the holy elephant, but it was gray. _____

_____

3. Barnum insisted "that there is no such thing as a pure white elephant." He put the Burmese beast on exhibition. _____

_____

4. The public was disappointed in Barnum's elephant. They flocked to see a competitor's white elephant called "The Light of Asia." _____

_____

5. The elephant certainly was white. The color was painted on—the exhibition was a fraud. _____

_____

A Word About Words

The king of Siam owned all of the rare and sacred albino elephants in the country. Supposedly, when he wanted to punish a member of his court, the king gave him a white elephant. The beast would cost a fortune to feed and maintain. This story may be the source of the expression *a white elephant*—meaning any possession, but especially a house, that is a useless waste of money.

PLACING MODIFIERS WITH PRECISION

The location of a modifier can greatly affect the meaning of a sentence. For example, notice how moving the word *just* affects the meaning of this sentence:

Just Bill gave his wife a kiss on the cheek.
Bill *just* gave his wife a kiss on the cheek.
Bill gave *just* his wife a kiss on the cheek.
Bill gave his *just* wife a kiss on the cheek.
Bill gave his wife *just* a kiss on the cheek.
Bill gave his wife a kiss *just* on the cheek.

We'll look at ways of placing modifiers to clearly express the meanings you intend.

Misplaced Modifiers

Who's hanging by the tail in these sentences?

Hanging by the tail, Bill laughed as the monkey made faces at his wife.
Bill laughed as the monkey made faces at his wife *hanging by the tail.*

If neither Bill nor his wife has grown a new body part, these sentences need to be revised. Place the modifier directly before or after the word it truly describes—or rewrite the modifier:

Bill laughed as the monkey, *hanging by the tail,* made faces at his wife.
Bill laughed as the monkey made faces at his wife *as it hung by the tail.*

Spotting and correcting misplaced modifiers aren't easy tasks because they're not always so funny. But your skill will improve with practice.

EXERCISE 6	Placing Modifiers Correctly

Each of the following sentences contains a misplaced modifier. Underline the modifier, and then draw a caret (^) in the spot where it belongs.

1. Barnum cared^about gathering crowds for his shows <u>only</u>, and he didn't mind fooling the public to do it.

2. For example, a man entered his office to beg for a job, and Barnum hired him one time for a dollar and a half a day.

3. Each day, the man would attract crowds by placing five bricks without saying a word on the street, then walking from one to the other, and exchanging them.

4. Within thirty minutes, to figure out what was happening, hundreds of people would gather.

5. Every hour, the "brick man" would go into Barnum's museum, followed, of course, by citizens who paid the admission fee to find out what the man was doing out of curiosity.

6. This kind of stunt was ideal for Barnum, showing great ingenuity and costing almost nothing.

Dangling Modifiers

Sometimes the word the modifier describes is missing from the sentence, so the modifier dangles unattached, describing nothing. This common error is known as a **dangling modifier**:

Sitting on the beach in July, the sun was very hot. (*Who* was sitting on the beach? It certainly wasn't the sun.)
Visiting New York, there are many sights to see. (*Who* is visiting New York? The sentence doesn't say.)

You cannot shift around a dangling modifier to make a sentence clear. You must rewrite the sentence, adding the word the modifier actually describes.

> *Sitting on the beach in July,* I felt the hot sun on my face.
> There are many sights for *you* to see on a visit to New York.

When trying to avoid dangling modifiers, keep in mind that a phrase beginning with an *–ing* word at the start of a sentence must modify the subject of the sentence. If it does not, it dangles.

EXERCISE 7	Eliminating Dangling Modifiers

Underline the dangling modifier in each sentence that follows, and then revise the sentence to eliminate the problem. If necessary, change a phrase into a dependent clause.

1. <u>Overwhelming the museum</u>, Barnum had to figure out how to handle such large crowds. *Barnum had to figure out how to handle such large crowds that were overwhelming the museum.*

2. Unable to get the crowds to leave the museum, new customers had to be turned away. _____

3. After pondering this dilemma, the perfect solution presented itself. _____

4. Seeing the scene painter at work on the stage, the man was told by Barnum to immediately paint a huge sign that said "To the Egress." _____

5. Seizing the brush, the sign was painted in fifteen minutes and then nailed over the door leading to the alleyway. _____

6. Unaware that *egress* meant *exit*, the alleyway was soon filled, leaving room for new customers. _____

Collaborative Activity 2

Adding Modifiers
Write four simple sentences in which the subject is performing an action. Exchange papers and add two or three modifiers—phrases or clauses, or both—to each sentence. Then check to be sure that these modifiers aren't misplaced or dangling. Discuss any problems in your group.

IN SUMMARY | Strengthening Modifiers

An Adjective Clause Modifier
1. begins with *who, which,* or *that.*
2. can often be condensed to a phrase by eliminating *who, which,* or *that* and recasting the remainder of the clause.

An Adverb Clause Modifier

1. begins with joining words such as *when, while, if, although,* or *because.*
2. can often be condensed to a phrase by eliminating the joining words plus the subject and beginning the phrase with a present or past participle.

But Any Modifier

1. must directly precede or follow the word it describes to avoid being a misplaced modifier.
2. must refer to a word in the sentence that it modifies to avoid being a dangling modifier.

EDITING FOR MASTERY

Mastery Exercise 1

Correcting Errors in Modifiers

The following passage contains eight misplaced or dangling modifiers and dependent clauses that could be phrases. Write your revisions on the lines following each sentence. If a sentence doesn't need revision, write "no change" on the lines that follow. The first sentence—which has two revisions—has been completed for you.

P. T. Barnum's Cardiff Giant—A Giant Hoax

1. George Hull, who was a tobacco farmer and cigar maker from a small town in New York, created one of the greatest hoaxes ever perpetrated on the American public in 1869. *In 1869, George Hull, a tobacco farmer and cigar maker from a small town in New York, created one of the greatest hoaxes ever perpetrated on the American public.*

2. A year earlier, after arguing with a preacher about references to giants in the Bible, the idea occurred to Hull of making a giant manlike figure out of stone and claiming it was a petrified man. _____

_____

_____

3. Hull and a partner acquired a five-ton block of stone and hired two sculptors with Hull serving as the model to carve a statue 10½ feet tall. _____

_____

_____

4. The giant was then shipped to his cousin William Newell's farm, where it was buried in a five-foot-deep grave behind the barn which was outside Cardiff, New York. _____

_____

_____

5. A year later on October 16, 1869, two workmen were hired to dig a well behind the barn, where they unearthed the giant. _____

_____

_____

6. A furor was created in the neighborhood that soon spread throughout the nation. _____

_____

7. Newell immediately erected a tent and began charging fifty cents for a look at the object, which was soon called the "Cardiff Giant." _____

_____

_____

8. But while people rushed to see the giant, suspicions that it was a phony grew greater. _____

_____

_____

Collaborative Activity 3

Comparing Corrections
Review your corrections in Mastery Exercise 1 with your group. Report your findings to the entire class.

9. As all the evidence pointed toward a hoax, George Hull confessed to the fraud.

_____

_____

10. The public nonetheless came to see it in growing numbers and the giant for exhibition was moved to Albany and then to New York City. _____

_____

_____

11. Unable to buy the giant, an imitation was made and displayed in New York City by P. T. Barnum that soon outdrew the original one. _____

_____

_____

12. Finally in 1948 the Cardiff giant was brought to the Farmers' Museum, which is one of the museums administered by the New York State Historical Association of Cooperstown, where it is on display today. _____

_____

_____

Scorecard: Number of errors found and corrected _____

Mastery Exercise 2

Correcting Errors in Modifiers

The following passage contains eight misplaced or dangling modifiers and dependent clauses that could be phrases. Write your revisions on the lines following each sentence.

If a sentence doesn't need revision, write "no change" on the lines that follow. The first sentence has been completed for you.

Charles S. Stratton (1838–1883): P.T. Barnum's "General Tom Thumb"

1. The midget Charles S. Stratton was one of the most famous performers of P. T. Barnum, who never grew more than thirty-five inches tall. *The midget Charles S. Stratton, who never grew more than thirty-five inches tall, was one of the most famous performers of P. T. Barnum.*

2. After growing normally for the first six months of his life, fifteen pounds was all he weighed when he was five years old. _____

3. When he was six years old and only twenty-two inches tall, P.T. Barnum discovered Charles. _____

4. For three dollars a week plus expenses, Barnum hired the boy and his mother and brought them to New York. _____

5. Barnum billed Little Charles as "General Tom Thumb, a dwarf of eleven years of age, just arrived from England." _____

6. On stage, he appeared in many costumes and played the roles of Cupid, a soldier, David against Goliath, and even Napoleon. _____

7. Within a short time, from three dollars to fifty dollars a week, his performances were sold out and his salary climbed dramatically._____

8. Many people saw his performances over the next fourteen years, including three years in Europe, and he retired as a wealthy man. _____

9. At the age of twenty-three he met twenty-year-old Lavinia Warren, who was another star midget of P. T. Barnum, who was only thirty-two inches tall. _____

10. They fell madly in love and were soon married at a wedding and then cele-
brated their honeymoon night attended by thousands. _____

_____

_____

11. But, at the age of forty-three, ten thousand people attended Tom Thumb's funeral when he died. _____

_____

12. Lavinia later married again, and she lived to be seventy-eight years old. _____

_____

13. However, after she died, she did not choose to be buried next to her second
husband._____

_____

14. Instead, she found her final resting place beside Tom Thumb, and the words
that were on her tombstone said simply, "His Wife." _____

_____

Scorecard: Number of errors found and corrected _____

26 Using Apostrophes, Hyphens, and Capital Letters

The *apostrophe* ('), the *hyphen* (-), and the *capital letter* may seem like small things, but small things can distract your readers from the important one: the content of your writing. You should therefore pay close attention to these apostrophes, hyphens, and capitals as you edit your work. This chapter will help you

- learn the rules
- give you practice in applying them

APOSTROPHES [']

Apostrophes ['] serve two main functions: to signal possession with nouns or to indicate contractions. We'll look at both functions here, and one additional one, for making plurals of letters.

Possession

Using apostrophes simplifies stating that something belongs to something, or belongs to someone else. Compare these expressions:

the degree of the doctor	the doctor's degree

But where the apostrophe belongs—and whether it needs an added *s*—differs in different situations. The sections that follow show how **possessives**—words that show ownership or possession—are formed.

UNIT 4

Chapter 26

Composing with Confidence

©2003

GO ELECTRONIC!

Use the following electronic supplements for additional practice with your writing:

- For chapter-by-chapter summaries and exercises, visit the Composing with Confidence Companion Website at: http://www.ablongman.com/meyers.

- For work with the writing process, visit The Longman Writer's Warehouse at http://longmanwriterswarehouse.com (password needed).

- For additional practice in grammar, use The Writer's ToolKit Plus CD-ROM

Singular Possessive Nouns.   As you've just seen, you can shorten expressions of possession or ownership by adding an apostrophe. With singular nouns, you must always follow the apostrophe with *s*:

the dog that belongs to Henry	= Henry's dog
the stereo my friend owns	= my friend's stereo
the house of my brother	= my brother's house

Notice that although a dog, a stereo, and a house are concrete and easy to visualize, abstract concepts can also be possessed:

Brad's suggestion
the doctor's opinion

People don't own these concepts, but people are responsible for them. "The doctor's opinion" really means "the opinion *of* the doctor." "Brad's suggestion" really means "the suggestion *made by* Brad."

The examples you've seen are of singular possessive nouns. And all singular nouns—even those ending in *s*, such as *boss*, John *Keats*, and Ms. *Williams*—form their possessive by adding both the apostrophe and *s*.

the job of the boss	= the boss's job
the poems of John Keats	= Keats's poems
the work of Ms. Williams	= Ms. Williams's work

EXERCISE 1	Establishing Possession

A Word About Words

The Greek root of *grammar* (the rules of language) and *graph* (a type of drawing) is the same because written language was originally represented in pictures (and still is in languages such as Chinese).

Revise each of the following expressions, using 's.

1. the hat that belongs to Susan _Susan's hat_____

2. the jewelry that Tom owns _____

3. the friendliness of Lonell _____

4. the mistake made by Elizabeth _____

5. the radio that belongs to Mr. Willis _____

6. the question asked by the boss _____

Plural Possessive Nouns.   Possessives with plural nouns are a different matter. As you know, most plural nouns end in *s*:

book*s*	student*s*	glass*es*	the Pearson*s*
chair*s*	dollar*s*	cit*ies*	the Lopez*es*

To make clear to readers that these nouns are *both* plural and possessive, add only an apostrophe after the *s*:

the apartment that belongs to the Pearsons	= the Pearsons' apartment
the behavior of my brothers	= my brothers' behavior

Here are examples of singular and plural possessive nouns. Compare the placement of the apostrophe:

my brother's behavior	= singular
my brothers' behavior	= plural

But some plural nouns are irregular; they don't end in *s*. Form the possessive of an irregular plural noun by adding both the apostrophe and *s*:

children's books
the media's job

EXERCISE 2   Forming Possessives

TIPS

For Using Apostrophes

As some people learn to use the apostrophe, they mistakenly put it before or after almost every final *s*. Don't confuse the possessive *'s* or *s'* with the final *s* on plural nouns or third-person singular verbs.

Possessives:

my *friend's* hobby

the *nurses'* responsibilities

Plurals:

Three of my *friends* (not *friend's*)

The *nurses* (not *nurses'* or *nurse's*)

Verbs:

Lawrence *works* (not *work's*)

He *owns* (not *own's*)

Rewrite each of the following expressions, using 's *or* s'.

1. the friend of the man   *the man's friend* _____

2. the responsibility of the children _____

3. the uncle of the boy _____

4. the uncle of the boys _____

5. the briefcase that belongs to Carlos _____

6. the new car that the Simpsons bought _____

7. the Day that celebrates Father _____

Possessives for Things and Time. You can use apostrophes to show that objects possess things:

the right headlight *of* the car	= the car's right headlight
the top branches *of* the trees	= the trees' top branches

You can even use *'s* or *s'* in some time expressions. Here are some examples:

a vacation *of* a month	= a month's vacation
the work *of* several years	= several years' work

EXERCISE 3   Placing Apostrophes Correctly

Insert apostrophes to establish possession in the following sentences. Not every sentence requires an apostrophe.

1. On the island of Yap in western Micronesia, one bank⌃s doors are always unlocked, and the money is unguarded.

2. In fact, all of the depositors money is openly displayed and may be handled and studied by anyone with the village chiefs permission.

3. The bank, called Stone Money Bank of Balabat, contains only thirty large donut-shaped stones, which are the traditional form of currency for Yap.

4. While the people purchase most items with American dollars, the stone moneys purpose is reserved for expensive purchases.

5. However, because of the stones great size, no one can steal them, and when the ownership changes, the money remains in the bank.

6. A stones value is actually based not on size but on the difficulty involved in bringing it to Yap; most of the stones came from the Palau Islands, which are 275 miles away and many days journey by sea.

TIPS

For Keeping Contractions Straight

Be careful to distinguish between the contractions and their look-alike and sound-alike words. Note these comparisons:

Contraction	*Possessive word*
it's	its house
you're	your house
they're	their house
who's	whose house
we're	*Verb:* were
Place words:	there where

Contractions

A **contraction** is a shortened form of a word that's missing one or more letters, usually when it melds with another word. An apostrophe replaces the missing letters:

does not	= doesn't (apostrophe replaces *o*)
it is	= it's (apostrophe replaces *i*)
you are	= you're (apostrophe replaces *a*)
we have	= we've (apostrophe replaces *ha*)
I would	= I'd (apostrophe replaces *would*)

EXERCISE 4   Forming Contractions

Make the following pairs of words into contractions, placing apostrophes in the proper locations.

1. she is _she's_____   6. could not _____
2. they are _____   7. who is _____
3. I have _____   8. you would _____
4. we are _____   9. it has _____
5. does not _____   10. you are _____

EXERCISE 5   Adding Apostrophes

Add apostrophes where necessary in the following sentences.

1. That^s my coat.
2. The elevators arent working today.
3. Dont you know whats the matter?
4. Whos the fellow whose shirt is torn?
5. Your letter doesnt say what youre interested in.
6. I cant help you when you wont help yourself.

Plurals of Letters

Add *apostrophe* + *s* to make a letter or group of letters plural, so readers won't mistake the *s* for one of the letters:

How many A's did you get this term?
My youngest child already knows her ABC's.

EXERCISE 6	Making Letters Plural

Collaborative Activity 1

Making Possessives and Contractions

Write five sentences with singular and plural nouns that possess something, but omit the apostrophes. Also write five sentences with words that could be contracted, but don't contract them. Exchange papers by passing to the left and rewrite the sentences with possessives and contractions indicated. Have a third student check the work. Discuss any problems.

Revise each of the following sentences, making the letter or letter group plural. Use the words in parentheses as guides.

1. She got a B last semester. (all) _She got all B's last semester._

2. One student in my class has a very high IQ. (several students)

   _____

3. You need at least one I.D. to cash a check. (two)

   _____

4. The word *traveled* can be spelled with one *l*. (two)

   _____

5. The army wants to produce a new ICBM. (three)

   _____

6. Don't forget to dot the *i* and cross the *t*. (plural)

   _____

HYPHENS [-]

Hyphens [-] always join. They join two or more words to make one, or they keep words joined when you must break them at the end of a line.

Between Words

Hyphens join two or more words to function as one word. Typically, these combinations form numbers, add certain indicators to nouns, create single adjectives that precede nouns, or create compound nouns.

Two-Word Numbers.   In formal writing, you should hyphenate numbers from twenty-one through ninety-nine:

sixty-two	twenty-seven

But don't hyphenate two-word numbers for one hundred or above, and express numbers of three or more words as numerals:

six thousand	427
five million	6,901

Finally, hyphenate any fractions written as words:

> three-fifths
> seven-eighths

EXERCISE 7	Joining Numbers with Hyphens

Hyphenate the following numbers where necessary.

1. thirty-̂four

2. seven thousand

3. two thirds

4. fifty one

5. five hundred

6. ninety one

Prefixes Before Nouns.   A **prefix** is a short structure attached to the beginning of another word, called a **root word**, as in these examples:

> *un*happy
> *dis*agree

The prefixes *self-*, *all-*, and *ex-* (meaning "former") require hyphens:

> self-control
> all-world
> ex-spouse

Hyphens connect any prefix to a capitalized noun:

> pro-German
> anti-American

And hyphens join all expressions with *in-law:*

> brother-in-law
> my in-laws
> sisters-in-law (Note how the plural is formed.)

EXERCISE 8	Hyphenating Prefixes

Revise each of the following prefix/noun combinations, using hyphens when necessary. Not all items require hyphens.

1. self awareness ___self-awareness___

2. ex police officer _____

3. brothers in law _____

4. trans American _____

5. non violence _____

6. all conference _____

Adjective Phrases.   When two or more words form a single adjective before a noun, they're joined by hyphens. Consider, for example, the expression *a four-hour trip*. It is not a *four* trip or an *hour* trip, but a four-hour trip. The hyphen makes that clear. Here are further examples:

> a simple-minded idea
> a two-car accident
> a better-than-average runner

But don't hyphenate these word groups if they come after linking verbs:

> As a runner, he is better than average.

EXERCISE 9   Hyphenating Adjectives

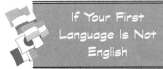

If Your First Language Is Not English

Unlike adjectives in many other languages, English adjectives don't have plural forms. So a hyphenated adjective before a noun is always singular:
a two-*star* movie (not *stars*)
a five-*foot* ladder (not *feet*)

Revise each of the following word groups, creating a two- or three-word adjective requiring hyphens. Eliminate plural noun forms where necessary.

1. a job for two persons   *a two-person job*

2. a suit with three pieces _____

3. a job that is long overdue _____

4. a board that is ten feet long _____

5. a situation meaning life or death _____

6. a pole that is five feet long _____

Compound Words.   When two complete root words are combined, they form a **compound word**, such as *background*. But be careful how you form compounds, for they can be written in three different ways. Check a dictionary when you need to.

1. As a single word:

Root word	Root word	New word
hand	made	handmade
head	ache	headache
note	book	notebook

Notice that both root words keep all of their letters in the compound word.

2. As hyphenated words (usually as nouns; verbs generally aren't hyphenated):

Root word	Root word	New word
president	elect	president-elect
give (and)	take	give-and-take
send	off	send-off (noun)
		send off (verb)

3. As two words (these are really not compound words):

master builder	heat wave	grand piano

If you're unsure whether to hyphenate a compound word, consult an up-to-date dictionary.

EXERCISE 10   Forming Compound Words

Combine a root word with each root word, using hyphens when necessary. Check a dictionary if necessary.

1. night _time_____

2. house _____

3. _____ worker

4. _____ ground

5. eye _____

6. _____ work

7. war _____

8. _____ book

Between Syllables

When you must divide a word at the end of a line, use a hyphen to signal that the two parts of the word are still joined. Divide the word only between **syllables**—one or more letters that include a single vowel sound (such as the three single vowel sounds in *un-der-stand*) or a vowel blend (such as *–sion* in *div-i-sion*). When you're in doubt, consult a dictionary. Don't divide single-syllable words such as *worked, through,* or *speak.*

> intell-igent
> com-munity
> pic-ture
> *But not*
> sty-le (one syllable)
> walk-ed (one syllable; the *–ed* has no vowel sound)

Syllable breaks often come after complete root words:
The syllable breaks also occur after prefixes or before **suffixes**—attachments to the ends of words:

> *un*-natural
> agree-*ment*
> usual-*ly*

And syllable breaks also come between two consonants—unless the consonants form a blended sound, such as *–ph, –th, –sh, –sc,* or *–ch,* or unless the consonants are part of a root word:

> *win*-ning
> *pen*-cil
> *paral*-lel
> *camp*-ing
> *like*-ly

TIPS

For Hyphenating on the Computer

You can ask word processing programs to automatically hyphenate words for you. But be careful. The program doesn't know the difference, for example, between *pre-sent (verb)* and *pres-ent (noun)* or *pro-ject (verb)* and *proj-ect (noun).* So proofread your paper carefully; you may be smarter than the computer.

Continued

spell-er
sad-ness

real-ly
   but
graph-ic
wash-ing
north-ern

Two hyphens in the same word are confusing, so break a hyphenated word only at its hyphen:

ex-wife   self-confidence

Finally, never hyphenate a contraction, and don't leave a single letter at the end of a line:

Wrong: does-   *Right:* doesn't
         n't
Wrong: a-   *Right:* aban-
         bandon   don

Again, consult a dictionary if you're unsure of where a hyphen break occurs.

EXERCISE 11 — Hyphenating Between Syllables

Rewrite the following words, dividing them between syllables. If a word can't be divided, don't rewrite it.

1. unnatural *unnat-ural*
2. reply
3. stopped
4. self-awareness
5. communication
6. happiness
7. truthfully
8. watch
9. baseball
10. adore

EXERCISE 12 — Combining with Hyphens

Combine each word that follows with a second word, using hyphens where they are needed. Consult a dictionary when necessary.

1. night *nighttime*   3. hand _____   5. sun _____
2. floor _____   4. dinner _____   6. house _____

7. prize _____   **9.** self _____   **10.** over _____

8. builder _____

CAPITALIZATION

Capitalized letters send signals: that a sentence is beginning, that someone or something has a proper name, or that someone has a title. We'll examine all the ways that capitalization works:

Begin every sentence with a capitalized word:

The sun sets at about 7:00 in mid-September. In summer, it sets much later.

Capitalize the pronoun *I*:

I *but* we he they his myself

Capitalize the names of people, places, courses, organizations, brand names, languages, and words formed from them:

William	Main Street
the Central Intelligence Agency	French
Texas	Texan
Italy	Italian
History 111 (the name of a course), *but* history (not a course name)	
Kleenex, *but* facial tissue	

EXERCISE 13	Capitalizing Proper Nouns

Underline the letters that should be capitalized.

1. african

2. james earl "jimmy" carter

3. the corner of central street and maple avenue

4. social science 101

5. sociology

6. california wine

7. you and i

8. the senate and the house of representatives

9. spanish

Capitalize a person's title before his or her name, but not after the name:

Mr. Gomez		
Ms. Yung		
President Truman	*but*	the president
Professor Lee	*but*	Who is your English professor?
Dr. Smith	*but*	She is a doctor.

Capitalize the names of areas or countries. But don't capitalize these terms when they mean only a direction:

The North won the war.	She is from the East.
but	*but*
We are traveling west.	Which way is northeast?

Capitalize the names of days, months, and holidays. But don't capitalize the seasons of the year:

Thursday		summer
May	*but*	
Memorial Day		fall

Capitalize all major words in titles. Don't capitalize little words—short prepositions, conjunctions, and articles—unless they are the first words in the title or subtitle:

A Farewell to Arms

Gone with the Wind

"Eight Days a Week"

Journal of the American Medical Association

"What Makes a Good Poem?"

If Your First Language Is Not English

Speakers of Spanish may confuse capitalization in English. Nationalities and names of languages aren't capitalized in Spanish, but they are in English. Here are some examples:

I speak *Spanish.*

He is *German.*

EXERCISE 14   Capitalizing Nouns

Underline the letters that should be capitalized.

1. friday

2. summer

3. july

4. the wild west

5. a doctor

6. dr. johnson

7. merriam webster's dictionary

IN SUMMARY   Apostrophes, Hyphens, and Capital Letters

Use Apostrophes

1. to make nouns possessive. Add apostrophe +*s* for all singular and irregular plural nouns; add the apostrophe after the *s* for all other plural nouns.

2. to form contractions. Place the apostrophe in the spot where letters have been omitted.

3. to form plurals of letters. Add apostrophe +*s*.

Use Hyphens

1. to join two-word numbers from twenty-one to ninety-nine.
2. to join the prefixes *self-*, *ex-*, and *all-* to root words, and join prefixes to capitalized nouns.
3. to join two-word adjectives before a noun.
4. to join some compound words.
5. to join the syllables of words divided at the end of a line.

Use Capital Letters

1. to begin every sentence.
2. with the personal pronoun *I*.
3. with the names of people, places, courses, organizations, languages, and words formed from them.
4. with personal titles before names, but not titles after the names or titles that stand alone.
5. with the names of countries and areas (but not directions).
6. with days, months, and holidays (but not seasons).
7. with all major words in titles.

EDITING FOR MASTERY

Mastery Exercise 1

Correcting Errors in Apostrophes, Hyphens, and Capital Letters

The following passage contains twenty errors in the use of apostrophes, hyphens, and capital letters in addition to the first two errors, which have been corrected for you as an example. Find and correct each error by making your changes above the line.

The Other Jonah

(1) Is the biblical tale of Jonah being swallowed by a whale just an ancient fish story? (2) Don^t be too sure, for it^s not the only case on record. (3) Theres another story that occurred about a Century ago.

(4) It happened in february 1891, when James Bartley, a young english sailor, was a crew member on the whaling ship *Star of the East*. (5) As the ship approached the Falkland Islands in the south Atlantic, the sailors spotted a huge sperm Whale. (6) Two small boats with crew-members—one of them Bartley—were sent out to kill the whale. (7) As a sailors harpoon struck the whale, the whale struck back with it's enormous V shaped tail. (8) The force of the blow capsized the boat. (9) Fortunately, the sailors on the other boat did'nt panic and soon killed the mammal.

(10) When the boat was righted, Bartley and another crewman had disappeared and were presumed to have drowned. (11) The crew pulled the animals carcass next to the whaling ship and worked until midnight removing the blubber. (12) The next morning, using the ships crane, they hoisted the stomach up on deck. (13) The men then noticed some movement in the whale's belly. (14) They opened it and found Bartley unconscious. (15) Several sailor's immediately bathed him in seawater. (16) Although this action revived Bartley, he was delirious and needed two weeks rest in the Captain's quarters to regain his sanity.

(17) Within a month, Bartley was fully recovered and able to describe his near death experience inside the belly of a whale. (18) He remembered seeing total darkness and then slipping along a smooth passage. (19) His hand's felt slime all around him. (20) In the unbearable heat of the stomach, he lost consciousness, and when he awoke he was in the captains' cabin.

(21) Bartley recovered his full mental powers, but he carried around physical evidence of his experience for the rest of his life. (22) His face, neck, and hands re-mained white-bleached by the whales digestive juices.

Scorecard: Number of Errors Found and Corrected _____

Collaborative Activity 3

Comparing Corrections
Review your corrections in Mastery Exercise 1 with your group. Report your findings to the entire class.

Mastery Exercise 2

Correcting Errors in Apostrophes, Hyphens, and Capital Letters

The following passage contains twenty errors in the use of apostrophes, hyphens, and capital letters in addition to the first error, which has been corrected for you as an example. Find and correct each error by making your changes above the line.

Rachel Carson (1907–1964): The First Ecologist

(1) Rachel Carson, with the publication of *Silent Spring* in 1962, transformed and energized the ecology movement when it wasn^'t even a movement.

(2) DDT was considered a wonder pesticide. (3) It had been called one of the greatest scientific leap's forward in history. (4) It's creator, Paul Muller, won a nobel Prize in 1948. (5) However, when Olga Owens Huckins, who was Rachel Carsons

friend, suggested that DDT might be dangerous, Carson began to research and collect data. (6) She concluded that pesticides build up in crops on which theyre sprayed and are then transferred to birds and other animals.

(7) DDT was actually a result of research conducted by the Military into biological warfare. (8) Researchers noticed that chemicals such as DDT, while not immediately poisonous to Humans, killed almost all insects. (9) In the previous two decades, it had widely been used as a pesticide on a many crops. (10) Crop yields were dramatically increased. (11) The battle against pest's that destroyed grains, fruits, and vegetables seemed about to be won in the midtwentieth-century.

(12) *Silent Spring* shattered that dream forever. (13) Whats the gain of greater crop yield's balanced against the poisoning of millions of birds? (14) The book raised issues that are important. (15) How do we balance our Industrial and agricultural needs with the dangers they create in the environment? (16) What is benefit of chemicals that increase agricultural production but also destroy the quality of life?

(17) Rachel Carson awakened the conscience of americans. (18) She was making them aware of a new term: ecology. (19) She argued that scientists and politicians must study the long term effects of pesticides on nature, not just the short-term economic benefits. (20) But her arguments appealed to everyday citizens as well. (21) As she states in the concluding chapter of *Silent Spring,* "It is our alarming misfortune that . . . a science had armed itself with the most modern and terrible weapons, and that in turning them against the insects it has also turned them against the earth."

(22) *Silent Spring* inspired the creation of the Environmental Defense Fund, which later became the Environmental Protection agency (the epa). (23) As a result, DDT was finally banned in the united states in 1972. (24) Other types of pesticides were banned in 1975.

Scorecard: Number of Errors Found and Corrected _____

27 Checking Punctuation

Punctuation marks—commas, periods, semicolons, and the like—are the stop-and-go signs that guide readers along their journey through your ideas. Some punctuation marks separate ideas; other punctuation marks join ideas. Therefore, incorrect punctuation can both annoy and confuse readers. This chapter will show you how to

- identify where to place punctuation marks
- select the right punctuation marks: commas, periods, question marks, exclamation points, semicolons, colons, dashes, parentheses, and quotation marks

THE COMMA [,]

Contrary to what some people think, **commas** do not merely indicate pauses in speech. Commas have five main uses—some to separate ideas, others to enclose them. Learn these uses, and you will know the proper signals to send your readers.

Three or More Items in a Series

When you write three or more items in a series, separate them with commas, and place *and* or another **coordinating conjunction**—*for, and, nor, but, or, yet, so* (FANBOYS)—before the last item. The comma before the conjunction is optional, but be consistent in using it. Either include or omit the comma each time:

> *José, Sammy,* and *I (subjects)*
> I *ran* to the station, *bought* my ticket, and *caught* the train just in time. *(verbs)*
> He is *short, ugly, obnoxious,* but *rich. (adjectives)*
> Not *on the grass, on the beach,* or *in the water. (phrases)*

GO ELECTRONIC!

Use the following electronic supplements for additional practice with your writing:

- For chapter-by-chapter summaries and exercises, visit the Composing with Confidence Companion Website at: http://www.ablongman.com/meyers.
- For work with the writing process, visit The Longman Writer's Warehouse at http://longmanwriterswarehouse.com (password needed).
- For additional practice in grammar, use The Writer's ToolKit Plus CD-ROM

EXERCISE 1	Adding Commas

Place commas where they are needed in the following groups of words. Some groups need no commas.

1. a jug of wine ˄ a loaf of bread ˄ and you

2. The Mad Dipper at the amusement park is exciting funny and scary.

3. You can take the crosstown bus the elevated train or the subway.

4. All I see in the mail are bills bills bills.

5. The government of the people by the people and for the people shall not perish from the earth.

6. The dog ran wildly around the kitchen crashed into a chair in the dining room tore a curtain in the living room and wet the bedroom rug.

Independent Clauses Joined by a Coordinating Conjunction

Remember that an **independent clause** contains a subject and a verb and can be a sentence by itself. When you join two independent clauses, signal to your readers that the clauses are separate by placing a comma before the conjunction that joins them (see Chapter 9).

> California was a remote area with very little population, *but* the gold rush of 1849 changed that situation in a hurry.
> Word of the discovery of gold spread quickly, *so* thousands of fortune hunters journeyed west to find the "gold in them thar hills."

Don't confuse two independent clauses with two verbs, which are simply two items in a series and should not be separated by a comma:

Incorrect:	People made fortunes in a day, *and* then gambled them away at night.
Correct:	People made fortunes in a day *and* then gambled them away at night.
Correct:	People made fortunes in a day, *and* then they gambled them away at night.

EXERCISE 2	Joining Independent Clauses

Join each of the following pairs of independent clauses by inserting an appropriate coordinating conjunction, preceded by a comma. You don't have to use every conjunction.

Joshua Abraham Norton (1819–1880): "The Emperor of the United States"

1. During and after the gold rush of 1849, San Francisco attracted many odd characters ˄ ,but one man rose to become perhaps the most successful eccentric in American history: Norton I, Emperor of the United States and Protector of Mexico.

2. In the first forty years of his life, Joshua Abraham Norton did not behave oddly he was both a shrewd and respected businessperson.

3. He was born in England he lived and worked in South Africa and Brazil until the age of thirty.

4. Hearing of the discovery of gold in San Francisco, he arrived there in 1849 with $40,000 he opened an office on the town's main street.

5. He may have been new to town he was no stranger to investing wisely.

6. Other men trusted his sharp judgment they asked him to be their agent in business deals.

EXERCISE 3	Punctuating Joined Clauses

Some—but not all—of the sentences in the following paragraph require a comma before the conjunction. Add commas where they are necessary.

The Collapse of Norton's Business Career

(1) Joshua Norton bought property and goods at cheap prices and then sold them at large profits. (2) Within a few years, he had earned a quarter of a million dollars so the town leaders greatly respected him. (3) In the end, however, one of Norton's risky investments caused his downfall but it also led to his rise to royalty. (4) In 1853, he was sure that he could corner the market in rice so he bought every grain of it already in the city or on its way there. (5) When unexpected shiploads of rice sailed into port, prices crashed and Norton and his friends lost a fortune. (6) Up to that point, no one in San Francisco had more energy or ambition but during the long, painful lawsuit that followed, Norton seemed to lose heart.

Sentence Interrupters

Words, phrases, or clauses often interrupt the flow of a grammatically complete sentence. Compare the two versions of the following sentence, the first without the interrupter and the second with it:

Joshua Norton dropped out of sight for two years.
Joshua Norton, *therefore,* dropped out of sight for two years.

Alert your readers to a sentence interrupter by enclosing it in two commas—in the same spots where parentheses would go. Here's another example:

One day, looking and acting quite differently, Norton suddenly reappeared.

A true sentence interrupter can be removed without seriously affecting the sentence's meaning. Use these tests to help you decide whether to enclose a structure in commas:

1. See if the structure fits logically in parentheses; or
2. Temporarily remove it and see if the sentence still makes sense.

Be careful to enclose an interrupter in *two* commas. Many people mistakenly punctuate by ear, putting in only one comma where they hear a pause. A single comma in these cases is misleading and confusing:

Incorrect:	Norton, who had been a conservative in dress and action was a strange sight to behold. (This looks like a sentence fragment.)
Incorrect:	Norton who had been a conservative in dress and action, was a strange sight to behold. (The comma in this sentence seems to separate the subject and verb: *Norton . . . was.*)
Correct:	Norton, who had been a conservative in dress and action, was a strange sight to behold.

EXERCISE 4 | Editing for Missing Commas

The following sentences contain only one comma before or after a sentence interrupter. Place the second comma where it's needed.

1. Depressed about his bad luck, Norton had spent two years in a cheap boarding-house. As time passed, however⌃ he became deeply troubled by the worsening political situation of the country.

2. Because of growing tensions between the North and South, a war, it seemed to him was unavoidable.

3. A democracy, which was unpredictable and inefficient could not handle the conflicts between the slave states and the free states.

4. Only a king, such as the one that Norton had lived under as a British citizen could guarantee peace.

5. What America needed Norton concluded, was a ruler with strong powers.

6. He had made this argument so often to his friends that they began to refer to him, jokingly of course as "His Gracious Highness" and "Emperor."

7. One day, therefore he asked himself: Why not?

TIPS

For Placing Commas

If you aren't sure if a group of words needs a comma, remember this simple rule:

When in doubt, leave commas out.

Introductory Expressions

When a sentence begins with an introductory expression, a comma signals to your readers that a complete statement will follow. The introductory expression may be a single word, a phrase, or a dependent clause:

Single Word:	*However,* Norton seemed to have lost his mind.
Phrase:	*In San Francisco's business community,* he had been a prominent and respected figure.
Dependent clause:	*After Norton reappeared,* all of that changed.

A comma is usually unnecessary at the end of a sentence, unless the comma precedes an afterthought or a contrasting idea:

The city had changed considerably *in those two years.*
Norton seemed to have lost his mind, *however.* (a contrast)
Norton had never been married, *incidentally.* (an afterthought)

EXERCISE 5	Punctuating Sentence Interrupters

Revise each of the following sentences, inserting the sentence interrupter (indicated in parentheses) in the most logical place. Be sure to use commas where they are needed.

The Rise of the Emperor

1. A dignified gentleman appeared in the offices of a San Francisco newspaper. (one day in September 1859) *One day in September 1859, a dignified gentleman appeared in the offices of a San Francisco newspaper.*

2. He gave the editor a proclamation that began: "At the . . . request and desire of a large majority of the citizens of these United States, I, Joshua Norton . . . declare and proclaim myself emperor . . ." (quietly and seriously) _____
   _____
   _____

3. The editor ran it without comment. (amused by this unusual feature story) _____
   _____
   _____

4. Very few people in the city paid much attention, even though the proclamation also abolished Congress and the Supreme Court. (at first) _____
   _____
   _____

5. When Norton began appearing in the streets in an odd uniform, the townsfolk began to take notice. (however) _____
   _____

6. There was some jeering, but people soon stopped. (of course)_____
   _____

7. The emperor created a sensation. (in his blue jacket with gold medallions and brass buttons, red general's cap, and navy boots) _____

_____

_____

EXERCISE 6	Punctuating a Paragraph

Correctly punctuate the sentence interrupters where necessary in the following passage.

(1) Soon growing used to this oddly dressed monarch, the public gave Norton "appropriate" respect. (2) He marched up and down the streets showing himself to his subjects and accepting their bows with the dignity of a true ruler. (3) Without fail each day he attended public gatherings and continued to issue proclamations concerning his empire. (4) Furthermore his concern for the people, his dignity, and his graciousness soon completely won over the city. (5) For twenty years the citizens of San Francisco cheerfully supported him in his madness. (6) The local merchants always honored the royal bonds he issued in the amount of fifty cents. (7) His former business associates routinely paid the taxes always for small amounts of money he levied against them.

Two or More Adjectives

Piled-up adjectives after a noun should be separated by commas like any other items in a series. But before a noun, commas may or may not be needed.

If you can reverse the order of the adjectives before a noun, separate them with a comma:

> A handsome, charming man (a charming, handsome man)
> A shy, awkward child (an awkward, shy child)

But if you cannot reverse the adjectives, don't separate them with a comma:

> A large red pencil (*not* a red large pencil)
> A powerful racing car (*not* a racing powerful car)

EXERCISE 7	Punctuating Adjectives

Place commas where they are needed in the following phrases.

1. a good-looking,ᐱ talented singer

2. a clever old thief

3. a disgusting slimy worm

4. a dirty worn-out shirt

5. a magnificent still-life drawing

6. a large yellow balloon

404 UNIT 4 Troubleshooting

EXERCISE 8	Editing for Comma Use

Some commas are missing or misplaced in the following passage. Insert commas where they're needed, and cross out those incorrectly placed.

Emperor Norton's Reign

(1) Norton I ate and drank for free at the best restaurants and saloons in the city. (2) Furthermore he was often invited to speak at political rallies where he was received, often ironically of course by the applause of his admiring subjects. (3) When the state legislature met a large comfortable chair was always reserved for him. (4) The city directory, listed him as "Norton, Joshua, Emperor." (5) And when the genuine Emperor Dom Pedro II of Brazil, visited the city in 1876 San Francisco proudly presented its own emperor to him with appropriate pomp and circumstance.

(6) Once when the emperor's uniform wore out the public, contributed money for a replacement. (7) On a similar occasion, later the board of supervisors voted him city funds. (8) Several tailors, who made and contributed uniforms proudly displayed cards in their windows that read: "By appointment to His Majesty." (9) His loyal subjects gave him a variety of hats a magnificent walking stick, and a big three-color, Chinese umbrella to keep his imperial self dry on rainy days. (10) When someone, attempted to have him committed to a mental institution, the judge dismissed the hearing into the emperor's sanity with the remark that Norton was "just about the best going in the king line."

Collaborative Activity 1

Looking at Commas

Write ten sentences that require commas—but leave all the commas out. In your group, exchange papers by passing to the left and add the missing commas. Return the papers to the original author and check over the sentences. Discuss any disagreements.

THE PERIOD [.]

Periods have two functions: to signal the end of sentences and to mark abbreviations.

Statements

End every complete statement with a period:

Emperor Norton had a long, fruitful reign. His subjects treated him kindly.

Abbreviations

Use periods for most abbreviations:

Mr., Ms., Mrs., Dr., Rev.
A.M., P.M.
etc.

But don't use periods for *acronyms*. Each letter of an acronym represents a word, and the acronym is often a word itself. Here are a few examples:

> *FBI*—the Federal Bureau of Investigation
>
> television or radio stations (*WLS*—once owned by Sears, which modestly used the letters to represent the World's Largest Store)
>
> *scuba*—self-contained underwater breathing apparatus

Consult your dictionary when you are not sure whether the word is an abbreviation or acronym.

THE QUESTION MARK [?]

A **question mark** indicates the end of a question; it cannot represent anything else. Therefore, place a question mark at the end of a **direct question**, but don't place a question mark at the end of an **indirect question**, which is contained within a larger statement and uses the word order of a statement:

> Why *did* this change in Norton *occur*? (A direct question, using the word order of *helping verb-subject-verb*)
>
> > *but*
>
> I'd like to know *why this change occurred*. (Indirect question, using the order of a statement: *subject-verb*)

THE EXCLAMATION POINT [!]

An **exclamation point** signals excitement, anger, fear, or other strong emotions—whether in full sentences or in partial sentences:

> You can't be serious!
> He ate three whole pizzas!
> Help! Police!

Don't overuse exclamation points! Too many of them will bombard your readers! (Like these.)

EXERCISE 9	Adding End Punctuation to Sentences

Place a period, question mark, or exclamation point at the end of each of the following sentences.

1. Just who was that masked man?

2. I want to know what is supposed to happen at the meeting

3. We are planning the agenda now

4. Paul asked if we could meet next Thursday

5. Sally will be taking care of her sick dog

6. She always gives that same ridiculous excuse

7. Is it possible to change the date of the meeting

8. Paul wanted to know how long the meeting would last

9. Not more than an hour, please

10. Is this the end of the exercise, or are there more sentences

THE SEMICOLON [;]

The **semicolon** has two uses: to join independent clauses and to separate items that have internal punctuation.

Joining Independent Clauses

You can use a semicolon to join two independent clauses whose ideas are closely related:

> We cannot afford any further delay; the problem must be stopped immediately.
>
> Everyone agrees upon the solution; *however,* no one can agree about how best to implement it.

Notice in the second example that a comma follows the introductory word *however* after the semicolon. You should treat this and similar introductory words just like a sentence interrupter at the beginning of a sentence. Also see Chapter 20 for further discussion of semicolons and transitional words.

Separating Items in a Series That Contains Internal Commas

As you know, commas separate three or more items in a series. But when these items also contain commas used for other purposes, more commas won't keep the items straight. You need to use semicolons:

> The only nine cities in the United States with populations larger than one million are New York, New York; Los Angeles, California; Chicago, Illinois; Houston, Texas; Philadelphia, Pennsylvania; Phoenix, Arizona; San Antonio, Texas; San Diego, California; and Dallas, Texas.

EXERCISE 10	Punctuating with Semicolons

Place semicolons and commas where they are needed in the following sentences.

1. Our reading list for this term includes Herman Melville‸ *Moby Dick*‸ Mark Twain‸ *The Adventures of Huckleberry Finn*‸ Nathaniel Hawthorne‸ *The Scarlet Letter*‸ and Henry James‸ *The Europeans.*

2. We will be visiting St. Louis Missouri Springfield Illinois Louisville Kentucky and Jackson Tennessee.

3. The winners of the election were Wendell Smith president Laury Jackson vice president Casey Redlinski secretary and Billy Hanson treasurer.

4. The most popular songs last year were "Boogie Boogie Hot and Heavy" "All I Want Is You You You" "Susie Lulu and Me" "Let's Do It Again Again and Again" and "I Can't Get No Education."

5. Mr. and Mrs. Williams adopted six children: Jon who was born in South Africa Ahn who was a native of Vietnam Marita who grew up in Argentina and Chile Tanveer who left Pakistan when he was four months old Eleni who was a victim of famine in Ethiopia and Frank who was born in San Francisco California.

THE COLON [:]

The **colon** acts almost like a mark of end punctuation because what comes before it must be a complete statement. But the colon signals that the complete statement is introducing either a long quotation, a list, an example, or an explanation.

Long Quotations

Long quotations, especially those that contain several sentences, should be introduced by a colon:

> When the federal government ignored Emperor Norton's decree to abolish Congress, he issued a second decree: "We do hereby Order and Direct Major General Scott, the Commander-in-Chief of our Armies, immediately on receipt of this our Decree, to proceed with suitable force and clear the halls of Congress."

Lists

Here's an example of a colon introducing a list:

> Norton's room in the boardinghouse contained only a few simple pieces of furniture: a table and a chair set on a faded rug, an outdoor camping cot, and a pitcher and a basin resting on a broken stand.

But remember that a colon can come only at the end of a complete statement:

> *Incorrect:*   Norton's room in the boardinghouse contained: a table and a chair set on a faded rug . . .

Don't use a colon after any form of *to be*, which leaves the statement incomplete:

> *Incorrect:*   The three winners of awards *were:* Wilson Rand, Judi Johnson, and Diego Ramos.
>
> *Correct:*   The three winners of awards *were* Wilson Rand, Judi Johnson, and Diego Ramos.

TIPS

For Keeping Semicolons and Colons Straight

Don't confuse semicolons with colons. Readers expect semicolons to join independent clauses or to separate items that have internal commas. Readers expect colons to introduce long quotations or lists:

Semicolons: Ask not what your country can do for you; ask what you can do for your country.

Semicolons: You can visit the most famous cities of the world without leaving the United States if you go to Paris, Texas; Cairo, Illinois; New London, Connecticut; Venice, Illinois; or Toledo, Ohio.

Colons: On your world tour, be sure to visit these cities: Paris, Cairo, London, Venice, and Toledo.

EXERCISE 11	Punctuating with Colons and Semicolons

Use either a colon or semicolon—whichever is required—in each of the following sentences.

Emperor Norton's Continuing Rule

1. Emperor Norton paid almost nothing for all of his necessities and entertainment his room and board, meals at restaurants, streetcar fares, laundry, and even his drinks in saloons.

2. Each day, he followed a rather casual routine rising late, allowing a fellow boarder to help dress him, strolling to the nearest bar for a light meal, and setting out on foot to observe his subjects.

3. Once an elderly lady, a fellow passenger on a streetcar, could not find her five-cent fare however, Norton rescued her by announcing to the conductor, "Let her be a guest of the empire."

4. On his daily walks he rarely went without company wild-eyed children and two faithful old dogs of less than aristocratic pedigree followed along.

5. One dog, a black mongrel, was known as Bummer for his habit of begging meals at taverns the other, a dark-yellow collie, was known as Lazarus because he had come back to life after a near fatal fight.

6. On his strolls, the emperor fulfilled a number of kingly duties inspecting government buildings, chatting with attractive women, discussing law enforcement with police, worshipping in a different church every week, and attending all political discussions and meetings.

THE DASH [—]

TIPS

For Making Dashes

On most typewriters and some word processors, you must create a dash by striking the hyphen key (-) twice (--). Most word processing programs also include a special command for creating dashes.

Dashes usually come in pairs and function like two commas that enclose sentence interrupters. But dashes are more dramatic; they tell readers that you want to emphasize and call attention to the sentence interrupter. Note the following example:

Norton's evening meals—*always at the best restaurants and free of charge*—were full-course affairs.

An interrupter can come at the beginning or end of a sentence, of course. When it comes at the beginning or end, use only one dash:

Norton's evening meals were full-course affairs—*always at the best restaurants and free of charge.*
Eating well—that was one luxury Norton often enjoyed.

PARENTHESES ( )

While dashes emphasize a sentence interrupter, **parentheses** do just the opposite; they deemphasize a sentence interrupter. They indicate that some information is merely incidental to a sentence (a short explanation, a definition, or some examples—such as the material you are reading right now). Notice the parentheses in the following sentences:

> On his daily walks, Emperor Norton was sure to chat with his subjects (especially attractive women).
>
> Joshua Norton's father, John Norton, helped found the city of Algoa Bay (now known as Port Elizabeth) in South Africa.

The parentheses are part of the sentence in which they appear, so the period that ends the sentence goes after the final parenthesis (like this one).

EXERCISE 12 | *Punctuating Sentence Interrupters*

Each of the following sentences contains an interrupter. Enclose it in two dashes (or use one dash for an interrupter at the beginning or end of the sentence) if the interrupter should be emphasized. Enclose it in parentheses if it provides incidental information and should be deemphasized.

Collaborative Activity 2

Using Punctuation

Write ten sentences that should include semicolons, colons, dashes, parentheses, and periods—but omit all punctuation and capitalization. Exchange papers and add the punctuation marks and capitalization. Decide which sentences should be joined by semicolons and which should be separated by periods. Then have a third student check your work. Discuss your changes with the entire group.

1. As emperor, Norton issued many proclamations ∧ on every subject, whether national or international ∧ and sent them off to the newspapers or other leaders.

2. Early in his reign, he decided that Mexico was unfit to govern itself it was in fact fighting for independence at that time and declared himself "protector of Mexico."

3. However, after Mexico's actual ruler was brutally executed a rather dangerous precedent Norton withdrew his protectorship on the grounds that the people were too "unsettled" to deserve it.

4. During the Civil War 1861–1865 Norton ordered President Abraham Lincoln and President Jefferson Davis of the Confederacy to come to California to negotiate an end to the fighting.

5. When they ignored his imperial command, he addressed a similar proclamation to the leaders of the two armies Generals Grant and Lee.

QUOTATION MARKS [" "]

Quotation marks tell readers that you are borrowing someone else's exact words. Use quotation marks in the following situations.

Titles of Short Works

Put quotation marks around the titles of poems, magazine articles, newspaper articles, songs, and other short works:

"The Road Not Taken" (poem)

"Yesterday" (song)

TIPS

For Handling Your Own Titles

Quotation marks and underlining tell readers that you are discussing someone else's work, so don't use them with the titles of your own essays. The one exception is if you discuss the title of one of your papers in another paper.

But underline the titles of books, the names of magazines, the names of newspapers, and other complete longer works. If you are composing on the computer, you may italicize (instead of underlining) these titles:

<u>Life</u> (magazine)	*or*	*Life*
<u>New York Times</u> (newspaper name)		*New York Times*
<u>Tom Sawyer</u> (book title)		*Tom Sawyer*
<u>Antz</u> (movie title)		*Antz*

Here are some titles of short works contained within longer ones:

"A Rising Star in the East," *Life*

"President Proposes Tax Cut," *New York Times*

"Using Important Punctuation Marks," in *Composing with Confidence*

EXERCISE 13   *Punctuating Titles*

Underline or quote the following titles.

1. <u>New York Daily News</u>

2. Time (magazine)

3. Titanic (movie)

4. Fierce Storm Strands Thousands (title of article) in the Los Angeles Times (newspaper)

5. My favorite poem from Modern American Poetry (book) is Walt Whitman's I Sing the Body Electric.

6. Did you see the play Rent when it appeared here?

Definitions

Quote (or underline or italicize) the word you want to define and quote its definition. (Either practice is acceptable.) For example:

"Villain" once meant "a resident of a village," but the meaning of the word has since changed.

Paleontology is defined as "the study of early life forms as revealed in fossils."

Speech and Other People's Writing

Let readers know when you're borrowing a speaker's or writer's exact words by quoting them. Put quotation marks around direct quotations, which reproduce these words exactly. But do not put quotation marks around reported speech, which summarizes or restates without using the exact words. See Chapter 22 for a full discussion of direct quotations and reported speech.

Direct quotation:	Norton once told a candidate for office who rose to appeal for votes: "You don't have to speak further because I hereby appoint you United States senator."
Reported speech:	Norton once told a candidate for office who rose to appeal for votes that the candidate didn't have to speak further because Norton was appointing him a United States senator.

The words identifying the speaker or writer are not part of the quotation, so don't place them in quotation marks. The words *that, if,* or *whether* introduce reported speech.

EXERCISE 14   Punctuating Quotations and Reported Speech

Put quotation marks around only the direct quotations in the following sentences.

1. Early in Norton's reign when a few newspapers made fun of him, he responded angrily, calling the attacks ^"scurrilous and untrue articles."^

2. At another time when the emperor's authority was challenged, a local newspaper wrote, Since he has worn the imperial purple, he has shed no blood, robbed nobody, and despoiled the country of no one, which is more than can be said of any of his fellows in that line.

3. Once a newly hired policeman said that he was going to arrest Norton on a charge of vagrancy.

4. However, the officer changed the charge to insanity after the enraged Norton shouted that he was not a vagrant since he had five dollars in his pocket.

5. The moment that the chief of police heard of the mistaken arrest, he personally released the monarch and said, Your Majesty, I apologize for this indignity visited upon your royal personage.

Collaborative Activity 3

Writing Dialogue

With another member of your group, write a short dialogue between two people on a humorous subject—gossip about a date, giving and misunderstanding directions, or whatever you wish. Include at least five exchanges between the speakers. Then, have two other members of the group check your work for correct use of quotation marks, punctuation, and paragraphing. Discuss areas of disagreement.

Capitalizing and Punctuating Quotations.   Capitalize the first word of a quoted sentence, regardless of whether it precedes or follows the identification of the speaker or writer.

Robert Louis Stevenson wrote, "Of all our visitors, I believe I preferred Emperor Norton."

"Of all our visitors, I believe I preferred Emperor Norton," wrote Robert Louis Stevenson.

Place commas and periods in quotations as follows:

1. When the identifying words introduce a quotation, place a comma after the introduction and place a period inside the final quotation mark. (See the first example above.)

2. When the sentence begins with the quotation, place a comma inside the quotation marks. (See the second example above.)

3. But when the quotation is a question or an exclamation, replace the end comma with a question mark or exclamation point, as in these examples:

"Who is Emperor Norton the First?" a politician asked.

"I don't pay for my meals!" Norton shouted at a waiter who was ignorant of the royal stature of the person he was serving.

---

4. When you quote only part of a sentence after the identifying words, don't capitalize the first word of the quotation:

On December 31, 1879, Norton published a proclamation welcoming in the new year and offering up "prayers of thanksgiving to Almighty God."

Note that all periods and commas go inside the final quotation mark, whether they are part of the quotation or not. Question marks and exclamation points go inside the final quotation mark when they are part of the quotation, but outside the final quotation mark when they are not part of the quotation:

Have you read the poem "Sailing to Byzantium"?

He asked, "Have you read any poems by William Butler Yeats?"

Punctuating Longer Quotations.   When quoting more than one sentence, use only two quotation marks—one at the beginning of the quotation and the other one at the end. Don't quote each sentence separately, or your readers may think that the sentences are spoken by different persons. (Note that a colon introduces the longer quotation.)

In praise of San Francisco, Robert Louis Stevenson wrote: "In what other city would a harmless madman who supposed himself emperor of the two Americas have been so fostered and encouraged? Where else would even the people of the streets have respected the poor man's illusion?"

But you can split a quotation from the same speaker with identifying words. Notice the punctuation and capitalization in the following examples:

"There were many hats," reported a newspaperman who visited Norton's room after the emperor's death. "There was an old stovepipe hat. Directly above, hanging in a row on the wall, were three more."

"On the wall opposite, over the bed," the reporter added, "hung the well-known sword of the emperor."

In the first example, the identifying words interrupt two complete sentences, so the first word of the second quotation is capitalized. In the second example, the identifying words split a single quoted sentence in the middle, so the quotation resumes without capitalization.

Paragraphing Dialogue.   In quoted dialogue, begin new paragraphs each time the speaker changes so readers can easily identify the speakers:

> Once a streetcar conductor said to an elderly woman, "Lady, if you can't pay the five-cent fare, you'll have to get off."
>
> "Let her be the guest of the empire," Norton said, and he advised the conductor to move on.

EXERCISE 15	Punctuating Quotations and Reported Speech

Correctly punctuate and capitalize the following passages containing quotations or reported speech.

1. When the genuine Emperor Dom Pedro II of Brazil visited the city in 1876, Joan Parker wrote in *American Heritage,* ^San Francisco proudly presented its own to him with fitting pomp and circumstance.^

2. Once Norton participated in a discussion of free love sponsored by a local organization. He began by claiming that 82 percent of infants born in America were destroyed. Said Norton take 25 miles of land. Let it rain on that land 24 hours. Then turn every one of those drops of water into a baby. How many babies will there be? Norton expected an answer to this question, but when the dazed audience offered none, the emperor marched out of the meeting.

3. When Norton was arrested by the rookie cop, the chief of police personally released the monarch and asked that Norton accept his apology.

4. Why are you wearing the uniform you have on an old friend of Norton's from South Africa once asked.

5. After the friend had promised to keep the secret, Norton confided that he had been born of French royalty and had been sent to South Africa for safety, with someone named John Norton as his guardian.

IN SUMMARY	Punctuation

Use Commas

1. to separate three or more items in a series.
2. to separate two independent clauses joined by *for, and, nor, but, or, yet, so* (FANBOYS).
3. to enclose a sentence interrupter.
4. to separate most introductory words or phrases (and some concluding words or phrases) from the rest of a sentence.
5. to separate two or more adjectives before a noun when their order can be reversed.

Use Periods

1. to end complete statements.
2. to end abbreviations.

Use Question Marks

to end direct questions, not indirect questions.

Use Exclamation Points

at the end of statements expressing strong emotions.

Use Semicolons

1. to join independent clauses that aren't joined by conjunctions.
2. to separate items in a series containing internal punctuation.

Use Colons

to introduce a long quotation, a list, an example, or an explanation.

Use Dashes

to enclose a sentence interrupter you want to emphasize.

Use Parentheses

to enclose a sentence interrupter you want to deemphasize.

Use Quotation Marks

1. for titles of short works or works contained within longer works.
2. for words you're defining and for their definitions.
3. for quoting a speaker or writer's exact words, according to the following rules:
   a. Capitalize the first word of a quoted sentence.
   b. Place a comma after the words introducing a quotation.
   c. When identifying words follow the quotation, end quoted statements with a comma, quoted questions with a question mark, and quoted exclamations with an exclamation point. Don't capitalize the identifying words.
   d. Place all periods and commas inside the final quotation mark.
   e. Place question marks and exclamation points inside the final quotation mark if they're part of the quotation, outside the final quotation if they're not part of the quotation.
   f. Place quotation marks around the entire quotation, not around each sentence of the quotation.
   g. Each time you quote a new speaker, begin a new paragraph.

EDITING FOR MASTERY

Mastery Exercise 1

Correcting Errors in Punctuation

The following passage contains twenty errors (plus one more that has been corrected as an example) in punctuation—commas, semicolons, colons, dashes, parentheses, and quotation marks. In some cases, the punctuation is missing. In other cases, the punctuation is incorrect. Find the errors and make your corrections above the lines.

The Death of the Emperor

(1) On the evening of January 8, 1880ˌ Norton went out in a drizzle to attend a debate. (2) He was in full uniform, and in a fine mood. (3) Even though he was sixty-two

years old and in poor health he still walked confidently. (4) Those who saw him observed, as Robert Louis Stevenson wrote, a "portly rather flabby man, with the face of a gentleman, rendered unspeakably pathetic and absurd by the great saber at his side and the peacock's feather in his hat. (5) As he approached the building where the debate was held; he suddenly tumbled and collapsed. (6) A passerby ran to his aid and propped him up while shouting for others "that they should get a carriage." (7) Norton was unconscious, when he was taken to the hospital; he was dead a few minutes later. (8) His pockets were emptied later in the morgue. (9) The contents spoke more eloquently than any biography; $3 in silver coins a gold piece worth $2.50 a French franc note dated 1828, messages signed by many foreign rulers, a certificate of ownership of 98,200 shares of stock in a mine, and several copies of his own imperial writing.

(10) The next morning, the headline of the San Francisco "Chronicle" announced, "Le Roi Est Mort" ("The King is Dead.") (11) As he lay in the morgue a crowd began to gather. (12) All classes of people were represented—from the rich to the poor, from the well dressed to the ragged, and by noon the crowd was so large that the police had to be called. (13) "He is dead, wrote the <u>Morning Call</u> newspaper, and no citizen of San Francisco could have been taken away who would be more generally missed."

(14) However more than fifty years later; there was another funeral. (15) In 1934, when the city expanded to swallow up the Masonic Cemetery the emperor's remains were dug up, and buried at another cemetery. (16) The mayor placed a wreath on the grave, while the municipal band played and a military battalion fired a volley in salute. (17) A fine granite monument was set in place. (18) It read:

NORTON I, EMPEROR OF THE UNITED STATES,

PROTECTOR OF MEXICO,

JOSHUA A. NORTON 1818–80

(19) As one historian has noted, there were no quotation marks around the inscription.

Scorecard: Number of Errors Found and Corrected _____

> ### Collaborative Activity 4
>
> **Comparing Corrections**
> Review your corrections in Mastery Exercise 1 with your group. Report your findings to the entire class.

Mastery Exercise 2

Correcting Errors in Punctuation

The following passage contains twenty errors (plus two more that have been corrected as examples) in punctuation—commas, semicolons, colons, dashes, parentheses, and quotation marks. In some cases, the punctuation is missing. In other cases, the punctuation is incorrect. Find the errors and make your corrections above the lines.

"Le Roi Est Mort"
Adapted and Abridged from the San Francisco Chronicle
January 11, 1880

(1) Imperial Norton is dead and turned to clay.

(2) His funeral₍ₓ₎ took place yesterday afternoon₍ₓ₎ from the undertaking establishment on "O'Farrell Street." (3) Thousands flocked there for a last look at the man; whose peculiarities of mind, garb, and person had rendered him familiar to all.

(4) The man of imaginary majesty, Emperor of the United States narrowly escaped burial in a plain redwood box. (5) Some people (noting the odd manner of life of the old man) have unkindly concluded, that his hallucination was simulated and that he had adopted his strange life to hide a hoard of unaccountably acquired wealth. (6) When his effects were searched; it was found that he had no means.

(7) He has no personal effects of any value, and—(without the help of people of means who knew Norton when he was a citizen of standing, he would have had a pauper's funeral at the city's expense. (8) A subscription paper to procure a funeral fund was drawn up and taken to the Pacific Club: where the sponsors soon had all the money they deemed necessary.

(9) After the autopsy Friday; the body was prepared for burial. (10) It was clothed in a black robe with a white shirt and black tie, then it was placed in a neat rosewood casket. (11) The general interest felt in the deceased was soon apparent. (12) Early in the afternoon of Friday, people who remembered the remarkable old man kindly—many of them gratefully and affectionately, began to call and ask to be allowed a last glance at the familiar face. (13) Among them were: several ladies whose dress revealed prosperity. (14) Some of them brought bouquets to be placed

on the coffin. (15) One, the daughter of a former well-known officer of the city government, brought a delicate boutonniere and pinned it to the lapel of the burial robe.

(16) This lady appeared in deep mourning, and betrayed the deepest feeling of any who gathered about the bier. (17) She stated that "she had known the deceased from her childhood when he was prosperous had received many and great kindnesses at his hands. (18) When she was a little girl he used to present her with flowers (that were very costly at that time.)

(19) The stream of visitors to the bier began, early yesterday morning. (20) By seven o'clock quite a number had dropped in; some of them laborers who had got off the car on their way to the shops to view the remains of the kindly man, others businessmen who stopped on their way downtown for a similar purpose. (21) Soon the number began to increase and there was a steady stream of people pressing through the office to the little back room where the remains lay in state; and filing out at the side exit to make room for the constantly increasing throng of visitors. (22) By noon there were hundreds of people gathered on sidewalk waiting their turn. (23) Policemen were called in to regulate the entrance.

Scorecard: Number of Errors Found and Corrected _____

28 Checking Sound-alike and Look-alike Words

Many writers confuse words that look alike or sound alike—and therefore confuse their readers. So be sensitive to such errors as you revise and proofread. It helps if you know the errors you are most likely to commit. Try to focus on one word in a look-alike or sound-alike pairing—the one that occurs or confuses you most often.

This chapter helps you distinguish between the most common (and troublesome) look-alike and sound-alike words by

- identifying the most commonly confused words
- showing you ways to keep them straight

CONTRACTION CONFUSION

Certain contractions deserve special attention because so many writers confuse them with similar looking or sounding words:

Contractions	Possessive words	Place words	Past tense
it's = *it is* (and *it has*)	its		
who's = *who is* (and *who has*)	whose		
he's = *he is* (and *he has*)	his		
they're = *they are*	their	there	
you're = *you are*	your		
we're = *we are*		where	were

- Notice that each contraction contains both a subject pronoun and a verb (*is, are,* or *has*), so each is always the subject and the verb of a sentence or clause.

UNIT 4

Chapter 28

Composing with Confidence

©2003

- Notice, too, that possessive pronouns—in contrast to possessive nouns—don't contain an apostrophe (').
- Notice that the place words—*there* and *where*—contain the word *here*.

EXERCISE 1	Identifying Contractions

Label each of the italicized words in the sentences below as C (contraction), P (possessive), Pl (place), or PT (past tense). If the word is a contraction, write out the words the contraction represents.

<u>C</u>   **1.** *It's* eight o'clock. <u>It is</u>

_____ **2.** The cat lost *its* collar. _____

_____ **3.** *They're* friends of mine. _____

_____ **4.** They got *their* grades yesterday. _____

_____ **5.** It was *there* a while ago. _____

_____ **6.** *You're* just in time for dinner. _____

_____ **7.** Is *your* biology class interesting? _____

_____ **8.** *Who's* seen my book? _____

_____ **9.** *Whose* hat is this? _____

_____ **10.** *We're* happy to see you. _____

_____ **11.** *Where* is it? _____

_____ **12.** *Were* you in the house? _____

Collaborative Activity 1

Writing and Checking Sentences

Write a sentence for each of the following words: *there, their, they're, your, you're, its, it's, who's, whose, were, where.*

THE *–d* DILEMMA

Because the sounds of the letters *d* and *t* are almost identical, many people drop the final *d* on a word in speech when the next word begins with *t*. But you can't do that in writing. Notice the spelling of the following phrases:

suppose*d* to	I'm suppose*d* to work later.
use*d* to	He use*d* to get up late, but now he's use*d* to getting up early.

Be careful to distinguish between *use* and *used to*. *Use* can be a verb in any tense—or even a noun:

> I *use* at least eight sheets of paper every time I write a one-paragraph essay. (present-tense verb)
>
> In fact, I revised the last paragraph so often that I *used* a dozen sheets of paper. (past-tense verb)
>
> But I find a *use* for the scrap paper; I give it to my children to draw on. (a noun)

Used to, however, has two meanings.

It can describe an action in the past that no longer occurs:

> When I was a child, I *used to* swim every week, but I don't swim anymore.

Or it can mean *accustomed to* when preceded by a form of *be*:

> Bill is *used to* working a double shift on Friday.

Many people also confuse the adjective *prejudiced* with the noun *prejudice*. You must put a final *d* on the adjective:

> *Adjective:*   He is *prejudiced* against people who hate others.
> *Noun:*   Racial *prejudice* shouldn't exist in this country.

EXERCISE 2   **Writing Correct Word Forms**

Supply the appropriate form of use, suppose, *or* prejudice *in each sentence.*

1. (use) For centuries, sap from the rubber tree _used_____ to have only a few uses, and very few Europeans knew about them.

2. (use) The Indians of Central and South America, who weren't _____ to the clothes that Europeans wore, _____ the hardened sap to make clothes and bottles.

3. (suppose) One day around 1820, Thomas Hancock of London devised another use for the rubber bottles, which were only _____ to hold water.

4. (suppose) He _____ that if he sliced the bottle into strips, they could be put into garters and waistbands.

5. (prejudice) About twenty-five years later, another Englishman named Stephen Perry, who wasn't _____ against stealing someone else's invention, patented the rubber band.

Collaborative Activity 2

Writing and Checking Sentences
Write a sentence that correctly uses *used to*, another that correctly uses *supposed to*, and one more that correctly uses *prejudiced*. Then exchange your sentences with another student and check each other's work.

THE *of* OFFENSE

In speech, many people contract *have* as –*'ve* after a helping verb:

could've	= could have
should've	= should have
would've	= would have
might've	= might have
must've	= must have

Because this contraction sounds like the preposition *of*, some people mistakenly write *could of* when they mean *could have*, and so forth. But *of* never follows the words *could, should, would, might,* and *must*:

> *Incorrect:*   He *must of* done it.
> *Correct:*   He *must have* done it.
>
> *Incorrect:*   I *might of* gone.
> *Correct:*   I *might have* gone.

EXERCISE 3	Writing Correct Word Forms

Complete each of the following sentences using might have, would have, could have, must have, *or* should have.

Collaborative Activity 3

Writing and Checking Sentences

Write a sentence using each of the following phrases: *could have, should have, might have, must have, would have.* Then exchange your sentences with another student and check each other's work.

1. If I had known you were coming, *I would have baked a cake.*

2. It started to rain while I was walking to work. I _____

   _____

3. Barry wasn't in school yesterday. He _____

   _____

4. You didn't have to take a cab to my house. You _____

   _____

5. Susan's tennis game is much better than it was. She _____

   _____

OTHER COMMONLY CONFUSED WORDS

A Word About Words

More evidence that English words are confusing:

1. I had to subject the subject to a series of tests.
2. The bandage was wound around the wound.
3. The insurance was invalid for the invalid.
4. Why do people recite at a play and play at a recital?

Now let's look at some other sound-alikes and look-alikes that may confuse you.

Accept/Except

Accept means *to agree to receive:*

> We are happy to *accept* your invitation.

Except means *excluding* or *but:*

> All my brothers and sisters *except* one have been to college.

EXERCISE 4	Writing Correct Word Forms

Supply the appropriate word in each of the blank spaces.

Collaborative Activity 4

Writing and Checking Sentences

Write a sentence that correctly uses *accept* and another that correctly uses *except.* Then exchange your sentences with another student and check each other's work.

1. When the fork was introduced in England in 1608, the English were slow to *accept* _____ the new invention.

2. The English ate with their hands and did not use any silverware, _____ knives for cutting meat they couldn't tear with their teeth.

3. They gradually began to _____ the fork after King James (1566–1625) began eating with one.

4. In the American colonies, however, forks weren't _____ until the eighteenth century.

Advice/Advise

Advice is a noun:

> What *advice* can you offer me?

Advise is a verb:

> He *advised* me to get a lawyer.

EXERCISE 5   Writing Correct Word Forms

Supply the appropriate word in each of the blank spaces.

1. In Florence, Italy, in 1306, a priest named Giordano *advised* _____ the members of his monastery to improve their eyesight by getting "disks for the eyes" from a glassmaker whose name today is unknown.

2. His _____ is the earliest record of what were later called eyeglasses. Giordano claimed he had met the glassmaker about twenty years earlier, which would put the date of the invention at around 1280 to 1286.

3. Giordano's _____ didn't help every person with poor eyesight, however, for the spectacles were only for the farsighted.

4. Today, if you are both farsighted and nearsighted, you would be well-_____ to wear bifocals, which were invented in 1785 by a famous American, Benjamin Franklin.

> **Collaborative Activity 5**
>
> **Writing and Checking Sentences**
>
> Write a sentence that correctly uses *advice* and another that correctly uses *advise*. Then exchange your sentences with another student and check each other's work.

Affect/Effect

Affect, a verb, means to *influence* or *change*:

> The cold *affected* her breathing ability.

Effect, a noun, is the result of a cause:

> We don't know what the *effect* of his decision will be.

EXERCISE 6   Writing Correct Word Forms

Supply the appropriate word in each of the blank spaces.

1. In 1827, an English chemist named John Walker accidentally struck a stick coated with potash and antimony against the floor and created a surprising *effect.* _____

2. The stick burst into flames, and the resulting invention has greatly _____ our lives.

3. Seeing the _____, Walker began to manufacture the first friction matches.

4. Although Walker never patented his invention, this didn't _____ his success, for he continued to produce and sell matches throughout his life.

Buy/By

Buy means *to purchase:*

> We *buy* our groceries at Save-A-Lot.

By, a preposition, has several meanings:

> He is standing *by* the door.
> I will be home *by* nine.
> He finished his term paper *by* working all weekend.

| EXERCISE 7 | Writing Correct Word Forms |

Supply the appropriate word in each of the blank spaces.

1. False teeth were invented *by* _____ the Etruscans around 700 B.C.

2. These early dentures were carved from bone or ivory or were taken from the mouths of young cattle. They were held together _____ gold bands.

3. _____ the eighteenth century A.D., certain improvements had been added. A Parisian dentist named Pierre Fauchard joined together upper and lower false teeth _____ using steel springs.

4. However, not everyone would _____ his invention, for the springs made it difficult for a wearer to close his mouth.

5. Porcelain teeth were introduced into the United States in 1785 _____ Dr. John Greenwood of New York City.

6. George Washington was one of the first to _____ Greenwood's product.

Conscience/Conscious

Your *conscience* monitors your behavior:

> My *conscience* bothers me about telling a lie.

Conscious means that you are awake and aware:

> The man was *conscious* for only a few minutes after his stroke and then fell into a coma.

| EXERCISE 8 | Writing Correct Word Forms |

Supply the appropriate word in each of the blank spaces.

1. Locks and keys have been around so long that few people are _conscious_____ of how or when they first were invented.

2. Devices have always been needed to stop people whose _____ won't prevent them from breaking into houses.

3. _____ of the problem, a man named Joseph Bramah introduced the padlock in 1784. He offered a large reward to anyone who could open the four-inch iron device; many tried, but no one succeeded.

Fine/Find

As an adjective, *fine* means *acceptable* or *excellent*. As a noun, it means *a penalty to pay:*

> This desk is *fine* for my purposes.
> We had a *fine* meal at Maxwell's restaurant.
> There is a $25 *fine* for parking here illegally.

Find means *to discover or locate:*

> Did you *find* the watch you lost?

| EXERCISE 9 | Writing Correct Word Forms |

Supply the appropriate word in each of the blank spaces.

1. No one could _find_____ a way to pick Bramah's padlock because there were 494 million combinations of the notches.

2. Finally, sixty-seven years later, an American locksmith named Alfred Charles Hobbs was able to _____ a way to pick the lock, after a month's work.

3. So _____ is Bramah's original design that you can still _____ variations of it in use today.

Know/No; Knew/New

Know means *to be familiar with* or *to understand.* Its past tense is *knew:*

> I *know* a lot about skiing. I *knew* how to ski when I was eight.

No is a negative word, and *new* is the opposite of old.

> We have *no* car at the moment. We have sold our old car and are going to buy a *new* one soon.

EXERCISE 10 — Writing Correct Word Forms

Supply the appropriate word in each of the blank spaces.

1. As we all ___*know*___, there is nothing more sinfully delicious than a Swiss chocolate bar.

2. But did you _____ that chocolate originated in France and Italy in the late eighteenth century? This _____ delicacy was made in rolls and sheets that were cut into smaller pieces for sale to local consumers who _____ about it.

3. Then in 1819, a Swiss named François-Louis Cailler, who _____ of the public's great desire for the sweet stuff, mass-produced chocolate in a block shape.

4. Cailler's son-in-law added milk to chocolate in 1875, and he thus perfected the candy that _____ one can resist.

Collaborative Activity 10

Writing and Checking Sentences

Write a sentence that correctly uses each of the following words: *know, knew, no, new*. Then exchange your sentences with another student and check each other's work.

Led/Lead

Led is the past tense of the verb *lead*:

> Marco and Tina always *lead* backpackers in the summer.
> The trail they took last year *led* to a river.

Lead is a heavy metal:

> The pipe is made of *lead*.

EXERCISE 11 — Writing Correct Word Forms

Supply the appropriate word in each of the blank spaces.

1. In 1908, women in Paris began wearing wrist bracelets with watches attached to them. Men continued to carry pocket watches made of gold, silver, or even ___*lead*___.

2. It was war, not fashion, that _____ men to change their habits.

3. In World War I, the generals who _____ the troops realized that soldiers could consult wristwatches more quickly than pocket time-pieces during battle.

4. Today, fancy watch designers _____, and fashion follows.

Collaborative Activity 11

Writing and Checking Sentences

Write a sentence that correctly uses each of the following words: *lead* (present-tense verb), *led* (past-tense verb), *lead* (heavy metal). Then exchange your sentences with another student and check each other's work.

Lie/Lay

Lie doesn't take an object:

I am going to *lie* down.
The pen is *lying* on top of the book.

Its forms are as follows:

Present tense	Past tense	Past participle
lie, lies	lay	lain

Lay is something you do to an object:

I am going to *lay* this book on the table.

Its forms are as follows:

Present tense	Past tense	Past participle
lay, lays	laid	laid

EXERCISE 12   **Writing Correct Word Forms**

Supply the appropriate word in each of the blank spaces.

Collaborative Activity 12

Writing and Checking Sentences
Write a sentence that correctly uses each of the following words: *lie, lay* (present tense), *lay* (past tense), *laid, lain*. Then exchange your sentences with another student and check each other's work.

1. Would-be inventors have long dreamed of creating a machine so efficient that, once it was started, would keep going indefinitely with no consumption of fuel. The beginning of the search for such an invention _lies_____ at the very beginning of civilization.

2. In Egypt around 3500 B.C., slaves aboard ships _____ down their oars when wind filled the newly invented sails.

3. In northern Greece during the first century B.C., water turned the blades of a wheel that _____ in a stream, powering the first water mill.

4. In England in 1191 A.D., Dean Herbert invented the first English windmill and used it to grind corn. Prior to then, corn had to be ground slowly by hand, resulting in the loss of many bushels that had simply _____ unharvested in the fields.

5. The sail, the water mill, and the windmill depend on external and unreliable energy sources, so the true secret of perpetual motion still _____ undiscovered. (See Exercise 13 for more about the search.)

Lose/Loose

Lose, a verb, means *to misplace* or *not to win:*

> Did you *lose* your wallet?
> Who *lost* the game?

Loose is an adjective meaning *not tight:*

> These pants are very *loose* on me.

EXERCISE 13	Writing Correct Word Forms

Supply the appropriate word in each of the blank spaces.

Collaborative Activity 13

Writing and Checking Sentences

Write a sentence that correctly uses *lose* and another that correctly uses *loose.* Then exchange your sentences with another student and check each other's work.

1. In Italy around 1500, Leonardo da Vinci envisioned a large and delicate wheel with flat, curved spokes, which would never _lose_____ momentum.

2. Inside the rim and between each pair of spokes was a heavy metal ball. When the wheel turned, the balls on the high end of the rim would be set _____ and then roll toward the rim on the low end.

3. In theory, this would create enough force to carry the balls on the low side back to the top, turning the wheel indefinitely. However, each time Leonardo spun the wheel, it would _____ speed and then grind to a halt.

Mine/Mind

Mine is a possessive word:

> This book is *mine.*

Mind as a noun means your *intellect.* As a verb, it means *to object:*

> The human *mind* is still much smarter than a computer.
> Do you *mind* if I smoke?

EXERCISE 14	Writing Correct Word Forms

Supply the appropriate word in each of the blank spaces.

1. We don't _mind_____ paying for traveler's checks when we take a vacation because the checks protect our money.

2. If the checks are lost or stolen, you can get your money back, and I can get _____.

3. Prior to 1792, an inefficient system of "letters of credit" existed to protect travelers. Then, a better idea popped into the _____ of an Englishman

named Robert Harries. He introduced "circular notes," which were accepted in ninety cities throughout the world.

4. However, Marcellus Berry was the master _____ of the modern system of traveler's checks. In 1891, he devised the idea of signing the checks twice.

Passed/Past

Passed is the past tense and past participle of the verb *pass:*

> I *passed* the sign without noticing it.

Past as a preposition means *beyond.* As a noun or adjective, *past* means *before the present:*

> Be careful not to go *past* Seventh Street, or you will get lost.
> You can't forget the *past,* but you have to live in the present.

EXERCISE 15   **Writing Correct Word Forms**

Supply the appropriate word in each of the blank spaces.

1. Sixty-one years *passed* _____ between the conception of the ballpoint pen and its production.

2. In 1888, an American named John Loud patented a pen that used a rotating ball to deliver ink, but he never got _____ the technical problems that made its writing messy and blurred.

3. In 1919, the Hungarian brothers Lasalo and Georg Biro reintroduced the ballpoint, but it still leaked and smeared. After fleeing France and setting up shop in Argentina during World War II, they introduced a new design that overcame many of the defects of _____ versions.

4. Finally, in 1949, Franz Seech of Austria joined their company and perfected a new ink, which was highly concentrated and dried on contact with the page. That same year, ballpoint sales sur _____ those of fountain pens.

Quiet/Quite

Quiet means *not noisy:*

> The children were very *quiet* as they watched the movie.

Quite means *very:*

> Stretch Johnson is *quite* tall.

| EXERCISE 16 | Writing Correct Word Forms |

Supply the appropriate word in each of the blank spaces.

1. There were _quite_____ a few inventors responsible for the modern escalator, which has changed considerably since its inception.

2. The first escalator was patented in March 1892 by an American named Jesse W. Reno and was known as the Reno Inclined Elevator. The grooved wooden slats attached to its inclined conveyor belt made it less _____ than modern ones, but the rubber cleats on the slats dampened the sound _____ a bit.

3. Two years later, Harrod's Department Store of London installed a Reno Elevator, complete with a porter at the top serving brandy down to passengers who were _____ nervous anticipating the ride.

4. Charles A. Wheeler patented a model in August 1892 that added flat steps, but its ride still wasn't very _____ or smooth. Six years later, Charles D. Seeberger further improved the design to create the first practical _____ "moving staircase."

5. The Otis Elevator Company of New York exhibited this model at the Paris Exhibition of 1900, where it was _____ a hit. Parisians called this device the escalator.

Collaborative Activity 16

Writing and Checking Sentences

Write a sentence that correctly uses *quiet* and another that correctly uses *quite*. Then exchange your sentences with another student and check each other's work.

Rise/Raise

Rise means *to get up without help:*

> The sun *rises* in the morning.

Raise as a verb means *to lift something* or *to increase something*. As a noun, it means *an increase in pay:*

> He *raised* the window to let in more air.
> The Ritz restaurant has *raised* prices again. I will need a *raise* in salary before I can afford to go there.

| EXERCISE 17 | Writing Correct Word Forms |

Supply the appropriate word in each of the blank spaces.

1. The first appearance of the diminutive bathing suit at a Paris fashion show on July 5, 1946, _raised_____ a public outcry.

2. This explosive debut came four days after a mushroom cloud, following an atomic bomb test, finished _____ above Bikini Atoll, so the creator of the two-piece bathing suit, Louis Reard, named it the *bikini.*

Collaborative Activity 17

Writing and Checking Sentences

Write a sentence that correctly uses each of the following words: *rise, raise* (verb), *raise* (noun). Then exchange your sentences with another student and check each other's work.

3. The first bikini was cotton and was worn by dancer Micheline Bernardi. Each time a newspaper printed her photograph, it would _____ the number of fan letters she received.

Sit/Set

Sit means *to seat yourself:*

Please *sit* over here.

Set means *to put something down* or *to establish something:*

You can *set* your books on this chair.
The rules were *set* many years ago.

EXERCISE 18   Writing Correct Word Forms

Supply the appropriate word in each of the blank spaces.

Collaborative Activity 18

Writing and Checking Sentences

Write a sentence that correctly uses *sit* and another that correctly uses *set*. Then exchange your sentences with another student and check each other's work.

1. People have been _setting_ words on paper for a long time, but the developing commercial world at the beginning of the nineteenth century needed fast and easy "duplicates of writing."

2. One day in 1806, Ralph Wedgwood of England decided to _____ down and invent a way to satisfy the need.

3. He soaked thin paper with ink and _____ it out to dry between sheets of blotting paper, producing a substance he patented under the name *carbon paper.* He _____ up a shop at 4 Rathbone Place, Oxford Street, London, where he sold his product in the 1820s.

Then/Than

Then is a time expression meaning *afterward* or *later:*

We stayed for a while, and *then* we left.

Than is used in a comparison:

He smells worse *than* a goat.

EXERCISE 19   Writing Correct Word Forms

Supply the appropriate word in each of the blank spaces.

1. There has been no more important advance in the treatment of ordinary pain _than_ the development of aspirin.

Collaborative Activity 19

Writing and Checking Sentences

Write a sentence that correctly uses *then* and another that correctly uses *than*. Then exchange your sentences with another student and check each other's work.

2. It was formulated in 1853 by Karl Gerhardt but was _____ ignored until 1899, when another scientist published a paper on its power to relieve pain.

3. _____ Dr. Felix Hoffman, who worked for a German firm, the Bayer AG, succeeded in manufacturing aspirin in a form pure enough to be used as a medical remedy.

4. Bayer began retailing aspirin tablets in 1915, and since _____ they have been used more _____ any other over-the-counter drug.

Too/Two/To

Too means *more than enough* or *also:*

> He is *too* fat; he must lose weight.
> His brother should lose weight, *too.*

Two is the number:

> He ate *two* whole chickens.

To is used in all other cases:

> I walked all the way *to* the library.
> I want to talk *to* you.

EXERCISE 20   Writing Correct Word Forms

Write the appropriate word—too, two, or to—in each blank space.

Collaborative Activity 20

Writing and Checking Sentences

Write a sentence that correctly uses each of the following words: *too, two, to.* Then exchange your sentences with another student and check each other's work.

1. In 1867, a chef at the Saratoga Springs hotel in Florida was paying _*too*_____ little attention _*to*_____ his work; consequently, he dropped a small quantity of thinly sliced potatoes into hot cooking oil.

2. _____ the rich and fashionable people who came _____ the Saratoga, it was a new delicacy that they called the Saratoga chip.

3. Stopping with one or _____ chips was _____ hard _____ do, so these elegant people would eat large quantities of them at a time. (See Exercise 21 for more about the chips.)

Whether/Weather

Whether suggests a choice; it is used in the same way as *if* in indirect questions:

> I don't know *whether* it will rain.
> He asked me *whether* I could come.

Weather refers to the temperature and atmospheric conditions:

It is supposed to rain tonight, but the *weather* will be better tomorrow.

EXERCISE 21	Writing Correct Word Forms

Supply the appropriate word in each of the blank spaces.

Collaborative Activity 21

Writing and Checking Sentences

Write a sentence that correctly uses *whether* and another that correctly uses *weather*. Then exchange your sentences with another student and check each other's work.

1. *Whether* _____ strolling down the wide avenues or sitting on the huge porch of the famous hotel, such rich and fashionable people as the Vanderbilts daintily ate potato chips from paper cups.

2. Each year, the wealthy would return to the Saratoga Springs hotel to escape the winter _____ and enjoy their chips.

3. Finally, in 1925, the first plant devoted exclusively to the making of potato chips was built in Albany, New York. Without mass production, who knows _____ the elegant potato chip would have ever become a commonplace household item?

IN SUMMARY   To Distinguish Sound-alikes and Look-alikes from Each Other

1. Contractions with *to be,* such as *it's* and *they're,* should not be confused with similar words such as *its* or *their.*

2. The final *d* in the expressions *used to, supposed to,* and *accustomed to,* as well as the final *d* of the adjective *prejudiced,* should not be omitted.

3. The contraction for *have, 've,* sounds like *of* but should not be replaced with *of.*

4. Other words discussed in this chapter can be confused, but if you follow the tips and are careful in your word choice, you can avoid picking the wrong word.

EDITING FOR MASTERY

Mastery Exercise 1

Correcting Errors in Sound-alike and Look-alike Words

The following passage contains twenty errors related to sound-alike and look-alike words, in addition to the first two errors that have been corrected as examples. Correct these errors by making any necessary changes above the lines.

The Life of Mao Zedong

(1) Of all twentieth-century leaders Mao Zedong has had a deeper and more di-
       effect   *than*
rect ^affect on more people on the planet ^then anyone else. (2) Mao was born to a

peasant family on December 26, 1893—the Chinese year of the snake—in a tiny village in Hunan Province. (3) But he rose from near the bottom of Chinese society to its very top. (4) He lead a revolution and dragged the planet's most populous nation into the twentieth century. (5) He had a cunning, razor-sharp mine, and his conscious never bothered him as he jailed, tortured, and killed his enemies.

(6) In spite of his peasant upbringing, Mao was an early and passionate reader. (7) Although the university would not except a peasant like him, he did manage to enroll in a teacher's training school and would later describe his primary role in life as that of a teacher.

(8) Mao joined the Communist Party in 1921 and had a quick raise to power. (9) When he assumed full control as it's chairman and ruler of the country after World War II, he attacked the problems of land reform, as well as bringing China into the modern era in industrial production. (10) He wasn't quiet successful.

(11) Mao was always an original thinker. (12) In 1956, he started a movement called the Hundred Flowers and the Hundred Schools. (13) The Hundred Flowers were suppose to encourage growth in the arts, and the Hundred Schools were intended to create a wide variety of philosophies. (14) Mao said there would be room in China for all beliefs. (15) But when these experiments failed, his opponents criticized and attacked him.

(16) As he had throughout the passed, Mao struck back, launching the Cultural Revolution in 1966. (17) He urged China's youth, who's average age was fifteen to nineteen, to destroy all Western influence and rid the country of impure "traitors" to the cause. (18) Many important leaders we're humiliated and attacked. (19) Finally, Mao stopped the movement, and China more or less returned to normal by 1969.

(20) Mao's personal habits created nightmares for his doctor. (21) The Chairman loved to gorge on fatty pork and lamb, as well as fish and vegetables swimming in cooking oil. (22) He chain-smoked English cigarettes and ignored his doctor's advise to cut down. (23) "Smoking is also a form of deep-breathing exercise, don't you think?" Mao said.

(24) Like many Chinese peasants, Mao didn't brush his teeth, preferring to rinse his mouth out with tea and than chew the leaves. (25) His teeth turned green and would have provided a fortune in work for a dentist. (26) But Mao dismissed any treatment saying, "Does a tiger brush his teeth?"

(27) He also considered bathing a waste of time and took only an occasional rubdown with wet towels provided buy servants while he worked. (28) Doctor Li, Mao's personal physician, said that the Chairman's peasant background preached a three-bath philosophy: "a bath at birth, one before marriage, and one at death."

(29) In public, Mao had a Puritanical image, so the public didn't no he was an amazing sexual athlete. (30) Although he fathered many children by his three wives, his spouses weren't his only partners. (31) He believed that the more women he slept with, the longer he would live. (32) At the rate he took on sexual partners, he could of lived forever! (33) When he contracted a venereal disease, he wouldn't set still for treatment. "Why are you getting so excited?" he asked his doctor. (34) "If it doesn't bother me, it doesn't matter."

(35) Even the indestructible Mao could not last forever. (36) In 1972, he was suffering from pneumonia, congestive heart disease, swelling of the internal organs, and Lou Gehrig's disease. (37) Nevertheless, he pulled his last great political surprise—opening contact with the United States. (38) He refused treatment until three weeks before the summit, when he was almost to sick to move. (39) He received a crash program of medicine and therapy, new uniforms where made for his bloated body, and he managed to meet the American president.

(40) After Mao died in 1976, his embalmed body was placed on display and, according to Chinese officials, will lay in state forever.

Scorecard: Number of Errors Found and Corrected _____

Collaborative Activity 22

Comparing Corrections
Review your corrections in Mastery Exercise 1 with your group. Report your findings to the entire class.

Mastery Exercise 2

Correcting Errors in Sound-alike and Look-alike Words

The following passage contains twenty errors related to sound-alike and look-alike words, in addition to the first error that has been corrected as an example. Correct these errors by making any necessary changes above the lines.

Adolf Hitler's Early Years

(1) We will never ^no the reason that Adolf Hitler became such a madman, but its
                  know

probably in part because of his early childhood experiences. (2) Adolf was born

April 20, 1889, in a small town in Austria. (3) His father, Alois, was born out of wed-

lock and went buy the last name of Schicklgruber (his mother's maiden name) until

he changed it to Hitler in 1876. (4) Alois, once a shoemaker's apprentice, rose him-

self through the ranks of civil service to become a customs officer. (5) He had two

hobbies: beekeeping and womanizing. (6) After his second wife died, he married

there children's nursemaid, Klara Pilzl, a young country girl twenty-three years

younger then he, who was pregnant by him. (7) The baby died, but Adolf was born

four years later. (8) He had five brothers and sisters, but all of them accept his sister

Paula died in childhood.

(9) Hitler's mother was frail, gentle and quite, but his father was overweight and

hostile. (10) Adolf's sister Paula said Adolf "challenged my father to extreme harsh-

ness" and "got his sound thrashing every day." (11) Consequently, Hitler's madness

could have arisen because of this conflict.

(12) According to one biographer, Hitler had "the classic desire of a whipped

child: the need for revenge, the still unformulated search for an enemy to punish."

(13) After his father retired at age sixty, the family moved to the outskirts of

Linz, capital of upper Austria. (14) Adolf met August Kubizek their, who was his

friend from the age of fifteen to nineteen. (15) Kubizek described Hitler's "eternal

guerrilla warfare with his teachers." (16) At first, he won all A's at Lambach

Benedictine monastery school, but then he seemed to loose all interest in school.

(17) Sometime during this time, Adolf contracted encephalitis, which may have

affected his personality and ability to learn. (18) Some Hitler experts have wondered weather he had a learning disorder.

(19) By the time Hitler quite school at age sixteen, his only good grade was in drawing. (20) He stayed with his mother, not doing to much accept for dreaming about being an artist and reading books on art, history, and the military. (21) His mother use to indulge him, cooking for him and fussing over him.

(22) When in October 1907, Hitler learned that his mother was dying of breast cancer, he nursed her until she past away on December 21. (23) Klara Hitler's doctor later said, "In all my forty-odd years of practice I had never seen a young man so broken by grief and bowed down by suffering as young Adolf Hitler was on that day."

(24) Then Hitler moved to Vienna and began living among loners and losers. (25) By the end of February 1908, he shared a room with August Kubizek, who studied music at the conservatory in Vienna. (26) Hitler pretended to be going to classes, but then told August of his rejection the school. (27) August later recalled that Hitler seemed to be loosing his grip: "Choking with his catalog of hates, he would pour his fury over everything, against mankind in general who did not understand him, who did not appreciate him and by whom be was persecuted."

(28) After Hitler tried and failed to reenter the school, he moved out of his room. (29) He lead a truly marginal life, setting in public libraries to read, living in cheap rooms. (30) When he ran out of money in mid-September 1909, he skipped out on his rent. (31) He could not fine a place to live, so he slept in coffeehouses, on park benches, and in flophouses. (32) He joined and remained in the army until 1920, and joined the German Workers' Party (later the Nazi Party) in Munich in 1919. (33) That year he became conscience of the fact that he "could make a good speech" that could hypnotize the masses.

(34) When he was nineteen, Hitler spoke about murdering Jews. (35) The solution to all of Germany's problems, to his mine, was a national dictatorship to remilitarize the

nation and "cleanse" it of its internal enemies. (36) By 1923 he had become the center

of a cult of leadership, considered above criticism—the dictator of the Nazi Party.

Scorecard: Number of Errors Found and Corrected _____

Use this checklist as you edit your paragraphs and essays.
Read over your drafts more than once, checking for a different
group of items each time. As the term progresses, you should
become more efficient in this practice. Highlight the items on
the lists that especially apply to you, and narrow your focus to
those items in the repeated readings.

SENTENCE BOUNDARIES AND STRUCTURE

☐ Are my sentences complete? (see pages 272-287)

☐ Have I joined sentences correctly, using coordination
and subordination? (see pages 288-306)

☐ Is my end punctuation (. ! ?) correct?
(see pages 404-406)

☐ Is my sentence structure correct—especially
parallelism? (see pages 75-79)

☐ Have I placed modifiers correctly? (see pages 377-379)

☐ Have I changed lengthy modifiers into phrases?
(see pages 372-377)

WORD FORMS AND WORD CHOICES

☐ Do my subjects and verb agree? Are my noun plural endings correct?
(see pages 307-309)

☐ Are my past-tense verbs and past-participle forms correct?
(see pages 322-336)

☐ Have I used the correct pronoun forms? Do my pronouns have antecedents?
Do my pronouns agree with their antecedents? (see pages 340-342)

☐ Are my verb tenses correct and consistent? (see pages 311-315)

☐ Is my word choice correct? (see pages 97-103)

PUNCTUATION AND SPELLING

☐ Is my handling of quotations correct? Is my handling of
reported speech correct? (see pages 348-349, 409-413)

☐ Have I capitialized correctly? (see pages 393-394)

☐ Have I used apostrophes correctly with possessives and
contractions? (see pages 384-388)

☐ Have I used hyphens correctly? (see pages 388-393)

☐ Have I used commas, colons, semicolons, parentheses, and
dashes correctly? (see pages 398-413)

Reading Selections

To write well, you need to read well—and often. Reading familiarizes you with a variety of sentence structures, expands your vocabulary, provides you with models of writing, and broadens your awareness of the experiences, thoughts, and knowledge of people you don't know and can know only through their words. Besides, reading is fun. It takes you on journeys into worlds you've never experienced—and even worlds that exist only in the imaginations of the people who created them. The following selections were chosen for the insights they offer into the lives of others—and our own.

Your instructor may ask you to read a selection at home and then discuss it in class or in your collaborative group—or to write about it. You can prepare for those discussions or writing assignments by *reading with a purpose*. The following advice should help you develop and improve your reading strategies—for these selections, for your reading in other courses, and for the reading you do on your own.

1. **Use the introductions as guides.** The introductions to each selection suggest what to look for as you read. Take these suggestions seriously. Make notes in the margins to show where these ideas and organizational strategies occur. The notes can be simple check marks, phrases ("important," "note this"), or short summaries of content.

2. **Expect to return to a selection after you've read it.** Purposeful reading includes reviewing what you've read to ensure that you understand its main points. That's especially important as you study. You don't have to reread every word, but you have to be able to locate the important ideas.

3. **Locate main ideas.** Look for and identify thesis statements and topic sentences, either by highlighting or by underlining them. When you return to the selection for further review and study, you can locate main ideas quickly.

4. **Make personal notes in the margins of the text.** In addition to noting the matters identified in the introduction, record your personal reactions to a sentence or a paragraph: statements of agreement or disagreement ("right!" or "yeah, right!"); reactions ("this is a key point," "that's his opinion"); objections ("but would every dock worker want to . . . ?"); and ideas to discuss in class or in writing ("how about the case of . . . ?"). Think of these reactions as a dialogue you're having with the writer. Someone else's ideas should stimulate your thinking; you shouldn't simply accept the ideas because "that's what the book says." It's what the *writer* of the book says—a human being with opinions, limits to his or her knowledge, and biases as well. Try to connect the reading to your own personal knowledge and experiences.

5. **Reread while reading.** If you don't understand a sentence or longer passage, stop and reread it, and reread the sentences preceding it. If the puzzling part still doesn't make sense, make a note in the margin so you can return to the passage later or perhaps discuss it with others.

6. **Circle or underline unfamiliar words, and look them up.** You can't fully comprehend an idea if you don't understand the language that presents it. And you can't build your vocabulary if you don't work on building it. Before looking up a word in the dictionary, however, try to determine its meaning in context. That is, reread the sentence the word appears in, as well as the ones before and after it. If you must look them up, do so after you finish reading,

441

and write the definition above the line or in the margin. Then reread the selection. You'll go much faster—and understand much more.

7. **Respond to readings in your journal.** If the selection raises questions or inspires ideas, record them in your journal. Discuss the questions in class, and use the ideas and questions as reminders when you study and write later on.

8. **Know how fast you read—in a variety of contexts.** Succeeding in school and in the working world depends greatly on budgeting your time effectively. Determine how long it takes you to read twenty pages in your social science text or twenty pages in biology. Time yourself. How many pages have you read in fifteen minutes or an hour? Once you know the answers, you can set aside enough time to complete your reading, and complete it carefully.

9. **Take frequent breaks.** Don't try to read a long, difficult selection straight through. Take a five- or ten-minute break every hour or so. But don't make the breaks too long, or you'll find them distracting rather than refreshing.

Buzzard
Bailey White

* * * *

We've all had moments when we mistake one person or thing for another. In this essay, Bailey White, a first-grade teacher in Georgia and regular commentator on the radio show, All Things Considered, *describes one such encounter. As you read it, notice how she quickly establishes the scene and blends the action with physical description. Consider her purpose. Does she want to tell you what the animal looks like, or does she assume that you already know? This essay first appeared in Ms. White's book* Mama Makes Up Her Mind.

1   There was something in the road. I drove closer to it. It was a buzzard eating a dead armadillo. I got closer. It was a big buzzard. And I'd never seen a buzzard's tail feathers so bleached and pale.

2   That buzzard better move, I thought. I'd never had to slow down for a buzzard before. They always lope out of the way. I got closer.

3   The buzzard turned his head and looked at me. He stood up on his big yellow legs. His head was snow white. His eyes were gold. He wasn't a buzzard. He was a bald eagle.

4   Then, not until after I had brought the car to a full stop, he spread his wings and with a slow swoop lifted himself into the air. He turned his head and gave me a long look through the car windshield with his level yellow eyes. Then he slowly wheeled up into the sky until he was just a black dot against the blue.

5   I turned the car off. I thought about that glare he had given me: What are you doing here? it had said. When I got started again, I drove slower and felt smaller. I think it does us all good to get looked at like that now and then by a wild animal.

Questions for Analysis

1. What is the setting for the encounter with the bird? What sentences and paragraphs establish the setting? Why doesn't Bailey White provide more detail about the setting?

2. Why does White first think the bird is a buzzard? What details reveal that it's actually a bald eagle?

3. White doesn't describe everything about the eagle's appearance. What parts of its body does she focus on, and why?

4. What actions of the eagle in the last two paragraphs reveal the eagle's attitude and character—if an animal can be said to have attitude and character?

5. In your own words, describe White's purpose—the point she seems to be making in this essay. What does she seem to feel is the relationship between the buzzard and humans? What do you think White means in her last paragraph?

Writing Assignments

1. Have you ever had an encounter with a wild animal? Describe what happened. What was the result?

2. Have you ever experienced a moment when an animal seemed almost human? Relate the experience.

3. Have you ever thought you were in control of a situation only to discover that you were the one being controlled? Describe the experience. What happened, and why did it happen?

4. Write an essay in which you explain what seems to be Bailey White's changing attitude toward the eagle. Support your analysis with details from her description.

from I Know Why the Caged Bird Sings
Maya Angelou

* * * *

Almost everyone has encountered prejudice of some sort—and many of us have been able to achieve our goals despite that prejudice. In the following passage from her most famous book, Maya Angelou—an African American writer, singer, dancer, and actor—describes an experience in which she was obviously being denied a job because of her race. As you read it, notice her emphasis on pride, her relationship with her mother, and her continuing efforts to achieve her goal.

1   My room had all the cheeriness of a dungeon and the appeal of a tomb. It was going to be impossible to stay there, but leaving held no attraction for me, either. The answer came to me with the suddenness of a collision. I would go to work. Mother wouldn't be difficult to convince; after all, in school I was a year ahead of my grade and Mother was a firm believer in self-sufficiency. In fact, she'd be pleased to think that I had that much gumption, that much of her in my character. (She liked to speak of herself as the original "do-it-yourself girl.")

2   Once I had settled on getting a job, all that remained was to decide which kind of job I was most fitted for. My intellectual pride had kept me from selecting typing, shorthand, or filing as subjects in school, so office work was ruled out. War plants and shipyards demanded birth certificates, and mine would reveal me to be fifteen, and ineligible for work. So the well-paying defense jobs were also out. Women had replaced men on the streetcars as conductors and motormen, and the thought of sailing up and down the hills of San Francisco in a dark-blue uniform, with a money changer at my belt, caught my fancy.

3   Mother was as easy as I had anticipated. The world was moving so fast, so much money was being made, so many people were dying in Guam and Germany, that hordes of strangers became good friends overnight. Life was cheap and death entirely free. How could she have the time to think about my academic career?

4   To her question of what I planned to do, I replied that I would get a job on the streetcars. She rejected the proposal with: "They don't accept colored people on the streetcars."

5   I would like to claim an immediate fury which was followed by the noble determination to break the restricting tradition. But the truth is, my first reaction was one of disappointment. I'd pictured myself, dressed in a neat blue serge suit, my money changer swinging jauntily at my waist, and a cheery smile for the passengers which would make their own work day brighter.

6   From disappointment, I gradually ascended the emotional ladder to haughty in-dignation, and finally to that state of stubbornness where the mind is locked like the jaws of an enraged bulldog.

7   I would go to work on the streetcars and wear a blue serge suit. Mother gave me her support with one of her usual terse asides, "That's what you want to do? Then— nothing beats a trial but a failure. Give it everything you've got. I've told you many times, 'Can't Do is like Don't Care!' Neither of them has a home."

8   Translated, that meant there was nothing a person can't do, and there should be nothing a human being didn't care about. It was the most positive encouragement I could have hoped for.

9   In the offices of the Market Street Railway Company, the receptionist seemed as surprised to see me there as I was surprised to find the interior dingy and drab. Somehow I had expected waxed surfaces and carpeted floors. If I had met no resis-tance, I might have decided against working for such a poor-mouth-looking concern. As it was, I explained that I had come to see about a job. She asked, was I sent by an agency, and when I replied that I was not, she told me they were only accepting appli-cants from agencies.

10 The classified pages of the morning papers had listed advertisements for mo-torettes and conductorettes and I reminded her of that. She gave me a face full of astonishment that my suspicious nature would not accept.

11 "I am applying for the job listed in this morning's *Chronicle* and I'd like to be pre-sented to your personnel manager." While I spoke in supercilious accents, and looked at the room as if I had an oil well in my own backyard, my armpits were being pricked by millions of hot pointed needles. She saw her escape and dived into it.

12 "He's out. He's out for the day. You might call him tomorrow and if he's in, I'm sure you can see him." Then she swiveled her chair around on its rusty screws and with that I was supposed to be dismissed.

13 "May I ask his name?"

14 She half turned, acting surprised to find me still there.

15 "His name? Whose name?"

16 "Your personnel manager."

17 We were firmly joined in the hypocrisy to play out the scene.

18 "The personnel manager? Oh, he's Mr. Cooper, but I'm not sure you'll find him here tomorrow. He's . . . Oh, but you can try."

19 "Thank you."

20 "You're welcome."

21 And I was out of the musty room and into the even mustier lobby. In the street I saw the receptionist and myself going faithfully through paces that were stale with familiarity, although I had never encountered that kind of situation before and, probably, neither had she. We were like actors who, knowing the play by heart, were still able to cry afresh over the old tragedies and laugh spontaneously at the comic situations.

22 The miserable little encounter had nothing to do with me, the me of me, any more than it had to do with that silly clerk. The incident was a recurring dream concocted years before by whites, and it eternally came back to haunt us all. The secretary and I were like people in a scene where, because of harm done by one ancestor to an-other, we were bound to duel to the death. (Also because the play must end some-where.)

23 I went further than forgiving the clerk; I accepted her as a fellow victim of the same puppeteer.

24 On the streetcar, I put my fare into the box and the conductorette looked at me with the usual hard eyes of white contempt. "Move into the car, please move on in the car." She patted her money changer.

25 Her Southern nasal accent sliced my meditation and I looked deep into my thoughts. All lies, all comfortable lies. The receptionist was not innocent and neither

was I. The whole charade we had played out in that waiting room had to do with me, black, and her, white.

26   I wouldn't move into the streetcar but stood on the ledge over the conductor, glaring. My mind shouted so energetically that the announcement made my veins stand out, and my mouth tighten into a prune.

27   I WOULD HAVE THE JOB. I WOULD BE A CONDUCTORETTE AND SLING A FULL MONEY CHANGER FROM MY BELT. I WOULD.

28   The next three weeks were a honeycomb of determination with apertures for the days to go in and out. The Negro organizations to whom I appealed for support bounced me back and forth like a shuttlecock on a badminton court. Why did I insist on that particular job? Openings were going begging that paid nearly twice the money. The minor officials with whom I was able to win an audience thought me mad. Possibly I was.

29   Downtown San Francisco became alien and cold, and the streets I had loved in a personal familiarity were unknown lanes that twisted with malicious intent. My trips to the streetcar office were of the frequency of a person on salary. The struggle expanded. I was no longer in conflict only with the Market Street Railway but with the marble lobby of the building which housed its offices, and elevators and their operators.

30   During this period of strain Mother and I began our first steps on the long path toward mutual adult admiration. She never asked for reports and I didn't offer any details. But every morning she made breakfast, gave me carfare and lunch money, as if I were going to work. She comprehended that in the struggle lies the joy. That I was no glory seeker was obvious to her, and that I had to exhaust every possibility before giving in was also clear.

31   On my way out of the house one morning she said, "Life is going to give you just what you put in it. Put your whole heart in everything you do, and pray, then you can wait." Another time she reminded me that "God helps those who help themselves." She had a store of aphorisms which she dished out as the occasion demanded. Strangely, as bored as I was with clichés, her inflection gave them something new, and set me thinking for a little while at least. Later when asked how I got my job, I was never able to say exactly. I only knew that one day, which was tiresomely like all the others before it, I sat in the Railway office, waiting to be interviewed. The receptionist called me to her desk and shuffled a bundle of papers to me. They were job application forms. She said they had to be filled out in triplicate. I had little time to wonder if I had won or not, for the standard questions reminded me of the necessity for lying. How old was I? List my previous jobs, starting from the last held and go backward to the first. How much money did I earn, and why did I leave the position? Give two references (not relatives). I kept my face blank (an old art) and wrote quickly the fable of Marguerite Johnson, aged nineteen, former companion and driver for Mrs. Annie Henderson (a White Lady) in Stamps, Arkansas.

32   I was given blood tests, aptitude tests, and physical coordination tests, then on a blissful day I was hired as the first Negro on the San Francisco streetcars.

33   Mother gave me the money to have my blue serge suit tailored, and I learned to fill out work cards, operate the money changer and punch transfers. The time crowded together and at an End of Days I was swinging on the back of the rackety trolley, smiling sweetly and persuading my charges to "step forward in the car, please."

34   For one whole semester the streetcars and I shimmied up and scooted down the sheer hills of San Francisco. I lost some of my need for the black ghetto's shielding-sponge quality, as I clanged and cleared my way down Market Street, with its honky-tonk homes for homeless sailors, past the quiet retreat of Golden Gate Park and along closed undwelled-in-looking dwellings of the Sunset District.

35   My work shifts were split so haphazardly that it was easy to believe that my superiors had chosen them maliciously. Upon mentioning my suspicions to Mother, she

said, "Don't you worry about it. You ask for what you want, and you pay for what you get. And I'm going to show you that it ain't no trouble when you pack double."

36   She stayed awake to drive me out to the car barn at four-thirty in the mornings, or to pick me up when I was relieved just before dawn. Her awareness of life's perils convinced her that while I would be safe on the public conveyances, she "wasn't about to trust a taxi driver with her baby."

37   When the spring classes began, I resumed my commitment with formal education. I was so much wiser and older, so much more independent, with a bank account and clothes that I had bought for myself, that I was sure I had learned and earned the magic formula which would make me a part of the life my contemporaries led.

38   Not a bit of it. Within weeks, I realized that my schoolmates and I were on paths moving away from each other. They were concerned and excited over the approaching football games. They concentrated great interest on who was worthy of being student body president, and when the metal bands would be removed from their teeth, while I remembered conducting a streetcar in the uneven hours of the morning.

Questions for Analysis

1. Who is the primary audience for this work?
2. What message would Maya Angelou like you to understand after reading this work? State it in your own words, in writing.
3. How would you characterize Angelou's personality? List several personality traits.
4. In paragraph 21, Angelou says of the receptionist and herself: "We were like actors who, knowing the play by heart, were still able to cry afresh over the old tragedies and laugh spontaneously at the comic situations." What does she mean? And who is the author of the play she mentions?
5. Why does Angelou originally want to be a conductorette? Later, her reason for wanting the job changes. Why?
6. Although it's unstated, what point is Angelou making about racism and her reaction to it? State that point in your own words, in writing.

Writing Assignments

1. Have you ever personally encountered prejudice? Relate what happened in one such instance.
2. Have you ever overcome an obstacle—either personal or social—to your success? Describe and explain how you overcame the obstacle.
3. Relate an incident in which you were treated like a number or an object instead of a human being. How did you react? What was the result?
4. Write an essay in which you explain Maya Angelou's motivations for becoming a streetcar conductor. Support your ideas with evidence from the story.

Reflections
Gloria Uduando

* * * *

Gloria Uduando was a student at Truman College who returned to school after working for many years as a secretary. As you read her story, notice how it divides into scenes, and notice how each scene begins by establishing when and where it occurred, and who was involved. Notice how dialogue and close attention to details play an important role in the development of the story. You'll probably want to reexamine that dialogue and those details after you finish reading.

1   The world of our neighborhood was small and poor. We knew everyone on the block and across the street, their habits, cooking smells, clothing styles, and cars. It was a cold day when any bit of gossip took longer than half an hour to get around the block.

2   My heart was pounding with excitement as I ran up the back stairs to the third floor of our old building. Shaking with impatience, I knocked at the door, thinking that I must be dreaming. When Donna opened the door, my words burst into her face. "Donna! Did you see it? Come on, come with me; they're taking it off the truck in front."

3   Donna's father owned the building, and the new tenants held a mysterious anticipation.

4   Hand in little hand, we stood mesmerized as the muscled men grunted and shouted orders at each other, carrying the beautiful baby grand piano up the flight of outside stairs to the second floor.

5   We held our breath as a large black car pulled up behind the moving van. Out popped a boy of about twelve or thirteen years old. We felt invaded and betrayed. We were both sure the baby grand would belong to a girl. Our curiosity now defunct, we silently crept into my basement apartment.

6   "Gloria, do you think we will be allowed to play with him?"

7   "He is living in our building so it must be okay."

8   Later that evening, the baby grand roared with classical music. My father was angry at not being able to hear the nightly fights on the radio, my mother's daily headache went migraine, and I was in heaven.

9   The next day we searched at school for our new future friend. We didn't find him. While doing our homework on the front porch, Donna and I watched the yellow school bus pull up in front of our building. Awkwardly he made his way toward us.

10   "Hello, my name is Gloria and this is Donna." His name was Michael.

11   Having moved from Michigan, his family planned to stay in our building for about a year until they found a house to buy on the Southwest Side of Chicago. He went to a special school to develop his musical talent.

12   He let his mom know he was home from school and quickly came back out, struggling with a bicycle built for two. As he was bouncing it down the stairs, his father angrily shouted behind him, "You know you can't ride your bike until you know every street name and location within three blocks of our house."

13   "But Dad, I am going to take Gloria with me, and she can teach me."

14   "All right Michael, but be back in an hour."

15   I didn't know how to ride a bike, and I didn't want Michael to know. While fear grabbed me tighter than my grip on the handlebars, Michael's soft voice behind me whispered, "Don't be afraid. Stay in the middle of the seat and steer. I will pedal and keep our balance." He knew I couldn't ride. I was ashamed. It would be twenty-five years later before I would ask him how he knew.

16   Pedaling past each house, I identified the owners by smell. Mrs. Letto used too much garlic, and the Johnsons from the South made wonderful smelling corn bread every night. We rode often that first week, reciting the names of every street. Soon Michael was at home and settled in the neighborhood.

17   With Michael giggling and nudging me through the door to his apartment, I became aware of Michael's reality. Surrounding the piano in the middle of the living room were bumpy sheets of music all around and books of every kind that would have made the library jealous. LP records were piled high in a corner next to the record player. There were no toys, no games. It was a cluttered sanctuary I would soon grow to love.

18 Michael sat at the piano, with both hands at his sides, closed his eyes, smiled, and proudly asked, "What can I play for you?"

19 "I don't know, Michael. Play anything."

20 His hands stretched, his fingers flexed, and then they gently rested on the keys. He began to play "Moonlight Sonata." The last note lingered in the air as Michael turned and calmly asked, "Did you like it?"

21 "It was beautiful."

22 The enchantment of the music, the room, and the serenity glowing from Michael's face as he played had created a magical state. At the age of eleven, I was in puppy love.

23 Donna was uneasy with Michael and left us to our friendship.

24 In the months that followed, Michael and I became inseparable, and he opened many doors in my mind. He read me stories from different countries; I wrote him poetry. He played and sang for me; I gave him colors. He gave with joy; I gave with gratitude.

25 As the big black car drove Michael away to his new home, sadness filled me as I knew I would probably never see him again or at least not for a long time.

26 Many years later, I started a new job as a secretary for a fire insurance investigation company. The first duty in the morning was to call the man from whom we would get the fire reports. A soft voice answered, "Hello. It's Mike. How can I help you?"

27 "Hi, Mike. This is Gloria, and I am calling from Freed's office for the fire reports."

28 As he spoke, my mind strained to recall where I had heard that voice before and why was it having such a strange effect on me.

29 "Here's one that started at 2:00 A.M. in my old neighborhood on Cleveland Avenue." Struck numb, I loudly blurted out, "Michael, it's Gloria!" Silence met my shouting. Again, but with a quiet knowing confidence, "Michael, it's Gloria, Gloria from Cleveland Avenue."

30 We excitedly made plans to have dinner at my apartment. He arrived by bus at 7:00 P.M. As I anxiously opened the door, there stood my childhood friend looking all of fifteen.

31 "Michael, you are disgusting. Will you never grow old?" He laughed, he reached out and hugged me, and we cried happy tears of reunion.

32 Dinner conversation overflowed of our experiences of the last twenty-five years. I had forgotten how fascinating it was to watch Michael eat. Every spoon had a level amount; every fork filled and emptied to the timing of a slowly set metronome.

33 After dinner we sat on the floor as we did as children. My mind whizzed with the question I had to ask. "Michael, how did you know I didn't know how to ride a bike?"

34 "I heard you swallow, and your breathing changed rhythm."

35 How simple. Of course, this was a part of Michael's magic.

36 "Gloria, I hope you will want to see me again. You are so beautiful to me, and I don't want to lose you again."

37 Many men will tell you that you are beautiful, and it's just a line they think you want to hear. When Michael said it, you would cherish and believe his words because Michael had been blind since birth and could only see with his heart.

Questions for Analysis

1. The ending of the story probably surprised you, but it is not a false surprise. The details throughout the story actually prepare for it. Go back and underline any clues—in description, action, and dialogue—that fulfill that role. Then discuss how they do so.

2. Notice how the dialogue is introduced in the story. Many times, the speakers are not identified with *I said, he said* tags. How are you able to keep track of who is speaking?

3. The fourth scene, which begins with "In the months that followed," is the shortest. Why? What function does it serve in the story?

4. Locate the remaining scenes, and examine the sentences at the beginning and end of each scene. How do they establish the setting of the scene and/or establish transitions?

Writing Assignments

1. Tell the story of a special friendship you had with someone. How did it begin? How did it develop? Like Gloria Uduando, divide the story into scenes. This may take some planning and multiple writing sessions over a period of several days or even weeks.

2. Do you know someone with a physical handicap who has been able to compensate for it in other ways? Describe what the person does.

3. If you had to lose one of your five senses, which one would you hate most to lose? Explain why.

4. Write an essay in which you explain why Gloria and Michael seemed to become such close friends. What made the relationship special?

What Is Poverty?
Jo Goodwin Parker

* * * *

An abstract definition can never convey the emotional impact of a specific example from one person's life. Here's one such powerful example. The following essay was delivered in a speech by Jo Goodwin Parker in Deland, Florida, on December 27, 1965. Professor George Henderson chose to include it in a book on children in schools outside of suburbia. As you read the essay, notice how each paragraph introduces a different aspect of poverty, and how that aspect is then illustrated and explained. Notice how Parker answers the questions or objections her audience might raise. And notice her appeal to her audience at the end of the essay.

1   You ask me what is poverty? Listen to me. Here I am, dirty, smelly, and with no "proper" underwear on and with the stench of my rotting teeth near you. I will tell you. Listen to me. Listen without pity. I cannot use your pity. Listen with understanding. Put yourself in my dirty, worn out, ill-fitting shoes, and hear me.

2   Poverty is getting up every morning from a dirt and illness-stained mattress. The sheets have long since been used for diapers. Poverty is living in a smell that never leaves. This is a smell of urine, sour milk, and spoiling food sometimes joined with the strong smell of long-cooked onions. Onions are cheap. If you have smelled this smell, you did not know how it came. It is the smell of the outdoor privy. It is the smell of young children who cannot walk the long dark way in the night. It is the smell of the mattresses where years of "accidents" have happened. It is the smell of the milk which has gone sour because the refrigerator long has not worked, and it costs money to get it fixed. It is the smell of rotting garbage. I could bury it, but where is the shovel? Shovels cost money.

3   Poverty is being tired. I have always been tired. They told me at the hospital when the last baby came that I had chronic anemia caused from poor diet, a bad case of worms, and that I needed a corrective operation. I listened, politely—the poor are always polite. The poor always listen. They don't say that there is no money for iron pills, or better food, or worm medicine. The idea of an operation is frightening and costs so much that, if I had dared, I would have laughed. Who takes care of my children? Recovery from an operation takes a long time. I have three children. When I left them with "Granny" the last time I had a job, I came home to find the

baby covered with fly specks, and a diaper that had not been changed since I left. When the dried diaper came off, bits of my baby's flesh came with it. My other child was playing with a sharp bit of broken glass, and my oldest was playing alone at the edge of a lake. I made twenty-two dollars a week, and a good nursery school costs twenty dollars a week for three children. I quit my job.

4   Poverty is dirt. You say in your clean clothes coming from your clean house, "Anybody can be clean." Let me explain about housekeeping with no money. For breakfast I give my children grits with no oleo or cornbread without eggs and oleo. This does not use up many dishes. What dishes there are, I wash in cold water and with no soap. Even the cheapest soap has to be saved for the baby's diapers. Look at my hands, so cracked and red. Once I saved for two months to buy a jar of Vaseline for my hands and the baby's diaper rash. When I had saved enough, I went to buy it and the price had gone up two cents. The baby and I suffered on. I have to decide every day if I can bear to put my cracked, sore hands into the cold water and strong soap. But you ask, why not hot water? Fuel costs money. If you have a wood fire, it costs money. If you burn electricity, it costs money. Hot water is a luxury. I do not have luxuries. I know you will be surprised when I tell you how young I am. I look so much older. My back has been bent over the wash tubs every day for so long, I cannot remember when I ever did anything else. Every night I wash every stitch my school age child has on—and just hope her clothes will be dry by morning.

5   Poverty is staying up all night on cold nights to watch the fire, knowing one spark on the newspaper covering the walls means your sleeping children die in flames. In summer poverty is watching gnats and flies devour your baby's tears when he cries. The screens are torn and you pay so little rent you know they will never be fixed. Poverty means insects in your food, in your nose, in your eyes, and crawling over you when you sleep. Poverty is hoping it never rains because diapers won't dry when it rains and soon you are using newspapers. Poverty is seeing your children forever with runny noses. Paper handkerchiefs cost money and all your rags you need for other things. Even more costly are antihistamines. Poverty is cooking without food and cleaning without soap.

6   Poverty is asking for help. Have you ever had to ask for help, knowing your children will suffer unless you get it? Think about asking for a loan from a relative, if this is the only way you can imagine asking for help. I will tell you how it feels. You find out where the office is that you are supposed to visit. You circle that block four or five times. Thinking of your children, you go in. Everyone is very busy. Finally, someone comes out and you tell her that you need help. That never is the person you need to see. You go see another person, and after spilling the whole shame of your poverty all over the desk between you, you find that this isn't the right office after all—you must repeat the whole process, and it never is any easier at the next place.

7   You have asked for help, and after all it has a cost. You are again told to wait. You are told why, but you don't really hear because of the red cloud of shame and the rising black cloud of despair.

8   Poverty is remembering. It is remembering quitting school in junior high because "nice" children had been so cruel about my clothes and my smell. The attendance officer came. My mother told him I was pregnant. I wasn't, but she thought that I could get a job and help out. I had jobs off and on, but never long enough to learn anything. Mostly I remember being married. I was so young then. I am still young. For a time, we had all the things you have. There was a little house in another town, with hot water and everything. Then my husband lost his job. There was unemployment insurance for a while and what few jobs I could get. Soon, all our nice things were repossessed and we moved back here. I was pregnant then. This house didn't look so bad when we first moved in. Every week it gets worse. Nothing is ever fixed. We now had no money. There were a few odd jobs for my husband, but everything went for food then, as it does now. I don't know how we lived through three years

and three babies, but we did. I'll tell you something, after the last baby I destroyed my marriage. It had been a good one, but could you keep on bringing children in this dirt? Did you ever think how much it costs for any kind of birth control? I knew my husband was leaving the day he left, but there were no good-byes between us. I hope he has been able to climb out of this mess somewhere. He never could hope with us to drag him down.

9   That's when I asked for help. When I got it, you know how much it was? It was, and is, seventy-eight dollars a month for the four of us; that is all I ever can get. Now you know why there is no soap, no needles and thread, no hot water, no aspirin, no worm medicine, no hand cream, no shampoo. None of these things forever and ever and ever. So that you can see clearly, I pay twenty dollars a month rent, and most of the rest goes for food. For grits and cornmeal, and rice and milk and beans. I try my best to use only the minimum electricity. If I use more, there is that much less for food.

10   Poverty is looking into a black future. Your children won't play with my boys. They will turn to other boys who steal to get what they want. I can already see them behind the bars of their prison instead of behind the bars of my poverty. Or they will turn to the freedom of alcohol or drugs, and find themselves enslaved. And my daughter? At best, there is for her a life like mine.

11   But you say to me, there are schools. Yes, there are schools. My children have no extra books, no magazines, no extra pencils, or crayons, or paper and the most important of all, they do not have health. They have worms, they have infections, they have pink-eye all summer. They do not sleep well on the floor, or with me in my one bed. They do not suffer from hunger, my seventy-eight dollars keeps us alive, but they do suffer from malnutrition. Oh yes, I do remember what I was taught about health in school. It doesn't do much good. In some places there is a surplus commodities program. Not here. The county said it cost too much. There is a school lunch program. But I have two children who will already be damaged by the time they get to school.

12   But, you say to me, there are health clinics. Yes, there are health clinics and they are in the towns. I live out here eight miles from town. I can walk that far (even if it is sixteen miles both ways), but can my little children? My neighbor will take me when he goes; but he expects to get paid, *one way or another.* I bet you know my neighbor. He is that large man who spends his time at the gas station, the barbershop, and the corner store complaining about the government spending money on the immoral mothers of illegitimate children.

13   Poverty is an acid that drips on pride until all pride is worn away. Poverty is a chisel that chips on honor until honor is worn away. Some of you say that you would do *something* in my situation, and maybe you would, for the first week or the first month, but for year after year after year?

14   Even the poor can dream. I dream of a time when there is money. Money for the right kinds of food, for worm medicine, for iron pills, for toothbrushes, for hand cream, for a hammer and nails and a bit of screening, for a shovel, for a bit of paint, for some sheeting, for needles and thread. Money to pay *in money* for a trip to town. And, oh, money for hot water and money for soap. A dream of when asking for help does not cast away the last bit of pride. When the office you visit is as nice as the offices of other governmental agencies, when there are enough workers to help you quickly, when workers do not quit in defeat and despair. When you have to tell your story to only one person, and that person can send you for other help and you don't have to prove your poverty over and over and over again.

15   I have come out of my despair to tell you this. Remember I did not come from another place or another time. Others like me are all around you. Look at us with an angry heart, anger that will help you help me. Anger that will let you tell of me. The poor are always silent. Can you be silent too?

Questions for Analysis

1. Jo Goodwin Parker begins her essay by saying, "I cannot use your pity." What does she want?

2. Paragraphs 2–10 contain topic sentences. Underline them. What helps you identify them?

3. In paragraph 11, Parker no longer defines poverty but responds to questions she anticipates from her audience. Why?

4. In paragraph 12, Parker says, "I bet you know my neighbor" and then describes him. What is her purpose in that description?

5. Parker suggests that one cause of poverty leads to another cause in a downward spiral. Write, in your own words, an explanation of that link between causes.

6. Parker begins her definition of poverty by focusing on smell in paragraph 2. Why?

7. Although Parker discusses actions and events more than feelings, at some points she does include words that describe her feelings. Find them. What are her feelings?

Writing Assignments

1. Parker defines poverty in a rural area almost four decades ago. Write a definition of poverty in an urban area today. Focus on three or four points.

2. Write a definition of any of the following: middle class; suburban; or your own ethnic group, nationality, or race. Focus on three or four points.

3. If your daily life is especially hectic or difficult, write an essay in which you define what your life is like. Divide the definition into categories, as Parker does.

4. Write an essay in which you discuss the causes of Jo Goodwin Parker's problems. Who or what is responsible?

5. Write an essay in which you offer some solutions to Jo Goodwin Parker's problems. What could be done to make her life better?

A Tale of Two Gravies
Karen P. Bellitto

* * * *

Grandparents play an important role in our lives. They establish a connection with our past, and in many cases spoil us in ways that our parents cannot—and should not—do. In the following essay, Karen P. Bellitto, a social work assistant in a nursing home for the elderly, describes her relationship with her two grandmothers. As you read the essay, notice the comparisons and contrasts between the grandmothers. Notice how those comparisons and contrasts are made specific through the use of narrative. Notice how the events are seen through the eyes of a child. And notice the obvious affection she feels toward her two grandmothers.

1   "Come on kids! We're going to Grandma's."

2   "Which one?"

3   During my childhood, these words were typical in my home almost every Saturday and Sunday afternoon. On Saturday, we'd go a few blocks to Grandma Ruth's, my father's mother; on Sunday, my mother would answer, "Grandma Meatball," her mom, and we'd drive to the suburbs. Each of those visits was enormously different, at least from the eyes of the little girl I was. I always wondered then why Grandma Ruth's "gravy" was thick and brown and poured over mashed

potatoes, but Grandma Meatball's was tomato sauce that she ladled over macaroni, sausage, and beef. As I grew up, however, I began to understand that Grandma Ruth and Grandma Meatball, who came from entirely diverse worlds, were more alike than I ever imagined.

4   "Come on kids. We're going to Grandma's."

5   "Which one?"

6   It was Saturday. "Grandma Ruth's." She lived only five minutes away, in an apartment building off Allerton Avenue in the Bronx. When she knew we were coming she would poke her head out the window so she could point out the best parking space when we got closer to the apartment. The building was old and there was no elevator. We climbed the five flights of stairs that led to my Grandma's apartment, for some still unknown reason marked "2E."

7   The doorbell was much higher than my reach and my dad would lift me up so I could ring it. The kitchen was about three feet from the door, so it wasn't long before Grandma Ruth came rushing out. She wasn't that tall, only about five-four, and slender, but she still smothered me and my sister, Tami. Looking at pictures of her when she was younger you'd say she never changed. She had begun to gray when she was only sixteen and the years in between made her wispy hair bright white. Grandma Ruth, in my mind's eye, will always be one of those young old people: young in mind and spirit with a body that just couldn't keep up.

8   Grandma Ruth was born in New York and was a city girl her whole life. She had three raucous boys. Grandma Ruth loved to talk and laugh; she was always having "company" over. My father remembers sitting at the kitchen table stuffing fundraising envelopes she'd brought home from work so they could make a little extra money. Grandma Ruth would tell him stories of her family picnics in upstate New York. These became family lore for me, too.

9   Grandma Ruth's Saturday meals were spectacular. The smells coming from the kitchen made the two hours before dinner almost unbearable. Roast beef with gravy, mashed potatoes, creamed onions, mashed turnips, and string beans were the usuals. The roast beef was sometimes replaced by a roast pork or leg of lamb. Whatever the main course, it was meat, and there was always bread and butter. The weekend after Grandma Ruth died, my mother made this exact meal. It was our way of saying good-bye—and thanks.

10   Years ago, while we waited for her dinner, we'd get bored with the grown-up conversation. I would sit at my grandmother's desk by the phone and play secretary with her datebook. She had a desk set of those marble pen holders where the pen is attached by a chain. This became my telephone since I wasn't allowed to use the real one. When even this got boring, I would begin to wander around the house looking for the next thing to keep my interest. The dining room had all kinds of cool stuff in it so I would usually end up there. Trinkets and books lined long shelves that spanned one entire wall of the room; there was plenty to explore and keep my imagination busy.

11   The dining room table was set with white dishes with green flowers on the edges. Even the glasses were frosted white with matching green flowers. The kiddy bridge table was just off to the left, but it was set the same way so we wouldn't feel left out. The adults drank wine; we drank Hoffman's lemon soda. It always amazed me how much the adults could talk while they ate, though my mother told me not to talk when we chewed. The laughter and chatter never ceased. After dinner, my folks would sprawl out on her bed and take a nap. My sister and I would look out the window, just like Grandma.

12   "Come on kids, we're going to Mass, then we're going to Grandma's."

13   "Which one?"

14   Sunday: "Grandma Meatball."

15   After ten o'clock Mass we'd pile into my father's long, tired Pontiac for the forty-five-minute trip to Long Island. For as long as I could remember, Grandma Meatball

and Grandpa lived in Uncle Vinny's basement apartment. In marked contrast to Grandma Ruth, Grandma Meatball was very Old World Italian. She was a quiet woman who spoke more with the smiling silence of her eyes; her house was filled with religious paintings and statues. When she did talk, she'd amaze us with her stories of Arthur Avenue, a noisy Italian section of town, where she and Grandpa raised a brood of seven children in a three-room apartment. She'd remember life in the Italian countryside before she came to America. Simply thinking that this wise old woman was once a little girl, like me, who barely knew English was not something I could picture.

16   When we arrived, stir crazy from the long trip, Tami and I would swing around to the backyard of the house where Grandpa was fussing with his vegetable garden. He knew we were coming and he wanted to have a bag of tomatoes ready to go home with us. Then we'd go down the concrete steps to the basement where Grandma was standing by the stove stirring her "gravy." The minute we'd walk in, she'd say hello with her quiet eyes; we'd literally get lost in her round hugs, stronger than a man's. After the long greeting—she never let go easily, even years later as she lay in her hospital bed—she'd lead us over to the stove where the bowl of meatballs was waiting for us. Grandma would always fry extra meatballs for us to eat when we got there. She had to make a double batch, because half went into the gravy and the rest got eaten one by one by whoever walked into the kitchen.

17   Macaroni didn't have to get thrown in until the last minute before we ate, so we were basically waiting for the gravy meat to cook. While Grandma put out bread, cheese, wine, and fruit to pick at before dinner, my cousins came down from upstairs and we played. Grandma's basement apartment was perfect for hide and seek: there were nooks and crannies all over the place. The closets were enough to keep us busy until we were called to eat, but the laundry room was off limits ever since my cousin John got thrown in the dryer by his brothers. It was on at the time.

18   There wasn't enough room for everyone to eat downstairs, so we would carry the meal up to Aunt Mary and Uncle Vinny's kitchen because it was bigger. I had five aunts and uncles all together, so if everyone was on Long Island at once there was absolutely no way we could fit everyone, even in the larger kitchen. The kids would be in the living room sitting at the bridge table. There was no room for us to make our own plate, so each mother would make one up for her kids. We didn't feel left out because we were in the other room. Everyone talked so loudly we were able to contribute from where we were.

19   The autumn my grandmothers died, I thought often about those big weekend dinners. When I was a kid, all I was able to see were the differences between these women. Looking back, I realize that the cultural, emotional, even personal disparity fascinated me at that time. But as I grew and learned more about their lives, I came to understand that Grandma Ruth and Grandma Meatball were much more alike than I had ever imagined.

20   They loved and protected their children and grandchildren passionately. The good family values that are so often missing from today's world were daily lessons in their homes: they taught my mother and father to keep a family together, to put each other and their children first, and to understand that a family that stuck together no matter what could never be poor. By educating my parents, each of my grandmothers, unique as they were, contributed to my growth as a young woman in these same ways. They each loved me in their own language and expressed that love on their own terms. Their separate worlds merged together to make me the whole that I am. They taught me that where I stand depends on where they stood before me. A little girl sees the old fashioned ways of her grandmothers. The young woman understands the underlying importance, even timeliness, of their commitment to be matriarchs to their families. To remember their stories and pass them on to my own family, then, is to honor them. That is their legacy, and my responsibility.

Questions for Analysis

1. The essay is about far more than the "two gravies" of the title and first paragraph; what larger ideas or themes do the two gravies represent? What sentences or phrases in the first paragraph introduce the topic ideas?

2. Does Karen Bellitto employ a whole-to-whole or part-to-part organization in drawing contrasts between her grandmothers? Why? When discussing their similarities near the end of the essay, which organization does she use? Why?

3. Make your own list of the contrasts between the two grandmothers. Are the contrasts introduced in the same order? Is each trait of one grandmother contrasted to a trait of the other grandmother?

Writing Assignments

1. Like Karen Bellitto, compose a story about two relatives whose lives and personalities were quite different but who shared some important similarities. Discuss what a typical experience with them was like, but don't limit yourself merely to narration. Like Bellitto, analyze or explain the similarities between the two relatives.

2. Write about a time when you were present at an occasion—a wedding, a funeral, a party, or any other event—that included practices or rituals unfamiliar to you. Describe the experience, and contrast it to practices you know.

3. Describe two different happy (or unhappy) events from your childhood that were in some ways similar. Tell the story of both, and make a point in comparing or contrasting them.

4. Write an essay in which you describe the most important values that Karen Bellitto's grandmothers taught her. Cite examples from Bellitto's essay to support your thesis.

From a Grandpa, Above and Beyond
Bob Greene

* * * *

Sometimes, heroism comes from small kindnesses done for strangers. The following story, which first appeared in the Chicago Tribune *on March 11, 1990, describes one such act of heroism. Its author, Bob Greene, is a syndicated columnist and frequent commentator on television and radio. As you read the story, notice how Greene lets the participants relate and interpret the events in their own words.*

1 When Bernie Meyers, who was seventy years old and who lived in Wilmette, Illinois, went into the hospital last September, his family at first did not know how serious his illness was. Thus his ten-year-old granddaughter, Sarah Meyers, was not taken to see him.

2 "He hadn't been feeling well for some time," said Sarah's mother, Ann Meyers. "He went into the hospital for some tests. Just to find out what was wrong."

3 What was wrong was Lymphoma—a cancer of the lymphatic system. In Bernie Meyers's case, the Lymphoma was advanced and irreversible. He died within two weeks.

4 Sarah Meyers never got a chance to say good-bye to her grandfather.

5 "Sarah saw him regularly, because we live close to where he lived," her mother said. "This was her first experience with death. We could tell that, as upset as she was, she was additionally upset that she didn't see him in those days before he died. She didn't get to have one last talk with him."

6   Sarah didn't say much about what she was feeling. But in October she came home from a friend's birthday party. The other children at the party had been given helium balloons as favors. Sarah had hers with her—a bright red balloon.

7   "She went into the house," her mother said. "When she came back out, she was carrying the balloon—and an envelope."

8   Inside the envelope was a letter she had written to her grandfather. The envelope was addressed to "Grandpa Bernie, in Heaven Up High." In the letter, Sarah wrote: "Hi Grandpa. How are you? What's it like up there?" The letter ended with Sarah telling her grandfather that she loved him, and that she hoped somehow he could hear what she was telling him.

9   "I'm not sure what Sarah's concept of heaven is," her mother said. "But I do know that she printed our return address on the envelope. I didn't ask her about it. She punched a hole in the envelope, and tied the envelope to the balloon. Then she let it go.

10   "That balloon seemed so fragile to me. I didn't think it would even make it past the trees. But it did. We watched the balloon sail away, and then we went back inside."

11   Two months passed; the weather got cold. Then one day a letter arrived addressed to "Sarah Meyers + Family." The letter bore a York, Pa., postmark, and had been mailed by a man named Donald H. Kopp.

12   The letter began:

13   *Dear Sarah, Family & Friends—*

14   *Your letter to Grandpa Bernie Meyers apparently reached its destination and was read by him. I understand they can't keep material things up there, so it drifted back to earth. They just keep thoughts, memories, love and things like that.*

15   Donald Kopp wrote that he had found the balloon and letter while hunting and hiking in a Pennsylvania state forest near the Maryland border. That is almost six hundred miles from Wilmette—the balloon had floated over Illinois, probably parts of Michigan and Indiana, Ohio and all the way across Pennsylvania before settling in the forest.

16   Donald Kopp's letter to Sarah continued:

17   *Whenever you think or talk about your grandpa, he knows and is very close by with overwhelming love. Sincerely, Don Kopp. (also a grandpa)*

18   Sarah said that after she had tied her letter to the balloon and let it float away, "At night I would think about it. I just wanted to hear from Grandpa somehow. In a way, now I think that I have heard from him."

19   Donald Kopp, who is sixty-three and retired from his job as a shipping clerk, said the other day that the red balloon, which had almost completely deflated, was resting on a blueberry bush the afternoon he found it.

20   "That's pretty dense woods," he said. "It was cold and windy that day. I walked over to see what the balloon was. I could tell it was a child's handwriting on the envelope. I didn't have my reading glasses on, and I thought it was addressed to someone at 'Haven High.' A high school or something.

21   "I put it in my pocket. When I got back home, I saw that it wasn't addressed to Haven High. It was addressed to Sarah's grandfather, in 'Heaven Up High.'"

22   So he decided to write his letter to Sarah. "It was important to me that I write to her," he said. "But I'm not very good at writing; I don't do it that often. It took me a couple of days to think of what to put in the letter. Then I mailed it.

23   "Like I said in the letter—I'm a grandfather, too."

Greene's column was abridged and adapted for inclusion in Reader's Digest *in its November 1990 issue. See if it tells the same story.*

Love Finds a Way
Bob Greene

* * * *

1   When seventy-year-old Bernie Meyers of Wilmette, Ill., died suddenly of cancer, his ten-year-old granddaughter Sarah Meyers didn't have a chance to say good-by

to him. For weeks Sarah said little about what she was feeling. But then one day she came home from a friend's birthday party with a bright-red helium balloon. "She went into the house," her mother recalls, "and came out carrying the balloon—and an envelope addressed to 'Grandpa Bernie, in Heaven Up High.'"

2   The envelope contained a letter in which Sarah told her grandfather that she loved him and hoped somehow he could hear her. Sarah printed her return address on the envelope, tied the envelope to the balloon and let it go. "The balloon seemed so fragile," her mother remembers. "I didn't think it would make it past the trees. But it did."

3   Two months passed. Then one day a letter arrived addressed to "Sarah Meyers & Family" and bearing a York, Pa., postmark.

4   "Dear Sarah, Family & Friends: Your letter to Grandpa Bernie Meyers apparently reached its destination and was read by him. I understand they can't keep material things up there, so it drifted back to Earth. They just keep thoughts, memories, love and things like that. Sarah, whenever you think about your grandpa, he knows and is very close by with overwhelming love. Sincerely, Don Kopp (also a grandpa)."

5   Kopp, a sixty-three-year-old retired receiving clerk, had found the letter and the nearly deflated balloon while hunting in northeastern Pennsylvania—almost six hundred miles from Wilmette. The balloon had floated over at least three states and one of the Great Lakes before coming to rest on a blueberry bush.

6   "Though it took me a couple of days to think of what to say," Kopp notes, "it was important to me that I write to Sarah."

7   Says Sarah, "I just wanted to hear from Grandpa somehow. In a way, now I think I *have* heard from him."

Questions for Analysis

1. Consider the title of the first Bob Greene story. Does it have more than one meaning? Compare it to the title of the *Reader's Digest* version. Do the titles imply the same ideals?

2. In the first, longer version, Donald Kopp tells Greene, "I'm not very good at writing. . . . It took me a couple of days to think of what to put in the letter." That may be true, but Kopp probably had other reasons for deliberating so long over what to say. What do you think these reasons were?

3. Greene tells the story from the point of view of the Meyers family and from Donald Kopp's point of view. What would be lost if Greene omitted Kopp from his telling of the story?

4. In condensing the original article, what does *Reader's Digest* omit or change?

5. The endings of the two stories are different. What points do they make? Are the points the same or different?

6. The two treatments differ in organization and structure. How? What effects do the changes have on your reactions?

Writing Assignments

1. As a child, did you experience the loss of someone you loved? Write an essay in which you narrate and describe how you attempted to cope with the loss.

2. Have you ever performed, benefited from, or witnessed an act of kindness from a stranger? Write an essay that describes the experience.

3. After Bob Greene's column was published, many people in York, Pennsylvania, wrote letters and articles about Donald Kopp, calling him a hero. Write an essay in which you define heroism, using Mr. Kopp as one example.

4. Like Bob Greene, tell someone else's story—and have someone tell your story, too. Here's how to do it. Everyone in your class will write a short, one-paragraph summary of an unusual or important event in his or her life. This summary should

not be very detailed. Next, exchange summaries with a classmate. Look over each other's summary and consider what else you want to know about the event: who was involved, what happened, what people said and did, and how your classmate felt (or feels) about the event. Then interview your classmate, who will also interview you. Take notes, including phrases and sentences you think might be worth quoting when you tell the story. Make arrangements for a second interview later, for when you begin writing, you'll probably think of more things you want to know. Then write the story.

Baby Birds
Gale Lawrence

* * * *

Finding an infant animal may elicit our most tender feelings. Gale Lawrence, a naturalist, offers advice on how to treat "baby birds" in this essay from The Beginning Naturalist, *a collection of fifty-two essays on her encounters with nature. As you read it, notice her specific, step-by-step advice. Notice her clear explanation of the process of caring for the birds, her explicit transitions, and her emphasis on practical, realistic procedures for the care and feeding of the animals.*

1   Every spring the "baby bird crisis" occurs. By May many birds have hatched their first broods and are feeding them in the nest while they grow their feathers and learn to fly. Baby birds have a way of tumbling out of their nests, and children have a way of finding them and bringing them home. What should a family do if faced with this "crisis"?

2   First, take the baby bird back to the exact spot where it was found. Look carefully for a nest nearby. If you find the nest and it is accessible, put the bird gently back into the nest. Contrary to popular belief, the mother bird will not reject a baby that has been handled by human beings. A deer, which has a keen sense of smell and fears the human scent, will reject a fawn that has been handled, but birds are different. If you find the nest and return the baby, you have done the best you can do.

3   As a next-best measure, tie a small box onto a branch of a tree or shrub near where the bird was found, and put the baby bird in the box. The bird will thus be off the ground and out of the reach of neighborhood cats and dogs.

4   The third best thing you can do is simply leave the bird in the exact spot where it was found. Parent birds are accustomed to having their young fall out of the nest, and they will feed them on the ground. Of course, the baby bird is more vulnerable on the ground than it is in the nest or in a box, but it still stands a better chance of surviving under its own parents' care than under human care. If the baby bird is found near a house, it is better to keep pet dogs and cats indoors than to bring the baby bird indoors in an attempt to protect it.

5   If the baby is truly abandoned or orphaned—something you can learn only by watching it from a distance for an hour or more—you have a decision to make. You can leave it there to die a natural death—which might in fact be the most humane thing to do. Or you can take it indoors. If you decide to care for it yourself, you are making a substantial commitment. And, even if you live up to your commitment, there is no guarantee that the bird will survive.

6   Two major problems are involved in trying to parent a baby bird. One is feeding it, and the other is preparing it for life in the wild. Parent birds do it all as a matter of course, but a human parent will have to drop other activities for a period of weeks and perhaps install a screened porch or aviary to do the job right.

7   Before you can even address yourself to the problem of feeding, however, you have the more immediate problem of the bird's shock and fright to contend with. Perhaps this is the time to send one member of the family for a book on the care of

wild animal young, while another rigs up a heating pad or hot water bottle to warm the baby bird. One good book is *Care of the Wild Feathered and Furred: A Guide to Wildlife Handling and Care* (Santa Cruz: Unity Press, 1973) by Mae Hickman and Maxime Guy. Another is Ronald Rood's *The Care and Feeding of Wild Pets* (New York: Pocket Books, 1976). A third book that is specifically about birds is *Bird Ambulance* (New York: Charles Scribner's Sons, 1971) by Arline Thomas.

8   Now comes the problem of feeding. The warm milk in an eye dropper that seems to be everyone's immediate impulse when it comes to feeding animal young may be appropriate for baby mammals, but it will come as a complete surprise to the baby bird. Its parents were probably feeding it mashed worms, caterpillars, insects, and other delicious odds and ends. Therefore, you'll need to do the same. At first you should supply the baby bird with protein-rich foods. Eventually you're going to have to identify the species and learn something about its food habits in the wild if you want the bird to grow up properly. Whether the bird is a seed eater, an insect eater, or a predator will make a difference.

9   Parent birds feed their babies about every ten or fifteen minutes from sunrise to sunset. They also feed them exactly what they need to keep their bowels regulated and their bodies growing properly. They also keep the nest clean by removing the babies' excrement, which usually appears shortly after each feeding. In brief, between finding and preparing appropriate food, feeding, and cleaning up after meals, you're not going to have much time for anything else for a while if you decide to parent a baby bird.

10   If you do manage to keep the young bird fed properly and growing, your next problem is providing it with enough space for it to practice flying. You cannot expect a bird to go from your kitchen to the wild with one swoop of its wings. You will need to continue feeding and protecting the bird while it is adjusting to the outdoors. If it had stayed with its parents, it would have had adult birds to follow and imitate, but, with nothing but human beings to encourage it, it will have to make sense out of its environment alone. The young bird that has been raised by humans is at a disadvantage when it comes to competing for food and avoiding the attacks of predators. So even if you do manage to raise a fledgling to adulthood, you have not guaranteed its survival in the wild.

11   If you think I'm trying to sound discouraging, I am. The adoption of a baby bird will probably result in failure. You might even cause a death that would not have occurred had you left the baby bird where it was. Your intentions might be good; the ethical impulse that motivates your actions might be of the best kind. But you should know that even experienced veterinarians have a low success rate in caring for wild animals.

12   Perhaps the most important thing a child or adult can learn from an encounter with a baby bird is the difference between wild animals and domestic pets. Whereas puppies and kittens warm to human attention and become very much a part of the family, a wild bird never will. Attempting to make a pet out of a wild animal is a serious disservice to that animal—so serious, in fact, that there are laws against it. Life in the wild does not consist of friendly humans, readily available meals, and a protected environment. Wild animals must remain wild to survive.

13   Rather than adopt a baby bird, why not "adopt" a whole bird family—from a distance? Chances are there is a bird's nest somewhere near your home. Or you can build birdhouses to attract birds to your yard. Learn to watch the bird family from a distance. If human beings get too close, the parent birds won't come to the nest. So practice sitting quietly, perhaps with a pair of binoculars, far enough away from the nest that the adult bird won't feel threatened.

14   Watching birds in the wild is a much healthier and more realistic activity than fantasizing that a bird will become your special friend because you raised it. Unfortunately, movies, television, and children's books have created a "Bambi syndrome" in us. The young of most species are precious and adorable, but the desire

to fondle and caress and make pets out of wildlings is dangerously romantic. It should not be encouraged. We'd be much wiser if we were content to be observers of wildlife. If we truly care about wild animals, we should be protectors of their wildness, which enables the best of them to survive.

Questions for Analysis

1. Is the purpose of this essay merely to inform? If not, what other purpose does it have?
2. The essay makes a number of points. What is its most important point?
3. Who is the audience for this essay? What does Gale Lawrence expect the readers to do with the information she provides?
4. What is the primary method of the development Lawrence uses—description, narration, process analysis, cause-effect? Does that method of development change at the end of the essay? Why or why not?
5. There are several major divisions in the essay. Locate the sentences that introduce each of the divisions. What words or phrases relate the ideas to the ideas that have preceded?

Writing Assignments

1. Like Gale Lawrence, write an essay in which you advise people about some practical matter. For example, assume you're a high school counselor who advises seniors about how to adjust to college life. Consider any (but not necessarily all) of these issues: living with roommates, budgeting time, budgeting money, taking and organizing notes.
2. Describe a time when you found a wild or abandoned animal. What did you do? If you decided to care for the animal, how did you do it? If you decided to have some agency handle the problem, what did you do? What was the result?
3. Explain the process of house training a dog, cat, or other domestic pet. Or describe a process you've gone through in taking care of a sick animal.
4. Gale Lawrence says, "The adoption of a baby bird will probably result in failure." Do you find that statement shocking? Did Lawrence convince you of its truth? Write an essay in which you examine your responses to Lawrence's essay in light of your own experiences and observations.

Neat People vs. Sloppy People
Suzanne Britt

* * * *

Neatness is usually considered a virtue, but the following essay, which first appeared in Suzanne Britt's collection of essays, Show and Tell *(Raleigh, N.C., 1983), has a little fun with that idea. As you read it, notice how she develops a whole-to-whole comparison, beginning with sloppy people and then drawing comparisons to neat people. Notice how she introduces each point in the comparison by beginning with the words "Neat people" or "Sloppy people." And notice her exaggeration in order to create humor.*

1   I've finally figured out the difference between neat people and sloppy people. The distinction is, as always, moral. Neat people are lazier and meaner than sloppy people.

2   Sloppy people, you see, are not really sloppy. Their sloppiness is merely the unfortunate consequence of their extreme moral rectitude. Sloppy people carry in their mind's eye a heavenly vision, a precise plan, that is so stupendous, so perfect, it can't be achieved in this world or the next.

3   Sloppy people live in Never-Never Land. Someday is their *métier* [vocation or special talent]. Someday they are planning to alphabetize all their books and set up home catalogs. Someday they will go through their wardrobes and mark certain items for tentative mending and certain items for passing on to relatives of similar shape and size. Someday sloppy people will make family scrapbooks into which they will put newspaper clippings, postcards, locks of hair, and the dried corsage from their senior prom. Someday they will file everything on the surface of their desks, including the cash receipts from coffee purchases at the snack shop. Someday they will sit down and read all the back issues of *The New Yorker*.

4   For all these noble reasons and more, sloppy people never get neat. They aim too high and wide. They save everything, planning someday to file, order, and straighten out the world. But while these ambitious plans take clearer and clearer shape in their heads, the books spill from the shelves onto the floor, the clothes pile up in the hamper and closet, the family mementos accumulate in every drawer, the surface of the desk is buried under mounds of paper, and the unread magazines threaten to reach the ceiling.

5   Sloppy people can't bear to part with anything. They give loving attention to every detail. When sloppy people say they're going to tackle the surface of a desk, they really mean it. Not a paper will go unturned; not a rubber band will go unboxed. Four hours or two weeks into the excavation, the desk looks exactly the same, primarily because the sloppy person is meticulously creating new piles of papers with new headings and scrupulously stopping to read all the old book catalogs before he throws them away. A neat person would just bulldoze the desk.

6   Neat people are bums and clods at heart. They have cavalier attitudes toward possessions, including family heirlooms. Everything is just another dust-catcher to them. If anything collects dust, it's got to go and that's that. Neat people will toy with the idea of throwing the children out of the house just to cut down on the clutter.

7   Neat people don't care about process. They like results. What they want to do is get the whole thing over with so they can sit down and watch the rasslin' on TV. Neat people operate on two unvarying principles: Never handle any item twice, and throw everything away.

8   The only thing messy in a neat person's house is the trash can. The minute something comes to a neat person's hand, he will look at it, try to decide if it has immediate use and, finding none, throw it in the trash.

9   Neat people are especially vicious with mail. They never go through their mail unless they are standing directly over a trash can. If the trash can is beside the mailbox, even better. All ads, catalogs, pleas for charitable contributions, church bulletins, and money-saving coupons go straight into the trash can without being opened. All letters from home, postcards from Europe, bills, and paychecks are opened, immediately responded to, then dropped in the trash can. Neat people keep their receipts only for tax purposes. That's it. No sentimental salvaging of birthday cards or the last letter a dying relative ever wrote. Into the trash it goes.

10   Neat people place neatness above everything, even economics. They are incredibly wasteful. Neat people throw away several toys every time they walk through the den. I knew a neat person once who threw away a perfectly good dish drainer because it had mold on it. The drainer was too much trouble to wash. And neat people sell their furniture when they move. They will sell a La-Z-Boy recliner while you are reclining in it.

11   Neat people are no good to borrow from. Neat people buy everything in expensive little single portions. They get their flour and sugar in two-pound bags. They

wouldn't consider clipping a coupon, saving a leftover, reusing plastic nondairy whipped cream containers, or rinsing off tin foil and draping it over the unmoldy dish drainer. You can never borrow a neat person's newspaper to see what's playing at the movies. Neat people have the paper all wadded up and in the trash by 7:05 A.M.

12   Neat people cut a clean swath through the organic as well as the inorganic world. People, animals, and things are all one to them. They are so insensitive. After they've finished with the pantry, the medicine cabinet, and the attic, they will throw out the red geranium (too many leaves), sell the dog (too many fleas), and send the children off to boarding school (too many scuff-marks on the hardwood floors).

Questions for Analysis

1. What is thesis of Suzanne Britt's essay? Underline it.
2. What is the effect of beginning sentences with the word "Someday" in the third paragraph?
3. Britt claims in the second paragraph that sloppy people have "extreme moral rectitude." What does she mean by this? (Notice her explanation that follows this claim.).
4. Britt uses a whole-to-whole comparison. What sentence signals the beginning of the discussion of neat people? Does it begin a paragraph or end one? Why?
5. Britt also claims that neat people "are bums and clods at heart." What does she mean by this?
6. Britt is joking in her comparison, but is there any truth to what she says? What points do you think are really valid?

Writing Assignments

1. Are you a neat or a sloppy person? Describe your routines for organizing your room, your kitchen, your files, your closet, or your desk.
2. Perhaps people who can easily make decisions are neat, but people who are indecisive are therefore sloppy. Develop this argument using some of Britt's ideas and details to support it.
3. What is the neatest part of your life, and what is the messiest? Why? Write an essay comparing and explaining these parts.
4. Suzanne Britt, of course, is not serious in her "criticism" of neat people, who actually have a number of positive traits. Write an essay that describes those traits, and cite examples from Britt to support your thesis.

Death of a Moth
Annie Dillard

* * * *

Common sights in nature such as those of insects dying usually don't catch our attention, but Annie Dillard, an essayist and professor at Wesleyan University, has an amazing ability to notice the smallest details of such ordinary things. In the following essay, she focuses on the deaths of a variety of insects. As you read it, notice how she precisely describes the remains of dead insects and spiders, and then describes the fiery death of a moth. Notice how she moves back and forth in time from yesterday, to today, to two years ago, and then to the present. As you will see, too, Dillard is an avid reader; she makes reference in this essay to Arthur Rimbaud, a nineteenth-century French poet who did most of his writing before he was twenty years old.

1   I live alone with two cats, who sleep on my legs. There is a yellow one, and a black one whose name is Small. In the morning I joke to the black one, Do you remember last night? Do you remember? I throw them both out before breakfast, so I can eat.

2   There is a spider, too, in the bathroom, of uncertain lineage, bulbous at the abdomen and drab, whose six-inch mess of web works, works somehow, works miraculously, to keep her alive and me amazed. The web is in a corner behind the toilet, connecting tile wall to tile wall. The house is new, the bathroom immaculate, save for the spider, her web, and the sixteen or so corpses she's tossed to the floor.

3   The corpses appear to be mostly sow bugs, those little armadillo creatures who live to travel flat out in houses, and die round. In addition to sow-bug husks, hollow and sipped empty of color, there are what seem to be two or three wingless moth bodies, one new flake of earwig, and three spider carcasses crinkled and clenched.

4   I wonder on what fool's errand an earwig, or a moth, or a sow bug, would visit that clean corner of the house behind the toilet; I have not noticed any blind parades of sow bugs blundering into corners. Yet they do hazard there, at a rate of more than one a week, and the spider thrives. Yesterday she was working on the earwig, mouth on gut; today he's on the floor. It must take a certain genius to throw things away from there, to find a straight line through that sticky tangle to the floor.

5   Today the earwig shines darkly, and gleams, what there is of him: a dorsal curve of thorax and abdomen, and a smooth pair of pincers by which I knew his name. Next week, if the other bodies are any indication, he'll be shrunk and gray, webbed to the floor with dust. The sow bugs beside him are curled and empty, fragile, a breath away from brittle fluff. The spiders lie on their sides, translucent and ragged, their legs drying in knots. The moths stagger against each other, headless, in a confusion of arcing strips of chitin like peeling varnish, like a jumble of buttresses for cathedral vaults, like nothing resembling moths, so that I would hesitate to call them moths, except that I have had some experience with the figure moth reduced to a nub.

6   Two summers ago I was camped alone in the Blue Ridge Mountains of Virginia. I had hauled myself and gear up there to read, among other things, *The Day on Fire,* by James Ullman, a novel about Rimbaud that had made me want to be a writer when I was sixteen; I was hoping it would do it again. So I read every day sitting under a tree by my tent, while warblers sang in the leaves overhead and bristle worms trailed their inches over the twiggy dirt at my feet; and I read every night by candlelight, while barred owls called in the forest and pale moths seeking mates massed round my head in the clearing, where my light made a ring.

7   Moths kept flying into the candle. They would hiss and recoil, reeling upside down in the shadows among my cooking pans. Or they would singe their wings and fall, and their hot wings, as if melted, would stick to the first thing they touched—a pan, a lid, a spoon—so that the snagged moths could struggle only in tiny arcs, unable to flutter free. These I could release by a quick flip with a stick; in the morning I would find my cooking stuff decorated with torn flecks of moth wings, ghostly triangles of shiny dust here and there on the aluminum. So I read, and boiled water, and replenished candles, and read on.

8   One night a moth flew into the candle, was caught, burnt dry, and held. I must have been staring at the candle, or maybe I looked up when a shadow crossed my page; at any rate, I saw it all. A golden female moth, a biggish one with a two-inch wingspread, flapped into the fire, dropped abdomen into the wet wax, stuck, flamed, and frazzled in a second. Her moving wings ignited like tissue paper, like angels' wings, enlarging the circle of light in the clearing and creating out of the darkness the sudden blue sleeves of my sweater, the green leaves of jewelweed by my side, the ragged red trunk of a pine; at once the light contracted again and the moth's wings vanished in a fine, foul smoke. At the same time, her six legs clawed,

curled, blackened, and ceased, disappearing utterly. And her head jerked in spasms, making a spattering noise; her antennae crisped and burnt away and her heaving mouthparts cracked like pistol fire. When it was all over, her head was, so far as I could determine, gone, gone the long way of her wings and legs. Her head was a hole lost to time. All that was left was the glowing horn shell of her abdomen and thorax—a fraying, partially collapsed gold tube jammed upright in the candle's round pool.

9   And then this moth-essence, this spectacular skeleton, began to act as a wick. She kept burning. The wax rose in the moth's body from her soaking abdomen to her thorax to the shattered hole where her head should have been, and widened into flame, a saffron-yellow flame that robed her to the ground like an immolating monk. That candle had two wicks, two winding flames of identical light, side by side. The moth's head was fire. She burned for two hours, until I blew her out.

10   She burned for two hours without changing, without swaying or kneeling—only glowing within, like a building fire glimpsed through silhouetted walls, like a hollow saint, like a flame-faced virgin gone to God, while I read by her light, kindled, while Rimbaud in Paris burnt out his brain in a thousand poems, while night pooled wetly at my feet.

11   So. That is why I think those hollow shreds on the bathroom floor are moths. I believe I know what moths look like, in any state.

12   I have three candles here on the table which I disentangle from the plants and light when visitors come. The cats avoid them, although Small's tail caught fire once; I rubbed it out before she noticed. I don't mind living alone. I like eating alone and reading. I don't mind sleeping alone. The only time I mind being alone is when something is funny; then, when I am laughing at something funny, I wish someone were around. Sometimes I think it is pretty funny that I sleep alone.

Questions for Analysis

1. In the second paragraph, Dillard says that the spider amazes her. What description does she provide that might justify her amazement?

2. What are the stages in the process by which the moth dies? Near the end of the essay, Dillard explains why she describes the death. Why does she do so? Do you think her stated reason is the only one?

3. Dillard doesn't reveal her feelings about the death of the moth. How do you think she feels about her relationship with animals, big and small? What evidence can you cite from the essay to support you opinion?

4. The last paragraph of the essay is somewhat puzzling. What do you think Dillard means when she discusses things that are funny? She claims that she is alone, but perhaps she isn't. Who are her companions?

Writing Assignments

1. Describe a process in nature that you have observed—perhaps the birth of a kitten or puppy, the hatching of an egg, an animal grooming itself or another animal, a fight between two animals, or even the rituals a cat or dog goes through in getting ready to sleep or eat. Be specific.

2. Have you ever gone camping, hiking, fishing, or hunting? Describe one outdoor experience in detail.

3. Write an essay on what you enjoy about being alone. If you wish, you can focus on one experience. Specifically describe what you do or did.

4. Write an essay in which you explain Annie Dillard's apparent relationship with nature, citing evidence from the essay.

Living in Two Worlds
Marcus Mabry

* * * *

Many students who are the first in the families to enter college find themselves living in two worlds, especially if they come from impoverished environments. Marcus Mabry, a senior editor of Newsweek *magazine's international edition, explores the conflicts between those two worlds in the following essay. As you read it, notice his discussion of the mixed feelings he holds: guilt, helplessness, and embarrassment. Notice how he explores each of those feelings through examples. Finally, notice the conflict he introduces between his own feelings and those of his family and friends.*

1   A round, green cardboard sign hangs from a string proclaiming, "We built a proud new feeling," the slogan of a local supermarket. It is a souvenir from one of my brother's last jobs. In addition to being a bagger, he's worked at a fast-food restaurant, a gas station, a garage and a textile factory. Now, in the icy clutches of the Northeastern winter, he is unemployed. He will soon be a father. He is 19 years old.

2   In mid-December I was at Stanford, among the palm trees and weighty chores of academe. And all I wanted to do was get out. I joined the rest of the undergrads in a chorus of excitement, singing the praises of Christmas break. No classes, no midterms, no finals . . . and no freshmen! (I'm a resident assistant.) Awesome! I was looking forward to escaping. I never gave a thought to what I was escaping to.

3   Once I got home to New Jersey, reality returned. My dreaded freshmen had been replaced by unemployed relatives; badgering professors had been replaced by hard-working single mothers, and cold classrooms by dilapidated bedrooms and kitchens. The room in which the "proud new feeling" sign hung contained the belongings of myself, my mom and my brother. But for these two weeks it was mine. They slept downstairs on couches.

4   Most students who travel between the universes of poverty and affluence during breaks experience similar conditions, as well as the guilt, the helplessness and, sometimes, the embarrassment associated with them. Our friends are willing to listen, but most of them are unable to imagine the pain of the impoverished lives that we see every six months. Each time I return home I feel further away from the realities of poverty in America and more ashamed that they are allowed to persist. What frightens me most is not that the American socioeconomic system permits poverty to continue, but that by participating in that system I share some of the blame.

5   Last year I lived in an on-campus apartment, with a (relatively) modern bathroom, kitchen and two bedrooms. Using summer earnings, I added some expensive prints, a potted palm and some other plants, making the place look like the more-than-humble abode of a New York City Yuppie. I gave dinner parties, even a *soirée française* [an elegant French evening].

6   For my roommate, a doctor's son, this kind of life was nothing extraordinary. But my mom was struggling to provide a life for herself and my brother. In addition to working 24-hour-a-day cases as a practical nurse, she was trying to ensure that my brother would graduate from high school and have a decent life. She knew that she had to compete for his attention with drugs and other potentially dangerous things that can look attractive to a young man when he sees no better future.

7   Living in my grandmother's house this Christmas break restored all the forgotten, and the never acknowledged, guilt. I had gone to boarding school on a full scholarship since the ninth grade, so being away from poverty was not new. But my own growing affluence has increased my distance. My friends say that I should not feel guilty: what could I do substantially for my family at this age, they ask. Even though I know that education is the right thing to do, I can't help but feel, sometimes, that I have it too good. There is no reason that I deserve security and warmth, while my

brother has to cope with potential unemployment and prejudice. I, too, encounter prejudice, but it is softened by my status as a student in an affluent and intellectual community.

8   More than my sense of guilt, my sense of helplessness increases each time I return home. As my success leads me further away for longer periods of time, poverty becomes harder to conceptualize and feels that much more oppressive when I visit with it. The first night of break, I lay in our bedroom, on a couch that let out into a bed that took up the whole room, except for a space heater. It was a little hard to sleep because the springs from the couch stuck through at inconvenient spots. But it would have been impossible to sleep anyway because of the groans coming from my grandmother's room next door. Only in her early 60s, she suffers from many chronic diseases and couldn't help but moan, then pray aloud, then moan, then pray aloud.

9   This wrenching of my heart was interrupted by the 3 A.M. entry of a relative who had been allowed to stay at the house despite rowdy behavior and threats toward the family in the past. As he came into the house, he slammed the door, and his heavy steps shook the second floor as he stomped into my grandmother's room to take his place, at the foot of her bed. There he slept, without blankets on a bare mattress. This was the first night. Later in the vacation, a Christmas turkey and a Christmas ham were stolen from my aunt's refrigerator on Christmas Eve. We think the thief was a relative. My mom and I decided not to exchange gifts that year because it just didn't seem festive.

10   A few days after New Year's I returned to California. The Northeast was soon hit by a blizzard. They were there, and I was here. That was the way it had to be, for now. I haven't forgotten; the ache of knowing their suffering is always there. It has to be kept deep down, or I can't find the logic in studying and partying while people, my people, are being killed by poverty. Ironically, success drives me away from those I most want to help by getting an education.

11   Somewhere in the midst of all that misery, my family has built, within me, "a proud feeling." As I travel between the two worlds it becomes harder to remember just how proud I should be—not just because of where I have come from and where I am going, but because of where they are. The fact that they survive in the world in which they live is something to be very proud of, indeed. It inspires within me a sense of tenacity and accomplishment that I hope every college graduate will someday possess.

Questions for Analysis

1. What is the topic sentence of the third paragraph? Mabry provides a number of contrasts to support the topic sentence. Underline them.
2. What is the most important point of the fourth paragraph? How do the contrasts he draws in the fifth and sixth paragraphs support that point?
3. In paragraph 7, Mabry explores his sense of guilt. What makes him feel guilty?
4. And in the final paragraph, Mabry explains his "proud feeling." What is he proud of? How does this sense of pride contrast with the things he is proud of (or should be proud of)?

Writing Assignments

1. Have you ever experienced a time when you felt torn between two worlds? Focus on a single event to explain, and compare and contrast, the two worlds.
2. An African proverb says, "It takes a village to raise a child." How does this proverb apply to Mabry?
3. Mabry seems to feel guilty about his accomplishments. Should he feel that way? Write an essay in which you explore this issue, supporting your thesis with details from Mabry's essay.

The Myth of the Latin Woman
Judith Ortiz Cofer

* * * *

Prejudice and stereotyping are often the results of lack of knowledge. In the follow-
ing essay, taken from The Latin Deli: Prose and Poetry, *Judith Ortiz Cofer describes*
her encounters with stereotyping and prejudice through much of her life. Ms. Cofer
is a novelist and poet who was born in Puerto Rico but did her graduate work at
Oxford University in England. As you read it, notice how she tells the story of an em-
barrassing experience in the present time, then returns to her past to describe other
such embarrassing moments. Notice how she examines the reasons behind many
practices and customs of Puerto Rican women that are misinterpreted by non-
Hispanics. And notice how she discusses her own attempts to clear up some of
these misconceptions.

1   On a bus trip to London from Oxford University where I was earning some graduate credits one summer, a young man, obviously fresh from a pub, spotted me and
as if struck by inspiration went down on his knees in the aisle. With both hands over
his heart he broke into an Irish tenor's rendition of "Maria" from *West Side Story.* My
politely amused fellow passengers gave his lovely voice the round of gentle applause it deserved. Though I was not quite as amused, I managed my version of an
English smile: no show of teeth, no extreme contortions of the facial muscles—I was
at this time of my life practicing reserve and cool. Oh, that British control, how I cov-
eted it. But "Maria" had followed me to London, reminding me of a prime fact of my
life: you can leave the island, master the English language, and travel as far as you
can, but if you are a Latina, especially one like me who so obviously belongs to Rita
Moreno's gene pool, the island travels with you.

2   This is sometimes a very good thing—it may win you that extra minute of someone's attention. But with some people, the same things can make you an island—not
a tropical paradise but an Alcatraz, a place nobody wants to visit. As a Puerto Rican
girl living in the United States and wanting like most children to "belong," I resented
the stereotype that my Hispanic appearance called forth from many people.

3   Growing up in a large urban center in New Jersey during the 1960s, I suffered
from what I think of as "cultural schizophrenia." Our life was designed by my parents
as a microcosm of their *casas* on the island. We spoke in Spanish, ate Puerto Rican
food bought at the *bodega,* and practiced strict Catholicism at a church that allotted
us a one-hour slot each week for mass, performed in Spanish by a Chinese priest
trained as a missionary for Latin America.

4   As a girl I was kept under strict surveillance by my parents, since my virtue and
modesty were, by their cultural equation, the same as their honor. As a teenager I
was lectured constantly on how to behave as a proper *senorita.* But it was a conflicting message I received, since the Puerto Rican mothers also encouraged their
daughters to look and act like women and to dress in clothes our Anglo friends and
their mothers found too "mature" and flashy. The difference was, and is, cultural; yet
I often felt humiliated when I appeared at an American friend's party wearing a
dress more suitable to a semiformal than to a playroom birthday celebration. At
Puerto Rican festivities, neither the music nor the colors we wore could be too loud.

5   I remember Career Day in our high school, when teachers told us to come
dressed as if for a job interview. It quickly became obvious that to the Puerto Rican
girls "dressing up" meant wearing their mothers' ornate jewelry and clothing, more
appropriate (by mainstream standards) for the company Christmas party than as
daily office attire. That morning I had agonized in front of my closet, trying to figure
out what a "career girl" would wear. I knew how to dress for school (at the Catholic
school I attended, we all wore uniforms), I knew how to dress for Sunday mass, and I
knew what dresses to wear for parties at my relatives' homes. Though I do not recall

the precise details of my Career Day outfit, it must have been a composite of these choices. But I remember a comment my friend (an Italian American) made in later years that coalesced my impressions of that day. She said that at the business school she was attending, the Puerto Rican girls always stood out for wearing "everything at once." She meant, of course, too much jewelry, too many accessories. On that day at school we were simply made the negative models by the nuns, who were themselves not credible fashion experts to any of us. But it was painfully obvious to me that to the others, in their tailored skirts and silk blouses, we must have seemed "hopeless" and "vulgar." Though I now know that most adolescents feel out of step much of the time, I also know that for the Puerto Rican girls of my generation that sense was intensified. The way our teachers and classmates looked at us that day in school was just a taste of the cultural clash that awaited us in the real world, where prospective employers and men on the street would often misinterpret our tight skirts and jingling bracelets as a "come-on."

6   Mixed cultural signals have perpetuated certain stereotypes—for example, that of the Hispanic woman as the "hot tamale" or sexual firebrand. It is a one-dimensional view that the media have found easy to promote. In their special vocabulary, advertisers have designated "sizzling" and "smoldering" as the adjectives of choice for describing not only the foods but also the women of Latin America. From conversations in my house I recall hearing about the harassment that Puerto Rican women endured in factories where the "boss-men" talked to them as if sexual innuendo was all they understood, and worse, often gave them the choice of submitting to their advances or being fired.

7   It is custom, however, not chromosomes, that leads us to choose scarlet over pale pink. As young girls, it was our mothers who influenced our decisions about clothes and colors—mothers who had grown up on a tropical island where the natural environment was a riot of primary colors, where showing your skin was one way to keep cool as well as to look sexy. Most important of all, on the island, women perhaps felt freer to dress and move more provocatively since, in most cases, they were protected by the traditions, mores, and laws of a Spanish/Catholic system of morality and machismo whose main rule was: *You may look at my sister, but if you touch her I will kill you.* The extended family and church structure could provide a young woman with a circle of safety in her small pueblo on the island; if a man "wronged" a girl, everyone would close in to save her family honor.

8   My mother has told me about dressing in her best party clothes on Saturday nights and going to the town's plaza to promenade with her girlfriends in front of the boys they liked. The males were thus given an opportunity to admire the women and to express their admiration in the form of *piropos:* erotically charged street poems they composed on the spot. (I have myself been subjected to a few *piropos* while visiting the island, and they can be outrageous, although custom dictates that they must never cross into obscenity.) This ritual, as I understand it, also entails a show of studied indifference on the woman's part; if she is "decent," she must not acknowledge the man's impassioned words. So I do understand how things can be lost in translation. When a Puerto Rican girl dressed in her idea of what is attractive meets a man from the mainstream culture who has been trained to react to certain types of clothing as a sexual signal, a clash is likely to take place. I remember the boy who took me to my first formal dance leaning over to plant a sloppy, overeager kiss painfully on my mouth; when I didn't respond with sufficient passion, he remarked resentfully: "I thought you Latin girls were supposed to mature early," as if I were expected to ripen like a fruit or vegetable, not just grow into womanhood like other girls.

9   It is surprising to my professional friends that even today some people, including those who should know better, still put others "in their place." It happened to me most recently during a stay at a classy metropolitan hotel favored by young professional couples for weddings. Late one evening after the theater, as I walked toward my room with a colleague (a woman with whom I was coordinating an arts program),

a middle-aged man in a tuxedo, with a young girl in satin and lace on his arm, stepped directly into our path. With his champagne glass extended toward me, he exclaimed "Evita!"

10   Our way blocked, my companion and I listened as the man half-recited, half-bellowed "Don't Cry for Me, Argentina." When he finished, the young girl said: "How about a round of applause for my daddy?" We complied, hoping this would bring the silly spectacle to a close. I was becoming aware that our little group was attracting the attention of the other guests. "Daddy" must have perceived this too, and he once more barred the way as we tried to walk past him. He began to shout-sing a ditty to the tune of "La Bamba"—except the lyrics were about a girl named Maria whose exploits rhymed with her name and gonorrhea. The girl kept saying, "Oh, Daddy," and looking at me with pleading eyes. She wanted me to laugh along with the others. My companion and I stood silently waiting for the man to end his offensive song. When he finished, I looked not at him but at his daughter. I advised her calmly never to ask her father what he had done in the army. Then I walked between them and to my room. My friend complimented me on my cool handling of the situation, but I confessed that I had really wanted to push the jerk into the swimming pool. This same man—probably a corporate executive, well-educated, even worldly by most standards—would not have been likely to regale an Anglo woman with a dirty song in public. He might have checked his impulse by assuming that she could be somebody's wife or mother, or at least *somebody* who might take offense. But, to him, I was just an Evita or a Maria: merely a character in his cartoon-populated universe.

11   Another facet of the myth of the Latin woman in the United States is the menial, the domestic—Maria the housemaid or countergirl. It's true that work as domestics, as waitresses, and in factories is all that's available to women with little English and few skills. But the myth of the Hispanic menial—the funny maid, mispronouncing words and cooking up a spicy storm in a shiny California kitchen—has been perpetuated by the media in the same way that "Mammy" from *Gone with the Wind* became America's idea of the black woman for generations. Since I do not wear my diplomas around my neck for all to see, I have on occasion been sent to that "kitchen" where some think I obviously belong.

12   One incident has stayed with me, though I recognize it as a minor offense. My first public poetry reading took place in Miami, at a restaurant where a luncheon was being held before the event. I was nervous and excited as I walked in with notebook in hand. An older woman motioned me to her table, and thinking (foolish me) that she wanted me to autograph a copy of my newly published slender volume of verse, I went over. She ordered a cup of coffee from me, assuming that I was the waitress. (Easy enough to mistake my poems for menus, I suppose.) I know it wasn't an intentional act of cruelty. Yet of all the good things that happened later, I remember that scene most clearly, because it reminded me of what I had to overcome before anyone would take me seriously. In retrospect I understand that my anger gave my reading fire. In fact, I have almost always taken any doubt in my abilities as a challenge, the result most often being the satisfaction of winning a convert, of seeing the cold, appraising eyes warm to my words, the body language change, the smile that indicates I have opened some avenue for communication. So that day as I read, I looked directly at that woman. Her lowered eyes told me she was embarrassed at her *faux pas* [in French, literally a "false step"], and when I willed her to look up at me, she graciously allowed me to punish her with my full attention. We shook hands at the end of the reading and I never saw her again. She has probably forgotten the entire incident, but maybe not.

13   Yet I am one of the lucky ones. There are thousands of Latinas without the privilege of an education or the entrées into society that I have. For them life is a constant struggle against the misconceptions perpetuated by the myth of the Latina. My goal is to try to replace the old stereotypes with a much more interesting set of

realities. Every time I give a reading, I hope the stories I tell, the dreams and fears I examine in my work, can achieve some universal truth that will get my audience past the particulars of my skin color, my accent, or my clothes.

14   I once wrote a poem in which I called all Latinas "God's brown daughters." This poem is really a prayer of sorts, offered upward, but also, through the human-to-human channel of art, outward. It is a prayer for communication and for respect. In it, Latin women pray "in Spanish to an Anglo God/ with a Jewish heritage," and they are "fervently hoping/ that if not omnipotent,/ at least He be bilingual."

Questions for Analysis

1. Who is the primary audience for this essay?
2. What is Judith Ortiz Cofer's purpose in writing this essay? What does she want her readers to know and do? Write an explanation of that purpose in your own words.
3. List the common stereotypes about Puerto Rican women that Cofer identifies.
4. Throughout the essay, Cofer contrasts false perceptions about Latin women with actual realities. What are those perceptions? How is life on the island of Puerto Rico different from life on the mainland?
5. In paragraph 3, Cofer says she suffered from "cultural schizophrenia." Write, in your own words, what she means.
6. Why, according to Cofer, do Puerto Rican women dress in ways that "Anglo" men find provocative?

Writing Assignments

1. Have you ever been stereotyped by another person and treated rudely—or worse? Describe the experience, and try to explain why the person acted as he or she did.
2. Do you follow some custom that people from outside your culture, religion, nationality, or race might not understand? Explain the custom and the reasons behind it.
3. Do your parents or caregivers have attitudes or beliefs that you don't share? Contrast those beliefs or attitudes with yours, and try to explain why they differ.
4. Cofer discusses a somewhat conflicting set of morals and values that her parents taught her. How do these values compare to the ones your parents or caregivers taught you? Write an essay in which you examine these comparisons.

Mother Tongue
Amy Tan

* * * *

We use language to communicate—to bring us together so we understand each other better. But we also use language to separate ourselves from others: we classify people into groups according to the way they speak or write. Amy Tan is well aware of this issue. The author of several novels about Chinese immigrant women and the first-generation American daughters, she has explored the conflicts and connections between the generations—especially as the conflicts and connections relate to language and what the language represents.

As you read the following essay, notice the contrasts it draws between the language Tan uses with the general public and with her mother. Notice its point about how language does not reflect intelligence, and about how rudely people treat those who don't speak in standard ways. Notice, too, Tan's account of how and why she became a writer.

1   I am not a scholar of English or literature. I cannot give you much more than personal opinions on the English language and its variations in this country or others.

2   I am a writer. And by that definition, I am someone who has always loved language. I am fascinated by language in daily life. I spend a great deal of my time thinking about the power of language—the way it can evoke an emotion, a visual image, a complex idea, or a simple truth. Language is the tool of my trade. And I use them all—all the Englishes I grew up with.

3   Recently, I was made keenly aware of the different Englishes I do use. I was giving a talk to a large group of people, the same talk I had already given to half a dozen other groups. The nature of the talk was about my writing, my life, and my book, *The Joy Luck Club.* The talk was going along well enough, until I remembered one major difference that made the whole talk sound wrong. My mother was in the room. And it was perhaps the first time she had heard me give a lengthy speech, using the kind of English I have never used with her. I was saying things like, "The intersection of memory upon imagination" and "There is an aspect of my fiction that relates to thus and thus"—a speech filled with carefully wrought grammatical phrases, burdened, it suddenly seemed to me, with nominalized forms, past perfect tenses, conditional phrases, all the forms of standard English that I had learned in school and through books, the forms of English I did not use at home with my mother.

4   Just last week, I was walking down the street with my mother, and I again found myself conscious of the English I was using, the English I do use with her. We were talking about the price of new and used furniture and I heard myself saying this: "Not waste money that way." My husband was with us as well, and he didn't notice any switch in my English. And then I realized why. It's because over the twenty years we've been together I've often used that same kind of English with him, and sometimes he even uses it with me. It has become our language of intimacy, a different sort of English that relates to family talk, the language I grew up with.

5   So you'll have some idea of what this family talk I heard sounds like, I'll quote what my mother said during a recent conversation which I videotaped and then transcribed. During this conversation, my mother was talking about a political gangster in Shanghai who had the same last name as her family's, Du, and how the gangster in his early years wanted to be adopted by her family, which was rich by comparison. Later, the gangster became more powerful, far richer than my mother's family, and one day showed up at my mother's wedding to pay his respects. Here's what she said in part:

6   "Du Yusong having business like fruit stand. Like off the street kind. He is Du like Du Zong—but not Tsung-ming Island people. The local people call putong, the river east side, he belong to that side local people. That man want to ask Du Zong father take him in like become own family. Du Zong father wasn't look down on him, but didn't take seriously, until that man big like become a mafia. Now important person, very hard to inviting him. Chinese way, came only to show respect, don't stay for dinner. Respect for making big celebration, he shows up. Mean gives lots of respect. Chinese custom. Chinese social life that way. If too important won't have to stay too long. He come to my wedding. I didn't see, I heard it. I gone to boy's side, they have YMCA dinner. Chinese age I was nineteen."

7   You should know that my mother's expressive command of English belies how much she actually understands. She reads the *Forbes* report, listens to *Wall Street Week,* converses daily with her stockbroker, reads all of Shirley MacLaine's books with ease—all kinds of things I can't begin to understand. Yet some of my friends tell me they understand 50 percent of what my mother says. Some say they understand 80 to 90 percent. Some say they understand none of it, as if she were speaking pure Chinese. But to me, my mother's English is perfectly clear, perfectly natural. It's my mother tongue. Her language, as I hear it, is vivid, direct, full of observation and imagery. That was the language that helped shape the way I saw things, expressed things, made sense of the world.

8   Lately, I've been giving more thought to the kind of English my mother speaks. Like others, I have described it to people as "broken" or "fractured" English. But I wince when I say that. It has always bothered me that I can think of no way to describe it other than "broken," as if it were damaged and needed to be fixed, as if it lacked a certain wholeness and soundness. I've heard other terms used, "limited English," for example. But they seem just as bad, as if everything is limited, including people's perceptions of the limited English speaker.

9   I know this for a fact, because when I was growing up, my mother's "limited" English limited my perception of her. I was ashamed of her English. I believed that her English reflected the quality of what she had to say. That is, because she expressed them imperfectly her thoughts were imperfect. And I had plenty of empirical evidence to support me: the fact that people in department stores, at banks, and at restaurants did not take her seriously, did not give her good service, pretended not to understand her, or even acted as if they did not hear her.

10   My mother has long realized the limitations of her English as well. When I was fifteen, she used to have me call people on the phone to pretend I was she. In this guise, I was forced to ask for information or even to complain and yell at people who had been rude to her. One time it was a call to her stockbroker in New York. She had cashed out her small portfolio and it just so happened we were going to go to New York the next week, our very first trip outside California. I had to get on the phone and say in an adolescent voice that was not very convincing, "This is Mrs. Tan."

11   And my mother was standing in the back whispering loudly, "Why he don't send me check, already two weeks late. So mad he lie to me, losing me money."

12   And then I said in perfect English, "Yes, I'm getting rather concerned. You had agreed to send the check two weeks ago, but it hasn't arrived."

13   Then she began to talk more loudly. "What he want, I come to New York tell him front of his boss, you cheating me?" And I was trying to calm her down, make her be quiet, while telling the stockbroker, "I can't tolerate any more excuses. If I don't receive the check immediately, I am going to have to speak to your manager when I'm in New York next week." And sure enough, the following week there we were in front of this astonished stockbroker, and I was sitting there red-faced and quiet, and my mother, the real Mrs. Tan, was shouting at his boss in her impeccable broken English.

14   We used a similar routine just five days ago, for a situation that was far less humorous. My mother had gone to the hospital for an appointment, to find out about a benign brain tumor a CAT scan had revealed a month ago. She said she had spoken very good English, her best English, no mistakes. Still, she said, the hospital did not apologize when they said they had lost the CAT scan and she had come for nothing. She said they did not seem to have any sympathy when she told them she was anxious to know the exact diagnosis, since her husband and son had both died of brain tumors. She said they would not give her any more information until the next time and she would have to make another appointment for that. So she said she would not leave until the doctor called her daughter. She wouldn't budge. And when the doctor finally called her daughter, me, who spoke in perfect English—lo and behold—we had assurances the CAT scan would be found, promises that a conference call on Monday would be held, and apologies for any suffering my mother had gone through for a most regrettable mistake.

15   I think my mother's English almost had an effect on limiting my possibilities in life as well. Sociologists and linguists probably will tell you that a person's developing language skills are more influenced by peers. But I do think that the language spoken in the family, especially in immigrant families which are more insular, plays a large role in shaping the language of the child. And I believe that it affected my results on achievement tests, IQ tests, and the SAT. While my English skills were never judged as poor, compared to math, English could not be considered my strong suit. In grade school I did moderately well, getting perhaps B's, sometimes B-pluses, in English and scoring perhaps in the 60th or 70th percentile on achievement tests.

But those scores were not good enough to override the opinion that my true abilities lay in math and science, because in those areas I achieved A's and scored in the 90th percentile or higher.

16   This was understandable. Math is precise; there is only one correct answer. Whereas, for me at least, the answers on English tests were always a judgment call, a matter of opinion and personal experience. Those tests were constructed around items like fill-in-the-blank sentence completion, such as, "Even though Tom was _____, Mary thought he was _____." And the correct answer always seemed to be the most bland combinations of thoughts, for example, "Even though Tom was shy, Mary thought he was charming," with the grammatical structure "even though" limiting the correct answer to some sort of semantic opposites, so you wouldn't get answers like, "Even though Tom was foolish, Mary thought he was ridiculous." Well, according to my mother, there were very few limitations as to what Tom could have been and what Mary might have thought of him. So I never did well on tests like that.

17   The same was true with word analogies, pairs of words in which you were supposed to find some sort of logical, semantic relationship—for example, "*Sunset* is to *nightfall* as _____ is to _____." And here you would be presented with a list of four possible pairs, one of which showed the same kind of relationship: *red* is to *stoplight, bus* is to *arrival, chills* is to *fever, yawn* is to *boring.* Well, I could never think that way. I knew what the tests were asking, but I could not block out of my mind the images already created by the first pair, "*sunset* is to *nightfall*"—and I would see a burst of colors against a darkening sky, the moon rising, the lowering of a curtain of stars. And all the other pairs of words—red, bus, stoplight, boring—just threw up a mass of confusing images, making it impossible for me to sort out something as logical as saying: "A sunset precedes nightfall" is the same as "a chill precedes a fever." The only way I would have gotten that answer right would have been to imagine an associative situation, for example, my being disobedient and staying out past sunset, catching a chill at night, which turns into feverish pneumonia as punishment, which indeed did happen to me.

18   I have been thinking about all this lately, about my mother's English, about achievement tests. Because lately I've been asked, as a writer, why there are not more Asian-Americans represented in American literature. Why are there few Asian-Americans enrolled in creative writing programs? Why do so many Chinese students go into engineering? Well, these are broad sociological questions I can't begin to answer. But I have noticed in surveys—in fact, just last week—that Asian students, as a whole, always do significantly better on math achievement tests than in English. And this makes me think that there are other Asian-American students whose English spoken in the home might also be described as "broken" or "limited." And perhaps they also have teachers who are steering them away from writing and into math and science, which is what happened to me.

19   Fortunately, I happen to be rebellious in nature and enjoy the challenge of disproving assumptions made about me. I became an English major my first year in college, after being enrolled as pre-med. I started writing nonfiction as a freelancer the week after I was told by my former boss that writing was my worst skill and I should hone my talents toward account management.

20   But it wasn't until 1985 that I finally began to write fiction. And at first I wrote using what I thought to be wittily crafted sentences, sentences that would finally prove I had mastery over the English language. Here's an example from the first draft of a story that later made its way into *The Joy Luck Club,* but without this line: "That was my mental quandary in its nascent state." A terrible line, which I can barely pronounce.

21   Fortunately, for reasons I won't get into today, I later decided I should envision a reader for the stories I would write. And the reader I decided upon was my mother, because these were stories about mothers. So with this reader in mind—and in fact she did read my early drafts—I began to write stories using all the Englishes I grew up with: the English I spoke to my mother, which for lack of a better term might be

described as "simple"; the English she used with me, which for lack of a better term might be described as "broken"; my translation of her Chinese, which could certainly be described as "watered down"; and what I imagined to be her translation of her Chinese if she could speak in perfect English, her internal language, and for that I sought to preserve the essence, but neither an English nor a Chinese structure. I wanted to capture what language ability tests can never reveal: her intent, her passion, her imagery, the rhythms of her speech and the nature of her thoughts.

22   Apart from what any critic had to say about my writing, I knew I had succeeded where it counted when my mother finished reading my book and gave me her verdict: "So easy to read."

Questions for Analysis

1. What, according to Amy Tan, made her self-conscious about the English she "had learned in school or through books"?
2. Tan says her mother's language "is vivid, direct, full of observation and imagery." Did Tan always feel that way? Why or why not?
3. Tan also claims that the English spoken in her home affected her school performance, test scores, and choice of possible careers. How were these things affected, and why? What does Tan think causes many Chinese to enter engineering programs?
4. Conversely, how did the language of her mother affect Tan's creativity? According to Tan, can this creativity be measured by standardized tests?
5. Tan implies the point of her essay in the last two paragraphs. What is that point? Does the point apply only to herself and her mother?

Writing Assignments

1. Is there a "generation gap" between you and one of your relatives? Describe how you differ, and why.
2. Have you ever overcome a lack of skill in some area? Trace the process you went through to overcome this deficiency. Explain why you chose to overcome it.
3. Do you perceive your parents or caregivers differently now than the way you did as a child? Compare and contrast the ways your perceptions have changed or remained the same.
4. Do you have two or more oral "languages," even if they are just different varieties of English? Which do you use more often, and under what circumstances? Why? Which is easier for you to use? Explain in an essay.
5. Tan's attitude toward her mother changed over time. Write an essay in which you describe that change and explain why you think it happened.

When Bright Girls Decide That Math Is "A Waste of Time"
Susan Jacoby

* * * *

What determines "intelligence" or "talent"? Is it only some trait we are born with, or is it partially influenced by society's expectations toward what we are capable of doing? In the following essay, Susan Jacoby, the author of numerous books, including Wild Justice: the Evolution of Revenge, *and* Half-Jew: A Daughter's Search for Her Family's Buried Past, *examines whether social factors encourage girls to think that they cannot succeed in mathematics or the sciences. As you read it, notice the comparisons Jacoby makes between skill in English and skill in mathematics, as well as the comparisons between attitudes in the 1930s and attitudes today. Notice her discussion of the role of adolescence in influencing girls' attitudes toward mathematical ability. Finally, notice her analysis of traditional views of "masculine" and "feminine" knowledge.*

The person she mentions in paragraph 7 is Joseph Stalin, a Russian dictator who killed millions of his own citizens and imprisoned many more.

1   Susannah, a sixteen-year-old who has always been an A student in every subject from algebra to English, recently informed her parents that she intended to drop physics and calculus in her senior year of high school and replace them with a drama seminar and a work-study program. She expects a major in art or history in college, she explained, and "any more science or math will just be a waste of my time."

2   Her parents were neither concerned by nor opposed to her decision. "Fine, dear," they said. Their daughter is, after all, an outstanding student. What does it matter if, at age sixteen, she has taken a step that may limit her understanding of both machines and the natural world for the rest of her life?

3   This kind of decision, in which girls turn away from studies that would give them a sure footing in the world of science and technology, is a self-inflicted female disability that is, regrettably, almost as common today as it was when I was in high school. If Susannah had announced that she had decided to stop taking English in her senior year, her mother and father would have been horrified. I also think they would have been a good deal less sanguine about her decision if she were a boy.

4   In saying that scientific and mathematical ignorance is a self-inflicted female wound, I do not, obviously, mean that cultural expectations play no role in the process. But the world does not conspire to deprive modern women of access to science as it did in the 1930s, when Rosalyn S. Yalow, the Nobel Prize-winning physicist, graduated from Hunter College and was advised to go to work as a secretary because no graduate school would admit her to its physics department. The current generation of adolescent girls—and their parents, bred on old expectations about women's interests—are active conspirators in limiting their own intellectual development.

5   It is true that the proportion of young women in science-related graduate and professional schools, most notably medical schools, has increased significantly in the past decade. It is also true that so few women were studying advanced science and mathematics before the early 1970s that the percentage increase in female enrollment does not yet translate into large numbers of women actually working in science.

6   The real problem is that so many girls eliminate themselves from any serious possibility of studying science as a result of decisions made during the vulnerable period of midadolescence, when they are most likely to be influenced—on both conscious and subconscious levels—by the traditional belief that math and science are "masculine" subjects.

7   During the teen-age years the well-documented phenomenon of "math anxiety" strikes girls who never had any problem handling numbers during earlier schooling. Some men, too, experience this syndrome—a form of panic, akin to a phobia, at any task involving numbers—but women constitute the overwhelming majority of sufferers. The onset of acute math anxiety during the teen-age years is, as Stalin was fond of saying, "not by accident."

8   In adolescence girls begin to fear that they will be unattractive to boys if they are typed as "brains." Science and math epitomize unfeminine braininess in a way that, say, foreign languages do not. High-school girls who pursue an advanced interest in science and math (unless they are students at special institutions like the Bronx High School of Science where everyone is a brain) usually find that they are greatly outnumbered by boys in their classes. They are, therefore, intruding on male turf at a time when their sexual confidence, as well as that of the boys, is most fragile.

9   A 1981 assessment of female achievement in mathematics, based on research conducted under a National Institute for Education grant, found significant differences in the mathematical achievements of ninth and twelfth graders. At age thirteen girls

10   were equal to or slightly better than boys in tests involving algebra, problem solving and spatial ability; four years later the boys had outstripped the girls.

10   It is not mysterious that some very bright high-school girls suddenly decide that math is "too hard" and "a waste of time." In my experience, self-sabotage of mathematical and scientific ability is often a conscious process. I remember deliberately pretending to be puzzled by geometry problems in my sophomore year in high school. A male teacher called me in after class and said, in a baffled tone, "I don't see how you can be having so much trouble when you got straight A's last year in my algebra class."

11   The decision to avoid advanced biology, chemistry, physics and calculus in high school automatically restricts academic and professional choices that ought to be wide open to anyone beginning college. At all coeducational universities women are overwhelmingly concentrated in the fine arts, social sciences and traditionally female departments like education. Courses leading to degrees in science- and technology-related fields are filled mainly by men.

12   In my generation, the practical consequences of mathematical and scientific illiteracy are visible in the large number of special programs to help professional women overcome the anxiety they feel when they are promoted into jobs that require them to handle statistics.

13   The consequences of this syndrome should not, however, be viewed in narrowly professional terms. Competence in science and math does not mean one is going to become a scientist or mathematician any more than competence in writing English means one is going to become a professional writer. Scientific and mathematical illiteracy—which has been cited in several recent critiques by panels studying American education from kindergarten through college—produces an incalculably impoverished vision of human experience.

14   Scientific illiteracy is not, of course, the exclusive province of women. In certain intellectual circles it has become fashionable to proclaim a willed, aggressive ignorance about science and technology. Some female writers specialize in ominous, uninformed diatribes against genetic research as a plot to remove control of childbearing from women, while some well-known men of letters proudly announce that they understand absolutely nothing about computers, or, for that matter, about electricity. This lack of understanding is nothing in which women or men ought to take pride.

15   Failure to comprehend either computers or chromosomes leads to a terrible sense of helplessness, because the profound impact of science on everyday life is evident even to those who insist they don't, won't, can't understand why the changes are taking place. At this stage of history women are more prone to such feelings of helplessness than men because the culture judges their ignorance less harshly and because women themselves acquiesce in that indulgence.

16   Since there is ample evidence of such feelings in adolescence, it is up to parents to see that their daughters do not accede to the old stereotypes about "masculine" and "feminine" knowledge. Unless we want our daughters to share our intellectual handicaps, we had better tell them no, they can't stop taking mathematics and science at the ripe old age of sixteen.

Questions for Analysis

1. The thesis statement of the essay does not appear in the first two paragraphs. What is the thesis statement of the essay? Underline it. What is the function of the first two paragraphs?

2. In the fourth paragraph, why does Jacoby say that culture doesn't play as large a role as it used to in influencing women to abandon math and science? How does this idea relate to the last sentence in the paragraph?

3. Where does Jacoby introduce her view of the real problem, and what is that problem?

4. What, in her view, is the most important reason that girls decide not to do well in math and science?

Writing Assignments

1. Have you ever been discouraged from doing something you thought you could do? Describe what happened and explain why it happened.

2. Have you—or someone you know—done something that didn't fit the traditional "masculine" or "feminine" stereotypes? Describe what you did and explain why you did it.

3. Do adolescent girls (or boys) ever "play dumb" in order to be accepted by their peers? Or do they ever assume roles in order to be accepted? Support your argument with evidence from Jacoby.

4. Write an essay in which you describe, using Jacoby's term, a "self-inflicted disability" that you have had—or that someone you know has had. Give examples to support your description.

5. Amy Tan, in the essay that precedes this one, makes almost the opposite argument about women's abilities in mathematics and science. Write an essay that contrasts her views with Jacoby's and explain why they differ.

Friends, Good Friends—and Such Good Friends
Judith Viorst

* * * *

Probably one of the most clichéd topics for writing is a definition of a "true friend." Judith Viorst, a contributing editor of Redbook *magazine and the author of a number of books for children, avoids that cliché in her essay on friendship. She classifies friends into various types. As you read her essay, note the classifications and examples of each. Note her use of quotations from friends to illustrate her points. And notice how the essay leads, in climax order, up to a definition of a best friend.*

The people she refers to in the second paragraph are Ingmar Bergman, a Swedish director; Albert Camus, a French philosopher; and Lawrence Welk, a television show bandleader.

1   Women are friends, I once would have said, when they totally love and support and trust each other, and bare to each other the secrets of their souls, and run—no questions asked—to help each other, and tell harsh truths to each other (no, you can't wear that dress unless you lose ten pounds first) when harsh truths must be told.

2   Women are friends, I once would have said, when they share the same affection for Ingmar Bergman, plus train rides, cats, warm rain, charades, Camus, and hate with equal ardor Newark and Brussels sprouts and Lawrence Welk and camping.

3   In other words, I once would have said that a friend is a friend all the way, but now I believe that's a narrow point of view. For the friendships I have and the friendships I see are conducted on many levels of intensity, serve many different functions, meet different needs and range from those as all-the-way as the friendship of the soul sisters mentioned above to that of the most nonchalant and casual playmates.

4   Consider these varieties of friendship:

5   **1. Convenience friends.** These are women with whom, if our paths weren't crossing all the time, we'd have no particular reason to be friends: a next-door neighbor, a woman in our car pool, the mother of one of our children's closest friends or maybe some mommy with whom we serve juice and cookies each week at the Glenwood Co-op Nursery.

6   Convenience friends are convenient indeed. They'll lend us their cups and silverware for a party. They'll drive our kids to soccer when we're sick. They'll take us to

pick up our car when we need a lift to the garage. They'll even take our cats when we go on vacation. As we will for them.

7   But we don't, with convenience friends, ever come too close or tell too much; we maintain our public face and emotional distance. "Which means," says Elaine, "that I'll talk about being overweight but not about being depressed. Which means I'll admit being mad but not blind with rage. Which means that I might say that we're pinched this month but never that I'm worried sick over money." But which doesn't mean that there isn't sufficient value to be found in these friendships of mutual aid, in convenience friends.

8   **2. Special-interest friends.** These friendships aren't intimate, and they needn't involve kids or silverware or cats. Their value lies in some interest jointly shared. And so we may have an office friend or a yoga friend or a tennis friend or a friend from the Women's Democratic Club.

9   "I've got one woman friend," says Joyce, "who likes, as I do, to take psychology courses. Which makes it nice for me—and nice for her. It's fun to go with someone you know and it's fun to discuss what you've learned, driving back from the classes." And for the most part, she says, that's all they discuss.

10   "I'd say that what we're doing *is doing* together, not being together," Suzanne says of her Tuesday-doubles friends. "It's mainly a tennis relationship, but we play together well. And I guess we all need to have a couple of playmates."

11   I agree.

12   My playmate is a shopping friend, a woman of marvelous taste, a woman who knows exactly *where* to buy *what,* and furthermore is a woman who always knows beyond a doubt what one ought to be buying. I don't have the time to keep up with what's new in eyeshadow, hemlines and shoes and whether the smock look is in or finished already. But since (oh, shame!) I care a lot about eyeshadow, hemlines and shoes, and since I don't *want to* wear smocks if the smock look is finished, I'm very glad to have a shopping friend.

13   **3. Historical friends.** We all have a friend who knew us when . . . maybe way back in Miss Meltzer's second grade, when our family lived in that three-room flat in Brooklyn, when our dad was out of work for seven months, when our brother Allie got in that fight where they had to call the police, when our sister married the endodontist from Yonkers and when, the morning after we lost our virginity, she was the first, the only, friend we told.

14   The years have gone by and we've gone separate ways and we've little in common now, but we're still an intimate part of each other's past. And so whenever we go to Detroit we always go to visit this friend of our girlhood. Who knows how we looked before our teeth were straightened. Who knows how we talked before our voice got un-Brooklyned. Who knows what we ate before we learned about artichokes. And who, by her presence, puts us in touch with an earlier part of ourselves, a part of ourselves it's important never to lose.

15   "What this friend means to me and what I mean to her," says Grace, "is having a sister without sibling rivalry. We know the texture of each other's lives. She remembers my grandmother's cabbage soup. I remember the way her uncle played the piano. There's simply no other friend who remembers those things."

16   **4. Crossroads friends.** Like historical friends, our crossroads friends are important for *what was*—for the friendship we shared at a crucial, now past, time of life. A time, perhaps, when we roomed in college together; or worked as eager young singles in the Big City together; or went together, as my friend Elizabeth and I did, through pregnancy, birth and that scary first year of new motherhood.

17   Crossroads friends forge powerful links, links strong enough to endure with not much more contact than once-a-year letters at Christmas. And out of respect for those crossroads years, for those dramas and dreams we once shared, we will always be friends.

18   **5. Cross-generational friends.** Historical friends and crossroads friends seem to maintain a special kind of intimacy—dormant but always ready to be revived—and though we may rarely meet, whenever we do connect, it's personal and intense. Another kind of intimacy exists in the friendships that form across generations in what one woman calls her daughter-mother and her mother-daughter relationships.

19   Evelyn's friend is her mother's age—"but I share so much more than I ever could with my mother"—a woman she talks to of music, of books and of life. "What I get from her is the benefit of her experience. What she gets—and enjoys—from me is a youthful perspective. It's a pleasure for both of us."

20   I have in my own life a precious friend, a woman of sixty-five who has lived very hard, who is wise, who listens well; who has been where I am and can help me understand it; and who represents not only an ultimate ideal mother to me but also the person I'd like to be when I grow up.

21   In our daughter role we tend to do more than our share of self-revelation; in our mother role we tend to receive what's revealed. It's another kind of pleasure—playing wise mother to a questing younger person. It's another very lovely kind of friendship.

22   **6. Part-of-a-couple friends.** Some of the women we call our friends we never see alone—we see them as part of a couple at couples' parties. And though we share interests in many things and respect each other's views, we aren't moved to deepen the relationship. Whatever the reason, a lack of time or—and this is more likely—a lack of chemistry, our friendship remains in the context of a group. But the fact that our feeling on seeing each other is always, "I'm so glad she's here" and the fact that we spend half the evening talking together says that this too, in its own way, counts as a friendship.

23   Other part-of-a-couple friends are the friends that came with the marriage, and some of these are friends we could live without. But sometimes, alas, she married our husband's best friend; and sometimes, alas, she is our husband's best friend. And so we find ourselves dealing with her, somewhat against our will, in a spirit of what I'll call reluctant friendship.

24   **7. Men who are friends.** I wanted to write just of women friends, but the women I've talked to won't let me—they say I must mention man–woman friendships too. For these friendships can be just as close and as dear as those that we form with women. Listen to Lucy's description of one such friendship:

25   "We've found we have things to talk about that are different from what he talks about with my husband and different from what I talk about with his wife. So sometimes we call on the phone or meet for lunch. There are similar intellectual interests—we always pass on to each other the books that we love—but there's also something tender and caring too."

26   In a couple of crises, Lucy says, "he offered himself for talking and for helping. And when someone died in his family he wanted me there. The sexual, flirty part of our friendship is very small, but *some*—just enough to make it fun and different." She thinks—and I agree—that the sexual part, though small, is always *some,* is always there when a man and a woman are friends.

27   It's only in the past few years that I've made friends with men, in the sense of a friendship that's mine, not just part of two couples. And achieving with them the ease and the trust I've found with women friends has value indeed. Under the dryer at home last week, putting on mascara and rouge, I comfortably sat and talked with a fellow named Peter. Peter, I finally decided, could handle the shock of me minus mascara under the dryer. Because we care for each other. Because we're friends.

28   There are medium friends, and pretty good friends, and very good friends indeed, and these friendships are defined by their level of intimacy. And what we'll reveal at each of these levels of intimacy is calibrated with care. We might tell a medium friend, for example, that yesterday eve we had a fight with our husband. And we might tell a pretty good friend that this fight with our husband made us so

29   mad that we slept on the couch. And we might tell a very good friend that the reason we got so mad in that fight that we slept on the couch had something to do with that girl who works in his office. But it's only to our very best friends that we're willing to tell all, to tell what's going on with that girl in his office.

29   The best of friends, I still believe, totally love and support and trust each other, and bare to each other the secrets of their souls, and run—no questions asked—to help each other, and tell harsh truths to each other when they must be told.

30   But we needn't agree about everything (only twelve-year-old girls agree about *everything*) to tolerate each other's point of view. To accept without judgment. To give and to take without ever keeping score. And to *be* there, as I am for them and as they are for me, to comfort our sorrows, to celebrate our joys.

Questions for Analysis

1. Judith Viorst wrote this essay for *Redbook* magazine, which appeals primarily to women. How does awareness of audience affect her choice of subject matter, her purpose, the examples she includes, and her writing style?

2. What criterion or criteria does Viorst use in classifying friends? (Locate her formal statement of classification.) Are there any overlapping categories?

3. What type of information does Viorst use to support and illustrate her categories?

4. What transitional expressions and other devices does Viorst use to label the categories and introduce explanations and examples?

5. At various points in the essay, Viorst contrasts and compares two categories. Why? In other words, what function do these comparisons and contrasts serve?

Writing Assignments

1. Assume you are writing for a magazine read primarily by men. Following Judith Viorst's model about women friends, compose an entertaining classification of the types of friends men have. Illustrate the categories with people you know—but don't use their real names.

2. Relate an event that revealed who your best-of-friends were—the ones who helped you or made some sacrifice at a critical time in your life.

3. Describe a cross-generational friendship you have, and illustrate it through examples of how you and this older or younger friend interact.

4. Write, in your own words, what you take to be Viorst's point. Support your thesis with examples from her essay.

from The Way to Rainy Mountain
N. Scott Momaday

* * * *

Although in recent years, our society has made an effort to understand the history and rich culture of the many branches of Native Americans, there is still much to learn. In the following essay, N. Scott Momaday, a Kiowa, describes his return to the homeland of his grandmother—and his ancestors—and teaches his readers much about its culture. As you read the essay, notice the connection he makes between the land and the people. Notice the connection he makes between the past and present. And notice the significance of his grandmother in his life.

1   A single knoll rises out of the plain in Oklahoma, north and west of the Wichita Range. For my people, the Kiowas, it is an old landmark, and they gave it the name

Rainy Mountain. The hardest weather in the world is there. Winter brings blizzards, hot tornadic winds arise in the spring, and in summer the prairie is an anvil's edge. The grass turns brittle and brown, and it cracks beneath your feet. There are green belts along the rivers and creeks, linear groves of hickory and pecan, willow and witch hazel. At a distance in July or August the steaming foliage seems almost to writhe in fire. Great green-and-yellow grasshoppers are everywhere in the tall grass, popping up like corn to sting the flesh, and tortoises crawl about on the red earth, going nowhere in the plenty of time. Loneliness is an aspect of the land. All things in the plain are isolate; there is no confusion of objects in the eye, but *one* hill or *one* tree or *one* man. To look upon that landscape in the early morning, with the sun at your back, is to lose the sense of proportion. Your imagination comes to life, and this, you think, is where Creation was begun.

2   I returned to Rainy Mountain in July. My grandmother had died in the spring, and I wanted to be at her grave. She had lived to be very old and at last infirm. Her only living daughter was with her when she died, and I was told that in death her face was that of a child.

3   I like to think of her as a child. When she was born, the Kiowas were living that last great moment of their history. For more than a hundred years they had controlled the open range from the Smoky Hill River to the Red, from the headwaters of the Canadian to the fork of the Arkansas and Cimarron. In alliance with the Comanches, they had ruled the whole of the southern Plains. War was their sacred business, and they were among the finest horsemen the world has ever known. But warfare for the Kiowas was preeminently a matter of disposition rather than of survival, and they never understood the grim, unrelenting advance of the U.S. Cavalry. When at last, divided and ill-provisioned, they were driven onto the Staked Plains in the cold rains of autumn, they fell into panic. In Palo Duro Canyon they abandoned their crucial stores to pillage and had nothing then but their lives. In order to save themselves, they surrendered to the soldiers at Fort Sill and were imprisoned in the old stone corral that now stands as a military museum. My grandmother was spared the humiliation of those high gray walls by eight or ten years, but she must have known from birth the affliction of defeat, the dark brooding of old warriors.

4   Her name was Aho, and she belonged to the last culture to evolve in North America. Her forebearers came down from the high country in western Montana nearly three centuries ago. They were a mountain people, a mysterious tribe of hunters whose language has never been positively classified in any major group. In the late seventeenth century they began a long migration to the south and east. It was a long journey toward the dawn, and it led to a golden age. Along the way the Kiowas were befriended by the Crows, who gave them the culture and religion of the Plains. They acquired horses, and their ancient nomadic spirit was suddenly free of the ground. They acquired Tai-me, the sacred Sun Dance doll, from that moment the object and symbol of their worship, and so shared in the divinity of the sun. Not least, they acquired the sense of destiny, therefore courage and pride. When they entered upon the southern Plains, they had been transformed. No longer were they slaves to the simple necessity of survival; they were a lordly and dangerous society of fighters and thieves, hunters and priests of the sun. According to their origin myth, they entered the world through a hollow log. From one point of view, their migration was the fruit of an old prophecy, for indeed they emerged from a sunless world.

5   Although my grandmother lived out her long life in the shadow of Rainy Mountain, the immense landscape of the continental interior lay like memory in her blood. She could tell of the Crows, whom she had never seen, and of the Black Hills, where she had never been. I wanted to see in reality what she had seen more perfectly in the mind's eye, and traveled fifteen hundred miles to begin my pilgrimage.

6   Yellowstone, it seemed to me, was the top of the world, a region of deep lakes and dark timber, canyons and waterfalls. But, beautiful as it is, one might have the sense of confinement there. The skyline in all directions is close at hand, the high

wall of the woods and deep cleavages of shade. There is a perfect freedom in the mountains, but it belongs to the eagle and the elk, the badger and the bear. The Kiowas reckoned their stature by the distance they could see, and they were bent and blind in the wilderness.

7   Descending eastward, the highland meadows are a stairway to the plain. In July the inland slope of the Rockies is luxuriant with flax and buckwheat, stonecrop and larkspur. The earth unfolds and the limit of the land recedes. Clusters of trees and animals grazing far in the distance cause the vision to reach away and wonder to build upon the mind. The sun follows a longer course in the day, and the sky is immense beyond all comparison. The great billowing clouds that sail upon it are shadows that move upon the grain like water, dividing light. Farther down, in the land of the Crows and Blackfeet, the plain is yellow. Sweet clover takes hold of the hills and bends upon itself to cover and seal the soil. There the Kiowas paused on their way; they had come to the place where they must change their lives. The sun is at home on the plains. Precisely there does it have the certain character of a god. When the Kiowas came to the land of the Crows, they could see the dark lees of the hills at dawn across the Bighorn River, the profusion of light on the grain shelves, the oldest deity ranging after the solstices. Not yet would they veer southward to the caldron of the land that lay below; they must wean their blood from the northern winter and hold the mountains a while longer in their view. They bore Tai-me in procession to the east.

8   A dark mist lay over the Black Hills, and the land was like iron. At the top of a ridge I caught sight of Devil's Tower upthrust against the gray sky as if in the birth of time the core of the earth had broken through its crust and the motion of the world was begun. There are things in nature that engender an awful quiet in the heart of man; Devil's Tower is one of them. Two centuries ago, because they could not do otherwise, the Kiowas made a legend at the base of the rock. My grandmother said:

Eight children were there at play, seven sisters and their brother. Suddenly the boy was struck dumb; he trembled and began to run upon his hands and feet. His fingers became claws, and his body was covered with fur. Directly there was a bear where the boy had been. The sisters were terrified; they ran, and the bear after them. They came to the stump of a great tree, and the tree spoke to them. It bade them climb upon it, and as they did so, it began to rise into the air. The bear came to kill them, but they were just beyond its reach. It reared against the tree and scored the bark all around with its claws. The seven sisters were borne into the sky, and they became the stars of the Big Dipper.

9   From that moment, and so long as the legend lives, the Kiowas have kinsmen in the night sky. Whatever they were in the mountains, they could be no more. However tenuous their well-being, however much they had suffered and would suffer again, they had found a way out of the wilderness.

10   My grandmother had a reverence for the sun, a holy regard that now is all but gone out of mankind. There was a wariness in her, and an ancient awe. She was a Christian in her later years, but she had come a long way about, and she never forgot her birthright. As a child she had been to the Sun Dances; she had taken part in those annual rites, and by them she had learned the restoration of her people in the presence of Tai-me. She was about seven when the last Kiowa Sun Dance was held in 1887 on the Washita River above Rainy Mountain Creek. The buffalo were gone. In order to consummate the ancient sacrifice—to impale the head of a buffalo bull upon the medicine tree—a delegation of old men journeyed into Texas, there to beg and barter for an animal from the Goodnight herd. She was ten when the Kiowas came together for the last time as a living Sun Dance culture. They could find no buffalo; they had to hang an old hide from the sacred tree. Before the dance could begin, a company of soldiers rode out from Fort Sill under orders to disperse the tribe. Forbidden without cause the essential act of their faith, having seen the wild herds slaughtered and left to rot upon the ground, the Kiowas backed away forever

from the medicine tree. That was July 20, 1890, at the great bend of the Washita. My grandmother was there. Without bitterness, and for as long as she lived, she bore a vision of deicide.

11   Now that I can have her only in memory, I see my grandmother in the several postures that were peculiar to her: standing at the wood stove on a winter morning and turning meat in a great iron skillet; sitting at the south window, bent above her beadwork, and afterwards, when her vision had failed, looking down for a long time into the fold of her hands; going out upon a cane, very slowly as she did when the weight of age came upon her; praying. I remember her most often at prayer. She made long, rambling prayers out of suffering and hope, having seen many things. I was never sure that I had the right to hear, so exclusive were they of all mere custom and company. The last time I saw her she prayed standing by the side of her bed at night, naked to the waist, the light of a kerosene lamp moving upon her dark skin. Her long, black hair, always drawn and braided in the day, lay upon her shoulders and against her breasts like a shawl. I do not speak Kiowa, and I never understood her prayers, but there was something inherently sad in the sound, some merest hesitation upon the syllables of sorrow. She began in a high and descending pitch, exhausting her breath to silence; then again and again—and always with the same intensity of effort, of something that is, and is not, like urgency in the human voice. Transported so in the dancing light among the shadows of her room, she seemed beyond the reach of time. But that was illusion; I think I knew then that I should not see her again.

Questions for Analysis

1. Who is the primary audience for this essay?
2. In the first paragraph, N. Scott Momaday says, "the hardest weather in the world is here," but ends the paragraph by saying, "this . . . is where Creation began." What is the connection between these ideas?
3. He says in paragraph 4 that his grandmother "belonged to the last culture to evolve in North America." What does he mean?
4. He also says in the same paragraph that his grandmother's people engaged in a "long journey toward the dawn, and it led to a golden age." Write in your own words what he means, using details from the paragraph to support your explanation.
5. He says in paragraph 10 that his grandmother "bore a vision of deicide"—or the killing of a god. What does he mean, and why does he say that?
6. What does the death of his grandmother represent to him?
7. What is the purpose of his essay?

Writing Assignments

1. Have you ever returned after a long absence to a place where you spent an important part of your childhood? Describe the experience of returning, contrasting it to your experiences as a child.
2. Does your family ever discuss a legend or repeat a story about a "legendary" figure from "the old country" or from the olden days? Relate the legend or tell the story, explaining its significance to the family and/or to you.
3. Have you witnessed a great change in your surroundings, in your family's traditions, or your own behavior in recent years? Compare the before and after, and explain and account for the change.
4. Momaday says, "The sun is at home on the plains." Write an essay in which you analyze Momaday's relationship to nature, using this statement as a point of departure.

Answers to Chapter Exercises

(Odd Numbered Items Only) and to Mastery Exercise 1 in All Chapters

Chapter 2

Exercise 1

3. to persuade

5. to inform

Exercise 2

3. a. pros: getting the job because of one's language skills; communicating easily with clients and colleagues; being able to function easily in daily life in the foreign country.

   cons: having to study hard to master the language.

   b. pros: learning the structure of one's own language by learning another; learning another culture through the language; perhaps reading literature or technical material in another language.

   cons: having to study hard to master the language.

Exercise 3

1. a magazine article; evidence: use of the informal *you* and the informal use of conjunctions to begin sentences

3. to inform

Chapter 3

Exercise 1

Possible answers, as examples.

3. The struggle to pay tuition.

5. Unsolicited and unwanted email.

Exercise 2

Paragraph C The first sentence

Paragraph E The last sentence

Paragraph G The first sentence

Exercise 3

Possible answers, as examples.

3. My job at the bank is never dull.

5. My three cats are very independent.

Chapter 4

Exercise 1

1. The first paragraph is the introduction. Paragraphs B-E are the body. The last sentence of Paragraph E serves as the conclusion.

3. B. Just like the fictional character, William Brodie changed identities in the nighttime. C. Until Brodie let his ego overcome his caution, his many crimes went undetected for almost two decades.

   D. With the police on his tail, Brodie tried to escape but didn't succeed.

   E. Although the man of two lives plotted for a third, his attempt to cheat the hangman failed.

5. The contrast between Brodie's identity in the day and identity at night. The second part of the contrast is introduced by "But Brodie's dark side emerged when the sun set."

Questions for Analysis

1. All the sentences leading up to "The person I am today is very different . . ."

5. Probably not, because he still respects those values, worries about losing them, and hopes to stay the same person on the inside.

Chapter 5

Exercise 1

The topic sentences are 4 (or 1 if 4 is considered introductory) and 6.

Exercise 2

Typical predictions.

1. How were the generals different? How were they alike?

3. What makes it like a house? How is food served? How do astronauts go to the bathroom?

Chapter 6

Exercise 1

Paragraph C . . . appeared <u>everywhere . . .</u> <u>because it appeared everywhere . . . fought under . . . fought under</u>

<u>The marines did not adopt the flag until 1876; the U. S. Cavalry did not adopt it until 1887.</u>

Exercise 2

Possible answers, as examples.

3. I walk to the bathroom, rubbing the sleep out of my eyes. I get dressed, pulling the clothes over my tired arms and legs. I stumble into the kitchen, bumping into walls and chairs as I enter.

Exercise 4

Only odd numbered items identified.

(3) antecedent: *the song*   pronoun: *its*

(5) antecedent: *the song*   pronoun: *it*

(7) antecedent: *the lyrics*   pronoun: *they*

Exercise 5

Only odd numbered items identified.

(1) banner, pole, hoisted

(3) "hoisted"

(5) storm flag

Exercise 6

Only odd numbered items identified.

(3) the British (the Parliament, the British government)

(5) the taxes

(7) the colonists

Exercise 7

Possible answers. Only odd numbered items identified.

(3) stories

(7) passion

(9) job . . . one

Exercise 9

had just ended <u>in February.</u> . . . invaded Philadelphia <u>on June 20.</u> . . . in the Old City Hall <u>that day.</u> . . .

carried on <u>for many years.</u> . . . <u>In 1790,</u> . . . midway between North and South <u>at that time.</u>

Exercise 10

Passage C At noon, In the afternoon, In the evening, At night

Exercise 11

Only odd numbered items identified.

(3) therefore,

(7) However,

(9) Second,

(13) Furthermore,

Chapter 7

Exercise 1

3. snatched, grabbed, swiped, stole

5. created, baked, whipped up

Exercise 2

3. When I was a child, my cat slept on my bed every night.

5. My father sits in his favorite chair every night.

Exercise 6

Possible answers.

3. can write

5. blue

7. facts

Exercise 7

Possible answers.

3. The imported cars from Japan and Europe are supposed to be better than American cars.

5. Today's athletes are overpaid.

Exercise 8

Possible answers.

3. Most of my coworkers are lazy.

5. A large truck crashed into the rear of the automobile, causing considerable damage.

Exercise 11

Possible answers.

3. My father wakes up at sunrise to go to work.

5. Only occasionally does something infuriate me.

7. I worked hard outside all day.

Chapter 8

Exercise 2

3. Late*r in the century,* King Charles V . . .

5. *Then* customs ever so slowly began to change.

Exercise 4

Possible changes.

3. a. *Instead of eating properly with knife and fingers,* she *stupidly* . . .

   b. *Stupidly,* she ordered . . . *instead of eating properly with knife and fingers.*

Exercise 9

3. Thick porridge *and thick soupy foods* . . .

5. Upper-class *Greeks and Romans* used spoons of bronze and silver, *while poorer people* carved spoons from wood.

Exercise 11

3. The spoons cost a fortune *and were highly popular.*

5. came from this custom *and meant* . . .

Exercise 13

3. the Latin *furca, a farmer's pitchfork.*

5. Duc de Richelieu, *cardinal and chief minister to the king in seventeenth-century France.*

Exercise 15

3. at the dinner table *picking their teeth . .*

5. follow his example, *placing orders for knives with rounded ends.*

Exercise 17

3. Towel-like napkins *later called "serviettes" were* used . . .

5. to the courses *eaten by people at the table.*

Chapter 9

Questions for Analysis

1. The first sentence

3. Beginning with the third sentence and continuing throughout the body of the paragraph.

5. Because it reveals some other information supporting the topic idea of "one of the earth's great natural wonders."

Exercise 2

Possible arrangements.

Paragraph A 2, 4, 6, 3, 7, 4, 5, 1

"The Decadent": Questions for Analysis

1. Yet the other day I had a strange mystical experience on the subway . . . As I looked toward the sunlight . . .

3. Yes, it does resemble the diagram, but its topic sentence and conclusion occupy separate paragraphs.

5. Adjectives of unpleasantness: meager, dirty, gloomy, dingy, sick, leprous, nauseating, stale, dry, condemned, unspeakable, congealed, dubious, mutilated, filthy, abominable, dirt-laden

   Adjectives of fascination and joy: strange, mystical, transforming, unique, peculiar

"The Beauty of My Town": Questions for Analysis

1. The town is filled with great natural beauty and the spiritual culture of the Mayan Indians.

3. The sight of Mayan Indians riding, his walk along the woodland trails, the singing of birds, his exchanging greetings with the Mayans, wandering along the river with its water

running, the Indians wearing and selling costumes, children playing in the square, the band playing and people dancing.

Chapter 10

Questions for Analysis

1. The first sentence. It should make readers want to read on because it establishes suspense: what happened to James Worson?

3. A quarter of the way through the race

   Wise said later

   When the men returned to Leamington

   And for years after his disappearance

Exercise 1

Paragraph A 2, 1, 3, 5, 4

Paragraph C 1, 3, 4, 2

Paragraph E 6, 2, 5, 3, 1, 7, 4

"The Footsteps in the House": Questions for Analysis

1. To create suspense.

3. (Paragraph 2) The first night . . . At around one o'clock . . . It was then . . . As I listened . . . After a moment of silence . . . I knew it was morning

   (Paragraph 3) The next night . . . Again

   (Paragraph 4) The third time . . . but this time . . . As the footsteps walked by my door, . . .

   (Paragraph 5 doesn't contain transitions of time)

   (Paragraph 6) this was the first time . . . That night as I went upstairs to bed, . . .

   Suddenly . . . I'm not sure how long I went on . . . As I went to bed that night

   (Paragraph 7) right now

5. (Paragraph 1) unmistakable warmth

   (Paragraph 2) some noise . . . listening to all the creaks and moans . . . heard footsteps . . . rather light and steady . . . I heard them start toward my door . . . I felt my heart pounding

   (Paragraph 3) sound of steps again . . .

   (Paragraph 5) seemed to bathe my house in warm glow

(Paragraph 6) I was surrounded by a warm breeze. The hair on my arms and neck stood on end. . . . I could smell her touch of lavender, and her warmth swept over me like a cloud.

These details create a sense of immediacy and drama. They make the presence of a supernatural being seem quite possible.

"A Death": Questions for Analysis

1. Jillian begins by revealing the end to entice readers to find out how the woman died. The actual climactic moments occur much later when Jillian approaches the cabin and feels relieved, and then when she enters the cabin and finds the body.

3. They create a sense of loss—of death amongst living things.

5. (Paragraph 5) I had seen her many times in town, the first when I was sixteen.

   (Paragraph 8) The winter that year was unusually mild.

   These are the two main transitional moments.

Chapter 11

Questions for Analysis

1. The first sentence.

3. Three, as labeled by "Your first surprise," "Your second surprise," and "Finally—and this may not be a surprise."

Questions for Analysis

1. Readers who might want to photograph wild animals, which the writer expects them perhaps to do.

3. Lens opening and shutter speed.

Exercise 1

Paragraph A 4, 3, 5, 2

"How to Write a Personal Letter": Questions for Analysis

1. The essay is entertaining, but it provides useful advice. The tone is lighthearted, warm, and friendly. Keillor takes this attitude probably because it reflects his personality, but also because he wishes to establish the tone that he wants writers to use in their letters.

3. Getting over the guilt of not writing, choosing writing instruments, writing the salutation, starting the letter, continuing the letter—and then providing advice on what to avoid.

5. Yes, especially the advice on being comfortable and not worrying about form and exact word choice, which often applies to first drafting of most writing.

"Let's Talk About It": Questions for Analysis

1. Essentially, that alcoholism is not limited to the less privileged but is a disease affecting everyone. It must be confronted openly, not concealed behind polite excuses.

3. The mother tried Alcoholics Anonymous and dryout clinics. She didn't succeed because she couldn't get the appropriate support from family members and friends.

5. This is not a set of instructions on how to do something, but a description of her own experiences and the experiences of others in her family who had to deal with alcoholism.

Chapter 12

Questions for Analysis

1. The second sentence is probably a more specific statement of the point than the first. The third sentence introduces the contrasts.

3. It's successful because it sticks to what it does best, and everything it does is for a practical reason. It's also successful because it continues to offer a product that customers want.

Questions for Analysis

1. Its purpose is to sell Omicrons. The intended audience is people interested in buying a new car.

3. A rear-mounted electric motor that is pollution free and economical—achieving the equivalent of 75 miles per gallon; top speed of 140 miles per hour; no tune-ups or oil changes; extremely reliable magnetic braking system; plastic alloy frame and panels. Transitions: Unlike, compared to, safest car you can drive, far exceed, four times stronger than, unsurpassed protection.

5. The same next-to-last sentence.

Exercise 1

Possible arrangements

Part-to-part	Whole-to-whole
A1-B4	A1, A3, A5, A2, A4
A3-B1	B4, B1, B5, B3, B2
A5-B5	
A2-B3	
A4-B2	

"Matinee Idler": Questions for Analysis

1. That he, like his father, has a fantasy life that he doesn't take too seriously.

3. He praises his acting ability while all he does is sit in a courtroom. He claims he gives a "nuanced performance" of "stunning invisibility." He tells his wife he's involved in a Hollywood blockbuster while he is merely an extra. He imagines Harrison Ford taking stage directions about being playful, with a hint of menace, as his wife had responded to him. He imagines sitting with his children as they watch his "major" role but cannot in actuality recognize him in the crowd.

Hughes's attitude toward himself is complex. He knows that his participation in the movie is trivial, but nonetheless enjoys the experience. He knows he is nothing like Harrison Ford, but nonetheless relishes the chance to pretend he is. He knows he sounds foolish, but is laughing at his foolishness along with the readers.

"Lady in the Telephone": Questions for Analysis

1. Whole-to-whole. The major transition begins with "Today's modern technology," then repeats "Today's" of "Today" at the beginning of the subsequent two paragraphs. The essay returns to the first use of the telephone with the transitional phrase "The first operator was not broken, so why fix her?"

3. Mostly to entertain, but at the end of the essay she makes a persuasive appeal (perhaps tongue-in-cheek) to picket AT&T and lobby senators.

Chapter 13

Questions for Analysis

1. The third sentence, beginning, "In terms of prestige."

3. Prestige, and often pay.

5. From the most prestigious to the least—so the similarities among the rankings, and then the differences, are clear.

7. Teachers to members of the military.

Exercise 1

Classification C number (or absence) of legs

Classification E degree to which beliefs are based on empirical (that is, clearly observable) evidence

Exercise 2

Possible arrangements.

Classification C cost of houses

  I. Expensive

    a. four-or-more bedrooms

    b. new

    c. older, but renovated

  II. Inexpensive

    a. two-bedroom

    b. older

  III. Moderately priced

    a. three-bedrooms

    b. middle-aged, without renovation

    c. new, but built with cheaper materials and more efficient building practices

"Darkness at Noon": Questions for Analysis

1. (a) Those who assume he can't hear, (b) those who think he can't talk, and (c) those who assume he can't see. The criterion is the assumptions people make about his abilities.

3. Amused, bordering on sarcastic. Examples: his discussion of the reluctance of the ticket agents "to inform me of my condition of which I may not have been previously unaware"; the hospital personnel's desire to "interpret" for him when he was admitted to an English hospital; and his story about the basketball game with his father. He is not serious about his "saint-like disposition," but uses the description for humorous effect.

"A Wake": Questions for Analysis

1. The third sentence, beginning with "I decided there are three types." The criterion is their closeness to the deceased.

3. They may be thinking about past experiences with the dead person and regretting they didn't say something to him or her before the death.

5. He cites himself as an example. He was somewhat indifferent to and uncomfortable with the death because he didn't know the person who died.

Chapter 14

Questions for Analysis

1. The first sentence.

3. The examples begin with the words "Without it, a person who fails" and continue to the end of the paragraph. The definitions would be abstract and unclear without the examples.

5. The distinction is important.

  Another example comes from everyday life.

Questions for Analysis

1. It shows how the meaning of the word changed over time—and how Chauvin probably doesn't deserve to have his name associated with the negative meanings of the word today.

3. They occur in the two sentences prior to the last sentence of the paragraph. They both place the word in a category ("extreme devotion" and "excessive defense") and then expand on that categorization in a short phrase ("to a name or cause" and "of men's 'privileges'"). The definitions contrast in both their intent (devotion and defense) and specificity—the current meaning is much more specific. The connotation of the current meaning is far more negative.

5. They suggest that societal changes lead to changes in the meaning of words; society shapes (or invents new ones) to fit its needs at various points in history.

Exercise 1

Possible synonyms

1. a buffalo

3. to chew

5. liar

Exercise 2

Possible definitions

3. A satellite is an object in space that orbits another object.

Exercise 3

Possible answers.

3. *Method of Development:* historical process; *Details:* artificial insemination, surrogate motherhood, cesarean section

Exercise 4

Possible arrangement: 4, 5, 3, 6, 7, 2

"Play It as It Lays": Questions for Analysis

1. His purpose is to give men advice and reassurance about their role as fathers. His likely audience is therefore fathers or soon-to-be fathers.

3. They came home, didn't help their wives, and demanded to be waited on.

5. To show that the unfamiliar act of diaper changing is easier than the familiar act of waxing a car.

7. The new American father must share equally in the parenting tasks formerly assumed to belong to women. The father must not beat his children, try to interfere in and resolve each conflict, or (at least in Cosby's experience) hope to become an acceptable cook.

"What Is a Strong Marriage": Questions for Analysis

1. In the opening paragraph, the formal definition is in the first sentence, and the preview is in the last sentence.

3. She contrasts battle and union to emphasize her point that marriage is a compromise.

5. That people enter marriage idealistically but must learn to deal with it as a realistic partnership, that marriage is a sharing relationship in which both people can develop their best traits.

Chapter 15

Questions for Analysis

1. "The explanations can be found in ancient mythology."

5. It states the result of the cause and concludes the paragraph strongly.

Questions for Analysis

1. "The only solution to weight reduction is a serious program of aerobic exercise."

3. Five. Transitions: First, Second, Third, Fourth, Finally

5. In climax organization, leading up to the strong concluding statement.

Exercise 1

3. a. causes; a. chronological order

5. a. causes; a. chronological order (or b. climax order)

Exercise 3

Paragraph B 2, 5, 1, 3, 6, 4

Paragraph C 3, 1, 4, 2, 5

Exercise 4

Possible answers.

4. For example,

2. Therefore,

6. Third,

9. Finally,

7. Fourth,

8. Thus,

3. Second,

5. Furthermore,

"Don't Worry, Be Hapa": Questions for Analysis

1. The final sentence.

3. She first encounters constant prejudice, and doesn't understand how she is different from other people, who make many wrong assumptions about her heritage. In high school, she feels ashamed of her identity and tries to deny it.

5. It refers to both cultures inside her and the changes in attitudes toward bi-racialism. The punch is the "all-American girl."

"Liquid Revenge": Questions for Analysis

1. He wants the readers to experience his discomfort of dealing with the effects of alcohol before making his point, which he states in the final paragraph.

3. Nausea, disorientation, headache. He creates a narrative rather than an analysis.

5. He likens his experience to hell and his search for relief as salvation at the temple door. He uses the metaphor to show the punishment one suffers for such sinful behavior.

Chapter 16

Questions for Analysis

1. Probably nonsmokers.

3. Answers will vary.

Questions for Analysis

1. To disarm a potentially hostile audience.

3. In the second paragraph she proposes that heroin be made legal.

5. Statistics in the second paragraph; and allusions to respected members of the community in the third paragraph.

7. Politicians may be afraid of being "pro-drugs," or organized crime may be buying off politicians.

Exercise 1

Thesis Statement C 1. Why should the age be lowered? 2. What would be the benefits? 3. Who would oppose it? 4. Why would those people oppose it?

Exercise 4

Paragraph A ineffective

Paragraph C ineffective

"Strike Out Little League": Questions for Analysis

1. His audience is the parents of Little League players, many of whom probably oppose any changes, and many of whom feel changes should be made.

3. I'll try to explain why. (third paragraph)

   These games are played at this hour because . . . (fourth paragraph)

   will never understand this. As a result . . . (fifth paragraph)

   This may be sound baseball, but it does nothing to help a youngster develop his hitting. (sixth paragraph)

5. He proposes that baseball for children begin after the school year ends and that it be played with a softball. Transition: If I'm going to criticize such a popular program, I'd better have some thoughts on what changes I'd like to see.

7. The end returns to the beginning, which provides a punch line and creates a satisfying sense of closure.

"The Schick Protector": Questions for Analysis

1. Men who shave. Raphael appeals to their pride in getting a comfortable, close shave.

3. The bulleted list of features he found on the blue casing of the shaver.

5. He first appeals to the pride of his audience and their presumed dissatisfaction with other razors. Then he gives a specific account of his own prior experiences with unsatisfactory razors. He emphasizes the importance of the "safety wires to protect the skin and eliminate cuts," and then provides his own testimonial.

7. He essentially follows a chronological organization. He could have organized it through a series of contrasts.

Chapter 17

Questions for Analysis

1. The first sentence uses essentially the same wording as the question.

3. Each is a topic sentence, introducing a point mentioned in the preview found in the first paragraph.

5. This structure establishes a climax organization, emphasizing each point, and especially emphasizing the difference. The difference serves as a dramatic ending.

Exercise 3

Possible answers.

1. *Thesis Statement:* The U.S. government is divided into three equally powerful branches, each of which performs its own role.

   Topic Sentences: The legislative branch, or Congress, is responsible for making the laws. The executive branch, or the president and the cabinet, is responsible for enforcing the laws. The judiciary branch, or the courts, is responsible for interpreting the laws.

3. *Thesis Statement:* Advertising plays three important roles in marketing a new product, such as a dishwashing detergent.

   Topic Sentences: The first role of advertising is to make consumers aware of the existence of the product. The second role is often to show consumers that they actually need the product. The third and final role is to show how the product differs from others like it in the marketplace.

Chapter 19

Exercise 1

3. Freedom

5. tailor

7. drinking and singing

9. authorities

Exercise 2

3. She quit . . . and continued

5. enlistment began

7. recruits did (not) expect

Exercise 4

3. bulges looked

5. voice sounded

Exercise 8

3. S F Many fights were terrible to witness and even more terrible to participate in.

5. S

7. S F F The Revolutionary War ended in 1783 with the defeat of the British and the victory of the thirteen colonies.

Exercise 9

3. people protected *because* . . . people did (not) believe

5. *Although* Deborah received . . . she could . . . conceal

Editing for Mastery

Possible answers.

(4) . . . carried to a **hospital**, . . . [join to (5)] **she** was examined by a doctor.

(6) . . . to feel her **pulse** . . . [join to (7)] **and** found . . .

(8) . . . **shocked**, [join to (9)] **not** only . . .

(10) . . . the **nurse**, [join to (11)] **who** helped . . .

(12) . . . the **infirmary**, [join to (13)] **the doctor** . . .

(14) . . . a **letter**, [join to (15)] **which** was addressed . . .

(17) . . . **the information**, [join to (18) and omit *he*] **summoned** Private Deborah . . .

(19) . . . faithful, [join to (20)] **and** in many respects, . . . [join to 21] **I** would . . .

(23) . . . his **sentence**, [join to (24)] **tears** came . . .

(25) . . . to Massachusetts, [join to (26)] **still** in men's clothing.

(28) Benjamin **Gannett**, [join to (29)] **who** stirred . . .

Chapter 20

Exercise 1

3. , but (yet)

5. , so

7. , or

9. , and

11. , nor was he ever wounded . . .

Exercise 4

Possible combinations.

3. . . . the Oglala; *consequently,* he joined . . .

5. . . . heavily armed; *however,* the surveyors . . .

7. . . . the treaty of 1868; *moreover,* he began to construct . . .

Exercise 6

Some possibilities.

C. S.   3.   . . . land, *and* white hunters.

C. S.   5.   . . . cow, *so* a foolish . . .

C. S.   7.   . . . broke out, *and* Native Americans . . .

C. S.   9.   . . . in Montana, *so* the army began . . .

Exercise 7

Some possibilities.

3. *After* the Native Americans . . . , they suggested . . .

5. *Although* the government ordered . . . at once, most of them . . .

7. . . . and Cheyenne, *although* they had never . . .

Exercise 8

Some possibilities.

3. . . . cooperation, *which* led . . .

5. The action, *which* would trap the hostile Native Americans between the two forces, had been used . . .

Exercise 9

3. . . . a Native American village <u>that was located</u> . . .

5. . . . this group<u>, which included Crazy Horse, Sitting Bull, and other great leaders,</u> was probably . . .

7. . . . his commanders<u>, who could not join or rescue him.</u>

9. . . . in a field <u>that lay about four miles away.</u>

Editing for Mastery

Possible answers.

(3) . . . starved them out, **(delete semicolon and insert comma)** many of the reservation . . .

(4) Nevertheless, **(delete semicolon and insert comma)** Crazy Horse . . .

(5) . . . attacked Miles in southern Montana, **[delete period, insert comma, and join to (6)]** The troops opened . . .

(7) . . . withdrew to the hills**; (insert semicolon)** then they . . .

(8) Finally, General Crook, **(insert comma)** whom the Native Americans respected for his integrity, **(insert comma)** . . .

(9) . . . , **(insert comma)** if he surrendered, his people . . .

(10) . . . agreed on May 5, 1877**, and** he led . . .

(11) . . . for Crazy Horse, **(delete either *although* or *but*) he** was unable . . .

(13) After some false rumors spread **(delete comma)** that . . .

(14) . . . to stop him, **(delete semicolon and insert comma)** Crazy Horse agreed . . .

(15) . . . peaceably; nevertheless, soldiers . . . **(delete comma and add semicolon, and add comma after *nevertheless*)**

(16) . . . people, which was the beginning . . . **[join to sentence (15), adding comma]**

(20) . . . to help Little Big Man, **(delete either *as* or *and*)** one of the soldiers . . . ,

(21-22) . . . Crazy Horse died **[delete period and join to (21)]** after asking his parents . . .

(23) . . . the following morning **(delete comma)** and soon vanished into the hills.

Chapter 21

Exercise 1

1. eat

3. hatch, takes, shakes

5. peer, travels

Exercise 2

(3) magnificent *birds* . . . , with *feathers* . . .

(6) stand for sixty *days* . . . (7) he switches *feet* . . .

(8) find some *fish* . . .

Exercise 3

3. need

5. wish

Exercise 4

(1) come (3) begin, become, decline (5) equals (7) lose

Exercise 5

(3) stomach and intestines *are* . . . (5) This churning is . . . (7) *are* mixed together . . . , the result *is* . . .

Exercise 6

3. When *they're* attacked . . .

5. Very high concentrations of Vitamin A *are* . .

7. The koala bear and the panda *are* not . . .

9. since *they're* both marsupials . . .

Exercise 7

(3) do

(5) does (7) does

Exercise 8

3. don't

5. don't

7. doesn't

Exercise 9

(3) has (5) have (don't have)

Exercise 10

3. come

5. win

Exercise 11

(3) is (5) is (7) Does . . . do . . . is (9) Does

Exercise 12

(3) pounds ~~of skin~~ are (5) skin ~~from this shedding action~~ is

Exercise 13

(3) shrinks, hardens (5) begins

Editing for Mastery

1. which *is* prepared . . . The *mice* . .

2. . . . that *is* held . . . and then *drink* . . .

3. . . . 200 people *die* . . . the fish *has* . . . a cook who *doesn't* . . .

4. Chicken feathers *are* . . . Georgia *have* found . . . A panel who *has* tasted . . .

5. . . . 160 *people* . . . of four *chefs.*

6. . . . ate 28 *worms.*

7. . . . Wapensky *describes* . . . There *are* several steps . . . a cup of ants *is* fried . . . in preparing the ants *is* to remove . . . After *they're* dry . . . Then the ants *are* fried . . . *they're* served . . .

Chapter 22

Exercise 1

3. P

5. P

Exercise 2

(3) programs *demonstrated* . . . (5) These flights provided the knowledge that *prepared* . . .

Exercise 3

3. Were

5. Were

Exercise 4

3. They *could* live . . .

5. On July 10, 1969, astronauts Neil Armstrong and Buzz Aldrin *could* . . . before their fuel supply *would* run out.

Exercise 5

(3) spun (5) came

(7) had, did

(9) rose (11) lay, gave

(13) became, grew (15) was, spoke

(17) was

(19) tore

(21) blew, became (23) lost

Exercise 6

3. My friend Claudio *has flown* to Ecuador . . .

5. Elmer *has taken* a bath . . . every Saturday . . .

Exercise 7

3. had taken

5. had walked

Exercise 8

3. had been

5. have been

Exercise 10

Possible answers.

3. was given

5. be completed

Exercise 11

Possible answers.

3. disappointed, shaken, saddened, annoyed

5. thrilled, pleased, delighted, shocked, saddened, disgusted, amused

Exercise 12

Possible answers.

3. (in either place) fried, scrambled, boiled, poached, deviled

5. torn, worn-out, frayed, faded, ragged

7. called, known as

9. left

Editing for Mastery

(1) a spaceship *powered* by the Saturn V rocket. (2) They *were* on their way . . . man *would* set foot . . . (3) The spacecraft *shot* along . . .

(6) the astronauts had *traveled* 244,930 miles . . . (7) It *circled* the moon . . . (9) Collins *flew* . . . (10) Armstrong *announced*, . . .

(12) then *drew* closer . . . (14) . . . computer had *begun* to fail, . . . (15) Armstrong *fired* the engines . . . (17) When the Lunar Module *touched* . . . Armstrong *could* see a sheet of moon dirt *blown* upward . . . (19) He seemed calm, but his heart *beat* . . .

(20) The two men were *supposed* . . .

(21) Houston agreed and *let* . . . to sleep, . . . they could skip the rest period. (22) Armstrong *led* the way . . . (23) he *turned* on a television camera. (24) his foot *made* contact

Chapter 23

Exercise 1

3. her, it, his

5. he, his, they

7. them

Exercise 3

(3) *it is* incredibly hungry. (5) why *it sleeps* . . . if *they* disturb it.

(7) pick *it* up . . . and toss *it* around and *he or she* won't awaken *it.*

Exercise 4

3. and *distrusted* anything they *didn't* understand.

5. *were* thought to be four-legged witches.

7. to exterminate the cats *began* . . . King Louis XIII *stopped* . . .

Exercise 6

(5) the animal *sticks* it out . . . not because the dog *needs* to sweat.

Exercise 7

1. a relaxing day

3. to be refreshed and ready to go

5. a popular girl

Exercise 9

Paragraph B (1) or simply to express joy (3) and announce their domains

Paragraph C (4) And they do not frighten other animals when they howl. (6) lambs, and calves

Paragraph D (1) and fascination as snakes. (6) And in the fifteenth and sixteenth centuries, the word serpent could refer to many creatures, including both salamanders and crocodiles.

Exercise 10

3. Dr. Smith told Bill, "You can turn in the paper on Tuesday."

5. The doctor warned me not to go to work until tomorrow.

Exercise 12

Rewritten: "... *I will have* to stop a further portion of the allowance."

Rewritten: (remove quotation marks) ... and *he gave* them the same wages and employment opportunities as male cats.

Rewritten: ... most weeks, Kojak leaves a couple of rats on *his* desk as well as an array of mice.

Editing for Mastery

(4) where no person would ever risk *his life* ... (or *no people* ...) (5) *was* to search ... (6) he *performed* (or *would perform*) many truly eccentric feats. (7) Everyone who learned of his exploits did not believe everything he or she *heard.*

(8) *he* had spotted ... (9) He never wore shoes or *put* on boots ... (10) the natives *had* pinned ... (11) and *placed* the sack ... (12) *He* could hear ... apparently *did* not object ...

(13) his helpers *couldn't* pull ... (14) said, *"I see the animal is in a state of fear."* (or said that he saw the animal was in a state of fear.) [counts as two errors] (15) and *jumped* on the animal's back. (16) he *said,* "and twisted ...

(17) *he* was ever on a crocodile's back.

(18) so he *decided* to let them drink some of his. (19) purposely *slept* with one foot exposed. (20) Waterton was frustrated.

Chapter 24

Exercise 1

3. no errors

5. no errors

Exercise 2

Possible answers.

3. José runs faster than they do.

5. Mom always liked you more than she liked me.

Exercise 3

Answers will vary, but here are some possibilities.

He was a colonel by 1864. ...

Though the *enemy* killed ...

he (the young colonel) kept on fighting.

His twentieth birthday was spent ... but *the young man* was soon back ... *he* triumphantly planted ...

watched as *an enemy* soldier ... wounded *him* in the side and hip.

A month later the twenty-year-old *leader* was appointed a brigadier general.

He was the youngest ... and *he* was still not twenty-one.

he remained in the army.

The general later refused ... where *he* died on October 1, 1916.

Exercise 4

Possible revisions.

3. All the people involved are doing their best to make the party successful.

5. None of the people have left their books on the desk.

Exercise 6

3. You must talk to the person who sets the policy for admissions.

5. We all need a close friend [whom] we can discuss our problems with. (*or* with whom we can discuss our problems).

Exercise 7

3. ourselves

5. I

Exercise 8

3. Those, this (that)

5. this

Exercise 9

Possible changes.

3. A car

5. This *action* would solve ...

Editing for Mastery

Possible revisions.

(3) built *this machine* for Maria Theresa . . .
(5) sat at a *chest* [delete comma] that had a built-in chessboard. (6) *Someone* could open the doors of the robot . . . [*The doors of the robot could be opened* . . .]

(8) *He* and the robot . . . then went on tour, . . . (9) it could play so much better than *they could.* (10) However, while *Maelzel and his robot* were . . . (13) *The machine* was . . . (14) *People* wondered, however, . . .

(16) *It* was not a robot at all. (17) explained *that once the doors were closed* . . . *himself* inside . . . (19) *This deception* had been kept a secret . . .

Chapter 25

Exercise 1

3. Joice Heath, *supposedly* the oldest living person at 161 years of age.

5. Barnum, *touring with* a circus in 1836, encountered several ministers who were denouncing his activities as immoral.

Exercise 2

3. old and weak animals, *hardly able to move* . . .

5. the ferryboat owners, *who agreed* to take the public . . .

7. the first batch of spectators, *who called out* from their boats . . .

Exercise 3

3. *Refusing to part with any money so quickly,* Barnum consulted . . .

5. no change

7. no change

Exercise 4

3. *To emphasize the mermaid's natural origins,* Barnum put up . . .

5. to all the newspaper publishers *in order to explain* . . .

7. *In the face of evidence that the mermaid was a fraud, Barnum* . . .

Exercise 5

3. *Insisting "that there is no such thing as a pure white elephant," Barnum* put . . .

5. The elephant certainly was white, *but* the color was painted on . . .

Exercise 6

3. by placing five bricks *on the street* without saying a word . . .

5. . . . who paid the admission fee *out of curiosity to see* . . .

Exercise 7

Possible answers.

3. <u>After pondering this dilemma,</u> he thought of the perfect solution.

5. <u>Seizing the brush,</u> the man painted the sign in fifteen minutes and then nailed it over the door leading to the alleyway.

Editing for Mastery

2. references to giants in the Bible, *Hull had the idea of making* . . .

3. two sculptors *to carve the statue* with Hull serving as the model.

4. his cousin William Newell's farm *outside Cardiff, New York,* . . .

5. no error

6. A furor *that soon spread throughout the nation* was created . . .

7. the object, *soon called* "the Cardiff Giant."

8. no error

9. no error

10. to Albany and then to New York City *for exhibition.*

11. Unable to buy the giant, *P. T. Barnum* made and displayed in New York City an imitation that soon outdrew the original one.

12. the Farmers' Museum, *one of the museums* . . .

Chapter 26

Exercise 1

3. Lonell's friendliness

5. Mr. Willis's radio

Exercise 2

3. the boy's uncle

5. Carlos's briefcase

7. Father's Day

Exercise 3

3. no change

5. the *stones'* great size . . .

Exercise 4

3. I've

5. doesn't

7. who's

9. it's

Exercise 5

3. Don't, what's

5. doesn't, you're

Exercise 6

3. You need at least two I.D.'s to cash a check.

5. The army wants to produce three new *ICBM's.*

Exercise 7

3. two-thirds

5. five hundred

Exercise 8

3. brothers-in-law

5. nonviolence

Exercise 9

3. a long-overdue job

5. a life-or-death situation

Exercise 11

3. stopped

5. com-mun-i-ca-tion

7. truth-ful-ly

9. base-ball

Exercise 14

3. July

5. no change

7. Merriam Webster's Dictionary

Editing for Mastery

(3) *There's* another . . . *century* ago

(4) It happened in *February* . . . young *English* sailor . . . (5) in the *South* Atlantic . . . sperm *whale.* (6) with *crew members* . . . (7) As the *sailor's* harpoon . . . *its* enormous *V-shaped* tail. (9) on the other boat *didn't* panic . . .

(11) the *animal's* carcass . . . (12) using the *ship's* crane . . . (15) Several *sailors* . . .

(16) needed two *weeks'* rest in the *captain's* quarters . . .

(17) his near-death . . . (19) His *hands* . . . (20) . . . the *captain's* cabin.

(22) bleached by *the whale's* digestive juices.

Chapter 27

Exercise 1

3. crosstown **bus, the** elevated **train, or** the subway.

5. of the **people, by** the **people, and** for the people . . .

Exercise 2

3. England, *but* he lived and worked . . .

5. to town, *but* he was no stranger . . .

Exercise 3

(1) no change (3) his **downfall, but** it also . . . (5) crashed, *and* Norton and his friends lost . . . .

Exercise 4

3. A democracy, which was unpredictable and **inefficient, could** . . .

5. What America **needed, Norton** concluded, was . . .

7. One day, **therefore, he** asked . . .

Exercise 5

Possible answers.

3. The **editor, amused by this unusual feature story, ran** it . . .

5. in a gaudy **uniform, however, the** citizenry . . .

7. **In his blue jacket with gold medallions and brass buttons, red general's cap, and navy boots, the** emperor . . .

Exercise 6

(3) Without **fail, each** day he attended . . .
(5) For twenty **years, the** citizens of San Francisco
. . . (7) the **taxes, always** for small amounts of **money,** he levied against them.

Exercise 7

3. a **disgusting, slimy** worm

5. no change

Exercise 8

(3) legislature **met, a large, comfortable** chair . . .
(5) of **Brazil visited** the city in **1876, San** Francisco proudly presented . . .

(7) **On a similar occasion later, the** board . . .
(9) . . . a variety of **hats, a** magnificent walking stick, and a **big, three-color Chinese** umbrella . . .
[This last comma is a debatable change.]

Exercise 9

3. now.

5. dog.

7. meeting?

9. please!

Exercise 10

3. Wendell Smith, president**;** Laury Jackson, vice president**;** Casey Redlinski, secretary**;** and Billy Hanson, treasurer.

5. **Jon, who** was born in South **Africa; Ahn,** who was a native of **Vietnam; Marita, who** grew up in Argentina and **Chile; Tanveer, who** left Pakistan when he was four months **old; Eleni, who** was a victim of famine in **Ethiopia; and Frank, who** was born in San **Francisco, California.**

Exercise 11

3. five-cent **fare; however,** Norton . . .

5. at **taverns; the other,** a dark-yellow collie . . .

Exercise 12

3. brutally **executed—a** rather dangerous **precedent—Norton** . . .

5. the leaders of two **armies—Generals** Grant and Lee.

Exercise 13

3. <u>Titanic</u>

5. My favorite poem in <u>Modern American Poetry</u> is Walt Whitman's "I Sing the Body Electric."

Exercise 14

3. no quotation marks

5. . . . and **said, "Your** Majesty, I apologize for this indignity visited upon your royal **personage."**

Exercise 15

3. no change

5. no change

Editing for Mastery

(2) full **uniform and** in a fine mood. (3) Even as a sixty-two-year old man and in poor **health, he** . . . (4) "**portly, rather** flabby man . . . at his side and the peacock's feather in his **hat.**" (5) the debate was **held, he** suddenly . . . (6) while shouting for others **that** they should get a **carriage.** (7) **unconscious when** he was taken to the hospital . . . (8) no change (9) any **biography:** $3 in silver **coins, a** gold piece worth **$2.50, a** French franc note dated 1828, a batch of cables signed by many foreign **rulers, a** certificate of ownership of 98,200 shares of stock in a mine, and . . .

(10) The next morning, the San Francisco **Chronicle** announced, "Le Roi Est **Mort,**" that is, "The King <u>Is</u> Dead." (11) the **morgue, a crowd** began to gather. (12) the well-dressed to the **ragged—and** by noon . . . (13) **"He is dead,"** wrote the <u>**Morning Call**</u> newspaper "**and** no citizen . . ."

(14) **However,** more than fifty years **later, there** . . . (15) swallow up the Masonic **Cemetery, the** emperor's remains were dug **up and** buried . . .

(16) . . . the mayor placed a wreath on the **grave while the** municipal band . . . (17) no change (18) It **read:** . . . (19) no change

Chapter 28

Exercise 1

3. C, They are

5. Pl

7. P

9. P

11. Pl

Exercise 2

3. supposed

5. prejudiced

Exercise 4

3. accept

Exercise 5

3. advice

Exercise 6

3. effect

Exercise 7

3. By, by

5. by

Exercise 8

3. Conscious

Exercise 9

3. fine, find

Exercise 10

3. knew

Exercise 11

3. led

Exercise 12

3. lay

5. lies

Exercise 13

3. lose

Exercise 14

3. mind

Exercise 15

3. past

Exercise 16

3. quite

5. quite

Exercise 17

3. raise

Exercise 18

3. set, set

Exercise 19

5. then, than

Exercise 20

3. two, too, to

Exercise 21

3. whether

Editing for Mastery

(4) He led a revolution . . . (5) He had a cunning, razor-sharp *mind,* and his *conscience* never bothered him . . .

(7) Although the university would not *accept* a peasant . . .

(8) had a quick *rise* to power. (9) When he assumed full control as *its* Chairman . . . (10) He wasn't *quite* successful.

(13) The Hundred Flowers were *supposed* to encourage growth . . .

(16) As he had throughout the *past,* . . . (17) He urged China's youth, *whose* average age . . . (18) Many important leaders *were* humiliated and attacked.

(22) ignored his doctor's *advice* to cut down.

(24) and *then* chew the leaves.

(27) provided *by* servants while he worked.

(29) so the public didn't *know* he was an amazing sexual athlete. (32) he could *have* lived forever! (33) he wouldn't *sit* still for treatment.

(38) when he was almost *too* sick to move. (39) new uniforms *were* made for his bloated body . . .

(40) will *lie* in state forever.

Quotations and Proverbs

Here's a list of proverbs and sayings. You can use them as topics for writing or simply for inspiration. Or read and enjoy them.

Marriage and Family Life

My childhood should have taught me lessons for my own parenthood, but it didn't because parenting can be learned only by people who have no children.
—**Bill Cosby,** actor, author and comedian, from *Childhood*, 1991

Kids' views are often just as valid as the teachers'. The best teachers are the ones that know that.
—**Morley Saefer,** journalist, on "Politically Incorrect," 1995

There are three ways to get something done: do it yourself, hire someone, or forbid your kids to do it.
—**Monta Crane**

Don't marry for money. You can borrow it cheaper.
—**Scots proverb**

Where there is love, there is pain.
—**Spanish proverb**

Love is a kind of military service.
—**Latin proverb**

Eat and drink with your relatives; do business with strangers.
—**Greek proverb**

Responsibilities

We have the Bill of Rights. What we need is a Bill of Responsibilities.
—**Bill Maher,** comedian and commentator, 1995

If you don't run your own life, somebody else will.
—**John Atkinson**

No problem is so big and complicated that it can't be run away from.
—**Linus** (Peanuts character by Charles Schulz)

Leadership

Take calculated risks. That is quite different from being rash.
—**General George S. Patton**

When you are right, you cannot be too radical; when you are wrong, you cannot be too conservative.
—**Martin Luther King, Jr.**

When you have a number of disagreeable duties to perform, always do the most disagreeable first.
—**Josiah Quincy**

If you treat people right they will treat you right—ninety percent of the time.
—**Franklin D. Roosevelt**

Whenever you are asked if you can do a job, tell 'em, "Certainly, I can!" Then get busy and find out how to do it.
—**Theodore Roosevelt**

Don't hit at all if it is honorably possible to avoid hitting; but never hit soft.
—**Theodore Roosevelt**

What you cannot enforce, do not command.
—**Socrates**

Keep your fears to yourself, but share your courage with others.
—**Robert Louis Stevenson**

Remember that when an employee enters your office, he is in a strange land.
—**Erwin H. Schell**

If you want work well done, select a busy man—the other kind has no time.
—**Elbert Hubbard**

Advice

Never trust the advice of a man in difficulties.
—**Aesop**

Don't ask the barber whether you need a haircut.
—**Daniel Greenberg**

Never take the advice of someone who has not had your kind of trouble.
—**Sidney J. Harris**

Beware of the young doctor and the old barber.
—**Benjamin Franklin**

When in doubt, tell the truth.
—**Mark Twain**

Ask the experienced rather than the learned.
—**Arab proverb**

Ambition and Competition

Sometimes something worth doing is worth overdoing.
—**David Letterman,** CBS Late Show, 1994

When your dreams turn to dust, vacuum.
—**Anon.**

If you can't win, make the fellow ahead of you break the record.
—**Anon.**

When you are an anvil be patient; when a hammer, strike.
—**Arab proverb**

You can get a lot more done with a kind word and a gun than you can with a kind word alone.
—**Al Capone**

Win any way as long as you can get away with it. Nice guys finish last.
—**Leo Durocher**

Never contend with a man who has nothing to lose.
—**Baltasar Gracian**

The secret of business is to know something nobody else knows.
—**Aristotle Onassis**

If you don't try to win you might as well hold the Olympics in somebody's back yard.
—**Jesse Owens**

Keep your eyes on the stars, and your feet on the ground.
—**Theodore Roosevelt**

Wisdom

If you look at life one way, there is always cause for alarm.
—**Elizabeth Bowen**

Never use intuition.
—**General Omar Bradley**

When you see a snake, never mind where he came from.
—**W. G. Benham**

You cannot acquire experience by making experiments. You cannot create experience. You must undergo it.
—**Albert Camus**

To know the road ahead, ask those coming back.
—**Chinese proverb**

No man ever listened himself out of a job.
—**Calvin Coolidge**

Wait till it is night before saying it was a fine day.
—**French proverb**

Remember that happiness is a way of travel, not a destination.
—**Roy Goodman**

To a quick question, give a slow answer.
—**Italian proverb**

You can fool all of the people all of the time if the advertising is right and the budget is big enough.
—**Joseph E. Levine**

Never try to reason the prejudice out of a man. It wasn't reasoned into him, and cannot be reasoned out.
—**Sydney Smith**

Measure a thousand times and cut once.
—**Turkish proverb**

All things good to know are difficult to learn.
—**Greek proverb**

Criticism

Never mind whom you praise, but be very careful who you blame.
—**Edmund Gosse**

Never judge a work of art by its defects.
—**Washington Allston**

The nail that sticks out is hammered down.
—**Japanese proverb**

Glossary

A

Action verb: a verb that states what a subject does, did, or will do.

Active voice: a sentence structure in which the subject performs the action of the verb.

Adjective: a word or group of words that describe a noun.

Adverb: a word or group of words that describe a verb (or a word formed from a verb such as an *-ing word* or an *infinitive*), telling *when, where, why, how,* or *how often* the action happens or happened. Adverbs can also describe adjectives or other adverbs, especially adverbs such as *very, really, too,* and *somewhat.*

Adverb clause: a clause beginning with a subordinating conjunction such as *if, because, when,* or *before* that functions as an adverb.

Antecedent: the word or words that come before a pronoun and which the pronoun refers to.

Apostrophe: a punctuation mark ['] that shows possession before or after *-s* on nouns, replaces omitted letters in contractions, or forms the plurals of letters before adding *-s.*

Appositive: a noun that adds identifying information about a noun that precedes it.

B

Body: the central part of a paragraph or essay that develops and explains the topic sentence of the paragraph or the thesis statement of the essay.

Brainstorming: a part of prewriting in which you list thoughts as they come to you.

C

Call for action: a persuasive appeal for the reader to do something.

Case: the grammatical role of a pronoun as subject, object, possessive, and so on.

Causal analysis: an organization that examines the causes of an event or the results of an event. It is also called cause-effect organization.

Cause-effect organization: see *causal analysis.*

Chronological order: an organization of events according to when they occur in a time sequence. This organization is found most often in narratives, process analysis, and cause-effect papers.

Classification: an organization that divides the subject matter into categories determined by one criterion, or standard.

Clause: a group of words containing both a subject and a verb. Every sentence must contain at least one clause, although many sentences contain more than one.

Cliché: a tired and overused expression.

Climax order: an organizational arrangement going from the least important to the most important information and often ending dramatically.

Clustering: a part of prewriting in which you explore and organize your thoughts in a chart. Begin by writing and circling the topic in the middle of the page, then draw lines (or branches) to circles in which you write related ideas. You can also draw branches and attach circles to each of the related ideas until you fill up the whole page.

Coherence: a quality in which the relationship between ideas is clear throughout a paragraph or essay.

Collective noun: a noun such as *class, orchestra,* or *team* that represents a group of people or things. Most—but not all—collective nouns are grammatically singular.

Colon: a punctuation mark [:] that functions like an equal sign. It is most often used to show that the last words of a grammatically complete statement are equal to what follows—usually a list, long quotation, example, or explanation.

Comma: a punctuation mark [,] used for separating ideas or, with two commas, enclosing ideas.

Comma-spliced sentence: a sentence containing two independent clauses incorrectly joined by a comma. This is a serious, but common, grammatical error.

Common noun: a noun that represents but does not name something and is therefore not capitalized.

Comparison-contrast: an organization that shows similarities and differences between two or more subjects. The organization can be whole-to-whole or part-to-part.

Complex sentence: a sentence containing an independent clause and a dependent clause that begins with a word such as *after, because, if, who, that,* or *which.*

Composing: a process of exploring, organizing, and adjusting your ideas in writing until they express what you want them to.

Composition: a complete multi-paragraph discussion of one main subject or idea, often expressed in a thesis statement.

Compound predicate: a predicate containing two or more verbs.

Compound sentence: a sentence containing two independent clauses, each of which could be a sentence by itself.

Compound subject: a subject consisting of two or more nouns and/or pronouns joined by *and.*

Compound word: a word formed by joining two complete words—sometimes with a hyphen and sometimes without.

Conclusion: the last sentence of a paragraph or last paragraph of an essay, which ties together the preceding ideas and gracefully ends the work.

Conjunction: a joining word or phrase. There are two types: coordinating conjunctions and subordinating conjunctions.

Conjunctive adverb: a word (often following a semicolon) that explains how two clauses or ideas are logically related. A conjunctive adverb, also called a *transitional word*, may appear in a sentence with just one clause.

Contraction: a joining of two words that requires the omission of a letter or several letters from the second word. An apostrophe occupies the spot of the missing letter(s).

Coordinating conjunction: a word that joins grammatically equal structures. There are only seven coordinating conjunctions: *for, and, nor, but, or, yet, so.*

Coordination: the joining of two or more grammatically equal structures, usually with a coordinating conjunction or a semicolon.

Countable nouns: nouns that can be either singular or plural.

Criterion: the method used in classifying things—such as by size, frequency, or age.

D

Dangling modifier: a modifier that does not modify any idea in a sentence.

Dash: a punctuation mark [—] used to separate and enclose items that dramatically interrupt a sentence. Internal items require two dashes, while end items require one.

Definition: an organization that explains the meaning of a term, often by providing examples and contrasting it with similar terms.

Demonstrative adjectives: the pronouns *this, that, these,* and *those,* which go before nouns—as in "this man" or "these cars."

Demonstrative pronouns: the pronouns *this, that, these,* and *those* when used without nouns (see *demonstrative adjectives*).

Dependent clause: a clause that cannot stand alone as a sentence but must be joined to an independent clause to complete its meaning. Most dependent clauses begin with words such as *because, although, if, that, which,* or *who.*

Detail: a smaller part of something larger. Details usually support generalizations.

Description: to draw a verbal picture of something or someone. Good description allows the reader to visualize the subject matter clearly, and it may involve the senses of sound, touch, motion, and smell in addition to the sense of sight.

Direct question: a question that forms a complete sentence ending in a question mark and usually places the verb (or first helping verb) before the subject.

Direct quotation: the exact words of a speaker or writer, placed in quotation marks.

Double negative: a type of grammatical error in which two negative words express one negative idea. Only one negative word should be used.

E

Editing: one of the last steps in the writing process in which you check over your second (or later draft) for misspelled words, words left out or repeated, grammatical errors, missing word endings, incomplete sentences, and incorrect punctuation.

Effect: the result of some action or event (see *causal analysis*).

Emphatic order: an arrangement in which the most important elements or events are discussed first, often used in a résumé.

Essay: an organized discussion of a topic in a series of paragraphs—usually at least five paragraphs and often many more. Ideally, the introductory paragraph attracts the readers' attention, states the thesis of the essay, and outlines its structure. The body paragraphs present each main supporting point of the thesis. The concluding paragraph summarizes the ideas and brings the paper to a graceful end.

Essay examination: an examination in which you must answer each question by writing a long answer—either a single paragraph or a full essay.

Example: a specific illustration of a concept.

Exclamation point: a punctuation mark [!] that ends an expression of strong emotion, often stated in an *exclamatory sentence.*

Exclamatory sentence: a statement of strong emotion ending in an exclamation point [!].

Explanation: a discussion of the reasoning behind some idea: how, why, when, in what way, with what result, and so on.

Expository writing (exposition): informative writing, the primary purpose of which is to explain something.

Extended definition: a definition that is explained and exemplified in one or more full paragraphs.

F

Fact: a statement that can be proven to be true.

Figure: a number or percentage.

Fragment: an incomplete sentence because (1) it is missing either a subject, a verb, or both; (2) the verb is incomplete; or (3) it is only a dependent clause and must be attached to an independent clause.

Freewriting: exploring your ideas in paragraph form without concern for grammar, spelling, or organization.

G

Generalization: a broad, abstract statement that usually must be developed through narrower and more specific statements and/or examples.

H

Helping verb: the parts of the verb before the main verb, conveying important information about verb tense or mood.

Hyphen: a punctuation mark [-] used for joining words and for separating words between syllables at the end of a line.

I

Imperative sentence: also called a command, in which the reader is told to do or not do something, and which the subject pronoun (you) is omitted.

Indefinite pronoun: a pronoun such as *everyone, nowhere,* or *something* that does not refer to a specific person, place, or thing.

Independent clause: a clause that can stand alone as a sentence.

Indirect question: a question contained within a larger statement that uses the word order of a statement. An indirect question does not end with a question mark.

Infinitive: a word formed from a verb but which does not have a tense and which functions as an adjective, adverb, or noun. Infinitives are of two types: full infinitives, which include the word *to* (such as *to be, to know,* and *to get*) and partial infinitives, which omit the word *to* (such as *be*).

–ing word: a word formed from a verb that functions either as a noun, an adjective, or an adverb. An *-ing* word can also be part of a verb if some form of *to be* precedes it, such as *is going, was going,* or *will be going.*

Introduction: the beginning of a paragraph or essay that attracts the readers' interest and usually states the point of the paragraph in a topic sentence or, for an essay, in a thesis statement.

Irregular nouns: nouns that do not form plurals by adding *-s.*

Irregular verbs: (1) verbs that do not simply add *-s* for present-tense subject-verb agreement but make larger changes, or (2) verbs that do not form the past tense or past participle by adding *-ed.* These verbs change internally or do not change form at all.

J

Job application letter: a letter intended to persuade its reader that he or she should interview you for a job.

L

Linking verb: a verb that does not express action but merely links the subject to the word or words that describe the subject. The most common linking verbs are *to be* (*is, am, was, were,* etc.) and the verbs representing the five senses: *look, feel, smell, sound,* and *taste.*

M

Main verb: the last word in a verb phrase, conveying important information about the action the verb expresses.

Metaphor: a way to making writing livelier by discussing your actual topic (such as *thinking*) in terms of another (*brewing up* or *cooking up ideas*).

Misplaced modifier: a modifier that has been placed incorrectly, therefore seeming to describe something other than the word or phrase it was intended to describe.

Modifier: a word or group of words that function as an adjective or an adverb.

N

Narration: a story, usually told in chronological order, or a sequence of consecutive events that build to a climax, which ends the story. A narration often includes dialogue.

Nonrestrictive relative clause: a clause that provides information not essential to the meaning of the noun it relates to, so two commas enclose the clause.

Noun: a word that functions as a subject or an object and can be replaced with a pronoun. A noun usually represents a person, place, idea, or thing.

Number: the singular or plural forms of nouns or pronouns.

O

Object-case pronoun: a pronoun form (*me, us, you, him, her, it,* or *them*) that follows verbs, prepositions, or words formed from verbs.

P

Paragraph: a group of sentences that discuss a topic. A paragraph can contain ten or more sentences or as few as one sentence, especially when used for dialogue in a story. In most circumstances, paragraphs are smaller divisions of an essay.

Parallel construction (parallelism): the repetition of the same grammatical structure for coherence or emphasis.

Paraphrase: to restate ideas in your own words and sentence structure—as opposed to quoting the ideas.

Parentheses: punctuation marks [( )] that enclose incidental information in a sentence. They always come in pairs.

Part-to-part organization: a way of making comparisons and contrasts between subjects by examining one part of each subject, then examining the second part of each, and so on.

Passive voice: a clause in which the subject does not act but is acted upon. The passive voice is formed from *be* and the past participle in any tense, such as *is done, was done,* or *will be done.*

Past participle: a verb form that ends in *-ed* for regular verbs, although there are more than a hundred irregular forms. The past participle functions as the main verb in perfect tenses (such as the present-perfect *has known,* or the

past-perfect *had known*), in the passive voice (such as *is known* or *was known*). The past participle is also used as an adjective (a *well-known man*).

Past-perfect tense: a tense used to describe past action or events occurring prior to a later time in the past. The past-perfect tense is formed with *had* plus the main verb's past participle.

Past tense: a tense used to discuss completed actions in the past. All regular past-tense verbs end in *-ed.* There are more than a hundred irregular past-tense verbs.

Period: a punctuation mark [.] that ends a complete statement or is included in an abbreviation.

Person: a way of classifying personal pronouns: first person, *I* and *we*; second person, *you*; third person: *he, she, it,* and *they.*

Personal pronoun: a pronoun such as *I, we, me, us, she, her,* or *them* that refers to a particular person or persons.

Persuasion: the attempt to get your readers to accept your viewpoint.

Phrase: any group of two or more words. A phrase may also be a clause.

Plagiarism: the use of another person's language as if it were your own. The person's language instead may be quoted or *paraphrased,* and the source of the information should be acknowledged.

Plural: more than one. Most plural nouns end in *s,* but two or more nouns or pronouns can be joined to make a plural using *and.* Present-tense plural verbs do not end in *-s.*

Possessive: a word that shows ownership or possession.

Possessive adjective: a possessive word—actually a pronoun, such as *my, our, your, his, her, its, their*—that shows possession before a noun (see *possessive pronoun*).

Possessive noun: a possessive word formed by adding *'s* to singular nouns or *'s* to plural nouns ending in *-s.*

Possessive pronoun: a possessive word such as *mine, ours, yours, his, hers, its,* and *theirs* that replaces a possessive noun or possessive adjective and the noun.

Predicate: the words that make a statement or ask a question about the subject. A predicate begins with a verb.

Prefix: an addition to the beginning of a root word.

Preposition: a small word such as *in, of, on, at,* or *around* that precedes a noun or pronoun (for example: *on* the roof, *by* the road, *under* the rug, *in* a year). The group of words, called a *prepositional phrase,* modifies a noun or a verb.

Present participle: an *-ing* word that functions as an adjective or adverb.

Present-perfect tense: a tense used to describe an action or condition in the past that continues up to or relates to the present. The tense is formed with *has/have* and the past participle.

Present tense: a tense used to discuss habitual actions, states, facts, or conditions that are true of the present. All third-person singular present-tense verbs end in *-s.*

Prewriting: the step in the writing process in which you think about your topic, purpose, and audience, and then explore your ideas through brainstorming, clustering or freewriting.

Process analysis: an organizational structure that explains how to do something or how something works.

Pronoun: a word that replaces a noun as a subject, object, or possessive word. Some pronouns have additional functions: *relative pronouns, demonstrative pronouns,* and *reflexive pronouns.*

Proof: evidence, such as facts and figures, that supports a statement.

Proofreading: the last step in the writing process, in which you examine the final copy for small errors and omissions.

Proper noun: a noun that names someone or something and is therefore capitalized.

Q

Question mark: a punctuation mark [?] that ends direct questions.

Quotation marks: punctuation marks [" "] that enclose direct quotations, titles of short works, definitions, and words used in special ways.

R

Reflexive pronoun: a pronoun that both performs and receives the action of the verb (such as "I looked at *myself*"), or is used for emphasis (such as "I *myself* wouldn't do that.") The pronoun's singular forms end in *-self,* and its plural forms end in *-selves.*

Regular verb: a verb that ends in *-ed* in the past tense or past participle, or that forms its third-person singular form by adding *-s* or *-es.*

Relative clause: a clause that functions like an adjective, relating its information back to the noun that, in most cases, immediately precedes it.

Relative pronoun: the word that begins a relative clause, which relates its information back to a noun preceding the clause. The most common relative pronouns are *who, which, that,* and *whom.*

Reported speech: a retelling in your own words of what the speaker or writer says or said. Reported speech never uses quotation marks.

Restrictive relative clause: a clause that provides essential information about the noun it relates to, so the clause is not enclosed in commas.

Résumé: a summary of your qualifications for a job, divided into categories such as work experience, education, activities and awards, special skills, and any other category you think will enhance your chances of being hired.

Reverse chronological order: an arrangement in which the most recent events or activities are listed first, often done in a resume.

Rhetorical question: a question that you don't expect to be answered. The question is usually used to create interest or as part of a persuasive strategy.

Root word: a word to which a suffix or prefix may be added.

Run-on sentence: a sentence containing two independent clauses with nothing joining them together. This is a very serious grammatical error.

S

Semicolon: a punctuation mark [;] that most commonly joins two independent clauses or less commonly separates items in a series that contains internal commas.

Sentence: a complete statement or question containing a subject (usually a noun or subject pronoun) and a verb.

Sequential order: an organization in which ideas are presented in consecutive steps, or a sequence.

Sexual bias: the use of pronouns that discuss general categories of people but that do not include both sexes. An example is a *person/he* instead of a *person/he or she* or *people/they.*

Simile: a comparison using *like* or *as,* such as "He ran *like a deer.*"

Singular: only one. Singular nouns usually do not end in *-s,* but the present-tense verbs that agree with them do end in *-s.*

Spatial order: an organization that presents details in space according to some arrangement such as top to bottom, left to right, or front to back. This organization occurs most often in description.

Subject: the topic (*who* or *what*) a clause makes a statement or asks a question about. Most often the subject is a noun or subject pronoun. In statements, the subject usually precedes the verb; in most questions, a helping verb precedes the subject.

Subject-case pronoun: a word that replaces a noun as the subject of a verb. The subject pronouns are *I, we, you, he, she, it,* and *they.*

Subject pronoun: a word that replaces a noun subject.

Subject-verb agreement: matching of singular subjects with singular verbs or plural subjects with plural verbs. With the exception of *to be (was/were)* in the past tense, only present-tense verbs change form to agree with their subjects.

Subordinating conjunction: a word that joins two clauses by making one clause less important and dependent on the second clause. The other clause is independent and completes the meaning of the dependent clause.

Substitute: a word or phrase that represents another word or phrase, such as *our first president* for *George Washington.*

Suffix: an ending added to a root word.

Syllable: a grouping of one or more letters that contains a single vowel sound.

Synonym: a word with the same or nearly the same meaning as another word.

T

Tense: the form of the verb that shows when an action or idea occurs or occurred—in the *present, past, future,* and so on. In two-, three-, or four-word verbs, the first word always indicates the tense (*doesn't want*—simple present; *didn't want*—simple past; *is going*—present continuous; *was going*—past continuous; and so on).

Thesis statement: a sentence included in the introductory paragraph of an essay that states the central point of the essay and often outlines the organization of the essay.

Tone: the attitude you show toward your readers—addressing them formally, casually, angrily, sarcastically, and so on.

Topic sentence: a sentence that states the main idea, or point, of a paragraph, which the body of the paragraph then develops. Most topic sentences come at the beginning of a paragraph.

Transitional word: a word that explains how or in what way two ideas are logically related (see also, *conjunctive adverb*).

U

Uncountable nouns: nouns that cannot be counted such as *air, water,* or *furniture.*

Unity: a quality in which each sentence of a paragraph develops the main idea, or topic, which is often expressed in the topic sentence.

V

Verb: a word or phrase that usually follows the subject (or usually precedes the subject in a question) and expresses the action the subject performs. A few verbs also link descriptive words back to the subject. Verbs generally have a tense (present, past, future, etc.) and can contain as many as four words.

W

Whole-to-whole organization: a way of making comparisons and contrasts between subjects by examining everything about one subject and then everything about the other.

Credits

LITERARY

CHAPTER 1 From *The Facts on File Encyclopedia of Word and Phrase Origins* by Robert Hendrickson. Copyright © 1997 by Robert Hendrickson. Reprinted by permission of Facts on File, Inc.

CHAPTER 2 From *The Facts on File Encyclopedia of Word and Phrase Origins* by Robert Hendrickson. Copyright © 1997 by Robert Hendrickson. Reprinted by permission of Facts on File, Inc.

CHAPTER 3 From *The Facts on File Encyclopedia of Word and Phrase Origins* by Robert Hendrickson. Copyright © 1997 by Robert Hendrickson. Reprinted by permission of Facts on File, Inc.; From *The People's Almanac Presents the Twentieth Century* by David Wallechinsky. Copyright © 1995 David Wallechinsky. Reprinted with the kind permission of the author.; From BIRD BY BIRD by Anne Lamott. Copyright © 1994 by Anne Lamott. Used by permission of Pantheon Books, a division of Random House, Inc.

CHAPTER 4 From *The Facts on File Encyclopedia of Word and Phrase Origins* by Robert Hendrickson. Copyright © 1997 by Robert Hendrickson. Reprinted by permission of Facts on File, Inc.; From BIRD BY BIRD by Anne Lamott. Copyright © 1994 by Anne Lamott. Used by permission of Pantheon Books, a division of Random House, Inc.

CHAPTER 5 From *The Facts on File Encyclopedia of Word and Phrase Origins* by Robert Hendrickson. Copyright © 1997 by Robert Hendrickson. Reprinted by permission of Facts on File, Inc.

CHAPTER 6 From *The Facts on File Encyclopedia of Word and Phrase Origins* by Robert Hendrickson. Copyright © 1997 by Robert Hendrickson. Reprinted by permission of Facts on File, Inc.

CHAPTER 7 From *The Facts on File Encyclopedia of Word and Phrase Origins* by Robert Hendrickson. Copyright © 1997 by Robert Hendrickson. Reprinted by permission of Facts on File, Inc.

CHAPTER 8 From *The Facts on File Encyclopedia of Word and Phrase Origins* by Robert Hendrickson. Copyright © 1997 by Robert Hendrickson. Reprinted by permission of Facts on File, Inc.

CHAPTER 9 From *The Facts on File Encyclopedia of Word and Phrase Origins* by Robert Hendrickson. Copyright © 1997 by Robert Hendrickson. Reprinted by permission of Facts on File, Inc.; From *TALENT AND GENIUSES* by Gilbert Highet. Copyright © 1957 by Gilbert Highet. Reprinted by permission of Curtis Brown, Ltd.

CHAPTER 10 From *The Facts on File Encyclopedia of Word and Phrase Origins* by Robert Hendrickson. Copyright © 1997 by Robert Hendrickson. Reprinted by permission of Facts on File, Inc.

CHAPTER 11 From *The Facts on File Encyclopedia of Word and Phrase Origins* by Robert Hendrickson. Copyright © 1997 by Robert Hendrickson. Reprinted by permission of Facts on File, Inc.

CHAPTER 12 From *The Facts on File Encyclopedia of Word and Phrase Origins* by Robert Hendrickson. Copyright © 1997 by Robert Hendrickson. Reprinted by permission of Facts on File, Inc.; From "Matinee Idler" by Robert Hughes from **Parents**, May, 1994. Copyright © 1994 Gruner+ Jahr USA Publishing. Reprinted from PARENTS magazine by permission.

CHAPTER 13 From *The Facts on File Encyclopedia of Word and Phrase Origins* by Robert Hendrickson. Copyright © 1997 by Robert Hendrickson. Reprinted by permission of Facts on File, Inc.

CHAPTER 14 From *The Facts on File Encyclopedia of Word and Phrase Origins* by Robert Hendrickson. Copyright © 1997 by Robert Hendrickson. Reprinted by permission of Facts on File, Inc.

CHAPTER 19 From *That's Not In My American History Book* by Thomas Ayres. Copyright © 2000 by Taylor Publishing Company. Reprinted by permission of Roman & Littlefield.

CHAPTER 20 From *That's Not In My American History Book* by Thomas Ayres. Copyright © 2000 by Taylor Publishing Company. Reprinted by permission of Roman & Littlefield.

CHAPTER 21 From *The People's Almanac* by David Wallechinsky.

Copyright © 1975. Reprinted with the kind permission of the author.

CHAPTER 22 From *The Facts on File Encyclopedia of Word and Phrase Origins* by Robert Hendrickson. Copyright © 1997 by Robert Hendrickson. Reprinted by permission of Facts on File, Inc.; From Space Hab NASA HUMAN SPACE FLIGHT http://spaceflight.nasa.gov/shuttle/archives/sts-95/ Reprinted by permission of NASA.; From John Glenn - Space Pioneer, Return to Orbit. http://www.grc.nasa.gov/WWW/PAO/html/johnglen.htm Reprinted by permission of NASA Glenn Research Center.

CHAPTER 23 From *The People's Almanac* by David Wallechinsky. Copyright © 1975. Reprinted with the kind permission of the author.

CHAPTER 24 From *The Twentieth Century* by David Wallechinsky. Copyright © 1995. Reprinted with the permission of Ed Victor, Ltd. on behalf of the author.

CHAPTER 25 From *The Facts on File Encyclopedia of Word and Phrase Origins* by Robert Hendrickson. Copyright © 1997 by Robert Hendrickson. Reprinted by permission of Facts on File, Inc.

From *The People's Almanac* by David Wallechinsky. Copyright © 1975. Reprinted with the kind permission of the author.

CHAPTER 26 From *The Twentieth Century* by David Wallechinsky. Copyright © 1995. Reprinted with the permission of Ed Victor, Ltd. on behalf of the author.

CHAPTER 27 "Le Roi Est Mort." San Francisco, California: *San Francisco Chronical*, 1880.

CHAPTER 28 From *The Twentieth Century* by David Wallechinsky. Copyright © 1995. Reprinted with the permission of Ed Victor, Ltd. on behalf of the author.

READINGS "Buzzard" from MAMA MAKES UP HER MIND AND OTHER DANGERS OF SOUTHERN LIVING by Bailey White. Copyright © 1993 by Bailey White. Reprinted by permission of Perseus Books Publishers, a member of Perseus Books, L.L.C.; From *I Know Why the Caged Bird Sings* by Maya Angelou. Copyright © 1969 and renewed 1997 by Maya Angelou. Used by permission of Random House, Inc.; Jo Goodwin Parker. "What is Poverty?" from *America's Other Children: Public Schools Outside Suburbia* by George Henderson. Reprinted by permission of University of Oklahoma Press.; "From a Grandpa, Above and Beyond" by Bob Greene from *The Chicago Tribune*, March 11, 1990. © Tribune Media Services, Inc. All Rights Reserved. Reprinted with permission.; From "Loves Finds a Way" by Bob Greene from *The Chicago Tribune*, March 11, 1990. © Tribune Media Services, Inc. All Rights Reserved. Reprinted with permission. Reprinted with permission from the November 1990 Reader's Digest.; "Neat People vs. Sloppy People" from *Show and Tell* by Suzanne Britt. Copyright ©1983 by Suzanne Britt. Reprinted by permission of the author.; "Death of a Moth" originally published in *Harper's Magazine* by Anne Dillard. Copyright © 1976 by Anne Dillard. Reprinted by permission of the author.; "Living in Two Worlds" by Marcus Mabry from *Newsweek on Campus*, April 1988. Copyright © 1988, Newsweek, Inc. All rights reserved. Reprinted by permission.; "The Myth of a Latin Woman" from THE LATIN DELI: PROSE & POETRY by Judith Ortiz Cofer. Copyright ©1993 by Judith Ortez Cofer. Reprinted by permission of the University of Georgia Press.; "When Bright Girls Decide That Math is a 'Waste of Time'" by Susan Jacoby. Copyright © 1983 by Susan Jacoby. Originally published in *The New York Times*. Reprinted by permission of Georges Borchardt, Inc. for the author.; From THE WAY TO RAINY MOUNTAIN by Scott Mornaday. Reprinted by permission of University of New Mexico Press.

PHOTO CREDITS

p. 39, Photo by Walter Chandoha p. 73, Library of Congress p. 126, © Bernie Boston Photography p. 175, Rube Goldberg, Self-Watering Palm Tree. Reprinted with special permission of King Features Syndicate, Inc.

Index